IMMIGRATION LAW

Kevin Browne, LLB, Solicitor

Published by

College of Law Publishing,
Braboeuf Manor, Portsmouth Road, St Catherines, Guildford GU3 1HA

British Library Cataloguing-in-Publication Data

A catalogue record for this book is available from the British Library.

ISBN 978 1 914219 70 2

Typeset by Style Photosetting Ltd, Mayfield, East Sussex

Tables and index by Moira Greenhalgh, Arnside, Cumbria

Preface

This book is intended to provide an introduction to immigration law and practice. I hope that it will be of use to students studying in this area, as well as practitioners who are new to the various topics covered or who wish to update their knowledge.

After a short, practical introduction in **Chapter 1** (which includes a list of useful websites at **1.2.8**), the book deals with British nationality and the right of abode in the United Kingdom in **Chapter 2**. This is followed by a detailed analysis of immigration controls in **Chapter 3**. The unique immigration status of EEA nationals and their family members is considered in **Chapter 4**, along with how a family member of a British citizen who has engaged Treaty rights might use EU rather than domestic law to enter the UK. The next four chapters then address the key immigration categories of entry to the UK. Asylum seekers and refugees are considered in **Chapter 9**. Enforcement of immigration law, the appeals system and judicial review are dealt with in the last three chapters. In each chapter I have tried to present the information in a logical, structured order with practical examples. I would welcome comments from readers which can be sent via CLP (clponline.co.uk).

Immigration law and practice constantly change. In this edition, I have included developments in section 3C IA 1971 leave, overstayers, rough sleeping as a ground for refusal, the Common Travel Area, EEA nationals and the EU Settlement Scheme, the new student Graduate route, the new Appendix Global Talent: Prestigious Prizes, Skilled Workers and tradeable points, UKVI guidance on sole responsibility for children, the Istanbul Protocol and asylum seekers, safe third country exceptions for asylum seekers, appeals and administrative review.

New cases include *Akinola v Upper Tribunal* [2021] (s 3C IA 1971 leave), *Kalsi v Secretary of State for the Home Department* [2021] (overstayers) and *R (Mungur) v Secretary of State for the Home Department* [2021] (long residence), *NA (Bangladesh) v Secretary of State for the Home Department* [2021] (private life), *NF v Secretary of State for the Home Department* [2021] (Article 1F.(c) exclusion), *HA (Iraq) v Secretary of State for the Home Department* [2020] (ECHR Article 8 private life), *Mobeen v Secretary of State for the Home Department* [2021] (ECHR Article 8 family life), *KM v Secretary of State for the Home Department* [2021] and *Sanambar v Secretary of State for the Home Department* [2021] (deportation), *R (Begum) v Special Immigration Appeals Commission* [2021] (appeals).

In the interests of brevity, the masculine pronoun has been used to include the feminine.

I would like to thank David Stott, Sue Hall and the team at CLP for all their hard work on this title.

I would also like to thank my wife, children, colleagues and past students for their help and inspiration.

This edition is dedicated to Alistair, Mary, Chris, Tom, Phil, Harry and Rene. All much missed.

Kevin Browne
The University of Law,
London

Contents

Table of Cases

S

Table of Statutes

Page numbers in **bold** refer to text of legislation in the Appendices

Table of Secondary Legislation

Page numbers in **bold** refer to text of legislation in the Appendices

Table of Abbreviations

AI(TC)A 2004	Asylum and Immigration (Treatment of Claimants, etc) Act 2004
BNA 1981	British Nationality Act 1981
BOCs	British overseas citizens
BOTCs	British overseas territories citizens
CAS	Confirmation of Acceptance for Studies
CPR 1998	Civil Procedure Rules 1998
CUKC	citizen of the UK and colonies
DCB	designated competent body
DfWP	Department for Work and Pensions
ECHR	European Convention on Human Rights
ECtHR	European Court of Human Rights
ECJ	European Court of Justice
ECO	Entry clearance officer
EEA	European Economic Area
EU	European Union
FCA	Financial Conduct Authority
HA 1985	Housing Act 1985
HMRC	HM Revenue and Customs
HRA 1998	Human Rights Act 1998
IA	Immigration Act
IAA 1999	Immigration and Asylum Act 1999
IAC	Immigration and Asylum Chamber
IANA 2006	Immigration, Asylum and Nationality Act 2006
I(EEA) Regs 2016	Immigration (European Economic Area) Regulations 2016
IHS	Immigration health surcharge
ISC	Immigration Skills Charge
NHS	National Health Service
NIAA 2002	Nationality, Immigration and Asylum Act 2002
SIAC	Special Immigration Appeals Commission
TEU	Treaty on European Union
TFEU	Treaty on the Functioning of the European Union
UKVI	UK Visas and Immigration
UNHCR	United Nations High Commissioner for Refugees

CHAPTER 1

INTRODUCTION

1.1 PUBLIC LAW AND PRACTICAL PROBLEMS

This book aims to provide an introduction to immigration and nationality law and practice.

This is a public law subject, dealing with relations between the State and the individual, concerned fundamentally with the exercise of discretion by officials. It is easy to understand the practical problems which arise in this area of the law, as it concerns the individual's ability to live, work and enjoy family life in the country of his or her choice. In practice, it involves a great deal of client contact, argument with officials, advocacy in tribunals and familiarity with a wide range of legal sources. It therefore calls upon the full range of legal skills.

1.2 SOURCES OF IMMIGRATION LAW AND GENERAL PRINCIPLES

1.2.1 Legislation

The main piece of legislation dealing with immigration law is the Immigration Act 1971 (IA 1971). This replaced existing immigration controls and introduced the concept of the right of abode in the United Kingdom (UK). The starting point for any immigration practitioner is the following general principles set out in s 1:

    (1)   All those who are in this Act expressed to have the right of abode in the United Kingdom shall be free to live in, and to come and go into and from, the United Kingdom without let or hindrance except such as may be required under and in accordance with this Act to enable their right to be established or as may be otherwise lawfully imposed on any person.

    (2)   Those not having that right may live, work and settle in the United Kingdom by permission and subject to such regulation and control of their entry into, stay in and departure from the United Kingdom as is imposed by this Act ...

As to s 1(1) and the right of abode in the UK, see **1.4.1**.

Section 1(2) establishes what are known as immigration controls: see **1.4.2**.

The IA 1971 has been amended by numerous subsequent Acts, almost on an annual basis.

British nationality law is dealt with mainly in the British Nationality Act 1981 (BNA 1981) (as amended). This Act came into force on 1 January 1983 and Pt 1 sets out the provisions which determine whether or not a person is a British citizen. The date is significant, as different tests apply to determine British citizenship depending on whether or not the individual was born before 1983 (ie up to and including 31 December 1982) or after 1982 (ie from and including 1 January 1983). Note that British citizenship is also affected by whether or not the person was born in the UK. Full details are to be found in **Chapter 2**.

A British citizen has the right of abode in the UK. Therefore a British citizen is not subject to immigration controls. So a preliminary question for an immigration practitioner to answer when seeing a new client is whether or not the client is a British citizen.

1.2.2   The Immigration Rules

Whilst the IA 1971 (as amended) is the framework of immigration law, it does not contain any detail. This is because ss 1(4) and 3(2) permit rules to be laid down and amended by the Secretary of State as to the practice to be followed in the administration of the Act for regulating the entry into and stay in the UK of persons not having the right of abode. These are the Immigration Rules. A copy can be found in **Appendix 1**. Quickly skim through the contents to get some idea of their wide coverage.

The Immigration Rules structure the discretion given by the IA 1971 to grant permission to enter, to vary permission, or to make a deportation order. They bind immigration officers, but not the Home Secretary who, in the exercise of their discretion, may, in appropriate circumstances, depart from the Rules they have laid down, for instance granting permission to remain in the UK when the Rules would require refusal. They are, therefore, not rules of law in the strict sense (*R v Secretary of State for the Home Department, ex p Hosenball* [1977] 3 All ER 452; *Odelolar v Secretary of State for the Home Department* [2008] EWCA Civ 308). But as the Rules are laid before and approved by Parliament, published Government policy guidance cannot add requirements that are not in the Rules themselves: see *Secretary of State for the Home Department v Pankina* [2010] EWCA Civ 719 and *R (on the application of Alvi) v Secretary of State for the Home Department* [2012] UKSC 33.

Nevertheless, a lawyer can base his advice on the Rules because they are normally followed by the immigration authorities, and because failure to apply them may give grounds for appeal, administrative review or judicial review (see **Chapters 11** and **12**).

The current Rules are cited as the Statement of Changes in Immigration Rules 1994 (HC 395). As the Rules are not delegated legislation, they are cited as a House of Commons Paper and not as a statutory instrument. Later amendments to the Rules are cited similarly.

1.2.3   Home Office practices

Since the Home Office has considerable discretion not governed by the Rules, it is inevitable that informal practices evolve in order to ensure that comparable cases are treated in like ways. These practices are not generally binding, although under the administrative law doctrine of legitimate expectation, a decision which disregards them may be quashed as unreasonable (*R v Secretary of State for the Home Department, ex p Asif Mahmood Khan* [1984] 1 WLR 1337).

The Home Office has made public some of the internal instructions to staff on the handling of immigration cases. These are available via the Internet (see **1.2.8**).

1.2.4   Case law

Immigration cases have in recent years formed the largest single category of applications to the High Court for judicial review. In addition, cases may reach the higher courts by way of appeal. These cases may be reported in the standard series of law reports, but may also be found in the specialist *Immigration and Nationality Law Reports* (INLR), published six times a year by Jordans, and the *Immigration Appeal Reports* (Imm LR), published quarterly by The Stationery Office.

1.2.5   EU law

The UK is no longer a member of the European Union (EU). However, many British citizens hold dual nationality, some with a Member State of the EU, notably Ireland. Nationals of EU and EEA Member States (see the list in **Appendix 2**) have special rights under EU law (eg under Article 45 of the Treaty on the Functioning of the European Union (TFEU) (freedom of movement of workers)). These rights are set out in detail in EU Regulations and Directives.

Probably the most significant Directive is Directive 2004/38/EC of the European Parliament and Council. A copy appears at **Appendix 3**. This sets out the terms and limits of the right of free movement.

1.2.6 The European Convention on Human Rights and the Human Rights Act 1998

The Human Rights Act 1998 (HRA 1998) interprets, rather than incorporates, the European Convention on Human Rights (ECHR). Although the legislation requires UK courts to apply Acts of Parliament even if they are incompatible with the Convention, it contains a number of measures which will enable practitioners to rely on the Convention in immigration cases. In outline these are as follows.

Section 3 requires UK courts to try to interpret an Act of Parliament in a way which is compatible with listed Convention rights, whether or not the Act is ambiguous.

Section 4 enables the courts to make a declaration that an Act is incompatible with Convention rights. The court must still apply the Act in the case before it, but s 10 enables the Government to introduce fast-track delegated legislation to alter the law.

Section 6 is probably the most far-reaching provision. It states that it is unlawful for public authorities (such as the Home Office) to act in a way which infringes Convention rights, unless required to do so by Act of Parliament. So, when exercising a discretion, the Home Secretary must take Convention rights into account and, if statute permits it, must avoid decisions which infringe them. As the Immigration Rules themselves are made in the exercise of a discretion, both the Rules and decisions made under them are open to challenge if they infringe Convention rights. So, in applying the Rules and exercising powers, the Secretary of State must respect Convention rights, whether or not the Rules explicitly refer to them: see *R (Syed) v Secretary of State for the Home Department* [2011] EWCA Civ 1059.

So immigration lawyers need a good working knowledge of human rights. The main Convention rights that might be relevant are set out in **Appendix 5**. Detailed references to human rights cases and principles can be found in the **Chapters 9, 10** and **11**.

1.2.7 Practitioner texts

The practitioner in immigration law relies heavily on a limited number of secondary sources. These include:

(a) *Macdonald's Immigration Law and Practice* (Butterworths): the leading practitioner text;

(b) *Butterworths Immigration Law Service*: in the form of a loose-leaf encyclopaedia, particularly useful as a source for Home Office practices;

(c) *Tolley's Immigration and Nationality Law and Practice*: a quarterly journal;

(d) *Immigration, Nationality and Refugee Law Handbook* (Joint Council for the Welfare of Immigrants): an invaluable practical guide (JCWI Handbook);

(e) Fransman, *British Nationality Law* (Butterworths);

(f) Webb and Grant, *Immigration and Asylum Emergency Procedures* (Legal Action Group).

1.2.8 Websites

There are many useful websites, most of which have links to other, related sites. You might start with the following:

UK Visas and Immigration (Home Office): www.gov.uk/government/organisations/uk-visas-and-immigration

First-tier Tribunal (Immigration and Asylum): www.gov.uk/courts-tribunals/first-tier-tribunal-immigration-and-asylum

Upper Tribunal (Immigration and Asylum Chamber): www.gov.uk/courts-tribunals/upper-tribunal-immigration-and-asylum-chamber

European Court of Human Rights: www.echr.coe.int

Joint Council for the Welfare of Immigrants: www.jcwi.org.uk
UNHCR UN Refugee Agency: www.unhcr.org
Electronic Immigration Network: www.ein.org.uk
Free Movement: https://www.freemovement.org.uk

1.3 INSTITUTIONS

1.3.1 The Home Office

Under the IA 1971, the Home Secretary has overall responsibility for the administration of immigration control. The Act designates the Home Secretary as the person who makes the Immigration Rules, appoints immigration officers, and takes specific decisions such as the decision to deport. The law generally recognises that, in practice, the Home Secretary acts through civil servants (*Carltona Ltd v Commissioner of Works* [1943] 2 All ER 560).

1.3.2 UK Visas and Immigration (UKVI)

UKVI is a department within the Home Office that is responsible applications for British citizenship (see **Chapter 2**), the UK's visa service (see **Chapter 3**), applications from employers and educational establishments who want to join the register of sponsors (see **Chapter 7**), asylum claims (see **Chapter 9**) and appeals from unsuccessful applicants (see **Chapter 11**).

1.3.3 Border Force

Border Force is a law enforcement command within the Home Office. It carries out immigration and customs controls for people and goods entering the UK.

1.3.4 Immigration Enforcement

This is part of the Home Office. It is responsible for preventing abuse, tracking immigration offenders and increasing compliance with immigration law.

1.3.5 HM Passport Office

This is part of the Home Office. It issues UK passports.

1.3.6 The First-tier Tribunal (Immigration and Asylum Chamber)

Some, but far from all, of the decisions made by an official in an immigration context are appealable to the First-tier Tribunal (Immigration and Asylum Chamber). Any further appeal on a point of law is to the Upper Tribunal and the Court of Appeal. See further **Chapter 11**.

1.4 IMMIGRATION CONTROLS

1.4.1 Right of abode in the UK

As we have seen, a British citizen has a right of abode in the UK. So, if a British citizen leaves the UK, he is free to return at any point in time and enter the UK via an airport or a port. Subject to producing evidence of that right of abode, usually by way of a British passport, he is not subject to immigration controls. This applies equally to a British citizen born abroad who travels to the UK for the first time.

Note that certain Commonwealth citizens also have a right of abode in the UK (see **2.3**).

1.4.2 Entry clearance, permission (leave) to enter and permission (leave) to remain in the UK

Immigration controls are dealt with in detail in **Chapter 3**. However, it is important to grasp the following points at this stage. As a general rule, immigration controls may exist at three particular points in time, namely:

(a)   before a person travels to the UK. This is known as entry clearance, and most persons, apart from some people who wish to enter for less than six months, must obtain it;

(b)   on arrival in the UK at the port of entry. This is known as permission (or leave) to enter the UK. All people who are subject to immigration controls must obtain this permission to enter the UK when first arriving;

(c)   after arrival, if an extension of the initial limited time granted for the stay is required. This is known as permission (or leave) to remain in the UK.

1.4.3   Visa nationals

A 'visa national' is a person who always needs entry clearance in advance of travelling to the UK for whatever purpose. The entry clearance document he needs to obtain from the British High Commission or embassy in his own country before travelling is a visa, and this will state the purpose of the entry to the UK, for example as a visitor or student, etc. Most visas appear as a stamp in the person's passport. A list of countries whose nationals must obtain visas appears in Appendix Visitor: Visa National list to the Immigration Rules (see **Appendix 1** to this book).

Upon arriving at a UK port of entry, a visa national usually requires permission to enter the UK, that is, he must convince the immigration officer that entry is pursuant to the terms of his visa. If permission is given, a stamp to that effect is put in his passport.

EXAMPLE

Kim is Chinese. He is a visa national. He wishes to come to the UK for a holiday. If he is to be given permission to enter the UK, he must, as a general rule:

(a)   obtain a visa in China before travelling; and

(b)   on arrival in the UK, convince the immigration officer that he is entering as a genuine visitor.

1.4.4   Non-visa nationals

A non-visa national is a person who is not on the visa list. He does not require entry clearance in advance of travelling to the UK for short-term purposes, ie a stay of up to six months in the UK, such as a visitor (see **Chapter 5**). However, he will require it for long-term purposes (ie a stay of more than six months), for example as an employee or a businessman, or if he wishes to stay permanently in the UK. The entry clearance document he needs to obtain from the British High Commission or embassy in his own country before travelling is an entry certificate. This will state the purpose of the entry to the UK, for example 'settlement as spouse', and usually appears as a stamp in the person's passport.

Upon arriving at a UK port of entry, a non-visa national will require permission to enter the UK, ie he must convince the immigration officer that entry is pursuant to the Immigration Rules.

EXAMPLE

Bob is an American. He is a non-visa national. He wishes to come to the UK for a holiday (ie for up to six months). He does not have to obtain an entry certificate in America before travelling but, on arrival, he must convince the immigration officer that he is entering as a genuine visitor, if he is to be given permission to enter. But if Bob wanted to enter and stay for more than six months, he would need to obtain an entry certificate before travelling to the UK.

1.4.5   Settled status

A person with 'settled status' (also known as unconditional leave, permanent stay, permanent residence, indefinite leave and settlement) does not have the right of abode in the UK and so, in theory, can be deported (see **Chapter 10**). This is a person who is legally in the UK without any conditions or restrictions being placed on his residence. Hence, it is not limited in time. If a person with settled status leaves the UK, he will be subject to immigration control on return, ie he will need permission to enter the UK on the basis that he is returning to reside again (see **3.8.3**).

1.4.6   Summary: who does what?

- Entry clearance officer (ECO) – visas and entry certificates;
- Immigration officer – permission to enter the UK;
- Home Office – extension of stay in UK, including switching of category.

CHAPTER 2

British Nationality and Right of Abode

2.1 INTRODUCTION

The law relating to nationality or citizenship forms the background to immigration law because a person's right to live in the country of his choice often depends on his nationality. This is true in UK law, in that a British citizen has a right to live in the UK.

There are two categories of people who have a statutory 'right of abode in the UK': all British citizens (see **2.2**) and certain Commonwealth citizens (see **2.3**). A person with the right of abode can freely enter the UK (ie he is not subject to immigration controls (see **1.4** and **Chapter 3**)). Moreover, he cannot be excluded from the UK (ie he cannot be removed or deported (see **Chapter 10**)).

2.2 BRITISH CITIZENSHIP

British nationality law has changed considerably over the last century. For an historical analysis, see **2.4**. The BNA 1981 was implemented on 1 January 1983, thereby creating the nationality of British citizenship. The starting points for determining whether a person is a British citizen or not is to answer two questions:

(a)   was he born before 1983 or after 1982; and

(b)   was he born in the UK or elsewhere?

There is a summary of the key requirements at **Appendix 6**.

2.2.1 People born in the UK before 1983

A person is a British citizen if, before 1983 (ie, up to and including 31 December 1982), he was born in the UK. The fact of being born in any part of the UK (England, Wales, Scotland or Northern Ireland) before 1983 is sufficient. Their status is that of a British citizen otherwise than by descent (see **2.2.5.1** and **2.5**).

2.2.2 People born outside the UK before 1983

A person is a British citizen if, before 1983, he was born outside the UK and:

(a)   his father was born in the UK; *or*

(b)   his father was registered or naturalised (see **2.2.6.1** and **2.2.7**) as a British citizen in the UK before the child's birth (if a father becomes British after the child's birth, this does not retrospectively make the child British); *and*

(c)   his parents were married, or subsequently marry in a country where that marriage operates to legitimise the child.

So, before 1983, a father could pass on his British citizenship acquired in the UK only to his legitimate child. An illegitimate child could not 'inherit' British citizenship through his father.

EXAMPLES

1.   Joshua was born in 1962 in the UK. He is therefore a British citizen (see **2.2.1**). In 1980 he married Grace (who is not a British citizen). In 1981 their daughter, Sophie, was born outside the UK. Sophie is a British citizen as her father was born in the UK and married to her mother at the time of Sophie's birth.

2.   Harry was born in 1961 in the UK. He is therefore a British citizen (see **2.2.1**). In 1979 he started a relationship with Lynda (who is not a British citizen). In 1981 their son, Michael, was born outside the UK. In 1982 Harry and Lynda married in a country where their marriage operated to legitimise Michael who thereby became a British citizen.

3.   James was born in 1960 in the UK. He is therefore a British citizen (see **2.2.1**). In 1978 he started a relationship with Lilly (who is not a British citizen). In 1981 their daughter, Katie, was born outside the UK. James and Lilly never marry. Katie is not a British citizen on these facts.

Before 1983, a mother could not pass on her British citizenship acquired by her birth, registration or naturalisation in the UK to any child born outside the UK. However, in those circumstances, the Home Office allowed for the child to be registered as British, and this is now possible pursuant to BNA 1981, s 4C (see **2.2.6**).

EXAMPLE

Ruby was born in 1959 in the UK. She is therefore a British citizen (see **2.2.1**). In 1980 she married Gary (who is not a British citizen). In 1982 their son, Simon, was born outside the UK. Although Ruby is a British citizen at the time of her son's birth, she cannot pass that citizenship on to him. However, she could have applied to register him as a British citizen whilst he was a child, or he may do so as an adult: see **2.2.6.2**.

The fact of being born outside the UK before 1983 means that you have to look to the person's parents to see if they might be British. If they are, then their status is that of a British citizen by descent (see **2.2.5.2** and **2.5**).

2.2.3   People born in the UK after 1982

A person is a British citizen if, after 1982 (ie, from and including 1 January 1983), he was born in the UK and at the time of his birth either of his parents was:

(a)   a British citizen; or

(b)   settled in the UK. (As to settled status, see **1.4.5** and **3.8**. Note that for these purposes a Commonwealth citizen with the right of abode (see **2.3**) is treated as 'settled'.)

Note that until the Nationality, Immigration and Asylum Act 2002 (NIAA 2002) came into force on 1 July 2006, a 'parent' in this context did not include a father of a child who was not married to the child's mother. However, the BNA 1981, as amended by the NIAA 2002, provides at s 50(9A) that from 1 July 2006 a child's father is:

(a)   the husband, at the time of the child's birth, of the woman who gives birth to the child (and remember that if the parents subsequently marry that may operate to legitimise the child); or

(b)   where a person is treated as the father of the child under s 28 of the Human Fertilisation and Embryology Act 1990, that person; or

(c)   where neither paragraph (a) nor (b) applies, any person who is proven to be the natural father by the production of such evidence (eg a birth certificate, DNA test report or court order) as may satisfy the Secretary of State on this point.

This means that subject to satisfying (c) above, an illegitimate person born in the UK on or after 1 July 2006 is a British citizen if his father was either a British citizen or settled at that time. What if an illegitimate person can meet these requirements but he was born in the UK before July 2006? In these circumstances the person may apply to register as a British citizen under s 4F of the BNA 1981 (see **2.2.6.1**).

EXAMPLES

1.   Evie was born in 1965 in the UK. She is therefore a British citizen (see **2.2.1**). In 1990 she gave birth to her daughter, Charlotte, in the UK. Charlotte is a British citizen as her mother was a British citizen at the time of Charlotte's birth.

2.   Chloe was born outside the UK in 1967 as a visa national. In 1970 she entered the UK with her family for the purposes of settlement. She had indefinite leave to remain in the UK when she gave birth to her son, Lewis, in 1987 in the UK. Lewis is a British citizen as his mother was settled in the UK at the time of his birth.

3.   John was born in 1970 in the UK. He is therefore a British citizen (see **2.2.1**). In 1995 he married Helen (who is not a British citizen). In 1997 their daughter, Sally, was born in the UK. Sally is a British citizen as her father was a British citizen and married to her mother at the time of Sally's birth.

4.   Oliver was born outside the UK in 1980 as a visa national. In 1992 he entered the UK with his family for the purposes of settlement. He had indefinite leave to remain in the UK when his girlfriend, Jessica, gave birth to his son, Alfie, in 2008 in the UK. Jessica had limited leave to remain in the UK at that point in time. Alfie is a British citizen if Oliver and Jessica subsequently marry in a country where their marriage operates to legitimise him; or if the Secretary of State accepts evidence that Oliver is his father.

5.   What if, in Example 4, Alfie had been born before 1 July 2006? In those circumstances Alfie could be registered as a British citizen at the discretion of the Secretary of State. See further **2.2.6.1**.

Note that if, at any time after his birth but before he reaches 18, either of his parents becomes a British citizen or settled in the UK, he may be able to register as a British citizen (see **2.2.6.1**).

The fact of being born in the UK after 1982 means that you have to look to the person's parents to see if they might be British. If they are, then their status is that of a British citizen otherwise than by descent (see **2.2.5.1** and **2.5**).

2.2.4   People born outside the UK after 1982

A person is a British citizen if, after 1982, he is born outside the UK, and:

(a)   his father or mother was a British citizen otherwise than by descent by birth in the UK (see **2.2.5**); *or*

(b)   his father or mother was a British citizen otherwise than by descent (see **2.2.5**), having been registered or naturalised (see **2.2.6.1** and **2.2.7**) as a British citizen in the UK before the child's birth (if either parent becomes British after the child's birth, this does not retrospectively make the child British).

As noted at **2.2.3**, until the NIAA 2002 came into force on 1 July 2006, a 'parent' in this context did not include a father of a child who was not married to the child's mother.

This means that subject to satisfying condition (c) of s 50(9A) of the BNA 1981 (**2.2.3**), an illegitimate person born outside the UK on or after 1 July 2006 is a British citizen if his father was a British citizen otherwise than by descent (see **2.2.5**), or registered or naturalised as a British citizen before the child's birth. What if an illegitimate person can meet these requirements but he was born outside the UK before July 2006? In these circumstances he may apply to register as a British citizen under s 4G of the BNA 1981 (see **2.2.6.3**).

The fact of being born outside the UK after 1982 means that you have to look to the person's parents to see if they might be British. If they are, then their status is that of a British citizen by descent (see **2.2.5.2** and **2.5**). If that person goes on to have their own child born outside the UK, it will only be in limited circumstances that their child will be British (see the detailed requirements for second generation children born abroad at **2.2.5.2**).

EXAMPLES

1. Amelia was born in 1970 in the UK. She is therefore a British citizen otherwise than by descent (see **2.2.5.1**). In 1990 she gave birth to her son, Charles, outside the UK. Charles is a British citizen (by descent: see **2.2.5.2**) as his mother was a British citizen otherwise than by descent at the time of Charles's birth.

2. Benjamin was born in 1972 in the UK. He is therefore a British citizen otherwise than by descent (see **2.2.5.1**). In 1997 he married Adela, a visa national. In 1999 their daughter, Ramona, was born outside the UK. Ramona is a British citizen (by descent: **2.2.5.2**) as her father was a British citizen otherwise than by descent and married to her mother at the time of Ramona's birth.

3. Ethan was born in the UK in 1980. He is therefore a British citizen otherwise than by descent (see **2.2.5.1**). In 2007 his girlfriend, Alice, gave birth to his son, Zach, outside the UK. Alice is a visa national. Zach is a British citizen by descent (see **2.2.5.2**) if the Secretary of State accepts evidence that Ethan is his father.

2.2.5   British citizenship: what about subsequent generations?

2.2.5.1   British citizen otherwise than by descent

A person who acquires British citizenship by birth in the UK (see **2.2.1** and **2.2.3**), or as a child by registration in the UK (see **2.2.6.1**) or as an adult by naturalisation in the UK (see **2.2.7**), is classified as a *British citizen otherwise than by descent*. This means he can automatically pass on British citizenship to a child born outside the UK in the circumstances described at **2.2.2** and **2.2.4** above.

2.2.5.2   British citizen by descent

Where a person is born outside the UK (see **2.2.2** and **2.2.4**) and acquires British citizenship only because one or both of his parents is a British citizen, he is classified as a *British citizen by descent*. This means that he cannot automatically pass on British citizenship to any child who is also born abroad. However, some second-generation children can be registered abroad at the British consulate as British citizens (by descent) if:

(a)   one of the parents is a British citizen by descent; and

(b)   the British parent has a parent who is or was British otherwise than by descent; and

(c)   the British parent had at some time before the child's birth lived in the UK for a continuous period of three years, not being absent for more than 270 days in that period.

In these circumstances a child is registered as a British citizen by descent – the registration takes place outside the UK and is based not on any residence in the UK by the child but by his British parent in the past before the child's birth.

UKVI guidance gives the following example.

- The child's maternal grandfather was born in the UK in 1949.
- The child's mother was born in France in 1970 (and is a British citizen by descent). She lived in the UK from September 1989 to September 1992 (and was not outside the UK for more than 270 days during that time).
- The child, born in France in 2009, is not a British citizen but can be registered [under BNA 1981, s 3(2)].

What if (a) and (b) are met but not (c)? It will be possible to register the child in the UK as a British citizen if during his childhood his father and mother come and live in the UK with him for a continuous period of three years and are not absent during that time for more than 270 days. Note that the requirement is that both parents live in the UK unless one of them is dead or the couple have divorced or their civil partnership has ended. Both parents must consent to the child being registered as a British citizen, but if one of the parents has died then only the consent of the surviving parent is required. In these circumstances a child is registered as a British citizen otherwise than by descent because the registration takes place in the UK and is based on the family's residence in the UK.

EXAMPLE

James was born in Germany in 1975. His father, Larry, was born in London, England in 1945. Larry had married James's mother in 1965. In 1990, James married Steffi, a German national. In 2005, their son, Thomas, was born in Germany.

Larry was born before 1983 in the UK and is therefore a British citizen otherwise than by descent. His son, James, was born outside the UK before 1983 and is therefore British by descent. Thomas can be registered as a British citizen by descent if James has lived in the UK at some time for a continuous period of three years before Thomas's birth.

What if James has not lived in the UK for the requisite period before Thomas's birth or, alternatively, the family are just about to move to the UK to live there permanently? If James, Steffi and Thomas all come to live in the UK whilst Thomas is still a child, and do so for a continuous period of three years, Thomas may be registered as a British citizen otherwise than by descent under BNA 1981, s 3(5).

Can a British citizen by descent apply for naturalisation as a British citizen (see **2.2.7**) in order that his children born abroad automatically become British citizens? No, held the Court of Appeal in the case of R v *Secretary of State for the Home Department, ex p Azad Ullah* [2001] INLR 74.

2.2.6 Registration as a British citizen

2.2.6.1 Child born in the UK after 1982

A child can apply to register as a British citizen, pursuant to s 1(3) and (4) of the BNA 1981, if he was born in the UK after 1982 and, after his birth:

(a) one of his parents becomes a British citizen or settled in the UK (see **3.8**) before he is 18; or

(b) he remains in the UK for the first 10 years of his life and is not absent for more than 90 days each year during that period. By s 1(7), a longer period of absence may be acceptable.

As we saw at **2.2.3**, an illegitimate child born in the UK after 1982 and before July 2006, who would otherwise automatically be a British citizen, can apply for registration under s 4F of the BNA 1981.

Such a person is a British citizen otherwise than by descent (see **2.2.5.1**).

2.2.6.2 Child born outside the UK before 1983

As we saw at **2.2.2**, a British mother could not before 1983 transmit her British citizenship acquired in the UK to her child born outside the UK. However, by concession, the Home Office did allow such a child to be registered as British (by descent), provided the application was made before the child reached 18. What if no such registration occurred, given that the concession, by its very nature, expired at the end of 2000? Section 4C of the BNA 1981 now gives a right to such a person born before 1 January 1983 to apply to register as a British citizen.

Such a person is a British citizen by descent (see **2.2.5.2**).

2.2.6.3 Child born outside the UK after 1982

As we saw at **2.2.4**, an illegitimate child born outside the UK after 1982 and before July 2006, who would otherwise automatically be a British citizen, can apply for registration under s 4G of the BNA 1981.

Such a person is a British citizen by descent (see **2.2.5.2**).

2.2.7 Naturalisation

If a foreign national adult living in the UK has settled status (see **1.4.5** and **3.8**), he may wish to apply to become a British citizen (otherwise than by descent) by a process known as naturalisation. Under s 6 of the BNA 1981, the Home Secretary has a discretion to grant a certificate of naturalisation to any person aged 18 or over who is not a British citizen. The grant of British citizenship under s 6 is not a fundamental human right: *R v Secretary of State for the Home Department, ex p Al Fayed* [2001] Imm AR 134 and *R (AHK) v Secretary of State for the Home Department* [2009] EWCA Civ 287. As Blake J stated at first instance in AHK (in a judgment entitled *MH v Secretary of State for the Home Department* [2008] EWHC 2525, at [41]), 'In general terms … no claimant [under s 6] has a right to British citizenship, but only a right to have an application fairly considered under the statutory scheme.'

The requirements are slightly different, depending on whether or not the applicant is married to or in a civil partnership with a British citizen at the time the application is made. Broadly, those requirements are as follows.

2.2.7.1 If the applicant is married to, or in a civil partnership with, a British citizen

The applicant:

(a)   must be settled (see **3.8**) at the time of the application;

(b)   must have been living in the UK legally for at least three years continuously before making the application;

(c)   must have been physically present in the UK on the date three years before the application is made. The start of the qualifying period of three years is the day after the corresponding application date. So, for example, if the application is received by the Home Office on 7 January 2020, the three-year qualifying period starts on 8 January 2016;

(d)   must not have been absent for more than 270 days in total during the three-year qualifying period, and not more than 90 days in the year immediately before the application. Only a whole day's absence from the UK counts. So, an applicant who leaves the UK on 1 January and returns on 2 January is not treated as being absent, ie the day of leaving and the day of return are ignored. The Home Office has indicated that it will normally disregard 30 days and 10 days respectively over these limits, provided all the other requirements are met. If the absences are greater than that or occur in the final year of the application, see the Home Office guidance, 'Naturalisation Booklet – The

Requirements' on the Home Office website (see **1.2.8**). What is the purpose of this residence requirement? Home Office guidance is that it allows an applicant to demonstrate close links with, and commitment to, the UK, and enables the Home Secretary to assess the strength of that commitment as well as the applicant's suitability on the other grounds;

(e) must have (i) sufficient knowledge of the English language and (ii) sufficient knowledge about life in the UK. How can an applicant demonstrate this? The answer is to be found in the British Nationality (General) Regulations 2003 (SI 2003/548, as amended), reg 5A. Broadly, the requirements are that the applicant:

(i) demonstrates knowledge of the English language by:

(A) possessing a Home Office approved qualification or passing a Home Office prescribed test as specified in Sch 2A to the 2003 Regulations; or

(B) possessing a degree which the Home Office accepts was taught in English (see **7.3.4**); or

(C) having met this requirement when making an earlier, successful application for indefinite leave to remain (see **3.8.7**); or

(D) satisfying the Secretary of State that he is a national of a Home Office designated majority English speaking country (see the list of relevant nationalities at **7.3.4**);

(ii) demonstrates knowledge about life in the UK by passing the test known as the 'Life in the UK Test' administered by a Home Office approved educational institution.

What is the 'Life in the UK Test'? The test has to be taken on a computer and consists of 24 questions, such as: where is the Prime Minister's official home in London, and is it true or false that UK citizens can vote in an election at the age of 18? It is based on the Government handbook, 'Life in the United Kingdom: A Guide for New Residents'. It can be taken only at an official testing centre. Note that in Wales and Scotland the test can be taken in Welsh or Scottish Gaelic, as appropriate. Full details can be found in the Home Office Guidance: 'Knowledge of language and life in the UK' on its website (see **1.2.8**).

In what circumstances will the Home Office waive these requirements? If the applicant is suffering from a long-term illness or disability that severely restricts his ability to learn English or prepare for the Life in the UK test, or has a mental condition and is not able to speak or learn the relevant language.

What other physical conditions may prevent an applicant from meeting the requirement? The Home Secretary will consider how the condition would stop the applicant from taking the Life in the UK test or learning English, for example, if the applicant is deaf or without speech or has a speech impediment which limits his ability to communicate in the relevant language.

Life in the UK test centres and many colleges can cater for a variety of disabilities, such as blindness. An applicant may be able to do the test even if he produces evidence of a disability.

If an applicant wishes to seek a waiver of this requirement, their application must be accompanied by written confirmation in a prescribed form from a registered medical practitioner that the waiver applies and how; and

(f) must show good character. This requirement is not defined in the BNA 1981. In R (Thamby) v Secretary of State for the Home Department [2011] EWHC 1763 Parker J stated, at [41]:

> It is a term capable of carrying a range of meanings, and requires an exercise in evaluation to apply it. It is established that this means that the proper approach of the courts to considering the standard of good character adopted by the Secretary of State and the application of the concept in a particular case is to ask whether the standard and its application were such as could

reasonably be adopted in the circumstances: *ex p Al Fayed* [2001] Imm AR 134, [41] (Nourse LJ), [93] (Kennedy LJ) and [97] (Rix LJ). It is open to the Secretary of State, so long as she acts rationally, to adopt a high standard of good character, and one higher than other reasonable decision-makers might have adopted: *ex p Al Fayed* at [41] (Nourse LJ).

The onus is on the applicant to establish his good character (R *(on the application of DA (Iran)) v Secretary of State for the Home Department* [2014] EWCA Civ 654). Home Office guidance is that it will not normally consider an applicant to be of good character if there is information to suggest any of the following: he has not respected and/or is not prepared to abide by the law; he has been involved in or associated with war crimes, crimes against humanity or genocide, terrorism or other actions that are considered not to be conducive to the public good; his financial affairs are not in appropriate order; his activities are notorious and cast serious doubt on his standing in the local community; he has been deliberately dishonest or deceptive in his dealings with the UK Government; he has assisted in the evasion of immigration control or he has previously been deprived of citizenship.

The applicant must disclose on the application form details of all criminal convictions both within and outside the UK. Any overseas conviction or non-custodial sentence will be treated in the same way as one imposed in the UK unless it is for behaviour that is considered legitimate in the UK, such as homosexuality or membership of a trade union. So what convictions affect an application? **Table 2.1** gives examples of sentences, along with the relevant sentence-based threshold. In calculating the threshold, it is the prison sentence that counts, not the time served. Note that a suspended sentence counts as if it were a non-custodial sentence unless that sentence is subsequently activated.

Table 2.1 Criminality requirement

Sentence	Impact on nationality application
4 years' or more imprisonment	Application should be refused, regardless of when the conviction occurred
Between 12 months' and 4 years' imprisonment	Application should be refused unless 15 years have passed since the end of the sentence
Up to 12 months' imprisonment	Application should be refused unless 10 years have passed since the end of the sentence.
A non-custodial sentence or other out of court disposal	Application should be refused if the conviction occurred in the last 3 years.

What count as non-custodial sentences? These include community penalties, a fine and a conditional or absolute discharge.

What count as out of court disposals? These include a simple or conditional caution, youth caution, warning or reprimand. A fixed penalty notice, often imposed for traffic offences, will not normally result in refusal unless the applicant has failed to pay it or has unsuccessfully challenged the notice and there were subsequent criminal proceedings resulting in a conviction.

UKVI guidance is that there is no set number of non-custodial sentences or other out of court disposals that will lead to an application being refused. However, the higher the number, the more likely it is that the application will be refused, and a series of minor offences or disposals in a short space of time may be seen as a pattern of sustained anti-social behaviour or disregard for the law which will be relevant to the assessment of the applicant's character.

What other behaviour is likely to count against an applicant? UKVI guidance includes the following:

Where there is information to suggest on the balance of probabilities that bankruptcy fraud has taken place, the application will normally be refused.

The following matters should not normally, of themselves, be relevant to assessing good character:

- divorce, separation, or other marital or domestic problems
- promiscuity or sexual preference within the law
- drinking or gambling
- eccentricity, including beliefs, appearance and lifestyle
- unemployment, working habits or other legitimate means of support.

However, where there is evidence that [an applicant] has, by the scale and persistence of their behaviour, made themselves notorious in their local or the wider community, [a decision maker] must consider refusing the application. This may for example be evidenced through media reporting, items on social media or information provided by members of the public

An application will not normally be refused based on the actions of the [applicant's] child or children. This includes where the [applicant's] child has been convicted of a criminal offence, issued with an anti-social behaviour order [or given an out of court disposal]. However, an application will normally be refused where the evidence suggests that the [applicant] parent's own behaviour demonstrates that they are not of good character. [Refusal is normally] limited to cases where [applicant] parents encouraged or were complicit in the criminal activity or were particularly negligent in their dealings with the authorities.

Are there any exceptional cases where on the facts the application would normally be refused but there are sufficient mitigating circumstances to justify granting naturalisation? UKVI guidance gives three examples:

- the [applicant's] criminal conviction is for an offence which is not recognised in the UK or there is no comparable offence
- the [applicant] has one single non-custodial sentence which occurred within the first 2 years of the preceding 3 (such as the person has had no offences within the last 12 months), and there are strong factors which suggest the [applicant] is of good character in all other regards so the decision to refuse would be disproportionate
- the applicant has one single conviction but has lived in the UK all their life or since a very young age and the conviction was many years ago

2.2.7.2 If the applicant is neither married to, nor in a civil partnership with, a British citizen

The applicant:

(a) must have been settled (see **3.8**) for at least one year before the application;

(b) must have been living in the UK legally for five years continuously before making the application;

(c) must have been physically present in the UK on the date five years before the application is received by the Home Office;

(d) must not have been absent for more than 450 days in total during the five-year qualifying period, and not more than 90 days in the year immediately before the application is made (see **2.2.7.1(d)** for Home Office policy where this is exceeded);

(e) must have sufficient knowledge of the English language and sufficient knowledge about life in the UK (see **2.2.7.1(e)**);

(f) must show good character (see **2.2.7.1(f)**); and

(g) must show an intention to live in the UK. Home Office guidance is that this requirement is usually met if the applicant's stated intention is to have his home or, if more than one, his principal home in the UK. Factors affecting this will include whether a home here (owned or rented) has already been established and the reason for any past or intended future absences.

2.2.8   Formalities for registration and naturalisation

These are governed by the BNA 1981 and the British Nationality (General) Regulations 2003 (SI 2003/548). In particular, applicants of full age are required to make an oath of allegiance and pledge. The latter states that the person will respect the rights and freedoms of the UK and will uphold its democratic values, observe its laws, and fulfil the duties and obligations of citizenship.

2.2.9   Deprivation of citizenship obtained by registration or naturalisation

This is governed by s 40 of the BNA 1981 and the British Nationality (General) Regulations 2003 (SI 2003/548). The Secretary of State may by order deprive a person of his British citizenship status if satisfied that it would be conducive to the public good. Home Office guidance is that this can be done in cases involving national security, terrorism, serious organised crime, war crimes and unacceptable behaviour such as preaching *jihad*.

The Secretary of State may also by order deprive a person of his British citizenship status where it was obtained by registration or naturalisation, if satisfied that such was obtained by means of fraud, false representation or concealment of a material fact. But note that naturalisation obtained by fraudulent impersonation is null and void (R (*on the application of Hysaj) v Secretary of State for the Home Department* [2015] EWCA Civ 1195).

The Secretary of State may not normally make either of the above orders if it would make a person stateless, unless he reasonably believes that the person can acquire another nationality or citizenship: see *Al-Jedda v Secretary of State for the Home Department* [2010] EWCA Civ 212. The Court held that the burden is on the appellant to show on the balance of probabilities that he will become stateless. See also *B2 v Secretary of State for the Home Department* [2013] EWCA Civ 616 and *Pham v Secretary of State for the Home Department* [2015] UKSC 19 for discussion of the meaning of statelessness under the BNA 1981. If a person claims that the Secretary of State's decision renders him stateless, then that is a ground of appeal against the deprivation decision to the Special Immigration Appeals Commission (see R (*on the application of Islam) v Secretary of State for the Home Department* [2019] EWHC 2169 (Admin)).

Before making a deprivation order the Secretary of State must give the person concerned written notice specifying that a decision has been made to make the order and the reasons for it. The notice must also advise the person of his right to appeal (see **Chapter 11**). Does the fact that the person has to conduct his appeal from outside the UK render the exclusion decision procedurally unfair? No, held the Court of Appeal in *GI v Secretary of State for the Home Department* [2012] EWCA Civ 867. On appeal, the Commission has to ask itself 'does the evidence in the case establish that citizenship was obtained by fraud?' If it does then it has to answer the question 'do the other circumstances of the case point to discretionary deprival?' See *Arusha and Demushi (deprivation of citizenship – delay)* [2012] UKUT 80 (IAC).

In *BA (deprivation of citizenship: appeals) Ghana* [2018] UKUT 85 (IAC), it was held that where the Secretary of State has decided in the exercise of their discretion to deprive a person of their British citizenship, the Tribunal can allow an appeal only if satisfied that the reasonably foreseeable consequence of deprivation would violate the obligations of the UK government under the Human Rights Act 1998 and/or that there is some exceptional feature of the case which means the discretion should be exercised differently.

In *Pham v Secretary of State for the Home Department* [2018] EWCA Civ 2064, amongst other matters, the Court was asked whether a person can be deprived of his status as a British citizen on the basis that he has repudiated his obligation of loyalty, and whether a person can be deprived of that status on that basis if he does not pose a risk to national security. The Court answered both questions in the positive.

2.3 COMMONWEALTH CITIZENS WITH RIGHT OF ABODE

There are two categories of Commonwealth citizens who have the right of abode in the UK, ie the right to enter the UK without being subject to immigration controls (see **1.4** and **Chapter 3**). There is a list of Commonwealth countries in **Appendix 9**.

It is important to appreciate that, since 1 January 1983, the only way for any person to acquire the right of abode in the UK has been by becoming a British citizen (see **2.2**). This is because, as you will see below at **2.3.1**, **2.3.2** and **2.3.4**, only certain Commonwealth citizens could acquire the right of abode if they met key requirements on 31 December 1982.

2.3.1 Parental link

The first category concerns those Commonwealth citizens with a 'parental link' to the UK. The requirements (pursuant to IA 1971, s 2(1)(d)) are that:

(a)   the person was a Commonwealth citizen on 31 December 1982, and continues to be such; and

(b)   either parent was born in the UK. 'Parent' in this context includes the mother, but not the father, of an illegitimate child. Does it include the adoptive parents of a legally adopted child? Yes, where the adoption was by order of a UK court or in any country listed in the Schedule to the Adoption (Designation of Overseas Adoptions) Order 1973 or in the Adoption (Recognition of Overseas Adoptions) Order 2013.

> **EXAMPLE**
>
> Bill was born in New Zealand in 1979. His mother, Ada, was born in London, England. His father was a citizen of New Zealand. Assuming that Bill is a citizen of New Zealand under that country's nationality laws and so remained, Bill was a Commonwealth citizen on 31 December 1982. As a Commonwealth citizen, he has the right of abode in the UK by virtue of his mother's birth in the UK. Query if Ada registered him as British in these circumstances before he reached 18 or, if she failed to do so, whether he has applied himself or wishes to now apply (see **2.2.6.2**).

2.3.2 Acquired by marriage

The second category concerns those Commonwealth citizen women who acquired the right of abode by marriage. The requirements (pursuant to IA 1971, s 2(2)) are that:

(a)   the woman was a Commonwealth citizen on 31 December 1982 and continues to be such; and

(b)   on or before 31 December 1982, she married a man who at the time of the marriage was either:

(i)   born, registered or naturalised in the UK, or

(ii)   was a Commonwealth citizen with a right of abode through a parental link (see **2.3.1**).

Note that any subsequent divorce or the death of the husband does not affect her status.

> **EXAMPLES**
>
> 1.   Anna was a citizen of Barbados on 31 December 1982 and continues to be such. In 1980 she married Frank. He had been born in the UK in 1960. Anna acquired the right of abode in the UK by marrying Frank.

> 2.   Barbara was a citizen of Fiji on 31 December 1982 and continues to be such. In 1975 she married Luke. He had been born in Fiji in 1955 and was a Fijian national. His mother had been born in the UK. Provided Barbara can produce evidence that Luke was a Commonwealth citizen with the right of abode by his parental link (see **2.3.1**), she acquired the right of abode by marrying him. There is no requirement that Luke must have obtained his own certificate evidencing his right of abode.

2.3.3 Certificate of entitlement

A Commonwealth citizen with the right of abode will travel under his or her own country's passport. Before travelling to the UK for the first time, he or she should apply to the British High Commission for a certificate showing that right of abode.

To get the certificate in the first category, the applicant will need to produce:

(a)   evidence of being a Commonwealth citizen on 31 December 1982 and that he remains a Commonwealth citizen;

(b)   his own full birth certificate naming the appropriate parent;

(c)   the appropriate parent's full UK birth certificate; and

(d)   if claiming through the father, the parent's marriage certificate or evidence of relationship.

A check should always be made to see if the applicant can claim British citizenship (see **2.2.2**).

To get the certificate in the second category, the applicant will need to produce:

(a)   evidence of being a Commonwealth citizen on 31 December 1982 and that she remains a Commonwealth citizen;

(b)   her marriage certificate; and

(c)   evidence that her husband was either British by birth, registration or naturalisation in the UK (eg his UK birth, registration or naturalisation certificate), or a Commonwealth citizen with his own right of abode (as above).

2.3.4 Excluded Commonwealth nationals

It is important to note that as Cameroon, Mozambique, Namibia, Pakistan and South Africa were not members of the Commonwealth on 31 December 1982, nationals of those countries cannot take advantage of the above provisions.

2.3.5 Deprivation of right of abode

Section 2A of the IA 1971 gives the Secretary of State power to remove this right of abode if it is conducive to the public good to remove or exclude the Commonwealth citizen from the UK. There is a similar power for deprivation of British citizenship (see **2.2.9**).

There is a right of appeal to the IAC or, if issues of national security arise, to the Special Immigration Appeals Commission (see **Chapter 11**).

2.3.6 Flow diagram: summary

We have seen that before 1983 some Commonwealth citizens acquired the right of abode in the UK. The requirements are summarised in the flow diagram at **Appendix 10**.

2.4 HISTORICAL BACKGROUND

One of the difficulties in understanding the law in this area is that a person's citizenship may change over time. Someone born in the UK in 1940 would have had the status of 'British subject' at common law. Under the British Nationality Act 1948, he would have become a citizen of the UK and colonies (CUKC). Under the BNA 1981, he would become a British citizen. The problem is that his current citizenship status is defined in the legislation in terms of his earlier status. Thus, it is necessary to know a little of the history of citizenship law – in particular, three major developments, illustrated in the diagram that follows.

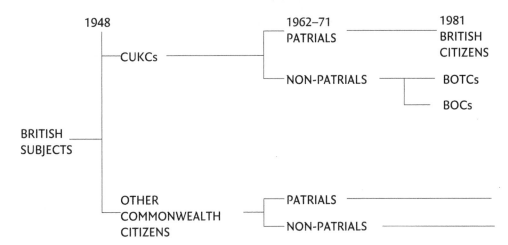

The terms used in the diagram have the broad meanings set out in **2.4.1** to **2.4.7** below.

2.4.1 British subjects

Before 1948, anyone who owed allegiance to the Crown, regardless of the Crown territory in which he was born.

2.4.2 CUKCs

After 1948, anyone connected with the UK or a Crown colony (such as Hong Kong).

2.4.3 Commonwealth citizens

After 1948, anyone having citizenship of an independent Commonwealth country, according to the law of that country. Independent Commonwealth countries included the former Dominions (eg Canada, Australia, New Zealand) and also former colonies (eg Jamaica) when they gained independence. On independence, existing citizens who were CUKCs might lose that status by becoming citizens of the newly independent Commonwealth country. The current list of countries whose citizens are Commonwealth citizens is given in **Appendix 9**. In addition, anyone who has British citizenship, British overseas territories citizenship or British overseas citizenship (see **2.4.5** to **2.4.7** below) is also a Commonwealth citizen.

2.4.4 Patrials

Anyone who under the IA 1971 had the right of abode in the UK. Until 1962, Commonwealth citizens and CUKCs could enter the UK freely. From that year, controls were introduced which were finally enacted in the 1971 Act. The controls extended to both CUKCs and Commonwealth citizens, but CUKCs and Commonwealth citizens who had a close connection with the UK were recognised as 'patrials', having the right of abode.

2.4.5 British citizens

Anyone who at 1 January 1983 was a CUKC with right of abode in the UK, and anyone who acquired British citizenship after that date (eg by birth in the UK, see **2.2.1**). British citizenship and the following categories of citizenship were created by BNA 1981.

2.4.6 British overseas territories citizens (BOTCs)

Anyone who at 1 January 1983 was a non-patrial CUKC, with a close connection with a colony, together with those later becoming BOTCs (eg by birth in the colony). The list of British overseas territories is given in **Appendix 11** to this book. By the Overseas Territories Act 2002, all BOTCs were granted British citizenship.

2.4.7   British overseas citizens (BOCs)

Anyone who at 1 January 1983 was a non-patrial CUKC, but without a close connection with a colony. This category included CUKCs living in a colony which gained independence, who did not acquire citizenship of the newly independent country (eg those of Asian origin in former colonies in East Africa).

This list is not exhaustive. There are other minor categories such as British protected persons, British nationals (overseas) and British subjects under the 1981 Act. In January 2021, the Government created a new category of Hong Kong BN(O) Visa for British nationals (overseas) citizens and their close family members who normally live in Hong Kong or the UK.

The following other major categories of citizens were unaffected by these changes in UK law.

2.4.8   Irish citizens

Citizens of the Republic of Ireland. They were not Commonwealth citizens under the British Nationality Act 1948. They are not subject to immigration controls (see **3.9**, Common Travel Area), but may be liable to deportation (see **Chapter 10**).

2.4.9   Aliens

Broadly, anyone who does not fall into the above categories. Immigration controls were introduced for aliens in 1905. They do not have the right of abode. However, UK law does permit dual nationality, so that someone who lacks the right of abode as an alien, may nevertheless have it if he can also claim British citizenship.

2.5   SUMMARY OF BRITISH CITIZENSHIP

A summary of British citizenship is set out in **Table 2.2** below.

Table 2.2 Summary of British Citizenship

	British citizen otherwise than by descent	British citizen by descent
Born in the UK before 1983	X	
Born in the UK after 1982 and either parent a British citizen or settled in the UK.	X	
Born in the UK after 1982 and subsequently either parent becomes a British citizen or settled in the UK before applicant is 18.	X	
Born in the UK after 1982 and remains in the UK for the first 10 years of life, and is not absent for more than 90 days each year during that period.	X	
Born outside UK before 1983 and father born, registered or naturalised in the UK and married to mother (or parents subsequently marry in a country where that marriage operates to legitimise the child).		X
Born outside UK before 1983 and mother born, registered or naturalised in the UK and registered child before reached 18 (or registers subsequently).		X
Born outside UK after 1982 and either parent a British citizen otherwise than by descent		X

	British citizen otherwise than by descent	British citizen by descent
Born outside UK after 1982 and one parent a British citizen by descent; and the British parent has a parent who is or was British otherwise than by descent; and the British parent had at some time before the child's birth lived in the UK for a continuous period of three years, not being absent for more than 270 days in that period.		X
Born outside UK after 1982 and one parent a British citizen by descent; and the British parent has a parent who is or was British otherwise than by descent; and the family lives in the UK during applicant's childhood for a continuous period of three years and is not absent during that time for more than 270 days.	X	
Naturalised in UK	X	

IMMIGRATION STATUS

3.1 IMMIGRATION CONTROLS

As we saw at **1.4**, a person with the right of abode in the UK (British citizens – see **2.2** – and certain Commonwealth citizens – see **2.3**) can enter without being subject to any immigration controls. All that person has to do is produce documentary evidence of that right of abode, usually a British passport or a Commonwealth country passport with a certificate of the right of abode.

Irish citizens are not subject to immigration controls (see **2.4.8**).

Everyone else is subject to immigration controls. Full details are given at **3.4**.

3.2 IMMIGRATION RULES

3.2.1 An overview

You will find it useful to take a brief look at the contents of the Immigration Rules. You will see that they start with a brief introduction, and importantly there are some useful definitions of key terms in para 6. The Rules are then divided into numbered Parts, each Part dealing with a discrete topic. So, for example, Part 1 sets out the general provisions regarding leave to enter or remain in the UK.

3.2.2 Structure

Parts 2 to 8 of the Rules and numerous Appendices set out the various different categories of entry to the UK. Why is the structure of the Rules for some categories different from others? This is because some categories require entry clearance, whilst a few do not for non-visa nationals. Also, some categories can lead to settlement, whilst others cannot.

Following the Law Commission's Report of January 2020 on Simplifying the Immigration Rules (Law Com No 388), the Government introduced in November the first tranche of new thematic rules. Until all the rules have been updated, the 'old' and 'new' terminology will have to sit side by side. The most common example is that of leave to enter and leave to remain, now often collectively referred to as permission.

3.2.3 Legal status of the requirements

After entering the UK an entrant does not commit a criminal offence by no longer meeting any particular requirement. For example, a student may no longer be following any course of study at all (see *OO v Secretary of State for the Home Department* [2008] EWCA Civ 747). However, if that comes to the attention of the Home Office, it may cancel the leave by what is still often called curtailment (see **3.7**). If an application is made to extend or vary the leave (see **3.6**), it is likely to be refused.

3.3 CONDITIONS OF LIMITED LEAVE (PERMISSION)

By s 3(1) of the IA 1971, a person granted limited leave (or permission) to enter or remain in the UK may be subject to all or any of the following conditions:

(a)   a condition restricting his employment or occupation in the UK;

(b)   a condition requiring him to maintain and accommodate himself, and any dependants of his, without recourse to public funds;

(c)   a condition requiring him to register with the police;

(d)   a condition requiring him to report to an immigration officer or the Secretary of State; and

(e)   a condition about residence.

3.3.1 Restricting employment or occupation

The category of entry will determine the nature of this condition, and the answer can be found by looking at the relevant paragraph under which leave (permission) is granted. For example, a student may work only within prescribed guidelines (see **6.6.4**). An innovator is not permitted to take employment other than working for the business or businesses that they have established (see **7.4**).

Note that para 6 defines 'employment' as including paid and unpaid employment, paid and unpaid work placements undertaken as part of a course or period of study, self-employment and engaging in business or any professional activity.

3.3.2 Not to have recourse to public funds

3.3.2.1 What are public funds?

All entrants with limited leave (permission) are subject to a condition not to have recourse to public funds. This is because all entrants are supposed to be self-sufficient and able to maintain and accommodate themselves and any dependants. So what count as public funds? All that follow:

(a)   housing of homeless persons under Pts VI or VII of the Housing Act 1996 and under Pt II of the Housing Act 1985;

(b)   the non-means tested welfare benefits of attendance allowance, carer's allowance, child benefit, personal independence payment, and disability living allowance;

(c)   the means-tested benefits of universal credit, income support, income-related employment and support allowance, income-based jobseeker's allowance, council tax benefit and a council tax reduction under a council tax reduction scheme, housing benefit, State pension credit, child tax credit and working tax credit; and

(d)   a Social Fund payment.

The following do not count as public funds:

(a)   the National Insurance-based welfare benefits of contribution-based jobseeker's allowance, contributory employment and support allowance, State pension and bereavement benefits;

(b)   National Health Service treatment (paid or unpaid), state-funded schooling in academy or maintained schools, and education in 16–19 academies.

As to (b), the Department for Health has its own rules on whether people who are not ordinarily resident in the UK can receive free NHS treatment (see the National Health Service (Charges to Overseas Visitors) Regulations 2015 (as amended)). NHS treatment does not count as public funds for the purposes of the Immigration Rules whether it is paid or unpaid. The law requires all children of compulsory school age to have access to education, meaning that compulsory school age education does not count as public funds for the purposes of the Immigration Rules.

3.3.2.2   Additional public funds

Very often entry to the UK is for the purposes of family reunion (see **Chapter 8**), for example a child joining a parent who is already settled in the UK. The person settled in the UK is often known as the 'sponsor'. If a sponsor already receives public funds, will entry clearance be refused? Paragraph 6 makes an important qualification to this condition. It states that

> For the purpose of these Rules, a person (P) is not to be regarded as having (or potentially having) recourse to public funds merely because P is (or will be) reliant in whole or in part on public funds provided to P's sponsor unless, as a result of P's presence in the United Kingdom, the sponsor is (or would be) entitled to increased or additional public funds (save where such entitlement to increased or additional public funds is by virtue of P and the sponsor's joint entitlement to benefits under the regulations referred to in paragraph 6B).

So, for example, if P seeks entry clearance to live permanently with his sponsor (S) in the UK, the application will not necessarily fail if S already receives one or more of the public funds. It will fail, however, if S becomes entitled either to an increase in the amount of his existing public funds, or to another public fund because of P's joining S in the UK.

Paragraph 6 then provides as follows:

> Subject to paragraph 6C, a person (P) shall not be regarded as having recourse to public funds if P is entitled to benefits specified under section 115 of the Immigration and Asylum Act 1999 by virtue of regulations made under subsections (3) and (4) of that section or section 42 of the Tax Credits Act 2002.

Normally a person with limited leave to enter or remain in the UK (permission) is excluded from claiming mainstream welfare benefits (including those on the public funds list) by s 115 of the IAA 1999. However, a claim might be made by such a person if he meets the exceptions in subsections (3) and (4). Also, if the person has a partner who is entitled to apply for child and/or working tax credits, uniquely the application can be made jointly, and both count when the tax credits are calculated under the 2002 Act.

Paragraph 6 also provides as follows:

> A person (P) making an application from outside the United Kingdom will be regarded as having recourse to public funds where P relies upon the future entitlement to any public funds that would be payable to P or to P's sponsor as a result of P's presence in the United Kingdom (including those benefits to which P or the sponsor would be entitled as a result of P's presence in the United Kingdom under the regulations referred to in to paragraph 6B).

What is the effect of the above provision? First, note that it only concerns an application by P for entry clearance. That application will be refused if P shows that he will be adequately maintained in the UK only by relying upon his or his sponsor's future entitlement to any public funds, including tax credits or those payable to him under the IAA 1999, s 115(3) and (4).

This form of sponsorship should not be confused with the more formal and detailed sponsorship of students, workers and family members under the Immigration Rules (see **Chapters 6,** 7 and **8**). Also see **3.4.4.**

3.3.3   Registration with the police

Adult nationals of certain countries are listed in Appendix 2 to the Immigration Rules (see **Appendix 1** to this book) as they are required to register with the police within seven days of arriving in the UK (see Part 10 of the Rules). To register they need to produce their passports and pay a registration fee.

3.3.4   Reporting to an immigration officer or Secretary of State

This condition and the next (**3.3.5**) were introduced by s 16 of the UK Borders Act 2007. The Government's view was that without these powers it was difficult for the Home Office to maintain contact with foreign nationals during the currency of their limited leave, and to enforce their removal should that leave (permission) be cancelled (see **3.7**). The Government stated that it would apply these conditions to foreign national criminals, who cannot currently be removed due to the ECHR, and to certain children about whom there are particular concerns or who have been placed on discretionary leave (see **9.10**) with a view to their removal when they reach 18.

3.3.5   Residence

See **3.3.4** above.

3.3.6   Consequences of breach of a condition

Although it is an offence under s 24(1)(b) of the IA 1971 for a person with limited leave knowingly to breach a condition of leave (permission), it is unusual for the Home Office to prosecute. Government policy is that if the breach is sufficiently serious, the person should be removed from the UK (see **10.4**).

3.4   ENTRY CLEARANCE

3.4.1   The general rule

The entry clearance procedure is, in effect, a form of pre-entry control, in which a UK official known as a visa or entry clearance officer (ECO) acts as an immigration officer, applying the Immigration Rules, but usually in the country in which the entrant is living before travel to the UK.

The form of clearance depends on the nationality of the entrant. The Immigration Rules specify countries whose nationals (known as 'visa nationals') require entry clearance in the form of a visa (usually stamped on the passport). A list of these countries is given in Appendix Visitor: Visa National list to the Immigration Rules (**Appendix 1** to this book). In the case of some 'non-visa nationals', entry clearance is required for a stay of more than six months (see **2.1**). In this case, the entry clearance is shown by a different stamp, known as an entry certificate (see para 25 of the Immigration Rules).

An applicant for entry clearance as a visitor must apply to a particular designated post. However, any other type of application must be made to the appropriate designated post in the country or territory where the applicant is living. Applicants from certain countries can apply on-line (see the details at <www.gov.uk/apply-to-come-to-the-uk>). Once they have submitted their on-line applications they are given an appointment to produce their original passports and supporting documents, and pay the appropriate fees if they have not already done so on-line. At that appointment the applicant's biographic and biometric data are collected (see **3.4.3**). These are then transmitted to the UK for checks.

Nationals listed in Appendix T of the Immigration Rules must undergo compulsory screening for active pulmonary tuberculosis if applying to enter the UK for more than six months.

Forms and guidance notes for making an application can be found at www.gov.uk/apply-to-come-to-the-uk.

3.4.2 Leave (permission) under the Immigration and Asylum Act 1999

The IAA 1999 provides for greater flexibility in the way permission to enter the UK and to remain may be granted. Instead of leave to enter always having to be given in writing at a port of entry, the IAA 1999 allows for additional ways of giving leave to enter to be specified, eg that a visa or other entry clearance is to be treated as leave to enter (permission). This means that holders of visas, for example, will be able to pass through the port control with only a quick check on identity and on the rightful ownership of the travel document and entry clearance, unless there is a need to examine for, among other matters, change of circumstances. Currently, citizens of an EU country, Australia, Canada, Iceland, Japan, Liechtenstein, New Zealand, Norway, Singapore, South Korea, Switzerland and the USA aged 12 or above are able to enter the UK by swiping their national passports in an electronic passport gate. By doing so they are automatically granted deemed leave for six months as a standard visitor (see art 8B of the Immigration (Leave to Enter and Remain) Order 2000 (as amended) and **5.2**).

Most entry clearance now takes effect as leave to enter (permission) as well. This means that there are two significant dates to look out for on a visa or entry certificate, namely, the *effective date* and the *expiry date*. In most cases, the effective date will be the date on which the entry clearance is issued. However, some people may not intend or be able to travel to the UK immediately following their application, and in these circumstances an ECO will usually exercise his discretion to defer the effective date for up to three months after entry clearance has been authorised. So, in order to avoid the cost of making an unnecessary application for an extension of stay, an applicant should always confirm his date of travel.

For applicants in categories that require a qualifying period to be met before applying for settlement, or who have a limit imposed on their total length of stay in that category, their leave to enter will normally begin on the date they arrive in the UK within the three-month limit. This ensures that the maximum leave to which they are entitled is given.

The expiry date on a visa or entry certificate reflects the date on which the entry clearance and leave to enter are no longer effective. After this date the entry clearance will not be valid for travel to the UK, neither will it confer leave to enter.

3.4.3 Biometric information

All applicants are now routinely required to provide 10-digit fingerscans and a digital photograph when applying for UK entry clearance. The applicant attends a pre-arranged appointment. Fingerprints are taken on a glass screen scan. A digital photograph is taken. The biometric data are stored on a central government database in the UK and checked against UK government records.

Where an applicant is issued with a visa exceeding six months, he will also receive a biometric residence permit. This is a standard credit card size (86mm x 54mm) and includes the applicant's name, date and place of birth, their fingerprints and a photograph of their face, their immigration status and any conditions of their stay.

3.4.4 Financial undertakings

Often entry clearance is sought for the purposes of immediate or ultimate settlement (eg child joining parent in UK, or grandparent joining grandchild in UK or spouse joining partner in UK, etc). The person based in the UK is usually known as 'the sponsor'. See the definition in Immigration Rules, para 6. This does not necessarily mean that that person has signed a written agreement with the DfWP to be financially responsible for the entrant. As para 35 of the Immigration Rules states, '[a] sponsor of a person ... may be asked to give an undertaking in writing to be responsible for that person's maintenance [and] accommodation'. However, it will always be required when the adult dependent relative of a British citizen or a person settled in the UK seeks entry clearance to settle in the UK (see **8.11.6**). As to what constitutes a written undertaking, see *Ahmed v Secretary of State for Work and Pensions* [2005] EWCA Civ 535.

The Home Office uses Sponsorship Undertaking Form SU07. It can be found on the Home Office website (see **1.2.8**).

3.4.5 Refusal of entry clearance and leave

3.4.5.1 Overview

The grounds for refusal of applications for entry clearance, leave (permission) to enter or remain in the UK are set out in Part 9 of the Immigration Rules. These apply equally to settlement. Suitability requirements apply to all routes of entry to the UK and must be met in addition to validity and eligibility requirements.

A person may also have their entry clearance or permission cancelled on suitability grounds.

Decisions on suitability are either mandatory (must) or discretionary (may) and must be compatible with the UK's obligations under the Refugee Convention and the European Convention on Human Rights, which are mainly provided for under other provisions in the Immigration Rules (see **Chapters 9, 10 and 11**).

The grounds of refusal are summarised below. In addition, see also **3.5.4** (additional grounds in respect of leave and permission to enter) and **3.6.5** (additional grounds in respect of leave and permission to remain). Also note that Section 5 of Part 9 sets out additional grounds for cancellation of entry clearance, permission to enter and permission to stay that include ceasing to meet a requirement of the Rules, withdrawal of sponsorship or endorsement grounds, a Student who does not start their course or ceases to study and a Skilled Worker who does not start work or ceases their employment.

Note that Part 9 does not apply to Appendix FM (see **Chapter 8**) save that paras 9.2.2, 9.3.2, 9.4.5, 9.9.2, 9.15.1, 9.15.2, 9.15.3, 9.16.2, 9.19.2, 9.20.1, 9.23.1 and 9.24.1 apply, and para 9.7.3 applies to permission to stay; and para 9.8.2(a) and (c) applies where the application is for entry clearance.

3.4.5.2 Exclusion or deportation order grounds

By para 9.2.1, an application must be refused where:

(a) the Secretary of State has personally directed that the applicant be excluded from the UK; or

(b) the applicant is the subject of an exclusion order; or

(c) the applicant is the subject of a deportation order, or a decision to make a deportation order.

Exclusion of a person from the UK is normally used in circumstances involving national security, international crimes (war crimes, crimes against humanity or genocide), corruption and unacceptable behaviour. The latter may include expressing views which provoke, justify or glorify terrorist violence in furtherance of particular beliefs, seek to provoke others to terrorist acts, provoke other serious criminal activity or seek to provoke others to serious criminal acts or foster hatred which might lead to inter-community violence in the UK.

Entry clearance or permission held by a person must be cancelled where the Secretary of State has personally directed that the person is to be excluded from the UK.

As to deportation, see **Chapter 10**.

3.4.5.3 Non-conducive grounds

By para 9.3.1, an application must be refused where the applicant's presence in the UK is not conducive to the public good because of their conduct, character, associations or other reasons (including convictions which do not fall within the criminality grounds). The Home Office gives the following examples: where a person's admission could adversely affect the conduct of foreign policy; where there is reliable evidence that a person has been involved in criminal activities, even though he has not been convicted; where the person's admission would be contrary to internationally agreed travel restrictions; where the person's admission might lead to infringement of UK law; where the person's admission might lead to an offence being committed by someone else; and where a person's activities are such that his presence in the UK is likely to cause a public order concern. What is involved is an evaluation of risk to the public. The question the ECO must answer is whether or not there is a substantial risk of disorder: see *CB (United States of America) v Entry Clearance Officer (Los Angeles)* [2008] EWCA Civ 1539.

Entry clearance or permission held by a person <u>must</u> be cancelled where the person's presence in the UK is not conducive to the public good.

3.4.5.4 Criminality grounds

By para 9.4.1, an application <u>must</u> be refused where the applicant:

(a) has been convicted of a criminal offence in the UK or overseas for which they have received a custodial sentence of 12 months or more; or

(b) is a persistent offender who shows a particular disregard for the law (see **10.3.6**); or

(c) has committed a criminal offence, or offences, which caused serious harm (see **10.3.5**).

By para 9.4.2, entry clearance or permission held by a person <u>must</u> be cancelled where the person:

(a) has been convicted of a criminal offence in the UK or overseas for which they have received a custodial sentence of 12 months or more; or

(b) is a persistent offender who shows a particular disregard for the law (see **10.3.6**); or

(c) has committed a criminal offence, or offences, which caused serious harm (see **10.3.5**).

What is a custodial sentence? It is defined in para 6 of the Immigration Rules as meaning a period of imprisonment, not including a suspended sentence.

By para 9.4.3, an application <u>may</u> be refused (where paras 9.4.2 and 9.4.4 do not apply) where the applicant:

(a) has been convicted of a criminal offence in the UK or overseas for which they have received a custodial sentence of less than 12 months; or

(b) has been convicted of a criminal offence in the UK or overseas for which they have received a non-custodial sentence, or received an out-of-court disposal that is recorded on their criminal record.

What count as non-custodial sentences? These include community penalties, a fine and a conditional or absolute discharge.

What count as out-of-court disposals recorded on a person's criminal record? These include a simple or conditional caution, youth caution, warning or reprimand. They do not include fixed penalty notices, penalty charge notices and penalty notices for disorder that have been imposed by the police or other authorised enforcement officers for traffic violations, environmental and civil violations.

By para 9.4.4, an application for entry clearance or permission to enter under Appendix V: Visitor (see **Chapter 5**), or where a person is seeking entry on arrival in the UK for a stay for less than six months, <u>must</u> be refused where the applicant:

(a)   has been convicted of a criminal offence in the UK or overseas for which they have received a custodial sentence of less than 12 months, unless more than 12 months have passed since the end of the custodial sentence; or

(b)   has been convicted of a criminal offence in the UK or overseas for which they have received a non-custodial sentence, or received an out-of-court disposal that is recorded on their criminal record, unless more than 12 months have passed since the date of conviction.

By para 9.4.5, entry clearance or permission held by a person may be cancelled (where para 9.4.2. does not apply) where the person:

(a)   has been convicted of a criminal offence in the UK or overseas for which they have received a custodial sentence of less than 12 months; or

(b)   has been convicted of a criminal offence in the UK or overseas for which they have received a non-custodial sentence, or received an out-of-court disposal that is recorded on their criminal record.

Are all overseas convictions relevant? Home Office guidance is that offences do not need to have an identically named provision or carry similar penalties as in the UK, provided that there is a comparable offence, for example homicide and murder. However, offences which do not constitute a criminal offence in the UK are ignored, such as homosexuality and proselytising (attempting to convert someone to another religion).

3.4.5.5   Exclusion from asylum or humanitarian protection grounds

By paras 9.5.1 and 9.5.2, respectively, an application may be refused and entry clearance or permission cancelled where an applicant has been refused asylum or humanitarian protection (see **Chapter 9**).

3.4.5.6   Involvement in a sham marriage or sham civil partnership grounds

By paras 9.6.1 and 9.6.2, respectively, an application may be refused and entry clearance or permission cancelled where the decision maker is satisfied that it is more likely than not that the applicant is, or has been, involved in a sham marriage or sham civil partnership (see **8.3.5.5**).

3.4.5.7   False representations, etc grounds

By para 9.7.1, an application may be refused where, in relation to the application, or in order to obtain documents from the Secretary of State or a third party provided in support of the application:

(a)   false representations are made, or false documents or false information submitted (whether or not relevant to the application, and whether or not to the applicant's knowledge); or

(b)   relevant facts are not disclosed.

Home Office guidance is that a false representation is made when an applicant or third party lies or makes a false statement in an application, either orally or in writing. It gives the following two examples of false representations:

(i)   A visa applicant states that he is a project manager for a company, earning a significant salary. It is discovered that he is in fact the cleaner for the company on a low salary.

(ii)   An applicant applies for entry clearance on the basis of his marriage to a British citizen, and states in his application form that he has never been married before. But a marriage certificate is received from another wife, which is verified, showing that he is already married.

Does a false statement mean one made dishonestly? Yes: see *AA (Nigeria) v Secretary of State for the Home Department* [2010] EWCA Civ 773. This is because 'a false representation stated in all innocence may be simply a matter of mistake, or an error short of dishonesty' (per Rix LJ at [68]).

What is a false document? Home Office guidance is that this includes a genuine document which has been altered or tampered with; a counterfeit document (one that is completely false); a genuine document that is being used by an impostor; a genuine document which has been fraudulently obtained or issued; and a genuine document which contains a falsified or counterfeit visa or endorsement.

Must the applicant have created the false document or even be aware that it is false? No, as Rix LJ observed in *Adedoyin v Secretary of State for the Home Department* [2010] EWCA Civ 773:

> 67. First, 'false representation' is aligned in the rule with 'false document'. It is plain that a false document is one that tells a lie about itself. Of course it is possible for a person to make use of a false document (for instance a counterfeit currency note, but that example, used for its clarity, is rather distant from the context of this discussion) in total ignorance of its falsity and in perfect honesty. But the document itself is dishonest. It is highly likely therefore that where an applicant uses in all innocence a false document for the purpose of obtaining entry clearance, or leave to enter or to remain, it is because some other party, it might be a parent, or sponsor, or agent, has dishonestly promoted the use of that document.

What about material facts that have not been disclosed? Here the ECO will need to show that the withheld information would have been relevant to his decision. Note that an ECO cannot refuse an applicant on this ground if he has not indicated to the applicant the kind of information that is relevant to the application. The Home Office gives the following example. The wife of a man in the UK who has limited leave to remain as a Skilled Worker (see **7.7**) applies to join her husband as his dependant, but does not mention that the marriage has broken down. The husband has sent a letter stating that the marriage no longer subsists.

By para 9.7.2, an application <u>must</u> be refused where the decision maker can prove that it is more likely than not the applicant used deception in the application.

By para 9.7.3, entry clearance or permission held by a person <u>may</u> be cancelled where, in relation to an application, or in order to obtain documents from the Secretary of State or a third party provided in support of the application:

(a)   false representations were made, or false documents or false information submitted (whether or not relevant to the application, and whether or not to the applicant's knowledge); or

(b)   relevant facts were not disclosed.

By para 9.7.4, permission extended under s 3C of the Immigration Act 1971 (see **3.6.2**) <u>may</u> be cancelled where the decision maker can prove that it is more likely than not that the applicant used deception in the application for permission to stay.

3.4.5.8   Previous breach of immigration laws grounds

By para 9.8.1, an application <u>must</u> be refused if:

(a)   the applicant has previously breached immigration laws; and

(b)   the application is for entry clearance or permission to enter and it was made within the relevant time period in para 9.8.7.

By para 9.8.2, an application <u>may</u> be refused where:

(a)   the applicant has previously breached immigration laws; and

(b)   the application was made outside the relevant time period in para 9.8.7; and

(c)   the applicant has previously contrived in a significant way to frustrate the intention of the rules, or there are other aggravating circumstances (in addition to the immigration breach), such as a failure to cooperate with the redocumentation process, such as using a false identity, or a failure to comply with enforcement processes, such as failing to report, or absconding.

By para 9.8.3, an application for permission to stay <u>may</u> be refused where a person has previously failed to comply with the conditions of their permission, unless permission has been granted in the knowledge of the previous breach.

Paragraph 9.8.4 provides that in paras 9.8.1 and 9.8.2 above, a person will only be treated as having previously breached immigration laws if, when they were aged 18 or over, they:

(a)   overstayed their permission and neither para 9.8.5 nor para 9.8.6. apply; or

(b)   breached a condition attached to their permission (see **3.3**) and entry clearance or further permission was not subsequently granted in the knowledge of the breach; or

(c)   were (or still are) an illegal entrant (see **10.4.2**); or

(d)   used deception in relation to an application (whether or not successfully).

By para 9.8.5, a period of overstaying will be disregarded for the purpose of para 9.8.4(a) where the person left the UK voluntarily, not at the expense (directly or indirectly) of the Secretary of State, and:

(a)   the person overstayed for 90 days or less, where the overstaying began before 6 April 2017; or

(b)   the person overstayed for 30 days or less, where the overstaying began on or after 6 April 2017; or

(c)   para 39E applied to the period of overstaying (see **3.6.5.2**).

By para 9.8.6, a period of overstaying will be disregarded for the purpose of para 9.8.4(a) where the overstaying arose from a decision to refuse an application, or cancellation of permission, which was subsequently withdrawn, or quashed, or reconsidered by direction of a court or tribunal, unless the legal challenge which led to the reconsideration was brought more than three months after the date of the decision to refuse or cancel.

By para 9.8.7, the relevant time period under paras 9.8.1 and 9.8.2 is as set out in **Table 3.1** (and where the person previously breached more than one immigration law, only the breach which leads to the longest period of absence from the UK will be taken into account).

Table 3.1   Relevant time periods

Time from date the person left the UK (or date of refusal of the entry clearance under row (f))	This applies where the applicant	And the applicant left the UK	And the applicant left the UK
(a) 12 months	left voluntarily	at their own expense	N/A
(b) 2 years	left voluntarily	at public expense	within 6 months of being given notice of liability for removal or when they no longer had a pending appeal or administrative review, whichever is later (see **Chapters 10** and **11**)

Time from date the person left the UK (or date of refusal of the entry clearance under row (f))	This applies where the applicant	And the applicant left the UK	And the applicant left the UK
(c) 5 years	left voluntarily	at public expense	more than 6 months after being given notice of liability for removal or when they no longer had a pending appeal or administrative review, whichever is later
(d) 5 years	left or was removed from the UK	as a condition of a caution issued in accordance with s 22 of the Criminal Justice Act 2003 (and providing that any condition prohibiting their return to the UK has itself expired)	N/A
(e) 10 years	was deported or removed from the UK	at public expense	N/A
(f) 10 years	used deception in an application for entry clearance (including a visit visa)	N/A	N/A

> **EXAMPLE**
>
> 1   Alan overstays his leave (permission) by 20 days in May 2017 before departing the UK voluntarily. He pays his own travel costs (so not at the expense (directly or indirectly) of the Secretary of State). As Alan overstayed for less than 30 days after 6 April 2017, any future application will not be subject to para 9.8.1 mandatory refusal.
>
> 2   Brenda overstays her leave (permission) by 100 days before departing the UK in January 2017. She voluntarily departs the UK but at the expense of the Secretary of State. She departs more than six months after being given notice of liability for removal. As Brenda overstayed for more than 90 days before 6 April 2017, any application she makes for entry clearance within five years of leaving the UK will, in these circumstances, be subject to para 9.8.1 mandatory refusal.

By para 9.8.8, permission (including permission extended under s 3C of the Immigration Act 1971 (see **3.6.2**)) <u>may</u> be cancelled where the person has failed to comply with the conditions of their permission (see **3.3**).

3.4.5.9   Failure to provide required information, etc grounds

By paras 9.9.1 and 9.9.2, respectively, an application <u>may</u> be refused and entry clearance or permission cancelled where a person fails without reasonable excuse to comply with a reasonable requirement to:

(a)   attend an interview; or

(b)   provide information; or

(c)   provide biometrics (whether or not requested as part of an application); or

(d)   undergo a medical examination; or

(e)   provide a medical report.

3.4.5.10   Admissibility to the Common Travel Area or other countries grounds

By para 9.10.1, an application <u>must</u> be refused where a person is seeking entry to the UK with the intention of entering another part of the Common Travel Area (see **3.9**) and fails to satisfy the decision maker that they are acceptable to the immigration authorities there.

By para 9.10.2, an application <u>may</u> be refused where a person seeking entry fails to satisfy the decision maker that they will be admitted to another country after a stay in the UK.

3.4.5.11   Debt to the NHS grounds

By para 9.11.1, an application <u>may</u> be refused where a relevant NHS body has notified the Secretary of State that the applicant has failed to pay charges under relevant NHS regulations on charges to overseas visitors (see **3.3.2.1**) and the outstanding charges have a total value of at least £500. Full details can be found in Home Office guidance.

3.4.5.12   Unpaid litigation costs grounds

By para 9.12.1, an application <u>may</u> be refused where a person has failed to pay litigation costs awarded to the Home Office. This ground is often referred to as 'litigation debt' as it concerns money owed to the Home Office where a court or Tribunal has ordered the applicant to pay legal costs. It most commonly arises from an unsuccessful appeal or judicial review. Full details can be found in Home Office guidance.

3.4.5.13   Purpose not covered by the Immigration Rules grounds

By para 9.13.1, an application <u>may</u> be refused where a person is seeking to come to or stay in the UK for a purpose not covered by the Immigration Rules.

3.5   LEAVE (PERMISSION) TO ENTER

3.5.1   The general rule

Leave (or permission) to enter the UK is dealt with in paras 7–11 of the Immigration Rules. Everyone must, on arrival in the UK, produce a passport or other document establishing his nationality and identity. On examination by an immigration officer, the entrant must furnish such information as may be required to enable the officer to decide whether he requires leave to enter, whether leave should be given, and the terms of leave. It is para 2(1) of Sch 2 to the IA 1971 which gives an immigration officer the power to examine any person who arrives in the UK and sets out the purpose for which such an examination is conducted, namely to determine whether:

(a)   he is or is not a British citizen; and, if not,

(b)   if he may or may not enter the UK without leave; and, if not,

(c)   if he has been given leave which is still in force, or should be given leave and for what period or on what conditions (if any), or should be refused leave.

If it is concluded that a person is a British citizen, the immigration officer takes no further action. If he is not a British citizen, however, he will be examined to determine whether or not he requires permission to enter the UK. If a person qualifies for permission (leave) to enter then the immigration officer will go on to decide the length of the leave and any conditions, such as permission to work, which will apply. Finally, if a person does not qualify for leave to enter then the immigration officer may refuse leave to enter.

These controls do not, however, apply to persons arriving from another part of the Common Travel Area (see **3.9**).

3.5.2 Documentary evidence

Documentary evidence to be produced to an immigration officer may include:

(a)   a UK passport: required to be produced by a British citizen as evidence of his right of abode;

(b)   a certificate of entitlement issued by the UK Government: evidence of right of abode which may be produced as an alternative to (a) above (by a Commonwealth citizen who has the right of abode, see **2.3**);

(c)   entry clearance in the form of a visa or entry certificate;

(d)   a non-UK passport or identity card: identity cards may be used as a substitute for a passport by EEA nationals.

3.5.3 Grant of limited leave

The immigration officer grants leave by written notice, usually in the form of a stamp on the entrant's passport. The stamp gives the date and port of entry, the time limit of the leave, and any conditions imposed, but does not indicate the Rule under which leave has been granted.

However, if a person's entry clearance also takes effect as leave to enter the UK (see **3.4.2**), an immigration officer may still question that person to establish that he is the rightful holder of the document, that the document does take effect as limited leave, that the passport is genuine and that there are no circumstances under which the entry clearance should be cancelled (see **3.5.4**).

3.5.4 Refusal of limited leave

An immigration officer may refuse leave to enter the UK on exactly the same grounds that an ECO may refuse entry clearance (see **3.4.5**).

Section 3 of Part 9 of the Immigration Rules sets out additional grounds for refusal of entry on arrival in the UK. These can be summarised as follows.

3.5.4.1 No entry clearance grounds

By para 9.14.1, permission to enter <u>must</u> be refused if the person seeking entry is required under these rules to hold on arrival entry clearance for the purpose for which entry is sought, or the person is a visa national, and the person does not hold the required entry clearance.

3.5.4.2 Failure to produce recognised passport or travel document grounds

By para 9.15.1, permission to enter <u>must</u> be refused if the person seeking entry fails to produce a passport or other travel document that satisfies the decision maker as to their identity and nationality, unless the person holds a travel document issued by the national authority of a state of which the person is not a national and the person's statelessness or other status prevents the person from obtaining a document satisfactorily establishing their identity and nationality.

By para 9.15.2, permission to enter <u>may</u> be refused if the person seeking entry produces a passport or other travel document which:

(a)   was issued by a territorial entity or authority which is not recognised by Her Majesty's Government as a state, or is not dealt with as a government by them; or

(b)   was issued by a territorial entity or authority which does not accept valid UK passports for the purpose of its own immigration controls; or

(c)   does not comply with international passport practice.

Paragraph 9.15.3 provides that entry clearance or permission held by a person <u>may</u> be cancelled where on arrival a person fails to produce a passport or other travel document that meets the requirements in para 9.15.1 or 9.15.2.

3.5.4.3 Medical grounds

By para 9.16.1, permission to enter <u>must</u> be refused where a medical inspector advises that for medical reasons it is undesirable to grant entry to the person, unless the decision maker is satisfied that there are strong compassionate reasons justifying admission.

Paragraph 9.16.2 provides that entry clearance or permission held by a person <u>may</u> be cancelled where a medical inspector advises that for medical reasons it is undesirable to grant entry to the person.

3.5.4.4 Consent for a child to travel grounds

By para 9.17.1, a child <u>may</u> be refused permission to enter if they are not travelling with their parent or legal guardian and, if required to do so, the child's parent or legal guardian fails to provide the decision maker with written consent to the child seeking entry to the UK.

3.5.4.5 Returning residents grounds

By para 9.18.1, a person seeking entry as a returning resident under para 18 of the Immigration Rules (see **3.8.3**) <u>may</u> be refused permission to enter if they fail to satisfy the decision maker that they meet the requirements of that paragraph, or that they are seeking entry for the same purpose as that for which their previous permission was granted.

3.5.4.6 Customs breaches grounds

By para 9.19.1, permission to enter <u>may</u> be refused where the decision maker is satisfied that a person has committed a customs breach, whether or not a criminal prosecution is pursued.

Paragraph 9.19.2 provides that were the decision maker is satisfied that a person has committed a customs breach, whether or not a criminal prosecution is pursued, any entry clearance or permission held by the person <u>may</u> be cancelled.

3.5.4.7 Change of circumstances or purpose grounds

By para 9.20.1, entry clearance or permission held by a person <u>may</u> be cancelled where there has been such a change in circumstances since the entry clearance or permission was granted that it should be cancelled.

Paragraph 9.20.2 provides that entry clearance or permission to enter held by a person on arrival in the UK <u>may</u> be cancelled where the person's purpose in seeking entry is different from the purpose specified in their entry clearance.

3.5.5 Immigration bail

Will a person be detained if a decision on whether or not to grant him leave cannot be made? It is Home Office policy that detention will only be used sparingly and as a last resort. There is a presumption in favour of not detaining and, wherever possible, alternatives to detention must be used. The most common alternative is to grant the person immigration bail pursuant to para 1 of Sch 10 to the Immigration Act 2016. Full details can be found in Home Office guidance notes on its website (see **1.2.8**).

3.5.6 Entry without a passport

By s 2(1) of the Asylum and Immigration (Treatment of Claimants, etc) Act 2004 (AI (TC)A 2004), a person commits an offence if, when seeking leave either to enter or remain in the UK or asylum, he does not have with him a passport (or similar immigration document) which is in force and satisfactorily establishes his identity and nationality or citizenship. By s 2(4) various defences may be raised, such as proving a reasonable excuse for not being in possession of the required document. The defendant has the legal burden of proving the defence on the balance of probabilities: see R v *Navabi and Embaye* [2005] EWCA Crim 2865.

However, note that by s 2(7) the fact that a document was deliberately destroyed or disposed of is not such a reasonable excuse unless it is shown that the destruction or disposal was for a reasonable cause, or that it was beyond the control of the person charged with the offence. So what is a 'reasonable cause'? By s 2(7)(b) this does not include the purpose of (i) delaying the handling or resolution of a claim or application or the taking of a decision, (ii) increasing the chances of success of a claim or application, or (iii) complying with instructions or advice given by a person who offers advice about, or facilitates, immigration into the UK, unless in the circumstances of the case it is unreasonable to expect non-compliance with the instructions or advice.

3.6 LEAVE (PERMISSION) TO REMAIN IN THE UK: EXTENSION AND VARIATION

3.6.1 Application made to Home Office

The general framework is laid down by s 3(3) of the IA 1971, which provides that limited leave (or permission) may be varied, whether by restricting, enlarging, or removing the time limit, or by adding, varying, or removing conditions. If the time limit is removed, the leave becomes indefinite and any conditions cease to have effect. Indefinite leave cannot be varied.

Application for variation is made to the Home Office. Immigration officers have no powers to deal with variations. Application should be made before expiry of the time limit on leave, because overstaying is a criminal offence, and may result in refusal of the application to extend leave.

If the application is granted, an appropriate entry is made in the applicant's passport and that is returned with a covering letter. Any refusal (see **3.6.5**) is notified to the applicant by letter, stating the reasons for the refusal and setting out any rights of review (see **Chapter 11**).

3.6.2 Effect of application on existing leave

By s 3C of the IA 1971, when a person applies for variation of his leave before that leave expires, but it then expires before a decision is taken, the leave is automatically extended to the point at which a decision is made or an appeal is determined or an administrative review is determined. This will protect the immigration status of that person and prevent him from becoming an overstayer. All conditions attached to the leave will still apply. So if a person who entered the UK as a fiancé(e) subsequently applies to stay as a spouse following the marriage, until the variation is granted by the Home Office, the applicant cannot lawfully work (see **8.4.10**). A person will not be able to submit further applications during the leave as extended under this section, although he would be able to vary his original application: this is to ensure that all issues raised are covered by one decision (see further **Chapter 11**).

What is the position of an applicant whose variation application is refused, they fail to appeal in time but the Tribunal allows the appeal to be accepted late? Their s 3C leave will be revived from the date the Tribunal allowed the appeal to be accepted late (see *Akinola v Upper Tribunal* [2021] EWCA Civ 1308).

Note that s 3C will not apply if the application is invalid: see R *(on the application of Mirza) v Secretary of State for the Home Department* [2016] UKSC 63, R *(on the application of Iqbal) v Secretary of State for the Home Department* [2015] EWCA Civ 838 and **3.6.4**.

3.6.3 Switching categories

In many cases, an entrant will apply to vary his leave by switching from one category of entry to another. For example, someone who has entered as a student may wish to remain as the spouse of someone living in the UK. In every case, it will be necessary to check the detailed provisions of the Rules relating to the new category.

Is there any danger in applying to switch categories? The danger is that the Home Office may refuse the application and cancel (curtail) the existing leave (see **3.7**).

3.6.4 Procedure for variation

3.6.4.1 Specified forms

Paragraphs 34 and 34A to 34J of the Immigration Rules lay down the procedure that must be followed for most applications to the Home Office (apart from EEA matters). First, certain applications must be made either by completing the relevant online application process (see para A34A) or on the form specified by the Home Office. An application form is specified when it is posted on the Visas and Immigration (Home Office) pages of the gov.uk website and it is marked on the form that it is a specified form for the purpose of the Immigration Rules. A form comes into force on the date specified on the form and/or in any accompanying announcement.

3.6.4.2 Following the specified forms procedure

It is absolutely vital that an applicant follows the specified form procedure or his application will be invalid. An invalid application is returned to the applicant and treated as if it was never made. Of course, if a valid application is not made in time, the applicant becomes an overstayer liable to removal from the UK (see **3.6.5** and **Chapter 10**).

What will make an application invalid? Any of the following:

(a) failing to use the specified form;

(b) failing to pay the specified fee, or paying it in a manner not specified in the form and/or guidance notes;

(c) failing to complete in full those parts of the specified form marked as mandatory. Every question in these parts of the form must be answered and all the information required given;

(d) failing to provide biographical or biometric information as required;

(e) failing to provide any photographs or documents specified as mandatory (see, for example, R (Fu) v Secretary of State for the Home Department [2010] EWHC 2922);

(f) failing to sign the form as required;

(g) failing to deliver the form in the manner stated on it.

As the requirements for an application to be valid are part of the Immigration Rules there is an element of discretion, but Home Office guidance is that this is limited to exceptional circumstances, such as where an applicant is unable to sign the form or to provide photographs because of a serious illness or accident.

It is vital that the Home Office receives the specified form before the applicant's current leave expires. If possible, therefore, it should be delivered by hand to the public enquiry office and a receipt obtained. If it is posted, the application is treated as made on the day it was posted by reference to the postmark.

If an application is rejected but then re-submitted, and fully complies with the requirements of para 34A, the date of application is the date that it is re-submitted.

UKVI guidance is that where an invalid application is received but a fee has been paid, even if it is the wrong fee, the Home Office will write to the applicant under the specified forms procedure in order to provide them with one opportunity to correct any omission or error. The applicant is given 10 business days to respond to the request. Where the requested information is received and the application is accepted as valid by the Home Office, then the application will be treated as valid from the date it was first made (and not the date the further information was received). The effect of this is that where the original application is made in time and the application is validated by the Home Office at a later date, the applicant's s 3C leave (see **3.6.2**) will start from the date when their extant leave expired, even if the correct fee is not received until after that date.

But what if the requested fee or further information is not received, or it is received but there is still no valid application? In those circumstances, leave will not have been extended by s 3C because the application was invalid from the date it was made, and as it was not validated by the Home Office, it does not give rise to s 3C leave.

EXAMPLE

Barnaby's limited leave expires on 7 January. He makes an application on 7 January to extend his leave but his application is invalid because he fails to include mandatory documents. The Home Office writes to Barnaby asking him to provide those missing documents. Barnaby provides the documents on 16 January and the application is validated. Barnaby's leave will have been extended by s 3C from 8 January.

In the alternative, assume that Barnaby does not provide the missing documents and that his application is rejected as invalid by the Home Office on 24 January. Barnaby will have been without leave (and thereby an overstayer) from 8 January as his leave expired on 7 January.

3.6.5 Refusal by Home Office

An immigration officer may refuse leave to enter the UK on exactly the same grounds that an ECO may refuse entry clearance (see **3.4.5**).

3.6.5.1 Procedural fairness

Where the Home Office is considering to refuse an application because of the applicant's dishonesty or other reprehensible conduct, then as a matter of procedural fairness the Secretary of State should indicate clearly to the applicant that they have this suspicion and give the applicant an opportunity to respond. The Secretary of State should take that response into account before drawing the conclusion that there has been such conduct (see *Secretary of State for the Home Department v Balajigari* [2019] EWCA Civ 673).

3.6.5.2 Overstayers

The provisions for refusal of an application for further leave to remain by an overstayer have changed over time.

From July 2012 until 23 November 2016, an application by an overstayer for further leave to remain after the previous leave had expired by less than 28 days was not refused on that basis.

From 24 November 2016, para 39E of the Immigration Rules provides that an application by an overstayer will not be refused but only if it was made within 14 days of the applicant's leave expiring (as interpreted in *Kalsi v Secretary of State for the Home Department* [2021] EWCA Civ 184) and the Secretary of State accepts that there was a good reason beyond the control of the applicant or his representative for the delay. The explanation for why the application could not be made in time must be provided in or with the application. How do caseworkers make a decision on the application? UKVI guidance is that they should consider the plausibility of the reasons, whether the reason was genuinely outside the applicant's control or whether the applicant has put forward difficulties that could realistically have been overcome, and the credibility of evidence provided. Whilst caseworkers must decide each case on its merits, the following are examples of reasons that might be considered beyond the control of applicants:

- the applicant was admitted to hospital for emergency treatment (evidenced by an official letter verifying the dates of admission and discharge and the nature of the treatment);
- a close family bereavement; or
- an educational institution was not sufficiently prompt in issuing a Confirmation of Acceptance for Studies for a Student – see **Chapter 6**.

3.6.5.3 Additional grounds for refusal

Section 4 of Part 9 of the Immigration Rules sets out two additional grounds for refusal of permission to stay. These can be summarised as follows.

Rough sleeping in the UK

By para 9.21.1, permission to stay <u>may</u> be refused where the decision maker is satisfied that a person has been rough sleeping in the UK and has repeatedly refused offers of suitable support, and has engaged in persistent anti-social behaviour. What is rough sleeping? According to para 6, it is sleeping, or bedding down, in the open air (for example on the street or in doorways) or in buildings or other places not designed for habitation (for example sheds, car parks or stations).

Paragraph 9.21.2 provides that where the decision maker is satisfied that a person has been rough sleeping in the UK and has repeatedly refused offers of suitable support, and has engaged in persistent anti-social behaviour, any permission held by the person <u>may</u> be cancelled.

UKVI guidance is that this ground is not intended to criminalise rough sleeping or to penalise those who inadvertently find themselves temporarily without a roof over their head. Instead, the rule will be applied to those who refuse to engage with the range of available support mechanisms and who engage in persistent anti-social behaviour.

Crew members

By para 9.22.1, where a person has permission to enter as a crew member, an application for permission to stay <u>may</u> be refused, unless permission to stay is granted to fulfil the purpose for which the person has permission to enter.

3.6.6 Overstaying: a summary

Note that by para 6 of the Immigration Rules, 'overstayed' and 'overstaying' mean that an applicant for leave to remain has stayed in the UK beyond the latest of:

(a)   the time limit attached to the last period of leave granted; or

(b)   the period that his leave was extended under ss 3C of the IA 1971 (see **3.6.2**); or

(c)   the date that an applicant receives the notice of invalidity declaring that an application for leave to remain is not a valid application, provided the application was submitted before the time limit attached to the last period of leave expired (see **3.6.4.2**).

3.7 CANCELLATION (CURTAILMENT) OF EXISTING LEAVE (PERMISSION) TO ENTER OR REMAIN

If a person enters the UK in one category and before his limited leave expires he applies to switch to another category, there is a danger not only that the application might be refused but also that the existing leave might be cancelled (or the applicant removed from the UK).

> **EXAMPLE**
>
> Bob enters the UK as a student with 12 months' limited leave. After three months he applies to remain in the UK as the spouse of a British citizen. The suspicion may well be that he never intended to leave the UK because he always intended to marry. Not only might his leave be cancelled, but alternatively he may be removed from the UK as an illegal entrant (see **Chapter 10**).

The power to cancel a person's leave is contained in s 3(3)(a) of the IA 1971. It may be used when a person has failed to comply with certain requirements of the Immigration Rules or has lost the justification for his presence here, eg an employee's job ends. It is only available when a person has limited leave. Guidance from the Home Office is that cancellation should not normally be used unless the person has at least six months' leave outstanding. For details of the grounds for cancellation, see **3.4.5**, **3.5.4** and **3.6.5**.

As cancellation is a matter of Home Office discretion it is not automatic. The burden of proof rests with the Secretary of State. Very often a person will be removed rather than his leave cancelled, eg where a person has failed to disclose relevant facts or has made false representations in order to obtain leave, consideration may be given to cancelling any subsisting leave, but it is more usual to proceed directly to administrative removal (see **Chapter 10**) or, in the case of leave to enter, removal for illegal entry (also **Chapter 10**). Equally, although leave may be cancelled where a person fails to observe the conditions of his leave to enter or remain, normally the Home Office proceeds direct to administrative removal for breach of conditions (see **Chapter 10**). Cancellation therefore is normally considered only where the person's actions are not so serious as to merit enforcement action, but where it would be inappropriate to let him remain for the duration of his leave.

3.8 SETTLEMENT

3.8.1 What is it?

A person is settled according to the definition in s 33(2A) of the IA 1971 if he is ordinarily resident in the UK without being subject under the immigration laws to any restriction on the period for which he may remain. The status will be acquired by a person given unlimited leave who satisfies the 'ordinary residence' test (see **3.8.2**). A person who has been given indefinite leave to remain in the UK would not be 'settled' in the UK under the IA 1971, if he has emigrated to another country and is no longer ordinarily resident in the UK.

A person who is settled in the UK has, subject to the Immigration Rules, the right to continue to live in the UK. Unlike a person with right of abode, he may be deported (see **Chapter 10**).

3.8.2 Ordinarily resident

This is a condition of settled status. It has a quite distinct meaning. Case law from various fields suggests that a person can be 'ordinarily resident' without having the right, or the intention, to reside here permanently. All that is necessary is that a person resides in a place with a 'settled purpose' (eg to undertake a course of education). It is possible to have ordinary residence in more than one place at the same time. A person may be ordinarily resident in the UK even though temporarily absent (eg on holiday). Generally, however, for purposes other than exemption from deportation, a person cannot be so resident at a time when he is in breach of immigration laws (eg overstaying) (see the IA 1971, s 33(2)).

> **EXAMPLES**
>
> (1) Erasmus has been in the UK for the last eight years, periodically renewing his leave to remain.
>
>   He is 'ordinarily resident' in the UK, but not 'settled' as he is subject to limited leave.

> (2)   Farooq was given indefinite leave to remain in the UK 10 years ago, but emigrated six years ago. He is now here for a holiday, having been admitted as a visitor.
>
> He is not 'ordinarily resident'. Neither is he 'settled', as his indefinite leave to remain was not renewed on his return to the UK.
>
> (3)   As (2), but Farooq has been admitted as a student, with 12 months' leave.
>
> He is 'ordinarily resident' but not 'settled'.

3.8.3   Returning resident rule

If a person with settled status leaves the UK and returns within two years, his leave will continue, leave to enter has to be given again and his settled status in effect confirmed. This is usually automatic under para 18 of the Rules, dealing with 'returning residents', provided that the entrant satisfies the immigration officer that he had indefinite leave to enter or remain in the UK when he last left, that he has not been away for longer than two years, and that he now seeks admission for the purpose of settlement. If a person is returning periodically only for a limited period simply to show residence in the UK within two years of each departure, then eventually he or she is likely to be denied the benefit of para 18 of the Immigration Rules.

What if a person with settled status does not return to the UK within two years of last leaving it? That person must apply for and be granted indefinite leave to enter the UK by way of entry clearance. What are the requirements? The applicant must demonstrate strong ties to the UK and the intention to make the UK their home. See para 19 of the Immigration Rules.

3.8.4   Who is treated as settled under the Immigration Rules?

Note that the Immigration Rules use the term 'settled' to cover British citizens (see **2.2**) and Commonwealth citizens who have the right of abode (see **2.3**), as well as those people who have indefinite leave.

3.8.5   Entry clearance

Only certain family members of a person already settled in the UK may apply for entry clearance for the purposes of settlement in the UK with that relative. These are dealt with in **Chapter 8**.

3.8.6   Switching where permitted

Some categories of entrants with limited leave are by their very nature temporary and so cannot lead to settlement, eg visitors (see **Chapter 5**) and students (see **Chapter 6**). However, most other categories may lead to settlement, and the answer is always found by studying the appropriate Immigration Rules. See further **Chapters 7** and **8**.

3.8.7   Knowledge of language and life in the UK

Any individual between the ages of 16 and 65, who has entered the UK with limited leave and subsequently applies for settlement, must satisfy the English language and life in the UK requirements detailed in Appendix KOL:UK of the Immigration Rules unless exempt because of a physical or mental condition (see **2.2.7.1(e)**). However, the following categories of people do not need to meet the requirement: victims of domestic violence (see **8.8**), bereaved spouses, civil partners, unmarried partners or same-sex partners of people present and settled in the UK (see **8.7**), adult dependent relatives (see **8.11**), people applying for settlement as a refugee (see **9.8.2**) or on the basis of humanitarian protection (see **9.10.1**) or discretionary leave (see **9.10.2**).

Note that if an applicant is aged between 60 and 64, the requirement is normally waived if the time needed to reach the required standard means the applicant would then be aged 65 or over.

3.8.8 The long-residence rules

Even where the requirements of the Immigration Rules for a switch to settled status are not met, it may be possible to obtain indefinite leave by virtue of long residence in the UK. Pursuant to the Immigration Rules, paras 276B and 276ADE, it is Home Office practice to consider this in cases where the applicant has been continuously resident in the UK either for 10 years lawfully (see **3.8.8.2**), or for most of his life (see **8.13**).

3.8.8.1 Key requirements

Both provisions share the key requirement of 'continuous residence'. By para 276A(a), this means residence in the UK for an unbroken period. Does that mean that the applicant must not have been absent from the UK at all? No, for these purposes a period is not considered broken where an applicant is absent from the UK for six months or less at any one time, provided that the applicant has existing limited leave to enter or remain on his departure and return. So in what circumstances is a period broken? This occurs if the applicant:

(a)   has been administratively removed or deported (see **Chapter 10**), or has left the UK having been refused leave to enter or remain here; or

(b)   has left the UK and, on doing so, evidenced a clear intention not to return; or

(c)   left the UK in circumstances in which he could have had no reasonable expectation at the time of leaving that he would lawfully be able to return (see R (Mungur) v Secretary of State for the Home Department [2021] EWCA Civ 1076); or

(d)   has been convicted of an offence and was sentenced to a period of imprisonment or was directed to be detained in an institution other than a prison (including, in particular, a hospital or an institution for young offenders), provided that the sentence in question was not a suspended sentence; or

(e)   has spent a total of more than 18 months absent from the UK during the period in question.

For the long residence provision based on 10 years' continuous residence (see **3.8.8.2**) there is an additional key requirement of 'lawful residence'. By para 276A(b), this means residence which is continuous residence pursuant to:

(a)   existing leave to enter or remain; or

(b)   temporary admission within s 11 of the 1971 Act (see **3.5.5**) where leave to enter or remain is subsequently granted; or

(c)   an exemption from immigration control, including where an exemption ceases to apply if it is immediately followed by a grant of leave to enter or remain. People exempt from immigration control include diplomats and members of the armed forces. These are beyond the scope of this book.

Time spent in the UK with the benefit of a visitor's visa counts as residence, including for the purposes of calculating continuous residence (see R (Mungur) v Secretary of State for the Home Department [2021] EWCA Civ 1076).

A period of overstaying does not necessarily break continuity of residence for the purpose of establishing 10 years' continuous lawful residence (see Hoque v Secretary of State for the Home Department [2020] EWCA Civ 135). Home Office guidance is that any period of overstaying for 28 days or less will be disregarded. If the period is longer but there are extenuating reasons for this, such as a postal strike, hospitalisation or an administrative error by the Home Office, caseworkers may exercise discretion to grant indefinite leave to remain, provided the application meets all the other requirements.

Continuous residence is considered to be broken by the Home Office if the applicant has:

(a)   been absent from the UK for a period of more than six months at any one time, or is absent from the UK for a shorter period but does not have valid leave to enter the UK on his return, or valid leave to remain on his departure from the UK; and/or

(b)   spent a total of 18 months outside the UK throughout the whole 10-year period.

Home Office guidance is that continuous residence is not broken if the applicant is absent from the UK for six months or less at any one time, or had existing leave to enter or remain when he left and when he returned (this can include leave gained at a port when returning to the UK as a non-visa national), or departed the UK after the expiry of his leave to remain but applied for fresh entry clearance within 28 days of that previous leave's expiring.

What about any time spent in prison by an applicant? Continuous residence is broken if he receives a custodial sentence by a court of law and is sent to prison, a young offender's institution or a secure hospital. So any leave accumulated before sentencing will be disregarded and only residence after release from custody counts. Note that continuous residence is not broken if an applicant receives a suspended sentence.

3.8.8.2   Ten years' residence provision

By para 276B, the requirements to be met by an applicant for indefinite leave to remain on the ground of long residence in the UK are that:

(a)   he has had at least 10 years' continuous lawful residence in the UK (see **3.8.8.1**);

(b)   having regard to the public interest, there are no reasons why it would be undesirable for him to be given indefinite leave to remain on the ground of long residence, taking into account his:

    (i)   age, and

    (ii)   strength of connections in the UK, and

    (iii)   personal history, including character, conduct, associations and employment record, and

    (iv)   domestic circumstances, and

    (v)   compassionate circumstances, and

    (vi)   any representations received on the person's behalf; and

(c)   the applicant does not fall for refusal under the general grounds for refusal (see **3.6.5**);

(d)   the applicant has sufficient knowledge of the English language and sufficient knowledge about life in the UK by passing the test known as the 'Life in the UK Test' (see **3.8.7**), unless he is under the age of 18 or aged 65 or over at the time he makes his application.

What is the Home Office guidance on the public interest factors in para 276B(ii) ((b) above)?

(a)   Age may be a relevant factor if the applicant is an unaccompanied child under the age of 18, or if the applicant or his dependants have spent their formative years in the UK and adapted to life here.

(b)   The family life a person has in the UK must be taken into account in assessing the strength of that person's connections to the UK. This may be particularly strong if he is married to or has established a similar relationship with a settled person. The person may have other close relatives settled in the UK. The strength and closeness of the relationship will determine how strong a factor this may be. Similarly, if a person's close relatives are not in the UK, this may call into question the strength of the person's connection to the UK.

    Owning property or a business may support the view that an applicant has shown long-term commitment and a connection to the UK. However, on its own, this would not be a significant factor. Factors such as the length of time the individual has owned the business or property, or whether the business is legally operating, must be considered.

If someone mentions his business interests as proof of commitment to the UK, he must provide supporting documentary evidence. The applicant will be required to show further proof of strong connections to the UK.

If the applicant has contributed positively to society, for example through significant investment or charitable work, this may be another factor in his favour, although this is unlikely to be decisive on its own.

(c)   Character, conduct and associations go beyond criminal convictions and enable the caseworker to consider whether the applicant's activities in the UK or abroad make it undesirable to grant indefinite leave. This could include concerns about the applicant on the basis of national security, war crimes, crimes against humanity and serious criminality, whether convicted or not. As to applicants with a conviction, see para 276B(iii).

A history of anti-social behaviour or low-level criminality might be a ground to refuse indefinite leave, especially if it has led to the issuing of an anti-social behaviour order (ASBO).

The applicant's employment record will often be a significant consideration. The caseworker must consider what the person has been doing while he has been in the UK, and what economic contribution, if any, he has made. Whilst not having a sound employment record is not in itself a reason to refuse leave, a sound employment record, along with strong ties with the UK, would count in a person's favour, if he has not been a burden on public finances but has, in fact, contributed through income tax and national insurance contributions.

(d)   If the applicant has dependent children who have adapted to life in the UK, this could be a factor against refusal. The presence of another settled person who is routinely dependent on the applicant, for example a disabled relative, might also be a factor against refusal.

(e)   It is not possible to define all potential compassionate circumstances, but it might, depending on the situation, include significant or serious illness, frailty and particularly difficult family circumstances.

(f)   All representations raised on behalf of the applicant must be carefully assessed, even if these have been dismissed in previous applications. The caseworker must weigh those factors against the compassionate circumstances, if any, and all the other circumstances of the case, and then decide whether a grant of indefinite leave would be against the public interest. In R (Balajigari) and Others v Secretary of State for the Home Department [2019] 1 WLR 4647, the Court of Appeal said that there must be: (i) reliable evidence of (ii) sufficiently reprehensible conduct; and (iii) an assessment, taking proper account of all relevant circumstances known about the applicant at the date of decision, of whether their presence in the UK is undesirable. This should include evidence of positive features of their character. The decision-maker must therefore conduct a balancing exercise informed by weighing all relevant factors, including such matters as any substantial positive contribution to the UK made by the applicant and also circumstances relating to the (mis)conduct in question, eg that it occurred a long time ago.

> In all but the most extreme cases, where the conduct complained of is such that on any view the balance must fall against an applicant, even where a sufficient character or conduct issue is proved, a balancing exercise is required. (per Irwin LJ in Yaseen v Secretary of State for the Home Department [2020] EWCA Civ 157 at [46])

Note that if the applicant cannot meet the requirements of paras 276B(iii) and/or (iv), he may under para 276A2 be granted an extension of his stay on the ground of long residence in the UK for a period not exceeding two years.

The application will be refused if the applicant does not meet the requirements for indefinite leave to remain or further leave to remain on the ground of long residence in the UK.

3.8.9 Windrush Scheme

The Windrush generation refers to immigrants who were invited to the UK after the Second World War from various Commonwealth countries. Whilst most had indefinite leave to remain under the law, many lacked formal immigration documentation, and a major news story broke in 2018 of large numbers being denied access to public services, detained in the UK or at the border or removed from, and refused re-entry to, the UK. In April 2018, the Government acknowledged that they had been treated unfairly. Under current policy, an applicant may be eligible to apply under the Home Office's Windrush Scheme if they are either:

(a)   a Commonwealth citizen (see **Appendix 9**) who settled in the UK before 1 January 1973 or has right of abode (see **2.3**); or

(b)   a child of a Commonwealth citizen parent who settled before 1 January 1973, where they were born in the UK or arrived in the UK before the age of 18; or

(c)   a person of any nationality who settled in the UK before 31 December 1988 and is settled in the UK.

Full details can be found on the UKVI website (see **1.2.8**).

3.8.10 Criminality requirement for settlement

In April 2011 the Government introduced a requirement that any person applying for settlement under the Immigration Rules must show that he does not have any relevant convictions as detailed in Part 9. Are criminal convictions imposed outside the UK relevant? Yes, as para 6 of the Immigration Rules provides that 'conviction' means conviction for a criminal offence in the UK or any other country. Home Office guidance is that offences do not need to have an identically named provision or carry similar penalties as in the UK, provided that there is a comparable offence, for example homicide and murder. However, offences which do not constitute a criminal offence in the UK are ignored, such as homosexuality and proselytising (attempting to convert someone to another religion). The details are in **Appendix 8**.

3.9   THE COMMON TRAVEL AREA

The Common Travel Area (CTA) is a longstanding administrative arrangement between the UK, Ireland and the Crown Dependencies of the Isle of Man, Guernsey and Jersey. It has been implemented in UK domestic law by s 1(3) of the IA 1971 which provides that persons arriving on local journeys to the UK from elsewhere in the CTA are not subject to immigration control, and no permission (leave) to enter is required. Control operates only on initial entry to the Area from outside. This is subject to some exceptions, for example under the Immigration (Control on Entry through the Republic of Ireland) Order 1972 (SI 1972/1610). This subjects some persons to immigration control (such as visa nationals without a visa for entry to the UK). If such persons enter the UK, for example, from Ireland, they are illegal entrants, even though they have never been examined by an immigration officer.

Under the CTA, British and Irish citizens can move freely and reside in either jurisdiction and enjoy associated rights and privileges, including the right to work, study and vote in certain elections, as well as to access social welfare benefits and health services.

Does the CTA still include Ireland given the UK has left the EU? Yes, the position is preserved by a memorandum of understanding signed in May 2019 between the two countries. Further, s 3ZA of the IA 1971 provides that Irish citizens do not require permission to enter or stay in the UK unless they are subject to a deportation order, exclusion decision or international travel ban (see **Chapter 10**).

Note that family members who are not Irish (or British) citizens are not covered by CTA arrangements, and UK domestic immigration law will apply to them unless they secured settlement in the UK under the EU Settlement Scheme (see **Chapter 4**).

3.10 IMMIGRATION HEALTH SURCHARGE

The immigration health surcharge (IHS) was introduced by s 38 of the IA 2014. The details can be found in the Immigration (Health Charge) Order 2015 (SI 2015/792) (as amended). Broadly, it must be paid by most applicants seeking entry clearance, limited leave to enter and limited leave to remain for more than six months. So, the largest group of entrants not liable to pay the IHS are standard visitors (see **5.2**) and those entering for settlement or applying in the UK for indefinite leave to remain.

Who is exempt from the IHS? The main groups are:

- Appendix FM domestic violence concession applicants (see **8.8**), and
- asylum seekers and applicants for humanitarian protection (see **Chapter 9**).

The IHS must be paid at the time of making the application. If it is not paid, the application will not be granted.

How much is the IHS? It costs £470 per year for a Student (see **Chapter 6**), a T5 (Temporary Worker) Youth Mobility Scheme Migrant (see **7.12.6**) and all children under the age of 18 at the date of the application. All other applicants and their dependants aged 18 or over at the date of the application pay £624 per year.

The specified annual amount is payable for each year of the maximum period of leave to enter or remain that can be granted to the applicant under the Immigration Rules. What if that period will be less than a year or include part of a year? If the part year is six months or less, the amount payable for that part is half of the specified annual amount; but if it is more than six months, the amount payable for that part is the full specified annual amount.

EXAMPLE 1

Alan applies for entry clearance as a Student (see **Chapter 6**). Assume that under the Immigration Rules the maximum amount of leave that he can be granted for the length of his course is 1 year and 5 months.

As a Student, Alan's annual IHS is £470. So, his total IHS will be calculated as follows: £470 for the first 12 months and £235 for the remaining 5 months (being less than 6 months and so amounting to half the annual amount) = £705.

Adult dependants usually pay the same amount as the applicant. All children pay £470.

EXAMPLE 2

Chloe applies for entry clearance in the Start-up category (see **7.3**) for herself, her husband, Max and their 6-year-old son, Adam. The maximum initial leave that she will be granted in this category is 2 years.

Chloe's annual IHS is £624. So her total IHS payable on her application is £1,248 for herself (2 x £624) plus £1,248 for Max (2 x £624) plus £940 (2 x £470) for Adam.

3.11 EVIDENTIAL FLEXIBILITY FOR THE POINTS-BASED SYSTEM

Some immigration categories are dealt with by way of a points-based system. These include Students (see **6.3**), Tier 1 Investor Migrants (see **7.5**), Skilled Workers (see **7.8**) and T5 Temporary Worker Migrants (see **7.12**). The requirements for each of these routes, including the documents specified for submission with the application, are set out in the Immigration Rules. This policy of evidential flexibility means that applicants may be asked to provide further evidence at a later stage, or, if when considering the application it is clear that the applicant has made an error or omission with the supporting evidence provided, they should be contacted and invited to provide additional information as set out in the detailed UKVI guidance that can be found on its website (see **1.2.8**).

Note the following example included in UKVI guidance as to where a decision maker should apply evidential flexibility:

> An application has been made under Appendix Student [see **Chapter 6**] and the applicant meets the requirements of the Immigration Rules but has not provided the specified evidence in relation to finance. For example, where there are one or more bank statements missing. [The decision maker has] assessed the application and believe[s] the applicant meets all the other requirements of the relevant Immigration Rules. Even if [the decision maker is] not certain the missing evidence exists, for example, if the missing bank statement is from the end of the series covering the relevant time period, [they] should employ evidential flexibility and request the missing evidence in relation to finance.

Note the following example included in UKVI guidance as to where a decision maker should not apply evidential flexibility.

> An application has been made under Appendix Student of the Immigration Rules and the CAS confirms that the applicant has passed the relevant English Language requirements. The CAS contains all the relevant detail as required and the application contains all the evidence required by the Immigration Rules except for a copy of the English Language Certificate. However, [the decision maker has] assessed the case and, having carried out an interview, [has] decided that the applicant does not meet the requirements of the genuine student rule. In this case [the decision maker does] not need to apply evidential flexibility and the refusal notice should explain why ....

EEA NATIONALS

4.1 WHO ARE EEA NATIONALS?

'EEA nationals' are nationals of the Member States of the European Union together with Iceland, Liechtenstein and Norway (which are parties to the European Economic Area Agreement). See **Appendix 2** to this book for the full list of relevant countries. As from 31 January 2020, the UK has not been a member of the EU. However, many British citizens hold dual nationality, some with a Member State of the EU, notably Ireland. This short chapter will therefore introduce the basic concepts of immigration within the EU by EEA nationals and provide a reminder of how EEA nationals and their family members may have historically acquired settled status in the UK.

Note that by an Agreement on the Free Movement of Persons made between the EC (now EU) and the Swiss Confederation (Cm 4904), Swiss nationals and their family members were from 1 June 2002 given broadly similar rights of entry to and residence in the EU as are enjoyed by EEA nationals.

Note that all references in this chapter to EEA nationals include Swiss nationals.

4.2 WHAT IS THEIR IMMIGRATION STATUS?

Nationals of the EEA have a hybrid status. They have their own immigration rights under their own national laws in their country of nationality. But they have rights of entry to, and residence in, other EU Member States while exercising rights in EU law (see **4.3**).

4.3 RIGHTS UNDER EU LAW

Article 20 TFEU states that:

1. Citizenship of the Union is hereby established. Every person holding the nationality of a Member State shall be a citizen of the Union. Citizenship of the Union shall be additional to and not replace national citizenship.

2. Citizens of the Union shall enjoy the rights and be subject to the duties provided for in the Treaties.

Article 21(1) TFEU provides that:

Every citizen of the Union shall have the right to move and reside freely within the territory of the Member States, subject to the limitations and conditions laid down in the Treaties and by the measures adopted to give them effect.

It can be seen that Article 21 TFEU provides for a right of residence and movement of EEA nationals throughout the EU. Directive 2004/38/EC of the European Parliament and Council of 29 April 2004 sets out the terms and limits of this right of movement. It is a consolidation and modernisation of existing EU secondary legislation in this area. A copy of the Directive is set out in **Appendix 3**.

More detailed treatment of this topic is to be found in Part III of **Legal Foundations**. The following is a summary of the main principles.

4.3.1 Free movement of workers

Article 45 TFEU requires free movement for workers within the Union. Article 45(3) TFEU provides that this entails the right to:

(a)   accept offers of employment;

(b)   move freely within the EU for this purpose;

(c)   stay in a Member State for employment;

(d)   remain after employment, subject to conditions.

4.3.2 Self-employed activities and establishment of businesses

Article 49 TFEU requires abolition of restrictions on the freedom of establishment of EU nationals. This freedom includes the right to pursue activities as self-employed persons, and to set up and manage undertakings such as companies or firms.

4.3.3 Provision of services

Article 56 TFEU requires abolition of the restrictions on freedom to provide services within the Union in respect of nationals of Member States who are established in a State of the Union other than that of the person for whom the services are intended.

Article 57 TFEU states that the provider of a service (including industrial, commercial, craft, and professional activities) may temporarily pursue his activity in a State where the service is provided. Permanent provision of the service would involve 'establishment'.

Freedom of movement extends not only to the providers, but also to the recipients of services. In Joined Cases 286/82 and 26/83 *Luisi (Graziana) and Carbone (Giuseppe) v Ministero del Tesoro* [1984] ECR 377, the ECJ held that this covered tourists, and those who travel for medical treatment, education or business.

Does the EEA national have to travel to another EEA country and provide services there? 'No', held the ECJ in *Alpine Investments BV v Minister van Financiën* (Case C-384/93) [1995] ECR I-1141 – an offer to provide services over the telephone to potential recipients established in other Member States is sufficient. On a proper construction, Article 56 applies to services which a provider supplies, without moving from the Member State in which he is established, to recipients established in other Member States.

4.3.4 When the 2004 Directive applies

The 2004 Directive applies only to EEA nationals exercising Treaty rights. So a non-EEA national cannot directly benefit from it. This is because the Directive determines how, and under what conditions, EEA citizens can exercise their right to freedom of movement within the territory of the Member States. Accordingly, the Directive concerns the travel and residence of an EEA citizen in a Member State other than that of which he is a national: see *McCarthy (European citizenship)* [2011] 3 CMLR 10. A non-EEA national may only indirectly benefit from the Directive if he is the family member of an EEA national (see **4.4.6**).

An EEA national will exercise his Treaty rights by, for example, moving to another EEA country and living there. This is the combined effect of Articles 20 and 21 TFEU (see **4.3**). The EEA national might take employment pursuant to Article 45 TFEU (see **4.3.1**), or run a business under Article 49 (see **4.3.2**). His right of entry to and residence in the host EEA country will be governed by the 2004 Directive.

> **EXAMPLES**
>
> (1) Abdus is a citizen of Pakistan. He is a single man. He travelled from Pakistan and entered Spain, an EEA country, pursuant to domestic Spanish immigration laws. Abdus is not an EEA national. He cannot exercise Treaty rights.
>
> (2) Marie is a French national living in Paris. She is single and an EEA national. She has a right of entry to and residence in the other EEA countries. She travels to Madrid, Spain (an EEA country) and starts working there. She is thereby exercising her Treaty rights.
>
> (3) Boris is a German national living in Berlin. He travels to Jamaica and works there for several years. He marries Alisha, a Jamaican national. The couple decide that they want to live together in Germany. As Jamaica is not an EEA country, Boris has not exercised his Treaty rights. Alisha will have to comply with domestic German law to enter and live with Boris there.
>
> (4) Marie, from example (2) above, meets Abdus from example (1) in Spain. They fall in love and marry. The couple subsequently decide to live together in France. As Marie is an EEA national who has exercised her Treaty rights, Abdus, as her spouse, can benefit indirectly. Rather than applying under domestic French immigration law to enter France with Marie, he can choose to rely on EU law and enter as the spouse of an EEA national.

4.4 THE IMMIGRATION (EUROPEAN ECONOMIC AREA) REGULATIONS 2016

The I(EEA) Regs 2016 enacted EU law rights of free movement in UK law. A copy may be found at **Appendix 4** to this book as parts may still be relevant to practitioners. In order to understand how certain EEA nationals and their family members historically acquired settlement in the UK, the following provisions of the 2016 Regs should be noted.

4.4.1 Right of admission for EEA nationals (reg 11(1))

An EEA national had to be admitted to the UK if they produced on arrival a valid national identity card or passport issued by an EEA State.

4.4.2 Right of admission for family members of EEA nationals (reg 11(2))

A person who was not an EEA national had to be admitted to the UK if they were the family member of an EEA national and produced on arrival a valid passport or an EEA family permit (see **4.4.7**), a residence card (see **4.4.8**) or a permanent residence card (see **4.4.10**).

The family member may be travelling with the EEA national to the UK, or joining the EEA national who is already in the UK. If the family member is travelling independently of the EEA national and not joining him in the UK then the Immigration Rules apply.

4.4.3 Initial right of residence for three months (reg 13)

An EEA national and their family member(s) were entitled to reside in the UK for a period not exceeding three months. The only condition was that the EEA national and their family member must not become an unreasonable burden on the social assistance system of the UK (see further **4.4.5.4**).

4.4.4 Residence beyond three months (reg 14)

An EEA national was entitled to reside in the UK for a period exceeding three months if they were a qualified person. Indeed, they had the right to reside in the UK for as long as they remained a qualified person. Their family member(s) had the same right.

It is important to appreciate that the family member's right to reside was dependent upon the EEA national's having a right to reside. The problem that arose if the EEA national died or left the UK, etc is considered at **4.4.11**.

4.4.5 Who was a qualified person? (reg 6)

A qualified person was an EEA national who was in the UK in any of the following categories:

(a)   a jobseeker;

(b)   a worker;

(c)   a self-employed person;

(d)   a self-sufficient person; or

(e)   a student.

4.4.5.1 Jobseeker

A 'jobseeker', as defined in reg 6(5), was an EEA national who either:

(a)   entered the UK in order to seek employment; or

(b)   was now present in the UK seeking employment immediately after enjoying a right to reside as a qualified person in another category.

In addition, they had to provide evidence that they were seeking employment and had a genuine chance of being engaged.

4.4.5.2 Worker

Regulation 4(1)(a) defined a worker by a simple cross-reference to Article 45 TFEU (see **4.3.1**), namely an employee.

Also note the definition of a worker who had ceased activity in reg 5(2)–(5).

4.4.5.3 Self-employed person

Regulation 4(1)(b) defined a self-employed person by a simple cross-reference to Article 49 TFEU (see **4.3.2**).

Note that by reg 6(3), an EEA national who was temporarily unable to work due to illness or accident retained the status of a self-employed person.

Also note the definition of a self-employed person who had ceased activity in reg 5(2)–(5) and that in the limited circumstances set out in reg 6(4), where a person who was no longer in self-employment would continue to be treated as a self-employed person.

4.4.5.4 Self-sufficient person

A 'self-sufficient person', as defined in reg 4(1)(c), was an EEA national who had (i) sufficient resources not to become a burden on the social assistance system of the UK during his period of residence; and (ii) comprehensive sickness insurance cover in the UK.

4.4.5.5 Student

A 'student', according to reg 4(1)(d), was an EEA national who:

(a)   was enrolled, for the principal purpose of following a course of study (including vocational training), at a public or private establishment which was financed from public funds; or otherwise recognised by the Secretary of State as an establishment which had been accredited for the purpose of providing such courses or training within the law or administrative practice of the part of the UK in which the establishment was located;

(b)   had comprehensive sickness insurance cover in the UK; and

(c)   assured the Secretary of State, by means of a declaration, or by such equivalent means as the person may choose, that they had sufficient resources not to become a burden on the social assistance system of the UK during their period of residence.

4.4.6   Who was a family member of an EEA national?

Under reg 7, as a general rule, the following were family members of an EEA national:

(a)   his spouse or his civil partner;

(b)   direct descendants (children, grandchildren, etc) of him, his spouse or his civil partner who were:

    (i)   under 21, or

    (ii)   dependants of him, his spouse or his civil partner;

(c)   dependent direct relatives in his ascending line (parents, grandparents, etc) or that of his spouse or his civil partner.

'Children' included step-children, and adopted children provided that the adoption was recognised by the UK.

What about direct descendants (children, etc) aged 21 or over, or direct relatives in the ascending line (parents, etc) who could not show dependency? What about other relatives, such as brothers and sisters, uncles and aunts, cousins, etc? These might fall within reg 8, which dealt with 'extended family members'. These were any of the following:

(a)   a person who was a relative of an EEA national and:

    (i)   who was residing in a country other than the UK and who was either dependent upon the EEA national or a member of his household,

    (ii)   who satisfied the condition in para (i) and was accompanying the EEA national to the UK or wished to join him here, or

    (iii)   who satisfied the condition in para (i), had joined the EEA national in the UK and continued to be either dependent upon him or a member of his household;

(b)   a person who was a relative of an EEA national and, on serious health grounds, who strictly required the personal care of the EEA national;

(c)   a person who was a relative of an EEA national and who would meet the requirements in the Immigration Rules (other than those relating to entry clearance) for indefinite leave to enter or remain in the UK as a dependent relative of the EEA national were the EEA national a person present and settled in the UK (see **8.11**);

(d)   a person who was the partner of an EEA national (other than a civil partner) and who could prove to the decision maker that he was in a durable relationship akin to marriage or a civil partnership with the EEA national.

Some of the above categories had a test of dependency on the EEA national. Guidance from the Home Office was that the dependency could be one of choice rather than necessity, but the definition of 'dependency' included only financial dependency and not emotional dependency. Financial dependency might be shown by the family member being unemployed.

4.4.7   Did a family member need a travel document? (reg 12)

To be admitted to the UK, a family member should apply to an ECO for a travel document known as an EEA family permit before travelling to the UK. It was required only where the family member was not an EEA national.

4.4.8   How could an EEA national or family member confirm a right of residence?

Under regs 17 and 18, an EEA national or a non-EEA family member entitled to residence could apply to the Secretary of State for a residence certificate or residence card respectively. A residence certificate or card was normally valid for five years.

4.4.9   Permanent right of residence in UK (reg 15)

The following persons could acquire the right to reside in the UK permanently:

(a)   an EEA national who had resided in the UK in accordance with the 2016 Regs for a continuous period of five years;

(b)   a family member of an EEA national (who was not himself an EEA national) who had resided in the UK with the EEA national in accordance with the 2016 Regs for a continuous period of five years;

(c)   a worker or self-employed person who had ceased activity;

(d)   the family member of a worker or self-employed person who had ceased activity;

(e)   a person who was the family member of a worker or self-employed person where:

   (i)   the worker or self-employed person had died,

   (ii)   the family member resided with him immediately before his death, and

   (iii) the worker or self-employed person had resided continuously in the UK for at least the two years immediately before his death, or the death was the result of an accident at work or an occupational disease;

(f)   a person who:

   (i)   had resided in the UK in accordance with the 2016 Regulations for a continuous period of five years; and

   (ii)   was, at the end of that period, a family member who had retained the right of residence.

Could the right of permanent residence be lost once acquired? Yes, but only through absence from the UK for a period exceeding two consecutive years.

4.4.10   How could an EEA national or family member confirm permanent residence?

Under reg 19, an EEA national or non-EEA family member entitled to permanent residence could apply to the Secretary of State for a document certifying permanent residence or a permanent residence card respectively.

A document certifying permanent residence did not have an expiry date. A permanent residence card was valid for 10 years and was renewable.

4.4.11   What was the status of a family member who had not acquired permanent residence on the death or departure from the UK of the qualified person, or the termination of marriage or civil partnership?

Until a family member acquired his own right of permanent residence he was in a vulnerable position: what if the qualified person died or left the UK? If his right of residence was dependent on marriage to, or on a civil partnership with, a qualified person, what was his immigration status when that relationship formally ended?

The answer was to be found in reg 10, which allowed certain family members to retain the right of residence.

4.4.12   British citizens who exercised Treaty rights and then returned to the UK (reg 9)

If a British citizen travelled to another EEA country to work or otherwise exercise Treaty rights, he was entitled to be accompanied by, or later joined by, his family members. Equally, if a British citizen travelled to the UK from an EEA country after exercising Treaty rights there as a worker or self-employed person, his family could accompany him. So, for example, the Indian spouse of a British citizen who had worked in another EEA country could take advantage of Article 44 TFEU, acquiring rights of residence in the UK itself beyond those given by UK immigration law – see R v Immigration Appeal Tribunal and Surinder Singh, ex p Secretary of State for the Home Department [1992] 3 CMLR 358. This decision was largely given effect to in reg 9.

4.5 EEA NATIONALS AND BREXIT

Before the UK left the EU, the UK government set about constructing an EU Settlement Scheme. It can still be found in Appendix EU of the Immigration Rules. The Scheme covered two periods: first, in respect of those EEA citizens and their family members resident here before the UK left the EU; and, secondly, in respect of those EEA nationals and their family members who arrived in the UK during the so-called implementation period to 31 December 2020.

Broadly, the Scheme provided as follows:

- EEA citizens and their family members who, by 31 December 2020, had been continuously resident in the UK for five years could apply for settled status (indefinite leave to remain in the UK).

- EEA citizens and their family members who arrived by 31 December 2020, but would not have been continuously resident here for five years, would be eligible for a newly created form of limited leave called 'pre-settled status'. This allows them to stay until they have reached the five-year threshold and then apply for settled status.

- Close family members (defined as a spouse, civil partner, durable partner, dependent child or grandchild, and dependent parent or grandparent) living overseas are still able to join an EEA citizen resident here after the end of the implementation period, where the relationship existed on 31 December 2020 and continues to exist when the person comes to the UK. Future children are also protected.

What was the deadline for applications to the Scheme? It was 30 June 2021. However, late applications may be considered on 'reasonable grounds', such as medical reasons or being the victim of domestic abuse.

Note that for the following applicants, a later deadline applies:

- An application must be made on behalf of a child born or adopted in the UK on or after 1 April 2021 (who is not a British citizen) within 90 days of their birth or adoption.

- A family member of a British citizen who lived with them in an EEA country by 30 December 2020 and returns to the UK with them (see **4.4.12**) must apply by 29 March 2022.

Over the next few years, those applicants granted pre-settled status should apply for settled status once they have resided in the UK, the Channel Islands or the Isle of Man continuously for five years. The Home Office gives the following example.

> An applicant came to the UK on 2 March 2018 and got pre-settled status on 15 January 2020. The applicant will become eligible to apply for settled status on 2 March 2023, after they have lived in the UK for five years. The latest they can apply for settled status will be on 14 January 2025, just before their pre-settled status expires.

Note that continuous residence may be lost if the applicant spends more than six months outside the UK in a 12-month period. In those circumstances, the applicant may be granted a further period of five years pre-settled status if the time they spent outside the UK was before 31 December 2020 and they were resident in the UK by 31 December 2020.

As to appeal rights under the Scheme, see **11.10**.

VISITORS

5.1 INTRODUCTION – WHO IS A VISITOR?

A person may want to enter the UK temporarily as a visitor for many different reasons – for a holiday, to visit family or friends, to conduct some sort of business, to have private medical treatment, get married or enter into a civil partnership, etc. Appendix V: Visitor to the Immigration Rules deals with these different routes into the UK for a visitor, and we shall look at the key categories in this chapter.

5.1.1 Entry clearance

Except in the case of visa nationals (see **1.4.3**), no entry clearance is normally required for a visit to the UK of up to six months. So it is possible for non-visa nationals (see **1.4.4**) to arrive at a UK port and seek leave to enter from an immigration officer. It may, however, reduce any potential problems for those who are not simply tourists if entry clearance is obtained in advance. In addition, there are some exceptions to the normal rule, as a non-visa national must apply for entry clearance if (a) visiting the UK to marry or to form a civil partnership, or to give notice of this (see **5.10**), unless they are an EEA national or a national of Switzerland (see **Chapter 4**), or (b) when seeking to visit the UK for more than six months.

5.1.2 Leave (permission) to enter and conditions

Most kinds of visitors under Appendix V: Visitor will be given leave to enter the UK for a period not exceeding six months, subject to a condition prohibiting employment (see **3.3.1**), but this does not prohibit any work-related permitted activities (see **5.4**). There will also be a condition of no study, although this does not prohibit the incidental study allowed by the permitted activities (see **5.4.15**). Like all limited leave entrants, visitors will be subject to the condition not to have recourse to public funds (also see **3.3.2**).

There is a useful chart at para V 17.2 of Appendix V: Visitor to the Immigration Rules that summarises the types and lengths of visit visa and leave to enter or remain.

Note that within the period for which a visit visa is valid, a visitor may enter and leave the UK multiple times, unless the visit visa is endorsed as a single or dual entry visa (see **5.2.4**).

5.1.3 Frequency of visits

Is there any restriction on the number of visits a person may make to the UK? Is there any requirement that a specified period of time must elapse between successive visits? The answer to both these questions is 'No'. Home Office guidance is that a person who has made a series of visits to the UK with only brief intervals between them would not, in the absence of any other relevant factors, be refused entry as a visitor. However, an immigration officer will consider the stated purpose of a visit in light of the length of time that has elapsed since previous visits. See further *Sawmynaden (Family visitors – considerations)* [2012] UKUT 00161 (IAC).

Note that the Home Office accepts that, occasionally, a visitor carrying out a permitted activity associated with business (see **5.4**) may be required to stay for a period of weeks or even months in the UK, for example where machinery is being installed or faults are being diagnosed and corrected. An immigration officer should be satisfied, however, that a person's presence in the UK on business for more than six out of any 12 months does not mean that he is basing himself here and holding down a specific post which constitutes employment, and which would therefore require the individual to seek entry under the points-based system (see **Chapter 7**).

Home Office guidance accepts that there is no specified maximum time a visitor can spend in the UK in any period, such as '6 months in 12 months'. However, if it is clear from a visitor's travel history that he is making the UK his home, the application will be refused (see further **5.2.2.2**).

> **EXAMPLE**
>
> Chelsea is a non-visa national. Every time that Chelsea arrives in the UK for a visit, she will have to satisfy the immigration officer that she meets the visit visa requirements. Provided that she does so, she will be granted leave to enter for six months on each occasion. As long as she does not stay for more than six months on each visit, there is no cumulative maximum time over a year or otherwise that she is allowed to spend in the UK.

5.2 STANDARD VISITOR

All visitors must meet the general entry, validity and suitability requirements set out in Parts V1 and V3 of Appendix V: Visitor to the Immigration Rules.

5.2.1 Suitability

Visitors are subject to the general grounds for refusal in Part 9 of the Immigration Rules (see **3.4.5**).

5.2.2 Genuineness and credibility

5.2.2.1 Requirements

Paragraph V 4.2 provides that an applicant must be a 'genuine' visitor. This means that the applicant:

(a)   will leave the UK at the end of his visit; and

(b)   will not live in the UK for extended periods through frequent or successive visits, or make the UK his main home; and

(c)   is genuinely seeking entry for a purpose permitted by Appendix V: Visitor; and

(d)   will not undertake any prohibited activities (see **5.3**).

5.2.2.2 Home Office policy

What should have struck you when reading the above requirements for a standard visitor is that they concern the applicant's intention. So he must *genuinely* be seeking entry as a visitor and *intend* to leave the UK at the end of his visit, and he must *not intend* to make the UK his main home, etc. The burden of proof is on the applicant, but to what standard? It is the balance of probabilities. Home Office guidance to its decision makers is that the following factors may be relevant:

- the applicant's previous immigration history, including visits to the UK and other countries
- the duration of previous visits, and whether this was significantly longer than originally stated on the applicant's visa application or on arrival
- the applicant's financial circumstances, as well as his family, social and economic background
- the applicant's personal and economic ties to his country of residence
- the cumulative period of time the applicant has visited the UK and his pattern of travel over the last 12-month period; and decision makers should assess whether this amounts to 'de facto' residence in the UK
- whether the information and the reasons for the visit provided by the applicant are credible and correspond to his personal, family, social and economic background
- the applicant's country of residence and/or country of nationality, including information on immigration non-compliance by individuals who applied for a visit visa from the same geographical region as the applicant.

Whilst visitors can undertake multiple activities whilst they are in the UK, Home Office guidance is that an applicant should be able to explain at the visa application stage and on entry his main reason for coming to the UK. So when might an ECO and/or an immigration officer doubt an applicant's intentions in visiting the UK? This may include the following circumstances:

- the applicant has few or no family and economic ties to his country of residence and has several family members in the UK
- the political, economic and security situation in the applicant's country of residence, including whether it is politically unstable, a conflict zone or at risk of becoming one, may lead to doubts about the applicant's intention to leave the UK at the end of his visit
- the applicant, his sponsor (if he is visiting a friend or relative) or other immediate family member has, or has attempted to, deceive the Home Office in a previous application for entry clearance, leave to enter or leave to remain
- there are discrepancies between the statements made by the applicant and the statements made by the sponsor, particularly on points where the sponsor could reasonably be expected to know the facts but does not
- it has not been possible to verify information provided by the applicant despite attempts to do so
- the information that has been provided or the reasons stated by the applicant are not credible
- a search of the applicant's baggage and vehicle at the border reveals items that demonstrate an intention to work and/or live in the UK.

5.2.3 Maintenance and accommodation

5.2.3.1 Requirements

Paragraph V 4.2(e) provides that an applicant must have sufficient funds to cover all reasonable costs in relation to his visit without working or accessing public funds (see **3.3.2**).

This includes the cost of the return or onward journey, any costs relating to dependants and the cost of any planned activities such as private medical treatment.

An applicant must have access to sufficient resources to maintain and accommodate himself adequately for the whole of his planned visit to the UK. Is there a set level of funds for an applicant to show this? No. So what are the key questions to be answered? These will include:

(a)   where the applicant will be staying;

(b)   the costs likely to be incurred, including any on-going financial commitments the applicant may have in his country of residence, such as rent or mortgage payments and any dependants whom the applicant supports financially, including those who are not travelling with him;

(c)   the sources of revenue that are available to the applicant.

Home Office guidance is that an applicant's income or savings, minus his financial commitments, must be sufficient to meet the likely costs he will incur in the UK and be reasonable expenditure in light of his financial situation.

5.2.3.2 Third party assistance

Paragraph V 4.3 provides that an applicant's travel, maintenance and accommodation may be provided by a third party, as long as that third party:

(a)   has a genuine professional or personal relationship with the visitor; and

(b)   is not, or will not be, in breach of UK immigration laws at the time of decision or the visitor's entry to the UK; and

(c)   can and will provide support to the applicant for the intended duration of his stay.

Typical third parties include family members, friends and business associates.

Home Office guidance is that when assessing whether the relationship is genuine and whether the third party intends to provide support, the decision maker should consider the relationship between the applicant and the third party sponsor (including, if appropriate, where they met, and how often and by what method they communicate), and the third party's previous history of 'sponsoring' visitors (as previous failures to support visitors may call into question the sponsor's intention and ability to do so for this applicant).

If the third party sponsor is an individual, such as a friend or family member providing financial support for the visitor, he must demonstrate that he has enough funds available to adequately support himself, and anyone normally dependent on him, as well as the applicant.

The third party may be asked to give an undertaking in writing to be responsible for the visitor's maintenance and accommodation during the visitor's stay (see **3.3.2**).

EXAMPLE

Ada, aged 22, is a non-visa national. She arrives in the UK without an entry certificate. She informs the immigration officer that she is visiting her sister in the UK for six months. When questioned, she discloses that:

(a)   she recently lost her job;

(b)   she will be looking after her sister's children whilst she is in the UK, because her sister and brother-in-law have just got jobs;

(c)   her sister will not pay her but will provide her with food and accommodation;

(d)   she has only a few pounds in cash on her;

(e)   her sister bought her a one-way ticket to the UK.

The immigration officer may decide that she does not meet the requirements for a standard visitor, as follows:

(a) Ada is not genuinely seeking entry as a standard visitor for six months; rather, her purpose is to enter the UK to be a child-minder for her sister and brother-in-law indefinitely.

(b) Ada does not intend to leave the UK after six months, especially as she has no return ticket and no apparent means of saving enough money to buy one whilst in the UK.

(c) Ada intends to take unpaid employment.

(d) Ada has no evidence to support her claim that she will be maintained and accommodated adequately by her sister.

(e) Ada has no evidence that she can meet the cost of her return journey after six months.

In particular, the immigration officer will take into account Home Office guidance that states, 'Where a family member is coming to look after a child in the UK, this is permitted provided it is for a short visit and does not amount to the relative being employed as a child-minder. You must be satisfied that the visit is of a short duration and the relative is a genuine visitor.'

5.2.4 Multi-entry visa

Visit visas are normally valid for six months. However, if a person needs to visit the UK regularly over a longer period, they can apply for a long-term standard visitor visa that lasts two, five or 10 years.

A visit visa is valid for unlimited journeys within its period of validity. However, a person with a visit visa may remain in the UK for a maximum of only six months on any one visit, or until the visa expires if less than six months.

> **EXAMPLE**
>
> Florence is a visa national. She is granted a five-year long-term standard visitor visa that is valid from 1 February 2020 to 1 February 2025. This multi-entry visa allows Florence to come to the UK as many times as she likes during this time, as long as she does not stay for longer than six months on any visit. She must also not stay beyond 1 February 2025. Every time that Florence enters the UK, she will have to satisfy the immigration officer that she meets the visit visa requirements.

5.3 PROHIBITED ACTIVITIES

5.3.1 Work

An applicant must not intend to work in the UK. This includes:

- taking employment in the UK
- doing work for an organisation or business in the UK
- establishing or running a business as a self-employed person
- doing a work placement or an internship
- direct selling to the public and providing goods and services.

Are there any exceptions? Yes, where expressly allowed by the permitted activities (see **5.4**). However, permitted activities must not amount to the applicant's taking employment, or doing work which amounts to his filling a role or providing short-term cover for a role within a UK-based organisation. In addition, where the applicant is already paid and employed outside of the UK, he must remain so. Payment may only be allowed in the specific circumstances set out below.

5.3.2 Payment

The applicant must not receive payment from a UK source for any activities undertaken in the UK, except for the following:

(a)   reasonable expenses to cover the cost of the applicant's travel and subsistence, including fees for directors attending board-level meetings;

(b)   prize money;

(c)   billing a UK client for the applicant's time in the UK, where the applicant's overseas employer is contracted to provide services to a UK company and the majority of the contract work is carried out overseas. Payment must be lower than the amount of the applicant's salary;

(d)   where the applicant is employed by a multi-national company that, for administrative reasons, handles payment of its employees' salaries from the UK;

(e)   where the applicant is engaged in Permitted Paid Engagements (see **5.11**), provided the applicant holds a visa or leave to enter in this category;

(f)   paid performances at a permit-free festival (see **5.4.11**); or

(g)   international drivers undertaking permitted activities (see **5.4.13(c)**).

5.4 PERMITTED ACTIVITIES

5.4.1 Tourism and leisure

Traditionally this route has been used for applicants to visit friends and family and/or come to the UK for a holiday.

5.4.2 Volunteering

A visitor can undertake 'incidental volunteering'. What is that? It means that the applicant may volunteer for no more than 30 days in total of his visit for a charity that is registered with either the Charity Commission for England and Wales, or the Charity Commission for Northern Ireland or the Office of the Scottish Charity Regulator.

As to entering the UK as a charity voluntary worker, see **7.12.2**.

5.4.3 Business: general activities

What sort of general business activities can a visitor in the UK undertake? Appendix Visitor: Permitted Activities, para PA 4 to the Immigration Rules provides that a visitor may:

(a)   attend meetings, conferences, seminars, interviews;

(b)   give a one-off or short series of talks and speeches, provided these are not organised as commercial events and will not make a profit for the organiser;

(c)   negotiate and sign deals and contracts;

(d)   attend trade fairs, for promotional work only, provided the visitor is not directly selling;

(e)   carry out site visits and inspections;

(f)   gather information for the visitor's employment overseas;

(g)   be briefed on the requirements of a UK-based customer, provided that any work for the customer is done outside of the UK.

Home Office guidance is that the decision maker should assess whether the period of leave requested is credible in view of the activities the applicant is seeking to carry out. For example, as to conferences and seminars falling within (a), these will usually be formal, speaker-led events lasting for a couple of days and focused on a specific topic or sector, but they can also include familiarisation programmes for people coming to learn about UK practices on law, finance, etc. However, they must not amount to the person's undertaking work experience or longer study.

5.4.4 Business: intra-corporate activities

What activities can an employee of an overseas-based company undertake whilst in the UK in this category? In relation to a specific internal project with UK employees of the same corporate group, provided no work is carried out directly with clients, the employee may:

(a)   advise and consult;

(b)   trouble-shoot;

(c)   provide training; and

(d)   share skills and knowledge.

Home Office guidance is that these activities should be of a short duration, linked to a specific project and not involve the visitor in working directly with or for clients. The applicant should be mainly based at the company's offices in the UK and not at client sites, unless that it is for meetings.

An internal auditor may also carry out regulatory or financial audits at a UK branch of the same group of companies as the visitor's employer overseas. Are there any restrictions on the nature of the regulatory audits? No, as long as they are internal to the group of companies, including a branch or subsidiary. Home Office guidance gives the example of an auditor inspecting the quality of car productions at a manufacturing plant.

5.4.5 Transit

A visitor may transit the UK, provided they meet additional requirements (see **5.12**).

5.4.6 Manufacturing and supply of goods to the UK

An employee of a foreign manufacturer or supplier may install, dismantle, repair, service or advise on equipment, computer software or hardware where it has a contract of purchase or supply or lease with a UK company or organisation.

Home Office guidance is that this activity should normally take less than one month to carry out, given that the applicant will be in employment overseas.

5.4.7 Clients of UK export companies

A client of a UK export company may be seconded to the UK company in order to oversee the requirements for goods and services that are being provided under contract by the UK company or its subsidiary company, provided that the two companies are not part of the same group. Employees may exceptionally make multiple visits to cover the duration of the contract, but there should be a clear end date for the work.

Home Office guidance is that there should be a contract of service between the two companies for the UK company to provide goods and/or services to the overseas company. An example given is that of a UK company contracting defence services to an overseas company.

5.4.8 Science, research and academia

Scientists and researchers may:

(a)   gather information and facts for a specific project that relates directly to their employment overseas; and

(b)   share knowledge or advise on an international project that is being led from the UK, provided the visitor is not carrying out research in the UK.

Researchers and scientists must remain paid and employed overseas, and may only carry out activities that are incidental to their jobs overseas. The Home Office gives the examples of providing advice on an international project, or sharing knowledge on research being conducted overseas.

Academics may:

(a)   take part in formal exchange arrangements with UK counterparts (including doctors);

(b)   carry out research for their own purposes if they are on sabbatical leave from their home institution; and

(c)   if they are eminent senior doctors or dentists, take part in research, teaching or clinical practice, provided this does not amount to filling a permanent teaching post.

An academic can carry out research for his own purposes, such as for a book or for his employment overseas, but the research should not be for commercial gain.

Eminent senior doctors or dentists must have been working for a number of years in their profession. They may come to the UK to take part in research, teaching or clinical practice, as long as this remains incidental to their employment overseas.

Also see **5.9**.

5.4.9   Legal

An overseas lawyer may enter in this category in order to advise a UK-based client on specific international litigation and/or an international transaction.

An expert witness may visit the UK to give evidence in a UK court.

A non-expert witness may visit the UK to attend a court hearing in the UK, but only if summoned in person by a UK court. The decision maker is likely to require evidence to confirm why the witness's attendance in person is necessary, and whether his evidence could be given by video-link instead.

5.4.10   Religion

A religious worker may visit the UK to preach or do pastoral work. The applicant must not be seeking to take up an office, post or appointment in the UK.

What are pastoral duties? Home Office guidance is that these include one-off engagements, such as conducting wedding ceremonies or funerals, provided the applicant will not receive payment and will continue to be in employment overseas.

5.4.11   Creative

An artist, entertainer, or musician may:

(a)   give performances as an individual or as part of a group;

(b)   take part in competitions or auditions;

(c)   make personal appearances and take part in promotional activities; and

(d)   take part in one or more cultural events or festivals on the list of permit-free festivals in Appendix Visitor: Permit Free Festival List to the Immigration Rules.

Who is an artist? Home Office guidance is that an artist can include anyone coming to the UK to undertake an activity that is connected to the arts. Amateur and professional artists are included, such as poets, film crew, photographers and designers.

Who is an entertainer according to the Home Office? The category includes dancers, comedians, members of circus acts and members of film crew.

Can personal or technical staff (such as conductors, choreographers, stage managers, make-up artists, personal bodyguards and press officers) accompany the artist, entertainer or musician to the UK? Yes, provided they are attending the same event as the applicant and are employed to work for the applicant outside of the UK.

Film crew (including actors, producers, directors and technicians) employed by an overseas company may visit the UK to take part in a location shoot for a film or programme, provided that it is produced and financed overseas.

5.4.12 Sport

A sportsperson may:

(a) take part in a sports tournament or sports event as an individual or part of a team;

(b) make personal appearances and take part in promotional activities;

(c) take part in trials, provided they are not in front of a paying audience;

(d) take part in short periods of training, provided he is not being paid by a UK sporting body; and

(e) join an amateur team or club to gain experience in a particular sport if he is an amateur in that sport.

Sportspersons are able to take part as visitors in tournaments or events in the UK, but not in a professional domestic championship or league, including where one or more of the fixtures or rounds takes place outside the UK. A professional sportsperson who is to be employed by a team based in the UK should apply under T2 or T5 of the points-based system (see **Chapter 7**).

Personal or technical staff of the sportsperson (such as physiotherapists, coaches, dieticians and press officers), as well as sports officials, including referees, assistant referees and umpires, may also enter for these permitted activities, provided they are attending the same event as the sports person.

5.4.13 Overseas business roles requiring specific activities in the UK

It is possible for the following types of professional workers to visit the UK to carry out their work in relation to their employment overseas:

(a) a translator and/or an interpreter may translate and/or interpret in the UK as an employee of an enterprise located overseas;

(b) personal assistants and bodyguards may support an overseas business person in carrying out permitted activities, provided they will attend the same event(s) as the business person and are employed by him outside the UK. They must not be providing personal care or domestic work for the business person;

(c) a driver on a genuine international route delivering or collecting goods or passengers from abroad to the UK;

(d) a tour group courier, contracted to a company with its headquarters outside the UK, who is entering and departing the UK with a tour group organised by that company;

(e) a journalist, correspondent, producer or cameraman gathering information for an overseas publication, programme or film;

(f) archaeologists taking part in a one-off archaeological excavation;

(g) a professor from an overseas academic institution accompanying students to the UK as part of a study abroad programme, who may provide a small amount of teaching to the students at the host organisation. However, this must not amount to filling a permanent teaching role for that institution.

5.4.14 Work-related training

Employees of an overseas company or organisation may receive training from a UK-based company or organisation in work practices and techniques required for their employment overseas and not available in their home country.

An employee of an overseas-based training company may deliver a short series of training to employees of a UK-based company, where the trainer is employed by an overseas business contracted to deliver global training to the international corporate group to which the UK-based company belongs.

What is training? Home Office guidance is that it should typically be class-room based and/or involve familiarisation or observation. Is practical training allowed? Yes, provided it does not amount to training on the job or the person filling a role. It is acceptable for a visitor to learn how to use a piece of equipment in the UK, but it must not amount to working for that company in the UK.

Overseas graduates from medical, dental or nursing schools may:

(a)   undertake clinical attachments or dental observer posts provided these are unpaid, and involve no treatment of patients; and

(b)   take certain Home Office-approved tests and examinations.

5.4.15   Study

As we saw at **5.1.2**, a standard visitor's limited leave is subject to a condition of no study, but this does not prohibit the incidental study allowed by the permitted activities. So what is incidental study? It is studying:

(a)   on educational exchanges or visits with a UK state or independent school; or

(b)   a total of up to 30 days on either –

(i)   recreational courses (but not English language training), or

(ii)   a short course (which includes English language training) at an accredited institution.

As to (a), the children must be in full-time education in their home country, and any teachers or other adults accompanying the group must be employed overseas. Home Office guidance is that exchanges and educational visits should be mainly about broadening horizons and deepening intercultural understanding.

For (b)(i), the Home Office give examples of a visitor coming to the UK for a holiday and undertaking a diving, horse-riding or dancing course. The Home Office accepts that any bona fide institution in the UK can offer recreational courses. However, courses that lead to formal qualifications are not normally considered recreational.

Must the permitted 30 days be completed in just one period? No, it may consist of multiple periods totalling no more than 30 days, for example study in two blocks of 15 days. However, the visitor must not make repeat visits in order to complete a longer course of study that should be carried out under the short-term student route (see **5.13**) or Student of the points-based system (see **Chapter 6**).

5.4.16   Medical treatment

As to when a visitor may enter the UK to receive private medical treatment, or act as an organ donor or be assessed as a potential organ donor to an identified recipient in the UK, see **5.6** and **5.7** respectively.

5.5   CHILD VISITOR

A child is a person under the age of 18 at the date of applying for a visitor visa. A child might be travelling to the UK alone or with an adult. Usually the purpose of the visit is to see family, but it may be for some short-term educational reason.

5.5.1   Requirements

In addition to meeting the requirements for a standard visitor (see **5.2**), a child applicant must demonstrate that adequate arrangements have been made for his travel to, reception in and care in the UK (see **5.5.1.1**).

What if the child applicant is not applying or travelling with a parent or guardian based in his home country or country of ordinary residence who is responsible for his care? Then that parent or guardian must confirm that he consents to the arrangements for the child's travel to, and reception and care in the UK. Where requested, this consent must be given in writing. What if the child's parents are divorced? Written consent must be given by the parent who has residence or legal custody, or sole responsibility for the child.

Where a child is travelling in the company of an adult, he must hold a visa that identifies the adult with whom he seeks to enter the UK. The identification is by way of the adult's passport number, initial and surname, which is included on the child's visa document.

5.5.1.1 Adequate travel, reception and care arrangements in UK

Where a child is applying to come to the UK as a visitor, he is not expected to have funds in his own name but instead will usually meet the requirement by showing that he has access to funds from his parents, guardians or a third party. Home Office guidance is that where there are no other factors giving cause for concern, this requirement may simply involve the inclusion of the child in the travel and accommodation arrangements of the parent(s), relative(s) or friend(s) accompanying him, or a letter from a relative or friend at the UK address, inviting the child to visit.

What evidence will an ECO require for entry clearance purposes? He will need the name, address and landline telephone number of the parent or carer in the child's home country, the host in the UK and the person accompanying the child. Where these details are missing or unclear, or other factors raise concerns about the child's welfare, further enquiries will be undertaken to confirm the identity and residence of the host, and that the child is expected in the UK. The application will be refused if the ECO remains concerned about the child's welfare in the UK.

Where an immigration officer considering leave to enter has concerns about the child's welfare, the Home Office's policy is that both the social service departments in the host's area and those local to the port of entry should be contacted, so that enquiries can be made to ascertain the host's suitability.

5.6 PRIVATE MEDICAL TREATMENT VISITOR

This provision allows a person who is genuinely seeking entry for the purpose of receiving private medical treatment in the UK to do so. The ECO and immigration officer must be satisfied that he does not intend to seek free treatment under the National Health Service; that he does not represent a danger to public health; that the treatment is of finite duration; and that he has sufficient funds available to pay for the cost of treatment and all other expenses until the treatment ends.

5.6.1 Requirements

An applicant must meet the requirements for a standard visitor (see **5.2**).

If the applicant is suffering from a communicable disease, he must satisfy a Home Office-appointed medical inspector that he is not a danger to public health (see **5.6.1.1**).

The applicant must arrange his private medical treatment before travelling to the UK, and must provide a letter from his doctor or consultant detailing:

(a) the medical condition requiring consultation or treatment;

(b) the estimated costs and likely duration of any treatment, which must be of a finite duration (see **5.6.1.2**); and

(c) where the consultation or treatment will occur.

In the alternative, if the applicant intends to receive NHS treatment under a reciprocal healthcare arrangement between the UK and another country, the applicant must produce an authorisation form issued by the government of that country.

If the applicant is applying for an 11-month visit visa for the purposes of private medical treatment, he must:

(a)   provide evidence from his medical practitioner in the UK that the proposed treatment is likely to exceed six months but not more than 11 months; and

(b)   if required under the Immigration Rules (para A39 and Appendix T, Part 1), provide a valid medical certificate issued by a Home Office-approved medical practitioner, confirming that he has undergone screening for active pulmonary tuberculosis and that this tuberculosis is not present in the applicant.

In the alternative, if the applicant intends to receive NHS treatment under a reciprocal healthcare arrangement between the UK and another country, the applicant must produce an authorisation form issued by the government of that country which clearly states that the proposed treatment is likely to exceed 6 months, but not more than 11 months.

5.6.1.1   No danger to public health

A person suffering from a communicable disease may be given leave to enter if he satisfies the medical inspector that there is no danger to public health. However, an applicant who otherwise meets all the requirements may still be refused entry under para 9.16.1 of the Immigration Rules (see **3.5.4.3**) if the medical inspector confirms that his admission is undesirable for medical reasons.

5.6.1.2   Proposed course of treatment is of finite duration

Home Office guidance is that a long period of treatment, for example 11 months, may be acceptable, provided there is a clear need for the patient to be in the UK to receive treatment and he has enough funds to meet all the costs. It is for the decision maker to assess how long treatment is likely to take, for example fertility treatment can go on for some years. With the applicant's consent, the decision maker may speak to the consultant who is due to treat him. If the treatment is open-ended, the application will be refused.

5.7   ORGAN DONOR VISITOR

This provision allows entry by a person who genuinely intends to donate an organ, or who is to be assessed as a potential organ donor to an identified recipient in the UK with whom he has a genetic or close personal relationship

5.7.1   Requirements

An applicant must meet the requirements for a standard visitor (see **5.2**).

An applicant must satisfy the decision maker that he genuinely intends to donate an organ, or that he is to be assessed as a potential organ donor to an identified recipient in the UK with whom he has a genetic or close personal relationship (see **5.7.1.1**).

The applicant must provide written confirmation of medical tests to show that he is a donor match to the identified recipient, or that he is undergoing further tests to be assessed as a potential donor to the identified recipient.

The applicant must provide a letter, dated no more than three months prior to his intended date of arrival in the UK, from either:

(a)   the lead nurse or co-ordinator of the UK's NHS Trust's Living Donor Kidney Transplant team; or

(b) a UK registered medical practitioner who holds an NHS consultant post, or who appears in the Specialist Register of the General Medical Council.

The letter must confirm that the applicant meets these requirements, and give details of when and where the planned organ transplant or medical tests will take place.

The applicant must be able to demonstrate, if required to do so, that the identified recipient is legally present in the UK, or will be at the time of the planned organ transplant.

5.7.1.1 Genetic or close personal relationship

Home Office guidance is that a genetic relationship exists where the donor is a blood relative to the identified recipient in the UK.

Close personal relationships typically include the visitor's spouse, partner or close friends. They do not extend to relations established via social media campaigns.

5.7.1.2 Persons accompanying a donor

Where a family member, friend or nurse is to accompany the applicant, he must apply as a standard visitor (see **5.2**).

5.8 APPROVED DESTINATION STATUS AGREEMENT VISITOR

The Approved Destination Status Agreement allows groups of Chinese tourists to enter the UK. A very limited number of designated tour operators have been accredited and trained by the British Embassy in China, and these may submit visa applications to the British Embassy for each member of the proposed tour group. The details are to be found in para V 6.1.

5.9 ACADEMIC VISITOR IN EXCESS OF SIX MONTHS

Academics who wish to apply for a 12-month visit visa, or an extension for up to 12 months, must be highly qualified within their field of expertise and working in that area before entering the UK. This will generally apply to people with at least a PhD in their field.

5.9.1 Requirements

An applicant must meet the requirements for a standard visitor (see **5.2**).

An applicant must satisfy the decision maker that he intends to carry out one or more of the permitted activities set out at **5.4.8**. In addition, he must be highly qualified within his own field of expertise, and currently working in that field at an academic institution or institution of higher education overseas.

If required under the Immigration Rules (para A39 and Appendix T Part 1), the applicant must provide a valid medical certificate issued by a Home Office-approved medical practitioner confirming that he has undergone screening for active pulmonary tuberculosis and that this tuberculosis is not present in the applicant.

5.10 MARRIAGE AND CIVIL PARTNERSHIP VISITOR

If a person wishes to enter the UK to marry or to enter into a civil partnership, this route may be used, provided, of course, that the couple do not intend to stay in the UK after the marriage or civil partnership ceremony.

If the couple wish to remain in the UK permanently, the applicant should apply as a fiancé(e) or proposed civil partner (see **8.7**).

5.10.1 Requirements

An applicant must meet the requirements for a standard visitor (see **5.2**).

An applicant must be aged 18 or over.

An applicant must satisfy the decision maker that he intends, within the validity period covered by his visit visa, to give notice of marriage or civil partnership, or to marry or form a civil partnership. That must not be a sham marriage or sham civil partnership (see **5.10.1.1**).

On arrival in the UK, a visitor coming to marry or form a civil partnership, or give notice of this in the UK, must have a valid visit visa endorsed with this purpose and the name of his or her fiancé(e) or proposed civil partner.

5.10.1.1   Sham marriage or sham civil partnership

What is the sham here? That the marriage or civil partnership is to be entered into for the purpose of avoiding the effect of one or more provisions of UK immigration law or the Immigration Rules (see further **8.3.5.5**).

5.11   PERMITTED PAID ENGAGEMENT (PPE) VISITOR

What if a UK higher education institution wants to pay a visiting academic to examine its students, chair a selection panel, or give one or more lectures? Or what if a person wants to pay an advocate to act for him at a court or tribunal hearing, arbitration or other form of alternative dispute resolution process in the UK? Or say that a UK-based arts or sports organisation or broadcaster wants to pay a professional artist, entertainer or sports person to carry out activities relating to his main profession. In these circumstances, but strictly limited to those activities listed in para V 13.3 of Appendix V: Visitor to the Immigration Rules, an applicant may apply as a PPE visitor.

5.11.1   Requirements

An applicant must meet the requirements for a standard visitor (see **5.2**).

An applicant must intend to do one or more of the permitted paid engagements set out in para V 13.3 of Appendix V: Visitor to the Immigration Rules. The activity must be:

(a)   arranged before the applicant travels to the UK,

(b)   declared as part of the application for a visit visa or leave to enter; and

(c)   evidenced by a formal invitation as required by para V 13.2.

In addition, the activity must relate to the applicant's area of expertise and occupation overseas.

An applicant must not be a child.

This is an alternative route to requiring sponsorship under the points-based system for these activities (see **Chapter 7**).

5.12   TRANSIT VISITOR

Who is a visitor in transit? This refers to any passenger whose sole purpose is to pass through the UK within 48 hours and who either:

(a)   arrives at one port or airport and needs to transfer to another port or airport to continue his journey; or

(b)   wishes to spend the time between his arrival and embarkation outside the transit area (ie pass through immigration controls at the port or airport).

Full details can be found in Appendix V: Visitor to the Immigration Rules.

5.13   SHORT-TERM STUDY VISA

There are three potential short-term study visa categories:

(a)   a short-term student (six months) for applicants aged 18 and over for a maximum of six months' study;

(b)   a short-term student (11 months) for applicants aged 18 and over for a maximum of 11 months' English language study only (see Appendix Short-term Student (English Language));

(c)   a short-term student (child) for applicants aged under 18 for a maximum of six months' study.

Full details can be found in relevant Home Office guidance.

STUDENTS AND GRADUATES

6.1 WHO IS A STUDENT?

6.1.1 Student and Child Student

There are two main types of student categories. First, an adult student, detailed in the Immigration Rules in Appendix Student. Here an adult is any person coming to the UK for post-16 education. We shall focus on this category in this chapter, as it attracts a large number of applicants. Secondly, a child student addressed in Appendix Child Student. This category covers children aged between 4 and 17 who wish to enter the UK for their education. Note that a child aged between 4 and 15 may be educated only at an independent fee-paying school. The details of this second category, which has a limited number of applicants, are beyond the scope of this book.

All students can enter to study at a Home Office-approved education provider only (see **6.2**). This is otherwise known as sponsorship.

Note that a Student after completing their studies may be able to switch to the Graduate route to stay in the UK to work or look for work (see **6.9**).

References to paragraphs in the Immigration Rules in this part of the chapter are to Appendix Student unless otherwise stated.

6.2 SPONSORSHIP: APPROVED EDUCATION PROVIDER

6.2.1 Obtaining a licence from the Home Office

All education providers that want to provide courses for international students need a licence from the Home Office. One key step is for the provider to obtain a satisfactory review or inspection by one of the publicly recognised inspection bodies approved for Student purposes (namely Ofsted and its equivalents in the devolved administrations, the Quality Assurance Agency for Higher Education and the Department for Education-approved inspectorates for independent schools). In addition, a provider must be able to show that it has allocated a number of key roles to its staff using the Home Office online sponsorship management system; it can comply with its sponsorship duties; and it has the appropriate human resource systems in place to be able to monitor its students' attendance.

For ease of reference, throughout the rest of this chapter we shall refer to an approved education provider as the 'sponsor'.

6.2.2   Sponsorship duties

The key duties of a sponsor are to keep copies of all students' passports, to keep up-to-date contact details for students, and to tell the Home Office if a student has any unauthorised absences, fails to enrol on their course or stops their studies.

6.2.3   Students register

Once a sponsor has a licence, it is added to the Students register with details of its name and location. The register can be found on the Home Office website (see **1.2.8**).

6.3   VALIDITY REQUIREMENTS

6.3.1   Entry clearance and permission to stay

Paragraph ST 1.1 provides that an applicant must apply on the specified form on gov.uk in accordance with **Table 6.1** below.

Table 6.1   Specified forms

Application	Form
EEA national with a chipped passport	Either: • Student using the UK Immigration: ID Check app; or • the forms listed below for applicants outside or inside the UK (as relevant)
Outside the UK	Student visa
Inside the UK	Student

The specified form process is detailed at **3.6.4**.

EEA nationals have passports that contain an electronic chip which stores their facial image and biographical data.

Paragraph 1.2 provides that an applicant must meet all the following requirements:

(a)   any fee (see **3.6.4.2**) and Immigration Health Charge (see **3.10**) must have been paid;

(b)   the applicant must have provided any required biometrics (see **3.4.3**);

(c)   the applicant must have provided a passport or other travel document which satisfactorily establishes their identity and nationality; and

(d)   the applicant must provide a Confirmation of Acceptance for Studies ('CAS') reference number (see **6.5.5.1**) that was issued to them no more than six months before the date of application.

What about switching in-country? By para 1.4 it is not possible to switch from the following categories: (a) a Visitor (see **Chapter 5**); (b) a Short-term Student (see **5.13**); (c) a Parent of an Appendix Child Student; or (d) a Seasonal Worker (see **7.12.7**).

Is there a minimum age requirement? Yes, para ST 1.5 provides that the applicant must be at least 16 years old on the date of application.

Any application which does not meet all these validity requirements is invalid and may be rejected and not considered.

6.4   SUITABILITY REQUIREMENTS

By para ST 2.1 an applicant must not fall for refusal under Part 9: grounds for refusal (see **3.5.4**).

Paragraph ST 2.2 provides that an applicant for permission to stay must not:

(a) be in the UK in breach of immigration laws, except that, where para 39E applies, any current period of overstaying will be disregarded (see **3.6.5**); or

(b) be on immigration bail (see **3.5.5**).

6.5 ELIGIBILITY REQUIREMENTS

6.5.1 Entry requirement

By para ST 3.1 entry clearance in this category is mandatory for all applicants.

Note that para ST 3.2 provides that any person applying for entry clearance for more than six months must meet the requirements for a tuberculosis certificate if the criteria specified in para A39 and in Appendix T of the Immigration Rules apply (see **3.4.1**).

6.5.2 Date of application requirement

By para ST 4.1 an application for entry clearance must be made no more than six months before the start date of the course stated on the CAS (see **6.5.5.1**).

Paragraph ST 4.2 provides that an application for permission to stay must be made no more than three months before the start date of the course on the Confirmation of Acceptance for Studies. By para ST 4.3 such an application must be for study on a course with a start date no more than 28 days after the expiry date of the applicant's previous permission.

6.5.3 Genuine Student requirement

By para ST 5.1 the applicant must be a genuine Student.

Home Office guidance is that when assessing whether the applicant is a genuine Student, the ECO must consider the application in the round and might take into account factors such as:

(1) The immigration history of the applicant and any dependant, in the UK and other countries, for example:
   - previous visa applications for the UK and other countries, including reasons for any visa refusals;
   - the amount of time the applicant has spent in the UK or other countries on previous visas, and for what purpose;
   - whether the applicant has complied with the terms of previous visas for the UK and other countries.

(2) The applicant's education history, study and post-study plans, for example:
   - the amount of time that has elapsed since the applicant last studied, and whether the applicant has sound reasons for returning to, or commencing, formal study in this area, particularly after any significant gap;
   - whether the applicant demonstrates sufficient commitment to the course;
   - whether the course represents academic progression;
   - the credibility of the applicant's rationale for, knowledge of, and level of research undertaken into, the proposed course of study and sponsoring institution, and living arrangements in the UK;
   - how the circumstances of any dependant may affect the ability or motivation of the applicant to study;
   - the relevance of the course to post-study plans in the UK or overseas;
   - whether the applicant intends to comply with the terms of their visa, including the requirement to leave the UK when their leave comes to an end (or, where lawful and appropriate, to apply to extend their leave as a Student or to switch to another immigration route).

(3)   The personal and financial circumstances of the applicant and any dependant, for example:

- the economic circumstances of the applicant and any dependant in their region in their home country;

- whether the applicant has credible funds to meet course fees, and living costs for themselves and any dependants for the duration of the course in the UK, in light of the fact that they may have limited or no ability to work in the UK;

- how the applicant was able to acquire the necessary funds for course fees, as well as accommodation in a UK city and living expenses in the UK for themselves and any dependant;

- the distance between the applicant's place of study and their proposed accommodation in the UK;

- the average monthly expenditure for the applicant and any dependant in the UK;

- the applicant's personal circumstances, where these might make it difficult to complete a full-time course of study.

(4)   The course provider and agents, for example:

- if the applicant is applying to study at an institution that is under investigation or has been identified by the Home Office as an institution of concern in relation to immigration compliance;

- where the application is being managed by an agent about whom the Home Office has concerns.

(5)   Where an applicant will be accompanied by a dependant or dependants and it appears that one of the main applicant's reasons for applying for a Student visa is employment, education or health care benefits for the dependants, the entry clearance officer or caseworker should consider particularly carefully whether they are satisfied that the applicant is a genuine Student.

(6)   The following are pull factors that are known to influence students' choice of the UK as their destination – they can give an indication of the Student's motivation in coming to the UK and whether they are a genuine Student:

- did they choose the UK because of the academic reputation of the UK's education institutions in comparison with those of other countries, for example, is the UK perceived to be the best for post-graduate study?

- was the ease of working during or after the course a deciding factor?

Home Office guidance is that a caseworker must not refuse an applicant based on an applicant's knowledge of the location where they will be studying, for example, if the applicant has a lack of knowledge of bus routes, or of the geography of the town or city.

If a caseworker has concerns over the applicant's English language ability potentially falling short of the required level, they should consider this when assessing the genuine Student requirement. However, the caseworker must clearly provide a justification in any refusal letter.

For those considered to be genuine Students, intention to leave the UK at the end of the course is not relevant as there are many bases on which an individual might lawfully remain in the UK.

6.5.4 Points requirement

By para ST 6.1 the applicant must be awarded a total of 70 points as per **Table 6.2** below.

Table 6.2   Points requirement

Points type	Relevant requirements to be met	Number of points
Study (must meet all)	Confirmation of Acceptance for Studies requirement Course requirement Approved qualification requirement Level of study requirement Place of study requirement	50
Financial	Financial requirement	10
English language	English language requirement	10

6.5.5   The study requirement

6.5.5.1   The Confirmation of Acceptance for Studies requirement

Once a sponsor has been granted a licence, the sponsor can access the Home Office's IT sponsorship management system. This may be used to create and assign a Confirmation of Acceptance for Studies (CAS). This is therefore not an actual certificate or paper document. It is a virtual document similar to a database record. Each CAS has a unique reference number. The CAS must contain the necessary information to confirm that all the relevant study requirements are met to secure the Student 50 points.

The CAS must state the cost of accommodation and fees (and any payment already made) so that the financial requirement (see **6.5.6**) can be assessed. In addition, it must show how the English language requirement has been met (see **6.5.7**).

6.5.5.2   Course requirement

Unless an exception applies (see the details in paras ST 8.2 and 8.4), the application must be for a course which is one of the following:

(a)   a full-time course at degree level or above that leads to an approved qualification (see **6.5.5.3**);

(b)   a full-time course below degree level involving a minimum of 15 hours per week of organised daytime study (08:00 to 18:00, Monday to Friday) that leads to an approved qualification (see **6.5.5.3**);

(c)   a full-time course involving a minimum of 15 hours per week of organised daytime study that is a pre-sessional course;

(d)   a part-time course above degree level that leads to an approved qualification (see **6.5.5.3**) where the CAS has been issued by a higher education provider with a four-year track record of compliance; or

(e)   a full-time course at degree level or above that is recognised by the UK's National Information Centre for the recognition and evaluation of international qualifications and skills (UK ENIC (www.enic.org.uk)) as being equivalent to a UK higher education course where the CAS has been assigned by an overseas higher education institution or a higher education provider with a four-year track record of compliance.

6.5.5.3   Approved qualification requirement

The course of study must lead to an approved qualification which is one of the following:

(a)   validated by Royal Charter;

(b)   awarded by a UK recognised body;

(c)   covered by a legal agreement between a UK recognised body and another education provider or awarding body, which confirms both: (i) the UK recognised body's independent assessment of the level of the Student sponsor's or awarding body's programme compared to the Regulated Qualifications Framework or its equivalents; and (ii) that the UK recognised body would admit any Student who successfully completes the education provider's or the awarding body's named course onto a specific or a range of degree-level courses it provides;

(d)   recognised by one or more recognised bodies through a formal articulation agreement with the awarding body;

(e)   in England, Wales and Northern Ireland, is at Regulated Qualifications Framework level 3 or above;

(f)   an overseas qualification that UK ENIC assesses as valid and equivalent to Regulated Qualifications Framework level 3 or above; or

(g)   an aviation licence, rating or certificate issued by the UK's Civil Aviation Authority.

6.5.5.4   Level of study requirement

The course must normally meet one of the following requirements:

(a)   the course will be studied in England, Wales or Northern Ireland and it is at Regulated Qualifications Framework level 3 or above;

(b)   the course is a short-term study abroad programme in the UK as part of the applicant's qualification at an overseas higher education institution outside of the UK, and that qualification is recognised as being at UK bachelor's degree level or above by UK ENIC;

(c)   the course is a pre-sessional course in English language at level B2 or above of the Common European Framework of Reference for Languages;

(d)   the course is a recognised Foundation Programme for postgraduate doctors or dentists;

(e)   the course is being delivered under a partnership between a higher education institution and a research institute and is accredited at Regulated Qualifications Framework level 7 or above.

6.5.5.5   Place of study requirement

As a general rule, all study that forms part of the course of study must take place on the premises of the sponsor or any partner institution.

6.5.6   The financial requirement

6.5.6.1   How much?

To score the required 10 points, the level of funds that the applicant will have to show is available will depend on where their course is being studied.

Table 6.3 below sets out the details regarding funds.

Table 6.3   Amount of funds required dependent on location

Location	Level of funds required
In London	Sufficient funds to pay any outstanding course fees as stated on the CAS and £1,334 for each month of the course up to a maximum of 9 months.
Outside London	Sufficient funds to pay any outstanding course fees as stated on the CAS and £1,023 for each month of the course up to a maximum of 9 months.

If the length of the applicant's course includes a part of a month, the time period will be rounded up to the next full month.

If the applicant has paid all or part of their course fees to their sponsor, this must be confirmed on the CAS, otherwise the applicant must provide a receipt issued by the sponsor confirming the amount of fees paid.

By para ST 12.4, if the applicant has paid a deposit to their sponsor for accommodation that the sponsor is providing (such as halls of residence), this deposit but only up to a maximum of £1,334 can be offset against the level of funds required.

When will a Student be studying in London? The answer is when their CAS confirms they will be studying at an institution wholly within the Greater London Area. If the applicant will be studying at more than one site, one or more of which is in Greater London Area and one or more outside, then the applicant will be considered to be studying in London if the applicant's CAS states that the applicant will be spending the majority of time studying at a site or sites situated within the Greater London Area.

EXAMPLE

Bryana applies for entry clearance as a Student. She has a CAS issued by a London-based sponsor. She has a place on a six-month (Home Office-approved) course. She does not have an official financial sponsor. She has paid her course fees as recorded in her CAS. She is arranging her own privately rented accommodation. What level of funds does she need? As she has already paid her course fees, she needs funds for the six months of her London-based course, that is £1,334 x 6 = £8,004.

EXAMPLE

Zach applies for entry clearance a Student. He has a CAS issued by a sponsor based outside London. He has a place on a three-year bachelor's degree course. He does not have an official financial sponsor. He has paid some of his course fees, leaving £5,500 due as recorded in his CAS. He has paid a deposit of £250 to his sponsor for accommodation in its halls of residence which is also recorded in his CAS. What level of funds does he need? He needs the balance of his course fees of £5,500 plus the Home Office set figure of £9,207 (as his course exceeds nine months and is based outside of London, ie £1,023 x 9). That totals £14,707. But he can deduct the £250 deposit paid towards the accommodation provided by his sponsor, leaving £14,457 required.

6.5.6.2   Evidence of the financial requirement

What records must a Student produce to show that they meet the required level of funds? Funds may be held in any form of personal bank or building society account (including current, deposit, savings, pension from which the funds can be withdrawn or investment account) provided the account allows the funds to be accessed immediately. However, funds held in other accounts or financial instruments such as shares, bonds, credit cards, pensions from which the funds cannot be withdrawn immediately, regardless of notice period, are not acceptable as evidence of funds.

The accounts relied on by the Student must be in their name, either alone or as a joint account holder, unless one of the following applies:

(a)   the account is in the name of the applicant's partner who is applying for entry clearance or permission to stay at the same time or has been granted permission; or

(b)   the account may be in the name of their parent, or their legal guardian. The Student must provide proof of this relationship and written consent from the parent or legal guardian to use the funds.

Overdraft facilities and promises of future third-party support are not acceptable as evidence of funds. So, what alternative sources do count? These include funds provided by an official financial sponsor, which must be Her Majesty's Government, the applicant's national government, the British Council or any international organisation, international company or University. In addition, a student loan counts if provided by a government; or a government sponsored student loan company; or an academic or educational loans scheme which is provided by a financial institution regulated for the purpose of issuing student loans by either the Financial Conduct Authority (FCA) and the Prudential Regulation Authority (PRA) or, in the case of overseas accounts, the official regulatory body for the country the institution is in and where the money is held.

Unless the applicant is relying on a student loan or an award from a government or international sponsorship agency, they must show that they have held the required level of funds for a 28-day period. The most recently dated piece of financial evidence produced by the Student must be dated within 31 days before the date of their application. The financial evidence provided must cover the whole 28-day period.

The applicant's financial documents must be from institutions acceptable to the Home Office. Appendix Finance para FIN 2.1 provides that funds will not be considered if they are held in a financial institution where (a) the decision maker is unable to make satisfactory verification checks; or (b) the financial institution is not regulated by the appropriate regulatory body for the country in which that institution is operating; or (c) the financial institution does not use electronic record keeping.

Applicants from a country listed in the differential evidence provision (see **6.5.8.2**) do not have to produce documentation required to meet the financial requirement, unless specifically required to do.

6.5.7 The English language requirement

6.5.7.1 What is required?

By para ST 13.1, the applicant must show English language ability on the Common European Framework of Reference for Languages in all four components of reading, writing, speaking and listening. To what level? At least level B2 if studying a course at UK Bachelor's degree level or above; or level B1 where studying a course below UK Bachelor's degree level.

6.5.7.2 How can the requirement be met?

The applicant must show that they meet the English language requirement as specified in Appendix English Language. Broadly, this can be done in any of the following six ways:

(a) If the applicant has already met the requirement at the required level in a previous successful application for entry clearance or permission.

(b) If the applicant is a national of any of the following majority-English-speaking countries:

Antigua and Barbuda • Australia • The Bahamas • Barbados • Belize • Canada • Dominica • Grenada • Guyana • Ireland • Jamaica • Malta • New Zealand • St Kitts and Nevis • St Lucia • St Vincent and the Grenadines • Trinidad and Tobago • United States of America.

(c) If the applicant has either (i) a Bachelor's degree, Master's degree or doctorate awarded in the UK; or (ii) a degree or degree-level qualification taught in a university or college in a majority-English-speaking country listed in (b) above but excluding Canada, which meets or exceeds the recognised standard of a Bachelor's degree, Master's degree or doctorate awarded in the UK; or (iii) a degree or degree level qualification which meets, or exceeds, the recognised standard of a UK Bachelor's degree, Master's degree or doctorate and was taught or researched in English.

If the relevant qualification was awarded by a body from outside the UK, confirmation must be obtained from UK ENIC that the qualification meets the requirement.

The Student will need to produce the certificate from their awarding body: or a transcript issued by the university or college that awarded their qualification; or an official letter from the university or college that awarded their qualification containing information equivalent to a degree certificate.

(d) If the applicant provides a valid digital reference number from an approved provider showing they have passed an approved English language test to the required level in the two years before the date of application. The list of approved tests and providers can be found on the Home Office website (see **1.2.8**).

(e) If the applicant has a GCSE, 'A' level, Scottish National Qualification at level 4 or 5 or Scottish Higher or Advanced Higher, in English (language or literature), that was awarded: (a) by an Ofqual (or SQA, Qualifications Wales or CCEA) regulated awarding body, and (b) following education in a UK school undertaken while they were aged under 18. The applicant will have to produce a certificate, or an official transcript issued by that awarding body.

(f) If the applicant is applying for a course of study at degree level or above and they are sponsored by a higher education provider with a 4-track record of compliance who states on the CAS that they have assessed the applicant's English language ability and how they have assessed it.

6.5.8 Documents used to obtain an offer requirement

6.5.8.1 What is required?

By para ST 20.1, the applicant must provide evidence of the qualifications or references they used to obtain the offer of a place on the course of study from their sponsor, unless either the applicant is applying for a course of study at degree level or above and is sponsored by a higher education provider with a four-year track record of compliance or para ST 22.1 applies (see **6.5.8.2**).

What evidence of each qualification must the applicant provide? It is one of the following: (a) the certificate(s) of qualification; (b) the transcript of results; or (c) a print out of the qualification or transcript results from the awarding body's online checking service (although the decision maker may require (a) or (b) in addition).

6.5.8.2 Differential evidence requirement

Nationals of certain countries are regarded as low risk and so do not have to meet this requirement (or produce documentation required to meet the financial requirement: see **6.5.6.2**) unless specifically required to do. What nationals are included? They are: holders of a valid passport which shows they are registered as a British National (Overseas), or which was issued by the competent authorities of Hong Kong SAR, Macau SAR or Taiwan (which includes the number of the identification card issued by the competent authority in Taiwan); or a national of any of the following:

Australia • Austria • Bahrain • Barbados • Belgium • Botswana • Brazil • Brunei • Bulgaria • Cambodia • Canada • Chile • China • Croatia • Republic of Cyprus • Czech Republic • Denmark • The Dominican Republic • Estonia • Finland • France • Germany • Greece • Hungary • Iceland • Indonesia • Ireland • Italy • Japan • Kazakhstan • Kuwait • Latvia • Liechtenstein • Lithuania • Luxembourg • Malaysia • Malta • Mauritius • Mexico • Netherlands • New Zealand • Norway • Oman • Peru • Poland • Portugal • Qatar • Romania • Serbia • Singapore • Slovakia • Slovenia • South Korea • Spain • Sweden • Switzerland • Thailand • Tunisia • United Arab Emirates • United States of America.

6.6 PERMISSION TO ENTER THE UK

6.6.1 Length of permission

If granted entry clearance, how long will a Student get as their permission to enter the UK? The starting point is the duration of their course as specified in their CAS. The total length of their permission will depend on the nature and length of the course, as set out in **Table 6.4** below.

Table 6.4   Amount of permission to enter

Type of course	Period granted before course start date	Period granted after course end date
A course of 12 months or longer	1 month	4 months
A course of 6 months or longer but shorter than 12 months	1 month	2 months

> **EXAMPLE**
>
> Chloe is granted entry clearance as a Student. Her CAS states that her course lasts 24 months. Her period of permission to enter the UK will be 29 months (24 months course plus a 1-month period before her course starts and a 4-month period after her course ends).

6.6.2   Conditions attached to permission

The grant of permission to a Student will be subject to the following conditions:

(a)   no access to public funds (see **3.3.2**);

(b)   no work except as specified in para ST 26 (see **6.6.2.1**);

(c)   no study except as specified in para ST 27 (see **6.6.2.2**); and

(d)   if Part 10 applies, the person will be required to register with the police (see **3.3.3**).

6.6.2.1   Work condition

An applicant's permission to enter the UK will be subject to the following employment conditions listed in **Table 6.5** below.

Table 6.5   Employment conditions

Type of study	Employment conditions
Student following a full-time course of degree level or above study, either: (a) sponsored by a higher education provider with a four-year track record of compliance; or (b) sponsored by an overseas higher education institution to undertake a short-term study abroad programme in the UK	20 hours per week during term time (full-time employment permitted outside of term time)
Student undertaking a full-time course below degree level study sponsored by a higher education provider with a four-year track record of compliance	10 hours per week during term time (full-time employment permitted outside of term time)
All other study	No employment permitted

Normally, a Student is not allowed to be self-employed, engage in business activity, work as a professional sportsperson (including as a sports coach), work as an entertainer or work in a position which would fill a permanent full-time vacancy.

6.6.2.2   Study

Generally, a Student must only study with the sponsor which assigned their CAS and on the course of study for which their CAS was assigned.

6.7 EXTENDING PERMISSION TO ENTER

6.7.1 When to apply

After finishing one course, a Student may wish to take another course. In these circumstances, an application for permission to stay must be made to study on a course with a start date no more than 28 days after the expiry date of the Student's current permission. In addition, the application for must be made no more than three months before the start date of the new course as stated on the CAS.

6.7.2 Financial requirement

Only if the Student has been in the UK with permission for less than 12 months will they have to meet the financial requirement (see **6.5.6**).

6.7.3 Academic progress requirement

By para ST 14.1, an applicant who has or previously had permission on the Student route and is applying for permission to stay as a Student must have successfully completed the course of study for which they were last granted permission on the Student route, unless an exception in para ST 14.4 applies, or they are applying to progress to a higher level course as specified in para ST 14.3(a) or (b).

In addition, by para ST 14.2, the applicant must show academic progress from the previous courses of study unless one of the exceptions in para ST 14.4 applies.

Paragraph ST 14.3 provides that an applicant will show academic progress if they are applying for any of the following:

(a)   to progress from a Bachelor's to Master's level course which is part of an integrated Master's course, where the applicant has been offered a place on a higher-level course by the student sponsor after an assessment of their academic ability;

(b)   to progress from a Master's to a PhD which is part of an integrated master's and PhD programme, where the applicant has been offered a place on a higher-level course by the student sponsor after an assessment of their academic ability; or

(c)   a course which is above the level of the previous course of study for which they were last granted permission unless: (i) the student sponsor is a higher education provider with a four-year track record of compliance; and (ii) the course is at degree level or above; and (iii) the new course is at the same level as the previous course of study; and (iv) the student sponsor confirms that either: (1) the new course of study is related to the applicant's previous course of study (meaning that it is either connected to the previous course, part of the same subject group, or involves deeper specialisation); or (2) the combination of the previous course of study and the new course of study support the applicant's genuine career aspirations.

By para ST 14.4, an applicant does not need to show academic progress where they are applying to re-sit examinations or repeat modules under para ST 14.5; or have previously re-sat examinations or repeated modules under para ST 14.5 and are applying to complete the course for which those examinations were re-sat or modules repeated. Paragraph ST 14.5 provides that if the applicant is re-sitting examinations or repeating a module of a course, the applicant must not previously have re-sat the same examination or repeated the same module more than once (they can only do so twice).

6.7.4 Maximum period of study requirement

By para ST 19.1, if the applicant is applying for a course that is below degree level, the grant of permission must not lead to the applicant being granted more than two years on this route to study courses below degree level from the age of 18 unless it is a regulatory requirement of the

Maritime and Coastguard Agency that the applicant spends at least 12 months at sea as a part of that course.

Paragraph ST 19.3 provides that if the course is at degree level, the grant of permission must not lead to the applicant being granted more than five years on the Student route from the age of 18 to study courses at degree level unless the course of study is one of the following:

(a)   architecture;

(b)   medicine;

(c)   dentistry;

(d)   veterinary medicine and science;

(e)   music at a music college that is a member of Conservatoires UK;

(f)   law, where the applicant has completed a course at degree level or above and is applying for a course of study which is a law conversion course validated by the Solicitors Regulation Authority and the Bar Standards Board in England and Wales.

6.8   FAMILY MEMBERS OF A STUDENT

6.8.1   Who are family members?

If subject to immigration controls, the spouse, civil partner, fiancé(e) or proposed civil partner, or unmarried partner ('the partner') and children under 18 of a Student will require entry clearance in order to enter the UK as a family member. If relevant, they should subsequently apply for an extension at the same time as the Student.

A child must be under the age of 18 at the date of application, unless they were last granted permission as a dependent child of the parent who has or is applying for entry clearance or permission to stay as a Student or as a dependant partner of a student (regardless of the route under which the parent had permission at the time the child's last permission was granted).

6.8.2   Which family members?

Can all Students bring their family members to the UK? No. So who can? The partner or child of a person who is:

(a)   a Student who has received an award from a government or international sponsorship agency and has, or is applying for, permission to study on a full-time course of six months or longer; or

(b)   a full-time Student who has, or is applying for, permission to study a postgraduate level course of nine months or longer at a higher education provider with a 4-track record of compliance; or

(c)   a Student who has, or had within the last three months before the date of application, permission to study on a full-time course of six months or longer, and is now applying for permission to study a full-time course of six months or longer where either: (i) the partner or child already has, or had within the last three months before the date of application, permission as a dependent partner or dependent child of the Student; or (ii) the child was born since the last grant of permission to the Student, where the Student and partner or child are applying at the same time.

See para ST 31.2 in respect of a child born to a Student whilst they are studying in the UK.

6.8.3   Validity requirements

The applicant must apply on the specified form on gov.uk in accordance with **Table 6.6** below.

Table 6.6   Specified forms

Applicant	Specified Form
EEA national with a chipped passport	Either (as applicable): • Dependant partner or dependant child using the UK Immigration: ID Check app; or • the forms listed below for dependant applicants outside or inside the UK as relevant.
Outside the UK	Dependant partner visa Dependant child visa
Inside the UK	If the dependant is applying at the same time as the Student, they can be included in the form Student where the form allows dependants to be added. Otherwise: Dependant partner Dependant child

Location of partner or child	Nationality	Form
Outside the UK	EEA national with a chipped passport	Either (as applicable): • Dependant partner or Dependant partner visa • Dependant child or Dependant child visa
	Other applicants	Dependant partner visa Dependant child visa
Inside the UK	All applicants	If the dependant is applying at the same time as the Student applicant, they can be included in the form Student where the form allows dependants to be added. Otherwise: Dependant partner Dependant child

The applicant must meet all the following requirements:

(a)   any fee (see **3.6.4.2**) and Immigration Health Charge (see **3.10**) must have been paid;

(b)   the applicant must have provided any required biometrics (see **3.4.3**); and

(c)   the applicant must have provided a passport or other travel document which satisfactorily establishes their identity and nationality.

An applicant who is in the UK on the date of application must not have, or have last been granted, permission as a Visitor (see **Chapter 5**), or a Short-term Student (see **5.13**), or a Parent of a Child Student, or a Seasonal Worker (see **7.12.7**).

6.8.4   Suitability requirements

An applicant must not fall for refusal under Part 9: grounds for refusal (see **3.5.4**).

An applicant must not:

(a)   be in the UK in breach of immigration laws, except that, where para 39E applies, any current period of overstaying will be disregarded (see **3.6.5**); or

(b)   be on immigration bail (see **3.5.5**).

6.8.5 Relationship requirement for dependent partner of a Student

The applicant and their Student partner must both be aged 18 or over at the date of application.

If the applicant and their Student partner are not married or in a civil partnership, all the following requirements must be met:

(a)   they must have been living together in a relationship similar to marriage or civil partnership for at least the two years before the date of application;

(b)   any previous relationship of the applicant and their partner with another person must have permanently broken down; and

(c)   the applicant and their partner must not be so closely related that they would not have been allowed to marry in the UK (see **8.3.5.3**).

The relationship must be genuine and subsisting (see **8.3.5.5**).

The applicant and their Student partner must intend to live together throughout the applicant's stay in the UK.

The applicant must not intend to stay in the UK beyond any permission granted to their student partner.

As to any financial requirement, see **6.8.7**.

6.8.6 Relationship requirement for dependent child of a Student

The applicant must be the child of a parent who has, or is at the same time being granted permission as a Student or the partner of a Student.

Each of the applicant's parents must either be applying at the same time as the applicant or have permission to be in the UK (other than as a visitor) unless:

(a)   the parent with permission as a Student or as a partner of a Student is the sole surviving parent;

(b)   the parent with permission as a Student or as a partner of a Student has sole responsibility for the child's upbringing (see **8.9.4.3**); or

(c)   the decision maker is satisfied that there are serious and compelling reasons (see **8.9.4.4**) to grant the child entry clearance or permission to stay with the parent who has permission on the Student route or as a dependent partner of a Student.

The child must live with a parent who has permission on the Student route during their stay in the UK, unless they can demonstrate a valid reason why they should not live with that parent but they have not been leading an independent life. There must be suitable arrangements for the child's care and accommodation in the UK which must comply with relevant UK legislation and regulations.

If the child is aged 16 or over at the date of application, they must not be leading an independent life (see **8.9.4.6**).

6.8.7 Financial requirement for dependent partner and child of a Student

Where the partner and/or child is applying for entry clearance or permission to stay and they have been in the UK less than 12 months, the Student, that partner or child must have funds specified in **Table 6.7** below up to a total of nine months or for the period of permission applied for by the partner and/or child, whichever is the shorter.

Table 6.7   Funds

Place of Student's study	Funds required
Studying in London	£845 per month
Studying outside London	£680 per month

These funds must be in addition to the funds required by the Student to meet their own financial requirement (see **6.5.6**) as well as the funds required for any other dependent of the Student who is applying at the same time or is already in the UK as a dependant.

Unless the applicant is relying on financial sponsorship from a government or international sponsorship agency that covers living costs of the Student and their partner and/or dependent child, the applicant must show that they have held the required level of funds for a 28-day period. The most recently dated piece of financial evidence produced by the applicant must be dated within 31 days before the date of their application. The financial evidence provided must cover the whole 28-day period.

EXAMPLE 1

Anne applies for entry clearance as a Student. She has a CAS issued by a London-based sponsor. She has a place on a 24-month Master's degree course. She does not have an official financial sponsor. She has paid her course fees as recorded in her CAS. Her civil partner, Brenda, will be travelling with her. They will be living in privately rented accommodation. In addition to meeting the non-financial requirements above, what funds must she have available? Anne needs £12,006 to cover her own living costs for the first nine months in the UK (£1,334 x 9: see **6.5.6.1**). As she will get 29 months' leave (see **6.6.1**), there must be the maximum additional amount available for Brenda of £7,605 (£845 x 9).

EXAMPLE 2

Lewis applies for entry clearance as a Student. He has a CAS issued by a sponsor based outside London. He has a place on a 12-month Master's degree course. He does not have an official financial sponsor. He has not yet paid his course fees. He is not using accommodation arranged by his sponsor. His wife, Alice, and 6-year-old son, John, will be travelling with him. In addition to meeting the non-financial requirements above, what funds does he need to have available? Lewis needs the amount of his course fees and £9,207 to cover his own living costs for the first nine months in the UK (£1,023 x 9: see **6.5.6.1**). As he will get 17 months' leave (see **6.6.1**), there must be the maximum additional amount available for his wife, Alice, of £6,120 (£680 x 9) and also the maximum additional amount available for his son, John, of £6,120 (£680 x 9).

6.8.8   Length of permission

A partner will be granted permission which ends on the same date as the Student's permission. A child will be granted permission which ends on the same date as whichever of their parents' permission ends first.

6.8.9   Conditions of permission

The grant of permission to a partner or child will be subject to all the following conditions:

(a)   no access to public funds (see **3.3.2**);

(b)   work, including self-employment and voluntary work, is generally permitted (see para ST 39.3(b) for the exceptions);

(c)   study is permitted (subject to the ATAS condition in Appendix ATAS if the study will commence when the partner or child is aged over 18); and

(d)   if Part 10 applies, the person will be required to register with the police (see **3.3.3**).

6.9   THE GRADUATE ROUTE

References to paragraphs in the Immigration Rules in this part of the chapter are to Appendix Graduate unless otherwise stated.

This route is for a Student in the UK who wants to work, or look for work, following their successful completion of an eligible course of study at UK bachelor's degree-level or above. The study must have been with a higher education provider with a track record of compliance.

Does a Graduate need a sponsor? No.

A Graduate visa lasts for 2 years unless the Student has a PhD or other doctoral qualification, when it will last for 3 years. The visa cannot be extended and it cannot lead to settlement. However, the Graduate might be able to switch categories, eg to a Skilled Worker (see **7.8**).

Can an existing dependant of a Student who is applying on this route also apply to extend their permission as a dependant on this route? Yes. The detailed requirements can be found in paras GR 9.1 to GR 14.2.

6.10   VALIDITY REQUIREMENTS

Paragraph GR 1.1 provides that an applicant must apply on the specified 'Graduate' form on gov.uk.

The specified form process is detailed at **3.6.4**.

Paragraph GR 1.2 provides that an applicant must meet all the following requirements:

(a)   any fee (see **3.6.4.2**) and Immigration Health Charge (see **3.10**) must have been paid;

(b)   the applicant must have provided any required biometrics (see **3.4.3**);

(c)   the applicant must have provided a passport or other travel document which satisfactorily establishes their identity and nationality; and

(d)   the applicant must be in the UK.

An applicant must have, or have last had, permission as a Student. An applicant must not have been previously granted permission as a Graduate.

If an applicant has, in the 12 months before their application, been awarded a scholarship or sponsorship by a government or international scholarship agency, covering both course fees and living costs for study in the UK (eg a Chevening or Marshall scholarship), they must provide written consent from their financial sponsor to the application for permission to stay in the UK as a Graduate.

6.11   SUITABILITY REQUIREMENTS

By para GR 2.1, an applicant must not fall for refusal under Part 9: grounds for refusal (see **3.5.4**).

Paragraph GR 2.2 provides that an applicant for permission to stay must not:

(a)   be in the UK in breach of immigration laws, except that, where para 39E applies, that period of overstaying will be disregarded (see **3.6.5**); or

(b)   be on immigration bail (see **3.5.5**).

6.12 ELIGIBILITY REQUIREMENTS

6.12.1 Points

By para GR 3.1, the applicant must be awarded a total of 70 points by meeting all of the following requirements: successful completion of course (see **6.12.2**), relevant qualification (see **6.12.3**) and study in the UK (see **6.12.4**).

6.12.2 Successful completion requirement

By para GR 4.1, the applicant must have last been sponsored by a Student sponsor which is a higher education provider with a track record of compliance on the date of application.

By para GR 4.2, the applicant must have successfully completed the course of study which was undertaken during their last grant of permission to study on the Student route (where the applicant was allowed to change their course of study without applying for further permission as a Student, this requirement only applies to the course to which they changed).

The student sponsor must have notified the Home Office, by the date of application, that the applicant has successfully completed the course of study in para GR 4.2. However, if the notification has not been received from the Student Sponsor, but the applicant's CAS (see **6.5.5.1**) shows that the applicant had been studying a qualifying qualification (see **6.12.3**), the caseworker must not refuse the application if it would otherwise be granted. Instead, the caseworker must contact the Sponsor asking for confirmation that the student has successfully completed the course of study.

6.12.3 Qualification requirement

By para GR 5.1, the applicant will meet the qualification requirement if they have successfully completed a course of study for which they have been or will be awarded a UK bachelor's degree, a UK postgraduate degree, or successfully completed a relevant qualification listed in para GR 5.2.

Paragraph GR 5.2 provides that a relevant qualification is one of the following:

(a) a law conversion course validated by the Joint Academic Stage Board in England and Wales; or

(b) the Legal Practice Course in England and Wales, the Solicitors Course in Northern Ireland, or a Diploma in Professional Legal Practice in Scotland; or

(c) the Bar Practice Course in England and Wales, or the Bar Course in Northern Ireland; or

(d) a foundation programme in Medicine or Dentistry; or

(e) a Postgraduate Certificate in Education (PGCE) or Postgraduate Diploma in Education (PGDE); or

(f) a professional course requiring study at UK bachelor's degree level or above in a profession with reserved activities that is regulated by UK law or UK public authority.

6.12.4 Study in the UK requirement

Paragraph GR 6.1 provides that the applicant must have studied in the UK for a minimum period of the course for which they were last granted permission to study on the Student route (the relevant period), as in the table below.

Table 6.8   Study requirement

Total length of course	Relevant period of Student permission granted during which all study took place in the UK (apart from permitted study abroad programmes)
12 months or less	Full duration of course
Longer than 12 months	At least 12 months

How is the total length of a course calculated? A course with a start date of 30 September 2021 and an end date of 29 September 2022 is 12 months long. A course is longer than 12 months if it starts on 30 September 2021 and ends on 30 September 2022 or later.

What if a course lasting longer than 12 months was completed by the applicant using a combination of immigration routes? To meet this requirement, the applicant must have spent the minimum required time as a Student in the most recent period of permission. So, an applicant who studied their whole course whilst holding permission on a route other than the Student route, for example, a student who undertook a master's degree whilst holding permission as a dependant, will not meet this requirement.

The caseworker must consider all periods of Student permission which were granted to study the relevant qualification that the applicant subsequently successfully completed. This means that an applicant who could not complete their studies in one period of Student permission, for reasons such as maternity leave or sickness, and who consequently deferred their studies and completed the course of studies at a later date with Student permission, will have all those periods counted.

Note that distance learning that took place during the Covid-19 pandemic period of 24 January 2020 and 27 September 2021 may qualify (see paras GR 6.2 and GR 6.3).

6.12.5   Length of permission

How long will a Graduate get as their permission to remain in the UK? See **Table 6.9** below which is based on para GR 8.1.

Table 6.9   Amount of permission

Type of qualification	Period granted from date of decision
PhD or other doctoral qualification	3 years
All other qualifications	2 years

6.12.6   Conditions attached to permission

The grant of permission to a Graduate will be subject to the following conditions:

(a)   no access to public funds (see **3.3.2**);

(b)   work (including self-employment and voluntary work) is permitted, apart from work as a professional sportsperson;

(c)   study is permitted, except study with an education provider which is a Student sponsor, and which would meet the approved qualification and level of study requirements of the Student route which are set out in Appendix Student;

(d)   study is subject to the ATAS condition in Appendix ATAS; and

(e)   if Part 10 applies, the person will be required to register with the police (see **3.3.3**).

CHAPTER 7

EMPLOYMENT, BUSINESS AND INVESTMENT

7.1 INTRODUCTION

7.1.1 Who can work, conduct business or invest in the UK?

In this chapter we will consider entry to the UK for the specific purpose of working, conducting business or investing.

A general visitor (see **5.1.2**) is prohibited from working. A student (see **6.6.2.1**) is restricted as to what work they may do. But the following people may freely carry out any of these activities:

(a)   anyone admitted for settlement (see **Chapter 8**);

(b)   anyone given limited leave with a view to settlement, eg spouses, civil partners and those in a non-marital relationship (see **Chapter 8**);

(c)   refugees and those granted humanitarian protection (see **Chapter 9**);

(d)   anyone admitted, without prohibition on employment, as the dependant of someone with limited leave in the UK, eg the spouse, civil partner, unmarried or same sex partner of a Tier 1 Investor, Start-up or Innovator migrant (see **7.3**, **7.4** and **7.5**).

7.1.2 Overview of the categories covered in this chapter

A person seeking to enter the UK may fall into one of the following categories:

(a)   A talented and promising individual in the field of science, engineering, medicine, humanities, digital technology, arts or culture (including film and television, fashion design and architecture) who wishes to work in the UK may be able to apply in the Global Talent category detailed in Appendix Global Talent to the Immigration Rules.

UKVI guidance is that applicants will be leaders in their field, or have the potential to be leaders, as determined by an endorsing body that is approved by the Home Office. Settlement may be granted after three or five years according to which requirements an applicant meets. See further **7.2**.

(b)   New entrepreneurs seeking to establish a business in the UK for the first time may apply to enter or remain in the Start-up category detailed in Appendix Start-up to the Immigration Rules. UKVI guidance is that applicants must have an innovative, viable and scalable business idea which has been assessed and supported by a letter from a Home Office-approved endorsing body. The maximum length of leave in this category is two years. It cannot lead to settlement. See further **7.3**.

(c)   An experienced entrepreneur, with an idea for a viable new business with potential for growth and who wants to set up or run that business in the UK, may apply to enter or remain in the Innovator category detailed in Appendix Innovator to the Immigration Rules. In all cases, an applicant must be endorsed by a Home Office-approved endorsing body and must have at least £50,000 in available investment funds. Initial leave is normally for three years after which an application for settlement may be possible, or otherwise extensions of three years may be granted and settlement obtained once the Innovator can meet the requirements. See further **7.4**.

(d)   The Tier 1 or T1 Investor category is a points-based route of entry to the UK detailed in the Immigration Rules for high net worth individuals prepared to make a substantial financial investment in the UK. How much is required? The investor must have money of their own, under their control, held in a regulated financial institution, which is disposable in the UK, amounting to not less than £2 million and must have opened an account with a UK regulated bank for the purposes of investing not less than £2 million in the UK. Entry clearance is normally granted for three years and four months. Settlement may be granted after two, three or five years according to which requirements an Investor can meet. See further **7.5**.

(e)   A Skilled Worker, an Intra-Company routes migrant, T2 Minister of Religion or Sportsperson. These applicants form part of a points-based system detailed in the Immigration Rules. Each applicant must be sponsored to do a specific job, which meets skill and salary requirements, by an employer that has been licensed by the Home Office. A Skilled Worker may be granted initial leave of up to five years depending on their job start and end dates, with the possibility of extending that leave and applying for settlement. An Intra-Company routes migrant cannot obtain settlement in that category. A T2 Minister of Religion or Sportsperson may be granted initial leave of up to three years depending on the start and end dates of their jobs, with the possibility of extending for a further three years and applying for settlement. See further **7.8**.

(f)   Temporary work in the creative and sporting sector, charity and religious workers, government authorised exchange workers, workers under an international agreement, workers under a youth mobility scheme and seasonal workers. These are known as T5 Migrants. Each category has its own sponsorship arrangements. As this tier provides for temporary work only, leave is usually limited to a number of months or years and cannot lead to settlement. See further **7.12**.

(g)   A sole representative of an overseas business who will establish a wholly-owned subsidiary or branch in the UK. This is a long-standing category. The requirements are set out in Appendix Representative of an Overseas Business of the Immigration Rules. A person who meets the requirements is given three years' limited leave. That may be extended for two years, followed by an application for settlement. See further **7.13**.

(h)   A Commonwealth citizen with a UK-born grandparent. This is a long-standing category reflecting the UK's historical links with the Commonwealth. The requirements are set out in Appendix UK Ancestry of the Immigration Rules. A person who meets the requirements may enter the UK to look for, or take up, work; five years' limited leave is given, after which an application for settlement can be made. See further **7.14**.

7.2 GLOBAL TALENT

7.2.1 Overview

This category allows a person with exceptional talent or exceptional promise, a leader or potential leading talent in the field of science, medicine, humanities, engineering, the arts and culture (including television and film, fashion and architecture) or digital technology to work in the UK, provided they have the official endorsement of a Home Office-specified Designated Competent Body (DCB). UKVI guidance is that this category is designed to ensure the most talented people from around the world are able to come to the UK, for example those that have won internationally renowned awards such as a Nobel prize, an Oscar or the Stirling Prize.

EXAMPLE

Nicole recently won the International Mathematical Olympiad. She has a PhD and significant experience in industrial and clinical research. She is regarded as a leader in her field and has a personal recommendation from an eminent person resident in the UK supporting her application. Nicole has the endorsement of The Royal Society, a Home Office-specified DCB.

For an initial application, there are usually two applications stages. First, a DCB assesses the applicant's skills, abilities and achievements. It then advises the Home Office if the applicant is endorsed. The endorsing bodies' details and requirements are set out in Appendix Global Talent. However, applicants who have reached the pinnacle of their careers can bypass this endorsement requirement and instead qualify if they have been awarded any of the relevant prizes listed in Appendix Global Talent: Prestigious Prizes. Secondly, the Home Office considers the immigration aspects of the application.

All applicants must meet the minimum age requirement of 18. In addition, an applicant must not fall for refusal under the general grounds for refusal (see **3.4.5**), must not have been in breach of immigration laws, except for any period of overstaying permitted by the Immigration Rules (see **3.6.5**) and must not be on immigration bail (see **3.5.5**).

An applicant must pay the immigration health surcharge for themselves and any family members when making their application (see **3.10**).

An applicant can choose how much leave they want to apply for, up to a maximum of five years in each grant. They can subsequently apply to extend their leave if further limited leave in the UK is required. Is there a maximum limit on the time a person can spend in the UK in this category? No, provided they meet the requirements for leave to remain. However, it is usual to apply for settlement after holding leave in this category for five years.

Applicants can find the specified application forms and guidance notes on the Home Office website (see **1.2.8**).

The evidential flexibility rules will apply to the application (see **3.11**).

7.2.2 Endorsement

An applicant making an initial application must score 70 points (unless applying as an applicant awarded any of the relevant prizes listed in Appendix Global Talent: Prestigious Prizes). To do so, they must be issued with an endorsement letter by a DCB; the date of application must be no more than three months after the date of their endorsement letter; and the endorsement must not have been withdrawn by the DCB.

What DCBs have been specified by the Home Office? These include: Arts Council England for arts, culture, film and television applications; The British Fashion Council for fashion; The Royal Institute of British Architects for architecture; The British Academy for humanities and social science applications; The Royal Society for natural sciences and medical science research applications; The Royal Academy of Engineering for engineering applications; and Tech Nation for digital technology applications.

So, what steps must an applicant take? An application must be submitted on the specified form to the Home Office and not to the DCB. The Home Office sends the relevant documentation to the applicant's chosen DCB, which will advise the Home Office whether the applicant meets the relevant endorsement criteria. If so, the Home Office will then consider the application, taking into account whether the DCB has endorsed the applicant, make its decision and notify the applicant of the result.

7.2.3 Post-entry: extension

Where the initial leave granted is less than five years, an application should be made to extend it.

An applicant will fail if their application is liable to be refused under the general grounds in Part 9 of the Immigration Rules (see **3.4.5**), they are in the UK in breach of immigration laws, except for any period of overstaying that may be ignored under para 39E of the Immigration Rules (see **3.6.5**) or they are on immigration bail (see **3.5.5**).

The applicant must score 70 points. To do so, they must have earned money in the UK as a result of employment or self-employment in their expert field as endorsed by their DCB; and the DCB must not have withdrawn its endorsement. See Appendix Global Talent and the UKVI guidance as to the types of documents the applicant should produce.

The applicant must pay the immigration health surcharge for themselves and any family members when making their extension application (see **3.10**).

7.2.4 Post-entry: settlement

Once a person has spent the appropriate continuous period in the UK, an application may be made for settlement. **Table 7.1** below sets out the appropriate qualifying continuous periods.

Table 7.1   Global Talent – qualifying periods for settlement

3 years if endorsed by the Royal Society, British Academy, Royal Academy of Engineering or UKRI.
3 years if awarded a prize set out in Appendix Global Talent: Prestigious Prizes or endorsed under the exceptional talent criteria by Arts Council England or Tech Nation.
5 years if endorsed under the exceptional promise criteria by Arts Council England or Tech Nation.

In addition, the applicant will have to show that they:

(a) do not fall for refusal under the general grounds for refusal (see **3.4.5**), are not in the UK in breach of immigration laws, except for any period of overstaying that may be ignored under para 39E of the Immigration Rules (see **3.6.5**) and are not on immigration bail (see **3.5.5**);

(b) have spent a continuous period of three or five years, as appropriate, lawfully in the UK with permission on any of (or any combination of) the following routes: Global Talent, Innovator, Skilled Worker, T2 Minister of Religion, T2 Sportsperson or Tier 1 Investor Migrant. As to the meaning of continuous, see Appendix Continuous Residence;

(c) have earned money in the UK as a result of employment or self-employment in their expert field as endorsed by their DCB and the DCB has not withdrawn its endorsement; and

(d)   have sufficient knowledge of the English language (see **7.3.4**) and sufficient knowledge about life in the UK (see **3.8.7**).

If an applicant has any family members (spouse, civil partner, unmarried or same sex partner and children under 18) living with them, they may be able to apply for settlement at the same time (see further **7.6** and **7.7**).

7.3 START-UP

7.3.1 Overview

This route is for early-stage, high potential, entrepreneurs who are starting a business in the UK for the first time. An applicant may have already begun setting up their business, but it should not yet have commenced trading. Applicants must have an innovative, viable and scalable business idea which has been assessed and supported by a Home Office-approved endorsing body. Only after securing endorsement can an application be made for entry clearance or leave to remain.

An applicant must be at least 18 years old (Appendix Start-up, para SU 1.3).

All applicants must meet the requirements for points (see **7.3.2**), endorsement (see **7.3.3**), English language (see **7.3.4**), finance funds (see **7.3.5**) and genuineness (see **7.3.6**). In addition, an applicant must not fall for refusal under the general grounds for refusal in Part 9 (see **3.4.5**), must not have been in breach of immigration laws, except for any period of overstaying permitted by the Immigration Rules (see **3.6.5**) and must not be on immigration bail (see **3.5.5**).

A person applying for entry clearance or permission to stay on the Start-up route must apply online on the gov.uk website on the appropriate specified form.

An applicant must pay the appropriate fees and the immigration health surcharge for themselves and any family members when making their application (see **3.10**).

An applicant must have been issued with an endorsement letter by an endorsing body dated no more than three months before the date of application and that endorsement must not have been withdrawn. How long is entry clearance or leave to remain normally granted for in this category? The maximum is two years or the remaining balance of two years if the applicant has previously held leave in this category. Whilst this category cannot lead to settlement, a person may be able to switch to the Innovator route (see **7.4**) and ultimately settlement in that category.

Can an applicant bring family members to the UK? Yes, a spouse, civil partner, unmarried or same sex partner (see **7.6**) and children under 18 (see **7.7**) may be eligible.

7.3.2 The points requirement

The applicant must be awarded a total of 70 points from **Table 7.2** below which is reproduced from Appendix Start-up, para SU 4.1.

Table 7.2   **Points requirement**

Requirement (mandatory)	Points available
Business is innovative, viable and scalable	25
The applicant has not previously established a business in the UK	25
English Language at level B2 (see **7.3.4**)	10
Financial requirement (see **7.3.5**)	10
Total number of points required	**70**

7.3.2.1 Business is innovative, viable and scalable

An applicant will meet the innovative, viable and scalable business venture requirement and score 25 points if all the following requirements (**Table 7.3**) are met:

Table 7.3   Innovative, viable and scalable

Innovation	Viability	Scalability
The applicant has a genuine, original business plan that meets new or existing market needs and/or creates a competitive advantage.	The applicant's business plan is realistic and achievable based on the applicant's available resources. The applicant has, or is actively developing, the necessary skills, knowledge, experience and market awareness to successfully run the business.	There is evidence of structured planning and of potential for job creation and growth into national markets.

7.3.2.2 The applicant has not previously established a business in the UK

In order to score these 25 points, the applicant must not have previously established any business in the UK which commenced trading, unless this business commenced trading during the applicant's last period of permission and that permission was for any of the following routes: (a) Start-up; or (b) Tier 1 Graduate Entrepreneur (a route that no longer exists); or (c) Student on the doctorate extension scheme.

7.3.3 Endorsement requirement

All applicants for entry clearance or leave to remain must have been endorsed in this category by a Home Office-approved endorsing body. A list of these can be found on the Home Office UKVI website (see **1.2.8**). The bodies are divided into two groups: business and higher education. The list contains links to the relevant web page of each body.

Endorsement is by way of a letter from the endorsing body (Appendix Start-up, para SU 10.1). It must include:

(a)   the name of the endorsing body; and

(b)   the endorsement reference number; and

(c)   the name, telephone number, email and workplace address of a person at the endorsing body who will verify the contents of the letter to the Home Office if requested; and

(d)   the date of endorsement; and

(e)   the applicant's name, date of birth, nationality and passport or other travel document number; and

(f)   a short description of the applicant's business venture and the main products or services it will provide to its customers; and

(g)   confirmation that in the view of the endorsing body the applicant's business is innovative, viable and scalable; and

(h)   confirmation that the endorsing body is satisfied that the applicant will spend the majority of their working time in the UK on developing their business venture; and

(i)   confirmation that the endorsing body is satisfied the applicant is either the sole founder of the business or an instrumental member of the founding team; and

(j)   confirmation that the endorsing body is satisfied the applicant has created and is relying on their own business plan.

How might an endorsing body determine if an applicant meets the innovative, viable and scalable criteria? UKVI guidance suggests the following questions should be answered:

Innovation	Viability	Scalability
Is the business offering something more than merely competing with similar local traders?	Is there evidence of market research?	Is the business likely to gain sufficient traction?
Is there a need for the business in the UK market that is not already being fulfilled?	Does the applicant have realistic, sustainable, product goals?	Is it a business with a potential for growth?
Is the idea bringing something new to the pre-existing UK/global business market?	Is there a long-term plan for the business?	Would this business successfully scale to be a part of the national market?

An electronic copy of the endorsement letter must be sent to the Home Office.

Securing an endorsement letter is the first major immigration obstacle that an applicant must overcome. Next, they must use it within three months to make their entry clearance or, if switching, leave to remain application.

7.3.4   English language

The applicant must show English language ability on the Common European Framework of Reference for Languages in all four components (reading, writing, speaking and listening) of at least level B2.

The applicant must show that they meet the English language requirement as specified in Appendix English Language. Broadly, this can be done in any of the following five ways.

(a)   If the applicant has already met the requirement at the required level in a previous successful application for entry clearance or permission.

(b)   If the applicant is a national of any of the following majority-English-speaking countries:

> Antigua and Barbuda • Australia • The Bahamas • Barbados • Belize • Canada • Dominica • Grenada • Guyana • Ireland • Jamaica • Malta • New Zealand • St Kitts and Nevis • St Lucia • St Vincent and the Grenadines • Trinidad and Tobago • United States of America.

(c)   If the applicant has either (i) a Bachelor's degree, Master's degree or doctorate awarded in the UK; or (ii) a degree or degree-level qualification taught in a university or college in a majority-English-speaking country listed in (b) above but excluding Canada, which meets or exceeds the recognised standard of a Bachelor's degree, Master's degree or doctorate awarded in the UK; or (iii) a degree or degree-level qualification which meets, or exceeds, the recognised standard of a UK Bachelor's degree, Master's degree or doctorate and was taught or researched in English.

If the relevant qualification was awarded by a body from outside the UK, confirmation must be obtained from UK ENIC (see **6.5.5.2**) that the qualification meets the requirement.

The applicant will need to produce the certificate from their awarding body; or a transcript issued by the university or college that awarded their qualification; or an official letter from the university or college that awarded their qualification containing information equivalent to a degree certificate.

(d) If the applicant provides a valid digital reference number from an approved provider showing they have passed an approved English language test to the required level in the two years before the date of application. The list of approved tests and providers can be found on the Home Office website (see **1.2.8**).

(e) If the applicant has a GCSE, 'A' level, Scottish National Qualification at level 4 or 5 or Scottish Higher or Advanced Higher, in English (language or literature), that was awarded: (a) by an Ofqual (or SQA, Qualifications Wales or CCEA) regulated awarding body, and (b) following education in a UK school undertaken while they were aged under 18. The applicant will have to produce a certificate, or an official transcript issued by that awarding body.

7.3.5 Financial requirement

If an applicant is applying for entry clearance or has been in the UK for less than 12 months at the date of application, they must have funds of at least £1,270.

The applicant must show that they have held the required level of funds for a 28-day period and as set out in Appendix Finance unless their endorsing body confirms they have been awarded funding of at least £1,270.

Unless the applicant is relying on their endorsing body's funding, as above, they must show that they have held the required level of funds for a 28-day period. The most recently dated piece of financial evidence produced by the applicant must be dated within 31 days before the date of their application. The financial evidence provided must cover the whole 28-day period.

Funds may be held in any form of personal bank or building society account (including current, deposit, savings, pension from which the funds can be withdrawn or investment account) provided the account allows the funds to be accessed immediately. Funds held in other accounts or financial instruments such as shares, bonds, credit cards, pensions from which the funds cannot be withdrawn immediately, regardless of notice period, will not be accepted as evidence of funds.

The applicant's financial documents must be from institutions acceptable to the Home Office. Appendix Finance, para FIN 2.1 provides that funds will not be considered if they are held in a financial institution where (a) the decision maker is unable to make satisfactory verification checks; or (b) the financial institution is not regulated by the appropriate regulatory body for the country in which that institution is operating; or (c) the financial institution does not use electronic record keeping.

Overdraft facilities are not counted towards meeting the financial requirement. Promises of future third-party support are not accepted as evidence of funds unless made by way of the applicant's endorsing body's funding, as above.

7.3.6 Genuine Start-up requirement

UKVI guidance is that a caseworker will not normally need to carry out a genuineness assessment for Start-up applications because an endorsing body will already have assessed an applicant's business plan. So, what is the point of the requirement to be found in Appendix Start-up, para SU 7.1? Why should a decision maker be satisfied that (i) the applicant genuinely intends to undertake, and is capable of undertaking, any work or business activity in the UK stated in their application; (ii) the applicant does not intend to work in the UK in breach of their conditions; and (iii) any money which the applicant claims to be available is genuinely available as described, and the applicant intends to use it for the purposes described in the application? UKVI guidance is that this power is primarily intended to be used where the Home Office has information that would not otherwise have been considered by an endorsing body when it assessed a migrant's suitability for endorsement.

7.3.7 Conditions and period of grant

A successful applicant will be granted permission for a maximum period of two years, and a person must not be granted further permission which would result in them spending more than two years with permission on the Start-up route.

The grant will be subject to all the following conditions:

(a)   no access to public funds (see **3.3.2**); and

(b)   work (including self-employment and voluntary work) permitted except for employment as a professional sportsperson, including as a sports coach; and

(c)   study is permitted, subject to the ATAS condition in Appendix ATAS; and

(d)   if Part 10 applies, the applicant will be required to register with the police (see **3.3.3**).

7.4   INNOVATOR

7.4.1   Overview

Experienced businesspersons seeking to establish a business in the UK can apply for entry in this category. Indeed, a novice entrepreneur may have entered the UK via the Start-up route (see **7.3**) and, having gained two years' experience, seek to switch into this category.

Applicants must have an innovative, viable and scalable business idea which has been assessed and supported by a Home Office-approved endorsing body. Only after securing endorsement can an application be made for entry clearance, leave to remain and settlement. A person applying for entry clearance or permission to stay as an Innovator must apply online on the gov.uk website on the appropriate specified form.

An applicant must be at least 18 years old (Appendix Innovator, para INN 1.3).

Applicants will usually need a minimum of £50,000 funding available to invest in their business. Does this have to be provided by their endorsing body? No, although some endorsing bodies choose to offer funding.

All applicants must meet the requirement for points (see **7.4.2**). The English language requirement and the financial requirement are the same as for the Start-up category (see **7.3.4** and **7.3.5**, respectively). In addition, an applicant must not fall for refusal under the general grounds for refusal in Part 9 (see **3.4.5**), must not have been in breach of immigration laws, except for any period of overstaying allowed under the Immigration Rules (see **3.6.5**) and must not be on immigration bail (see **3.5.5**).

An applicant must pay the appropriate fees and the immigration health surcharge for themselves and any family members when making their application (see **3.10**).

Can an applicant bring family members to the UK? Yes, a spouse, civil partner, unmarried or same sex partner (see **7.6**) and children under 18 (see **7.7**) may be eligible.

Applicants can find application forms and guidance notes on the Home Office website (see **1.2.8**).

7.4.2   Points requirement

An applicant must be awarded 70 points from the table below (**Table 7.4**) that is reproduced from Appendix Innovator para INN 5.1. It is important to note that 50 points must be scored either under the new business criteria or under the same business criteria, but not both.

Table 7.4   Points requirement

Requirement	New or same business	Points available
Business plan.	New Business	10
Business venture is innovative, viable and scalable.	New Business	20
£50,000 available funds to invest or having been invested.	New Business	20
Applicant's previous permission was in the Innovator or Start-up route and they are pursuing a business assessed by a Home Office approved endorsing body either for the previous endorsement or at a contact point.	Same Business	10
Business is active, trading and sustainable and demonstrates significant achievements against the business plan.	Same Business	20
Applicant is active in day-to-day management and development of business.	Same Business	20
English Language requirement at level B2 (see **7.3.4**).	Mandatory for all applicants	10
Financial requirement (see **7.3.5**).	Mandatory for all applicants	10
Total number of points required		**70**

7.4.2.1   New Business: Business plan

The applicant must have an endorsement letter from an endorsing body which confirms that: (a) the applicant has either generated, or made a significant contribution to, the ideas in their business plan; (b) the applicant will have a day-to-day role in carrying out the business plan; and (c) the applicant is either the sole founder or an instrumental member of the founding team.

7.4.2.2   New Business: Business is innovative, viable and scalable

The applicant must be supported by an endorsing body for this route which confirms in their endorsement letter that they consider that the applicant meets the following requirements (**Table 7.5**).

Table 7.5   Innovative, viable and scalable

Innovation	Viability	Scalability
The applicant has a genuine, original business plan that meets new or existing market needs and/or creates a competitive advantage.	The applicant's business plan must be realistic and achievable based on the applicant's available resources. The applicant must have, or be actively developing, the necessary skills, knowledge, experience and market awareness to successfully run the business.	There is evidence of structured planning and of potential for job creation and growth into national and international markets.

7.4.2.3 New Business: Investment funds

The applicant must show that they have at least £50,000 of funds available to invest, or which have been invested, in their business by one of the following:

(a)   providing confirmation from the endorsing body that it is providing the funds of at least £50,000; or

(b)   providing confirmation from the endorsing body that it has verified the funds are available from other sources (which can include the applicant); or

(c)   providing confirmation from the endorsing body that it has verified that at least £50,000 has already been invested in the applicant's business; or

(d)   providing evidence that the £50,000 of funds are available from another source.

An applicant may demonstrate that they meet the funding requirements in the following ways (**Table 7.6**).

Table 7.6   Funding

Source of funds	Evidence required
Endorsing body that has verified the funds are available	Endorsement letter confirms available or prior investment of £50,000.
A UK organisation employing at least 10 people	A letter which confirms: • how they know the applicant; and • the amount of funding they are making available in pounds sterling (£); and • that this funding has not been promised to any other person or business for another purpose; and • the name and contact details (telephone number, email and workplace address) of an individual at the organisation who can verify the contents of the letter to the Home Office, if requested.
An overseas organisation, a UK organisation which employs less than 10 people or an individual third party	A signed declaration from the funding provider, dated no more than three months before the date of application, setting out: • how they know the applicant; and • the amount of funding they are making available in pounds sterling (£); and • confirmation that this funding has not been promised to any other person or business for another purpose; and • the name and contact details (telephone number, email and workplace address) of an individual at the organisation who can verify the contents of the letter to the Home Office, if requested. A letter from a legal representative (who is registered to practise legally in the country where the third party or the money is), confirming that the declaration and signature in the signed declaration is genuine. A bank letter, dated no earlier than one month before the date of application, confirming that the funds are held in a regulated financial institution(s), and if the institution is outside the UK, the letter must also confirm that the funds are transferrable to the UK.

Source of funds	Evidence required
Funds held by the applicant	Either: Bank statements, showing that the funds are held in the UK in an institution regulated by the Financial Conduct Authority. The statements must cover a consecutive three months, ending no earlier than one month before the date of application. Or: A bank letter, dated no earlier than one month before the date of application, and if the institution is outside the UK, the letter must also confirm that the funds are transferrable to the UK. If these documents do not show that the applicant has held the funds for at least three months, the applicant must also provide all the evidence from the source of the funds as set out for an overseas organisation or a UK organisation which employs less than 10 people.
Funds already invested in business	Either of the following documents which must show the amount that has been invested: Business accounts, showing the name of the accountant and the date they were produced. Or: Business bank statements.

Any evidence of funds not shown in pounds sterling (£) must be converted on the date of application using the spot exchange rate that appears on the OANDA website (<www.oanda.com>).

Funds must be from institutions acceptable to the Home Office. Appendix Finance, para FIN 2.1 provides that funds will not be considered if they are held in a financial institution where (a) the decision maker is unable to make satisfactory verification checks; or (b) the financial institution is not regulated by the appropriate regulatory body for the country in which that institution is operating; or (c) the financial institution does not use electronic record keeping.

7.4.2.4 Same Business: Business previously assessed by an endorsing body requirement

The applicant must be supported by an endorsing body which confirms that they are endorsing the application on the basis of a business they or another endorsing body have previously assessed while the applicant had permission on the Innovator or Start-up route.

7.4.2.5 Same Business: Business is active, trading and sustainable

The applicant's business must be active, trading and sustainable and the applicant must have made significant progress against their business plan. The applicant's business must be registered with Companies House and the applicant must be listed as a director or member of that business. The applicant must be supported by an endorsing body which has assessed the applicant's business and confirmed that it meets these requirements.

7.4.2.6 Same Business: Day-to-day management and development

The applicant must be involved in the day-to-day management and development of their business and provide a letter confirming this from an endorsing body.

7.4.3 Period and conditions of grant

The applicant will be granted permission for a maximum period of three years.

The grant will be subject to the following conditions:

(a)   no access to public funds (see **3.3.2**); and

(b)   no work, other than working for the business(es) the applicant has established. What does that mean? Working for the business(es) does not include any apprenticeship or any work pursuant to a contract of service, whether express or implied and whether oral or written, with another business (which means successful applicants cannot fill a position or hire their labour to another business, even if the work is undertaken through contracting with the applicant's own business or through a recruitment or employment agency); and

(c)   study is permitted, subject to the ATAS condition in Appendix ATAS; and

(d)   if Part 10 applies, the applicant will be required to register with the police (see **3.3.3**).

7.4.4   Settlement

7.4.4.1   Overview

Once an applicant has spent at least three years continuously in the UK with permission on the Innovator route, they may apply for settlement. In addition to the usual validity and suitability requirements, the applicant must meet the Knowledge of Life in the UK requirement as set out in Appendix KOL UK (see **3.8.7**). The main requirement concerns endorsement (see **7.4.4.2**).

7.4.4.2   Endorsement

The applicant must provide an endorsement letter issued by an endorsing body, which includes all of the following information:

(a)   the name of the endorsing body; and

(b)   the endorsement reference number; and

(c)   the date of issue, which must be no earlier than three months before the date of application; and

(d)   the applicant's name, date of birth, nationality and passport number; and

(e)   a short description of the applicant's business venture and the main products or services it has provided; and

(f)   the name and contact details (telephone number, email and workplace address) of an individual at the endorsing body who will verify the contents of the letter to the Home Office if requested; and

(g)   confirmation that the applicant has shown significant achievements, judged against the business plan assessed in their previous endorsement; and

(h)   confirmation that the applicant's business is registered with Companies House and the applicant is listed as a director or member of that business; and

(i)   confirmation the business is active and trading; and

(j)   confirmation that the business appears to be sustainable for at least the following 12 months, based on its assets and expected income, weighed against its current and planned expenses; and

(k)   confirmation the applicant has demonstrated an active key role in the day-to-day management and development of the business; and

(l)   confirmation the applicant's business venture has met at least two of the following requirements:

   (i)   at least £50,000 has been invested into the business and actively spent furthering the business; or

(ii) the number of the business's customers has at least doubled within the most recent three years and is currently higher than the mean number of customers for other UK businesses offering comparable main products or services; or

(iii) the business has engaged in significant research and development activity and has applied for intellectual property protection in the UK; or

(iv) the business has generated a minimum annual gross revenue of £1 million in the last full year covered by its accounts; or

(v) the business is generating a minimum annual gross revenue of £500,000 in the last full year covered by its accounts, with at least £100,000 from exporting overseas; or

(vi) the business has created the equivalent of at least 10 full-time jobs for settled workers; or

(vii) the business has created the equivalent of at least five full-time jobs for settled workers, each of which has a mean salary of at least £25,000 a year (gross pay, excluding any allowances).

Can an applicant qualify under any combination of two requirements in provision (l) above, even if they are similar? Yes. For example, an applicant will have met two criteria if their business has an annual revenue of £1 million [(iv) above], with at least £100,000 from exporting overseas [(v) above]. But an applicant cannot qualify by relying on the same criterion twice. For example, an applicant who has invested £100,000 (2 x £50,000) in their business venture will be considered to have met only one criterion [(i) above].

Are there any additional points to consider if the applicant is relying on the criteria for creating jobs [(vi) and (vii) above]? Yes. First, the jobs must have existed for at least 12 months and comply with all relevant UK legislation, including (but not limited to) the National Minimum Wage Regulations in effect at the time and the Working Time Regulations 1998. Secondly, each of the jobs must involve an average of at least 30 hours of paid work per week. Can two or more part-time jobs that add up to 30 hours per week be combined to represent the equivalent of a single full-time job? Yes, as long as each of the jobs has existed for at least 12 months. However, a single full-time job of more than 30 hours of work per week does not count as more than one full-time job. In addition, UKVI guidance is that any reference to jobs means posts filled, rather than employees. So, if a single job has been filled over 12 months by different employees at different times, that counts as the job having existed for at least 12 months.

7.5 TIER 1 INVESTOR

7.5.1 Overview

This category is for an individual aged 18 or over who is able to make a substantial financial investment of at least £2 million in the UK.

An applicant does not have to meet on entry any English language requirement because they are investing in the UK and may choose whether or not they want to work. However, the English language requirement (including the Life in the UK test) will apply when settlement is sought (see **7.5.4**). In addition, given the level of investment, the applicant does not have to demonstrate that they have enough money to maintain themselves (and any dependants).

The applicant must not fall for refusal under the general grounds for refusal under Part 9 (see **3.4.5**) and must be at least 18 years old to apply.

The applicant must pay the immigration health surcharge for themselves and any dependants when making the application (see **3.10**).

The applicant and any adult dependants must provide an overseas criminal record certificate for any country they have resided in continuously for 12 months or more in the 10 years prior to the application.

If entry clearance is granted, it will be for a period of three years and four months.

Applicants can find application forms and guidance notes on the Home Office website (see **1.2.8**).

The evidential flexibility rules will apply to the application (see **3.11**).

7.5.2 The investor attributes

An applicant must score 75 points for having: (a) access to £2 million that is in a regulated financial institution and disposable in the UK, set out in Table 7 of Appendix A to the Immigration Rules (see **Appendix 1** to this book); and (b) opened an account with a UK regulated bank for the purposes of investing not less than £2 million in the UK.

The applicant must show that they can make an investment of at least £2 million in the UK. The money may already be in the UK or held overseas at the time of application. If it is not in pounds sterling, the applicant must convert its value into that using the Oanda website (see **7.4.2.4**) on the date on which the application is made.

The applicant must open an account with a UK regulated bank for the purposes of investing not less than £2 million in the UK. The applicant must provide with their application an original letter issued by that bank on its official letter-headed paper, which is dated within the three months immediately before the date of the application. The letter must state the applicant's name as the account holder and include the account number. It must also confirm that the applicant opened the account for the purposes of investing not less than £2 million in the UK, that the bank is regulated by the Financial Conduct Authority for the purposes of accepting deposits and that the bank has carried out all required due diligence checks and Know Your Customer enquiries in relation to the applicant.

Can an applicant rely on money that they own jointly with their spouse, civil partner, unmarried or same sex partner? Yes – see paras 61 and 61-SD of Appendix A to the Immigration Rules.

An applicant must have held the money relied on in their application for at least a consecutive two-year period of time, ending no earlier than one calendar month before the date of application, and produce the documents specified in para 64A-SD of Appendix A to the Immigration Rules to earn 75 points by this route. In summary, these include:

(a) A portfolio report or breakdown of investments in a letter produced by a UK regulated financial institution covering a consecutive two-year period of time, ending no more than one calendar month before the date of application. Where the applicant manages their own investments or has a portfolio manager who does not operate in the UK, they must produce documentary evidence of their holdings. This may include certified copies of bonds, share certificates and audited accounts. All documents must cover a consecutive two-year period of time, ending no earlier than one calendar month before the date of application.

Where money has already been invested in the UK before the date of application, points will only be awarded if it was invested in the UK no more than 12 months before the date of application.

(c) If the funds are in a bank account, the applicant must provide personal bank statements from a bank that is regulated by the official regulatory body for the country in which the institution operates and the funds are located. These must show the amount of money available in the name of the applicant and/or their spouse, civil partner, unmarried or same sex partner. Consecutive bank statements covering a consecutive two-year period of time, ending no earlier than one calendar month before the date of application, are needed. Alternatively, a letter from that bank may be acceptable.

What if the money has not been held in a portfolio or bank account covering a consecutive two-year period of time, ending no earlier than one calendar month before the date of application? Then the applicant will have to provide evidence of the source of the money as outlined in **Table 7.7** below.

Table 7.7   Investor – sources of funds

Source of funds	Supporting evidence key points
Gift	The original irrevocable memorandum of gift and a letter from a legal adviser confirming that it is valid and binding according to the laws of the country in which it was made.
Deeds of sale	The original deeds of sale of assets (such as property or business) and a letter from a legal adviser confirming that the sale was genuine and that the money is available to the applicant.
Evidence from a business	Business accounts and a letter from a legal adviser confirming that the applicant can lawfully extract the money from the business.
Will	A notarised copy of the will and a letter from a legal adviser confirming the validity of the will.
Divorce settlement	A notarised copy of the terms of the divorce settlement and a letter from a legal adviser confirming that the document is valid.
Award of winnings	A letter from the organisation issuing the financial award or winnings and a letter from a legal adviser confirming that the money has been transferred.

In all other cases the applicant will need to produce documentation as evidence of the source of the money, together with independent supporting evidence. For example, if the money was received as a result of court action, the Home Office requires documents in the form of a letter of confirmation of the court proceedings and a suitable letter from the applicant's solicitor.

(d)   Applicants who have funds that are not held in the UK, or who have a portfolio of investments that are not in the UK, must provide a letter from their bank or financial institution confirming that the money can be transferred into the UK.

An ECO may refuse the application if there are reasonable grounds to believe that the applicant is not in control of the investment funds; the funds were obtained unlawfully (or by means which would be unlawful if they happened in the UK); or the character, conduct or associations of a party providing the funds means that approving the application is not conducive to the public good.

In R (JW and Others) v Secretary of State for the Home Department (Tier 1 Investor; control; investments) [2019] UKUT 393 (IAC), the Tribunal held that 'control' is to be interpreted in accordance with its natural and ordinary meaning, namely that a person has the authority to manage and/ or direct the use of the money, asset or investment (depending on the context). It includes not just a question of legal or beneficial ownership but includes an element of choice of use. The money must be under a person's control at the point of investment.

7.5.3   Post-entry: extension

Just before the initial three years' limited leave of an investor expires, an application should be made to extend it under para 245ED of the Immigration Rules (unless the applicant is in a position to apply for settlement at this stage: see **7.5.4**).

Funds held in a financial institution that is listed in Appendix P as not satisfactorily verifying financial statements will not count.

An applicant will fail if their application is liable to be refused under the general grounds in Part 9 of the Immigration Rules (see **3.5.4**), they are an illegal entrant (see **10.2.2**) or they are in the UK in breach of immigration laws, except for any period of overstaying that may be ignored under para 39E of the Immigration Rules (see **3.6.5**).

The applicant must pay the immigration health surcharge for themselves and any family members when making their extension application (see **3.10**).

Where an extension is granted, it will be for a period of two years.

Basically, the applicant has to demonstrate that the original requirements have been met, ie the investor has made the required investment, and the applicant must again score at least 75 points. The attributes are set out in Table 8A of Appendix A to the Immigration Rules (see **Appendix 1** to this book), as shown in **Table 7.8** below.

Table 7.8   Investor – attributes for extension

Money and investment	Points
The applicant has invested not less than £2 million in the UK by way of share capital or loan capital in active and trading UK registered companies (see **Appendix 12**), subject to the restrictions set out in para 65 (see **7.5.3.1**). The investment referred to above was made:	75
(1) within three months of the applicant's entry to the UK, if they were granted entry clearance as a Tier 1 (Investor) Migrant and there is evidence to establish their date of entry to the UK, unless there are exceptionally compelling reasons for the delay in investing, or	
(2) where there is no evidence to establish their date of entry in the UK or where the applicant was granted entry clearance in a category other than Tier 1 (Investor) Migrant, within three months of the date of the grant of entry clearance or leave to remain as a Tier 1 (Investor) Migrant, unless there are exceptionally compelling reasons for the delay in investing, or	
(3) where the investment was made prior to the application which led to the first grant of leave as a Tier 1 (Investor) Migrant, no earlier than 12 months before the date of such application,	
and in each case the level of investment has been at least maintained for the whole of the remaining period of that leave.	
'Compelling reasons for the delay in investing' must be unforeseeable and outside of the applicant's control. Delays caused by the applicant failing to take timely action will not be accepted. Where possible, the applicant must have taken reasonable steps to mitigate such delay.	

7.5.3.1 Investment

By para 65 of Appendix A to the Immigration Rules, certain investments do not count. These include an offshore company or trust; open ended investment companies; investment trust companies or pooled investment vehicles; companies mainly engaged in property investment, property management or property development; deposits with a bank, building society or other enterprise whose normal course of business includes the acceptance of deposits; ISAs, premium bonds and saving certificates issued by the National Savings and Investment Agency; and UK Government bonds.

By para 245ED(g), no points from Appendix A will be awarded if the Secretary of State has reasonable grounds to believe that (a) the applicant is not or was not in control of and at liberty to freely invest the money specified in their application for the purposes of meeting the requirements of Appendix A; or (b) any of the money specified in the application was acquired by means of conduct which is unlawful in the UK, or would constitute unlawful conduct if it occurred in the UK, or has been or will be transferred internationally by means which are unlawful in any of the countries involved; or (c) where any of the money specified in the application has been made available by another party and the character, conduct or associations of that party are such that approval of the application would not be conducive to the public good.

7.5.3.2 Maintaining the level of investment

By para 65C(a) of Appendix A to the Immigration Rules, points for maintaining the level of investment for the specified continuous period of leave are only to be awarded:

(a)   if the applicant has purchased a portfolio of qualifying investments for a price of least £2 million (or £5 million or £10 million, as appropriate); and

(b)   where any part of the qualifying investments in the portfolio is sold (whether at a gain or at a loss) during the specified continuous period of leave, their gross proceeds are reinvested in qualifying investments before the end of the next reporting period, or within six months of the date of completion of the sale, whichever is sooner.

7.5.4 Post-entry: settlement

Once an investor has spent a continuous period of five years in the UK in this category (or a shorter period of two or three years in the circumstances set out in **Table 7.9** below – this is known as accelerated settlement), an application can be made for settlement under para 245EF of the Immigration Rules. As to the meaning of continuous, see **7.4.6.1**.

The applicant will have to show that they:

(a)   do not fall for refusal under the general grounds for refusal (see **3.5.4**), are not an illegal entrant (see **10.4.2**) and are not in the UK in breach of immigration laws except for any period of overstaying that may be ignored under para 39E of the Immigration Rules (see **3.6.5**);

(b)   score 75 points from Appendix A for specific attributes (see **7.5.4.1**); and

(c)   have sufficient knowledge of the English language and sufficient knowledge about life in the UK (see **3.8.7**).

No points are awarded under Appendix A where the specified documents relied on by the applicant show that the funds are held in a financial institution with which the Home Office is unable to make satisfactory verification checks.

Like an extension application, para 245EF(f) will see no points awarded from Appendix A if the Secretary of State has reasonable grounds to believe that the applicant is not or was not in control of and at liberty to freely invest the money specified in their application for the purposes of meeting the requirements of Appendix A, etc as per para 245ED(g) detailed at **7.5.3.1**.

If an applicant has any spouse, civil partner, unmarried or same sex partner (see **7.6**) and children under 18 (see **7.7**) living with them, they may be able to apply for settlement at the same time. Home Office guidance is that the partner of an investor may apply for settlement at the same time as the investor, provided they have lived together in the UK for at least five years before applying for settlement. An investor's child may apply for settlement at the same time as the investor, as long as the child meets the requirements of the Immigration Rules.

7.5.4.1   Specific attributes for settlement

An applicant must score 75 points for specific attributes in relation to the investment steps they have taken since entering the UK. The details are set out in Table 9A of Appendix A to the Immigration Rules (see **Appendix 1** to this book), as shown in **Table 7.9** below.

Table 7.9   Investor – attributes points for indefinite leave to remain

Row	Money and investment	Points
1	The applicant has invested money of their own under their control amounting to at least: (a) £10 million; or (b) £5 million; or (c) £2 million in the UK by way of share capital or loan capital in active and trading UK registered companies (see **Appendix 12**), subject to the restrictions set out in para 65 (see **7.5.3.1**).	40
2	The applicant has spent the specified continuous period lawfully in the UK, with absences from the UK of no more than 180 days in any 12 calendar months during that period. The specified continuous period must have been spent with leave as a Tier 1 (Investor) Migrant. The specified continuous period is: (a) two years if the applicant scores points from row 1(a) above; (b) three years if the applicant scores points from row 1(b) above; or (c) five years if the applicant scores points from row 1(c) above.	20
3	The investment referred to above was made no earlier than 12 months before the date of the application which led to the first grant of leave as a Tier 1 (Investor) Migrant. The level of investment has been at least maintained throughout the relevant specified continuous period referred to in row 2, other than in the first three months of that period, and the applicant has provided the specified documents to show that this requirement has been met. When calculating the specified continuous period, the first day of that period will be taken to be the later of: (a) the date the applicant first entered the UK as a Tier 1 (Investor) Migrant (or the date entry clearance was granted as a Tier 1 (Investor) Migrant) or the date the applicant first entered the Bailiwick of Guernsey, the Bailiwick of Jersey or the Isle of Man with leave in a category equivalent to Tier 1 (Investor) if this is earlier; or (b) the date three months before the full specified amount was invested in the UK, or before the full required amount in an equivalent category was invested in the Bailiwick of Guernsey, the Bailiwick of Jersey or the Isle of Man.	15

7.6 PARTNERS OF A GLOBAL TALENT, START-UP, INNOVATOR, TIER 1 INVESTOR

7.6.1 Entry clearance and leave to remain

If subject to immigration controls, the spouse, civil partner, unmarried or same sex partner ('the Partner') of a Global Talent (see **7.2**) or Start-up (see **7.3**) or Innovator Migrant (see **7.4**) or Tier 1 (Investor) Migrant (see **7.5**) ('the Migrant') will require entry clearance in order to enter the UK, and should usually subsequently apply for an extension at the same time as their sponsor.

7.6.1.1 Partner

Broadly, the requirements are as follows:

(a) The applicant must produce suitable criminal record certificates (see **7.2.2.8**) and not fall for refusal under the general grounds for refusal (see **3.5.4**), and if applying for leave to remain must not be an illegal entrant (see **10.4.2**) nor in the UK in breach of immigration laws, except for any period of overstaying that may be ignored under para 39E of the Immigration Rules (see **3.6.5**).

(b) The applicant must be the spouse or civil partner, unmarried or same sex partner of a person who:

   (i) has valid leave to enter or remain as a Migrant; or

   (ii) is, at the same time, being granted entry clearance or leave to remain as a Migrant.

(c) An applicant who is the unmarried or same sex partner of a Migrant must also meet the following requirements:

   (i) any previous marriage or civil partnership, or similar relationship by the applicant or the Migrant with another person must have permanently broken down;

   (ii) the applicant and the Migrant must not be so closely related that they would be prohibited from marrying each other in the UK (see **8.3.5.3**); and

   (iii) the applicant and the Migrant must have been living together in a relationship similar to marriage or civil partnership for a period of at least two years (see further **8.3**).

(d) The marriage or civil partnership, or relationship similar to marriage or civil partnership, must be subsisting at the time the application is made (see **8.3.5.5**).

(e) The applicant and the Migrant must intend to live with the other as their spouse or civil partner, unmarried or same sex partner throughout the applicant's stay in the UK (see **8.3.5.9**).

(f) The applicant must not intend to stay in the UK beyond any period of leave granted to the Migrant.

(g) If the applicant's partner is a Start-up or Innovator Migrant, there must be a sufficient level of funds available to the applicant as follows:

   (i) There must be £285 in funds.

   (ii) The relevant amount of funds must be available to either the applicant or the Migrant.

   (iii) Where the Migrant is applying for entry clearance or leave to remain at the same time as the applicant, the amount of funds available to the applicant must be in addition to the level of funds required separately by the Migrant.

   (iv) Sufficient funds will be deemed to be available where the Migrant's endorsing body has confirmed in their endorsement letter that funding has been awarded that is at least sufficient to cover the required maintenance funds for the Migrant, the applicant and any other dependants (and any investment funds that an Innovator is required to have in that category).

> **EXAMPLE**
>
> Adam applies for entry clearance as an Innovator. His civil partner, Brian, will be travelling with him. In addition to meeting the requirements above, what financial funds do they need to have available? Adam needs £1,270 for himself (see **7.3.5**) and an additional £285 available for Brian.

If the application is successful, leave will be subject to conditions not to have recourse to public funds and registration with the police, if this is required (see **3.3.2** and **3.3.3** respectively). The partner will be free to work in the UK, but not as a professional sportsperson (including as a sports coach).

7.6.2 Settlement by a partner

Once a Tier 1 Investor or a Global Talent or Innovator Migrant ('the Migrant') is in a position to apply for settlement, the applicant's partner may apply for settlement at the same time, provided the couple have lived together for at least five years (or later when that requirement is met). This is because a partner must complete a five-year probationary period before they qualify for settlement. So, if the Migrant is granted indefinite leave to remain before their partner has completed their five-year probationary period, the partner can apply for further leave to remain for up to three years.

Broadly, the requirements are as follows:

(a) The applicant must not fall for refusal under the general grounds for refusal (see **3.5.4**) and must not be an illegal entrant (see **10.4.2**) and is not in the UK in breach of immigration laws except for any period of overstaying that may be ignored under para 39E of the Immigration Rules (see **3.6.5**).

(b) The applicant must be the spouse or civil partner, unmarried or same sex partner of a person who is being, or has been, granted indefinite leave to remain as a Migrant (or who has subsequently become a British citizen).

(c) The applicant must have, or have last been granted, leave as the partner of the Migrant who is being or has been granted indefinite leave to remain (or who has subsequently become a British citizen).

(d) The applicant and the Migrant must have been living together in the UK in a marriage or civil partnership, or in a relationship similar to marriage or civil partnership, for a period of at least five years. During that time the applicant must have had continuous leave as the partner of the Migrant and met all of the relevant requirements. In addition, the applicant must not have been absent from the UK for more than 180 days during any 12-month period in the continuous period.

(e) The marriage or civil partnership, or relationship similar to marriage or civil partnership, must be subsisting at the time the application is made (see **8.3.5.5**).

(f) The applicant and the Migrant must intend to live permanently with the other as spouse or civil partner, unmarried or same sex partner. See further **8.3.5.9**.

(g) The applicant must have sufficient knowledge of the English language and sufficient knowledge about life in the UK (see **3.8.7**) (unless the applicant is aged 65 or over at the time the application is made).

7.7 CHILDREN OF A GLOBAL TALENT, START-UP, INNOVATOR, TIER 1 INVESTOR

7.7.1 Entry clearance and leave to remain

If subject to immigration controls, the child of a Tier 1 (Investor) (see **7.5**), or a Global Talent (see **7.2**) or Start-up (see **7.3**) or Innovator Migrant (see **7.4**) ('the Migrant') will require entry clearance in order to enter the UK, and should usually subsequently apply for an extension at the same time as their sponsor.

7.7.2 Child

The requirements are broadly as follows:

(a) The applicant must not fall for refusal under the general grounds for refusal (see **3.5.4**), and if applying for leave to remain must not be an illegal entrant (see **10.4.2**) nor in the UK in breach of immigration laws, except for any period of overstaying that may be ignored under para 39E of the Immigration Rules (see **3.6.5**).

(b) The applicant must be the child of either:

(i) one parent who has valid leave to enter or remain as a Migrant, or is, at the same time, being granted entry clearance or leave to remain as a Migrant where:

   (1) that parent is the applicant's sole surviving parent, or

   (2) that parent has and has had sole responsibility for the applicant's upbringing (see **8.9.4.3**), or

   (3) there are serious and compelling family or other considerations which would make it desirable not to refuse the application and suitable arrangements have been made for the applicant's care (see **8.9.4.4**); or

(ii) parents:

   (1) one of whom has valid leave to enter or remain as a Migrant and one of whom has leave as the partner of a Migrant, or

   (2) who are at the same time being granted entry clearance or leave to remain as a Migrant and as the partner of a Migrant, or

   (3) where one parent has valid leave to enter or remain as the partner of a person who has either limited leave to enter or remain as a Migrant, indefinite leave to remain as a Migrant, or who has subsequently become a British citizen.

(c) The applicant must be under the age of 18 on the date the application is made, or if over 18 and applying for leave to remain, must have, or have last been granted, leave as the child of a Migrant.

(d) The applicant must not be married or in a civil partnership, must not have formed an independent family unit, and must not be leading an independent life. See further **8.9.4.6**.

(e) The applicant must not intend to stay in the UK beyond any period of leave granted to the Migrant parent.

(f) An applicant who is applying for leave to remain must have, or have last been granted, leave as the child of a parent who had leave under any category of the Immigration Rules.

(g) If the applicant is a child born in the UK to a Migrant and their partner, the applicant must provide a full UK birth certificate showing the names of both parents.

(h) All arrangements for the child's care and accommodation in the UK must comply with relevant UK legislation and regulations.

(i) If the applicant's parent is a Start-up or Innovator Migrant, there must be a sufficient level of funds available to the applicant, namely £315 for the first child in the UK or applying to come to the UK and £200 for each additional child in the UK or applying to come to the UK.

It is important to note the effect of (c) above in respect of a child now aged 18 or over. That child will still qualify for an extension of leave in this category, provided they had previously obtained such leave when under 18.

> **EXAMPLE**
>
> Mona applies for entry clearance as an Innovator. Her daughter, Janice, will be travelling with her. Janice's father is dead. In addition to meeting the requirements above, what financial funds need to be available? Mona needs £1,270 for herself (see **7.3.5**) and £315 available for Janice.

7.7.3 Settlement by a child

Once a Tier 1 Investor, Global Talent or Innovator ('the Migrant') is in a position to apply for settlement, the applicant's children may apply for settlement at the same time, provided the following requirements are met:

(a) The applicant must not fall for refusal under the general grounds for refusal (see **3.5.4**) and must not be an illegal entrant (see **10.4.2**) and is not in the UK in breach of immigration laws except for any period of overstaying that may be ignored under para 39E of the Immigration Rules (see **3.6.5**).

(b) The applicant must be the child of:

    (i) a parent who has been granted or is at the same time being granted indefinite leave to remain as a Migrant where:

        (1) that parent is the applicant's sole surviving parent, or

        (2) that parent has and has had sole responsibility for the applicant's upbringing (see **8.9.4.3**), or

        (3) there are serious and compelling family or other considerations which would make it desirable not to refuse the application and suitable arrangements have been made for the applicant's care (see **8.9.4.4**); or

    (ii) a parent who is at the same time being granted indefinite leave to remain as the partner of a person who has indefinite leave to remain as a Migrant, or who has subsequently become a British citizen.

(c) The applicant must have, or have last been granted, leave as the child of the Migrant who is being granted indefinite leave to remain.

(d) The applicant must not be married or in a civil partnership, must not have formed an independent family unit, and must not be leading an independent life (see **8.9.4.6**).

(e) Both of an applicant's parents must either be lawfully present in the UK, or being granted entry clearance, limited leave to remain, or indefinite leave to remain at the same time as the applicant, unless:

    (i) the Migrant is the applicant's sole surviving parent;

    (ii) the Migrant has and has had sole responsibility (see **8.9.4.3**) for the applicant's upbringing; or

    (iii) there are serious and compelling family or other considerations which would make it desirable not to refuse the application, and suitable arrangements have been made for the applicant's care (see **8.9.4.4**).

(f) The applicant must have sufficient knowledge of the English language and sufficient knowledge about life in the UK (see **3.8.7**), unless the applicant is under the age of 18 at the time the application is made.

(h) All arrangements for the child's care and accommodation in the UK must comply with relevant UK legislation and regulations.

7.8 SKILLED WORKERS

7.8.1 Introduction

7.8.1.1 Profile

The Skilled Worker category is a points-based route of entry to the UK. An applicant must have a job offer in an eligible skilled occupation from a UK-based employer which holds an appropriate sponsor's licence from the Home Office. The detailed requirements can be found in Appendix Skilled Workers.

Full details of sponsorship are beyond the scope of this book, and the Home Office-published guidance on its website (see **1.2.8**) should be consulted. In outline, a prospective sponsor must apply for a licence and indicate the number of certificates of sponsorship that it intends to issue. The application must be made online, the applicant must pay a prescribed fee and submit certain specified documents. Once licensed, a sponsor can issue certificates of sponsorship up to a set number. A licence lasts for four years, unless it is withdrawn or surrendered before then.

A licensed sponsor is rated A or B according to the Home Office's assessment of any risk posed. A sponsor that is B-rated must comply with a time-limited action plan, which will set out the steps it needs to take in order to gain or regain an A-rating. If the sponsor does not comply with this action plan, it is likely to lose its licence altogether.

7.8.1.2 Validity and suitability requirements

An application for entry clearance or permission to stay as a Skilled Worker must be made online on the gov.uk website on the appropriate specified form.

An applicant must meet all the following requirements:

(a)   any fee (see **3.6.4.2**) and Immigration Health Charge (see **3.10**) must have been paid;

(b)   the applicant must have provided any required biometrics (see **3.4.3**);

(c)   the applicant must have provided a passport or other travel document which satisfactorily establishes their identity and nationality; and

(d)   the applicant must have a Certificate of Sponsorship (see **7.8.2.2**) that was issued to them by their sponsor no more than three months before the date of application.

What about switching in-country? It is not possible to switch from the following categories: (a) a Visitor (see **Chapter 5**); (b) a Short-term Student (see **5.13**); (c) a Parent of a Child Student; or (d) a Seasonal Worker (see **7.12.7**).

Is there a minimum age requirement? Yes, Appendix Skilled Worker, para SW 1.3 provides that the applicant must be at least 18 years old on the date of application.

Finally, note that an applicant must not fall for refusal under Part 9: grounds for refusal (see **3.5.4**). In addition, an applicant for permission to stay must not be in the UK in breach of immigration laws (except that, where para 39E applies, any current period of overstaying will be disregarded (see **3.6.5**)) nor be on immigration bail (see **3.5.5**).

7.8.1.3 Entry requirement

Entry clearance in this category is mandatory for all applicants. In addition, any person applying for entry clearance for more than six months must meet the requirements for a tuberculosis certificate if the criteria specified in para A39 and in Appendix T of the Immigration Rules apply (see **3.4.1**).

7.8.2   Points requirements

7.8.2.1   How many points are required?

The applicant must be awarded 50 mandatory points from **Table 7.10** reproduced below that appears at Appendix Skilled Worker, para SW 4.1.

Table 7.10   **Mandatory points**

Mandatory points requirements	Relevant rules	Points
Sponsorship	SW 5.1 to SW 5.7	20
Job at an appropriate skill level	SW 6.1 to SW 6.5	20
English language skills at level B1 (intermediate)	SW 7.1 to SW 7.3	10

See further **7.8.2.2** to **7.8.2.4**.

In addition, the applicant must be awarded 20 tradeable points from **Table 7.11** reproduced below that appears at Appendix Skilled Worker, para SW 4.2. Whilst the points are described as tradeable, it is important to note that an applicant can only be awarded points for one of the six Options in the table. See further **7.8.2.5** to **7.8.2.10**.

Table 7.11   **Tradeable points**

Option	Tradeable points requirements for each option	Relevant rules	Points
A	The applicant's salary equals or exceeds all of the following: • £25,600 per year; • £10.10 per hour; and • the going rate for the occupation code.	SW 8.1 to SW 8.5 and SW 14.1 to SW 14.5	20
B	Educational qualification: PhD in a subject relevant to the job and the applicant's salary equals or exceeds all of the following: • £23,040 per year; • £10.10 per hour; and • 90% of the going rate for the occupation code. For this Option, 10 points may be awarded for the educational qualification and 10 points for the applicant's salary.	SW 9.1 to SW 9.10 and SW 14.1 to SW 14.5	20
C	Educational qualification: PhD in a STEM subject relevant to the job and the applicant's salary equals or exceeds all of the following: • £20,480 per year; • £10.10 per hour; and • 80% of the going rate for the occupation code.	SW 10.1 to SW 10.6 and SW 14.1 to SW 14.5	20

Option	Tradeable points requirements for each option	Relevant rules	Points
D	Job in a shortage occupation and the applicant's salary equals or exceeds all of the following: • £20,480 per year; • £10.10 per hour; and • 80% of the going rate for the occupation code.	SW 11.1 to SW 11.6 and SW 14.1 to SW 14.5	20
E	Applicant is a new entrant to the labour market and their salary equals or exceeds all of the following: • £20,480 per year; • £10.10 per hour; and • 70% of the going rate for the occupation code.	SW 12.1 to SW 12.7 and SW 14.1 to SW 14.5	20
F	Job in a listed health or education occupation and the applicant's salary equals or exceeds both: • £20,480 per year; and • the going rate for the occupation code. An applicant with a job in a listed health or education occupation can only be awarded tradeable points from Option F.	SW 13.1 to SW 13.7 and SW 14.1 to SW 14.5	20

So, an applicant must score 70 points in total by a combination of 50 mandatory points and 20 points from only one Option.

7.8.2.2 Mandatory 20 points: Sponsorship

Once a sponsor has been granted a licence, the sponsor can access the Home Office's IT sponsorship management system. This may be used to create and assign a Certificate of Sponsorship (COS). This is therefore not an actual certificate or paper document. It is a virtual document similar to a database record. Each COS has a unique reference number.

To be valid, a COS must:

(a)   confirm the applicant's name, that they are being sponsored as a Skilled Worker, details of the job and salary the sponsor is offering them and PAYE details if HM Revenue and Customs (HMRC) requires income tax and National Insurance for the sponsored job to be paid via PAYE; and

(b)   if the application is for entry clearance, have been allocated by the Home Office to that sponsor for the specific job and salary details shown; and

(c)   include a start date, stated by the sponsor, which is no more than three months after the date of application; and

(d)   not have been used in a previous application which was either granted or refused (but can have been used in a previous application which was rejected as invalid, made void or withdrawn); and

(e)   not have been withdrawn by the sponsor or cancelled by the Home Office.

The sponsor must be authorised by the Home Office to sponsor the job in question under the Skilled Worker route. That sponsor must be listed as A-rated on the Home Office's register of licensed sponsors, unless the applicant was last granted permission as a Skilled Worker and is applying to continue working for the same sponsor as in their last permission.

The sponsor must have paid in full any required Immigration Skills Charge (see **7.8.2.11**).

The relationship between the sponsor, as employer, and the applicant, as employee, must be genuine. So, the decision maker must not have reasonable grounds to believe the job the applicant is being sponsored to do does not exist; or is a sham; or has been created mainly so the applicant can apply for entry clearance or permission to stay. In addition, the decision maker must not have reasonable grounds to believe that the job amounts to the hire of the applicant to a third party who is not the sponsor to fill a position with that party, whether temporary or permanent; or contract work to undertake an ongoing routine role or to provide an ongoing routine service for a third party who is not the sponsor, regardless of the nature or length of any arrangement between the sponsor and the third party.

7.8.2.3 Mandatory 20 points: Skill level

The Office of National Statistics produces a multi-purpose common classification of occupations for the UK. This classification, known as the Standard Occupational Classification, has been adopted by the Home Office. Jobs are classified by way of a code in terms of their skill level and skill content. For example, code 1115 addresses chief executives and senior officials; code 2111 deals with chemical scientists; and code 3111 applies to laboratory technicians.

An applicant must be sponsored for a job in an eligible occupation code listed in Appendix Skilled Occupations. In addition to the occupation code, there are related job titles. For example, code 4112 applies to national government administrative occupations where the related job titles are an administrative assistant (courts of justice), administrative officer (government), civil servant (EO), clerk (government) and revenue officer (government).

The sponsor must choose an appropriate occupation code. Points will not be awarded if the decision maker has reasonable grounds to believe the sponsor has chosen a less appropriate occupation code because, for example, the most appropriate occupation code is not eligible under the Skilled Worker route. In applying this test, the decision maker may, in particular, consider: (a) whether the sponsor has shown a genuine need for the job as described; and (b) whether the applicant has the appropriate skills, qualifications and experience needed to do the job as described; and (c) the sponsor's history of compliance with the immigration system including, but not limited to, paying its sponsored workers appropriately; and (d) any additional information from the sponsor.

7.8.2.4 Mandatory 10 points: English language

An applicant must show English language ability on the Common European Framework of Reference for Languages in all four components (reading, writing, speaking and listening) of at least level B1 (intermediate) in accordance with the requirements set out in Appendix English Language. The applicant must show that they meet the English language requirement as specified in Appendix English Language. Broadly, this can be done in any of the following five ways.

(a) If the applicant has already met the requirement at the required level in a previous successful application for entry clearance or permission.

(b) If the applicant is a national of any of the following majority-English-speaking countries:

> Antigua and Barbuda • Australia • The Bahamas • Barbados • Belize • Canada • Dominica • Grenada • Guyana • Ireland • Jamaica • Malta • New Zealand • St Kitts and Nevis • St Lucia • St Vincent and the Grenadines • Trinidad and Tobago • United States of America.

(c) If the applicant has either (i) a Bachelor's degree, Master's degree or doctorate awarded in the UK; or (ii) a degree or degree-level qualification taught in a university or college in a majority-English-speaking country listed in (b) above but excluding Canada, which meets or exceeds the recognised standard of a Bachelor's degree, Master's degree or doctorate awarded in the UK; or (iii) a degree or degree-level qualification which meets, or exceeds, the recognised standard of a UK Bachelor's degree, Master's degree or doctorate and was taught or researched in English.

If the relevant qualification was awarded by a body from outside the UK, confirmation must be obtained from UK ENIC (see **6.5.5.2**) that the qualification meets the requirement.

The applicant will need to produce the certificate from their awarding body: or a transcript issued by the university or college that awarded their qualification; or an official letter from the university or college that awarded their qualification containing information equivalent to a degree certificate.

(d)   If the applicant provides a valid digital reference number from an approved provider showing they have passed an approved English language test to the required level in the two years before the date of application. The list of approved tests and providers can be found on the Home Office website (see **1.2.8**).

(e)   If the applicant has a GCSE, 'A' level, Scottish National Qualification at level 4 or 5 or Scottish Higher or Advanced Higher, in English (language or literature), that was awarded: (a) by an Ofqual (or SQA, Qualifications Wales or CCEA) regulated awarding body, and (b) following education in a UK school undertaken while they were aged under 18. The applicant will have to produce a certificate, or an official transcript issued by that awarding body.

7.8.2.5   Option A points

To be awarded 20 points under Option A, the applicant must:

(a)   be sponsored for a job in an appropriate eligible occupation code listed in Table 1 of Appendix Skilled Occupations (see **7.8.2.3**); and

(b)   the salary for the job for which the applicant is being sponsored must equal or exceed all of the following: (i) £25,600 per year, (ii) £10.10 per hour, and (iii) the going rate for the occupation code.

> **EXAMPLE**
>
> Alex is a chief medical officer. His sponsor will pay him a salary of £70,000 per annum (£34.50 per hour). Alex falls within the occupation code 1115 for chief executives and senior officials. Subject to checking that all his salary qualifies, he meets the salary requirement as the going rate for his job is £67,300.

As to what constitutes 'salary', see **7.8.2.12**.

7.8.2.6   Option B points

Option B allows for 10 or 20 points. Obviously, the full 20 points are needed. However, the first 10 points are met by having an appropriate educational qualification and this test is also used for acquiring points under Option C (see **7.8.2.7**).

First, an applicant may be awarded 10 points for their educational qualification if they are being sponsored for a job in an appropriate occupation code listed as being 'eligible for PhD points' in Table 1 of Appendix Skilled Occupations (see **7.8.2.3**). The applicant must have a UK PhD or other academic doctoral qualification, or an overseas academic qualification which UK ENIC (see **6.5.5.2**) confirms meets the recognised standard of a UK PhD.

The applicant's sponsor must provide a credible explanation of how the qualification is relevant to the job for which the applicant is being sponsored.

Note that the applicant may only be awarded points for one qualification.

Second, an applicant may be awarded 10 points if the salary for the job they are being sponsored for equals or exceeds all of the following: (i) £23,040 per year, (ii) £10.10 per hour, and (iii) 90% of the going rate for the occupation code that is listed in Table 1 of Appendix Skilled Occupations (see **7.8.2.3**).

> **EXAMPLE**
>
> Beatrice is an engineering manager. Her sponsor will pay her a salary of £31,000 per annum (£15.20 per hour). Beatrice falls within the occupation code 1121 for production managers and directors in manufacturing. Beatrice has a PhD awarded by a UK university. Beatrice's sponsor can provide a credible explanation of how her qualification is relevant to the job for which she is being sponsored.
>
> Beatrice cannot be awarded points under Option A as her salary does not reach the required going rate of £33,000. However, she will be awarded 10 points under Option B for her educational qualification as her code 1121 job is eligible for PhD points. Subject to checking that all her salary qualifies, she meets the salary requirement for which she will be awarded a further 10 points as 90% of the going rate for her job is a salary of £29,700.

As to what constitutes 'salary', see **7.8.2.12**.

7.8.2.7   Option C points

An applicant will be awarded 20 points under Option C if:

(a)   they meet the requirements for 10 educational qualification points under Option B (see **7.8.2.6**); and

(b)   the applicant's sponsor can provide a credible explanation that the qualification in question is in a Science, Technology, Engineering or Mathematics (STEM) subject; and

(c)   the salary for the job the applicant is being sponsored for must equal or exceed all of the following: (i) £20,480 per year, (ii) £10.10 per hour, and (iii) 80% of the going rate for the occupation code that is listed in Table 1 of Appendix Skilled Occupations (see **7.8.2.3**).

> **EXAMPLE**
>
> Claudette is a Games programmer. Her sponsor will pay her a salary of £27,000 per annum (£13.30 per hour). Claudette falls within the occupation code 2136 for programmers and software development professionals. She has a PhD in Intelligent Games & Game Intelligence awarded by a UK university. Her sponsor can provide credible explanations of how her qualification is relevant to the job for which she is being sponsored and that it is a Technology subject.
>
> Claudette cannot be awarded points under Option A as her salary does not reach the required going rate of £33,300. She does meet the requirements to be awarded 10 points under Option B for her educational qualification as her code 2136 job is eligible for PhD points, but she does not meet the salary requirement for a further award of 10 points under Option B as 90% of the going rate for her job is a salary of £29,970. However, subject to checking that all her salary qualifies, she does meet the salary requirement for Option C, and so she will be awarded 20 points under Option C as 80% of the going rate for her job is a salary of £26,400.

As to what constitutes 'salary', see **7.8.2.12**.

7.8.2.8   Option D points

An applicant will be awarded 20 points under Option D if:

(a)   they are sponsored for a job in an appropriate eligible occupation code listed in Appendix Shortage Occupation List as being a shortage occupation in the nation of the UK where that job is based; and

(b)   the salary for the job the applicant is being sponsored for must equal or exceed all of the following: (i) £20,480 per year, (ii) £10.10 per hour, and (iii) 80% of the going rate for the occupation code that is listed in Table 1 of Appendix Skilled Occupations (see **7.8.2.3**).

For many years the UK has had a shortage of workers in certain occupations – that is to say, there are not enough resident workers to fill available jobs in particular sectors of the UK's economy. Historically this has included various healthcare and teaching jobs. The Appendix Shortage Occupation List is updated regularly, usually following recommendations from the Migration Advisory Committee.

EXAMPLE

Dexter is a hydrogeologist. He has a Master's degree in environmental engineering. His sponsor will pay him a salary of £30,000 per annum (£14.80 per hour). Dexter falls within the occupation code 2113 for physical scientists. Under the Appendix Shortage Occupation List, the job of hydrogeologist in the construction related ground of the engineering industry qualifies.

Dexter cannot be awarded points under Option A as his salary does not reach the required going rate of £36,500. He does not meet the requirements to be awarded 10 points under Option B for his educational qualification as he does not have a PhD. However, subject to checking that all his salary qualifies, he does meet the salary requirement for Option D as 80% of the going rate for his job is a salary of £29,200.

As to what constitutes 'salary', see **7.8.2.12**.

7.8.2.9   Option E points

An applicant will be awarded 20 points under Option E if:

(a)   they are sponsored for a job in an appropriate eligible occupation code listed in Table 1 of Appendix Skilled Occupations (see **7.8.2.3**); and

(b)   they meet one or more of the requirements set out in Appendix Skilled Worker, para SW 12.2 which include that:

     (i)   the applicant is under the age of 26 on the date of application; or

     (ii)   the job offer must be for a postdoctoral position in any of the following occupation codes:

        • 2111 Chemical scientists • 2112 Biological scientists and biochemists • 2113 Physical scientists • 2114 Social and humanities scientists • 2119 Natural and social science professionals not elsewhere classified • 2311 Higher education teaching professionals; or

     (iii)   the job offer must be in a UK regulated profession and the applicant must be working towards a recognised professional qualification for that profession; or

     (iv)   the applicant must be working towards full registration or chartered status with the relevant professional body for the job they are being sponsored for; and

(c)   the salary for the job the applicant is being sponsored for must equal or exceed all of the following: (i) £20,480 per year, (ii) £10.10 per hour, and (iii) 70% of the going rate for the occupation code that is listed in Table 1 of Appendix Skilled Occupations (see **7.8.2.3**).

EXAMPLE

Emma, aged 24, is a product development manager. She has a Bachelor's degree in marketing. Her sponsor will pay her a salary of £26,000 per annum (£12.80 per hour). Emma falls within the occupation code 3545 for sales accounts and business development managers.

Emma cannot be awarded points under Option A as her salary does not reach the required going rate of £35,400. She does not meet the requirements to be awarded points under Options B or C as she does not have a PhD. She cannot be awarded points under Option D as her job is not on the Appendix Shortage Occupation List. However, she is under the age of 26 and, subject to checking that all her salary qualifies, she meets the salary requirement for Option E as 70% of the going rate for her job is a salary of £24,780.

As to what constitutes 'salary', see **7.8.2.12**.

7.8.2.10   Option F points

This Option is only concerned with applicants in health and education eligible occupation codes listed in Table 2 of Appendix Skilled Occupations. These include, for example, code 2211 medical practitioners where the related job titles are those of anaesthetist, consultant (hospital service), doctor, general practitioner, medical practitioner, paediatrician, psychiatrist, radiologist and surgeon.

To score points under Option F, the salary for the job for which the applicant is being sponsored must equal or exceed both: (a) £20,480 per year; and (b) the going rate for the occupation code.

7.8.2.11   Immigration Skills Charge (ISC)

An employer normally has to pay to the government the ISC when it assigns a COS to a Skilled Worker. Full details and the limited exceptions can be found in the Immigration Skills Charge Regulations 2017 (SI 2017/499).

How much is the ISC? It depends on the size of the sponsor's organisation and the period of prospective employment in respect of which the certificate of sponsorship is assigned. Small and charitable sponsors pay £364 for the first 12 months and £182 for each additional six months. All other sponsors pay £1,000 for the first 12 months and £500 for each additional six months. The figures are set out in **Table 7.12** below.

Table 7.12   ISC

Length of employment	Small or charitable sponsor	All other sponsors
12 months or less	£364	£1,000
More than 12 months, but no more than 18 months	£546	£1,500
More than 18 months, but no more than 24 months	£728	£2,000
More than 24 months, but no more than 30 months	£910	£2,500
More than 30 months, but no more than 36 months	£1,092	£3,000
More than 36 months, but no more than 42 months	£1,274	£3,500
More than 42 months, but no more than 48 months	£1,456	£4,000
More than 48 months, but no more than 54 months	£1,638	£4,500
More than 54 months, but no more than 60 months	£1,820	£5,000

What is a small or charitable sponsor? It is a company that is subject to the small companies' regime under s 381 of the Companies Act 2006; a charity within the meaning of s 1 of the Charities Act 2011; or a company or a person who employs no more than 50 employees.

7.8.2.12 What constitutes 'salary'?

For the purposes of all of the Options, an applicant's salary only includes guaranteed basic gross pay before income tax and including employee pension and national insurance contributions.

Salary does not include other pay and benefits, such as any of the following:

(a)   pay which cannot be guaranteed because the nature of the job means that hours fluctuate; or

(b)   additional pay such as shift, overtime or bonus pay (whether or not it is guaranteed); or

(c)   employer pension and employer national insurance contributions; or

(d)   any allowances, such as accommodation or cost of living allowances; or

(e)   in-kind benefits, such as equity shares, health insurance, school or university fees, company cars or food; or

(f)   one-off payments, such as 'golden hellos'; or

(g)   any payments relating to immigration costs, such as the fee or Immigration Health Charge; or

(h)   payments to cover business expenses, including (but not limited to) travel to and from the applicant's country of residence, equipment, clothing, travel or subsistence.

Points are only awarded for up to a maximum of 48 hours a week, even if the applicant is sponsored to work more than this. For example, if the applicant will earn £14 per hour, working 60 hours per week, the salary taken into account is £34,944 (£14 x 48 x 52) and not £43,680 (£14 x £60 x 52).

Going rates for occupation codes listed in Table 1 of Appendix Skilled Occupations are based on a 39-hour week and therefore must be pro-rated if different hours are to be worked by the applicant. How? Appendix Skilled Worker, para SW 14.4 provides as follows:

(a)   (the going rate for the occupation code stated in Table 1 of Appendix Skilled Occupations) x (the number of weekly working hours stated by the sponsor ÷ 39)

Note that the applicant's full weekly hours must be included when checking their salary against the pro-rated going rate, even if they work more than 48 hours a week.

(b)   Where an applicant's salary is required to be 70%, 80% or 90% of the going rate, the resulting figure from the calculation in (a) above must be multiplied by 0.7, 0.8 or 0.9 as appropriate, to calculate the required salary.

In addition, the applicant's hourly salary must be calculated to check that the applicant is being paid at least at the minimum rate of £10.10 per hour.

EXAMPLE

Frank is a logistics manager. His sponsor will pay him a salary of £30,000 per annum. This will be his guaranteed basic gross pay before income tax and including employee pension and national insurance contributions. It will include £1,000 travel expenses.

Frank will be sponsored to work 45 hours a week. Frank falls within the occupation code 1162 for managers and directors in storage and warehousing. The going rate for his job is £24,300.

Can Frank score 20 points under Option A (see **7.8.2.5**)? As he is working more than 39 hours a week, his pro-rated going rate is £28,038 (£24,300 x 45 hours ÷ 39). As Frank's qualifying salary will be £29,000 (£30,000 – £1,000 non-eligible travel expenses) and his hourly rate of pay is £12.39 (£29,000 ÷ 52 ÷ 45), he should score 20 points under Option A.

Home Office guidance gives the following example:

> An applicant is sponsored to work 42 hours a week as a senior care worker for a salary of £21,000. The applicant is claiming 20 points under option D for a job in a shortage occupation. [The job falls within occupation code 6146: see Immigration Rules Appendix Shortage Occupation List.] Their annual pay [£21,000] exceeds the reduced general annual threshold of £20,480 and equates to £9.62 per hour [£21,000 ÷ 52 ÷ 42]. This is higher than the 80% of the going rate they need under option D [£13,520: see Immigration Rules Appendix Skilled Occupations], but lower than the £10.10 minimum hourly rate. They are not awarded the 20 tradeable points.

7.8.3 Financial requirement

7.8.3.1 How much?

If the applicant is applying for entry clearance, or has been in the UK for less than 12 months on the date of their application, either:

(a) the applicant must have funds of at least £1,270; or

(b) the sponsor must certify that they will, if necessary, maintain and accommodate the applicant up to the end of the first month of their employment, to an amount of at least £1,270.

7.8.3.2 Evidence required

Unless the applicant is relying on their sponsor's certificate (see **7.8.3.1**), they must show that they have held the required level of funds for a 28-day period. The most recently dated piece of financial evidence produced by the applicant must be dated within 31 days before the date of their application. The financial evidence provided must cover the whole 28-day period.

Funds may be held in any form of personal bank or building society account (including current, deposit, savings, pension from which the funds can be withdrawn or investment account) provided the account allows the funds to be accessed immediately. Funds held in other accounts or financial instruments such as shares, bonds, credit cards, pensions from which the funds cannot be withdrawn immediately, regardless of notice period, will not be accepted as evidence of funds.

The applicant's financial documents must be from institutions acceptable to the Home Office. Appendix Finance, para FIN 2.1 provides that funds will not be considered if they are held in a financial institution where (a) the decision maker is unable to make satisfactory verification checks; or (b) the financial institution is not regulated by the appropriate regulatory body for the country in which that institution is operating; or (c) the financial institution does not use electronic record keeping.

Overdraft facilities are not counted towards meeting the financial requirement. Promises of future third-party support are not accepted as evidence of funds unless made by way of a sponsor's certificate (see **7.8.3.1**).

7.8.4 Criminal record certificate requirement

If the applicant is applying for entry clearance and is being sponsored for a job in any of the occupation codes listed in Appendix Skilled Worker, para SW 16.1, they must provide a criminal record certificate from the relevant authority in any country in which they have been present for 12 months or more (whether continuously or in total) in the 10 years before the date of application, and while aged 18 or over.

7.8.5 Period and conditions of grant for a Skilled Worker

An applicant will be granted entry clearance or permission to stay until 14 days after the end date of their COS. This may be up to a maximum of five years after the start date of their COS.

The grant will be subject to all the following conditions:

(a)   no access to public funds (see **3.3.2**); and

(b)   work is permitted only in the job the applicant is being sponsored for, subject to (c) to (e); and

(c)   supplementary employment is permitted, providing the person continues to work in the job for which they are being sponsored; and

(d)   voluntary work is permitted; and

(e)   working out a contractual notice period is permitted, for a job the applicant was lawfully working in on the date of application; and

(f)   study is permitted, subject to the ATAS condition in Appendix ATAS; and

(g)   if Part 10 applies, the applicant will be required to register with the police (see **3.3.3**).

7.8.6   Settlement as a Skilled Worker

7.8.6.1   Validity requirements

A person applying for settlement as a Skilled Worker must apply online on the gov.uk website on the specified form, 'Settle in the UK in various immigration categories: form SET(O)'.

The applicant must meet all the following requirements:

(a)   any fee must have been paid; and

(b)   the applicant must have provided any required biometrics (see **3.4.3**); and

(c)   the applicant must have provided a passport or other travel document which satisfactorily establishes their identity and nationality; and

(d)   the applicant must be in the UK on the date of application; and

(e)   the applicant must have, or have last been granted, permission as a Skilled Worker.

7.8.6.2   Suitability requirements

An applicant must not fall for refusal under Part 9: grounds for refusal (see **3.5.4**).

An applicant must not:

(a)   be in the UK in breach of immigration laws, except that, where para 39E applies, any current period of overstaying will be disregarded (see **3.6.5**); or

(b)   be on immigration bail (see **3.5.5**).

7.8.6.3   Qualifying period requirement

The applicant must have spent a continuous period of five years in the UK with permission on any of, or any combination of, the following routes: (a) Skilled Worker; or (b) Global talent; or (c) Innovator; or (d) T2 Minister of Religion; or (e) T2 Sportsperson; or (f) Representative of an Overseas Business; or (g) as a Tier 1 Investor Migrant.

7.8.6.4   Knowledge of life in the UK

The applicant must meet the Knowledge of Life in the UK requirement as set out in Appendix KOL UK.

7.8.6.5   Sponsorship and salary requirement

The sponsor in the applicant's most recent permission must still be approved by the Home Office to sponsor Skilled Workers on the date of decision. In addition, the sponsor must confirm that they still require the applicant to work for them for the foreseeable future, and that the applicant is paid, and will be paid for the foreseeable future, at least the general salary requirement or the going rate requirement listed in **Table 7.13** below taken from Appendix Skilled Worker, para SW 24.3, whichever is higher.

Table 17.13   Settlement salary requirement

	Applicant's circumstances	General salary	Going rate
A	All cases where row B does not apply.	Salary of at least £25,600 per year	At least the going rate
B	The applicant was sponsored in their most recent permission for a job in a shortage occupation or a health or education occupation code listed in Table 2 of Appendix Skilled Occupations	Salary of at least £20,480 per year	At least the going rate

As to what constitutes 'salary', see **7.8.2.12**.

7.8.7   Entry by the dependants of a Skilled Worker

7.8.7.1   Validity requirements

A person applying for entry clearance or permission to stay as a dependent partner or dependent child of a Skilled Worker must apply online on the gov.uk website on the appropriate specified form. The applicant must meet all the following requirements:

(a)   any fee (see **3.6.4.2**) and Immigration Health Charge (see **3.10**) must have been paid; and

(b)   the applicant must have provided any required biometrics (see **3.4.3**); and

(c)   the applicant must have provided a passport or other travel document which satisfactorily establishes their identity and nationality; and

(d)   if the applicant is applying as a dependent partner, they must be aged 18 or over on the date of application.

7.8.7.2   Suitability requirements

An applicant must not fall for refusal under Part 9: grounds for refusal (see **3.5.4**).

If applying for permission to stay the applicant must not be: (a) in breach of immigration laws, except that where paragraph 39E applies, that period of overstaying will be disregarded (see **3.6.5**); or (b) on immigration bail (see **3.5.5**).

7.8.7.3   Relationship requirement for a dependent partner

The applicant must be the partner of a person (P) where one of the following applies:

(a)   P has permission on the Skilled Worker route; or

(b)   P is, at the same time, applying for (and is granted) entry clearance or permission on the Skilled Worker route; or

(c)   P is settled or has become a British citizen, providing P had permission on the Skilled Worker route when they settled, and the applicant had permission as P's partner at that time.

If the applicant and their Skilled Worker partner are not married or in a civil partnership, all of the following requirements must be met:

(a)   they must have been living together in a relationship similar to marriage or civil partnership for at least the two years before the date of application (see **8.3**); and

(b)   any previous relationship of the applicant or their Skilled Worker partner with another person must have permanently broken down; and

(c)   the applicant and their Skilled Worker partner must not be so closely related that they would not be allowed to marry or form a civil partnership in the UK (see **8.3.5.3**); and

(d)   the relationship between the applicant and their Skilled Worker partner must be genuine and subsisting (see **8.3.5.5**); and

(e)   the applicant and their Skilled Worker partner must intend to live together throughout the applicant's stay in the UK (see **8.3.5.9**).

7.8.7.4 Relationship requirement for a dependent child

The applicant must be the child of a parent (P) where one of the following applies:

(a)   P has permission on the Skilled Worker route; or

(b)   P is, at the same time, applying for (and is granted) entry clearance or permission on the Skilled Worker route; or

(c)   P is settled or has become a British citizen, providing P had permission on the Skilled Worker route when they settled, and the applicant had permission as P's child at that time.

The applicant's parents must each be either applying at the same time as the applicant or have permission to be in the UK (other than as a visitor) unless:

(a)   the parent with permission as a Skilled Worker is the sole surviving parent; or

(b)   the parent with permission as a Skilled Worker has sole responsibility for the child's upbringing (see **8.9.4.3**); or

(c)   the decision maker is satisfied that there are serious and compelling reasons to grant the child entry clearance or permission to stay with the parent who has permission as a Skilled Worker (see **8.9.4.4**).

If the applicant is aged under 18 on the date of application, there must be suitable arrangements for the child's care and accommodation in the UK, which must comply with relevant UK legislation and regulations.

The child must be under the age of 18 on the date of application, unless they were last granted permission as the dependent child of their parent or parents.

If the child is aged 16 or over at the date of application, they must not be leading an independent life (see **8.9.4.6**).

7.8.7.5 Financial requirement for a dependent partner or dependent child

How much is needed? The funds required are as follows:

(a)   £285 for a dependent partner in the UK or applying for entry clearance; and

(b)   £315 for the first dependent child in the UK or applying for entry clearance; and

(c)   £200 for any other dependent child in the UK or applying for entry clearance.

If the applicant is applying for entry clearance, or has been in the UK for less than 12 months on the date of application, either:

(a)   the applicant and/or their partner or parent(s) must have funds of at least the appropriate amount required; or

(b)   the sponsor of the Skilled Worker must certify that they will, if necessary, maintain and accommodate the dependent partner and/or any dependent child as well as the Skilled Worker, up to the end of the first month of each of their grants of permission, to at least the appropriate amounts required.

The funds held for the applicant (see **7.8.3.1**) must be held in addition to these funds. The evidence required is the same as for the Skilled Worker (see **7.8.3.2**).

7.8.7.6 Period and conditions of grant for a dependent partner or dependent child

A partner will be granted permission which ends on the same date as their partner's permission as a Skilled Worker or three years' permission if the Skilled Worker was (or is being) granted settlement as a Skilled Worker.

A child will be granted permission which ends on the same date as whichever of their parents' permission ends first, unless both parents have (or are being granted) settlement or British Citizenship, in which case the child will be granted permission for three years.

The grant will be subject to all the following conditions:

(a) no access to public funds (see **3.3.2**); and

(b) work (including self-employment and voluntary work) is permitted, except as a professional sportsperson (including as a sports coach); and

(c) study is permitted, subject to the ATAS condition in Appendix ATAS, if the applicant is over the age of 18; and

(d) if Part 10 applies, the applicant will be required to register with the police (see **3.3.3**).

7.8.8 Settlement by the dependants of a Skilled Worker

Broadly, the applicant must have spent a continuous period of five years in the UK with permission as a dependant of the Skilled Worker.

Unless an exemption applies, the applicant must show English language ability on the Common European Framework of Reference for Languages in speaking and listening to at least level B1.

The applicant must show they meet the English language requirement as specified in Appendix English Language.

If the applicant is aged 18 or over on the date of application, they must meet the Knowledge of Life in the UK requirement as set out in Appendix KOL UK.

7.9 INTRA-COMPANY ROUTES

7.9.1 Overview

There are two Intra-Company routes. First, the Intra-Company Transfer route. This is for established workers who are being transferred by the business they work for to do a skilled role in the UK. The second is the Intra-Company Graduate Trainee route. This is for workers who are being transferred by the business they work for to undertake a role in the UK as part of a structured graduate training programme.

The routes require knowledge from the outset of two important concepts. A 'High Earner' under Appendix Intra-Company routes is a person who is sponsored in a job with a gross annual salary of £73,900 or more (based on working a maximum of 48 hours per week) as confirmed by their sponsor. A 'Sponsor Group', under Appendix Intra-Company routes, means the sponsor and any business or organisation that is linked to the sponsor by common ownership or control, or by a joint venture on which the applicant is sponsored to work.

A dependent partner and dependent children can apply to come to the UK on these routes. The requirements are similar to those of a Skilled Worker (see **7.8.7**).

The Intra-Company routes cannot lead to settlement.

The detailed requirements can be found in Appendix Intra-Company routes.

7.9.2 Validity requirements

A person applying for entry clearance or permission to stay on either route must apply online on the gov.uk website on the appropriate specified form. The applicant must meet all the following requirements:

(a)   any fee (see **3.6.4.2**) and Immigration Health Charge (see **3.10**) must have been paid; and

(b)   the applicant must have provided any required biometrics (see **3.4.3**); and

(c)   the applicant must have provided a passport or other travel document which satisfactorily establishes their identity and nationality; and

(d)   the applicant must have a COS from an approved Sponsor that was issued to them no more than three months before the date of application; and

(e)   the applicant must be aged 18 or over on the date of application.

7.9.3 Suitability requirements

An applicant must not fall for refusal under Part 9: grounds for refusal (see **3.5.4**).

If applying for permission to stay the applicant must not be: (a) in breach of immigration laws, except that where para 39E applies, that period of overstaying will be disregarded (see **3.6.5**); or (b) on immigration bail (see **3.5.5**).

7.9.4 Points requirement

The applicant must be awarded 60 points from **Table 7.14** reproduced below that appears at Appendix Intra-Company routes, para IC 4.1.

Table 7.14   Points requirements

Points requirements	Relevant Rules	Points
Sponsorship	IC 5.1 to IC 5.10	20
Job at an appropriate skill level	IC 6.1 to IC 6.7	20
Salary at required level	IC 7.1 to IC 9.5	20

7.9.5 Sponsorship

The applicant must have a valid COS for the job they are planning to do, which must:

(a)   confirm the applicant's name, that they are being sponsored as an Intra-Company Transfer or Intra-Company Graduate Trainee, details of the job, salary and any allowances the sponsor is offering them and PAYE details if HM Revenue and Customs (HMRC) requires income tax and national insurance for the sponsored job to be paid via PAYE; and

(b)   include a start date for the job, stated by the sponsor, which is no more than three months after the date of application; and

(c)   not have been used in a previous application which was either granted or refused (but can have been used in a previous application which was rejected as invalid, made void or withdrawn); and

(d)   not have been withdrawn by the sponsor or cancelled by the Home Office; and

(e)   unless the applicant is a High Earner, confirm that the applicant has worked for the Sponsor Group for the requisite period (see below).

The sponsor must:

(a)   be authorised by the Home Office to sponsor the job in question under the Intra-Company routes; and

(b)   be listed as A-rated on the Home Office's register of licensed sponsors, unless the applicant was last granted permission under the Intra-Company routes and is applying to continue working for the same sponsor as in their last permission; and

(c)   have paid in full any required Immigration Skills Charge (see **7.8.2.11**).

An applicant on the Intra-Company Transfer route must be currently working for the Sponsor Group and unless they are applying as a High Earner must have worked outside the UK for the Sponsor Group for 12 months.

An applicant on the Intra-Company Graduate Trainee route must have worked outside the UK for the Sponsor Group for a continuous period of at least three months immediately before the date of application.

7.9.6   Job at appropriate skill level

The applicant will meet the job skill level requirement if they are being sponsored for a job in an occupation code listed in Appendix Skilled Occupations that is identified in the final column of Table 1 as eligible for the Intra-Company routes.

If the applicant is applying on the Intra-Company Graduate Trainee route, the job must be part of a structured graduate training programme, with clearly defined progression towards a managerial or specialist role within the sponsor organisation.

If the applicant is applying on the Intra-Company Graduate Trainee route, the sponsor must not have assigned more than 20 certificates of sponsorship, to Intra-Company Graduate Trainees, including the certificate of sponsorship assigned to the applicant, in the financial year (which begins on 6 April and ends on 5 April each year) in which the certificate of sponsorship is assigned.

7.9.7   Salary at required level

The salary for the job for which the applicant is being sponsored must equal or exceed both: (a) the general salary requirement (see **7.9.7.1**); and (b) the going rate requirement (see **7.9.7.2**).

7.9.7.1   General salary rate

If the applicant is being sponsored for a job in one of the occupation codes listed in Table 1 of Appendix Skilled Occupations, the general salary requirement is:

(a)   £41,500 per year if the applicant is applying on the Intra-Company Transfer route; or

(b)   £23,000 per year if the applicant is applying on the Intra-Company Graduate Trainee route.

If the applicant is being sponsored to work more than 48 hours a week, only the salary for the first 48 hours a week will be considered towards the general salary requirement. For example, an applicant who works 60 hours a week for £10 per hour will be considered to have a salary of £24,960 (£10 x 48 x 52) per year and not £31,200 (£10 x 60 x 52).

7.9.7.2   Going rate

If the applicant is being sponsored for a job in one of the occupation codes listed in Table 1 of Appendix Skilled Occupations, the going rate requirement is:

(a)   100% of the pro-rated going rate if the applicant is applying on the Intra-Company Transfer route, which will be calculated as 1 x (the going rate for the occupation code stated in Table 1 of Appendix Skilled Occupations) x (the number of weekly working hours stated by the sponsor ÷ 39); or

(b)   70% of the pro-rated going rate if the applicant is applying in the Intra-Company Graduate Trainee route, which will be calculated as 0.7 x (the going rate for the occupation code stated in Table 1 of Appendix Skilled Occupations) x (the number of weekly working hours stated by the sponsor ÷ 39).

Note that the applicant's full weekly hours are included when checking their salary against the going rate, even if they work more than 48 hours a week. For example, an applicant who works 60 hours a week in an occupation code with a going rate of £39,000 must be paid £54,000 (0.9 x £39,000 x 60 ÷ 39) per year, not £43,200 (0.9 x £39,000 x 48 ÷ 39).

7.9.7.3 What salary counts?

Salary under these requirements includes only:

(a)   guaranteed basic gross pay (before income tax and including employee pension and national insurance contributions); and

(b)   allowances which are guaranteed to be paid for the duration of the applicant's employment in the UK (such as London weighting) or are paid as a mobility premium or to cover the additional cost of living in the UK. Where an allowance is solely for the purpose of accommodation, it will only be taken into account up to a value of either 30% of the total salary package, where the applicant is applying in the Intra-Company Transfer route, or 40% of the total salary package, where the applicant is applying in the Intra-Company Graduate Trainee route.

Salary does not include other pay and benefits, such as any of the following:

(a)   flexible working where the nature of the job means that hours fluctuate and pay cannot be guaranteed; or

(b)   additional pay such as shift, overtime or bonus pay, whether or not it is guaranteed; or

(c)   employer pension and national insurance contributions; or

(d)   any allowances, other than those specified above; or

(e)   in-kind benefits, such as equity shares, health insurance, school or university fees, company cars or food; or

(f)   one-off payments, such as 'golden hellos'; or

(g)   any payments relating to immigration costs, such as the fee or Immigration Health Charge; or

(h)   payments to cover business expenses, including (but not limited to) travel to and from the applicant's country of residence, equipment, clothing, travel or subsistence.

7.9.8 Financial requirement

This is the same as for a Skilled Worker: see **7.8.3**.

7.9.9 Maximum length of assignments requirement

If the applicant is a High Earner, the grant of permission must not lead to the applicant being granted cumulative periods of permission in the Intra-Company routes totalling more than nine years in any 10-year period.

If the applicant is not a High Earner, the grant of permission must not lead to the applicant being granted cumulative periods of permission in the Intra-Company routes totalling more than five years in any six-year period.

So, how long may permission be granted at any one time? If the application is as an Intra-Company Transfer, permission will be granted for a period which is the shortest of the following:

(a)   five years after the start date of the job detailed in the COS; or

(b)   14 days after the end date of the job detailed in the COS; or

(c) if the applicant is a High Earner, the date at which the applicant will have had cumulative permission in the Intra-Company routes totalling nine years in any 10-year period; or

(d) if the applicant is not a High Earner, the date at which the applicant will have had cumulative permission in the Intra-Company routes totalling five years in any six-year period.

If the application is as an Intra-Company Graduate Trainee, the applicant will be granted permission until whichever is the shorter of 14 days after the end date of the job detailed in the COS or one year after the start date of the job stated on their COS.

7.10 T2 MINISTER OF RELIGION

7.10.1 Overview

This route is for a person who has a key leading role within their faith-based organisation or a religious order in the UK to carry out pastoral duties. Those duties include leading worship regularly and on special occasions; providing religious education for children and adults by preaching or teaching; officiating at marriages, funerals and other special services; offering counselling and welfare support to members of the congregation; recruiting, training and coordinating the work of any local volunteers and lay preachers.

In addition to the usual validity and suitability requirements (see Appendix T2 Minister of Religion), the points requirements follow below.

If the applicant is applying for entry clearance, permission will be granted for whichever is the shorter of: (a) up to 14 days after the period of employment stated on their COS; or (b) 3 years and 1 month.

If the applicant is applying for permission to stay, it will be granted for whichever is the shorter of: (a) up to 14 days after the period of employment stated on their COS; or (b) 3 years; or (c) the difference between 6 years and the period they have already been granted permission as a T2 Minister of Religion, T2 Sportsperson, or Skilled Worker (or any combination of these routes).

7.10.2 Points requirement

The applicant must score 70 points based on **Table 7.15** reproduced below from Appendix T2 Minister of Religion, para MOR 4.1.

Table 7.15 Points requirement

Offer of a job by an approved sponsor	50 points
Financial requirement	10 points
English language at level B2 (intermediate)	10 points

7.10.3 Offer of a job by an approved sponsor

The sponsor must be listed as A-rated on the Home Office's register of licensed sponsors, unless the applicant was last granted permission as a T2 Minister of Religion and is applying to continue working for the same sponsor as in their last permission.

The COS must confirm all the following:

(a) the applicant's name and details of the job and salary and any other remuneration of the applicant; and

(b) the job is as a T2 Minister of Religion; and

(c) the applicant is qualified to do the job of a T2 Minister of Religion; and

(d)   the applicant is a member of the sponsor's religious order (if the sponsor's organisation is a religious order); and

(e)   the applicant will perform religious duties within the sponsor's organisation or directed by the sponsor's organisation in the UK (which may include preaching, pastoral and non-pastoral work); and

(f)   the applicant's role will not involve mainly non-pastoral duties, such as school teaching, media production, domestic work or administrative and clerical work, unless the role is a senior position within the sponsor's organisation; and

(g)   that applicant will receive pay and conditions at least equal to those given to settled workers in the same role and compliant with the national minimum wage; and

(h)   that the applicant will be based in the UK; and

(i)   that if the application is successful, the applicant will comply with the conditions of their permission.

7.10.4 Financial and English language requirements

The financial requirement is the same as that for a Skilled Worker: see **7.8.3**.

The applicant must have English language ability on the Common European Framework of Reference for Languages in all four components (reading, writing, speaking and listening) of at least level B2. It can be met by any of the ways detailed at **7.8.2.4**.

7.11 T2 SPORTSPERSON

7.11.1 Overview

This category is for elite sportspersons and coaches who are internationally established at the highest level, whose employment will make a significant contribution to the development of their sport at the highest level in the UK, and who intend to base themselves in the UK. The applicant must be sponsored on a long-term contract by an appropriate Sports Governing Body.

The grant of permission is the same as for a T2 Minister of Religion (see **7.10.1**). In addition to the usual validity and suitability requirements (see Appendix T2 Sportsperson), the points requirements follow below.

7.11.2 Points requirement

The applicant must score 70 points based on **Table 7.16** reproduced below from Appendix T2 Sportsperson, para SP 4.1.

Table 7.16   Points requirement

Offer of a job by an approved sponsor	50 points
Financial requirement	10 points
English language at level A1	10 points

7.11.3 Offer of a job by an approved sponsor

The applicant must provide a letter from the relevant Sports Governing Body listed in Appendix M containing their endorsement number and confirming that (a) the applicant is internationally established at the highest level; and (b) the employment of the applicant will make a significant contribution to the development of their sport at the highest level in the UK.

The applicant's COS must confirm all the following:

(a)   the applicant's name and details of the job and salary and any other remuneration offered to the applicant; and

(b)   that the sponsor is sponsoring the worker as a T2 Sportsperson; and

(c)   the job is one the applicant is qualified to undertake; and

(d)   the applicant has been issued a unique endorsement number from the appropriate governing body specified in Appendix M; and

(e)   the applicant intends to be based in the UK; and

(f)   if the application is successful, the applicant will comply with the conditions of their permission.

7.11.4 Financial and English language requirements

The financial requirement is the same as that for a Skilled Worker: see **7.8.3**.

The applicant must have English language ability on the Common European Framework of Reference for Languages in all four components (reading, writing, speaking and listening) of at least level A1. It can be met by any of the ways detailed at **7.8.2.4**.

7.12 T5 TEMPORARY WORKERS

This tier covers temporary sponsored workers (and, where eligible, their family members) who can remain in the UK for no longer than six months (Seasonal workers) or 12 months (Sporting workers and Charity workers) or 24 months (Creative workers, Religious workers, Government authorised exchange workers, international agreement workers and workers under a Youth Mobility Scheme) or up to a maximum of 72 months (Government authorised exchange workers). We shall consider each type of worker briefly in turn.

Applicants can find detailed guidance and specified application forms on the Home Office website (see **1.2.8**).

7.12.1 Creative and Sporting worker

7.12.1.1 A profile

This category is for creative artists (performers and entertainers) and sportspeople who wish to work in the UK for up to 12 months. A Creative worker can apply to extend their stay up to a maximum of 24 months if they are still working for the same sponsor.

A Creative worker is someone who can make a unique contribution to the UK's rich cultural life, for example as an artist, dancer, musician or entertainer, or as a model contributing to the UK's fashion industry. Sportspeople should be internationally established at the highest level in their sport, and/or their employment in the UK should make a significant contribution to the development and operation of that particular sport in this country.

Full details are in Appendix T5 (Temporary Worker) Creative and Sporting Worker.

7.12.1.2 Sponsorship

If the applicant is a Creative Worker, the sponsor must ensure that:

(a)   the applicant complies with their relevant Code of Practice under Appendix T5 Creative Workers Codes of Practice, where one exists for their occupation; or

(b)   the role appeared in the shortage occupation list in Appendix Shortage Occupation Lists; or

(c)   before assigning the COS, the sponsor took into account the needs of the resident labour market in that field and was satisfied that the work could not be carried out by a settled worker.

If the applicant is a Sporting Worker, the sponsor must have an endorsement for the applicant from the appropriate governing body under Appendix M before assigning the COS which confirms both: (a) the player or coach is internationally established at the highest level and/or will make a significant contribution to the development of their sport at the highest level in the UK; and (b) the role could not be filled by a settled worker.

If the COS records that the applicant is being sponsored for more than one engagement by the same sponsor, there must be no more than 14 days between each individual engagement. In addition, if the applicant has consecutive engagements, each sponsor must assign its own COS to the applicant

7.12.1.3 Financial requirement

This is the same as for a Skilled Worker (see **7.8.3**).

7.12.2 Charity worker

7.12.2.1 A profile

This category is for a charity worker undertaking voluntary activity and not paid employment for no longer than 12 months in the UK.

Full details are in Appendix T5 (Temporary Worker) Charity Worker.

7.12.2.2 Sponsorship

The charity work the applicant is applying to be sponsored to do must meet all the following requirements:

(a)   it is voluntary fieldwork which contributes directly to the achievement or advancement of the sponsor's charitable purpose; and

(b)   it must be voluntary work and not be paid or otherwise remunerated, including receipt of benefits in kind, except for reasonable expenses as defined in the National Minimum Wage Act 1998; and

(c)   the applicant must not be filling a permanent position, including on a temporary basis.

7.12.2.3 Financial requirement

This is the same as for a Skilled Worker (see **7.8.3**).

7.12.3 Religious worker

7.12.3.1 A profile

The Religious worker route is for a person who wants to support the activities of religious institutions in the UK by conducting religious work such as working in a religious order or undertaking non-pastoral work for a religious organisation.

The role the applicant is applying for must meet all the following requirements:

(a)   the role must involve performing religious duties within, or directed by, the sponsor's organisation to support the activities of the religious institution; and

(b)   the religious duties must not include work which falls under a role of a Minister of Religion (which means the applicant must not have core duties of leading a congregation in performing the rites and rituals of the faith and in preaching the essentials of the creed).

A Minister of Religion must apply under the T2 Minister of Religion route (see **7.10**) if their engagement in the UK involves leading a congregation in performing rites, rituals and preaching the essentials of the creed as its core duties.

Full details are in Appendix T5 (Temporary Worker) Religious Worker.

7.12.3.2 Sponsorship

The COS must, amongst other matters, include

(a) confirmation of the applicant's name and that they are being sponsored as a Religious Worker;

(b) an outline of their duties involved in the role; and

(c) confirmation of whether the applicant is a member of the sponsor's order, if the sponsor is a religious order.

7.12.3.3 Resident labour market test

When issuing a COS, the sponsor must confirm that the migrant will not be displacing or denying an employment opportunity to a suitably qualified member of the resident labour force. Full details are in Appendix T5 (Temporary Worker) Creative and Sporting Worker, para RW 5.5.

7.12.3.4 Financial requirement

This is the same as for a Skilled Worker (see **7.8.3**).

7.12.4 Government authorised exchange worker

7.12.4.1 A profile

This category is for migrants coming to the UK through approved schemes that aim to share knowledge, experience and best practice for a period of no more than 12 or 24 months (depending on the scheme). It is for work experience. It cannot be used to fill a job vacancy.

Full details are in Appendix T5 (Temporary Worker) Government Authorised Exchange Worker.

7.12.4.2 Sponsorship

Sponsorship for this category is rather novel. Government policy is that in order to prevent potential abuse of this category and the formation of small individual schemes, employers and organisations cannot sponsor migrants. Instead, there will be an overarching body to administer the exchange scheme. This overarching body will be the sponsor and will need to apply for a licence. The scheme and the body must have the support of a UK government department. The body will issue certificates of sponsorship to migrants who meet the requirements of the scheme. A list of approved schemes can be found in Appendix N to the Immigration Rules.

The COS must include confirmation of all the following:

(a) the role meets the requirements of the individual exchange scheme as set out in Appendix N; and

(b) the role does not fill a vacancy in the workforce; and

(c) the role appears in Table 1 or Table 2 of Appendix Skilled Occupations.

> **EXAMPLE**
>
> The Law Society is an overarching body that can authorise eligible firms to issue certificates of sponsorship to prospective short-term migrants under internship and secondment programmes.

7.12.4.3 Financial requirement

This is the same as for a Skilled Worker (see **7.8.3**).

7.12.5   International agreement worker

This category is for migrants who are coming to the UK under contract to provide a service that is covered under international law, including the General Agreement on Trade in Services; similar agreements between the UK and another country; employees of overseas governments and international organisations; and private servants in diplomatic households.

This is a specialised category, the details of which are beyond the scope of this book.

7.12.6   Worker under a Youth Mobility Scheme

7.12.6.1   A profile

The Youth Mobility Scheme provides a cultural exchange programme that allows young adults from participating countries and territories to experience life in the UK for up to two years.

This is a novel category, as the sponsors under the youth mobility scheme are the national governments of the Home Office-approved participating countries listed in Annex Youth Mobility Scheme: eligible nationals. Places on the scheme for each of those countries are capped each year by the UK Government. Once the limit is reached, no further applications will be considered that year. In addition, British Overseas Citizens, British Overseas Territories Citizens or British National (Overseas) citizens may be eligible under the Scheme.

So how young does a national of an approved participating country have to be? The answer is between the ages of 18 and 30 inclusive when they apply.

A person can be granted leave in this category only once.

Full details are in Appendix T5 (Temporary Worker) Youth Mobility Scheme.

7.12.6.2   Financial requirement

The applicant must have funds of £2,530.

The applicant must not have any children aged under 18 who are either living with them or financially dependent upon them.

Apart from the above, the same details apply as for a Skilled Worker (see **7.8.3**).

7.12.7   Seasonal Worker

7.12.7.1   A profile

This category is for migrants coming to the UK as seasonal workers in the edible horticulture sector through a Home Office-approved scheme operator. What is seasonal work? It is employment which fluctuates or is restricted according to the season or time of the year.

The applicant must be no less than 18 years of age at the time of application.

Successful applicants can come to the UK for a maximum period of six months' employment in the UK within any 12-month period under the scheme.

Full details are in Appendix T5 (Temporary Worker) Seasonal Worker.

7.12.7.2   Sponsorship

The Certificate of Sponsorship must state the role is in the edible horticulture sector, which means those growing:

(a)   Protected Vegetables – those grown in glasshouse systems; or

(b)   Field Vegetables – those grown outdoors, including vegetables, herbs, leafy salads and potatoes; or

(c) Soft Fruit – those grown outdoors or under cover, eg in glasshouses or polytunnel. Includes strawberries, raspberries, blackcurrants, blueberries and all rabes and rubus species; or

(d) Top Fruit (Orchard Fruit) - trees that bear fruit, eg apples, plums, cherries, apricots; or

(e) Vine and Bines – both twining or climbing flexible stems of certain plants, eg hops is a bine, and grapes is a vine; or

(f) Mushrooms – typically covers *Agaricus bisporus* species but can also include more exotic species (typically grown indoors).

The COS must confirm that the role conforms with all relevant legislation, such as the National Minimum Wage Act 1998, the relevant Agricultural Wages Order rate where this applies, and the Working Time Regulations.

7.13 SOLE REPRESENTATIVE OF AN OVERSEAS FIRM

7.13.1 A profile

If an overseas firm has no branch, subsidiary or representative in the UK, it may wish to send one of its senior employees to the UK to establish a wholly-owned subsidiary or branch in the UK. This is a long-standing category and it is not part of the points system.

The usual validity and suitability requirements apply, including that an applicant must pay the immigration health surcharge for themselves and any dependants when making their application (see further **3.10**). The applicant must also not fall for refusal under the general grounds for refusal (see **3.4.5**).

The requirements otherwise are set out in Appendix Representative of an Overseas Business, as follows.

7.13.2 The Overseas Business

The applicant must have been recruited and taken on as an employee outside the UK by a business which has, and will continue to have, its headquarters and principal place of business outside the UK ('the Overseas Business').

The application will be refused if it is clear intention of the Overseas Business to move the main centre of the business to the UK and effectively cease trading outside the UK.

The Overseas Business must be active and trading. This is judged in the round, taking into account the length of time that the company has been established, its turnover, profitability, the number of employees, etc. It must be the intention that the business remains centred abroad. This does not mean, however, that an otherwise sound application is refused because of evidence of an intention to make the branch in the UK flourish so vigorously that it might, at some time in the longer term, overshadow the overseas parent company.

The Overseas Business must have no active branch, subsidiary or other representative in the UK for the purpose of representing that business in the UK. This means that the applicant must be the only representative of the employer present in the UK in this category. It is not possible for the Overseas Business to have two representatives.

Are there any circumstances in which an application may be granted when the Overseas Business has already conducted preliminary business activity in the UK? Yes, UKVI guidance is that if the Overseas Business has used any of the following in the UK, they are not regarded as an 'other representative' in line with this requirement provided that in all cases no one in the UK was directly employed by the Overseas Business:

- a broker or sales commission agent (either an individual or a business);
- a distributor, selling on a commission basis;
- a distributor buying the Overseas Business's products and on-selling; or

- an individual or a business finding sales leads and passing them back to the Overseas Business.

The applicant must establish and operate a registered branch or wholly owned subsidiary of the Overseas Business which will actively trade in the same type of business as the Overseas Business. A 'branch' is a part of a company which is organised so as to conduct business on behalf of the company. This means that a person is able to deal directly with the branch in the UK, instead of the company overseas. The UK branch must apply to register with Companies House within one month of opening. A wholly owned subsidiary is a separate corporate body and is not subject to these registration requirements, being treated in the same way as any other company incorporated in the UK. How will the UK business meet the requirement of conducting the same type of business as the Overseas Business? The most obvious way is by supplying a similar product or service. However, the UKVI accepts that an overseas manufacturing business can establish a UK branch or subsidiary for the sale or servicing of their products in the UK.

The registered branch or wholly owned subsidiary must not be established solely for the purpose of facilitating the entry and stay of the applicant.

7.13.3 Senior employee

The applicant must be a senior employee of the Overseas Business. A decision maker will judge this taking into account the applicant's contract of employment, the applicant's job description, the Overseas Business's business plans and other confirmation from the employer that, whilst in the UK, the applicant will have authority to take business decisions on behalf of the Overseas Business to establish and operate a registered branch or wholly owned subsidiary.

The applicant must be an existing senior employee of the Overseas Business who intends to be employed full time as a representative of that business and will not engage in business of their own or represent any other business's interest in the UK. The applicant is required to provide a document detailing the terms and conditions of their employment. The importance of the position should be reflected in the salary and other benefits. The Home Office expects a sole representative to be vested with the authority to take the majority of key operational decisions locally but accepts that it is unreasonable to expect them to take unilateral decisions on all matters.

Sole representatives are expected to base themselves in the UK and according to previous UKVI guidance need to spend a minimum of nine months of the year here. However, applications may be approved from those who intend to spend less time in the UK, provided that the additional absences are essential to the running of the UK business, for example if the UK office is to be the centre of European operations. Applicants who intend to spend less than four months of the year in the UK are unlikely to satisfy the Home Office that they are making genuine efforts to establish a commercial presence in the UK. Such persons should be advised to apply instead as business visitors (see **5.4**).

7.13.4 Skills, experience and knowledge

The applicant must have the skills, experience and knowledge of the business necessary to undertake their role and have the full authority to negotiate and take operational decisions on behalf of the Overseas Business.

7.13.5 Must not have a majority stake in, own or control the Overseas Business

The applicant must not have a majority stake in, or otherwise own or control, that Overseas Business, whether that ownership or control is by means of a shareholding, partnership agreement, sole proprietorship or any other arrangement. This means that an applicant will be ineligible if they:

- own more than 50% of the shares;
- control more than 50% of the voting rights;
- are the self-employed owner or the sole proprietor of that business; or
- are in a partnership agreement in which they own more than 50% of that business.

Sole representatives must not have entered into any arrangement in relation to the Overseas Business which makes them effectively the majority owner, controller, or the main beneficiary of the business, even though they may not actually own more than 50% of the business. The UKVI guidance gives the example of an applicant who would be ineligible if a silent partner owns the majority of the Overseas Business but has agreed to give majority control and profits to the applicant.

The Home Office accepts that as a senior employee, an applicant may have some amount of ownership or control of the Overseas Business. However, if that constitutes a substantial stake in the Overseas Business, albeit not more than 50%, the decision maker might request additional information or an interview with the applicant, especially if they have any other reason to suspect that the applicant might be the overall owner; for example, if the applicant founded the business and it is named after them.

Spouses and partners of sole representatives who own or control a majority of the Overseas Business are not eligible to apply for entry as the dependent partner of a sole representative (see **7.13.14**).

7.13.6   Full-time employment

The applicant must intend to work full time as the representative of the Overseas Business and must not intend to undertake work for any other business or engage in business of their own.

Sole representatives are required to work full time as such, but this is not linked to a set number of hours per week. The main consideration is that the Overseas Business should be paying a 'full-time' salary sufficient for the sole representative to support and accommodate themselves and any dependants without taking other work or resorting to public funds.

7.13.7   English language

The applicant must show English language ability on the Common European Framework of Reference for Languages in speaking and listening of at least level A1. It can be met by any of the ways detailed at **7.8.2.4**.

7.13.8   Maintenance and accommodation

The applicant must be able to maintain and accommodate themselves and any dependants adequately without recourse to public funds.

Sole representatives may be offered a remuneration package consisting of a basic salary and commission. This is acceptable to the Home Office as long as the salary element is sufficient to support the applicant and their family without recourse to public funds. As this category is not part of the points system, no set amount is prescribed for maintenance. Full details can be found at **8.3.6.10** and **8.3.7**.

7.13.9   Entry clearance

The applicant must hold a valid UK entry clearance for entry in this capacity.

7.13.10   Supporting documentation for entry clearance

The Home Office requires the following documents to support the application:

(a)   a full description of the Overseas Business's activities, including details of assets and accounts and the share distribution or ownership for the previous year; and

(b)   a letter which confirms the Overseas Business will establish a registered branch or wholly owned subsidiary in the UK in the same business activity as the overseas business; and

(c)   a job description, salary details and contract of employment for the applicant; and

(d)   a letter confirming the applicant has the relevant skills, experience, knowledge and authority; and

(e)   a notarised statement which confirms the applicant will be their sole representative in the UK, that the company has no other active branch, subsidiary or representative in the UK, and that its operations will remain centred overseas.

7.13.11   Extension

Leave is initially given for three years. Towards the end of that time an application may be made to the Home Office for a two-year extension of stay. This requires the following:

(a)   the applicant must have established the registered branch or wholly-owned subsidiary of the Overseas Business for which they were last granted permission under this route; and

(b)   the applicant must be engaged in full-time employment and must supervise the registered branch or wholly-owned subsidiary that they have established, and must be required by their employer to continue in that role; and

(c)   the applicant must provide all of the following:

(i)   evidence of business that has been generated, principally with firms in the UK, on behalf of their employer since their last permission, in the form of accounts, copies of invoices or letters from businesses with whom the applicant has done business, including the value of transactions; and

(ii)   a Companies House certificate of registration as a UK establishment (for a branch), or a certificate of incorporation (for a subsidiary), together with either a copy of the share register or a letter from the Overseas Business's accountant confirming that the UK business is wholly owned by the Overseas Business; and

(iii)   a letter from the applicant's employer confirming that the applicant supervises the UK branch or subsidiary and is required to continue in that employment; and

(iv)   evidence of salary paid by the employer in the 12 months immediately before the date of application.

7.13.12   Settlement

When a sole representative has remained in the UK for five years in this capacity, they may be eligible to apply for settlement. This requires that the sole representative:

(a)   has spent a continuous period of five years in the UK in this capacity;

(b)   is still required for the employment in question, as certified by their employer; and

(c)   has sufficient knowledge of the English language and sufficient knowledge about life in the UK (see **3.8.7**).

7.13.13   The genuineness requirement

When an applicant applies for entry clearance, leave to enter or leave to remain, they must demonstrate that they genuinely meet all the relevant requirements. Home Office guidance is that the following situations may raise doubts as to the genuineness of the application:

•   the Overseas Business has only a small number of staff or trading premises;

•   the Overseas Business only has a trading presence in one other country and no track record of international expansion;

•   the Overseas Business has only been set up recently;

- there is little evidence of the Overseas Business's trading presence and business activities (whether physical or internet-based);

- the applicant has previous activity in the UK that is not related to the business they now represent, or there is some similar reason to doubt they will work only in accordance with the conditions of their leave; or

- the domestic rules on business ownership in the country where the Overseas Business is located necessitate a request for non-standard information to determine whether the applicant owns or controls that business.

7.13.14 Family members of a sole representative

The spouse, civil partner, same sex or unmarried partner and children under 18 of an applicant will need to apply for entry clearance. They may also subsequently apply for settlement. See further **Chapter 8**.

7.14 COMMONWEALTH CITIZEN WITH UK ANCESTRY

7.14.1 A profile

A Commonwealth citizen (see the list at **Appendix 9**), aged 17 or over, who can show that one of their grandparents was born in the UK (and Islands) and who intends to take or seek employment in the UK and support themselves without needing public funds, may be granted entry clearance in this category. Entry clearance is compulsory and limited leave is given of five years. Thereafter an application can be made for settlement.

An applicant must pay the immigration health surcharge for themselves and any dependants when making their application (see further **3.10**).

The applicant must not fall for refusal under the general grounds for refusal (see **3.4.5**).

In this category an applicant does not need to meet the requirements of the points system under any of the tiers. Beyond the usual validity and suitability requirements, the additional requirements to be met are set out in the Immigration Rules, Appendix UK Ancestry.

7.14.2 A Commonwealth citizen

The applicant must satisfy the ECO that they are a citizen of a Commonwealth country at the date of the application.

7.14.3 Aged 17 or over

The applicant must satisfy the ECO that they are or will be at least 17 years of age when entering the UK.

7.14.4 Proof of ancestry

The applicant must be able to provide proof that one of their grandparents was born in the UK and Islands, and that any such grandparent is the applicant's blood grandparent or grandparent by reason of an adoption recognised by the laws of the UK relating to adoption.

As regards proof of birth in the UK and Islands, the applicant must be able to demonstrate that the grandparent on whom the claim is based was born in:

(a)   the UK;

(b)   Channel Islands;

(c)   the Isle of Man; or

(d)   if the grandparent was born before 31 March 1922, what is now the Republic of Ireland.

Home Office guidance is that birth on a British registered ship or aircraft also counts.

The applicant may be related to that grandparent in one of two ways. First, by blood. So, a qualifying connection can be made through a legitimate or an illegitimate line. Secondly, by adoption. An applicant who has been adopted, or whose parents were, can qualify if:

(a)   the applicant has been adopted by someone who has a UK-born parent; or

(b)   one of the applicant's parents was adopted by a person born in the UK; or

(c)   the applicant's natural grandparents were born in the UK.

Any adoption must be through an adoption process recognised as valid for the purposes of UK law (see generally the Adoption (Recognition of Overseas Adoptions) Order 2013, the Adoption (Designation of Overseas Adoptions) Order 1973 and the Adoption (Designation of Overseas Adoptions) (Variation) Order 1993).

No claim can be made through step-parents where no legal adoption has taken place.

What sort of proof of the relationship is required by an ECO? The applicant should produce their own full birth certificate; where appropriate the marriage certificates of their parents and appropriate grandparents (or, if unmarried, evidence of the relationship if the claim is made through the paternal line); if applicable the legal adoption papers of the applicant or their parents; and the full birth certificates of the parent and grandparent through whose ancestry they are making the application.

EXAMPLES

Charles is a Commonwealth citizen, aged 20. His mother, Florence, was not born in the UK. His grandmother, Rose, on his maternal side (ie Florence's mother) was born in the UK. What documents should Charles produce to prove this ancestral link? A minimum of three documents are required to confirm the following details:

(a)   his birth certificate naming Florence as his mother;

(b)   Florence's birth certificate naming Rose as her mother; and

(c)   Rose's UK birth certificate showing she was born in the UK.

Greg, aged 22, is a citizen of Australia and thereby a Commonwealth citizen. Greg's mother, Hayley, is an Australian citizen. Hayley was legally adopted in Australia when she was 6 by William and Amy. Her adoption is recognised in the UK. William is an Australian national. Amy is a British citizen having been born in the UK. What documents should Greg produce to prove this ancestral link? A minimum of three documents is required to confirm the following details:

(a)   Greg's birth certificate naming Hayley as his mother;

(b)   Hayley's legal adoption papers naming Amy as her adoptive mother; and

(c)   Amy's UK birth certificate showing that she was born in the UK.

7.14.5   Able to work and intends to take or seek employment in the UK

Entry clearance is for the purpose of work in the UK, not to study or visit. The applicant must satisfy the ECO that they have arranged employment in the UK already, or that they genuinely intend to seek employment or become self-employed and have a realistic prospect of securing it. Home Office guidance is that the ECO will consider such factors as the applicant's age and health, eg any medical problems that may prevent the applicant from taking employment.

The applicant only needs to demonstrate that they are able to work and genuinely intend to take or seek work (employed or self-employed) in the UK.

Evidence of this could include job offers from potential UK employers, registration with a recruitment agency, job applications, relevant education and training courses and a business plan if the applicant intends to be self-employed in the UK.

If an applicant proposes to undertake unpaid voluntary work in the UK, that will count as employment (see para 6 of the Immigration Rules). However, the ECO will pay particular attention as to how the applicant intends to maintain and accommodate themselves and any dependants adequately without recourse to public funds (see **7.14.6**).

There is no requirement that any employer must be based in the UK.

7.14.6   No recourse to public funds

The applicant must be able to maintain and accommodate themselves and any dependants adequately without recourse to public funds (see **3.3.2**). In assessing whether the applicant meets this financial requirement, the decision maker may take into account credible promises of financial support from a third party, such as a relative or friend of the applicant.

An applicant might produce as supporting evidence any relevant payslips, bank statements, proposed contract of employment, details of third-party support from relatives, job advertisements, tenancy agreement and details of property that might be rented.

As this category is not part of the points system, no set amount is prescribed for maintenance. See further **8.3.6.10** and **8.3.7**.

7.14.7   Holds a valid UK entry clearance for entry in this capacity

Entry clearance is mandatory for a person who wishes to enter the UK in this category.

It is not possible to switch into this category.

7.14.8   Settlement

Near to the end of the person's five years' limited leave, they should apply for settlement. The requirements are as follows:

(a)   the applicant has spent a continuous period of five years in the UK in this capacity; and
(b)   the applicant has sufficient knowledge of the English language and sufficient knowledge about life in the UK (see **3.8.7**);

Although (a) above requires the applicant to have resided continuously in the UK in this category for five years, there is no requirement that any employment taken must be continuous. Home Office guidance is that if the applicant is in employment at the time of the application then all that is required is a letter from their current employer confirming that the employment will continue. If, however, the applicant is not employed then they will need to produce evidence of their employment record throughout the five years and evidence of the attempts made to find employment. If it is clear that the applicant has not been in employment for any length of time over the five years, they will be asked to provide reasons as to why they have failed to obtain employment. Unless there is a very good reason for this, the application will be refused. The Home Office will also make enquiries as to how the applicant has been supporting themselves without a regular income.

7.14.9   Family members

The spouse, civil partner, same sex or unmarried partner and children under 18 of an applicant will need to apply for entry clearance. They may also subsequently apply for settlement. See further **Chapter 8**.

7.15   ILLEGAL WORKING IN THE UK

7.15.1   Employer's duties

The law on preventing illegal migrant working in the UK has evolved over time. An employer's legal responsibilities may therefore vary according to when it recruited its existing staff. There is a very useful summary of the previous legal requirements on the Home Office website (see

1.2.8). The current law may be found in ss 15 to 26 of the Immigration, Asylum and Nationality Act (IANA) 2006. This makes an employer liable to payment of a civil financial penalty of up to £20,000 if it employs a person aged 16 or over who is subject to immigration control and who has no permission to work in the UK, or who works in breach of their conditions of stay in the UK (see **3.3.1**).

Note that it is essential that any appeal against a civil penalty is made promptly as the court has no discretion to extend the time limits laid down in the IANA 2006: see *Massan v Secretary of State for the Home Department* [2011] EWCA Civ 686.

7.15.2 Civil penalty

How can an employer avoid civil liability? This is answered by the Immigration (Restrictions on Employment) Order 2007 (SI 2007/3290), as amended. The employer must obtain from the prospective employee certain original documents that need to be checked in accordance with art 6, for example, if the document contains a date of birth, the employer must be satisfied that this is consistent with the appearance of the prospective employee. So, what documents count? The employer can choose from documents in the Schedule. This consists of two lists: list A, which includes a British national's passport or a passport endorsed with indefinite leave to remain; and list B, Parts 1 and 2. Part 1 includes a biometric immigration document issued by the Home Office to the holder which indicates that the person named in it can stay in the UK and is allowed to do the work in question. Part 2 includes a Positive Verification Notice issued by the Home Office Employer Checking Service to the employer or prospective employer, which indicates that the named person may stay in the UK and is permitted to do the work in question.

Further details can be found in guidance on the Home Office website (see **1.2.8**).

7.15.3 Criminal offence

An employer commits a criminal offence if it employs a person who is disqualified from employment by reason of their immigration status and it had reasonable cause to believe that the employee was so disqualified.

A person is disqualified from employment by reason of their immigration status if they are an adult subject to immigration control and have not been granted leave to enter or remain in the UK; or their leave to enter or remain is invalid or has ceased to have effect (whether by reason of curtailment, revocation, cancellation, passage of time or otherwise) or is subject to a condition preventing them from accepting the employment.

What sentence might be imposed? An unlimited fine and/or a maximum of five years' imprisonment.

7.16 OFFENCE OF ILLEGAL WORKING

Section 24A of the Immigration Act (IA) 1971 (introduced by the IA 2016) makes it a criminal offence for a person disqualified from employment by reason of their immigration status (see **7.15.3**) to work at a time when they know or have reasonable cause to believe that they are so disqualified.

A person who is guilty of this offence is liable on summary conviction to imprisonment for a term not exceeding 51 weeks and/or an unlimited fine.

7.17 RIGHT TO RENT CHECKS

Just as employers have a duty to check that an employee has a right to work (see **7.15**), Chapter 1 of Part 3 of the IA 2014 imposes an obligation on landlords (and their agents) to check that any adult occupying premises under a residential tenancy agreement is not disqualified as a result of their immigration status. A failure to carry out the appropriate checks may incur a civil penalty of up to £3,000 per tenant.

A criminal offence is committed if the landlord knows or has reasonable cause to believe that the premises are occupied by an adult who is disqualified as a result of their immigration status. An unlimited fine and/or a maximum sentence of five years' imprisonment may be imposed.

Full details can be found in guidance on the Home Office website (see **1.2.8**).

Is the right to rent check scheme compatible with Article 14 ECHR in conjunction with Article 8 ECHR? Yes, held the Court of Appeal in R (*Joint Council for the Welfare of Immigrants*) v *Secretary of State for the Home Department* [2020] EWCA Civ 542.

7.18 BANK AND BUILDING SOCIETY ACCOUNT CHECKS

The Immigration Act 2014 prohibits banks and building societies from opening current accounts for individuals who are in the UK unlawfully. These powers were extended by the Immigration Act 2016 to prevent known illegal migrants from continuing to operate existing accounts. How is this done? Banks and building societies are required to check regularly whether they are operating a current account for a person known by the Home Office to be in the UK illegally. If a bank or building society establishes that a customer is an illegal migrant, it has a duty to report this to the Home Office along with the details of any other accounts it provides to that customer. The Home Office will then normally require the accounts to be closed. In addition, the Home Office has power to apply to the courts to freeze a current account until the illegal migrant leaves the UK. Use of this power is targeted towards hard-to-remove cases with significant funds in order to force cooperation with the removal process.

For further details, see ss 40A to 40H of the IA 2014 and the Home Office's Immigration Act 2014 Code of Practice: Freezing Orders (Bank Accounts Measures).

7.19 RECENTLY CLOSED CATEGORIES

In 2019, the Tier 1 (Entrepreneur) and Tier 1 (Graduate Entrepreneur) Migrant routes, respectively, were closed to new applicants. Anyone still concerned with either route should consult the current UKVI guidance on the Home Office website (see **1.2.8**) and the 2019 edition of this book.

In 2020, the Tier 1 (Exceptional Talent), Tier 2 Migrant and Intra-Company Transfer routes were closed. Anyone still concerned with these should consult the current UKVI guidance on the Home Office website (see **1.2.8**) and the 2020 edition of this book. These categories have been replaced with the Global Talent category (see **7.2**), Skilled Worker (see **7.5**) and Intra-Company routes (see **7.6**) respectively.

At the time of writing, the government intends as from October 2021 to close the T2 Sportsperson and T5 Sporting Worker routes and replace these with the new category of International Sportsperson (see Appendix International Sportsperson).

FAMILY REUNION

8.1 OVERVIEW

8.1.1 Background

Until July 2012, Part 8 of the Immigration Rules had dealt with most family reunion situations. Now the only significant group left in Part 8 are children seeking to join either a parent, both parents or a relative in the UK for the purposes of settlement (see para 297, detailed at **8.9** below). It is Appendix FM to the Immigration Rules that currently sets out the requirements for a person to enter or remain in the UK on the basis of his family life with a person who is a British citizen (see **2.2**), or settled in the UK (see **3.8**), or in the UK with limited leave as a refugee (see **9.8**) or a person granted humanitarian protection (see **9.10.1**).

Broadly, Appendix FM covers entry clearance, extensions and switching, as well as settlement by partners (see **8.3**), parents (see **8.10**) and adult dependent relatives (see **8.11**). It also provides for entry by a child of a parent already in the UK with limited leave as a partner or parent (see **8.12**).

In this chapter we shall also consider one other category, namely, a person allowed to remain in the UK and ultimately settle on the basis that he has established a private life here under Article 8 ECHR (see **8.13**).

8.1.2 Partners

8.1.2.1 Terminology

The member of the couple who is not a British citizen, nor settled in the UK nor in the UK with limited leave as a refugee or humanitarian protection, is known as the applicant. The applicant's spouse, civil partner, fiancé(e), proposed civil partner or the person with whom he is in a long-term heterosexual or same-sex relationship is known as the applicant's partner (or sometimes as his 'sponsor').

8.1.2.2 Immigration controls for a fiancé(e) or proposed civil partner

There is no provision for a person already in the UK to switch into the category of fiancé(e) or proposed civil partner. So the applicant must be outside the UK and will have to apply for entry clearance. If successful, he will be granted entry clearance for a period not exceeding six months. This will be subject to a condition of no recourse to public funds (see **3.3.2**), a prohibition on employment (see **3.3.1**) and, if appropriate, registration with the police (see **3.3.3**).

The applicant will therefore have six months in the UK for the marriage or civil partnership to take place. He should then apply to the Home Office for leave to remain in the UK as a spouse or civil partner (see **8.1.2.3**).

8.1.2.3 Immigration controls for all other partners

Where the applicant is outside the UK he will have to apply for entry clearance.

If successful, he will be granted entry clearance for an initial period not exceeding 33 months, subject to a condition of no recourse to public funds (see **3.3.2**) and, if appropriate, registration with the police (see **3.3.3**). The applicant will be free to work in the UK. Just before an applicant has completed 30 months with limited leave as a partner, he should make an application for further leave to remain for 30 months. After 60 months' leave in total he will be eligible to apply for indefinite leave to remain. This is known as the 'five-year family route'.

Note that if an applicant cannot meet the usual requirements for an extension of limited leave as a partner, it may be possible to remain by establishing a claim under Article 8 ECHR (see **8.1.7** and **8.14**). In those circumstances the applicant will have a longer route to settlement, namely, 10 years (granted in four periods of limited leave of 30 months, with a fifth application for indefinite leave to remain). This is known as the '10-year family route'.

These five- and 10-year limited leave periods are often called 'probationary periods'.

If a person is already in the UK, it may be possible for him to apply for leave to remain as a partner and so start on a five- or 10-year family route to settlement.

What if the applicant's partner dies before the relevant probationary period is completed? See **8.7**.

What if the couple separate due to domestic violence by the applicant's partner before the relevant probationary period is completed? See **8.8**.

8.1.3 Children

8.1.3.1 Entering for immediate settlement

A child may seek entry clearance and be granted indefinite leave to enter the UK to join one or both parents who are already settled in the UK. Exceptionally he might be joining a relative who is here and settled. See **8.9**.

8.1.3.2 Entering with or to join a parent who has limited leave

Note that if a child's parent has only limited leave to enter or remain in the UK, the child can apply under an associated Immigration Rule to travel with or join that parent during the parent's leave (see, eg, **7.6.1.2** and **8.12**).

8.1.3.3 Entering with limited leave

A child might enter the UK with limited leave in his own right under the Immigration Rules, eg as a student (see **Chapter 6**).

8.1.4 Parents

A parent with sole parental responsibility for, or access rights to, a British citizen child or settled child who is living in the UK, may apply for entry clearance and subsequently leave to remain under Appendix FM to the Immigration Rules.

A parent already in the UK may switch into this category. This most commonly occurs when a person has entered the UK with limited leave as the partner of a British citizen or settled person (see **8.3**) but can no longer remain in the UK in that category as the relationship has broken down. If that person has sole parental responsibility for, or is exercising access rights to, his British or settled child, an application may be made for leave to remain.

Ultimately it may be possible to apply for settlement in this category.

See **8.10**.

8.1.5 Adult dependent relatives entering for immediate settlement

This route allows an adult dependent relative of a British citizen in the UK or a person settled in the UK to enter and settle because, as a result of age, illness or disability, he requires a level of long-term personal care that can only be provided in the UK by his relative here. See **8.11**.

8.1.6 Immigration health surcharge (IHS)

Any applicant applying for limited leave to enter or remain in the UK must usually pay the IHS for himself and any dependants when making the application (see **3.10**).

8.1.7 Application of Article 8 ECHR

By para GEN.3.2, if an application for entry clearance or leave to remain under Appendix FM does not otherwise meet the relevant requirements of the Immigration Rules, the decision maker must go on to consider, on the basis of the information provided by the applicant, whether there are exceptional circumstances which would render refusal of the application a breach of Article 8 because it would result in unjustifiably harsh consequences for the applicant or his family. See further **8.14**.

Note, however, that this provision does not apply to an application for leave to remain as a bereaved partner (see **8.7**) or a victim of domestic violence (see **8.8**).

8.1.8 Best interests of a child

By para GEN.3.3, when considering an application under Appendix FM, the decision maker must take into account, as a primary consideration, the best interests of any child that is under the age of 18 years at the date of the application and, it is evident from the information provided by the applicant, would be affected by a decision to refuse the application.

8.2 EXEMPT GROUPS

Part 8 of and Appendix FM to the Immigration Rules do not apply to those people who do not need leave, or who are seeking entry under other provisions of the Immigration Rules. For example:

(a)   persons who already have the right of abode in the UK (see **2.2** and **2.3**);

(b)   persons with settled status re-entering as returning residents (see **3.8.3**);

(c)   persons who are entering in another category under the Rules (eg visitors, etc).

EXAMPLE 1

Ben is a citizen of Canada. He was born in Canada in 1972. Ben's father is Canadian but his mother was born in the UK and she is a British citizen. Ben has recently married Sue, a British citizen. The couple now wish to travel to the UK to set up home together in Manchester, England.

As a British citizen, Sue can freely enter the UK as she is not subject to immigration controls.

Ben is a Commonwealth citizen with right of abode in the UK. So Ben can enter the UK freely as he is not subject to immigration controls and therefore does not need to comply with the provisions in Appendix FM to the Immigration Rules. (Ben will need a 'certificate of entitlement' in his Canadian passport: see **2.3**. A check could also be made to see if he is registered as a British citizen and holds, or is entitled to, a British passport: see **2.2.6.2**.)

EXAMPLE 2

Carla is a citizen of The Philippines. She married Denis, a British citizen, whilst he was on holiday in The Philippines last month. Denis has just returned to the UK without Carla. She has not yet agreed to join him in the UK. She intends to apply for a visa to enter the UK as a standard visitor in order to decide whether she would wish to live in the UK with Denis.

In principle, Carla could obtain a standard visitor visa, but she would need to satisfy the ECO that she did intend to leave the UK at the end of her visit (see **5.2**).

8.3 ENTRY CLEARANCE AS A PARTNER

8.3.1 Who is a partner?

A partner, for the purposes of Appendix FM (see para GEN 1.2), is:

(a)   the applicant's spouse;

(b)   the applicant's civil partner;

(c)   the applicant's fiancé(e) or proposed civil partner; or

(d)   a person who has been living together with the applicant in a relationship akin to a marriage or civil partnership for at least two years prior to the date of application.

For (a) and (b) the parties must have entered into a valid marriage or valid civil partnership (see **8.3.5.6**).

For (c) the parties must intend to marry or enter into a civil partnership within six months of entering the UK (see **8.3.5.7**).

As to (d), Home Office guidance is that 'living together with' should be applied fairly tightly, in that the couple should show evidence of cohabitation for the preceding two-year period. Short breaks apart may be acceptable for good reasons, such as work commitments or looking after a relative, which take one partner away for a period of up to six months, where it was not possible for the other partner to accompany the first partner and it can be seen that the relationship continued throughout that period by visits, letters, etc. The phrase 'akin to a marriage or civil partnership' is said to refer to a relationship that is similar in its nature to a marriage or a civil partnership, which therefore includes both heterosexual and same-sex relationships. In order to demonstrate a two-year relationship, evidence of cohabitation is needed. In order to show a relationship akin to a marriage or a civil partnership, the Home Office looks for evidence of a committed relationship. The following type of supporting evidence might therefore be useful in this respect:

- joint commitments (such as joint bank accounts, joint investments, joint tenancy agreement, joint mortgage account, etc);

- if there are children of the relationship, a full birth or adoption certificate naming the parties as parents;

- correspondence which links them to the same address (eg household bills in joint names, etc); and

- any official records of their address (eg doctors and dentist records, government records, etc).

EXAMPLE 1

Zach and Yvonne are engaged to be married. Zach is a visa national. Yvonne is a British citizen. The couple are living in Zach's home country, but they now wish to travel to the UK to get married and set up home together.

Zach can apply to enter the UK under Appendix FM to the Immigration Rules as Yvonne's partner (fiancé), provided they intend to marry within six months of entering the UK.

EXAMPLE 2

David is a British citizen. He has worked abroad for several years and for the last 18 months has been living in the USA with John, an American citizen. David now wishes to return to the UK and John wishes to travel with him. If John is admitted to the UK he intends to live with David permanently, but the couple do not wish to enter into a civil partnership.

David and John are not civil partners, neither do they intend to enter into a civil partnership. They have not been living in a relationship akin to a civil partnership for at least two years prior to the date of John's wishing to make an application. So the couple's relationship will need to continue for another six months before John can apply under Appendix FM to the Immigration Rules as David's partner.

EXAMPLE 3

Alice and Brian are both citizens of New Zealand. They were both born there and have never been to the UK before. They have recently married and now wish to travel to the UK to set up home together. Whilst they are both Commonwealth citizens, neither has the right of abode in the UK.

Appendix FM to the Immigration Rules does not apply. Whilst the couple are partners (spouses), neither Alice nor Brian is a British citizen or settled in the UK, or in the UK with limited leave as a refugee or person granted humanitarian protection.

8.3.2 An overview of the requirements

The requirements in Appendix FM to be met for entry clearance as a partner (see para EC-P.1.1) are that:

(a) the applicant must be outside the UK;

(b) the applicant must have made a valid application for entry clearance as a partner;

(c) the applicant must not fall for refusal under any of the grounds in Section S-EC: Suitability–entry clearance (see **8.3.3**); and

(d) the applicant must meet all of the requirements of Section E-ECP: Eligibility for entry clearance as a partner (see **8.3.4**).

8.3.3 Suitability requirements in detail

Section S-EC, paras S-EC.1.2 to S-EC.1.9 set out the following mandatory grounds on which an ECO will refuse an application:

S-EC.1.2   The Secretary of State has personally directed that the exclusion of the applicant from the UK is conducive to the public good.

S-EC.1.3   The applicant is at the date of application the subject of a deportation order.

S-EC.1.4   The exclusion of the applicant from the UK is conducive to the public good because they have been convicted of an offence for which they have been sentenced to a period of imprisonment of (a) at least 4 years; or (b) at least 12 months but less than 4 years, unless a period of 10 years has passed since the end of the sentence; or (c) of less than 12 months, unless a period of 5 years has passed since the end of the sentence. Where this paragraph applies, unless refusal would be contrary to the Human Rights Convention or the Convention and Protocol Relating to the Status of Refugees, it will only be in exceptional circumstances that the public interest in maintaining refusal will be outweighed by compelling factors.

S-EC.1.5   The exclusion of the applicant from the UK is conducive to the public good or because, for example, the applicant's conduct (including convictions which do not fall within S-EC.1.4.), character, associations, or other reasons, make it undesirable to grant them entry clearance.

(For each of the above, see further **Chapter 10**.)

S-EC.1.6   The applicant has failed without reasonable excuse to comply with a requirement to –

(a)   attend an interview;

(b)   provide information;

(c)   provide physical data; or

(d)   undergo a medical examination or provide a medical report.

S-EC.1.7   It is undesirable to grant entry clearance to the applicant for medical reasons.

S-EC.1.8   The applicant left or was removed from the UK as a condition of a caution issued in accordance with section 22 of the Criminal Justice Act 2003 less than 5 years prior to the date on which the application is decided.

S-EC.1.9   The Secretary of State considers that the applicant's parent or parent's partner poses a risk to the applicant. That person may be considered to pose a risk to the applicant if, for example, they –

(a)   have a conviction as an adult, whether in the UK or overseas, for an offence against a child;

(b)   are a registered sex offender and have failed to comply with any notification requirements; or

(c)   are required to comply with a sexual risk order made under the Anti-Social Behaviour, Crime and Policing Act 2014 and have failed to do so.

Paragraphs S-EC.2.2, 2.4 and 2.5 set out the following discretionary grounds on which an ECO will normally refuse an application:

S-EC.2.2   Whether or not to the applicant's knowledge –

(a)   false information, representations or documents have been submitted in relation to the application (including false information submitted to any person to obtain a document used in support of the application); or

(b)   there has been a failure to disclose material facts in relation to the application.

S-EC.2.4   A maintenance and accommodation undertaking has been requested or required under paragraph 35 of these Rules or otherwise and has not been provided.

S-EC.2.5   The exclusion of the applicant from the UK is conducive to the public good because (a) within the 12 months preceding the date of the application, the person has been convicted of or admitted an offence for which they received a non-custodial sentence or other out of court disposal that is recorded on their criminal record; or (b) in the view of the Secretary of State (i) the person's offending has caused serious harm; or (ii) the person is a persistent offender who shows a particular disregard for the law.

Note that despite the wording of para S-EC.2.2, Home Office guidance on (b) is that refusal for failure to disclose material facts in relation to the application can be imposed only where the applicant acts with knowledge. An applicant must not therefore be refused on the grounds that he unknowingly failed to disclose material facts in relation to his application.

Note that para S-EC.3.1 provides that the applicant may be refused on grounds of suitability if he has failed to pay litigation costs awarded to the Home Office. In addition, para S-EC.3.2

provides for refusal if one or more relevant NHS bodies has notified the Secretary of State that the applicant has failed to pay charges of £500 or more in accordance with the relevant NHS regulations.

8.3.4 Eligibility requirements in outline

An applicant must meet all of the eligibility requirements in paras E-ECP.2.1 to E-ECP.4.2. Broadly these are as follows:

(a)   relationship requirements (see **8.3.5**);

(b)   financial requirements (see **8.3.6**)

(c)   accommodation requirements (see **8.3.7**); and

(d)   English language requirement (see **8.3.8**).

8.3.5 Relationship requirements (paras E-ECP.2.1 to E-ECP.2.10)

8.3.5.1 Immigration status of applicant's partner

By para E-ECP.2.1, the applicant's partner must be:

(a)   a British citizen in the UK; or

(b)   present and settled in the UK; or

(c)   in the UK with refugee leave or with humanitarian protection.

For (a) and (b), does this mean that the application will be refused if the British citizen or person settled in the UK is currently living abroad with his partner and will be travelling with the partner to the UK? No, because para GEN.1.3(b) provides that 'references to a person being present and settled in the UK also include a person who is being admitted for settlement on the same occasion as the applicant'. Paragraph 6 of the Immigration Rules also defines 'present and settled' as meaning that the person concerned is settled in the UK and, at the time that an application under the Rules is made, is physically present here or is coming here with or to join the applicant, and intends to make the UK his home with the applicant if the application is successful. In addition, note that para GEN.1.3(c) states that 'references to a British Citizen in the UK also include a British Citizen who is coming to the UK with the applicant as their partner'.

8.3.5.2 Minimum age

By paras E-ECP.2.2 and E-ECP.2.3, both the applicant and his partner must be aged 18 or over at the date of application.

8.3.5.3 Relationship not within prohibited degree

By para E-ECP.2.4, the applicant and his partner must not be within any prohibited degree of relationship. Three statutory provisions apply, as follows:

(a)   The Marriage Act 1949 prohibits a marriage by a man to any of the persons mentioned in **Table 8.1** below, and prohibits a marriage between a woman and any of the persons mentioned in **Table 8.2** below.

Table 8.1 Prohibited degrees for a man

Mother
Daughter
Father's mother
Mother's mother
Son's daughter
Daughter's daughter

Table 8.2 Prohibited degrees for a woman

Father
Son
Father's father
Mother's father
Son's son
Daughter's son

Sister
Father's sister
Mother's sister
Brother's daughter
Sister's daughter

Brother
Father's brother
Mother's brother
Brother's son
Sister's son

(b)   The Marriage (Prohibited Degrees of Relationship) Act 1986 prohibits a marriage between those listed in **Table 8.3** below until both parties are aged 21 or over, and provided that the younger party has not at any time before attaining the age of 18 been a child of the family in relation to the other party.

Table 8.3 Prohibited degrees

Daughter of former wife
Son of former husband
Former wife of father
Former husband of mother
Former wife of father's father
Former husband of father's mother
Former wife of mother's father
Former husband of mother's mother
Daughter of son of former wife
Son of son of former husband
Daughter of daughter of former wife
Son of daughter of former husband

(c)   The Marriage (Prohibited Degrees of Relationship) Act 1986 also prohibits a marriage between those listed in **Table 8.4** below.

Table 8.4 Prohibited degrees

Mother of former wife, until the death of both the former wife and the father of the former wife
Father of former husband, until after the death of both the former husband and the mother of the former husband
Former wife of son, until after the death of both his son and the mother of his son
Former husband of daughter, until after the death of both her daughter and the father of her daughter

8.3.5.4   The parties have met in person

Paragraph E-ECP.2.5 requires the applicant and his partner to have met in person. What does this mean?

The Home Office guidance, following *Meharban v ECO, Islamabad* [1989] Imm AR 57, is that 'met' requires the parties to have 'made the acquaintance of one another'. This need not have been in the context of marriage or a civil partnership. So if, for example, the parties had originally been childhood friends, perhaps going to the same school for several years, they may be said to have met in person and become acquainted.

'Met' implies a face-to-face meeting which results in the making of mutual acquaintance. There is a requirement of 'at least an appreciation by each party of the other in the sense of, for example, appearance and personality'. Therefore a relationship developed over the Internet by Facebook messages, Skype calls or the like would potentially satisfy this requirement, but only if it includes a personal face-to-face meeting between the couple which itself results in the making of their mutual acquaintance. Evidence of a face-to-face meeting might include travel documents, photographs, statements from witnesses, or relevant email or text message exchanges detailing meetings.

8.3.5.5   The relationship is genuine and subsisting

Paragraph E-ECP.2.6 requires the relationship between the applicant and his partner to be genuine and subsisting. Neither term is defined in the Immigration Rules or the Home Office guidance. However, in *GA ('Subsisting' marriage) Ghana* [2006] UKAIT 00046, the Tribunal held that the requirement that a relationship is subsisting requires more than just double-checking the legal status of that relationship. The nature and quality of the substance of the relationship – therefore including whether or not it is genuine – is under scrutiny. As the Tribunal indicated at para 14, this means that when assessing the subsistence of a relationship, the decision maker:

> will plainly have to bear in mind the cultural context and the wide differences that exist between individual lifestyles, whether by choice, or by circumstances, or by economic necessity. He will also be able to put the claim into the context of the history of the relationship and to assess whether and to what extent this illuminates the nature of the parties' present relationship and future intentions.

Home Office guidance to its decision makers is that they must be alert and sensitive to the extent to which religious and cultural practices may shape the factors present or absent in a particular case, particularly at the entry clearance and leave to remain stages. For example, a couple in an arranged marriage may have spent little, if any, time together prior to the marriage. For many faiths and cultures marriage marks the start of a commitment to a lifelong partnership and not the affirmation of a pre-existing partnership. Home Office guidance is that its decision makers must also take into account normal practices for marriages and family living according to particular religious and cultural traditions. In particular, evidence of pre-marital cohabitation and joint living arrangements can be a factor associated with a genuine relationship; equally, their absence can be too. In some cultures it is traditional for the household accounts, bills, etc to be in the name of the male head of the household (who could be the male partner, or his father or grandfather).

Home Office guidance makes it clear that its decision makers have discretion to grant or refuse an application based on their overall assessment, regardless of whether one or more of the factors contained in the guidance is, or is not, present in the case. As the guidance stresses, consideration of whether a relationship is genuine and subsisting is not a checklist or tick-box exercise.

It is for the applicant to show the requirement is met on the balance of probabilities: see *Naz (subsisting marriage – standard of proof) Pakistan* [2012] UKUT 00040.

In assessing whether a relationship is genuine and subsisting, Home Office guidance to its decision makers as to what factors might be taken into account is as follows:

Factors which may be associated with a genuine and subsisting relationship

(i)   The couple are in a current, long-term relationship and are able to provide satisfactory evidence of this.

(ii)   The couple have been or are co-habiting and are able to provide satisfactory evidence of this.

(iii)   The couple have children together (biological, adopted or step-children) and shared responsibility for them.

(iv)   The couple share financial responsibilities, eg a joint mortgage/tenancy agreement, a joint bank account and/or joint savings, utility bills in both their names.

(v)   The partner and/or applicant have visited the other's home country and family and are able to provide evidence of this. (The fact that an applicant has never visited the UK must not be regarded as a negative factor, but it is a requirement of the Immigration Rules that the couple have met in person).

(vi)   The couple, or their families acting on their behalf, have made definite plans concerning the practicalities of the couple living together in the UK.

(vii)   In the case of an arranged marriage, the couple both consent to the marriage and agree with the plans made by their families.

Factors which may prompt additional scrutiny

Further enquiries may be required to accept a marriage as valid for immigration purposes where:

- the marriage was a church marriage in a Muslim country
- it was a religious or a customary marriage which has not been registered with the civil authorities of the country in which it was celebrated
- the person's country of domicile is unclear, especially where their country of domicile would mean the type of marriage or civil partnership entered into would not be valid
- a previous marriage or civil partnership was ended by a divorce or dissolution obtained in a different country from the one where it was celebrated, and neither partner was:
  - habitually resident in the country where the divorce or dissolution was obtained
  - a national of the country where the divorce or dissolution was obtained or domiciled in the country (or US state) where the divorce or dissolution was obtained.
- the marriage or civil partnership took place in the UK, a report – of a suspicious sham marriage or civil partnership – was made by a registration officer under section 24 or 24A of the Immigration and Asylum Act 1999
- there is evidence from a reliable third party (for example the Forced Marriage Unit (FMU), police, social services, registration officer, or a minister of religion) which indicates that the marriage or civil partnership is, or may be a sham or a forced marriage or partnership of convenience (it may not be possible for this information to be used in any refusal notice)
- there is an allegation or other information suggesting that this is a forced marriage or that the marriage or civil partnership may not be genuine or that the couple are not living together
- the applicant or their partner does not appear to have the capacity to consent to the marriage, civil partnership or relationship, for example one has or both parties have learning difficulties
- there is evidence of unreasonable restrictions being placed on the applicant or partner, for example, being kept at home by their family, being subject to unreasonable financial restrictions, attempts to prevent the police or other agencies having reasonable, unrestricted access to the applicant or partner
- the applicant or partner fail to attend an interview, without reasonable explanation, where required to do so to discuss the application or their welfare, or seeking to undermine the ability of the Home Office to arrange an interview, for example unreasonable delaying tactics by the couple or a third party
- the couple is unable to provide any information about their intended living arrangements in the UK or about the practicalities of the applicant moving to the UK
- the circumstances of the wedding or civil ceremony or reception, for example, no or few guests and/or no significant family members present
- the couple are unable to provide accurate personal details about each other
- the couple are unable to communicate with each other in a language understood by them both
- there is evidence of money having been exchanged for the relationship to be contracted, unless it is part of a dowry
- there is a lack of appropriate contribution to the responsibilities of the marriage, civil partnership or relationship, for example, a lack of shared financial or other domestic responsibilities
- co-habitation is not maintained, or there is little or no evidence that they have ever co-habited
- the applicant is a qualified medical practitioner or professional, or has worked as a nurse or carer, and the partner has a mental or physical impairment which currently requires medical assistance or personal care in their own accommodation
- the partner has previously sponsored another partner to come to or remain in the UK or, if applicable, claimed to be married or in a civil partnership in reply to an asylum questionnaire

- the partner has previously been sponsored as a partner to come to or remain in the UK (for example, the partner obtained settlement on this basis) and that marriage, partnership or relationship ended shortly after the partner obtained settlement (excluding circumstances where the partner is a bereaved partner, or where the partner obtained settlement on the basis of domestic violence perpetrated by their former partner)
- the partner was married to or in a civil partnership with the applicant at an earlier date, married or formed a partnership with another person, and is now sponsoring the original partner to come to or remain in the UK
- the past history of the partner and/or the applicant contains evidence of a previous sham marriage, civil partnership or forced marriage, or of unlawful residence in the UK or elsewhere
- the applicant has applied for leave to enter or remain in the UK in another category and been refused prior to making their application on the basis of their relationship with a partner
- the marriage or civil partnership has taken place overseas in a country that is not an obvious or popular destination for a marriage or civil partnership and has no obvious links to the couple

When an application can be refused

Entry clearance or leave should be refused if a decision maker is satisfied the relationship is not genuine and subsisting because there is:

- a public statement (a disclosable statement that is not in confidence) made by the applicant or partner that their marriage or civil partnership is a sham or one of convenience or has broken down permanently
- a public statement (a disclosable statement that is not in confidence) made by the applicant or partner that they have been forced into marriage
- evidence that a sibling of the partner or applicant has been forced into marriage
- the applicant, partner or an immediate family member of either, is or has been the subject or respondent of a forced marriage protection order under the Forced Marriage (Civil Protection) Act 2007, or the Forced Marriage (Protection and Jurisdiction) (Scotland) Act 2011.

8.3.5.6 Valid marriage or civil partnership

Paragraph E-ECP.2.7 states that if the applicant and partner are married or in a civil partnership, it must be a valid marriage or civil partnership, as specified.

Home Office guidance is that the type of marriage must be recognised in the country in which it took place, it must satisfy the legal requirements of that country and there must not be anything in the law of either party's country of domicile that restricted their freedom to enter into the marriage.

Home Office guidance includes a list of countries where it recognises a civil partnership as valid.

8.3.5.7 Fiancé(e) or proposed civil partner entering UK for marriage or civil partnership

Paragraph E-ECP.2.8 states that if the applicant is a fiancé(e) or proposed civil partner, he must be seeking entry to the UK to enable his marriage or civil partnership to take place. The couple will usually need to produce adequate documentary evidence of the arrangements already made in the UK for the marriage or civil partnership ceremony.

8.3.5.8 Any previous relationship broken down permanently

Paragraph E-ECP.2.9 provides that if the applicant and/or his partner has previously been married or in a civil partnership, the applicant must provide suitable evidence that that relationship has ended (eg decree absolute of divorce, or dissolution order terminating a civil partnership), unless it is a polygamous marriage or civil partnership which falls within para 278(i) of the Immigration Rules. Home Office guidance includes further details.

In addition, if the applicant is a fiancé(e) or proposed civil partner, neither the applicant nor his or her partner must be married to, or in a civil partnership with, another person at the date of application.

8.3.5.9   Intention to live together permanently in the UK

By para E-ECP.2.10, the applicant and his partner must intend to live together permanently in the UK. Paragraph 6 of the Immigration Rules defines this as an intention to live together, evidenced by a clear commitment from both parties that they will live together permanently in the UK immediately following the outcome of the application in question or as soon as circumstances permit thereafter.

There is an obvious overlap here with the requirement in para E-ECP.2.6 that the relationship between the applicant and his partner is genuine and subsisting (see **8.3.5.5**), since a relationship that is found to be a sham is a relationship where the parties have no intention of living together at all.

A decision maker may question whether parties meet this requirement if they have lived apart following their marriage or civil partnership. Usually the couple will respond by producing an explanation for the separation, and details of letters sent and telephone calls made during this period, to illustrate their 'intervening devotion'.

In the case of *Amarjit Kaur* [1999] INLP 110, the Immigration Judge had found that the applicant's 'overriding wish was to marry someone from abroad. The letters and phone calls were evidence, not of intervening devotion, but merely of intervening contact'. No further evidence of letters or phone calls was produced to the Tribunal, and although the sponsor had visited his wife in India, the appeal was dismissed. The Immigration Judge had taken a dim view of the fact that the sponsor was a divorcée, 20 years older than the applicant, and that the applicant had turned down Indian-based suitors in order to marry the sponsor. The Tribunal did not demur from that.

Contrast *Amarjit Kaur* with the case of *Goudey (subsisting marriage – evidence) Sudan* [2012] UKUT 00041 (IAC). There the Tribunal concluded that the applicant and her partner were

> the right age for each other, and the [partner] as a young man would undoubtedly be of an age when he would want to have the company of a wife. She appears to have moved homes when the marriage was being arranged. He travelled to Egypt to meet his wife and there is some evidential support for the proposition given in his oral account that the relationship was conducted by telephone. We see no basis on which the judge could dismiss the consistent evidence that they intended to live together as man and wife as lacking in credibility.

The question whether parties intend to live together permanently in the UK is basically one of fact, and decisions often turn on the credibility of the available evidence.

8.3.6   Financial requirements (paras E-ECP.3.1 to 3.3)

8.3.6.1   Overview

When applying for entry clearance (and usually for leave to remain and settlement: see **8.4** and **8.6** respectively) the applicant will have to provide specified documentary evidence that a prescribed minimum gross annual income is available. Home Office guidance is that this sets a benchmark for financial stability and independence on the part of the couple. However, a different test will apply if the applicant's partner is at the time of the application in receipt of certain UK welfare benefits (see **8.3.6.9**).

To satisfy the financial requirement the applicant will have to meet all of the following:

(a)   the level of financial requirement applicable to the application under Appendix FM (see **8.3.6.2**); and

(b)   the requirements specified in Appendix FM and Appendix FM-SE as to:

(i)   the permitted sources of income and savings (see **8.3.6.3** to **8.3.6.7**);

(ii)   the time periods and permitted combinations of sources applicable to each permitted source relied on (see **8.3.6.3** to **8.3.6.7**); and

(iii) the documentary evidence required for each permitted source relied upon (see **8.3.6.8**).

8.3.6.2 The prescribed minimum gross annual income

Currently, by para E-ECP.3.1, the applicant must provide specified evidence, from the sources listed in para E-ECP.3.2, of a specified gross annual income of at least £18,600.

What if the applicant's child or children will be living with the couple in the UK? An extra £3,800 is required for the first child and a further £2,400 for each additional child.

EXAMPLE

Ivan, a citizen of Russia, has recently married Judith, a British citizen. Ivan and his 8-year-old twin daughters, Olga and Nina, are applying under Appendix FM to the Immigration Rules to enter the UK where they will live with Judith and her 6-year-old son, Mark. Both Judith and Mark are British citizens. What gross annual income must Ivan demonstrate?

The answer is £24,800 (£18,600 for Ivan; £3,800 for Olga; and £2,400 for Nina).

For these purposes, a 'child' means a dependent child of the applicant or the applicant's partner who is:

(a) under the age of 18 years, or who was under the age of 18 years when they were first granted entry under this route;

(b) applying for entry clearance as a dependant of the applicant or the applicant's partner, or is in the UK with leave as their dependant; and

(c) not a British Citizen or settled in the UK.

So, in the example above, Mark, a British citizen, although a dependent child of the applicant's partner, Judith, does not count as a 'child' when calculating Ivan's prescribed minimum gross income.

Note that the set amount of £18,600 was held in *MM (Lebanon) v Secretary of State for the Home Department* [2013] EWHC 1900 (Admin) to disproportionately interfere with the ability of partners to live together contrary to their rights under the Article 8 ECHR. However, the Government successfully overturned that decision in the Court of Appeal; see [2014] EWCA Civ 985. Subsequently, the Supreme Court ([2017] UKSC 10) also upheld the set amount but made certain recommendations for revisions to Appendix FM. The Secretary of State's response was to amend the Immigration Rules in July 2017 and these changes are included in this chapter.

8.3.6.3 Meeting the prescribed minimum gross annual income

Paragraph E-ECP.3.2 sets out the only financial resources that count, namely:

(a) income of the partner from specified employment or self-employment, which, in respect of a partner returning to the UK with the applicant, can include specified employment or self-employment overseas and in the UK;

(b) specified pension income of the applicant and partner;

(c) any specified maternity allowance or bereavement benefit received by the partner in the UK;

(d) other specified income of the applicant and partner; and

(e) specified savings of the applicant and partner.

It is clear from the above that certain financial resources on which a couple might wish to rely are excluded. Importantly, para E-ECP.3.2 has the effect of overruling the Supreme Court decision in *Ahmed Mahad (previously referred to as AM) (Ethiopia) v ECO* [2009] UKSC 16, as financial support from a third party, such as relatives or community groups, cannot be counted. If third parties wish to assist a couple, they might do so by gifting them money which can then count towards the couple's savings, provided it is received at least six months before the date of the application (see **Category D** below). There must be exceptional circumstances before third party support can be taken into account (see **8.3.6.8**).

Home Office guidance is that the allowable financial resources can be used to meet the financial requirements in seven different possible ways, which it categorises A to G as follows.

Category A: salaried employment for the last six months

Where the applicant's partner is resident in the UK and is in salaried employment at the date of the application and has been with the same employer for at least the last six months, the applicant can count the gross annual salary (at its lowest level in those six months if there has been any increase) towards the financial requirement.

If necessary to meet the level of the financial requirement applicable to the application, the applicant can add to this, as permitted, from Categories C, D and E (see below).

EXAMPLE OF SALARIED EMPLOYMENT IN UK

The applicant's partner, Alan, is employed in the UK, earning £20,000 gross a year. He has worked for the same firm for over a year. The applicant has no dependent children. Alan should meet the financial requirement under Category A (subject to checking all his salary counts: see **8.3.6.4**).

Note that if Alan had been promoted into his current role within the last six months from a salary of £18,000, he can only use that lower figure for Category A purposes. If he wants to use the higher figure, he will have to delay his application until it has been paid to him for at least six months. Whenever he makes his application, he can combine his Category A salary with any income available from Categories C, D and E.

But what if the applicant's partner meets the above requirement in respect of salaried employment *abroad* and is returning with the applicant to the UK to take up employment here? In these circumstances the partner must also have confirmed salaried employment to return to in the UK, starting within three months of their return. This must have an annual starting salary sufficient to meet the financial requirement applicable to the application either alone or in combination with any, or all, of the items in Categories C, D and E as permitted.

EXAMPLE OF SALARIED EMPLOYMENT OUTSIDE UK

The applicant's partner, Heidi, is currently employed abroad, earning £25,000 gross a year. She has worked for the same firm for the last nine months. She has no dependent children. She has a signed contract of employment with a UK-based employer which has a starting salary of £30,000 and a start date within three months of her planned return to the UK. Heidi should meet the financial requirement under Category A (subject to checking that all her salary counts: see **8.3.6.4**).

For what counts as salaried employment, see **8.3.6.4**.

Category B: salaried employment for less than the last six months

Under Category B, salaried employment at the date of the application with the same employer but for less than the last six months counts in the same way as Category A above, but only if an additional test is met. The couple must also have received in the 12 months prior to the application the level of income required to meet the financial requirement based only on:

(a)   the gross salaried employment income of the applicant's partner (and/or the applicant if he is in the UK with permission to work and applying for leave to remain or settlement);

(b)   the gross amount of any specified non-employment income received by the applicant's partner, the applicant or both jointly;

(c)   the gross amount of any State (UK or foreign) or private pension received by the applicant's partner or the applicant; and/or

(d)   the gross amount of any UK maternity allowance, bereavement allowance, bereavement payment and widowed parent's allowance received by the applicant's partner or the applicant.

EXAMPLE

The applicant's partner, Brenda, is employed in the UK. She started her current employment last month. Her gross annual salary is £32,500. Over the last 12 months she has had two other salaried jobs and earned £28,750 from these in total. The applicant has no dependent children.

Brenda will not qualify under Category A above as she has not been with the same employer for at least six months. However, she will qualify under Category B as she has earned more than £18,600 in the last 12 months from salaried employment and is currently in employment at a salary of at least £18,600. This is subject to checking that all her salary payments count: see **8.3.6.4**.

Category B operates differently where the applicant's partner is *abroad* and returning with the applicant to the UK to take up employment. The partner does not have to be in employment abroad at the date of application. Instead, the following two tests must be met.

First, the couple returning to the UK must have received in the 12 months prior to the application the level of income required to meet the financial requirement, based only on:

(a)   the gross salaried employment income overseas of the applicant's partner;

(b)   the gross amount of any specified non-employment income received by the applicant's partner, the applicant or both jointly;

(c)   the gross amount of any state (UK or foreign) or private pension received by the applicant's partner or the applicant; and/or

(d)   the gross amount of any UK maternity allowance, bereavement allowance, bereavement payment and widowed parent's allowance received by the applicant's partner or the applicant.

Secondly, the applicant's partner must in addition have confirmed salaried employment to return to in the UK (starting within three months of his return). This must have an annual starting salary sufficient to meet the financial requirement applicable to the application either alone or in combination with any, or all, of the items in Categories C, D and E as permitted.

For what counts as salaried employment, see **8.3.6.4**.

Category C: specified non-employment income

The specified non-employment income (see **8.3.6.5**) (excluding pension under Category E below) the applicant's partner and/or the applicant have/has received in the 12 months prior to the application can count towards the applicable financial requirement, provided they continue to own the relevant asset (eg property, shares, etc) at the date of application.

The gross amount of any UK maternity allowance, bereavement allowance, bereavement payment and widowed parent's allowance received by the applicant's partner or the applicant in the 12 months prior to the application can be used in combination with other income for that period as described.

Only the above UK welfare benefits count. So even if the applicant's partner receives other benefits, such as tax credits, child benefit, universal credit, council tax benefit, etc, these cannot count.

This income may also be used in combination with other categories as described.

Category D: cash savings

An amount based on any cash savings above £16,000 held by the applicant's partner, the applicant or both jointly for at least six months prior to the application and under their control, can count towards the applicable financial requirement.

At entry clearance and the leave to remain stages, the amount above £16,000 must be divided by 2.5 (to reflect the 2.5 year or 30-month period before the applicant will have to make a further application) to give the amount which can be used. Mathematically, the calculation is the following equation: $(S - £16,000) \div 2.5 = C$ where S is the total amount of cash savings under the control of the applicant, their partner, or both jointly for at least the 6 months prior to the date of the application of entry clearance or leave to remain and C is the amount of Category D cash savings which can be used towards the financial requirement.

On an application for indefinite leave to remain, the whole of the amount above £16,000 can be used. Mathematically, the calculation is the following equation: $(S - £16,000) = C$ where S is the total amount of cash savings under the control of the applicant, their partner, or both jointly for at least the 6 months prior to the date of the application for settlement and C is the amount of Category D cash savings which can be used towards the financial requirement.

The amount based on cash savings may also be used in combination with other categories as described. What follows is an example where Categories A, C and D are combined.

EXAMPLE

The applicant's partner, Janice, a British citizen, is in employment in the UK at the date of her husband's application for entry clearance under Appendix FM. The couple have no dependent children.

Janice has been working for the same employer for at least 6 months prior to the date of the application, earning a gross annual salary for the purposes of Category A of £10,100 during that time (subject to checking that all her salary counts: see **8.3.6.4**).

Janice receives non-employment income from a rental property that she owns, and continues to own, in Canada, and in the 12 months prior to the date of her husband's application she received for the purposes of Category C a gross rental income of £7,250.

Janice has cash savings of £25,000 in a UK bank account. She has held those savings for at least 6 months prior to the date of her husband's application. The amount of savings for the purposes of Category D that can be used towards the financial requirement is $(£25,000 - £16,000) \div 2.5 = £3,600$.

Janice's husband's application requires a prescribed minimum gross annual income of £18,600. That is met by using a combination of income categories A, C and D, namely £10,100 + £7,250 + £3,600 = £20,950.

For further details, see **8.3.6.6**.

Category E: pension

The gross annual income from any State (UK basic State pension and additional or second State pension, or foreign) or private pension received by the applicant's partner or the applicant can count towards the applicable financial requirement. The annual amount may be counted where the pension has become a source of income at least 28 days prior to the application. This income can also be used in combination with other categories as described.

The gross amount of any State (UK or foreign) or private pension received by the applicant's partner or the applicant in the 12 months prior to the application can be used, alone or in combination with other income, for that period as described.

Category F: self-employment (last financial year)

The applicant's partner (and/or the applicant if he is in the UK with permission to work and applying for leave to remain or settlement) must be in self-employment at the date of the application and in the last full financial year received self-employment and other income (salaried, specified non-employment and pension) sufficient to meet the applicable financial requirement.

Note that cash savings cannot be used in combination with Category F.

> **EXAMPLE**
>
> The applicant's partner, Noel, is currently self-employed in the UK and in the last full financial year earned £20,575. The applicant has no dependent children.
>
> Noel will qualify under Category F as he is currently self-employed and in the last full financial year earned at least £18,600.

Category G: self-employment (last two financial years)

The applicant's partner (and/or the applicant if he is in the UK with permission to work and applying for leave to remain or settlement) must be in self-employment at the date of the application and as an average of the last two full financial years received self-employment and other income (salaried, specified non-employment and pension) sufficient to meet the applicable financial requirement.

Note that cash savings cannot be used in combination with Category G.

8.3.6.4 Further details about Categories A and B

For the purposes of Categories A and B, what counts as salaried employment?

Employment may be full-time or part-time. It can also be permanent, a fixed-term contract or with an agency.

What counts as income from salaried employment for the purposes of Categories A and B?

Basic pay, skills-based allowances and UK location-based allowances will be counted as income provided that (i) they are paid under the employee's contract of employment and (ii) where these allowances make up more than 30% of the total salary, only the amount up to 30% will be counted.

Overtime, payments to cover travel time, commission-based pay and bonuses (which can include tips and gratuities paid via a tronc scheme registered with HMRC) will be counted as income, where they have been received in the relevant period of employment or self-employment relied on in the application.

What does not count as income from salaried employed for the purposes of Categories A and B?

Payments relating to the costs of (a) UK or overseas travel, including, for example, travelling or relocation expenses, (b) subsistence or accommodation allowances and (c) payments made towards the costs of living overseas will not be counted as income.

8.3.6.5 Further details about Category C

What income falls within Category C? The specified sources of non-employment income are:

(a)   dividends or other income from investments, stocks, shares, bonds and trust funds;

(b)   property rental income;

(c)   interest from savings;

(d)   maintenance payments from a former partner in relation to the applicant and former partner's child or children dependent on and cared for by the applicant; and

(e)   UK Maternity Allowance, Bereavement Allowance, Bereavement Payment and Widowed Parent's Allowance.

The income at (d) above is derived from the Immigration Rules, Appendix FM-SE, para A1.1.1(b)(i), which provides that:

> Existing sources of third party support will be accepted in the form of payments from a former partner of the applicant for the maintenance of the applicant or any children of the applicant and the former partner, and payments from a former partner of the applicant's partner for the maintenance of that partner.

EXAMPLE

Joanne, a visa national, is applying for entry clearance as a spouse under Appendix FM. Joanne will be accompanied by her visa national daughter from a previous marriage, Alice. Her sponsor is her British husband, Keith. He is living in the UK with his British son, Zach, from a previous marriage.

Joanne receives maintenance for both herself and her daughter from her ex-husband. Both of these maintenance payments will count for Category C purposes.

Keith receives maintenance for Zach from his ex-wife. As this maintenance is paid for the applicant's partner's child (Zach) rather than the applicant's partner himself (Keith), the maintenance payment will not count for Category C purposes.

These sources of income must be in the name of the applicant's partner, the applicant or both jointly.

The relevant asset such as shares, bonds, property, etc must be held by the applicant's partner, the applicant or both jointly at the date of application.

In what circumstances can rent received from a property count? The property, whether in the UK or overseas, must be owned by the applicant's partner, the applicant or both jointly, and must not be their main residence (therefore income from a lodger in that residence cannot be counted). If the applicant's partner or applicant shares ownership of the property with a third party, only income received from the applicant's partner's and/or applicant's share of the property can be counted. Income from property which is rented out for only part of the year, eg a holiday let, can be counted. The equity in a property cannot be used to meet the financial requirement.

EXAMPLE

The applicant's partner, William, has been employed in the UK by the same employer for the last 12 months, earning £16,000 gross a year. He also receives £9,000 a year in rent from a house that he lets out. The house was left to him by his grandfather several years ago. It is in his sole name. The applicant has no dependent children.

William should meet the financial requirement of £18,600 under a combination of Category A income of £16,000 (subject to checking all his salary counts: see **8.3.6.4**) and Category C income of £9,000, so totalling £25,000.

8.3.6.6 Further details about Category D

To be counted, the applicant's partner, the applicant or both jointly must have cash savings of more than £16,000, held by the applicant's partner, the applicant or both jointly (but not with a third party) for at least six months at the date of application and under their control.

The savings may be held in any form of bank or savings account such as a current, deposit or investment account. However, the account must be provided by a financial institution regulated by the appropriate regulatory body for the country in which that institution is operating. Moreover, where appropriate, the financial institution must be on an approved list or not appear on a list of excluded institutions under Appendix P to the Immigration Rules. In all cases the account must allow the savings to be accessed immediately.

Only the amount of cash savings *above* £16,000 can be counted against any shortfall in the £18,600 income threshold (see **8.3.6.2**) or the relevant higher figure where at least one child of the applicant is included (see **8.3.6.2**). How is this done? At the entry clearance and limited leave to remain stages, the amount above £16,000 is divided by 2.5 (to reflect the 2.5 year or 30-month period before the applicant will have to make a further application). On an application for settlement, the whole of the amount above £16,000 can be used.

> **EXAMPLE**
>
> Zach and Yvonne are engaged to be married. Zach is a visa national. Yvonne is a British citizen. The couple are living in Zach's home country but they now wish to travel to the UK to get married and set up home together. Zach has no dependent children.
>
> Zach applies for entry clearance under Appendix FM to the Immigration Rules as Yvonne's partner (fiancé). The couple have no income to count towards the financial requirement, but they do have £70,000 in cash savings which they have held in a joint account for at least the last six months. Will they qualify?
>
> Under Category D, Zach and Yvonne's cash savings exceed £16,000 by £54,000. That figure divided by 2.5 is £21,600. As they require £18,600, they meet the financial requirement, provided they can produce the specified documents for these cash savings.

The level of savings required to meet any shortfall income must be based on the level of employment-related and/or other income at the date of application.

Table 8.5 below sets out some examples of the minimum amount of savings required to meet a shortfall where £18,600 (applicant with no dependent children) is the prescribed minimum gross annual income.

Table 8.5 Minimum amount of savings required to meet shortfall

Income	Entry clearance and leave to enter or remain: minimum amount of savings required
No other relevant income	£62,500 (£16,000 + (shortfall of £18,600 x 2.5))
Other relevant income of £15,000	£25,000 (£16,000 + (shortfall of £3,600 x 2.5))
Other relevant income of £18,000	£17,500 (£16,000 + (shortfall of £600 x 2.5))

8.3.6.7 Further details about Categories F and G

What income from self-employment counts for the purposes of Categories F and G? Where the self-employed person is a sole trader, or is in a partnership or franchise agreement, the income taken into account is the gross taxable profits from that person's share of the business. Allowances or deductible expenses which are not taxed are not counted towards income. What if the self-employed person has set up his own registered company and is listed as a director of that company? The income that counts will then be any salary drawn from the post-tax profits of the company.

8.3.6.8 Exceptional circumstances and third party support

As we saw at **8.3.6.3**, the applicant and his or her partner are limited as to the financial resources that count towards meeting the prescribed minimum gross income. But what if the minimum cannot be met and the applicant is not exempt (see **8.3.6.9** for the limited grounds for exemption)? If it is evident from the information provided by the applicant that there are exceptional circumstances which could render refusal a breach of Article 8 ECHR because that could result in unjustifiably harsh consequences for the applicant, his or her partner or a relevant child (see **8.14**), the decision maker will consider whether the financial requirement is met through taking into account other sources of income, financial support and funds listed in para 21A(2) of Appendix FM-SE. These are:

(a)   a credible guarantee of sustainable financial support to the applicant or his or her partner from a third party;

(b)   credible prospective earnings from the sustainable employment or self-employment of the applicant or his or her partner; or

(c)   any other credible and reliable source of income or funds for the applicant or his or her partner, which is available to him or her at the date of application or which will become available to him or her during the period of limited leave applied for.

In determining the genuineness, credibility and reliability of these sources of income, financial support and funds, the decision maker will take into account such matters as follows.

(a)   *In respect of a guarantee of sustainable financial support from a third party:*
   (i)   whether the applicant has provided verifiable documentary evidence from the third party in question of their guarantee of financial support;
   (ii)   whether that evidence is signed, dated and witnessed or otherwise independently verified;
   (iii) whether the third party has provided sufficient evidence of their general financial situation to enable the decision maker to assess the likelihood of the guaranteed financial support continuing for the period of limited leave applied for;
   (iv)   whether the third party has provided verifiable documentary evidence of the nature, extent and duration of any current or previous financial support which they have provided to the applicant or his or her partner;
   (v)   the extent to which this source of financial support is relied upon by the applicant to meet the financial requirement; and
   (vi)   the likelihood of a change in the third party's financial situation or in their relationship with the applicant or the applicant's partner during the period of limited leave applied for.

(b)   *In respect of prospective earnings from sustainable employment or self-employment of the applicant or his or her partner:*
   (i)   whether, at the date of application, a specific offer of employment has been made, or a clear basis for self-employment exists. In either case, such employment or self-employment must be expected to commence within three months of the applicant's arrival in the UK (if the applicant is applying for entry clearance) or within three months of the date of application (if the applicant is applying for leave to remain);

(ii)   whether the applicant has provided verifiable documentary evidence of the offer of employment or the basis for self-employment, and, if so, whether that evidence:

    (A)   is on the headed notepaper of the company or other organisation offering the employment, or of a company or other organisation which has agreed to purchase the goods or services of the applicant or his or her partner as a self-employed person;

    (B)   is signed, dated and witnessed or otherwise independently verified;

    (C)   includes (in respect of an offer of employment) a signed or draft contract of employment;

    (D)   includes (in respect of self-employment) any of a signed or draft contract for the provision of goods or services; a signed or draft partnership or franchise agreement; an application to the appropriate authority for a licence to trade; or details of the agreed or proposed purchase or rental of business premises;

(iii) whether, in respect of an offer of employment in the UK, the applicant has provided verifiable documentary evidence:

    (A)   of a relevant employment advertisement and employment application;

    (B)   of the hours to be worked and the rate of gross pay, which that evidence must establish equals or exceeds the National Living Wage or the National Minimum Wage (as applicable, given the age of the person to be employed) and equals or exceeds the going rate for such work in that part of the UK; and

    (C)   which enables the decision maker to assess the reliability of the offer of employment, including in light of the total size of the workforce and the turnover (annual gross income or sales) of the relevant company or other organisation;

(iv)   whether the applicant has provided verifiable documentary evidence that, at the date of application, the person to be employed or self-employed is in, or has recently been in, sustained employment or self-employment of the same or a similar type, of the same or a similar level of complexity and at the same or a similar level of responsibility;

(v)   whether the applicant has provided verifiable documentary evidence that the person to be employed or self-employed has relevant professional, occupational or educational qualifications and that these are recognised in the UK;

(vi)   whether the applicant has provided verifiable documentary evidence that the person to be employed or self-employed has the level of English language skills such prospective employment or self-employment is likely to require;

(vii) the extent to which this source of income is relied upon by the applicant to meet the financial requirement; and

(viii) where an offer of employment is relied upon, and where the proposed employer is a family member or friend of the applicant or their partner, the likelihood of a relevant change in that relationship during the period of limited leave applied for.

(c)   *In respect of any other credible and reliable source of income or funds for the applicant or his or her partner:*

(i)   whether the applicant has provided verifiable documentary evidence of the source;

(ii)   whether that evidence is provided by a financial institution regulated by the appropriate regulatory body for the country in which that institution is operating, and is signed, dated and witnessed or otherwise independently verified;

(iii) where the income is or the funds are based on, or derived from, ownership of an asset, whether the applicant has provided verifiable documentary evidence of its current or previous ownership by the applicant, his or her partner or both;

(iv) whether the applicant has provided sufficient evidence to enable the decision maker to assess the likelihood of the source of income or funds being available to him or her during the period of limited leave applied for; and

(v) the extent to which this source of income or funds is relied upon by the applicant to meet the financial requirement.

Note that whilst any cash savings relied on by the applicant must at the date of application be in the name(s), and under the control, of the applicant, his or her partner or both, by concession those savings need not have been held for at least 6 months before the application was made.

An applicant granted leave under this provision will be on the 10-year route to settlement (see **8.1.2.3**) but can subsequently apply to enter the five-year route if he or she then meets the relevant requirements.

8.3.6.9   When applicant is exempt a maintenance test applies

By para E-ECP.3.3(a), the applicant is exempt from the financial requirement if the applicant's partner is receiving one or more of the following UK welfare benefits:

(a)   disability living allowance or personal independence payment;

(b)   severe disablement allowance;

(c)   industrial injury disablement benefit;

(d)   attendance allowance;

(e)   carer's allowance;

(f)   Armed Forces Independence Payment or Guaranteed Income Payment under the Armed Forces Compensation Scheme;

(g)   Constant Attendance Allowance, Mobility Supplement or War Disablement Pension under the War Pensions Scheme; and

(h)   Police Injury Pension.

Paragraph 12 of Appendix FM-SE requires the applicant to produce official documentation from the DfWP confirming the entitlement to the relevant benefit or allowance and the amount received, as well as at least one personal bank statement showing payment of the benefit or allowance into the partner's account.

If the applicant is exempt from the financial requirement then, by para E-ECP.3.3(b), the applicant must provide evidence that his partner is able to maintain and accommodate himself, the applicant and any dependants adequately in the UK without recourse to public funds (see **8.3.6.10**). As to public funds, see **3.3.2**; and as to accommodation, see **8.3.7**.

8.3.6.10   What is adequate maintenance?

By para 6 of the Immigration Rules, 'adequately' in relation to this maintenance requirement means that, after income tax, National Insurance contributions and housing costs have been deducted, there must be available to the family the level of income that would be available to them if the family was in receipt of income support.

Home Office guidance to its decision makers is that the following five steps should be taken:

Step 1   Establish the applicant's partner's (and/or the applicant's if he is in the UK with permission to work and applying for leave to remain or settlement) current income. The gross income should be established and if the income varies, an average should be calculated.

Income from disability benefits can be included as income. Job offers or the prospects of employment are not taken into account.

Promises of third party support are not acceptable as Home Office guidance is that the applicant and his partner must have the required resources under their own control, not somebody else's.

Evidence of employment might include wage slips, a letter from the employer (confirming the employment and annual salary) and bank statements showing where the salary has been paid in.

Evidence of income from benefits received by the applicant's partner, such as disability benefits, may include the notice of award, but the best evidence will be the applicant's partner's bank statement showing where it has been paid into the account (see *Ahmed (benefits: proof of receipt; evidence) Bangladesh* [2013] UKUT 84 (IAC)).

Step 2   Establish the applicant's partner's current housing costs from the evidence provided.

Step 3   Deduct the housing costs from the net income.

Step 4   Calculate how much the family would receive if they were on income support.

Note that the income support level in 2019/20 was £114.85 a week for a couple and £66.90 a week for a child.

Step 5   The gross income after deduction of housing costs must equal or exceed the income support rate.

Note that if on making any future application for leave or settlement the applicant's partner no longer receives an exempting welfare benefit, the financial requirement (**8.3.6.2**) will apply instead, unless para EX.1 then applies (see **8.5**).

8.3.6.11   Specified documents

Full details of the documents that must be produced in order to meet the financial requirement are set out in Appendix FM-SE to the Immigration Rules.

8.3.7   Accommodation requirements (para E-ECP.3.4)

8.3.7.1   Adequate accommodation

By para E-ECP.3.4, the applicant must provide evidence that there will be adequate accommodation, without recourse to public funds, for the family, including other family members who are not included in the application but who live in the same household, which the family own or occupy exclusively (see **8.3.7.2**).

Accommodation is not regarded as adequate if it is, or will be, overcrowded (or it contravenes public health regulations) (see **8.3.7.3**).

8.3.7.2   Owned or occupied exclusively

The couple will have to provide documentary evidence where the property is either owned or rented by them. This may be in the form of a letter from their mortgagee, if the property was bought with the aid of a mortgage, a copy of the property deeds and, in the case of rented accommodation, a rent book and tenancy agreement.

Where the accommodation is rented from a local authority or housing association, correspondence from the landlord is normally regarded as genuine and sufficient by the Home Office.

Can a third party provide accommodation for the couple? Yes, provided it is a firm arrangement. In *AB (Third-party provision of accommodation)* [2008] UKAIT 00018, the sponsor wife was living in premises provided by a relative. She contributed to the household bills but did not pay any rent. The relative was happy for this arrangement to continue if she was joined by her husband. The Tribunal indicated that the mere mention of a relative or friend who was prepared to accommodate the parties was probably not enough, but a real and stable arrangement for accommodation provided by another might be. In this case the offer of accommodation was a real and stable one. It was credible and practical, and satisfied the requirement. In these circumstances it obviously helps if the third party supplies a statement setting out the accommodation arrangements.

If the accommodation is not owned but shared, para 6 of the Immigration Rules provides that 'occupy exclusively' in relation to accommodation means that part of the property must be for the exclusive use of the family. But what does this mean in practice? In *KJ ('Own or occupy exclusively') Jamaica* [2008] UKAIT 00006, the Tribunal observed that

> it is clear that it cannot mean either 'alone' nor 'with a legal right to exclude all others' ... it ought not to be enough for an applicant to say that he will be accommodated by a series of friends allowing him to sleep on sofas, or that he has enough money to put up his dependants in hotels from time to time, or that he or they will find space in hostels. What appears to be required is that there is somewhere that the person or people in question can properly, albeit without any legal accuracy, describe as their own home. They may not own it; and they may share it; but it is adequate for them, it is in a defined place, and it is properly regarded as where they live, with the implications of stability that that phrase implies. (*per* Mr CMG Ockelton, Deputy President, at para 9)

Home Office guidance is that where accommodation is shared, a decision maker should expect to see evidence that the family unit of the applicant, the applicant's partner and any dependants will have exclusive use of at least the number of bedrooms required for the age and gender of the members of that family unit (see **8.3.7.3**).

8.3.7.3 Overcrowding

The Housing Act 1985 (HA 1985), s 324 contains two tests to determine whether or not accommodation is overcrowded. If by coming to live in the property the applicant will cause it to be overcrowded under either test, the application will fail. The provisions currently included in Home Office guidance are as follows:

324   Definition of overcrowding

A dwelling is overcrowded for the purposes of this Part when the number of persons sleeping in the dwelling is such as to contravene—

(a)   the standard specified in section 325 (the room standard), or

(b)   the standard specified in section 326 (the space standard).

325   The room standard

(1)   The room standard is contravened when the number of persons sleeping in a dwelling and the number of rooms available as sleeping accommodation is such that two persons of opposite sexes who are not living together as husband and wife must sleep in the same room.

(2)   For this purpose—

(a)   children under the age of ten shall be left out of account, and

(b)   a room is available as sleeping accommodation if it is of a type normally used in the locality either as a bedroom or as a living room.

326   The space standard

(1)   The space standard is contravened when the number of persons sleeping in a dwelling is in excess of the permitted number, having regard to the number and floor area of the rooms of the dwelling available as sleeping accommodation.

(2)   For this purpose—

(a)   no account shall be taken of a child under the age of one and a child aged one or over but under ten shall be reckoned as one-half of a unit, and

(b)   a room is available as sleeping accommodation if it is of a type normally used in the locality either as a living room or as a bedroom.

(3)   The permitted number of persons in relation to a dwelling is the number specified in the following Table but no account shall be taken for the purposes of the Table of a room having a floor area of less than 50 square feet.

Table

Number of rooms	Number of persons
1	2
2	3
3	5
4	7.5
5	10
6 or more	2 persons for each room

As you will have noted, the first test is called 'the room standard'. It means that a property is overcrowded if two people aged 10 or more of the opposite sex, other than the applicant and the applicant's partner, have to sleep in the same room. The second test is 'the space standard'. Basically, this determines whether or not the number of people sleeping in the property exceeds that permitted by the Act. The table sets out the limits. The applicant can meet the accommodation requirement only if both tests are satisfied.

Are there any circumstances when overcrowding is allowed by the Home Office? Yes, but only if it is due to a new-born child or a child who has just turned one of the specified ages above and alternative accommodation arrangements have not yet been made; or temporary, for example, because a non-resident member of the family comes to live in the home for a short time.

> **EXAMPLE**
>
> Ian lives in a house with three rooms that can be used for sleeping. Living with him is his son, Lionel, aged 12, and his daughter, Diane, aged 13. Ian's mother, Mary, also lives with them. Ian recently travelled to Moscow and married Vika, a Russian national. Will the house be overcrowded if she is allowed to join Ian in the UK?
>
> First, apply the room standard and answer the question: who can sleep in each room?
>
> By HA 1985, s 325(1), Ian and Vika, as husband and wife, can share one room.
>
> In light of HA 1985, s 325(1) and (2)(a), Lionel, aged 12, and Diane, aged 13, as two persons of 10 years old or more of the opposite sex, cannot share. So they must be in separate rooms. The house will not be overcrowded, therefore, if Diane shares with Mary (two persons of 10 years old or more but of the same sex) and Lionel has a room of his own.
>
> Secondly, apply the space standard and answer the question: will the permitted number of persons for this property be exceeded?
>
> Here, with three rooms available to sleep in, the limit under HA 1985, s 326(3) is five persons, and that will not be exceeded as there will be only five people in the household if Vika joins them, namely, Ian (an adult counts as one), Vika (an adult counts as one), Lionel (aged 12, so 10 years old or more and counts as one), Diane (aged 12, so 10 years old or more and counts as one) and Mary (an adult counts as one).
>
> A check should be made that each of the three rooms has a floor area of at least 50 square feet for the purposes of HA 1985, s 326(3).

8.3.8 English language requirement (para E-ECP.4.1)

8.3.8.1 Meeting the requirement

By para E-ECP.4.1, the applicant will meet the English language requirement if he provides specified evidence that he:

(a)   is a national of a Home Office-designated majority English-speaking country (see **7.3.4.2**);

(b)   has an academic qualification recognised by UK ENIC to be equivalent to the standard of a Bachelor's or Master's degree or PhD in the UK, which was taught in English (see **7.3.4.3**);

(c)   has passed an English language test in speaking and listening at a minimum of level A1 of the Common European Framework of Reference for Languages with a secure provider approved by the Home Office (SELT: see **7.3.4.1**). A list of Home Office-approved tests can be found on the Home Office website (see **1.2.8**); or

(d)   is exempt from the English language requirement (see **8.3.8.2**).

The requirement does not breach Article 8 ECHR: see R *(on the application of Bibi) v Secretary of State for the Home Department* [2013] EWCA Civ 322.

8.3.8.2   Exempt from English language requirement

By para E-ECP.4.2, the applicant is exempt from the requirement to provide a suitable English language test certificate if at the date of the application he is is aged 65 or over, or has a disability (physical or mental condition) which prevents him from meeting the requirement, or if there are exceptional compassionate circumstances which prevent him from meeting the requirement prior to entering the UK.

Home Office guidance is that exemption applies only where someone has a physical or mental impairment which prevents him from learning English and/or taking a test. This is not a blanket exemption, as some disabled people are capable of learning English and taking an English test. So the exemption is granted only on production of satisfactory medical evidence from a medical practitioner who is qualified in the appropriate field, which specifies the disability and from which it may be concluded that exemption is justified.

What exceptional compassionate circumstances might lead to exemption? Home Office guidance is that the applicant must demonstrate that as a result of his circumstances he is unable to access facilities for learning English before coming to the UK. Evidence of an inability to attend, prior or previous attendance, or attempts to access learning must be clearly provided. This evidence must be provided by an independent source, eg from an appropriately qualified medical practitioner, or alternatively must be independently verified by a decision maker.

Home Office guidance is that situations which might, subject to receipt of all necessary evidence in support, lead a decision maker to conclude that the applicant can properly claim exceptional compassionate circumstances, include the following:

(a)   if the applicant's partner in the UK is seriously ill and requires immediate support or care from the applicant whilst receiving medical attention in the UK, and there is insufficient time for the applicant to access learning and/or to take a test; and

(b)   where a country or region is affected by conflict or humanitarian disaster, the Home Office will consider whether the situation makes it unreasonable for individuals to learn English and/or to take a test. In such circumstances a decision maker will consider the nature of the situation, including the infrastructure affected, and whether it would be proportionate to expect an applicant to meet the English language requirement.

It will be extremely rare for exceptional circumstances to apply when the applicant is applying in the UK for leave to remain, as applicants already here will have access to a wide variety of facilities for learning English.

Financial reasons, or claims of illiteracy or limited education are not acceptable to the Home Office.

Note that if an applicant has been granted an exemption due to exceptional compassionate circumstances at entry clearance, he will be required to meet the English language requirement when he applies for further leave to remain after 30 months.

8.3.9 Decision on application

By para D-ECP.1.1, only an applicant who meets the requirements for entry clearance as a partner will be granted entry clearance. This will be for an initial period not exceeding 33 months and subject to a condition of no recourse to public funds. However, if the applicant is a fiancé(e) or proposed civil partner, the applicant will be granted entry clearance for a period not exceeding six months and subject to a condition of no recourse to public funds and a prohibition on employment.

By para D-ECP.1.2, where the applicant does not meet the requirements for entry clearance as a partner the application will be refused.

8.4 LEAVE TO REMAIN IN THE UK AS A PARTNER

8.4.1 Who can apply?

There are six different situations to be considered here, namely:

(a) where a person entered the UK as a partner under Appendix FM and now seeks an extension of his limited leave for a further 30 months;

(b) where a person entered the UK as a fiancé(e) or proposed civil partner under Appendix FM and now, following marriage or civil partnership, applies to switch to the category of a partner under Appendix FM;

(c) where a person is in the UK in a different immigration category has married or entered into a civil partnership and now wishes to switch to the category of a partner under Appendix FM;

(d) where a person switched in the UK to the category of a partner under Appendix FM and now applies for an extension of his limited leave for a further 30 months;

(e) where a person wishes to start on the 10-year family route to settlement under Appendix FM (see **8.1.2.3**) by relying on his Article 8 ECHR rights under para EX.1 (see **8.5**). This application might be made, for example, by an overstayer who has married a British citizen or a person settled in the UK, and who otherwise faces administrative removal from the UK (see **10.4**);

(f) where a person is on the 10-year family route to settlement under Appendix FM and now seeks an extension of his limited leave for a further 30 months.

8.4.2 An overview of the requirements

The requirements in Appendix FM to be met for leave to remain as a partner (see para R-LTRP.1.1) are that:

(a) the applicant and his partner must be in the UK;

(b) the applicant must have made a valid application for limited or indefinite leave to remain as a partner; and either

(c) (i) the applicant must not fall for refusal under Section S-LTR: Suitability – leave to remain, and

(ii) the applicant meets all of the requirements of Section E-LTRP: Eligibility for limited leave to remain as a partner;

or

(d) (i) the applicant must not fall for refusal under Section S-LTR: Suitability – leave to remain, and

(ii)   the applicant meets the eligibility requirements of paras E-LTRP.1.2–1.12 and E-LTRP.2.1, and

(iii) para EX.1 applies.

The suitability requirements are detailed at **8.4.3**, the eligibility requirements at **8.4.4** and para EX.1 at **8.5**.

8.4.3 Suitability requirements

Paragraphs S-LTR.1.2–1.8 and S-LTR.2.2, 2.4 and 2.5 set out respectively the mandatory and discretionary grounds on which the Home Office will normally refuse an application. You will see that broadly these are the same as for entry clearance (see **8.3.3**).

S-LTR.1.2   The applicant is at the date of application the subject of a deportation order.

S-LTR.1.3   The presence of the applicant in the UK is not conducive to the public good because he has been convicted of an offence for which he has been sentenced to imprisonment for at least four years.

S-LTR.1.4   The presence of the applicant in the UK is not conducive to the public good because he has been convicted of an offence for which he has been sentenced to imprisonment for less than four years but at least 12 months.

S-LTR.1.5   The presence of the applicant in the UK is not conducive to the public good because, in the view of the Secretary of State, his offending has caused serious harm or he is a persistent offender who shows a particular disregard for the law.

S-LTR.1.6   The presence of the applicant in the UK is not conducive to the public good because his conduct (including convictions which do not fall within paras S-LTR.1.3–1.5), character, associations, or other reasons, make it undesirable to allow him to remain in the UK.

S-LTR.1.7   The applicant has failed without reasonable excuse to comply with a requirement to attend an interview; provide information; provide physical data; or undergo a medical examination or provide a medical report.

S-LTR.1.8   The presence of the applicant in the UK is not conducive to the public good because the Secretary of State (a) has made a decision under Article 1F of the Refugee Convention to exclude the person from the Refugee Convention or under para 339D of these Rules to exclude them from humanitarian protection; or (b) has previously made a decision that they are a person to whom Article 33(2) of the Refugee Convention applies because there are reasonable grounds for regarding them as a danger to the security of the UK.

S-LTR.2.2   Whether or not to the applicant's knowledge: (a) false information, representations or documents have been submitted in relation to the application (including false information submitted to any person to obtain a document used in support of the application); or (b) there has been a failure to disclose material facts in relation to the application.

S-LTR.2.4   A maintenance and accommodation undertaking has been requested under para 35 of the Rules and has not been provided.

S-LTR.2.5   The Secretary of State has given notice to the applicant and their partner under section 50(7)(b) of the Immigration Act 2014 that one or both of them have not complied with the investigation of their proposed marriage or civil partnership.

Note that when the Secretary of State is considering whether the presence of the applicant in the UK is not conducive to the public good (see S-LTR.1.3–1.8 above), any legal or practical reasons why the applicant cannot presently be removed from the UK must be ignored.

In addition, para S-LTR.4.1 provides that the applicant may be refused on grounds of suitability if any of the following apply.

S-LTR.4.2   The applicant has made false representations or failed to disclose any material fact for the purpose of obtaining a previous variation of leave, or in order to obtain a document from the Secretary of State or a third party, required in support of a previous variation of leave.

S-LTR.4.3   The applicant has previously made false representations or failed to disclose material facts for the purpose of obtaining a document from the Secretary of State that indicates that he or she has a right to reside in the United Kingdom.

S-LTR.4.4   The applicant has failed to pay litigation costs awarded to the Home Office.

S-LTR.4.5   One or more relevant NHS bodies has notified the Secretary of State that the applicant has failed to pay charges in accordance with the relevant NHS regulations on charges to overseas visitors and the outstanding charges have a total value of at least £500.

8.4.4   Overview of eligibility requirements

If an applicant meets all of the eligibility requirements in paras E-LTRP.1.2–4.2, he may be granted limited leave to remain and proceed on the five-year family route to settlement. Alternatively, if the applicant can meet the eligibility requirements of paras E-LTRP.1.2–1.12 and E-LTRP.2.1, and also meets para EX.1 (see **8.5** below), he may be granted limited leave to remain and proceed on the 10-year family route to settlement.

The eligibility requirements are as follows:

(a)   relationship requirements (see **8.4.5**);

(b)   immigration requirements (see **8.4.6**);

(c)   financial requirements (see **8.4.7**);

(d)   accommodation requirements (see **8.4.8**); and

(e)   English language requirement (see **8.4.9**).

8.4.5   Relationship requirements

Paras E-LTRP.1.2–1.10 set out the same relationship requirements as for entry clearance (see **8.3.5**). Note that para E-LTRP.1.10 provides, in addition, that the applicant must produce evidence that, since entry clearance as a partner was granted or since the last grant of limited leave to remain as a partner, the applicant and his partner have lived together in the UK, or there is good reason, consistent with a continuing intention to live together permanently in the UK, for any period in which they have not done so.

Note that para E-LTRP.1.11 provides that if the applicant is in the UK with leave as a fiancé(e) or proposed civil partner and the marriage or civil partnership did not take place during that period of leave, there must be good reason why it did not, and evidence must be produced that it will take place within the next six months. In those circumstances any further leave will be for six months only and subject to a condition of no recourse to public finds and a prohibition on employment.

Paragraph E-LTRP.1.12 provides that the applicant's partner cannot be the applicant's fiancé(e) or proposed civil partner, unless the applicant was granted entry clearance as that person's fiancé(e) or proposed civil partner.

8.4.6   Immigration requirements

Paragraph E-LTRP.2.1 excludes certain people already in the UK from switching into this category, namely, a visitor (see **Chapter 5**), or a person with valid leave granted for a period of six months or less, unless that leave is as a fiancé(e) or proposed civil partner, or a person on temporary admission (see **3.5.5**).

By para E-LTRP.2.2(b), the applicant must not be in the UK in breach of immigration laws (any period of overstaying for a period of 14 days or less may be ignored (see **3.6.5**)), unless para EX. 1 applies (see **8.5**).

8.4.7 Financial requirements

Generally, by paras E-LTRP.3.1–3.3 the same financial provisions apply as for entry clearance (see **8.3.6**). The key differences to note are as follows:

(a) Income from specified lawful employment or self-employment (Categories A, B, F and G – see **8.3.6.3**) of the applicant can now be included to meet the financial requirement, provided he is in the UK with permission to work. The only partner prohibited from working is a fiancé(e) or proposed civil partner.

> **EXAMPLE**
>
> Luke is a visa national. Over two years ago he entered the UK as the partner (spouse) of Rachel, a British citizen. He was accompanied by his dependent child, Ambrose. Luke and Ambrose are now applying for leave to remain for a further 30 months under Appendix FM to the Immigration Rules. The financial requirement Luke must meet is a minimum gross annual income of £22,400 (ie £18,600 for himself and £3,800 for Ambrose).
>
> Both Rachel and Luke have had the same jobs for over a year. Luke produces the specified documents evidencing the following financial resources: his annual salary from employment of £11,750, plus Rachel's annual salary from employment of £13,250. Together that totals £25,000 and so the minimum gross annual income is met.

(b) An applicant does not have to meet the financial requirement, nor the alternative maintenance test (see **8.3.6.9**) if para EX.1 applies (see **8.5**).

8.4.8 Accommodation requirements

By para E-LTRP.3.4, the same accommodation provisions apply as for entry clearance (see **8.3.7**) unless para EX.1 applies (see **8.5**).

8.4.9 English language requirement

If the applicant has not already met this requirement in a previous application for leave as a partner, the applicant must now do so unless para EX.1 applies (see **8.5**). The details are the same as for entry clearance (see **8.3.8**). Note, however, that as from 1 May 2017, if the applicant only met the requirement previously by passing an English language test in speaking and listening at the minimum of level A1 of the Common European Framework of Reference for Languages, he must now pass it at level A2 or above.

8.4.10 Decision on application

If the applicant meets all the requirements he will be granted limited leave to remain for a period not exceeding 30 months and subject to a condition of no recourse to public funds. The applicant will be eligible to apply for settlement after a continuous period of at least 60 months (five years) with such leave (see **8.6**). This includes any period spent in the UK with entry clearance as a partner under para D-ECP1.1, but does not include any period of entry clearance or limited leave as a fiancé(e) or proposed civil partner.

A fiancé(e) or proposed civil partner will be able to work only once he has received notification from the Home Office that his application for leave to remain has been granted.

If the applicant can meet the suitability requirements, the eligibility requirements of paras E-LTRP.1.2–1.12 (the relationship requirements at **8.4.5**) and E-LTRP.2.1 (the first immigration requirement at **8.4.6**), and para EX.1 (see **8.5**) applies, he will be granted leave to remain for a period not exceeding 30 months. This will be subject to a condition of no recourse to public funds (unless there are exceptional circumstances set out in the application which require access to public funds to be granted on grounds of destitution). He will be eligible to apply for settlement after a continuous period of at least 120 months (10 years) with such leave (see **8.6**). This includes any period spent in the UK with entry clearance as a partner under para D-ECP1.1, but does not include any period of entry clearance or limited leave as a fiancé(e) or proposed civil partner.

8.5 PARAGRAPH EX.1

If the applicant can meet the suitability requirements (**8.4.3**) and the eligibility requirements of paras E-LTRP.1.2-1.12 (the relationship requirements at **8.4.5**) and E-LTRP.2.1 (the first immigration requirement at **8.4.6**), the application will be granted if para EX.1 applies. Broadly, this allows an applicant to remain in the UK on the basis of his family life with a child and/or a partner if it would breach Article 8 ECHR to remove the applicant. In these circumstances the applicant will have a longer route to settlement, namely 10 years, granted in four periods of 30 months' limited leave, with a fifth application for indefinite leave to remain.

Note that if the applicant is being deported having committed a criminal offence or criminal offences in the UK, and so does not meet the suitability requirements at **8.4.3**, then different considerations will apply instead of para EX.1: see **10.3.4**.

Further note that if the applicant is liable to being removed from the UK, perhaps as an overstayer, he may still meet the suitability requirements at **8.4.3**, and para EX.1 will then apply: see **10.4.6**.

8.5.1 Family life in UK with a child

Paragraph EX.1 applies if the applicant has a genuine and subsisting parental relationship with a child (under the age of 18 years) who is in the UK, who is a British citizen or who has lived in the UK continuously for at least the seven years immediately preceding the date of application, and, taking into account the child's best interests as a primary consideration, it would not be reasonable to expect that child to leave the UK.

8.5.1.1 Genuine and subsisting parental relationship

Home Office guidance to its decision makers is that when considering whether the relationship is genuine and subsisting, the following questions are likely to be relevant:

(a) Does the applicant have a parental relationship with the child? What is the relationship – biological, adopted, step-child, legal guardian? Is the applicant the child's *de facto* primary carer?

(b) Is it a genuine and subsisting relationship? Does the child live with the person? Where does the applicant live in relation to the child? How regularly do they see one another? Are there any relevant court orders governing access to the child?

(c) Is there any evidence or other relevant information provided within the application, eg the views of the child or other family members, or from social work or other relevant professionals? To what extent is the applicant making an active contribution to the child's life?

Factors which might prompt closer scrutiny include:

(a) that there is little or no contact with the child, or contact is irregular;

(b) any contact is only recent in nature;

(c) support is only financial in nature, there is no contact or emotional or welfare support;

(d) the child is largely independent of the person.

The 'parent' must have a 'subsisting' role in personally providing at least some element of direct parental care to the child. The focus of this exception is upon the loss, by deportation, of a parent who is providing, or is able to provide, 'care for the child' (see *Secretary of State for the Home Department v VC (Sri Lanka)* [2017] EWCA Civ 1967).

Each child falling within para EX.1 should be identified as a qualifying child (see *Reid v Secretary of State for the Home Department* [2021] EWCA Civ 1158: which concerned a similar provision in respect of deportation, dealt with at **10.3.7**).

8.5.1.2 Qualifying child is a British citizen or been in the UK for a continuous period of seven years

Home Office guidance is that its decision makers should establish the age and nationality of each qualifying child affected by the decision, and where they are foreign nationals their immigration history in the UK, eg how long they have lived in the UK and where they lived before.

In establishing whether a non-British citizen qualifying child has been in the UK continuously for more than seven years, the time spent in the UK with and without valid leave can be included. Short periods outside the UK, for example for holidays or family visits, would not count as a break in the seven years required. However, where a child has spent more than six months out of the UK at any one time, this normally should count as a break in continuous residence unless any exceptional factors apply.

8.5.1.3 It would be unreasonable to expect the qualifying child to leave the UK

Home Office guidance is that the starting point is that it would not normally expect a qualifying child to leave the UK. Why? Because it accepts that it is normally in a child's best interest for the whole family to remain together, which means that if the child is not expected to leave, then the parent or parents or primary carer of the child will also not be expected to leave the UK. Consideration of whether or not it is reasonable to expect a qualifying child to leave the UK must be given regardless of whether the child is actually expected to leave the UK (*Secretary of State for the Home Department v AB (Jamaica)* [2019] EWCA Civ 661). The provision calls for a fact-finding exercise so that the full background facts must be established against which the question can then be addressed. Once all the relevant facts have been found, the only question which arises is whether or not it would be reasonable to expect the child to leave the UK. The focus has to be on the child (see *Runa v Secretary of State for the Home Department* [2020] EWCA Civ 514).

If one parent has no right to remain, but the other parent does, that is the background against which the assessment is conducted. If neither parent has the right to remain, then that is the background against which the assessment is conducted. Thus, the ultimate question will be: is it reasonable to expect the child to follow the parent with no right to remain to the country of origin? (See *KO (Nigeria) v Secretary of State for the Home Department* [2018] UKSC 53.)

Home Office guidance is that it may be reasonable for a qualifying child to leave the UK with the parent or primary carer where, for example:

- the parent or parents, or child, are a citizen of the country and so able to enjoy the full rights of being a citizen in that country;
- there is nothing in any country specific information, including as contained in relevant country information, which suggests that relocation would be unreasonable;
- the parent or parents or child have existing family, social, or cultural ties with the country, and if there are wider family or relationships with friends or community overseas that can provide support:
    - the decision maker must consider the extent to which the child is dependent on or requires support from wider family members in the UK in important areas of their life and how a transition to similar support overseas would affect them;

- a person who has extended family or a network of friends in the country should be able to rely on them for support to help (re)integrate there;

- a parent or parents or a child who have lived in or visited the country before for periods of more than a few weeks should be better able to adapt, or the parent or parents would be able to support the child in adapting, to life in the country;

- the decision maker must consider any evidence of exposure to, and the level of understanding of, the cultural norms of the country. For example, a period of time spent living amongst a diaspora from the country may give a child an awareness of the culture of the country;

- the parents or child can speak, read and write in a language of that country, or are likely to achieve this within a reasonable time period. Fluency is not required – an ability to communicate competently with sympathetic interlocutors would normally suffice;

• removal would not give rise to a significant risk to the child's health; and

• there are no other specific factors raised by or on behalf of the child.

The parents' situation is a relevant fact to consider in deciding whether they themselves and therefore their child is expected to leave the UK. Home Office Guidance is that where both parents are expected to leave the UK, the natural expectation is that the child would go with them and leave the UK, and that expectation would be reasonable unless there are factors or evidence that means it would not be reasonable.

8.5.1.4 Exceptional factors

If para EX.1 does not apply the application is normally be refused. However, the Home Office accepts that there may be exceptional factors which would make refusal unreasonable. Its decision makers should consider any other exceptional factors raised in relation to the qualifying child's best interests and question whether refusal is still appropriate in light of those factors. In some cases it may be appropriate to grant leave on a short-term temporary basis to enable particular issues relating to the child's welfare to be addressed before return.

Home Office guidance is that whilst all cases are to an extent unique, those unique factors do not generally render them exceptional. Furthermore, a case is not exceptional just because the exceptions to para EX.1 have been missed by a small margin. Rather, the Immigration Rules establish the thresholds as determining when leave would be appropriate bar other factors. However, in assessing exceptionality the matters identified in para EX.1 need to be considered along with all other aspects of the case. The decision maker then needs to determine whether removal would have such severe consequences for the child that exceptionally refusal or return is not appropriate. Finally, the decision maker should be prepared to take into account any order made by the UK Family Court, but that is not determinative of the immigration decision. However, the judgment of the family court, with all the tools at its disposal (including the assistance of the Children and Family Court Advisory and Support Service (CAFCASS) and the opportunity to assess all the adults), could and should inform the decision maker: see *Mohan v Secretary of State for the Home Department* [2012] EWCA Civ 1363.

8.5.2 Family life in UK with a partner

Paragraph EX.1 additionally, or alternatively, applies if the applicant has a genuine and subsisting relationship (see **8.3.5.5**) with a partner who is in the UK and who is a British citizen, settled in the UK, or in the UK with refugee leave or humanitarian protection, and there are insurmountable obstacles to family life with that partner continuing outside the UK.

8.5.2.1   Insurmountable obstacles

In determining whether there are 'insurmountable obstacles', para EX.2 provides that the decision maker should consider if there are very significant difficulties that would be faced by the applicant or his partner in continuing their family life together outside the UK, and which could not be overcome or would entail very serious hardship for the applicant or his partner.

Home Office guidance emphasises that the assessment of whether there are 'insurmountable obstacles' is a different and more stringent assessment than whether it would be 'reasonable to expect' the applicant's partner to join him overseas. For example, a British citizen partner who has lived in the UK all of his or her life, has friends and family here, works here and speaks only English may not wish to uproot and relocate halfway across the world, and it may be very difficult for him or her to do so, but a significant degree of hardship or inconvenience does not amount to an insurmountable obstacle.

Sales LJ held, in *R (on the application of Agyarko) v Secretary of State for the Home Department* [2015] EWCA Civ 440:

> 21. The phrase 'insurmountable obstacles' as used in this paragraph of the Rules clearly imposes a high hurdle to be overcome by an applicant for leave to remain under the Rules. The test is significantly more demanding than a mere test of whether it would be reasonable to expect a couple to continue their family life outside the United Kingdom.

> 22. This interpretation is in line with the relevant Strasbourg jurisprudence. The phrase 'insurmountable obstacles' has its origin in the Strasbourg jurisprudence in relation to immigration cases in a family context, where it is mentioned as one factor among others to be taken into account in determining whether any right under Article 8 exists for family members to be granted leave to remain or leave to enter a Contracting State: see eg *Rodrigues da Silva and Hoogkamer v Netherlands* (2007) 44 EHRR 34, para [39] ('... whether there are insurmountable obstacles in the way of the family living together in the country of origin of one or more of them ...'). The phrase as used in the Rules is intended to have the same meaning as in the Strasbourg jurisprudence. It is clear that the ECtHR regards it as a formulation imposing a stringent test in respect of that factor, as is illustrated by *Jeunesse v Netherlands* [(2015) 60 EHRR 17] (see para [117]: there were no insurmountable obstacles to the family settling in Suriname, even though the applicant and her family would experience hardship if forced to do so).

The Court of Appeal decision in *Agyarko* was upheld by the Supreme Court ([2017] UKSC 11), which confirmed that the test is compatible with Article 8.

The Home Office states that Article 8 of the ECHR does not oblige the UK to accept the choice of a couple as to which country they would prefer to reside in.

Home Office guidance is that the lack of knowledge of a language spoken in the country in which the couple would be required to live would not usually amount to an insurmountable obstacle. Why? Because it is reasonable to conclude that the couple must have been communicating whilst in the UK. Therefore, it is possible for family life to continue outside the UK, whether or not the partner chooses to also learn a language spoken in the country of proposed return.

Does being separated from extended family members, such as might happen where the partner's parents and/or siblings live here, amount to an insurmountable obstacle? Would a material change in the quality of life for the applicant and his partner in the country of return, such as the type of accommodation they would live in, or a reduction in their income, amount to an insurmountable obstacle? No, answers the Home Office, not unless there were particular exceptional factors in either case.

According to the Home Office, the factors which might be relevant to the consideration of whether an insurmountable obstacle exists include, but are not limited to, the following:

(a)   The ability of the family to lawfully enter and stay in another country.

(b)   Cultural barriers where the partner would be so disadvantaged that he or she could not be expected to go and live in that country, for example, a same sex couple where the UK partner would face substantial societal discrimination, or where the rights and freedoms of the UK partner would be severely restricted.

(c)   Whether or not either party has a mental or physical disability, a move to another country may involve a period of hardship as the person adjusts to his or her new surroundings. But a physical or mental disability could be such that in some circumstances it could lead to very serious hardship, for example due to lack of health care.

(d)   In some circumstances, there may be particular risks to foreign nationals which extend to the whole of the country of return.

It is vital that an applicant produces evidence in support of the claim. For example, in *R (Mudibo) v Secretary of State for the Home Department* [2017] EWCA Civ 1949, the obstacles to family life, which were said to be insurmountable, were the applicant's [Mr Ali's] inability to work, his inability to support himself in his home country of Tanzania and the difference in standards of medical care for his condition in the UK and in Tanzania:

> It seems to me that the evidence on all these points was tenuous in the extreme. There was no evidence given by Mr Ali at all: he did not explain what work he had been accustomed to, what his skills were and what the real obstacles to employment were for him. There was no evidence from any quarter as to what obstacles there were to support for the couple in Tanzania and no explanation as to what the appellant's own employment prospects were. The medical evidence was brief and relatively old and nothing was provided to establish a case of lack of necessary medication and/or medical care in Tanzania ... the claim to 'insurmountable obstacles' amounted in reality to mere assertion. (per McCombe LJ at [31])

8.5.2.2   Exceptional circumstances

Where the applicant does not meet the requirements set out above, refusal of the application will be appropriate. However, leave may be granted outside the Rules where exceptional circumstances apply.

The Home Office decision maker needs to determine whether refusal or removal would have such severe consequences for the individual that this would not be proportionate given the nature of his family life, notwithstanding the fact that there are no insurmountable obstacles to family life with the applicant's partner continuing outside the UK. Home Office guidance is that is likely to be the case only very rarely.

In determining whether there are exceptional circumstances, the decision maker must consider all relevant factors, such as the following:

(a)   The circumstances around the applicant's entry to the UK and the proportion of the time he has been in the UK legally as opposed to illegally. Did he form his relationship with his partner at a time when he had no immigration status or this was precarious? Family life which involves the applicant putting down roots in the UK in the full knowledge that his stay here is unlawful or precarious should be given less weight, when balanced against the factors weighing in favour of removal, than family life formed by a person lawfully present in the UK.

(b)   Cumulative factors should be considered. For example, where the applicant has family members in the UK but his family life does not provide a basis for staying and he has a significant private life in the UK. Although under the Rules family life and private life are considered separately, when considering whether there are exceptional circumstances private and family life should be taken into account.

(c)   The public policy considerations in s 117A of the NIAA 2002 (see **10.3.4.2**).

If the application is granted because exceptional circumstances apply, leave outside the Immigration Rules for a period of 30 months is usually given.

8.6   INDEFINITE LEAVE TO REMAIN (SETTLEMENT) AS A PARTNER

8.6.1   Who can apply?

There are two different situations to be considered here, namely:

(a)   where a person has completed the five-year family route to settlement, ie two periods of 30 months' leave in the UK as a partner; and

(b)   where a person has completed the 10-year family route to settlement, ie four periods of 30 months' leave in the UK as a partner.

8.6.2   An overview of the requirements

The requirements in Appendix FM to be met for indefinite leave to remain as a partner (see para R-ILRP.1.1) are that:

(a)   the applicant and his partner must be in the UK;

(b)   the applicant must have made a valid application for indefinite leave to remain as a partner;

(c)   the applicant must not fall for refusal under any of the grounds in Section S-ILR: Suitability for indefinite leave to remain (see **8.6.3**);

(d)   the applicant must meet all of the requirements of Section E-LTRP: Eligibility for leave to remain as a partner (see **8.4.4**); and

(e)   the applicant must meet all of the requirements of Section E-ILRP: Eligibility for indefinite leave to remain as a partner (see **8.6.4**).

8.6.3   Suitability requirements for indefinite leave to remain

Paragraph S-ILR.1.1 provides that the application will be refused if any of the following apply:

S-ILR.1.2   The applicant is currently the subject of a deportation order.

S-ILR.1.3   The presence of the applicant in the UK is not conducive to the public good because they have been convicted of an offence for which they have been sentenced to imprisonment for at least four years.

S-ILR.1.4   The presence of the applicant in the UK is not conducive to the public good because they have been convicted of an offence for which they have been sentenced to imprisonment for less than four years but at least 12 months, unless a period of 15 years has passed since the end of the sentence.

S-ILR.1.5   The presence of the applicant in the UK is not conducive to the public good because they have been convicted of an offence for which they have been sentenced to imprisonment for less than 12 months, unless a period of seven years has passed since the end of the sentence.

S-ILR.1.6   The applicant has, within the 24 months prior to the date on which the application is decided, been convicted of or admitted an offence for which they received a non-custodial sentence or other out of court disposal that is recorded on their criminal record.

S-ILR.1.7   The presence of the applicant in the UK is not conducive to the public good because, in the view of the Secretary of State, their offending has caused serious harm or they are a persistent offender who shows a particular disregard for the law.

S-ILR.1.8   The presence of the applicant in the UK is not conducive to the public good because their conduct (including convictions which do not fall within paragraphs S-ILR.1.3. to S-ILR.1.6.), character, associations, or other reasons, make it undesirable to allow them to remain in the UK.

S-ILR.1.9   The applicant has failed without reasonable excuse to comply with a requirement to:

> (a)   attend an interview;
>
> (b)   provide information;
>
> (c)   provide physical data; or
>
> (d)   undergo a medical examination or provide a medical report.

Paragraph S-ILR.2.1 provides that the application will normally be refused if any of the following apply:

S-ILR.2.2 Whether or not to the applicant's knowledge:

> (a)   false information, representations or documents have been submitted in relation to the application (including false information submitted to any person to obtain a document used in support of the application); or
>
> (b)   there has been a failure to disclose material facts in relation to the application.

S-ILR.2.4 A maintenance and accommodation undertaking has been requested under paragraph 35 of these Rules and has not been provided.

When considering whether the presence of the applicant in the UK is not conducive to the public good, are any legal or practical reasons why the applicant cannot presently be removed from the UK ignored? Yes, see para S-ILR.3.1.

Finally, para S-ILR.4.1 provides that the application may be refused if any of the following apply.

S-ILR.4.2 The applicant has made false representations or failed to disclose any material fact for the purpose of obtaining a previous variation of leave, or in order to obtain a document from the Secretary of State or a third party, required in support of a previous variation of leave.

S-ILR.4.3 The applicant has previously made false representations or failed to disclose material facts for the purpose of obtaining a document from the Secretary of State that indicates that he or she has a right to reside in the United Kingdom.

S-ILR.4.4 The applicant has failed to pay litigation costs awarded to the Home Office.

S-ILR.4.5 One or more relevant NHS bodies has notified the Secretary of State that the applicant has failed to pay charges in accordance with the relevant NHS regulations on charges to overseas visitors and the outstanding charges have a total value of at least £500.

8.6.4 Eligibility requirements for indefinite leave to remain

Note that whilst the applicant must meet all of the requirements of Section E-LTRP: Eligibility for leave to remain as a partner (see **8.4.4**), where the financial requirement applies, any cash savings in Category D that exceed £16,000 are taken into account in full.

Table 8.6 below sets out some examples of the minimum savings required to meet a shortfall where £18,600 (applicant with no dependent children) is the prescribed minimum gross annual income.

Table 8.6 Minimum savings required to meet a shortfall

Income	Indefinite leave to remain: minimum savings required
No other relevant income	£34,600 (£16,000 + shortfall of £18,600)
Other relevant income of £15,000	£19,600 (£16,000 + shortfall of £3,600)
Other relevant income of £18,000	£16,600 (£16,000 + and shortfall of £600)

By para E-ILRP.1.2, the applicant must be in the UK with valid leave to remain as a partner (disregarding any period of overstaying for a period of 28 days or less).

By para E-ILRP.1.3, the applicant must have completed a continuous period of at least 60 months with limited leave as a partner (under para R-LTRP.1.1(a) to (c), or in the UK with entry clearance as a partner under para D-ECP.1.1), or a continuous period of at least 120 months with limited leave as a partner (under para R-LTR.P.1.1(a), (b) and (d), or in the UK with entry clearance as a partner under para D-ECP.1.1) or a continuous period of at least 120 months with limited leave as a partner under a combination of these paragraphs. Note that any period of entry clearance or limited leave as a fiancé(e) or proposed civil partner cannot be included.

By para E-ILRP.1.4, only those periods of limited leave when the applicant's partner is the same person can be taken into account.

By para E-ILRP.1.6, the applicant must have sufficient knowledge of the English language and sufficient knowledge about life in the UK (see **3.8.7** and **8.6.5**).

8.6.5   Absences from the UK

There is no requirement that the entire five- or 10-year leave periods, as appropriate, must be spent in the UK. Home Office guidance is that where an applicant has spent a limited period outside of the UK in connection with his or his partner's employment, this should not count against him. However, if he has spent the majority of the period overseas, there may be reason to doubt that all the requirements of the Immigration Rules have been met, eg that the couple intend to live together permanently in the UK (see **8.3.5.9**). The Home Office states that each case must be judged on its merits, taking into account reasons for travel, length of absence, and whether the applicant and his partner travelled and lived together during the time spent outside the UK. These factors will need to be considered against the relevant requirements of the Immigration Rules.

8.6.6   Decision on the application

By para D-ILRP.1.1, if the applicant meets all of the requirements at **8.6.2** he will be granted indefinite leave to remain unless para EX.1 applies (see **8.5**). Where paragraph EX.1 applies, the applicant will be granted further limited leave to remain as a partner for a period not exceeding 30 months under para D-ILRP.1.2 (see immediately below).

What if the applicant cannot meet all the requirements? Paragraph D-ILRP.1.2 has a limited concession. It provides that if the applicant does not meet the requirements for indefinite leave to remain as a partner only for one or both of the following reasons:

(a)   para S-ILR.1.5 or 1.6 applies; and/or

(b)   the applicant does not have sufficient knowledge of the English language and sufficient knowledge about life in the UK;

then the applicant will be granted further limited leave to remain as a partner for a period not exceeding 30 months and subject to a condition of no recourse to public funds (unless there are exceptional grounds requiring access to public funds on the basis that the applicant is destitute).

Where an applicant is granted further limited leave under para D-ILRP.1.2 he should be advised that should the reason at (a) and/or (b) be overcome, he can make a further application for settlement at any time within the 30-month period.

The application will be refused if the applicant does not meet all the eligibility requirements for indefinite leave to remain as a partner and does not qualify for further leave to remain as a partner under para D-ILRP.1.2 or for limited leave to remain as a partner in accordance with para R-LTRP.1.1(a), (b) and (d) (see **8.4.2**).

8.7 INDEFINITE LEAVE TO REMAIN (SETTLEMENT) AS A BEREAVED PARTNER

What if, before the relevant five- or 10-year probationary period is completed, the applicant's partner dies? In these circumstances, if the bereaved partner wishes to remain in the UK permanently, he should apply for settlement.

By para BPILR.1.1, the applicant will have to meet the following requirements:

(a)   the applicant must be in the UK;

(b)   the applicant must have made a valid application for indefinite leave to remain as a bereaved partner;

(c)   the applicant must not fall for refusal under any of the grounds in Section S-ILR: Suitability for indefinite leave to remain (see **8.6.3**); and

(d)   the applicant must meet all of the requirements of Section E-BPILR: Eligibility for indefinite leave to remain as a bereaved partner (see **8.7.1**).

8.7.1 Eligibility requirements

By para E-BPILR.1.2, the applicant's last grant of limited leave must have been as:

(a)   a partner (other than a fiancé(e) or proposed civil partner) of a British citizen or a person settled in the UK; or

(b)   a bereaved partner.

By para E-BPILR.1.3, the person who has died must have been the applicant's partner at the time the applicant was last granted limited leave under Appendix FM.

By para E-BPILR.1.4, at the time of the partner's death the relationship between the applicant and the partner must have been genuine and subsisting (see **8.3.5.5**), and each of the parties must have intended to live permanently with the other in the UK (see **8.3.5.9**).

Home Office guidance is that normally detailed enquiries as to the subsistence of the marriage, civil partnership or relationship will not be made unless there are already doubts expressed on the file. In most cases, provided the eligibility requirements are met, the application will be granted on sight of the partner's death certificate and without further enquiry.

In cases of doubt, for example where there were doubts expressed at the time of granting the initial period of leave to remain, or where allegations have since been made about the genuine and subsisting nature of the relationship, it may be appropriate to refuse the application. However, as the Home Office guidance recognises, it must be borne in mind that the burden of proof on the Secretary of State will be very high in view of the fact that the applicant will no longer be in a position to prove the subsistence of the relationship.

8.7.2 Timeliness of application

Home Office guidance is that this provision is intended to benefit only those whose sponsor has died during the probationary period and who make their application whilst they still have limited leave to enter or remain in the UK.

The provision is also applied where the sponsor dies after an application for settlement has been submitted but before a decision has been reached.

Is the fact that a sponsor dies during the very early stages of the probationary period considered by the Home Office as an adverse factor in reaching a decision? No: Home Office guidance is that where an applicant can meet the requirements, the application is to be granted regardless of how much of the probationary period has been completed.

What if the application is made after the applicant's existing leave has expired? Home Office guidance is that an applicant does not need to comply with the requirement not to have overstayed by more than 28 days (para E-LTRP 2.2 at **8.4.6**), provided that the circumstances of any period of overstaying relates to a period of bereavement and where compassionate circumstances therefore apply. Applications made out of time where all the other requirements are met should be considered sympathetically. An application should not normally be refused solely on the grounds that the applicant is here without leave. Acceptable reasons for the delay in making an application could be that the partner's death only occurred shortly before the application for settlement was due, or that the stress of the situation led the applicant to overlook the need to regularise his immigration status.

8.7.3 Decision on application

If the applicant meets all of the requirements set out at **8.7** above, he will be granted indefinite leave to remain.

But what if the applicant cannot meet all of the requirements? Paragraph D-BPILR.1.2 has a limited concession. It provides that if the only requirement not met is either para S-ILR.1.5 or 1.6, he will be granted further limited leave to remain for a period not exceeding 30 months (subject to a condition of no recourse to public funds). The applicant should be informed that if he is granted a further period of limited leave under para D-BPILR1.2, he can make a further application for settlement at any time within the 30-month period if the requirement is met.

If the applicant does not meet the requirements for indefinite leave to remain as a bereaved partner, or limited leave to remain as a bereaved partner under para D-BPILR.1.2, the application will be refused.

What if the applicant does not wish to settle in the UK but intends to leave the UK, eg to return to his country of origin? In these circumstances, Home Office guidance is that the applicant may be granted further leave to remain for six months, subject to the same conditions, to give him time to sort out his affairs.

8.8 INDEFINITE LEAVE TO REMAIN (SETTLEMENT) AS A PARTNER WHO IS A VICTIM OF DOMESTIC VIOLENCE

What if the couple separate due to domestic violence before the relevant probationary period is completed? In these circumstances, if the applicant wishes to remain in the UK permanently, he should apply for settlement.

By para DVILR.1.1, the applicant will have to meet the following requirements:

(a)   the applicant must be in the UK;

(b)   the applicant must have made a valid application for indefinite leave to remain as a victim of domestic violence;

(c)   the applicant must not fall for refusal under any of the grounds in Section S-ILR: Suitability for indefinite leave to remain (see **8.6.3**); and

(d)   the applicant must meet all of the requirements of Section E-DVILR: Eligibility for indefinite leave to remain as a victim of domestic violence (see **8.8.1**).

8.8.1 Eligibility requirements

By para E-DVILR.1.2, the applicant's last grant of limited leave must have been:

(a)   as a partner (other than a fiancé(e) or proposed civil partner) of a British citizen or a person settled in the UK;

(b)   granted to enable access to public funds pending an application under this provision; or

(c)   granted under para D-DVILR.1.2 (see **8.8.2**).

Paragraph E-DVILR.1.3 provides that the applicant must provide evidence that during the last period of limited leave as a partner, his relationship broke down permanently as a result of domestic violence. Note first that there needs to be a causal link between the infliction of domestic violence on the applicant and the permanent breakdown of the relationship. Secondly, consideration needs to be given as to what evidence might be available. Has the applicant's partner been convicted of assaulting the applicant or formally cautioned by the police? Many victims of domestic violence do not tell anyone. Whatever the circumstances, the detailed guidance issued by the Home Office on this requirement should be consulted.

8.8.2 Decision on application

If the applicant meets all of the requirements set out at **8.8**, he will be granted indefinite leave to remain.

But what if the applicant cannot meet all of the requirements? Paragraph D-DVILR.1.2 has a limited concession. It provides that if the only requirement not met is para S-ILR.1.5 or 1.6, he will be granted further limited leave to remain for a period not exceeding 30 months. The applicant should be informed that if granted a further period of limited leave under para D-DVILR.1.2, he can make a further application for settlement at any time within the 30-month period if the requirement is met.

If the applicant does not meet the requirements for indefinite leave to remain as a victim of domestic violence, or further limited leave to remain under para D-DVILR.1.2, the application will be refused.

8.9 CHILDREN ENTERING FOR IMMEDIATE SETTLEMENT

8.9.1 Who is a child?

A child is a person under the age of 18 at the date he applies for entry clearance. So it is irrelevant if he turns 18 before the ECO decides his application or before travelling to the UK under his visa or entry certificate (see paras 27 and 321(ii) respectively of the Immigration Rules).

This route is only available to a child outside the UK. A child cannot switch into this route whilst in the UK.

8.9.2 Exempt groups

A child will usually need to apply for entry clearance under Part 8 of the Immigration Rules to join a parent, both parents or a relative who is already settled in the UK. The child will need to apply for entry clearance, and if granted can enter the UK for the purposes of immediate settlement. However, those Rules will not apply to the following:

(a)   children who are British citizens (see **Chapter 2**);

(b)   children who have rights of entry to the UK as the family member of an EEA national with settled status under the EU Settlement Scheme (see **Chapter 4**).

> **EXAMPLE**
>
> Eva is a German citizen, aged 17. Her father, also German, is working in the UK. She is entitled to enter the UK in her own right (I(EEA) Regs 2016, reg 11). Whether she has any right of residence beyond three months (reg 14) depends on establishing a qualifying status under reg 6. In the alternative, she can enter and reside as the family member of her father who is an EEA national. The Immigration Rules do not apply.

8.9.3 Who is a parent?

The term 'parent', for the purposes of the Immigration Rules, is defined in para 6 and includes:

(a)   the step-father of a child whose father is dead, and the reference to 'step-father' includes a relationship arising through civil partnership;

(b)   the step-mother of a child whose mother is dead, and the reference to 'step-mother' includes a relationship arising through civil partnership;

(c)   the father, as well as the mother, of an illegitimate child where he is proved to be the father;

(d)   an adoptive parent (provided that the child was legally adopted in a country whose adoption orders are recognised by the UK – see **8.9.6**);

(e)   in the case of a child born in the UK who is not a British citizen, a person to whom there has been a genuine transfer of parental responsibility on the ground of the original parent's/parents' inability to care for the child.

8.9.4   Entry clearance requirements

Normally a child will be seeking entry clearance to join one or both parents who are already settled in the UK. Exceptionally, he might be joining a relative who is here and settled. Note that these people are often called the child's 'sponsor'.

The requirements are set out in para 297.

8.9.4.1   Overview of requirements

The starting point is to identify the parent, parents or relative the child is seeking to join in the UK, as listed in para 297(i)(a)–(f). Unless one of those categories is established, the application will fail at this first hurdle.

Then proceed to consider the remaining requirements in para 297(ii)–(v). The main issues normally concern the child's maintenance and accommodation in the UK.

As you would expect, there is a requirement to obtain entry clearance (see para 297(vi)).

8.9.4.2   Parent, parents or relative

There are four straightforward categories of entry for a child. These are listed in para 297(i), as follows:

(a)   both parents are present and settled in the UK; or

(b)   both parents are being admitted on the same occasion with the child for settlement; or

(c)   one parent is present and settled in the UK and the other parent is being admitted on the same occasion with the child for settlement; or

(d)   one parent is present and settled in the UK or being admitted on the same occasion with the child for settlement, and the other parent is dead.

As can be seen, (a)–(c) involve both parents; in (d) one parent is dead.

The remaining two categories impose additional tests. This is because one parent is alive but will not be involved in the family reunion. This is likely where the parents have never lived together, or have separated or divorced. On what basis will the child be allowed to join the one parent who is present and settled in the UK? This is provided for in para 297(i), as follows:

(e)   one parent is present and settled in the UK or being admitted on the same occasion with the child for settlement, and has had sole responsibility for the child's upbringing; or

(f)   one parent or a relative is present and settled in the UK or being admitted on the same occasion with the child for settlement, and there are serious and compelling family or other considerations which make exclusion of the child undesirable and suitable arrangements have been made for the child's care.

The sole responsibility test in (e) is discussed at **8.9.4.3**. The serious and compelling reasons test in (f) is examined at **8.9.4.4**.

You will have noted that the only way a child can join a relative other than a parent in the UK is under category (f).

8.9.4.3   Sole responsibility

According to Home Office guidance, sole responsibility reflects the situation where parental responsibility for a child, to all intents and purposes, rests chiefly with one parent. Such a situation is in contrast to the family unit where responsibility for a child's upbringing is shared between the two parents (although not necessarily equally).

> Sole parental responsibility means that one parent has abdicated or abandoned parental responsibility, and the remaining parent is exercising sole control in setting and providing the day-to-day direction for the child's welfare. It is unrealistic for a child to have contact with no other adult other than the parent exercising sole responsibility. We accept that the child will have contact with other adults, including relatives, and that these are likely to include some element of care towards the child, either generally or specifically such as taking the child to school. Actions of this kind that include looking after the child's welfare may be shared with others who are not parents, for example, relatives or friends, who are available in a practical sense, providing the applicant has overall responsibility, on their own, for the welfare of the child. You are not considering whether the applicant (or anyone else) has day-to-day responsibility for the child, but whether the applicant has continuing sole control and direction of the child's upbringing, including making all the important decisions in the child's life. If not, then they do not have sole parental responsibility for the child. (Home Office Family Policy guidance, June 2021)

In *Suzara Ramos v Immigration Appeal Tribunal* [1989] Imm AR 148, the Court of Appeal (per Dillon LJ) held that

> the words 'sole responsibility' have to carry some form of qualification in that the rule envisages that a parent who is settled in the United Kingdom will or may have had the sole responsibility for the child's upbringing in another country. Obviously there are matters of day-to-day decision in the upbringing of a child which are bound to be decided on the spot by whoever is looking after the child in the absence of the parent settled here, such as getting the child to school safely and on time, or putting the child to bed, or seeing what it has for breakfast, or that it cleans its teeth, or has enough clothing, and so forth. … The question must be a broad question.

> Direction and control of upbringing are … factors which are part of the total pattern of facts on which the adjudicator had to make his decision. Another matter was of course the extent of contact that the mother had had with the child since the mother went to the United Kingdom …

A parent claiming to have had 'sole responsibility' for a child must satisfactorily demonstrate that he has, for a period of time, been the chief person exercising parental responsibility. For such an assertion to be accepted by the Home Office, it must be shown that he has had, and still has, the ultimate responsibility for the major decisions relating to the child's upbringing, and provides the child with the majority of the financial and emotional support he requires. It must also be shown that he has had and continues to have care and control of the child.

In the case of *Nmaju v Entry Clearance Officer* (2000) *The Times*, 6 September, the Court of Appeal held that this requirement could be satisfied even where the parent in question had exercised sole responsibility only for a short period of time (namely, about two and a half months on the facts). The Court said that the question posed by the rules was: Had the parent settled in the UK sole responsibility for the upbringing of the child? In this case the Tribunal had found that the mother had had sole responsibility for the upbringing of the appellants. Having concluded that, the Tribunal was not at liberty under the rules to find that the appellants did not qualify for entry merely because that sole responsibility had not been assumed for a period of in excess of much over two months.

Home Office guidance is that a parent claiming to have had sole responsibility for a child must satisfactorily demonstrate this, usually for a 'substantial period of time'. This arguably fails to follow *Nmaju*, where the Court stated that:

> It is a mistake in my judgment to try and address the question of time on its own, asking questions such as were addressed to us in submissions 'can two months be substantial?' The proper course is to address the question posed by the rules, namely, has the parent settled in the United Kingdom had sole responsibility for the upbringing of the child? (per Schiemann LJ)

In *Nmaju*, the Court of Appeal indicated that:

> While legal responsibility under the appropriate legal system will be a relevant consideration, it will not be a conclusive one. One must also look at what has actually been done in relation to the child's upbringing by whom and whether it has been done under the direction of the parent settled here. (per Schiemann LJ)

In *Cenir v Entry Clearance Officer* [2003] EWCA Civ 572, Buxton LJ stated that the following was a useful rule of thumb:

> [A]ll the important decisions in the child's life, questions concerning health and place of abode, schooling and probably going as far as serious questions of behaviour, mode of dress and the like must be under the oversight of the parent claiming sole responsibility or delegated to someone obliged to consult and act upon her instructions. To have responsibility means to be answerable.

The following factors may be relevant when deciding this issue:

(a)   the period for which the parent in the UK has been separated from the child;

(b)   what the arrangements were for the care of the child before that parent migrated to the UK;

(c)   who has been entrusted with day-to-day care and control of the child since the sponsoring parent migrated here;

(d)   who provides, and in what proportion, the financial support for the child's care and upbringing;

(e)   who takes the important decisions about the child's upbringing, such as where and with whom the child lives, the choice of school, religious practice, health and medical treatment, holidays and recreational activities, etc;

(f)   the degree of contact that has been maintained between the child and the parent claiming sole responsibility;

(g)   what part in the child's care and upbringing is played by the parent not in the UK and any relatives.

The Home Office guidance is that in assessing whether the applicant has sole parental responsibility for a child, the decision maker must consider if evidence has been provided to show that:

- decisions have been taken and actions performed in relation to the upbringing of the child under the sole direction of the applicant, without the input of the other parent or any other person;
- the applicant parent is responsible for the child's welfare and for what happens to them in key areas of the child's life, and that others do not share this responsibility for the child; and
- the applicant parent has exclusive responsibility for making decisions regarding the child's education, health and medical treatment, religion, residence, holidays and recreation; protecting the child and providing them with appropriate direction and guidance; the child's property and the child's legal representation.

8.9.4.4   Serious and compelling reasons

Guidance from the Home Office on the meaning of 'serious and compelling reasons' in para 297(i)(f) states:

> [T]he objective of this provision is to allow a child to join a parent or relative in this country only where that child could not be adequately cared for by his parents or relatives in his own country. It has never been the intention of the Rules that a child should be admitted here due to the wish of or for the benefit of other relatives in this country. This approach is entirely consistent with the internationally accepted principle that a child should first and foremost be cared for by his natural parent(s) or, if this is not possible, by his natural relatives in the country in which he lives. Only if the parent(s) or relative(s) in his own country cannot care for him should consideration be given to him joining relatives in another country.

The degree to which these considerations should be taken into account, and whether they should relate solely to the child or include the circumstances of the sponsor, is determined by two factors, namely:

(a)   whether the sponsor is a parent or other relative of the child; and

(b)   whether or not the sponsor is settled here.

If the sponsor is not a parent but another relative (eg an aunt or grandparent), the factors which are to be considered relate only to the child and the circumstances in which he lives or lived prior to travelling to the UK. These circumstances should be exceptional in comparison with the ordinary circumstances of other children in his home country. It is not, for instance, sufficient to show he would be better off here by being able to attend a State school.

> The focus needs to be on the circumstances of the child in the light of his or her age, social background and developmental history and will involve inquiry as to whether: (i) there is evidence of neglect or abuse; (ii) there are unmet needs that should be catered for; (iii) there are stable arrangements for the child's physical care. The assessment involves consideration as to whether the combination of circumstances [is] sufficiently serious and compelling to require admission. (per Blake J in *Mundeba* (*s.55 and para 297(i)(f)*) [2013] UKUT 88 (IAC) at [37])

The circumstances relating to the sponsors here (eg the fact that they are elderly or infirm and need caring for) are not taken into account.

If the sponsor in the UK is one of the child's parents, consideration needs to be given to whether or not that parent is settled here or being admitted for settlement. If he is not, the relevant circumstances relate solely to the child (as detailed above). But if the child's sponsor is one of his parents and he is settled here (or being admitted for settlement), the considerations to be taken into account may relate either to the child and his circumstances in the country in which he lives or lived prior to travelling here, or to the parent who is settled here or being admitted for settlement.

The circumstances surrounding the child must be exceptional in relation to those of other children living in that country, but in this case, circumstances relating to the parent here, both of an emotional and of a physical nature, may be taken into account. Such circumstances may include illness or infirmity which requires assistance.

EXAMPLE

Marlene is the mother of Dora, aged 14. Both are citizens of Barbados. Marlene is divorced from Dora's father, who never contacts his daughter. He is still living in Barbados. When Dora was 8 years old, Marlene came to the UK and left Dora in Barbados in the care of her grandmother, who alone has supported her granddaughter financially. Marlene now has indefinite leave to remain in the UK. She wishes to know whether Dora can join her in the UK.

Marlene cannot establish her sole responsibility (see **8.9.4.3**) for Dora, as she has not provided any financial support for her from the UK. She must instead show that there are serious and compelling considerations which make Dora's exclusion undesirable (eg if Dora's grandmother becomes seriously ill and incapable of looking after her). If this requirement is not met, Dora cannot currently be admitted for settlement in the UK.

Marlene may be able to establish sole responsibility (see **8.9.4.3**) over the next few months if she provides all or the majority of Dora's financial and emotional support, and takes responsibility for the major decisions in Dora's life.

8.9.4.5   Age

By para 297(ii), the child must be under the age of 18. See further **8.9.1**.

8.9.4.6 Dependent life-style

By para 297(iii), the child must not be leading an independent life, must be unmarried and not a civil partner, and must not have formed an independent family unit.

Paragraph 6 of the Immigration Rules provides that 'must not be leading an independent life' means that the applicant:

(a)   does not have a partner as defined in Appendix FM (see **8.1.2.1**);

(b)   is living with his parents (except where he is at boarding school, college or university as part of his full-time education);

(c)   is not employed full-time (unless aged 18 years or over);

(d)   is wholly or mainly dependent upon his parents for financial support (unless aged 18 years or over); and

(e)   is wholly or mainly dependent upon his parents for emotional support.

Obviously the above general factors may have to be adapted when applied to the different categories of possible entry in para 297(i): see **8.9.4.2**.

8.9.4.7 Accommodation

By para 297(iv), the child must be accommodated adequately by the parent, parents or relative the child is seeking to join, without recourse to public funds, in accommodation which the parent, parents or relative the child is seeking to join own or occupy exclusively.

The equivalent provision for partners under Appendix FM is detailed at **8.3.7**.

EXAMPLE

In the case of *Loresco* [1999] INLP 18, three teenage children (one girl and two boys) sought to join their mother in the UK. Was her two-bedroomed flat, with a living room that was also available as sleeping accommodation, too small for her, her husband, their 1-year-old child and the three teenagers? The Tribunal said 'Yes'. Three rooms were available to sleep in. There was one room for the sponsor and her husband, one room for the girl over 10, and the third room for the two boys over 10. So the room standard was met.

Under the space standard, with only three available rooms, the permitted number of persons was five. But the child aged 1 year counted as half a unit, and as everyone else was aged 10 or over, that meant the total number of people in the flat would be five and a half persons with the three teenage children. Their application was therefore refused as the flat was overcrowded under the space standard (see **8.3.7.3**).

8.9.4.8 Maintenance

By para 297(v), the child must be maintained adequately by the parent, parents or relative the child is seeking to join, without recourse to public funds. As to public funds, see **3.3.2**.

The equivalent provision for partners under Appendix FM is detailed at **8.3.6.10**. However, as the application is made under Part 8 of the Immigration Rules rather than Appendix FM, the Home Office guidance on third party support and prospective earnings is different. The guidance currently reads as follows.

> Undertakings of third party support – If the applicant is unable to produce sufficient evidence to meet the adequate maintenance requirement, they may provide a written undertaking from members of their family that those members will support the applicant until they are able to support themselves from their own resources. The decision maker will need to assess and verify an offer of third party support in order to determine whether the applicant satisfies the requirement that they can be adequately maintained in the UK without recourse to public funds. The decision maker may request recent evidence of the third party's assets (e.g. original bank statements or a reasonable equivalent over

a period of at least three months). It is open to the decision maker to ask a third party offering long-term support to become a joint sponsor and to give an undertaking (under paragraph 35 of Part 1 of the Immigration Rules) to underwrite this commitment.

Prospective employment earnings – The application may rely on a confirmed job offer or an expectation of achieving income from employment based on the skills, qualifications or present employment of the sponsor, the applicant or both. These can be included if satisfactory evidence is provided that the job offer or prospect of obtaining employment is genuine, credible and realistic. Jobs that are unrealistic in the light of the applicant's skills or jobs that appear to have been manufactured and lack any prospect of continuing will not suffice.

8.9.4.9 General grounds for refusal

The application must not fall for refusal under the general grounds for refusal (see **3.4.5** and the criminality requirements in **Appendix 8**).

8.9.5 Adopted children

Adopted children are dealt with in paras 309A–316F of the Immigration Rules. The details are beyond the scope of this book.

8.10 PARENT OF A CHILD SETTLED IN THE UK

8.10.1 Who can apply?

A parent with sole parental responsibility for, or access rights to, a British citizen child or settled child who is living in the UK, can apply for entry clearance (see **8.10.2**) and leave to remain (see **8.10.3**) under Appendix FM to the Immigration Rules. Ultimately it may be possible to apply for settlement in this category (see **8.10.4**).

A parent already in the UK may switch into this category. This most commonly occurs when a person has entered the UK with limited leave as the partner of a British citizen or settled person (see **8.3**), but can no longer remain in the UK in that category as the relationship has broken down. If that person has sole parental responsibility for, or is exercising access rights to, his British or settled child, an application may be made for limited leave to remain (see **8.10.3**).

Who is a parent for these purposes? See **8.9.3**.

8.10.2 Entry clearance

By para EC-PT.1.1 of Appendix FM to the Immigration Rules, the requirements to be met for entry clearance as a parent are:

(a)   the applicant must be outside the UK;

(b)   the applicant must have made a valid application for entry clearance as a parent;

(c)   the applicant must not fall for refusal under any of the grounds in Section S-EC: Suitability – entry clearance; and

(d)   the applicant must meet all of the requirements of Section E-ECPT: Eligibility for entry clearance as a parent.

Note that the suitability requirements are the same as for a partner under Appendix FM, and these are detailed at **8.3.3**. As to the eligibility requirements, see **8.10.2.1**.

8.10.2.1 Eligibility requirements in outline

An applicant must meet all of the eligibility requirements in paras E-ECPT.2.1–4.2. Broadly these are as follows:

(a)   relationship requirements (see **8.10.2.2**);

(b)   financial requirements (see **8.10.2.3**)

(c)   accommodation requirements (see **8.10.2.4**); and

(d)   English language requirement (see **8.10.2.5**).

8.10.2.2   Relationship requirements (paras E-ECPT.2.1–2.4)

By para E-ECPT.2.1, the applicant must be aged 18 years or over.

Paragraph E-ECPT.2.2 provides that the child of the applicant must be:

(a)   under the age of 18 years at the date of application;

(b)   living in the UK; and

(c)   a British citizen (see **2.2**) or settled in the UK (see **3.8**).

By para E-ECPT.2.3, either:

(a)   the applicant must have sole parental responsibility for the child (see **8.9.4.3**); or

(b)   the parent or carer with whom the child normally lives must be –

    (i)   a British citizen in the UK or settled in the UK;

    (ii)   not the partner of the applicant; and

    (iii)   the applicant must not be eligible to apply for entry clearance as a partner under Appendix FM (see **8.3**).

By para E-ECPT.2.4, the applicant must provide evidence that he has either:

(a)   (i)   sole parental responsibility for the child; or

    (ii)   access rights to the child; and

(b)   the applicant must provide evidence that he is taking, and intends to continue to take, an active role in the child's upbringing.

What evidence is required?

Home Office guidance is that to demonstrate access rights, the applicant will need to produce either a residence or a contact order granted by a court in the UK, or a sworn affidavit from the UK resident parent or carer of the child confirming that the applicant can have access to the child and describing in detail the access arrangements. If the contact with the child is supervised, the supervisor must swear the statement.

How can an applicant show that he is taking, and intends to continue to take, an active role in his child's upbringing? The application form states:

> Please provide details of how you have been involved in the upbringing of your child(ren). You should include information on what role you played in choosing their care arrangements in the UK or which nursery/school they attend. What role have you played in choosing their academic options? How often do you speak to or see your child(ren)? Have you been present for key events in their lives eg religious events, birthdays etc? How do you keep in touch (telephone, email, letters etc)? Please provide any documentary evidence that you have to support your answer.

8.10.2.3   Financial requirements

By para E-ECPT.3.1, the applicant must provide evidence that he will be able to maintain and accommodate himself and any dependants in the UK adequately without recourse to public funds. As to public funds, see **3.3.2**.

The equivalent provision for partners under Appendix FM is detailed at **8.3.6.10**.

8.10.2.4   Accommodation requirements

By para E-ECPT.3.2, the applicant must provide evidence that there will be adequate accommodation in the UK, without recourse to public funds, for the family, including other family members who are not included in the application but who live in the same household, which the family own or occupy exclusively. Accommodation will not be regarded as adequate if:

(a)   it is, or will be, overcrowded; or

(b)   it contravenes public health regulations.

The equivalent provision for partners under Appendix FM is detailed at **8.3.7**.

8.10.2.5 English language requirement

The requirement in para E-ECPT.4.1 is exactly the same as for a partner seeking entry clearance under Appendix FM, and the details are at **8.3.8**.

8.10.2.6 Decision on application

If the applicant meets the requirements for entry clearance as a parent, he will be granted entry clearance for an initial period not exceeding 33 months and subject to a condition of no recourse to public funds.

8.10.3 Leave to remain

8.10.3.1 Who can apply?

There are five different situations to be considered here, namely:

(a)   where an applicant entered the UK as a parent under Appendix FM and now seeks an extension of his limited leave for a further 30 months;

(b)   where a person entered the UK in a different category, often a partner under Appendix FM, and now applies to switch to this category;

(c)   where a person switched in the UK to this category and now wants an extension of his limited leave for a further 30 months;

(d)   where a person seeks to start on the 10-year family route to settlement under Appendix FM by relying on his Article 8 ECHR rights under para EX.1 (see **8.5**). This application might be made, for example, by an overstayer with no partner in the UK but a child, and who otherwise faces administrative removal from the UK (see **10.4**);

(e)   where a person is on the 10-year family route to settlement under Appendix FM and now seeks an extension of his limited leave for a further 30 months.

8.10.3.2 An overview of the requirements

The requirements to be met for limited leave to remain as a parent (see para R-LTRPT.1.1) are that:

(a)   the applicant and the child must be in the UK;

(b)   the applicant must have made a valid application for limited leave to remain as a parent; and either

(c)   (i)   the applicant must not fall for refusal under Section S-LTR: Suitability – leave to remain (see **8.10.3.3**), and

　　　(ii)   the applicant must meet all of the requirements of Section E-LTRPT: Eligibility for leave to remain as a parent (see **8.10.3.4**), and

　　　(iii)   para EX.1 (see **8.5**) has not been applied; or

(d)   (i)   the applicant must not fall for refusal under Section S-LTR: Suitability – leave to remain, and

　　　(ii)   the applicant meets the eligibility requirements of paras E-LTRPT.2.2–2.4 and E-LTRPT.3.1; and

　　　(iii)   para EX.1 applies.

8.10.3.3   Suitability requirements

Paragraphs S-LTR.1.2–1.7 and S-LTR.2.1–2.4 set out the mandatory and discretionary grounds on which the Home Office will normally refuse an application. These are detailed at **8.4.3**.

8.10.3.4   Overview of eligibility requirements

If an applicant meets all of the eligibility requirements in paras E-LTRPT.1.2–5.2, he may be granted limited leave and proceed on a five-year route to settlement. If he meets the eligibility requirements of paras E-LTRPT.2.2–2.4 and E-LTRPT.3.1, and para EX.1 (see **8.5**) applies, he may be granted limited leave and proceed on a 10-year route to settlement.

The eligibility requirements are as follows:

(a)   relationship requirements (see **8.10.3.5**);

(b)   immigration requirements (see **8.10.3.6**);

(c)   financial requirements (see **8.10.3.7**)

(d)   accommodation requirements (see **8.10.3.8**); and

(e)   English language requirement (see **8.10.3.9**).

8.10.3.5   Relationship requirements

Paragraphs E-LTRPT.2.2–2.4 set out virtually the same relationship requirements as for entry clearance (see **8.10.2.2**). However, note that by para E-LTRPT.2.2 the following additional fourth category of child of the applicant is included, namely, where the child has lived in the UK continuously for at least the seven years immediately preceding the date of application and para EX.1 (see **8.5**) applies.

8.10.3.6   Immigration requirements

Paragraph E-LTRPT.3.1 excludes certain people already in the UK from switching into this category, namely, a visitor (see **Chapter 5**), or a person with valid leave granted for a period of six months or less, or a person on temporary admission (see **3.5.5**).

By para E-LTRPT.3.2, the applicant must not be in the UK in breach of immigration laws (any period of overstaying for a period of 14 days or less may be ignored (see **3.6.5**)), unless para EX. 1 (see **8.5**) applies.

8.10.3.7   Financial requirements

Paragraph E-LTRPT.4.1 set out the same financial requirements as for entry clearance (see **8.10.2.3**), unless para EX. 1 (see **8.5**) applies.

8.10.3.8   Accommodation requirements

Paragraph E-LTRPT.4.2 set out the same accommodation requirements as for entry clearance (see **8.10.2.4**), unless para EX. 1 (see **8.5**) applies.

8.10.3.9   English language requirement

Paragraph E-LTRPT.5.1 set out the same English language requirements as for entry clearance (see **8.10.2.5**), unless para EX. 1 (see **8.5**) applies.

8.10.3.10   Decision on application

If the applicant meets all the requirements for limited leave to remain as a parent, the applicant will be granted limited leave to remain for a period not exceeding 30 months and subject to a condition of no recourse to public funds. The applicant will be eligible to apply for settlement (see **8.10.4**) after a continuous period of at least 60 months with such leave or in the UK with entry clearance as a parent under para D-ECPT.1.1.

If the applicant can meet the suitability requirements, the eligibility requirements of paras E-LTRPT.2.2–2.4 (the relationship requirements at **8.10.3.5**) and E-LTRPT.3.1 (the first immigration requirement at **8.10.3.6**), and para EX.1 (see **8.5**) applies, he will be granted leave to remain for a period not exceeding 30 months. He will be eligible to apply for settlement (see **8.10.4**) after a continuous period of at least 120 months with such leave, with limited leave as a parent under para D-LTRPT.1.1, or in the UK with entry clearance as a parent under para D-ECPT.1.1.

8.10.4   Indefinite leave to remain (settlement) as a parent

8.10.4.1   Who can apply?

There are two different situations to be considered here, namely:

(a)   where a person has completed the five-year route to settlement, ie two periods of 30 months' leave as a parent; and

(b)   where a person has completed the 10-year route to settlement, ie four periods of 30 months' leave as a parent.

8.10.4.2   An overview of the requirements

The requirements in Appendix FM to be met for indefinite leave to remain as a parent (see para E-ILRPT.1.1) are:

(a)   the applicant must be in the UK;

(b)   the applicant must have made a valid application for indefinite leave to remain as a parent;

(c)   the applicant must not fall for refusal under any of the grounds in Section S-LTR: Suitability – leave to remain (see **8.4.3**);

(d)   the applicant must meet all of the requirements of Section E-LTRPT: Eligibility for leave to remain as a parent **(see 8.10.3.4)**; and

(e)   the applicant must meet all of the requirements of Section E-ILRPT: Eligibility for indefinite leave to remain as a parent (see **8.10.4.3**).

8.10.4.3   Eligibility requirements for indefinite leave to remain

By para E-ILRPT.1.2, the applicant must be in the UK with valid leave to remain as a parent (any period of overstaying for 14 days or less may be ignored (see **3.6.5**)).

Paragraph E-ILRPT.1.3 provides that the applicant must have completed a continuous period of at least 60 months with limited leave as a parent (under paras R-LTRPT.1.1.(a)–(c) or in the UK with entry clearance as a parent under para D-ECPT.1.1), or a continuous period of at least 120 months with limited leave as a parent (under paras R-LTRPT.1.1(a), (b) and (d) or in the UK with entry clearance as a parent under para D-ECPT.1.1) or a continuous period of at least 120 months with limited leave as a partner under a combination of these paragraphs.

By para E-ILRPT.1.4, the applicant must at the date of application have no unspent convictions (see **Appendix 8** and **8.10.4.4**).

Paragraph E-ILRPT.1.5 requires the applicant to have sufficient knowledge of the English language and sufficient knowledge about life in the UK (see **3.8.7** and **8.10.4.4**).

8.10.4.4   Decision on the application

By para D-ILRPT.1.1, if the applicant meets all of the requirements listed at **8.10.4.2**, he will be granted indefinite leave to remain unless para EX.1 applies. Where para EX.1 applies, the applicant will be granted further limited leave to remain as a parent for a period not exceeding 30 months under para D-ILRPT.1.2 (see immediately below).

But what if the applicant cannot meet all the requirements? Paragraph D-ILRPT.1.2 has a limited concession. It provides that if the applicant does not meet the requirements for indefinite leave to remain as a parent only for one or both of the following reasons:

(a)   the applicant has an unspent conviction; and/or

(b)   the applicant does not have sufficient knowledge of the English language and sufficient knowledge about life in the UK;

then the applicant will be granted further limited leave to remain as a parent for a period not exceeding 30 months and subject to a condition of no recourse to public funds.

Where an applicant is granted further limited leave under para D-ILRPT.1.2, he should be advised that should the reason at (a) and/or (b) be overcome, he can make a further application for settlement at any time within the 30-month period.

The application will be refused if the applicant does not meet the requirements for indefinite leave to remain as a parent, or further leave to remain as a parent under para D-ILRPT.1.2.

8.11   ADULT DEPENDENT RELATIVES ENTERING FOR IMMEDIATE SETTLEMENT

8.11.1   Who can apply?

The purpose of this route is to allow an adult dependent relative of a British citizen in the UK, a person settled in the UK, or a person in the UK with refugee leave or humanitarian protection, to enter and settle. On what basis? It must be demonstrated that the applicant, as a result of age, illness or disability, requires a level of long-term personal care that can only be provided in the UK by his relative here and without recourse to public funds.

Note that the applicant's qualifying relative in the UK is known as his 'sponsor'.

Not all relatives can apply. Only the sponsor's parent aged 18 years or over; grandparent; brother or sister aged 18 years or over; and son or daughter aged 18 years or over are able to apply.

Note that this route is available only to an applicant outside the UK. A person cannot switch into this route whilst in the UK.

8.11.2   Entry clearance requirements

By para EC-DR.1.1, the requirements to be met for entry clearance as an adult dependent relative are:

(a)   the applicant must be outside the UK;

(b)   the applicant must have made a valid application for entry clearance as an adult dependent relative;

(c)   the applicant must not fall for refusal under any of the grounds in Section S-EC: Suitability for entry clearance (see **8.3.3**); and

(d)   the applicant must meet all of the requirements of Section E-ECDR: Eligibility for entry clearance as an adult dependent relative (see **8.11.3**).

8.11.3   Eligibility requirements in outline

To meet the eligibility requirements for entry clearance as an adult dependent relative all of the requirements in paras E-ECDR.2.1–3.2 must be met. Broadly these are:

(a)   relationship requirements (see **8.11.4**);

(b)   care needs requirements (see **8.11.5**);

(c)   financial requirements (see **8.11.6**).

The requirements are compatible with Article 8 of the ECHR: see R *(on the application of Britcits) v Secretary of State for the Home Department* [2016] EWHC 956 (Admin).

8.11.4 Relationship requirements

By para E-ECDR.2.1, the applicant must be related to the sponsor in the UK in one of the following ways:

(a)   a parent aged 18 years or over;

(b)   a grandparent;

(c)   a brother or sister aged 18 years or over; or

(d)   a son or daughter aged 18 years or over.

Note that para E-ECDR.2.2 provides that if the applicant is the sponsor's parent or grandparent, he must not be in a subsisting relationship with a partner unless that partner is also the sponsor's parent or grandparent and is applying for entry clearance at the same time as the applicant.

Evidence of the family relationship should normally take the form of birth or adoption certificates.

By para E-ECDR.2.3, the sponsor must at the date of application be:

(a)   aged 18 years or over; and

(b)   (i)   a British citizen in the UK; or

     (ii)   present and settled in the UK; or

     (iii) in the UK with refugee leave (see **9.8**) or humanitarian protection (see **9.10.1**).

8.11.5 Care needs requirements

By para E-ECDR.2.4, the applicant (or, if the applicant and his partner are the sponsor's parents or grandparents, the applicant's partner) must, as a result of age, illness or disability, require long-term personal care to perform everyday tasks.

Home Office guidance is that everyday tasks include washing, dressing and cooking. In *Osman v ECO* (2013) Appeal Number: OA/18244/2012, the Upper Tribunal stated at [31] that the phrase has a wider meaning and includes, for example, the management of an individual's bodily functions, difficulties with mobility and communication. The inability to carry out these tasks may have started recently, eg due to a serious accident resulting in long-term incapacity, or it could be the result of deterioration in the applicant's condition over several years.

By para 34 of Appendix FM-SE, medical evidence that the applicant's physical or mental condition means that he cannot perform everyday tasks must be obtained from a doctor or other health professional. Note that paras 36–39 of the Immigration Rules give the ECO the power to refer the applicant for a medical examination, and to require that this is undertaken by a doctor or other health professional on a list approved by the British Embassy or High Commission.

Paragraph E-ECDR.2.5 provides that the applicant (or, if the applicant and his partner are the sponsor's parents or grandparents, the applicant's partner) must be unable, even with the practical and financial help of the sponsor, to obtain the required level of care in the country where he is living, because:

(a)   it is not available and there is no person in that country who can reasonably provide it; or

(b)   it is not affordable.

As to (a), Home Office guidance is that the ECO should consider whether there is anyone in the country where the applicant is living who can reasonably provide the required level of care. This might be a close family member such as a son, daughter, brother, sister, parent, grandchild or grandparent. But it can include any person who is able to provide care, eg a home-help, housekeeper, nurse, carer, or care or nursing home. If an applicant has more than one close relative in the country where he is living, those relatives may be able to pool resources to provide the required care.

The ECO should bear in mind any relevant cultural factors, such as in countries where women are unlikely to be able to provide support.

Evidence that the required level of care is not, or is no longer, available in the country where the applicant is living could be obtained from a central or local health authority, a local authority, or a doctor or other health professional. If the required care has been provided through a private arrangement, the applicant must provide details of that arrangement and why it is no longer available. See paras 35 and 36 of Appendix FM-SE.

In the *Osman* case, the Upper Tribunal stated at [33] that:

> This latter requirement undoubtedly imposes a significant burden of proof upon an individual to show that the required level of care is not available and no one can reasonably provide it in the individual's country. An example where that latter requirement might well be satisfied would be where the 'required level of care' needed requires a particular type of carer, for example a close family member, none of whom live in the individual's country. The evidence would have to establish, in such a case, the need for a particular type of carer such as a family member and not simply that the individual required personal care from someone. In many circumstances, the 'required level of care' to perform such everyday tasks as cooking, washing, and to assist mobility are likely to be capable of being performed not just by family members who do not live in that individual's country. But, it is equally possible to contemplate, having regard to cultural factors, that needed 'personal care' involving intimate or bodily contact may require a gender-specific carer from the individual's family. What is the 'required level of care' and who may appropriately provide it will depend upon the circumstances and the evidence in any given case.

Further guidance was given by the Court of Appeal in *Britcits v Secretary of State for the Home Department* [2017] EWCA Civ 368 per the Master of the Rolls at [59]:

> ... the provision of care in the home country must be reasonable both from the perspective of the provider and the perspective of the applicant, and the standard of such care must be what is required for that particular applicant. It is possible that insufficient attention has been paid in the past to these considerations, which focus on what care is both necessary and reasonable for the applicant to receive in their home country. Those considerations include issues as to the accessibility and geographical location of the provision of care and the standard of care. They are capable of embracing emotional and psychological requirements verified by expert medical evidence. What is reasonable is, of course, to be objectively assessed.

As to (b), if payment was made for arranging care, Home Office guidance is that the ECO should ask to see records and for an explanation of why this payment cannot continue. If financial support has been provided by the sponsor or other close family in the UK, the ECO should ask for an explanation of why this cannot continue or is no longer sufficient to enable the required level of care to be provided (see para 37 of Appendix FM-SE).

8.11.6   Financial requirements

By para E-ECDR.3.1, the applicant must provide evidence that he can be adequately maintained, accommodated and cared for in the UK by the sponsor without recourse to public funds.

The maintenance and accommodation requirements are similar to those for partners under Appendix FM, and are detailed at **8.3.6.10** and **8.3.7** respectively. However, in addition the ECO must be satisfied that the required level of care can and will be met by the sponsor in the UK without recourse to public funds.

Note that by para E-ECDR.3.2, if the applicant's sponsor is a British citizen or settled in the UK, the applicant must provide an undertaking signed by the sponsor confirming that the applicant will have no recourse to public funds, and that the sponsor will be responsible for his maintenance, accommodation and care, for a period of five years from the date the applicant enters the UK if he is granted indefinite leave to enter.

Home Office guidance is that maintenance may be provided by the sponsor, or by any combination of the funds available to the sponsor and the applicant. So if the applicant has a partner, their joint capital and income resources may be taken into account. However, the prospects of employment or better paid employment do not count. Promises of third party support will not be accepted, as these are vulnerable to a change in another person's circumstances or in the sponsor's or the applicant's relationship with that party. Cash savings which have originated in a gift (not a loan) from a third party may count towards the required maintenance, but those cash savings must be in an account in the name of the sponsor or the applicant and under that person's control.

What evidence should the sponsor provide? Home Office guidance is:

(a)   original bank statements covering the last six months;

(b)   other evidence of income – such as pay slips, income from savings, shares and bonds – covering the last six months;

(c)   relevant information on outgoings, eg council tax, utilities, etc, and on support for anyone else who is dependent on the sponsor;

(d)   a copy of a mortgage or tenancy agreement showing ownership or occupancy of a property; and

(e)   planned care arrangements for the applicant in the UK (which can involve other family members in the UK) and the cost of these (which must be met by the sponsor, without undertakings of third party support).

It can be seen from (e) above that the sponsor would be well advised to provide the applicant with a detailed written care plan to be submitted with the application. This should set out who will provide the care in the UK (which can include other family members) and any associated costs of doing so. The ECO must be satisfied that these care arrangements are adequate, so suitable cross-referencing should be made to the level of care required as detailed in the supporting medical evidence (see **8.11.5**).

8.11.7   Home Office example scenarios taken from guidance

Example 1

A person (aged 25) has a learning disability that means he cannot feed, wash or dress himself. His parents have recently died in an accident and his only surviving close relative is a brother in the UK who has been sending money to the family for some time. The person has been cared for temporarily by family friends since his parents' death, but they are no longer able to do this. The sponsor is unable to meet the costs of full-time residential care, but he and his family have sufficient financial and other means to care for the applicant in their home. **This could meet the criteria if the applicant can demonstrate that he is unable even with the practical and financial help of the sponsor to obtain the required level of care in the country where he is living because it not available and there is no person in that country who can reasonably provide it or it is not affordable and other relevant criteria are met.**

Example 2

A person (aged 30) has lived alone in Sri Lanka for many years. His parents are settled in the UK; other siblings live in the UK and USA. The person has recently been involved in a road accident and as a result has developed a long-term condition which means that he can no longer care for himself. The mother has been visiting Sri Lanka to care for her son, but needs to return to the UK to care for her younger children. **This could meet the criteria if the applicant can demonstrate that he is unable even with the practical and financial help of the sponsor to obtain the required level of care in Sri Lanka where he is living because it not** available and there is no person in that country who can reasonably provide it or it is not affordable and other relevant criteria are met.

Example 3

A husband and wife (both aged 70) live in Pakistan. Their daughter lives in the UK. The wife requires long-term personal care owing to ill health and cannot perform everyday tasks for herself. The husband is in good health, but cannot provide his wife with the level of care she needs. They both want to come and live in the UK. The daughter can care for her mother full time in her home as she does not work whilst her husband provides the family with an income from his employment. Her sister in the UK will also help with care of the mother. The applicant provides the ECO with the planned care arrangements in the UK. **This could meet the criteria if the applicant can demonstrate that she is unable even with the practical and financial help of her sponsor to obtain the required level of care in Pakistan because it not available and there is no person in that country who can reasonably provide it or it is not affordable and other relevant criteria are met.**

8.11.8 Decision on application

By para D-ECDR.1.1, if the applicant meets the requirements for entry clearance as an adult dependent relative of a British citizen or person settled in the UK, he will be granted indefinite leave to enter.

Paragraph D-ECDR.1.2 provides that if the applicant meets the requirements for entry clearance as an adult dependent relative and the sponsor has limited leave as a refugee or with humanitarian protection, the applicant will be granted limited leave of a duration which will expire at the same time as the sponsor's limited leave. This will be subject to a condition of no recourse to public funds. If the sponsor applies for further limited leave, the applicant may apply for further limited leave of the same duration, if the requirements in para EC-DR.1.1(c) and (d) (see **8.11.2**) continue to be met (again subject to no recourse to public funds). In due course an application could be made for settlement – see Section R-ILRDR of Appendix FM.

8.12 CHILD ENTERING WITH OR TO JOIN A PARENT WHO HAS LIMITED LEAVE

8.12.1 Where parent has limited leave as a partner or parent under Appendix FM

8.12.1.1 Entry clearance

By para EC-C.1.1, the requirements to be met for entry clearance as a child are:

(a)   the applicant must be outside the UK;

(b)   the applicant must have made a valid application for entry clearance as a child;

(c)   the applicant must not fall for refusal under any of the grounds in Section S-EC: Suitability for entry clearance; and

(d)   the applicant must meet all of the requirements of Section E-ECC: Eligibility for entry clearance as a child.

Note that the suitability requirements are the same as for a partner under Appendix FM, and these are detailed at **8.3.3**. As to the eligibility requirements, see **8.12.1.2**.

8.12.1.2 Eligibility requirements in outline

To meet the eligibility requirements for entry clearance as a child, all of the requirements of para E-ECC.1.2–2.4 must be met. Broadly these are:

(a)   relationship requirements (see **8.12.1.3**);

(b)   financial requirements (see **8.12.1.4**);

(c)   accommodation requirements (see **8.12.1.5**).

8.12.1.3 Relationship requirements

By para E-ECC.1.2, the applicant must be under the age of 18 at the date of application.

Paragraph E-ECC.1.3 provides that the applicant must not be married or in a civil partnership.

By para E-ECC.1.4, the applicant must not have formed an independent family unit.

Paragraph E-ECC.1.5 provides that the applicant must not be leading an independent life. See further **8.9.4.6**.

By para E-ECC.1.6, one of the applicant's parents must be in the UK with limited leave to enter or remain, or be applying, or have applied, for entry clearance as a partner (see **8.3**) or a parent (see **8.10**) under Appendix FM (the 'applicant's parent') and (a) the applicant's parent's partner is also a parent of the applicant or (b) the applicant's parent has had and continues to have sole responsibility for the child's upbringing (see **8.9.4.3**) or (c) there are serious and compelling family or other considerations which make exclusion of the child undesirable and suitable arrangements have been made for the child's care (see **8.9.4.4**).

8.12.1.4 Financial requirement

The equivalent provision for partners under Appendix FM applies, as detailed at **8.3.6**.

8.12.1.5 Accommodation requirements

The equivalent provision for partners under Appendix FM applies, as detailed at **8.3.6**.

8.12.1.6 Decision on application

If the applicant meets the requirements for entry clearance as a child, he will be granted entry clearance of a duration which will expire at the same time as the leave granted to the applicant's parent and subject to a condition of no recourse to public funds.

8.12.1.7 Leave to remain and settlement

When the applicant's parent applies for further leave to remain and settlement, the applicant should do so as well.

As to leave to remain, see generally Section R-LTRC, para 1.1 of Appendix A. As to settlement, see **8.6** and **8.10.4**.

8.12.2 Other provisions applying to children of parents with limited leave

There are separate requirements applying to children of a parent (or parents) in each of the other categories of limited leave already covered in this book.

8.13 PRIVATE LIFE IN THE UK

8.13.1 Limited leave to remain

8.13.1.1 Who can apply?

A person who has lived in the UK for at least 20 years continuously, lawfully or unlawfully, can apply to the Home Office for leave to remain in the UK on the basis of the Article 8 ECHR right to respect for private life. Alternative provisions allow an applicant to be granted limited leave to remain in the UK on the basis of private life after seven years' continuous residence if he is under the age of 18; or if he has spent at least half of his life in the UK if he is aged between 18 and 24; or if the applicant has less than 20 years' continuous residence in the UK but there would be very significant obstacles to the applicant's integration into his country of origin.

Most commonly an application will be made as an alternative to an asylum claim (see **Chapter 9**) and when opposing the administrative removal (see **10.4**) of the applicant.

8.13.1.2   Requirements for leave to remain

By para 276ADE(i)–(vi) of the Immigration Rules, the requirements to be met by an applicant for leave to remain on the grounds of private life in the UK are that at the date of application, the applicant:

(a)   does not fall for refusal under any of the grounds in Section S-LTR 1.1 to S- LTR 2.2 and S-LTR.3.1 to S-LTR.4.5 in Appendix FM (see **8.4.3**); *and*

(b)   has lived continuously in the UK (see **3.8.8.1**) for at least 20 years (discounting any period of imprisonment); *or*

(c)   is under the age of 18 years and has lived continuously in the UK for at least seven years (discounting any period of imprisonment) and it would not be reasonable to expect him to leave the UK; *or*

(d)   is aged 18 years or above and under 25 years, and has spent at least half of his life living continuously in the UK (discounting any period of imprisonment); *or*

(e)   is aged 18 years or above, has lived continuously in the UK for less than 20 years (discounting any period of imprisonment) but there would be very significant obstacles to the applicant's integration into the country to which he would have to go if required to leave the UK (see **8.13.1.3**).

Note that for the purposes of (c) above, the applicant must meet the seven years requirement at the date of their application: *Koori v Secretary of State for the Home Department* [2016] EWCA Civ 552. Home Office guidance is that the provision reflects the duty in s 55 of the Borders, Citizenship and Immigration Act 2009 to have regard to the need to safeguard and promote the welfare of children. The decision maker must have regard to the best interests of the child as a primary consideration. The guidance stresses that it is not the only or the paramount consideration. So, the decision maker must determine whether refusal of the application will mean or is likely to mean that the child will have to leave the UK, and, if so, whether, taking into account their best interests as a primary consideration, it is reasonable to expect the child to leave the UK. But the focus is not simply on the child but on all aspects of the public interest (see **10.3.4.2**). The decision maker must ask whether, paying proper regard to the best interests of the child and all other relevant considerations bearing on the public interest, including the conduct and immigration history of the applicant's parent or parents, it is not reasonable to expect the child to leave (see *MA (Pakistan) v Upper Tribunal* [2016] EWCA Civ 705, *AM (Pakistan) v Secretary of State for the Home Department* [2017] EWCA Civ 180, *KO (Nigeria) v Secretary of State for the Home Department* [2018] UKSC 53 and *NA (Bangladesh) v Secretary of State for the Home Department* [2021] EWCA Civ 953).

As to (d), being 'under 25 years' means the applicant has not at the date of their application reached their 25th birthday. It does not include an applicant who is aged 25 but has not yet reached their 26th birthday: *BG (Jamaica) v Secretary of State for the Home Department* [2015] EWCA Civ 960.

How does a decision maker assess the length of time that the applicant has resided in the UK? Home Office guidance is that an applicant needs to provide credible evidence from an independent source, for example letters from a housing trust, local authority, bank, school or doctor. The decision maker must be satisfied that the evidence provided has not been tampered with or otherwise falsified, and that it relates to the person who is making the application. In order to be satisfied that the applicant's residence in the UK was continuous, the decision maker should normally expect to see evidence to cover every 12-month period of the length of continuous residence and travel documents to cover the entire period, unless the decision maker is satisfied on the basis of a credible explanation provided as to why this has not been submitted. Note that continuous residence in this context allows for an applicant to be absent from the UK for a period of six months or less at any one time, provided they have existing limited leave to enter or remain on their departure and return.

8.13.1.3 The very significant obstacles to integration ground

As to the ground in para 276ADE(vi)(e) (in **8.13.1.2** above), how should a decision maker assess this? Home Office guidance is that the starting point is to assume that the applicant will be able to integrate into his country of return, unless he can demonstrate why that is not the case. The onus is on the applicant to show that there are very significant obstacles to that integration, not on the decision maker to show that there are not.

The decision maker will expect to see original, independent and verifiable documentary evidence of any claims made in this regard, and will place less weight on assertions which are unsubstantiated. Where it is not reasonable to expect corroborating evidence to be provided, consideration will be given to the credibility of the applicant's claims.

The Home Office states that a very significant obstacle to integration means something which would prevent or seriously inhibit the applicant from integrating into the country of return. The decision maker is looking for more than the existence of obstacles but whether those are 'very significant' obstacles. This is a high threshold. Very significant obstacles will exist where the applicant demonstrates that he would be unable to establish a private life in the country of return, or where establishing a private life in the country of return would entail very serious hardship for the applicant.

The decision maker must consider all the reasons put forward by the applicant as to why there would be obstacles to his integration in the country of return. These reasons must be considered individually and cumulatively to assess whether there are very significant obstacles to integration. In considering whether there are very significant obstacles to integration, the decision maker should consider whether the applicant has the ability to form an adequate private life by the standards of the country of return and not by UK standards. The decision maker will need to consider whether the applicant will be able to establish a private life in respect of all its essential elements, even if, for example, his job, or his ability to find work, or his network of friends and relationships may be differently constituted in the country of return.

The fact that the applicant may find life difficult or challenging in the country of return does not mean that there are very significant obstacles to integration. The decision maker must consider all relevant factors in the person's background and the conditions he is likely to face in the country of return.

The decision maker will need to consider the specific obstacles raised by the applicant. He will also need to set these against other factors in order to make an assessment in the individual case. Relevant considerations set out in Home Office guidance include the following:

(a) *Cultural background.* Is there evidence of the applicant's exposure to and level of understanding of the cultural norms in the country of return? Where the person has spent his time in the UK living mainly amongst a diaspora community from that country, then it may be reasonable to conclude that he has cultural ties with that country even if he has never lived there or has been absent from that country for a lengthy period. If the applicant has cultural ties with the country of return, then it is likely that it would be possible for him to establish a private life there. Even if there are no cultural ties, the cultural norms of that country may be such that there are no barriers to integration.

(b) *Length of time spent in the country of return.* Where the applicant has spent a significant period of time in the country of return, it will be difficult for him to demonstrate that there would be very significant obstacles to integration into that country. The decision maker must consider the proportion of the person's life spent in that country and the stage of life the person was at when in that country.

(c) *Family, friends and social network.* An applicant who has family or friends in the country of return should be able to turn to them for support to help him to integrate into that country. The decision maker must consider whether the applicant or his family have sponsored or hosted visits in the UK by family or friends from the country of return, or the applicant has visited family or friends in the country of return.

The decision maker must consider the quality of any relationships with family or friends in the country of return, but they do not have to be strong familial ties and can include ties that could be strengthened if the person were to return.

The Home Office guidance includes the following examples of common claims made under this provision:

(a)   That the applicant has no friends or family members in the country of return. Where there are no family, friends or social networks in the country of return, that is not in itself a very significant obstacle to integration. Why? Because many people successfully migrate to countries where they have no ties.

(b)   If there are particular circumstances in the applicant's case which mean that he would need assistance to integrate, it will also be relevant to consider whether there are any organisations in the country of return which may be able to assist with integration.

(c)   That the applicant has never lived in the country of return or only spent early years there. If an applicant has never lived in the country of return, or only spent his early years there, this will not necessarily mean that there are very significant obstacles preventing him from integrating, particularly if he can speak a language of that country, eg if the country of return is one where English is spoken or if a language of the country was spoken at home when he was growing up. For these purposes, fluency is not required – conversational level language skills or a basic level of language which could be improved on return would be sufficient. The cultural norms of the country and how easy it is for the person to adapt to them will also be relevant.

(d)   That the applicant cannot speak any language spoken in the country of return. Where there is credible evidence that an applicant cannot speak any language which is spoken in the country of return, this will not in itself be a very significant obstacle to integration unless he can also show that he would be unable to learn a language of that country, for example because of a mental or physical disability.

(e)   That the applicant would have no employment prospects on return. Lack of employment prospects is very unlikely to be a very significant obstacle to integration. In assessing a claim that an absence of employment prospects would prevent an applicant from integrating in the country of return, his circumstances on return should be compared to the conditions that prevail in that country and to the circumstances of the general population, not to his circumstances in the UK.

Less weight will be given to generalised claims about country conditions that have not been particularised to take account of the applicant's individual circumstances.

(f)   The applicant's private life in the UK. The degree of private life an individual has established in the UK is not relevant to the consideration of whether there are very serious obstacles to integration into the country of return. However, this will be relevant to the consideration of whether, where the applicant falls for refusal under the Immigration Rules, there are exceptional circumstances which would make refusal unjustifiably harsh for the applicant.

8.13.1.4   Decision on application

By para 276BE, limited leave to remain on the grounds of private life in the UK may be granted for a period not exceeding 30 months if the requirements in para 276ADE are met (or, in respect of the requirements in para 276ADE(iv) and (v) ((c) and (d) in **8.13.1.2**), were met in a previous application which led to a grant of limited leave to remain under this para). The applicant may be able to apply for further periods of leave in this category and settlement after 120 months (see **8.13.2**).

What if one or more requirement in para 276ADE is not met? Home Office guidance is that the decision maker should consider whether there are any exceptional circumstances (see **8.13.1.5**) which would make refusal and the removal of the applicant from the UK a breach of Article 8 ECHR.

8.13.1.5 Exceptional circumstances

If the requirements in para 276ADE (see **8.13.1.2**) are not met, what exceptional circumstances would make refusal and the requirement for the applicant to leave the UK a breach of Article 8 ECHR? Home Office guidance is that the decision maker should determine whether removal would have such severe consequences for the individual that refusal of the application and his removal from the UK would not be proportionate given the nature of his private life. The Home Office states that this will rarely be the case.

In determining whether a case is exceptional, the decision maker must consider all relevant factors, such as:

(a) The best interests of any child in the UK affected by the decision.

(b) The nature of the family relationships involved, such as the length of the applicant's marriage and how frequently he has contact with his children if they do not live with him. What evidence is there that the couple do or do not have a genuine family life?

(c) The immigration status of the applicant and his family members. The decision maker should take into account the circumstances around the applicant's entry to the UK and the proportion of the time he has been in the UK legally as opposed to illegally. Did he form his relationship with his partner at a time when he was in the UK unlawfully? Family life formed in the knowledge that his stay here is unlawful should be given less weight (when weighed against the public interest in his removal) than family life formed by a person lawfully present in the UK.

(d) The nationalities of the applicant and his family members. The nationality of any child of an applicant is a matter of particular importance given the intrinsic importance of citizenship, and the advantages of growing up and being educated in their own country.

(e) How long the applicant and his family members have lawfully lived in the UK, and how strong their social, cultural and family ties are with the UK.

(f) The likely circumstances the applicant's partner and/or child would face in the applicant's country of return. It is relevant to consider how long the applicant resided in the country of return and what social, cultural and family ties he has retained with that country, as well as the degree of exposure his partner and/or child has had to that country and to its language and culture.

(g) Whether there are any factors which might increase the public interest in removal, for example where the applicant has failed to meet the suitability requirements because of deception or issues around his character or conduct in the UK, or the fact that he does not speak English or is not financially independent.

(h) Cumulative factors should be considered, for example, where the applicant has family members in the UK but his family life does not provide a basis for stay and he has a significant private life in the UK. Although, under the Rules, family life and private life are considered separately, when considering whether there are exceptional circumstances, private and family life should be taken into account.

Cumulative factors weighing in favour of the applicant should be balanced against cumulative factors weighing in the public interest in deciding whether refusal would be unjustifiably harsh for the applicant or his family.

8.13.2 Indefinite leave to remain (settlement)

8.13.2.1 Who can apply?

Once an applicant has been granted four periods of 30 months' limited leave under para 276BE and so spent 10 years in the UK on that basis, he may apply for indefinite leave to remain.

8.13.2.2 Requirements

By para 276DE, the requirements to be met for the grant of indefinite leave to remain on the grounds of private life in the UK are:

(a)   the applicant has been in the UK with continuous leave on the grounds of private life for a period of at least 120 months;

(b)   the applicant meets the requirements of para 276ADE (see **8.13.1.2**);

(c)   the applicant does not fall for refusal under the general grounds for refusal (see **3.5.4**);

(d)   the applicant has sufficient knowledge of the English language and sufficient knowledge about life in the UK by passing the test known as the 'Life in the UK Test' (see **3.8.7 and 8.10.4.4**), unless the applicant is under the age of 18 or aged 65 or over at the time the applicant makes the application; and

(e)   there are no reasons why it would be undesirable to grant the applicant indefinite leave to remain based on the applicant's conduct, character or associations, or because the applicant represents a threat to national security.

8.13.2.3 Decision on the application

By para 276DF, if the applicant meets all of the requirements at **8.13.2.2** he will be granted indefinite leave to remain.

But what if the applicant cannot meet all the requirements? Paragraph 276DG has a limited concession. It provides that if the applicant does not meet the requirements for indefinite leave to remain only for one or both of the following reasons:

(a)   para S-ILR.1.5 or 1.6 applies (see **8.6.2(c)**); and/or

(b)   the applicant does not have sufficient knowledge of the English language and sufficient knowledge about life in the UK;

then the applicant may be granted further limited leave to remain on the grounds of private life in the UK for a period not exceeding 30 months.

Where an applicant is granted further limited leave under para 276DG, he should be advised that should the reason at (a) and/or (b) above be overcome, he can make a further application for settlement at any time within the 30-month period.

The application will be refused if the applicant does not meet the requirements for indefinite leave to remain, or further leave to remain on the grounds of private life in the UK under para 276DG.

8.14 CLAIMS UNDER ARTICLE 8 ECHR

What is the position if an application for entry clearance or limited leave to remain as a partner or child under Appendix FM does not meet the minimum income requirement (see **8.3.6**)? Normally, the application is refused unless the applicant is exempt from the requirement (see **8.3.6.9**). But what if otherwise the refusal of the application could result in unjustifiably harsh consequences for the applicant, his or her partner or a relevant child? In these exceptional circumstances, the decision maker will consider other credible and reliable sources of income, financial support or funds available to the couple in order to assess whether the minimum income requirement under Appendix FM is met (see **8.3.6.8**).

What if any other applicant for entry clearance or limited leave to remain under Appendix FM, for example a parent of a child settled in the UK (see **8.10**) or an adult dependent relative (see **8.11**), cannot meet the usual requirements? Again, the decision maker must go on to consider if there are exceptional circumstances arising if the refusal of the application could result in unjustifiably harsh consequences for the applicant, his or her partner or a relevant child. Note, however, that this provision does not apply to an application for leave to remain as a bereaved partner (see **8.7**) or a victim of domestic violence (see **8.8**).

So, what is meant by 'exceptional circumstances'? Home Office guidance is that 'exceptional' does not mean unusual or unique. For example, a case is not exceptional just because the criteria set out in the Immigration Rules have been missed by a small margin. It means circumstances in which refusal of the application could or would result in unjustifiably harsh consequences for the individual or his or her family such that refusal would not be proportionate under Article 8.

So, what are 'unjustifiably harsh consequences'? Home Office guidance is that, in the context of entry clearance, a key question in the assessment, taking into account as a primary consideration the best interests of any relevant child, will be: why can't the UK partner go or remain overseas to continue or maintain his or her family life with the applicant? Alternatively, is it proportionate to expect the family to separate or for existing separation to be maintained? The following factors may affect the answer to those questions:

(a)   the best interests of a relevant child (see below);

(b)   the ability to lawfully remain in or enter another country;

(c)   the nature and extent of the family relationships involved;

(d)   where relevant, the circumstances giving rise to the applicant being separated from his or her partner and or/child in the UK;

(e)   the likely impact on the applicant, his or her partner and/or child if the application is refused;

(f)   serious cultural barriers to relocation overseas;

(g)   the impact of a mental or physical disability or of a serious illness which requires ongoing medical treatment;

(h)   the absence of governance or security in another country;

(i)   the immigration status of the applicant and his or her family members; and

(j)   whether there are any factors which might increase the public interest in refusal.

In conducting this assessment, the decision maker must have regard to all of the information and evidence provided by the applicant and take into account, as a primary consideration, the best interests of any relevant child. The Supreme Court determined, in *ZH (Tanzania) v Secretary of State for the Home Department* [2011] UKSC 4, that the 'best interests of the child' broadly means their well-being, but their interests are not necessarily determinative and can be outweighed by public interest considerations. The Court also indicated that whilst British citizenship is not a 'trump card', it is of particular importance in assessing the best interests of a child. So, the decision maker will normally consider:

(a)   the age of the child at the date of application;

(b)   the child's nationality;

(c)   the child's current country of residence and length of residence there;

(d)   the family circumstances in which the child is living;

(e)   the physical circumstances in which the child is living.

(f)   the child's relationships with his or her parent(s) overseas and in the UK;

(g)   how long the child has been in education and what stage his or her education has reached;

(h)   the child's health;

(i)   the child's connection with the country outside the UK in which his or her parents are, or one of his or her parents is, currently living or where the child is likely to live if the child's parents leave the UK; and

(j)   the extent to which the decision will interfere with the child's family or private life.

ASYLUM-SEEKERS AND REFUGEES

9.1 OVERVIEW

People may flee their own countries for many different reasons – social, economic, political, religious, etc. On arrival in the UK or subsequently, they may claim that they do not wish to return to their country of nationality or habitual residence.

An asylum-seeker is a person who flees because of a fear of persecution in his own country and who, as a consequence, is seeking the protection of the UK Government. Such protection is granted if that person is given the immigration status of a refugee. Otherwise, on human rights grounds, he may be granted what is known as humanitarian protection or discretionary leave (see **9.10**).

9.2 LAW AND PROCEDURE

9.2.1 Relevant law

Set out below is a list of the key legal provisions referred to in this chapter:

(a) The United Nations' 1951 Convention and 1967 Protocol Relating to the Status of Refugees (generally known as 'the Refugee Convention').

(b) UNHCR *Handbook on Procedures and Criteria for Determining Refugee Status.*

(c) Parts 11 and 11B of the Immigration Rules.

(d) The Refugee or Person in Need of International Protection (Qualification) Regulations 2006 (SI 2006/2525) ('Qualification Regulations 2006'). A copy is reproduced at **Appendix 13.**

(e) UK and ECHR case law.

(f) Home Office asylum policy instructions and process guidance.

9.2.2 Procedure

Asylum claims are dealt with by the Home Office. Those who wish to have a detailed understanding of the procedures should consult the Home Office guidance, issued to its asylum staff and published on its website (see **1.2.8**).

Anyone in the UK can make an asylum claim, whatever his immigration status. He may be someone who has arrived without a visa or with forged documents, or someone who has obtained limited leave to enter for a different reason (eg as a visitor), an overstayer, or even an illegal entrant. The claim can be made on entry or after entry to the UK.

Government policy is not to allow asylum seekers to work whilst their claim is being considered. Instead, they are encouraged to volunteer whilst their claim is being considered. However, the Home Office may grant permission to work to a claimant whose claim has been outstanding for more than 12 months through no fault of their own.

9.3 WHAT IS AN ASYLUM CLAIM?

9.3.1 The Refugee Convention

The Immigration Rules, para 327 defines an applicant for asylum as a person who makes a request to be recognised as a refugee under the Refugee Convention on the basis that it would be contrary to the UK's obligations under that Convention for him to be removed from or required to leave the UK, or otherwise makes a request for international protection.

To be granted asylum, or the status of a refugee, a claimant must meet the following requirements as set out in Article 1 A. of the Refugee Convention:

> [The claimant,] owing to well-founded fear of being persecuted for reasons of race, religion, nationality, membership of a particular social group or political opinion, is outside the country of his nationality and is unable or, owing to such fear, is unwilling to avail himself of the protection of that country; or who, not having a nationality and being outside the country of his former habitual residence ... is unable, or owing to such fear, is unwilling to return to it.

By para 334 of the Immigration Rules, an asylum applicant will be granted asylum in the UK if the Secretary of State is satisfied that:

(a) he is in the UK or has arrived at a port of entry in the UK;

(b) he is a refugee falling within Article 1 A. (see **9.4**) and not excluded (see **9.5.1**);

(c) there are no reasonable grounds for regarding him as a danger to the security of the UK (see **9.5.2**);

(d) he does not, having been convicted by a final judgment of a particularly serious crime, constitute danger to the community of the UK (see **9.5.2**); and

(e) refusing his application would result in his being required to go (whether immediately or after the time limited by any existing leave to enter or remain) in breach of the Refugee Convention, to a country in which his life or freedom would be threatened on account of his race, religion, nationality, political opinion or membership of a particular social group.

9.3.2 Sources of persecution

Before we look in detail at each requirement of Article 1 A., and in particular at what may amount to persecution, we shall consider the possible source of that fear. It might be the government or State itself. Legislation may discriminate against or persecute a certain group, for example, laws may discriminate against women or homosexuals. Or the persecution might come from State bodies, like the police or the army, acting on government orders. Additionally, there may be persecution if the State fails to take steps to protect its citizens from officials who abuse their authority. This might include, for example, a policeman who rapes a woman for his own sexual gratification.

A person may also fear being persecuted by people who have nothing to do with the government. These are known as non-State actors (see further **9.4.1.5**). Common examples concern political or religious intolerance, such as where one section of society does not respect the political or religious beliefs of another. Here we need to remember that part of the Refugee Convention test is that the claimant is unwilling to avail himself of the protection of his country. The question is whether or not the State has a system of criminal law which makes attacks by non-State actors punishable *and* if the State is prepared to take reasonable steps to enforce that law.

9.4 MEETING THE REQUIREMENTS OF THE REFUGEE CONVENTION

9.4.1 Well-founded fear of persecution

9.4.1.1 Subjective and objective tests

The claimant must be in fear of persecution, but his claim can be rejected if there is no real risk or reasonable likelihood of persecution (R *v Secretary of State for the Home Department, ex p Sivakumaran and conjoined appeals (UN High Commissioner for Refugees Intervening)* [1988] 1 All ER 193). The main issue will be the credibility of the claimant's testimony (see also **9.6.2**) that he has a genuine fear (the subjective test), but the Home Office may rely on evidence of conditions in the country from which he is fleeing to show that there is insufficient basis for the fear (the objective test). The Home Office Country of Origin Information Service has produced assessments of certain countries that produce a significant number of asylum claims. These are used for background purposes by decision makers (see further **9.7**).

In some cases applicants may be able to provide some documentary evidence to support their claims, such as newspaper or Internet articles, passports or identity cards, political party membership cards, arrest warrants, photographs and medical reports. Organisations such as Amnesty International and the US Department of State (country reports) may be able to provide helpful evidence. As to medical evidence of torture, an applicant may be able to obtain a report from the charity Medical Foundation for the Care of Victims of Torture (see www.torturecare.org.uk). This organisation provides medical and social care, practical assistance and therapy to survivors of torture. If the applicant is already seeing a doctor or consultant, he may be able to provide a report.

Medical evidence of injury or scarring

When obtaining medical evidence of a claimant's injuries or scarring, it is important that the expert assesses how they were caused: see SA *(Somalia)* [2006] EWCA Civ 1302 and RT *(medical reports, cause of scarring) Sri Lanka* [2008] UKAIT 00009. Where the expert makes findings that there is a degree of consistency between the injuries or scarring and the claimant's allegations as to how they were caused by his persecutors, the expert should also include any other possible causes (whether many, few or unusually few), and gauge how likely they are, bearing in mind what is known about the individual's life history and experiences. Where possible an expert should be instructed in accordance with para 187 of the 'Manual on the Effective Investigation and Documentation of Torture and Other Cruel, Inhuman or Degrading Treatment or Punishment', usually known as the 'Istanbul Protocol', submitted to the UN High Commissioner for Human Rights in 1999, to consider the degree of consistency on the following scale:

(1)   *Not consistent*: the injury or scarring could not have been caused as alleged.

(2)   *Consistent with*: the injury or scarring could have been caused as alleged, but it is non-specific and there are many other possible causes.

(3)   *Highly consistent*: the injury or scarring could have been caused as alleged, and there are few other possible causes.

(4)   *Typical of*: this is an appearance that is usually found with this type of injury or scarring, but there are other possible causes.

(5)   *Diagnostic of*: this appearance could not have been caused in any way other than that alleged.

Paragraph 188 of the Istanbul Protocol states that, 'Ultimately, it is the overall evaluation of all lesions and not the consistency of each lesion with a particular form of torture that is important in assessing the torture story.'

> If on examining an applicant for asylum it appears to the medical expert that features of the scarring said to be corroborative of the applicant's account of torture indicate that there are medical issues which cast doubt on that account, it will be the duty of the expert witness to draw these issues to the attention of the Tribunal. For example, that might be because scarring of the kind in question is not compatible with the account given by the applicant of how it was inflicted or because features of the scarring indicate that it was inflicted at a time different from that stated by the applicant. Or if the injury relied upon as corroborative of torture is also familiar to the expert as a kind which is a common sporting injury, that might be the sort of thing which should be mentioned. (per Sales LJ at [95] in *KV (Sri Lanka) v Secretary of State for the Home Department* [2017] EWCA Civ 119)

It will be rare, in the absence of supporting medical evidence and in the face of medical evidence to the contrary, that a decision maker will find scars to have resulted from self-inflicted injuries, particular where somebody medically trained would have had to have been involved by administering anaesthetic and causing the injuries on a part of the body inaccessible to the claimant (see *KV (Sri Lanka) v Secretary of State for the Home Department* [2019] UKSC 10).

Home Office guidance on medical evidence in asylum claims directs its decision makers to give due consideration to the opinion of the medical expert on the degree of consistency between clinical findings and the account of torture or serious harm, on the understanding that this does not impinge on their duty to make an overall finding on credibility. A decision maker must have in mind the approach to assessing the credibility of past events set out in *Karanakaran v Secretary of State for the Home Department* [2000] EWCA Civ 11, which emphasises that evidence must not be excluded where some weight may be attached to it. Medical evidence in support of a claim of torture or serious harm must not be dismissed, or have little or no weight attached to it, when the overall assessment of the credibility of the claim is made. Unless exceptional circumstances apply, less weight will be accorded to evidence from a medical expert who has assessed the applicant's records and never assessed or treated the applicant directly.

9.4.1.2   Benefit of the doubt

Obviously, the applicant may find it difficult to provide evidence of events in his home country and many statements may be unsupported. According to the UNHCR *Handbook*, statements should not necessarily be rejected for that reason: 'If the applicant's account appears credible, he should, unless there are good reasons to the contrary, be given the benefit of the doubt' (para 196). Unsupported statements need not, however, be accepted if they are inconsistent with the general account put forward by the applicant (para 197).

9.4.1.3   Acts of persecution

'Persecution' is not defined in the Refugee Convention. The UNHCR *Handbook* suggests that while it will often involve a threat to life or liberty, it could extend to other threats, such as to the person, livelihood, identity and nationality. Discrimination against a particular group does not of itself amount to persecution; but it may do so if serious, for example if it stops someone practising his religion, or earning a livelihood. 'Persecution' does not mean 'punishment'. A person who fears punishment for commission of a common-law crime will not normally be regarded as a refugee, unless, for example, the law under which he is to be punished is seriously discriminatory.

Further examples of persecution are listed in reg 5(2) of the Qualification Regulations 2006. These include an act of physical or mental violence, including an act of sexual violence; a legal, administrative, police, or judicial measure which in itself is discriminatory, or which is implemented in a discriminatory manner; and prosecution or punishment which is disproportionate or discriminatory.

In R (Sivakumar) v Secretary of State for the Home Department [2003] 2 All ER 1097, the House of Lords held that it is the severity of the treatment inflicted on the applicant that has a logical bearing on the issues. Excessive or arbitrary punishment can amount to persecution. See further the discussion in the Court of Appeal case of MI (Pakistan) v Secretary of State for the Home Department [2014] EWCA Civ 826 at [55]–[58].

Regulation 5(1) of the Qualification Regulations 2006 provides that an act of persecution must be sufficiently serious by its nature or repetition as to constitute a severe violation of a basic human right, in particular a right from which derogation cannot be made under Article 15 ECHR. The basic human rights from which derogation cannot be made under the ECHR include Article 2 (right to life – save that derogation is permitted in respect of deaths resulting from lawful acts of war); Article 3 (prohibition of torture, inhuman or degrading treatment or punishment); Article 4(1) (prohibition of slavery) and Article 7 (no punishment without law). Alternatively, persecution may arise from an accumulation of various measures, including a violation of a human right which is sufficiently severe as to affect an individual in this manner.

A person does not have to be singled out for adverse treatment in order to be said to be persecuted (see R v Secretary of State for the Home Department, ex p Jeyakumaran (Selladurai) [1994] Imm AR 45). Discrimination may amount to persecution – this accords with the Tribunal decision of Padhu (12318), concerning the inability to work and deprivation of State benefits due to ethnic origin. What if the persecution feared comes from non-State actors? In the case of Gashi and Nikshiqi v Secretary of State for the Home Department (United Nations High Commissioner for Refugees Intervening) [1997] INLR 96, the Tribunal held that persecution includes the failure of a State to protect:

(a)   those rights which are non-derogative even in times of compelling national emergency (the right to life; prohibition against torture and cruel, inhumane or degrading treatment);

(b)   those rights which are derogative during an officially recognised life-threatening public emergency (freedom from arbitrary arrest and detention; fair trial);

(c)   some aspects of those rights which require States to take steps to the maximum of their available resources to realise rights progressively in a non-discriminatory manner (the right to earn a livelihood; the right to a basic education; the right to food, housing and medical care).

9.4.1.4   Current fear and past acts of persecution

Whilst there must be a current fear of persecution for a Convention reason upon return (see Adan v Secretary of State for the Home Department [1999] 1 AC 293), persecution suffered in the past is relevant to whether a person has a current, well-founded fear of persecution. This is recognised by para 339K of the Immigration Rules. It provides that the fact that a person has already been subject to persecution, or to direct threats of such persecution, will be regarded as a serious indication of the person's well-founded fear of persecution, unless there are good reasons to consider that such persecution will not be repeated. Equally, whilst a past history of no persecution is not determinative of future risks, unless circumstances in an asylum-seeker's return country have deteriorated or some other special factor is present, it is inevitable that an asylum-seeker will have difficulty in showing future risk in the absence of any finding of past persecution: see Becerikil v Secretary of State for the Home Department [2006] EWCA Civ 693.

9.4.1.5   Persecution by non-State actors

The applicable law as to persecution by non-State actors is the House of Lords' decision in *Horvath v Secretary of State for the Home Department* [2001] 1 AC 489. This established that persecution implied a failure by the State to make protection available against the ill-treatment or violence which had been suffered at the hands of the persecutors. In such a case, the failure of the State to provide protection was an essential element, and accordingly the person claiming refugee status had to show that the feared persecution consisted of acts of violence against which the State was unable or unwilling to provide protection. Such a conclusion was consistent with the principle of surrogacy which underpinned the Convention, namely that the protection afforded by the Convention was activated only upon the failure of protection by the home State. Moreover, the application of that principle rested upon the assumption that the home State was not expected to achieve complete protection against random and isolated attacks.

Accordingly, in determining whether the protection afforded by the applicant's home country was sufficient for the purposes of the Convention, the court had to apply a practical standard which took proper account of the duty owed by a State to all its nationals, rather than a standard which eliminated all risk. Thus, the sufficiency of State protection was to be measured not by the existence of a real risk of an abuse of human rights but by the availability of a system for the protection of the citizen and a reasonable willingness to operate that system. This is now reflected in reg 4 of the Qualification Regulations 2006.

9.4.1.6   Attacks on applicant's family members

Can an attack upon an applicant's spouse or close family member amount to persecution of the applicant for the purposes of an asylum claim, even though there was no direct threat to the applicant himself? 'Yes', said the Court of Appeal in *Frantisek Katrinak v Secretary of State for the Home Department* [2001] INLR 499. As Schiemann LJ said:

> If I return with my wife to a country where there is a reasonable degree of likelihood that she will be subjected to further grave physical abuse for racial reasons, that puts me in a situation where there is a reasonable degree of risk that I will be persecuted. It is possible to persecute a husband or a member of a family by what you do to other members of his immediate family. The essential task for the decision taker in these sort of circumstances is to consider what is reasonably likely to happen to the wife and whether that is reasonably likely to affect the husband in such a way as to amount to persecution of him.

9.4.1.7   Should the applicant have to change their behaviour to avoid persecution if returned?

Is a claimant required to take reasonable measures if returned home to avoid persecution? For example, where an applicant claims to have been persecuted due to their sexual orientation, is it relevant to take into account whether it would be reasonable to expect them to conceal it if returned? No, held the Supreme Court in *HJ (Iran) v Secretary of State or the Home Department* [2010] UKSC 31 when considering an application by a gay man. In considering such a claim, the Home Office must address the following issues:

(a)   Is it satisfied on the evidence that the applicant is gay or LGBQ, or that they would be treated as gay or LGBQ by potential persecutors in their country of nationality?

(b)   Is it satisfied on the available evidence that gay or LGBQ people who lived openly would be liable to persecution in the applicant's country of nationality?

(c)   What will the applicant do if returned to that country?

(d)   If the applicant would in fact live openly and thereby be exposed to a real risk of persecution, then the applicant has a well-founded fear of persecution – even if they could avoid the risk by living 'discreetly', ie concealing their sexual orientation.

(e)   If, on the other hand, the applicant would in fact conceal their sexual orientation and so avoid persecution, the question to be answered is why they would do so.

(f)   If the conclusion is that the applicant would choose to conceal their sexual orientation simply because that was how they would wish to live, or because of social pressures, eg not wanting to distress their parents or embarrass their friends, then the application should be rejected.

(g)   If, on the other hand, the material reason for the applicant concealing their sexual orientation on their return would be a fear of the persecution which would follow if they were to live openly as a gay or LGBQ person, then, other things being equal, their application should be accepted. Such a person has a well-founded fear of persecution. To reject the application on the ground that they could avoid the persecution by concealing their sexual orientation would be to defeat the very right which the Convention exists to protect, namely their right to live freely and openly as a gay or LGBQ person without fear of persecution.

See further the June 2018 paper by the UK Lesbian and Gay Immigration Group (https://uklgig.org.uk/) entitled, 'Applying HJ (Iran) and HT (Cameroon) to asylum claims based on sexual orientation'. The Home Office accepts that the case law test also applies to claims based on gender identity.

The case law test may potentially apply across all Convention grounds (see **9.4.2**). For example, as 'a general proposition a person found to have genuine political beliefs cannot be refused refugee status merely because they have declined to hide those beliefs, or to act "discreetly", in order to avoid persecution': per Carnwath LJ in *RT (Zimbabwe) v Secretary of State for the Home Department* [2010] EWCA Civ 1285 at [25].

9.4.1.8   Examples

EXAMPLE 1

Bela has fled from his own country which is engaged in civil war. His farm has been destroyed in a battle, and he has no other means of earning his living.

The Home Office may argue that Bela is a displaced person rather than a refugee, unless he can show, for example, that he is likely to suffer persecution if returned to his home country because he is identified with one of the sides in the civil war.

EXAMPLE 2

Chaka has left his country because high taxes and an economic crisis have caused his business to fail.

The Home Office may argue that he is an economic migrant rather than a refugee, unless he can show, for example, that the tax measures were directed at a particular ethnic group of which he is a member, designed to destroy their economic position.

9.4.2   'For reasons of race, religion, nationality, membership of a particular social group or political opinion'

9.4.2.1   Race

The concept of race includes, for example, colour, descent, or membership of a particular ethnic group. The fact that a claimant belongs to a certain racial group is not normally enough to prove a claim.

9.4.2.2   Religion

As to the meaning of the word 'religion', see *Omoruyi v Secretary of State for the Home Department* [2001] INLR 33. In the case the applicant was a Nigerian Christian persecuted by a group described variously as 'a secret cult … associated with idol worshipping to the extent of drinking blood', 'a mafia organisation involving criminal acts', and a 'devil cult' carrying out 'rituals', namely 'the sacrificing of animals to a graven image'. The court held that the persecution was not for a Convention reason (ie it was not related to the applicant's beliefs but to the fact that he had failed to comply with certain demands made by the cult) and therefore his application for asylum failed.

Note that reg 6(1)(b) of the Qualification Regulations 2006 provides that the concept of religion includes, for example, the holding of theistic, non-theistic and atheistic beliefs; the participation in, or abstention from, formal worship in private or in public, either alone or in community with others; other religious acts or expressions of view, or forms of personal or communal conduct based on or mandated by any religious belief.

9.4.2.3   Nationality

The term 'nationality' includes citizenship, or the lack of it, as well as membership of a group determined by such matters as its cultural, ethnic, or linguistic identity. Persecution for reasons of nationality may consist of adverse actions and measures against a national, ethnic or linguistic minority, and in certain circumstances the fact of belonging to such a minority may in itself give rise to a well-founded fear of persecution.

Note that nationals of certain countries may have their asylum claims certified by the Secretary of State as unfounded (see **11.15**).

9.4.2.4   Membership of a particular social group

Over recent years, the courts have given much consideration as to what is meant by the expression 'particular social group'. In the joint cases of *Islam (Shahana) v Secretary of State for the Home Department; R v Immigration Appeal Tribunal and Secretary of State for the Home Department, ex p Syeda Shah* [1999] INLR 144, the House of Lords had to decide if two Pakistani women, who had fled Pakistan after false allegations of adultery and violence by their husbands, were part of such a group. The House held that a 'particular social group' consists of a group of persons who share a common, immutable characteristic that either is beyond the power of an individual to change, or is so fundamental to the individual's identity or conscience that he ought not to be required to change it. Thus, as gender is an immutable characteristic that is beyond the power of the individual to change, and as discrimination against women is prevalent in Pakistan, in violation of fundamental rights and freedoms, women in Pakistan constitute a particular social group.

In the *Islam* and *Shah* appeals, Lord Hoffmann asked:

> What is the reason for the persecution which the appellants fear? Here it is important to notice that it is made up of two elements. First, there is the threat of violence to Mrs Islam by her husband and his political friends and to Mrs Shah by her husband. This is a personal affair, directed against them as individuals. Secondly, there is the inability or unwillingness of the State to do anything to protect them. There is nothing personal about this. The evidence was that the State would not assist them because they were women. It denied them a protection against violence which it would have given to men. These two elements have to be combined to constitute persecution within the meaning of the Convention.

See also *RG (Ethiopia) v Secretary of State for the Home Department* [2006] EWCA Civ 339, where it was held that women and girls in Ethiopia constitute a particular social group. The Court found institutionalised discrimination, since the penal law in Ethiopia legitimises the marriage of abducted and raped girls to their violators, which marriage then exempts the latter from punishment. This, and the evidence of a lack of protection of women against sexual abuse and serious discrimination, shows a degree of complicity by the State in the treatment of women in Ethiopia, sufficient to conclude that women constitute a particular social group.

Regulation 6(1)(d) of the Qualification Regulations 2006, as interpreted in *K v Secretary of State for the Home Department; Fornah v Secretary of State for the Home Department* [2006] UKHL 45, [2007] 1 All ER 671, provides two useful guidelines defining a particular social group. First, where members of that group share an innate characteristic, or a common background that cannot be changed, or share a characteristic or belief that is so fundamental to identity or conscience that a person should not be forced to renounce it. Secondly, where the group has a distinct identity in the relevant country, because it is perceived as being different by the surrounding society.

What about claims relating to sexual orientation or gender identity? Lesbian, gay, bisexual, trans, queer or intersex (LGBTQI+) people may be recognised as a member of a particular social group, if the decision maker concludes they are LGBTQI+, or would be treated as such, and LGBTQI+ people are perceived to have a distinct identity in their country of origin. The UNHCR Guidelines on International Protection No 9: Claims to Refugee Status based on Sexual Orientation and/or Gender Identity confirm that, as understood in refugee law, a particular social group can be based on sexual orientation. LGBTQI+ people in most countries will meet this definition. See also the ECJ joined Cases C-199/12 to C-201/12 [2013] WLR(D) 427, [2013] EUECJ C199/12.

In *DH (Particular Social Group: Mental Health) Afghanistan* [2020] UKUT 223 (IAC), the tribunal held that, depending on the facts, a person living with disability or mental ill health may qualify as a member of a particular social group (PSG) either as (i) sharing an innate characteristic or a common background that cannot be changed, or (ii) because they may be perceived as being different by the surrounding society and thus have a distinct identity in their country of origin. The key issue is how an individual is viewed in the eyes of a potential persecutor making it possible that those suffering no, or a lesser degree of, disability or illness may also qualify as a PSG.

9.4.2.5 Political opinion

To show persecution on grounds of political opinion, it is not enough for the claimant to establish that he holds opinions which his government opposes. He must show that that government will not tolerate his opinions, and that it is aware that he holds them. Where the claimant has committed criminal offences in the course of political opposition, he cannot base a claim to refugee status on fear of his country's normal punishment for that offence.

EXAMPLE

Enrico is a member of a minority linguistic group, and of the political party which represents it. The party is campaigning for language rights, for example in regional schools, and its political activities are permitted. His national government will not concede these rights and pursues discriminatory policies. Enrico has fled the country after setting fire to a school which refused to use the minority language.

The Home Office may argue that Enrico does not fear persecution on grounds of his political opinions, but rather punishment for an ordinary criminal offence. However, he may be able to show that his punishment would be excessive or arbitrary, which would amount to persecution. The discriminatory measures in themselves may not be sufficiently serious to amount to persecution on grounds of nationality.

In what circumstances may a person who objects to carrying out compulsory military service be granted asylum? In *Sepet v Secretary of State for the Home Department* [2003] 3 All ER 304, the House of Lords held that refugee status should be accorded to a person who refuses to undertake compulsory military service on the grounds that such service would or might require him to commit atrocities or gross human rights abuses, or participate in a conflict condemned by the international community, or where refusal to serve would earn grossly excessive or disproportionate punishment. In *PK (Draft evader; punishment; minimum severity)*

Ukraine [2018] UKUT 00241, the Tribunal held that a legal requirement for conscription and a mechanism for the prosecution or punishment of a person refusing to undertake military service is not sufficient to entitle that person to refugee protection if there is no real risk that the person will be subjected to prosecution or punishment. In addition, a person will only be entitled to refugee protection if there is a real risk that the prosecution or punishment they face for refusing to perform military service in a conflict that may associate them with acts that are contrary to basic rules of human conduct reaches a minimum threshold of severity.

Even if a claimant does not hold political views which his government opposes, it may well be that the government believes that he does. So a person to whom a political opinion is imputed may qualify for refugee status: see *Sivakumar v Secretary of State for the Home Department* [2002] INLR 310. Imputed political opinion may include those who are perceived to be members or supporters of an opposition party, as well as anyone who is unable to demonstrate support for, or loyalty to, the government regime or ruling political party: see *TM (Zimbabwe) v Secretary of State for the Home Department* [2010] EWCA Civ 916.

EXAMPLE

Alexander has fled from his own country because his brother has been imprisoned for political activities.

The Home Office may argue that Alexander's fear is not well founded, unless he can show that persecution is for an imputed political opinion or extends to the social group associated with the political activity.

9.4.3 'Is outside the country of his nationality'

No one can claim to be a refugee until he has left the country of which he is a citizen. This means that a claimant cannot normally obtain a visa from a UK entry clearance officer in his country, clearing him to enter the UK as a refugee. He must (somehow) find his way to the UK and make the claim on arrival. This may be difficult, as airlines are fined for carrying people without correct travel documents (Immigration (Carriers' Liability) Act 1987).

9.4.3.1 The internal flight alternative or internal relocation

The claimant must be outside his country owing to fear of persecution there. What if the persecution is to be feared in only part of the country? Paragraph 339O of the Immigration Rules provides that the Secretary of State will not grant asylum if in part of the country of origin a person would not have a well-founded fear of being persecuted, and the person can reasonably be expected to stay in that part of the country. So if someone would be safe only if he lived in a remote village, separated from his family, his flight from the country can still be said to be based on a fear of persecution there (see *R v Immigration Appeal Tribunal, ex p Jonah* [1985] Imm AR 7).

The House of Lords, in *Januzi v Secretary of State for the Home Department* [2006] UKHL 5, gave further guidance on this issue. Lord Hope of Craighead said (para 47):

> The question where the issue of internal relocation is raised can, then, be defined quite simply. As Linden JA put it in *Thirunavukkarasu v Canada (Minister of Employment and Immigration)* (1993) 109 DLR (4th) 682, 687, it is whether it would be unduly harsh to expect a claimant who is being persecuted for a Convention reason in one part of his country to move to a less hostile part before seeking refugee status abroad. The words 'unduly harsh' set the standard that must be met for this to be regarded as unreasonable. If the claimant can live a relatively normal life there judged by the standards that prevail in his country of nationality generally, and if he can reach the less hostile part without undue hardship or undue difficulty, it will not be unreasonable to expect him to move there.

The following checklist of key points was provided by the Court of Appeal in *AS (Afghanistan) v Secretary of State for the Home Department* [2019] EWCA Civ 873 at [61]:

- The ultimate question is whether in such a case 'taking account of all relevant circumstances pertaining to the claimant and his country of origin, ... it is reasonable to expect the claimant to relocate or whether it would be unduly harsh to expect him to do so'.

- The test so stated is one of great generality (save only that it excludes any comparison of the conditions, including the degree of respect for human rights, between those obtaining in the safe haven and those of the country of refuge). It requires consideration of all matters relevant to the reasonableness of relocation, none having inherent priority over the others.

- One way of approaching that assessment is to ask whether in the safe haven the applicant can lead 'a relatively normal life without facing undue hardship ... in the context of the country concerned'. It is a valuable way of approaching the reasonableness analysis. Its value is because if a person is able to lead in the safe haven a life which is relatively normal for people in the context of his or her own country, it will be reasonable to expect them to stay there.

- It may be reasonable, and not unduly harsh, to expect a refugee to relocate even if conditions in the safe haven are, by the standards of the country of refuge, very bad. It is vividly illustrated by the outcome of *AH (Sudan) v Secretary of State for the Home Department* [2006] UKHL 49, where the House of Lords upheld the decision of the tribunal that it was reasonable for Darfuri refugees to be expected to relocate to the camps or squatter slums of Khartoum. That may seem inconsistent with the suggested approach of asking whether the applicant would be able lead a 'relatively normal life' in the safe haven; but the reconciliation lies in the qualification 'in the context of the country concerned'. However, this does not mean that it will be reasonable for a person to relocate to a safe haven, however bad the conditions they will face there, as long as such conditions are normal in their country. Conditions may be normal but nevertheless unduly harsh.

- The assessment must in each case be conducted by reference to the reasonableness of relocation for the particular individual.

It is for the Home Office to demonstrate that internal relocation is reasonable and not unduly harsh, taking account of the means of travel and communication, cultural traditions, religious beliefs and customs, ethnic or linguistic differences, health facilities, employment opportunities, supporting family or other ties (including childcare responsibilities and the effect of relocation upon dependent children) and the presence and ability of civil society (eg non-governmental organisations) to provide practical support for the claimant.

9.4.3.2   Safe third country exception (AI(TC)A 2004, Sch 3)

Paragraph 345A of the Immigration Rules provides that an asylum application may be treated as inadmissible and not substantively considered if the Secretary of State determines that:

(i)   the applicant has been recognised as a refugee in a safe third country and they can still avail themselves of that protection; or

(ii)   the applicant otherwise enjoys sufficient protection in a safe third country, including benefiting from the principle of non-refoulement [the practice of not forcing refugees or asylum seekers to return to a country in which they are liable to be subjected to persecution]; or

(iii)   the applicant could enjoy sufficient protection in a safe third country, including benefiting from the principle of non-refoulement because:

   (a)   they have already made an application for protection to that country; or

   (b)   they could have made an application for protection to that country but did not do so and there were no exceptional circumstances preventing such an application being made, or

   (c)   they have a connection to that country, such that it would be reasonable for them to go there to obtain protection.

What is a safe third country? Paragraph 345B of the Immigration Rules provides that a country is a safe third country for a particular applicant, if:

(i)   the applicant's life and liberty will not be threatened on account of race, religion, nationality, membership of a particular social group or political opinion in that country;

(ii)   the principle of non-refoulement will be respected in that country in accordance with the Refugee Convention;

    (iii)   the prohibition of removal, in violation of the right to freedom from torture and cruel, inhuman or degrading treatment as laid down in international law, is respected in that country; and

    (iv)   the possibility exists to request refugee status and, if found to be a refugee, to receive protection in accordance with the Refugee Convention in that country.

Historically, and as still provided for in Part 2 of Sch 3 to the AI(TC)A 2004, members of the EU (see **Appendix 2** to this book) (apart from Croatia) together with Norway, Switzerland and Iceland are treated as safe third countries.

What happens when an application is treated as inadmissible? The Secretary of State will attempt to remove the applicant to the safe third country in which they were previously present or to which they have a connection, or to any other safe third country which may agree to their entry.

Note that when an application has been treated as inadmissible and either removal to a safe third country within a reasonable period of time is unlikely; or upon consideration of a claimant's particular circumstances the Secretary of State determines that removal to a safe third country is inappropriate, the Secretary of State will substantially consider the claim.

Note further that whilst there is no strict deadline by which an inadmissibility decision must be made, the Home Office normally applies a time limit of just over 6 months.

HOME OFFICE EXAMPLE

If it is believed that a claimant passed through Belgium before arriving in the UK and claiming asylum, a decision under paragraph 345A(iii)(b) may be appropriate. Such a decision would need to show that it was more likely than not that the claimant had been in that particular country and could reasonably have been expected to have made an application for protection there but did not (for example that there were no exceptional circumstances preventing such an application). The decision would also need to show that the country is safe for that particular individual.

Scenario 1: A passer-by in Kent seeing the claimant arriving in a small boat from an easterly direction would not, by itself, meet the standard of proof required under paragraph 345A(iii)(b).

Scenario 2: An admission from the claimant that they had spent a couple of weeks in Brussels staying with friends whilst trying to find an agent to bring them illegally to the UK would likely constitute evidence that they had been in that particular country and could reasonably have been expected to have applied for asylum there (absent any factors to the contrary). The decision would also need to show that the country is safe for that particular individual.

Scenario 3: Even without an admission, or even with a denial, material in the claimant's belongings such as receipts and tickets from Belgian shops, services and transport showing time and freedom of movement in Belgium would likely meet the standard of proof required under the Rule that they had been in that particular country and could reasonably have been expected to have applied for asylum there. However, this would need to be weighed against any other strong evidence that the receipts did not belong to the claimant and so did not connect them with Belgium, or that the claimant was under the coercive control of another person such that although they were indeed in that country, they were prevented from seeking protection there. The decision would also need to show that the country is safe for that particular individual.

9.4.3.3   Sur place claims

Can a claimant have a well-founded fear of being persecuted or a real risk of suffering serious harm based on events which take place after he leaves his country of origin and/or activities in which he engages since leaving his country of origin? Yes, this provision can be found in the Immigration Rules, para 339P. It will apply, in particular, where it is established that the activities relied upon constitute the expression and continuation of convictions or orientations held in the country of origin by the claimant. The most common example is a claimant who carries on political activities in the UK. However, the provision applies equally to a claimant who was a conformist before leaving his country of origin but who becomes politicised in exile, even if those political activities were designed to create or enhance an asylum claim. As Kay LJ stated in *KS (Burma) v Secretary of State for the Home Department* [2013] EWCA Civ 67 at [32], 'It is unpalatable that someone may become entitled to refugee status as a result of his cynical manipulation but if, objectively, he has a well-founded fear of persecution by reason of imputed political opinion, that may be the reality.'

In assessing a *sur place* claim, the key question is whether the claimant's activities create a real risk of persecution in his home country. The claim fails if the activities are not likely come to the attention of the authorities of that country or the authorities are likely to ignore them: see *TM (Zimbabwe) v Secretary of State for the Home Department* [2010] EWCA Civ 916.

How should a *sur place* claim be assessed? In *BA (Demonstrators in Britain – risk on return) Iran CG* [2011] UKUT 36 the Tribunal identified the following factors:

(i) *Nature of* sur place *activity*

- Theme of demonstrations – what do the demonstrators want (eg reform of the regime through to its violent overthrow); how will they be characterised by the regime?

- Role in demonstrations and political profile – can the person be described as a leader; mobiliser (eg addressing the crowd); organiser (eg leading the chanting); or simply a member of the crowd; if the latter is he active or passive (eg does he carry a banner); what is his motive, and is this relevant to the profile he will have in the eyes of the regime?

- Extent of participation – has the person attended one or two demonstrations, or is he a regular participant?

- Publicity attracted – has a demonstration attracted media coverage in the United Kingdom or the home country; nature of that publicity (quality of images; outlets where stories appear etc)?

(ii) *Identification risk*

- Surveillance of demonstrators – assuming the regime aims to identify demonstrators against it, how does it do so: through filming them, having agents who mingle in the crowd, reviewing images/recordings of demonstrations etc?

- Regime's capacity to identify individuals – does the regime have advanced technology (eg for facial recognition); does it allocate human resources to fit names to faces in the crowd?

(iii) *Factors triggering inquiry/action on return*

- Profile – is the person known as a committed opponent or someone with a significant political profile; does he fall within a category which the regime regards as especially objectionable?

- Immigration history – how did the person leave the country (illegally; type of visa); where has the person been when abroad; is the timing and method of return more likely to lead to inquiry and/or being detained for more than a short period and ill-treated (overstayer; forced return)?

(iv) *Consequences of identification*

- Is there differentiation between demonstrators depending on the level of their political profile adverse to the regime?

(v) Identification risk on return

- Matching identification to person – if a person is identified, is that information systematically stored and used; are border posts geared to the task?

9.4.4 'And is unable, or, owing to such fear, is unwilling to avail himself of the protection of that country'

A claimant would be unable to avail himself of his country's protection if, for example, it refused entry to him, or refused to issue him with a passport. A claimant who fears persecution will normally be unwilling to accept his government's protection, and it is inconsistent with his claim to refugee status if, for example, he wishes to retain his national passport.

9.5 EXCLUSION FROM REFUGEE STATUS

Even if an applicant meets the tests under the Refugee Convention, the UK Government will in certain circumstances refuse to grant him refugee status (**9.5.1**) or forcibily remove him (**9.5.2**). However, in either circumstance it must still go on to consider if it is appropriate to award the applicant humanitarian protection or discretionary leave (see **9.10**).

9.5.1 Exclusion under Article 1F.

Article 1F. of the Refugee Convention excludes the following claimants from asylum because they are considered not to be deserving of international protection. This is because there are serious reasons for considering that they:

(a)   have committed a crime against peace, a war crime or a crime against humanity; or

(b)   have committed a serious non-political crime outside the country of refuge prior to admission into that country; or

(c)   are guilty of acts contrary to the purposes and principles of the United Nations.

There is an evidential burden on the Secretary of State to establish serious reasons for considering that a claimant has committed an act under Article 1F. (see *JS (Sri Lanka) v Secretary of State for the Home Department* [2010] UKSC 15). However, it does not have to be shown to the criminal standard of proof, ie beyond reasonable doubt (see *Al-Sirri v Secretary of State for the Home Department* [2012] UKSC 54). Article 1F. of the Convention has to be applied with caution. It requires a close examination of the facts and a carefully reasoned decision as to precisely why the person is excluded from protection under the Convention (see *MAB (Iraq) v Secretary of State for the Home Department* [2019] EWCA Civ 1253).

So when does Article 1F. apply?

> I would hold an accused disqualified under Article 1F if there are serious reasons for considering him voluntarily to have contributed in a significant way to the organisation's ability to pursue its purpose of committing war crimes, aware that his assistance will in fact further that purpose. (per Lord Brown in *R (on the application of JS) (Sri Lanka) v Secretary of State for the Home Department* [2010] UKSC 15 at para 38)

9.5.1.1 Article 1F.(a)

What is a 'crime against humanity' for the purposes of Article 1F.(a)? The starting point is the following definition in Article 7(1) of the Rome Statute of the International Criminal Court 2002:

> 1.   ... any of the following acts when committed as part of a widespread or systematic attack directed against any civilian population, with knowledge of the attack:
>
> (a)   Murder;
>
> (b)   Extermination;
>
> ...
>
> (e)   Imprisonment or other severe deprivation of physical liberty ...;
>
> (f)   Torture;

...

(h)   Persecution ... on political, racial, national, ethnic, cultural, religious, gender ... grounds ...;

(i)   Enforced disappearance of persons;

...

(k)   Other inhumane acts of a similar character intentionally causing great suffering, or serious injury to body or to mental or physical health.

(See *SK (Zimbabwe) v Secretary of State for the Home Department* [2012] 1 WLR 2809.)

Article 25 of the Rome Statute 2002 regulates individual criminal responsibility for a crime against humanity falling within Article 7. Article 25(3) provides:

3.   In accordance with this Statute, a person shall be criminally responsible and liable for punishment for a crime within the jurisdiction of the Court if that person:

(a)   Commits such a crime, whether as an individual, jointly with another or through another person, regardless of whether that other person is criminally responsible;

(b)   Orders, solicits or induces the commission of such a crime which in fact occurs or is attempted;

(c)   For the purpose of facilitating the commission of such a crime, aids, abets or otherwise assists in its commission or its attempted commission, including providing the means for its commission;

(d)   In any other way contributes to the commission or attempted commission of such a crime by a group of persons acting with a common purpose. Such contribution shall be intentional and shall either:

(i)   Be made with the aim of furthering the criminal activity or criminal purpose of the group, where such activity or purpose involves the commission of a crime within the jurisdiction of the Court; or

(ii)   Be made in the knowledge of the intention of the group to commit the crime.

...

For a detailed discussion of this exclusionary provision, see *AA-R (Iran) v Secretary of State for the Home Department* [2013] EWCA Civ 835.

9.5.1.2   Article 1F.(b)

Note that reg 7(2) of the Qualification Regulations 2006 interprets the meaning of Article 1 F.(b) as follows:

The reference to 'serious non-political crime' includes a particularly cruel action, even if it is committed with an allegedly political objective. The reference to the crime being committed outside the country of refuge prior to his admission as a refugee shall mean the time up to and including the day on which a residence permit [signifying the grant of refugee status] is issued.

Note that in *AH (Article 1F (b) – 'serious') Algeria* [2013] UKUT 382 it was said: 'The examination of seriousness should be directed at the criminal acts when they were committed, although events in the supervening passage of time may be relevant to whether exclusion is justified: a formal pardon, or subsequent acquittal, or other event illuminating the nature of the activity may be relevant to this assessment.'

9.5.1.3   Article 1F.(c)

Also note that s 54 of the IANA 2006 interprets the meaning of Article 1F.(c). It provides that acts of committing, preparing or instigating terrorism, or encouraging or inducing others to do so, are included within the meaning of what constitutes 'acts contrary to the purposes and principles of the United Nations'.

The application of Article 1F.(c) will be straightforward in the case of an active member of an organisation that promotes its objects only by acts of terrorism. There will almost certainly be serious reasons for considering that he has been guilty of acts contrary to the purposes and principles of the United Nations. However, what if the organisation pursues its political ends in part by acts of terrorism and in part by military action directed against the armed forces of the government? A person may join such an organisation because he agrees with its political objectives and may be willing to participate in its military actions, but he may not agree with and may not be willing to participate in its terrorist activities. The higher up in the organisation a person is, the more likely will be the inference that he agrees with and promotes all of its activities, including its terrorism.

The correct approach to Article 1F.(c) was stated in *Al-Sirri v Secretary of State for the Home Department* [2012] UKSC 54 as follows:

> The article should be interpreted restrictively and applied with caution. There should be a high threshold 'defined in terms of the gravity of the act in question, the manner in which the act is organised, its international impact and long-term objectives, and the implications for international peace and security. And there should be serious reasons for considering that the person concerned bore individual responsibility for acts of that character … [I]t is our view that the appropriately cautious and restrictive approach would be to adopt para 17 of the UNHCR Guidelines: 'Article 1F(c) is only triggered in extreme circumstances by activity which attacks the very basis of the international community's coexistence. Such activity must have an international dimension. Crimes capable of affecting international peace, security and peaceful relations between states, as well as serious and sustained violations of human rights would fall under this category'. (per Lady Hale and Lord Dyson at [16] and [38])

In light of that approach, when might exclusion for 'encouraging [terrorism] or inducing others to [commit, prepare or instigate terrorism]' occur? This was considered by the Court of Appeal in *Youssef v Secretary of State for the Home Department* [2018] EWCA Civ 933. In the case, it was not alleged that the applicant had incited or encouraged any specific piece of violence, or that any specific act of terrorism could be shown to be linked to his incitement or encouragement. It was accepted by the Secretary of State that no such specific link could be made. Rather it was argued that, in a sustained fashion over a long period, the applicant had praised Al Qaeda and its leaders, often by individual name, and encouraged others to follow them and support them.

The Court held that individual responsibility for acts falling within Article 1F.(c) can arise solely by way of implicit or explicit encouragement of such acts, in the absence of evidence that an offence has been committed or attempted as a consequence of anything said or done by the applicant.

The Court pointed out that there is a high threshold before Article 1F.(c) is triggered. The activity must be capable of affecting international peace and security. The test is whether the 'resulting acts have the requisite serious effect'. In short, do the relevant acts have the necessary character and the necessary gravity? The Court suggested that it would be helpful to consider separately the quality of the acts in question and their gravity or severity:

> To adopt an illustration which arose in argument, it is easy to conceive of an immature 18 year old going on-line from his suburban bedroom, and using the most lurid terms in calling for international jihad. The nature or quality of this would, it seems to me, satisfy the requirements of Article 1F(c). It would represent active encouragement or incitement of international terror. However, it would be unlikely, without more, to be grave enough in its impact to satisfy the approach laid down in *Al-Sirri*. That might well require more: evidence of wide international readership, of large-scale repetition or re-tweeting, or citation by those who were moved to join an armed struggle, for example. (per Irwin LJ at [85])

EXAMPLE

Recently, Danilow, an asylum seeker, was convicted of six counts of possession of material for a purpose connected with the commission or preparation of an act of terrorism. The convictions were based on computer files discovered on two computers in his possession. The material included descriptions of how to establish a jihadist organisation, and how to make viable explosives or other dangerous material. In the course of sentencing him, the judge emphasised the degree of detail in the material found, including:

> ... an organisational chart for the establishment of terrorist cells and detailed and genuine instructions in relation to the making of harmful chemicals, explosive substances, detonators, explosive devices and bombs and the placing of such devices and the targeting of particular premises, public places and public figures.
>
> The sentencing judge also emphasised the context, and the conclusions he drew:
>
> > Your possession of this material has to be seen in the context of other features of the case. ... part of the background is formed also by your multiple identities, your different addresses, your coming to this country under an assumed name, the lies which you then told before and during the police inquiry into this case.
> >
> > Doubts remain as to who you really are and where you really come from. In my view the only reasonable conclusion to be drawn from these features of your case is that you were indeed as the prosecution contended, a sleeper for some sort of terrorist organisation.
>
> At the same time, it was accepted that it was not possible to demonstrate that Danilow had been involved in the commission, preparation or instigation of:
>
> > ... an act of terrorism, and there is no evidence you have done so. It is not known if, when and how you might have been called on to play your part.
>
> The acts of terrorism that Danilow must have contemplated would, if committed or attempted by him, have been sufficient to satisfy Article 1F.(c) (and indeed Article 1F.(a)). Are his acts preparatory for such substantive offending, but falling short of attempts or completed terrorist attacks, sufficient to satisfy the requirements of Article 1F.(c)? Yes, if his conduct is held to be sufficiently grave and serious that it would have had an effect upon international peace, security and relations between states.
>
> See NF v *Secretary of State for the Home Department* [2021] EWCA Civ 17.

9.5.2 Enforced removal under Article 33(2)

Article 33(2) of the Refugee Convention allows the UK Government to remove a person who is otherwise a refugee where there are reasonable grounds for regarding him as a danger to the security of the UK, or who, having been convicted by a final judgment of a particularly serious crime, constitutes a danger to the community of the UK.

Home Office guidance is that for a person to be a danger to the security of the UK, the actions or anticipated actions of that person need not create a direct threat to the UK's system of government or its people. The interests of national security could be threatened indirectly by activities directed against other States. Thus the definition of a threat to national security is very wide: for example, depending on the specific facts of the case, if someone is believed or known to be a terrorist then, due to the nature of international terrorism, and regardless of the immediate threat of his particular terrorist group, it may be reasonable to regard the person as a threat to the UK's national security.

What is a particularly serious crime such that the person constitutes a danger to the community of the UK? By s 72 of the NIAA 2002, there is a general presumption of this where the person was sentenced to a period of imprisonment of at least two years. Note, however, that in EN (Serbia) v *Secretary of State for the Home Department* [2009] EWCA Civ 630, the Court of Appeal held that the presumption is rebuttable and that the Nationality, Immigration and Asylum Act 2002 (Specification of Particularly Serious Crimes) Order 2004 (SI 2004/1910), which specifies a large number of offences as offences to which s 72 applies, irrespective of the sentence imposed, is ultra vires and unlawful. However, the Order remains in force.

The Court in EN (Serbia) stressed that the second ground for enforced removal under Article 33(2) requires two conditions to be met: first, that the refugee has been convicted by a final judgment of a particularly serious crime; and, secondly, that he constitutes a danger to the community. The presumption that each of these conditions is met is rebuttable. So, for example, if the refugee can demonstrate that he is not a danger to the community, Article 33(2) cannot apply. Note, however, that the Court indicated (at [45] and [46]) that where a person is convicted of a particularly serious crime, and there is a real risk of its repetition or the recurrence of a similar offence, he is likely to constitute a danger to the community. The Court also gave the example of a person convicted of a particularly serious offence of violence whom the Government can establish is a significant drug dealer as being one where removal under Article 33(2) is likely.

On an asylum appeal, the Secretary of State may issue a certificate pursuant to s 72(9)(b) that the presumption applies. Thereafter, the tribunal hearing the appeal must begin its substantive deliberation by considering the certificate. If, after giving the appellant the opportunity for rebuttal, it agrees that the presumption applies, it must dismiss the appeal in so far as it relies on the ground that to remove the appellant would breach the UK's obligation under the Refugee Convention. See further *Secretary of State for the Home Department v JR (Jamaica)* [2014] EWCA Civ 477.

9.6 CONSIDERATION OF CASES

9.6.1 The Home Office checklist

Home Office asylum case owners use the following checklist when assessing a claim:

(a)   What is the applicant's basis of claim?

(b)   Which of the applicant's claims about past events can be accepted?

Are the applicant's claims as to his past experiences consistent with objective country policy and information notes (see **9.7**) relating to the relevant period, including generally known facts?

Are the applicant's claims consistent with other evidence submitted, eg the evidence of other witnesses, family members or documents specifically referring to the applicant?

Are any of the applicant's claims about his past experiences not able to be corroborated by reference to country of origin information or other evidence? If so, can the benefit of the doubt be given to any of these claims? If not, why not?

After due consideration of the principle of the benefit of the doubt, which of the applicant's material claims can be accepted, and which can be rejected?

(c)   Taking into account the applicant's statements and behaviour, does the applicant have a subjective fear of persecution?

(d)   Objectively, are there reasonable grounds for believing that the harm feared might in fact occur in the applicant's country of origin?

Who are the actors of persecution? Do the authorities of the home country conduct the persecution, or support persecution committed by others?

How far is the State or organisations controlling the State (including international organisations) able to provide protection from persecution caused by others? What laws are in place and are they enforced effectively?

Has the applicant sought the protection of the authorities? If so, what was the outcome? If not, why not?

Considering the objective country of origin information, the past experiences of the applicant and the attitude of the State authorities, is there a reasonable likelihood that the applicant would experience harm if returned?

(e)   Can the applicant return to a part of the country in which he would not be subject to the harm feared (see **9.4.3.1**)?

(f)   Is the harm feared a form of persecution (see **9.4.1.3**)?

Is the harm of sufficient gravity to constitute persecution, or is it something less serious?

Does the cumulative effect of lesser prejudicial actions or threats amount to persecution?

If the applicant has a fear of prosecution or punishment for an offence, is the punishment discriminatory or disproportionate? Does this give rise to a fear of persecution?

If the fear of prosecution is due to draft evasion or desertion, special considerations may apply.

(g)   If the harm feared is serious enough to constitute persecution, would it be inflicted for one or more of the reasons set out in the Refugee Convention, ie race, religion, nationality, membership of a particular social group or political opinion? See further **9.4.2**.

(h)   In the light of (a)–(g) above, does the applicant satisfy all the criteria of the 1951 Convention?

(i)   Should the applicant be excluded from international protection by operation of the exclusion clauses of the Convention? See further **9.5**.

(j)   If an applicant fails to qualify for asylum, decision makers should consider whether to grant humanitarian protection or discretionary leave (see **9.10**).

9.6.2   Adverse inferences

9.6.2.1   Claimant's duties

The Immigration Rules (paras 339I–339N) list some factors which are taken into account. These start by imposing a duty on the claimant to submit to the Secretary of State, as soon as possible, all material factors needed to substantiate the asylum claim. These material factors include the claimant's statement of the reasons for making an asylum claim; all documentation at the claimant's disposal regarding his age, background, identity, nationality(ies), country(ies) and place(s) of previous residence, previous asylum applications, and travel routes; and identity and travel documents.

It is further the duty of the claimant to substantiate the claim. Paragraph 339L of the Immigration Rules provides that where aspects of the claimant's statements are not supported by documentary or other evidence, those aspects will not need confirmation when *all* of the following conditions are met:

(a)   the claimant has made a genuine effort to substantiate his asylum claim;

(b)   all material factors at the claimant's disposal have been submitted, and a satisfactory explanation regarding any lack of other relevant material has been given;

(c)   the claimant's statements are found to be coherent and plausible, and do not run counter to available specific and general information relevant to his case;

(d)   the claimant has made an asylum claim at the earliest possible time, unless he can demonstrate good reason for not having done so; and

(e)   the general credibility of the claimant has been established.

Paragraph 339M of the Immigration Rules provides that the Secretary of State may consider that a person has not substantiated his asylum claim if he fails, without reasonable explanation, to make a prompt and full disclosure of material facts, either orally or in writing, or otherwise to assist the Secretary of State in establishing the facts of the case. This includes, for example, a failure to attend an interview, failure to report to a designated place to be fingerprinted, failure to complete an asylum questionnaire or failure to comply with a requirement to report to an immigration officer for examination.

9.6.2.2   Statutory adverse inferences

Section 8(1) of the AI(TC)A 2004 includes similar guidelines for assessing the credibility of the claimant. The key provisions are as follows:

(1)   In determining whether to believe a statement made by or on behalf of a person who makes an asylum claim or a human rights claim, a deciding authority shall take account, as damaging the claimant's credibility, of any behaviour to which this section applies.

(2)   This section applies to any behaviour by the claimant that the deciding authority thinks—

(a)   is designed or likely to conceal information,

(b)   is designed or likely to mislead, or

(c)   is designed or likely to obstruct or delay the handling or resolution of the claim or the taking of a decision in relation to the claimant.

(3)   Without prejudice to the generality of subsection (2) the following kinds of behaviour shall be treated as designed or likely to conceal information or to mislead—

(a)   failure without reasonable explanation to produce a passport on request to an immigration officer or to the Secretary of State,

(b)   the production of a document which is not a valid passport as if it were,

(c)   the destruction, alteration or disposal, in each case without reasonable explanation, of a passport,

(d)   the destruction, alteration or disposal, in each case without reasonable explanation, of a ticket or other document connected with travel, and

(e)   failure without reasonable explanation to answer a question asked by a deciding authority.

(4)   This section also applies to failure by the claimant to take advantage of a reasonable opportunity to make an asylum claim or human rights claim while in a safe country.

(5)   This section also applies to failure by the claimant to make an asylum claim or human rights claim before being notified of an immigration decision, unless the claim relies wholly on matters arising after the notification.

(6)   This section also applies to failure by the claimant to make an asylum claim or human rights claim before being arrested under an immigration provision, unless—

(a)   he had no reasonable opportunity to make the claim before the arrest, or

(b)   the claim relies wholly on matters arising after the arrest.

9.6.2.3   How adverse?

What is the effect of s 8(1)? In *JT (Cameroon) v Secretary of State for the Home Department* [2008] EWCA Civ 878, the Court of Appeal held that the section lays down a framework of factors that may potentially damage a claimant's credibility. However, it is for the decision maker to decide the extent to which that person's credibility is damaged, if at all, and what weight should be given to any adverse finding of credibility. In this case the claimant had used false papers to enter the UK and false identities whilst in the UK. The Home Office refused the claimant asylum and the Tribunal determined that under s 8 the claimant's conduct had seriously damaged his credibility.

9.6.2.4   Reasonable explanation

What is a reasonable explanation for the purposes of s 8(3)(a) and (c)–(e)? Home Office guidance is that this may include exceptional situations where the applicant could not easily have disobeyed the instructions of an agent who facilitates immigration into the UK; cases where an adult is severely traumatised, or where cultural norms may make it difficult for a person to answer questions at interview or to disobey instructions, including instructions about documents; situations where a person can show that a document was destroyed or disposed of as a direct result of force, threats or intimidation, eg where an individual was forced at knifepoint to give a document to someone else; or where the document has been lost or stolen and the individual can substantiate such a claim, usually with a police report of the loss or theft.

As to what is a safe country for the purposes of s 8(4), see **9.4.3.2**. What is a reasonable opportunity to claim asylum in such a country? Home Office guidance is that the claimant could have approached the authorities at the border or internally, as long as there is no reason to think that the claim would not have been received. For example, it might be thought that someone who spent several weeks in France before coming to the UK must have had a reasonable opportunity to claim asylum there; but this would not be reasonable if the applicant was imprisoned by traffickers throughout that time. The true question is whether in any particular case there has in reality been such a reasonable opportunity. In making that assessment, the decision maker cannot infer its existence from mere presence in a nominally safe country identified by the 2004 Act. Just to give one example, there may well not have been an opportunity to claim asylum in a safe country through which a claimant has passed while concealed in the back of a lorry (see *KA (Afghanistan) v Secretary of State for the Home Department* [2019] EWCA Civ 914 at [52]).

As to s 8(6), Home Office guidance is that an applicant's credibility must be treated as damaged if the claim is made after the applicant's arrest under an immigration provision unless there was no reasonable opportunity to make the claim before the arrest, or the claimant relies wholly on matters arising after the arrest. An applicant has had a reasonable opportunity to claim asylum before being arrested if he could have approached the authorities at any time after his arrival in the UK. Each case should be considered on its merits. So, for example, someone who is apprehended by the police soon after getting out of a back of a lorry is less likely to have been able to make a claim before arrest than someone who passed through immigration control when arriving in the UK.

9.7 COUNTRY POLICY AND INFORMATION NOTES

The UKVI produces notes on over 40 countries used by Home Office staff as part of assessing a claim. The notes provide information on the general, political and human rights situations in those countries. The notes are often specific to particular types of claimants or issues, for example sexual orientation and gender issues, anti-government groups, prison conditions, internal relocation, ethnic minority groups, religious groups and human rights activists.

The notes are compiled on recommendations made by the Independent Chief Inspector of Borders and Immigration. A wide range of sources are used, such as BBC News, Freedom House, US Department of State Country Reports on Human Rights Practices, Amnesty International, international and national and local newspapers, statute law and case law.

Full details and the notes can be found at <www.gov.uk/government/collections/country-policy-and-information-notes>.

9.8 REFUGEE STATUS

9.8.1 Five years' limited leave

A refugee is normally granted five years' leave to remain in the UK. Pursuant to para 339Q(i) of the Immigration Rules, the Secretary of State issues what is known as a UK Residence Permit valid for five years. During this time the refugee is free to work and claim all mainstream welfare benefits.

9.8.2 Settlement

After holding limited leave for five years, a refugee may apply for settlement (see Appendix Settlement Protection of the Immigration Rules).

9.8.3   Review of status

A refugee's status is liable to a review which may lead to that status being withdrawn, cancelled or revoked. Such a step does not in itself affect the person's leave but, in practice, it will normally result in curtailment of any limited leave (see **3.7**) or revocation of any indefinite leave, and in action being taken to remove the person from the UK (see **Chapter 10**). Note that when deporting a refugee, the Secretary of State is not required to first take steps to revoke their refugee status: *RY (Sri Lanka) v Secretary of State for the Home Department* [2016] EWCA Civ 81.

9.8.3.1   Withdrawal of refugee status

Paragraph 339A of the Immigration Rules gives the Secretary of State power to withdraw refugee status from a person where:

(a)   he has voluntarily re-availed himself of the protection of the country of nationality;

(b)   having lost his nationality, he has voluntarily re-acquired it; or

(c)   he has acquired a new nationality, and enjoys the protection of the country of his new nationality;

(d)   he has voluntarily re-established himself in the country which he left or outside which he remained owing to a fear of persecution;

(e)   he can no longer, because the circumstances in connection with which he has been recognised as a refugee have ceased to exist, continue to refuse to avail himself of the protection of the country of nationality;

(f)   being a stateless person with no nationality, he is able, because the circumstances in connection with which he has been recognised a refugee have ceased to exist, to return to the country of former habitual residence.

Note that (a)–(d) are voluntary steps taken by the refugee. In respect of (e) and (f) the Secretary of State must issue a Ministerial Statement announcing that significant and non-temporary changes have occurred in a particular country such that nationals can be expected to return, or that there are exceptional circumstances for that.

As to (e), can the Ministerial Statement be based on the internal flight alternative or internal relocation? Yes – see *Secretary of State for the Home Department v MS (Somalia)* [2019] EWCA Civ 1345.

9.8.3.2   Cancellation of refugee status

Paragraph 339A of the Immigration Rules gives the Secretary of State power to cancel a person's refugee status where:

(a)   he should have been or is excluded from being a refugee in accordance with reg 7 of the Qualification Regulations 2006 (see **9.5.1**);

(b)   his misrepresentation or omission of facts, including the use of false documents, was decisive for the grant of asylum;

(c)   there are reasonable grounds for regarding him as a danger to the security of the UK (see **9.5.2**);

(d)   having been convicted by a final judgment of a particularly serious crime he constitutes danger to the community of the UK (see **9.5.2**).

9.8.3.3   Revocation of refugee status

Home Office guidance is that revocation of refugee status may be appropriate where a refugee's conduct is so serious that it warrants withdrawal of that status. Where there are serious reasons for considering that a person has committed a crime or act that falls within the scope of Article 1 F.(a) or (c) (see **9.5.1**), subsequent to the grant of asylum, it will be appropriate to revoke a person's refugee status.

9.9 HUMAN RIGHTS ISSUES

A person may claim that he should be allowed to remain in the UK as his removal would be a breach of his human rights and that he cannot reasonably be expected to return voluntarily.

9.9.1 Domestic and foreign cases

The House of Lords in R (Ullah) v Special Adjudicator; Do v Secretary of State for the Home Department [2004] UKHL 26 distinguished between what it called domestic and foreign cases. A domestic case is where an applicant alleges that the UK has acted in a way which infringes the applicant's enjoyment of a Convention right within the UK. The most common example is where a person claims that his removal would separate him from his family in the UK and so breach Article 8 ECHR.

A foreign case is where a person claims that requiring him to leave the UK will lead to a violation of his Convention rights in the country of return, ie the alleged violation of the Convention right will occur outside the UK. For example, an applicant may allege that on return he will suffer death contrary to Article 2; inhuman or degrading treatment in breach of Article 3; unlawful detention breaching Article 5; an unfair trial contrary to Article 6; or restrictions on his freedom of religion or expression in breach of Articles 9 and 10. Article 8 claims may arise in respect of a claimant's private life. For example, a person may claim that he would be unable to be openly homosexual in the receiving State because of societal prejudice and/or legislation banning homosexuality, and that his removal from the UK would therefore lead to a breach of his right to respect for private life in the receiving country.

9.9.2 Article 2 ECHR

Home Office guidance is that it will not normally seek to return a person to a country where there are substantial grounds for believing that there is a real risk he would be unlawfully killed either by the State, or through the State being unable or unwilling to protect him. In R (Ullah) v Special Adjudicator; Do v Secretary of State for the Home Department (**9.9.1** above), the House of Lords cited the decision of the ECtHR in Dehwari v Netherlands (2000) 29 EHRR CD 74, where the Court doubted whether a real risk was enough to resist removal under Article 2 and suggested that the loss of life must be shown to be a 'near-certainty'.

9.9.3 Article 3 ECHR

A person will not be removed from the UK to a country where there are substantial reasons for believing that he faces a real risk of serious harm or other treatment contrary to Article 3. This includes torture, as well as treatment or punishment that is degrading because it arouses in the victim feelings of fear, anguish or inferiority capable of humiliating and debasing him, and possibly breaking his physical and moral resistance. Severe discrimination based on race, sex or other grounds is also capable of constituting degrading treatment. For a review of the case law, see BB v Secretary of State for the Home Department [2015] EWCA Civ 9.

Ever since the ECtHR held in D v United Kingdom (1997) 24 EHRR 423 that the expulsion of an AIDS sufferer to St Kitts would breach Article 3 ECHR, the Strasbourg Court has sought to distinguish that case. In the case of D, the Court extended the reach of Article 3. The Court noted that Contracting States have the right, as a matter of well-established international law and subject to their treaty obligations including the ECHR, to control the entry, residence and expulsion of aliens. The Court applied Article 3 in what it described as the 'very exceptional circumstances' of that case, namely that the applicant was in the final stage of a terminal illness, AIDS, and had no prospect of medical care or family support on expulsion to St Kitts. In N(FC) v Secretary of State for the Home Department [2005] UKHL 31, [2005] 2 WLR 1124, the House of Lords was not persuaded to extend Article 3 any further. The House held that it must be shown that the applicant's medical condition has reached such a critical state that there are compelling humanitarian grounds for not removing him or her to a place which lacks the medical and social services which he or she would need to prevent acute suffering. This approach was confirmed when the case was appealed to the ECtHR: see N v UK [2008] LTL 28 May (App No 00026565/05).

It can be seen that the case of D v United Kingdom establishes that Article 3 may be engaged where the harm will not result from inhuman and degrading treatment by the receiving authority. For example, in Bensaid v United Kingdom [2001] ECHR 82, the applicant suffered from long-term schizophrenia. He claimed that his condition would seriously deteriorate if he were returned to his home country because of difficulties in obtaining suitable medication there. The Court stated, at para 37:

> Deterioration in his already existing mental illness could involve relapse into hallucinations and psychotic delusions involving self-harm and harm to others, as well as restrictions in social functioning (such as withdrawal and lack of motivation). The Court considers that the suffering associated with such a relapse could, in principle, fall within the scope of Article 3.

However, the Court went on to find that Article 3 would not be violated in this case as there were no exceptional circumstances. Ultimately, the question is whether what is likely to befall the claimant crosses the high threshold and the test of exceptionality (GS (India) v Secretary of State for the Home Department [2015] EWCA Civ 40). Whether or not the required level of severity is reached in a particular case for an adult or a child depends on all the circumstances of that case (AE (Algeria) v Secretary of State for the Home Department [2014] EWCA Civ 653).

In Paposhvili v Belgium (Application No 41738/10), 13 December 2016, [2017] Imm AR 867, the ECtHR at [183] said that it needed to clarify the approach to 'very exceptional cases'. The Court stated that this includes situations involving the removal of a seriously ill person in which substantial grounds have been shown for believing that he, although not at imminent risk of dying, would face a real risk, on account of the absence of appropriate treatment in the receiving country or the lack of access to such treatment, of being exposed to a serious, rapid and irreversible decline in his state of health resulting in intense suffering or to a significant reduction in life expectancy.

So, what factors affect this clarified test? The Court held at [189] that the authorities in the returning State must verify on a case-by-case basis whether the care generally available in the receiving State is sufficient and appropriate in practice for the treatment of the applicant's illness so as to prevent him being exposed to treatment contrary to Article 3. The benchmark is not the level of care existing in the returning State; it is not a question of ascertaining whether the care in the receiving State would be equivalent or inferior to that provided by the health-care system in the returning State. Nor is it possible to derive from Article 3 a right to receive specific treatment in the receiving State which is not available to the rest of the population.

The authorities must also consider the extent to which the individual in question will actually have access to this care and these facilities in the receiving State. The Court observed that it has previously questioned the accessibility of care and referred to the need to consider the cost of medication and treatment, the existence of a social and family network, and the distance to be travelled in order to have access to the required care. At [191] the Court concluded:

> Where, after the relevant information has been examined, serious doubts persist regarding the impact of removal on the persons concerned – on account of the general situation in the receiving country and/or their individual situation – the returning State must obtain individual and sufficient assurances from the receiving State, as a precondition for removal, that appropriate treatment will be available and accessible to the persons concerned so that they do not find themselves in a situation contrary to Article 3.

What is the practical effect of the decision in Paposhvili? The Supreme Court in AM (Zimbabwe) v Secretary of State for the Home Department [2020] UKSC 17 held that 'significant' means a 'substantial' reduction in life expectancy. The Court was persuaded to depart from the House of Lords decision in N(FC) above. As Lord Wilson observed at [31] and [33]:

> were a reduction in life expectancy to be less than substantial, it would not attain the minimum level of severity which article 3 requires. Surely the Court of Appeal was correct to suggest, albeit in words too extreme, that a reduction in life expectancy to death in the near future is more likely to be significant than any other reduction. But even a reduction to death in the near future might be significant for one person but not for another. Take a person aged 74, with an expectancy of life normal for that age. Were that person's expectancy be reduced to, say, two years, the reduction might well – in this context – not be significant. But compare that person with one aged 24 with an expectancy of life normal for that age. Were his or her expectancy to be reduced to two years, the reduction might well be significant.
>
> ... while it is for the applicant to adduce evidence about his or her medical condition, current treatment (including the likely suitability of any other treatment) and the effect on him or her of inability to access it, the returning state is better able to collect evidence about the availability and accessibility of suitable treatment in the receiving state. [The] obligation on the returning state [is] to dispel any serious doubts raised by the applicant's evidence.

Where a foreign national seeks to rely on Article 3 as an answer to an attempt by the UK Government to remove him to another country, the overall legal burden is on him to show that Article 3 would be infringed in his case by showing that there are substantial grounds for believing that he would face a real risk of being subject to torture or to inhuman or degrading treatment in that other country. However, note that in *Paposhvili*, at [186]–[187], the Grand Chamber of the ECtHR indicated that if a foreign national raises a prima facie case of infringement of Article 3 then that casts an evidential burden onto the defending State which is seeking to expel him (confirmed in *Secretary of State for the Home Department v PF (Nigeria)* [2019] EWCA Civ 1139 and *AM (Zimbabwe)* above).

See further **10.2.1**.

9.9.4   Other Convention Articles

When considering a foreign case involving an article other than Articles 2 and 3 ECHR, Home Office guidance is that case owners should assess the likelihood of the alleged treatment or conduct occurring on return and whether that would be a breach of the ECHR; then they should consider whether any breach would be sufficiently serious that it would amount to a flagrant violation of the relevant Convention right.

Where a claim is based on Article 8 ECHR, Home Office guidance is that pursuant to para 326B of the Immigration Rules, it should be considered in line with Appendix FM (family life) (see **8.5**) and paras 276ADE to 276DH (see **8.13**). If the claim for asylum (or humanitarian protection) is refused but the claimant qualifies for leave under either of these provisions, he should be granted leave to remain of 30 months, and he may be eligible to apply for settlement after 120 months of such leave.

9.10   HUMANITARIAN PROTECTION AND DISCRETIONARY LEAVE

9.10.1   Humanitarian protection

9.10.1.1   Overlap with asylum claim

The great majority of claims for humanitarian protection are likely to arise in the context of asylum claims. However, where an individual claims that although he is in need of international protection he is not seeking asylum, and the reasons given clearly do not engage the UK Government's obligations under the Refugee Convention (ie the fear of persecution is clearly not for one of the five Convention reasons: see **9.4.2**), then it is accepted as a stand-alone claim for humanitarian protection.

9.10.1.2 Paragraph 339C requirements

A person will be granted humanitarian protection in the UK if the Secretary of State is satisfied that the following requirements of para 339C of the Immigration Rules are met:

(a)   he is in the UK or has arrived at a port of entry in the UK; and

(b)   he does not qualify as a refugee (see **9.1**); and

(c)   substantial grounds have been shown for believing that the person concerned, if he returned to the country of return, would face a real risk of suffering serious harm and is unable, or, owing to such a risk, unwilling to avail himself of the protection of that country; and

(d)   he is not excluded from a grant of humanitarian protection. Exclusion is on the same grounds as that for asylum: see **9.5**.

For the purposes of (c) above, serious harm is defined as:

(a)   the death penalty or execution;

(b)   unlawful killing;

(c)   torture, or inhuman or degrading treatment or punishment of a person in the country of return; or

(d)   serious and individual threat to a civilian's life or person by reason of indiscriminate violence in situations of international or internal armed conflict.

In considering whether there are substantial grounds for believing that a person would face a real risk of suffering serious harm (para 339C(iii)), the standard of proof applied is that of a reasonable degree of likelihood or a real risk.

9.10.1.3 Grant of humanitarian protection

A person granted humanitarian protection is normally granted five years' leave to remain in the UK. Pursuant to para 339Q(i) of the Immigration Rules, the Secretary of State issues what is known as a UK Residence Permit, valid for five years. After holding limited leave for five years an application can be made for settlement. Life a refugee, this status is liable to a review, which may lead to its being withdrawn, cancelled or revoked (see **9.8.3**).

9.10.2 Discretionary leave

9.10.2.1 Overlap with asylum claim

The great majority of claims for discretionary leave are likely to arise in the context of asylum claims. However, a stand-alone human rights claim may also result in a grant of discretionary leave if the qualifying criteria are met.

9.10.2.2 Qualifying criteria for discretionary leave

In exceptional cases a person's medical condition, or severe humanitarian conditions in the country of return, can make his removal contrary to Article 3 ECHR. Home Office guidance is that the fact that the applicant is suffering from a distressing medical condition involving, say, a limited life expectancy or affecting his mental health, may not, in itself, be sufficient. An applicant will need to show exceptional circumstances that prevent return, namely that there are compelling humanitarian considerations, such as the applicant being in the final stages of a terminal illness without prospect of medical care or family support on return.

There may be some extreme, albeit rare, cases where a person would face such poor conditions if returned, like absence of water, food or basic shelter, that removal could be a breach of the UK's Article 3 obligations.

Home Office guidance is that discretionary leave may be appropriate where the breach would not give rise to a grant of humanitarian protection but where return would result in a flagrant denial of an ECHR right in the person's country of origin. However, it cautions that it will be rare for return to breach another Article of the ECHR in this way without also breaching Article 3.

9.10.2.3 Grant of discretionary leave

Where discretionary leave is granted, it is normally for 30 months (two-and-a-half years). Subsequent similar periods of leave may be granted if the applicant continues to meet the qualifying criteria. Once a person has held discretionary leave for 10 years, an application for settlement can be made.

Life a refugee and those granted humanitarian protection, this status is liable to a review, which may lead to its being withdrawn, cancelled or revoked (see **9.10.1.3**).

9.10.3 Asylum claims

All asylum claims are treated by the Home Office as containing an implied claim for humanitarian protection on the ground that the applicant will face a real risk of serious harm in the country of return, and/or a claim for discretionary leave on the basis that requiring the applicant to leave the UK will otherwise breach the UK's obligations under Article 3 because of the ill-treatment the applicant alleges he will suffer on return. In other words, all asylum claims should be treated as an implied Article 3 foreign case (see **9.9.1**); and if the asylum claim is refused, consideration should be given to whether return would breach the UK's obligations under Article 3, first by reference to the requirements for humanitarian protection and then by reference to any residual Article 3 issues that may entitle the applicant to discretionary leave.

9.11 CLAIMS CERTIFIED AS BEING UNFOUNDED

Section 94 of the NIAA 2002 allows the Secretary of State to certify that certain asylum or human rights claims are unfounded. The result is that there is no right of appeal in the UK. Further details are given at **11.11**.

9.12 DANGER OF UNSUCCESSFUL CLAIMS

In many cases, an entrant may feel that he has nothing to lose in making an asylum claim. However, his adviser should consider whether he has any other basis for remaining in the UK which might be prejudiced by an unsuccessful claim. If an applicant already has limited leave, the Home Office may, having refused asylum, proceed to consider whether he still meets the requirements of the Rules under which he was admitted to the UK. If he does not, his existing leave can be cancelled (curtailed) (see **3.7**) and he may then be removed from the UK.

EXAMPLE

Manuel was admitted to the UK as a student with 12 months' leave. Three months later he claims asylum. The Home Office refuses the claim. The Home Office may argue that he no longer meets the requirements of the Immigration Rules (see **6.2**), for example because he does not intend to leave the UK at the end of his studies. His leave can be cancelled (curtailed) (see **3.7**) so that he is required to leave his course before it ends.

9.13 ASYLUM APPEALS

A person refused asylum can appeal under s 82 of the NIAA 2002 (see **11.2**).

9.14 MAKING A 'FRESH' ASYLUM (OR HUMAN RIGHTS) CLAIM

What can a claimant do if his asylum (or human rights) claim has been refused by the Home Office and all his appeal rights (see **Chapter 11**) have been exhausted?

Successive UK Governments have taken the view that many failed asylum seekers attempt to prolong their stay in the UK by making more than one claim. This has led to two key powers being given to the Secretary of State. First, the ability to certify an asylum (or human rights) claim as clearly unfounded, with the result that no appeal can be made in the UK (see s 94 of the NIAA 2002 at **11.11**). Secondly, another possible bar to an appeal lies in s 96 of the NIAA 2002. This enables the Secretary of State (or an immigration officer) to issue a certificate preventing an appeal when a second asylum (or human rights) claim relies on a matter that should have been raised in an appeal against the first claim (see **11.5**).

Now let us answer the question we posed above. Further submissions in support of an asylum claim can be made to the Home Office. If these are accepted, asylum will be granted. But what if they are rejected? Is there any right of appeal in the UK? Only if the further submissions amount to a 'fresh claim' for the purposes of para 353 of the Immigration Rules. When will the submissions amount to a fresh claim? Only if they are 'significantly different from the material that has previously been considered' because:

(a)   the content has not already been considered; and

(b)   taken together with the previously considered material, the claim has a realistic prospect of success, notwithstanding its rejection.

Note that para 353B of the Immigration Rules provides that where further submissions have been made and the decision maker has established whether or not they amount to a fresh claim under para 353, the decision maker should decide if there are exceptional circumstances which mean that claimant's removal from the UK is no longer appropriate. In doing so the decision maker should take into account the claimant's:

(a)   character, conduct and associations, including any criminal record and the nature of any offence of which the migrant concerned has been convicted;

(b)   compliance with any conditions attached to any previous grant of leave to enter or remain, and compliance with any conditions of temporary admission or immigration bail where applicable; and

(c)   length of time spent in the UK spent for reasons beyond the claimant's control after the human rights or asylum claim has been submitted or refused.

If the Secretary of State concludes that a fresh claim has not been made, this can be challenged by way of judicial review on the traditional *Wednesbury* ground of irrationality: see R (*MN (Tanzania)*) *v Secretary of State for the Home Department* [2011] EWCA Civ 193. This will involve the tribunal answering two questions:

> First, has the Secretary of State asked himself the correct question? The question is not whether the Secretary of State himself thinks that the new claim is a good one or should succeed, but whether there is a realistic prospect of an [immigration judge], applying the rule of anxious scrutiny, thinking that the applicant will be exposed to a real risk of persecution on return ... The Secretary of State of course can, and no doubt logically should, treat his own view of the merits as a starting-point for that enquiry; but it is only a starting-point in the consideration of a question that is distinctly different from the exercise of the Secretary of State making up his own mind. Second, in addressing that question, both in respect of the evaluation of the facts and in respect of the legal conclusions to be drawn from those facts, has the Secretary of State satisfied the requirement of anxious scrutiny? If the court cannot be satisfied that the answer to both of those questions is in the affirmative it will have to grant an application for review of the Secretary of State's decision. (per Buxton LJ in *WM (DRC) v Secretary of State for the Home Department* [2006] EWCA Civ 1495)

See also **Chapter 12**.

9.15 ASYLUM CHECKLIST

Consider the following questions when advising an asylum claimant:

(a)   Can the applicant return to a part of the country in which he would not be subject to the harm feared (see **9.4.3.1**)?

(b)   Does the safe third country exception apply (see **9.4.3.2**)?

(c)   Is the harm feared a form of persecution (see **9.4.1.3**)? Identify acts of past persecution.

(d)   What ECHR Articles are engaged (see **9.9**)?

(e)   Is that fear of persecution well founded? Taking into account the applicant's statements and behaviour, does the applicant have a subjective fear of persecution (see **9.4.1**)?

(f)   Is that fear of persecution well founded? Objectively, are there reasonable grounds for believing that the harm feared might in fact occur in the applicant's country of origin (see **9.4.1**)?

(g)   What evidence is available or should be obtained (including medical reports)?

(h)   Are any adverse inferences to be drawn (see **9.6.2**)?

(i)   Check any relevant country policy and information notes (see **9.7**).

(j)   If the harm feared is serious enough to constitute persecution, would it be inflicted for one or more of the reasons set out in the Refugee Convention, ie race, religion, nationality, membership of a particular social group or political opinion (see **9.4.2**)?

(k)   Is the applicant saying he will change his behaviour to avoid persecution if returned (see **9.4.1.7**)?

(l)   Are there any relevant sur place activities (see **9.4.3.3**)?

(m)   Should the applicant be excluded from international protection by operation of the exclusion clauses of the Convention (see **9.5**)?

(n)   If an applicant fails to qualify for asylum, should he be granted humanitarian protection or discretionary leave (see **9.10**)?

If a claim is refused, check any appeal rights (see **9.13**).

CHAPTER 10

Deportation and Administrative Removal

10.1 DEPORTATION

10.1.1 Introduction

Under s 5 of the Immigration Act 1971 (IA 1971), the Secretary of State has a discretionary power to make a deportation order. This requires a person to leave the UK and prohibits him from lawfully re-entering while the order is in force. It also invalidates any existing leave (permission) to enter or remain.

British citizens and others with the right of abode in the UK (see **2.2** and **2.3**) cannot be deported. Some Commonwealth and Irish citizens are exempt from deportation (see **10.1.2**). Anyone else, including a person who is settled in the UK (see **3.8** and the example of *Samaroo and Sezek v Secretary of State for the Home Department* [2001] UKHRR 1150), is liable to deportation.

10.1.2 Exemption from deportation

The main exemptions from deportation are dealt with in s 7(1)(b) and (c) of the IA 1971. They apply only to Commonwealth or Irish citizens who had that citizenship at 1 January 1973 and were then ordinarily resident in the UK. Such persons are exempt from deportation on any ground if they have been ordinarily resident in the UK and Islands for five years before the date of the Secretary of State's decision to deport.

The term 'ordinarily resident' is considered in **3.8.2**. However, s 7(2) provides that, for the purpose of this exemption, if a person has at any time become ordinarily resident in the UK, he does not lose that status by remaining in breach of immigration laws. This means that a person who has overstayed, or broken conditions of entry, may nevertheless qualify for exemption.

10.1.3 Grounds for deportation

The Secretary of State may order that a person is to be deported, but only on the alternative grounds specified in s 3(5)(b) and (6) of the IA 1971. These are as follows:

(a) that the Secretary of State considers his deportation to be 'conducive to the public good' (see **10.1.4**);

(b) a person is a member of the family of a deportee (see **10.1.10**);

(c) a court has recommended deportation, in the case of a person aged 17 or over convicted of an offence punishable with imprisonment (but see the case of *R v Kluxen* at **10.1.5**).

As to the steps the Secretary of State should take to establish any ground, see *DA (Colombia) v Secretary of State for the Home Department* [2009] EWCA Civ 682.

10.1.4   When is deportation conductive to the public good?

In *OH (Serbia)* [2009] INLR 109 (approved by the Court of Appeal in *RU (Bangladesh) v Secretary of State for the Home Department* [2011] EWCA Civ 651) the court identified three important features of the public interest in deportation, namely:

(a)   the risk of re-offending by the person concerned;

(b)   the need to deter foreign nationals from committing serious crimes by leading them to understand that, whatever the other circumstances, one consequence for them may well be their deportation; and

(c)   the role of deportation as an expression of society's revulsion at serious crimes and in building public confidence in the criminal justice system's treatment of foreign citizens who have committed serious crimes.

As to (a), the risk of re-offending is normally addressed in the report prepared for sentencing and commented on by the trial judge when giving reasons for the sentence imposed.

The Secretary of State has traditionally determined that deportation is beneficial for the public good where a person has been convicted either of one serious crime or of a series of lesser offences. The former category has been largely superseded by the fact that foreign nationals sentenced to a period of imprisonment of at least 12 months are invariably deported 'automatically' (see **10.1.5**). But an offender who repeatedly commits minor offences, or a person who commits a single offence involving, for example, the use of false identity documents for which he receives a custodial sentence of less than 12 months, may be deported at the Secretary of State's discretion.

10.1.5   Automatic deportation of foreign criminals

By s 32 of the UK Borders Act 2007, the Secretary of State must, subject to limited exceptions in s 33, make a deportation order in respect of a foreign adult criminal. This is a person who is not a British citizen (see **2.2**), nor a Commonwealth citizen with the right of abode (see **2.3**) or exempt (see **10.1.2**), and who has been convicted in the UK of an offence for which he was sentenced to a period of imprisonment of at least 12 months.

Moreover, a person may appeal on the ground that his removal from the UK would breach his ECHR rights (see **10.2** and **10.3.4**) and/or the UK's obligations under the Refugee Convention (see, eg, *RU (Bangladesh) v Secretary of State for the Home Department* [2011] EWCA Civ 651; *AP (Trinidad & Tobago) v Secretary of State for the Home Department* [2011] EWCA Civ 551; **Chapter 9** and **11.3**).

A person liable to automatic deportation might seek to oppose it by claiming asylum in the UK. However, even if the asylum claim is accepted, the person may still be removed if he had been sentenced to a term of imprisonment of at least two years (see **9.5.2**).

What is the effect of s 32 on a criminal court's power to recommend deportation? The Court of Appeal, in *R v Kluxen* [2010] EWCA Crim 1081, held that:

(a)   in cases to which the 2007 Act applies, it is no longer necessary or appropriate to recommend the deportation of the offender concerned; and

(b)   in cases to which the 2007 Act does not apply (eg the foreign criminal does not receive any single custodial sentence of 12 months or more, or receives a non-custodial sentence), it will rarely be appropriate to recommend the deportation of the offender concerned. Those cases remain within the discretion of the Secretary of State (see **10.1.4**).

10.1.6 Effect

What are the effects of a deportation order? A person may not legally enter the UK whilst an order is in force. By para 9.2.1 of Part 9 of the Immigration Rules, entry clearance and leave to enter will be refused to such a person (see **3.4.5.2**).

See **10.1.9** as to revoking an order.

10.1.7 Procedure

The general procedure is described in paras 381, 382 and 384 of the Immigration Rules. Initially, the Home Office takes a decision to deport. Notice of this is then normally given to the deportee. He may then exercise his rights of appeal. If he fails to appeal, or loses his appeal, the Secretary of State may then sign the deportation order. Under Sch 3 to the IA 1971, the deportee may then be removed to the country of which he is a national, or to another country which is likely to receive him.

The deportee may be detained following the decision to deport. The power to detain a person who is subject to deportation action is set out in para 2 of Sch 3 to the IA 1971 and s 36 of the UK Borders Act 2007. This includes those whose deportation has been recommended by a court pending the making of a deportation order, those who have been served with a notice of intention to deport pending the making of a deportation order, those who are being considered for automatic deportation or pending the making of a deportation order as required by the automatic deportation provisions, and those who are the subject of a deportation order pending removal.

Note that a similar power to detain an illegal entrant or a person liable to administrative removal (or someone suspected to be such a person) (see **10.4**) is found in para 16(2) of Sch 2 to the IA 1971.

Rights of appeal against deportation decisions are dealt with in **Chapter 11**.

10.1.8 Voluntary departure

What if a person is subject to enforcement action but a deportation order has not yet been signed? As an order cannot be made against a person who is not in the UK, it is open to the person to leave the UK voluntarily. Enforcement action will cease if it is known that a person has embarked. The advantage is that the person is not subsequently debarred from re-entering the UK, although he must, of course, satisfy the requirements of the Immigration Rules for which he is seeking entry in the normal way.

10.1.9 Revocation of a deportation order

By para 390 of the Immigration Rules, an application may be made for revocation of a deportation order, and this will be considered in the light of all the circumstances, including the following:

(a) the grounds on which the order was made;

(b) any representations made in support of revocation;

(c) the interests of the community, including the maintenance of an effective immigration control; and

(d) the interests of the applicant, including any compassionate circumstances.

Note that by para 391, if an applicant was deported following conviction for a criminal offence then revocation will not occur:

(a) in the case of a conviction for an offence for which the person was sentenced to a period of imprisonment of less than four years, unless 10 years have elapsed since the making of the deportation order, or

(b)   in the case of a conviction for an offence for which the person was sentenced to a period of imprisonment of at least four years, at any time.

Can these prescribed periods be overridden? Yes, if, in either case, the continuation would be contrary to the European Convention on Human Rights or the Refugee Convention, or there are other exceptional circumstances that mean the continuation is outweighed by compelling factors.

> Decision-takers will have to conduct an assessment of the proportionality of maintaining the order in place for the prescribed period, balancing the public interest in continuing it against the interference with the applicant's private and family life; but in striking that balance they should take as a starting-point the Secretary of State's assessment of the public interest reflected in the prescribed periods and should only order revocation after a lesser period if there are compelling reasons to do so. (per Underhill LJ in *Secretary of State for the Home Department v ZP (India)* [2015] EWCA Civ 1197 at [24])

In other cases, revocation of the order will not normally be authorised unless the situation has materially altered, either by a change of circumstances since the order was made, or by fresh information coming to light which was not before the appellate authorities or the Secretary of State. The passage of time since the person was deported may also in itself amount to a change of circumstances justifying revocation of the order.

So, when the 10-year period applies, it will be very difficult for other factors to counterbalance the presumptive effect of the Secretary of State's policy:

> That is consistent with the decision of this court in *ZP (India)*. Once the ten year period has elapsed it becomes easier to argue that the balance has shifted in favour of revocation on the facts of a particular case because the presumption has fallen away; but that does not mean that revocation thereafter is automatic or presumed. The question of revocation of a deportation order will depend on the circumstances of the individual case. (per The Senior President in *EYF (Turkey) v Secretary of State for the Home Department* [2019] EWCA Civ 592 at [28])

Revocation of a deportation order does not entitle the person concerned to re-enter the UK. It merely renders him eligible to apply for admission under the Immigration Rules.

10.1.10   Family members of deportee

By s 5(4) of the IA 1971, the family members liable to be deported with the deportee are his spouse or civil partner and his or her children under 18. For these purposes an adopted child, whether legally adopted or not, may be treated as the child of the adopter and, if legally adopted, must be regarded as the child only of the adopter. Also an illegitimate child (unless adopted) is regarded as the child of the mother.

Note that no family deportation can be made once eight weeks have elapsed since any other family member was deported (see IA 1971, s 5).

This can be a controversial ground for deportation, as someone who is deported as the family member of the deportee may have committed no breach of immigration law or indeed any other laws. Remember, however, that it cannot be used to deport any family member who has the right of abode in the UK (see **2.2** and **2.3**) or is exempt (see **10.1.2**).

By para 365 of the Immigration Rules, the Secretary of State will not normally decide to deport the spouse or civil partner of a deportee where:

(a)   he has qualified for settlement in his own right; or

(b)   he has been living apart from the deportee.

By para 366 of the Immigration Rules, the Secretary of State will not normally decide to deport the child of a deportee where:

(a)   he and his mother or father are living apart from the deportee; or

(b)   he has left home and established himself on an independent basis; or

(c)   he married or formed a civil partnership before deportation came into prospect.

Note that para 389 of the Immigration Rules provides that a family member of a deportee may be able to seek re-admission to the UK under the Immigration Rules where:

(a)   a child reaches 18 (when he ceases to be subject to the deportation order); or

(b)   in the case of a spouse or civil partner, the marriage or civil partnership comes to an end.

As to arguments opposing deportation based on human rights see **10.2** and **10.3**.

For further details, see the UKVI criminal casework guidance on the deportation of family members of foreign national offenders on its website (see **1.2.8**).

10.1.11   Presumption that the public interest requires deportation

Paragraph 396 of the Immigration Rules provides that where a person is liable to deportation, the presumption shall be that the public interest requires deportation.

Paragraph 396 of the Immigration Rules also states that it is in the public interest to deport where the Secretary of State must make a deportation order in accordance with s 32 of the UK Borders Act 2007 (see **10.1.5**).

In what circumstances is the presumption rebutted? Paragraph 397 provides that a deportation order will not be made if the person's removal pursuant to the order would be contrary to the UK's obligations under the Refugee Convention (see **Chapter 9**) or the Human Rights Convention (see **10.2** and **10.3**). However, it is stressed that where deportation would not be contrary to these obligations, it will be only in exceptional circumstances that the public interest in deportation is outweighed.

10.2   HUMAN RIGHTS CHALLENGES TO DEPORTATION OTHER THAN ARTICLE 8 ECHR

10.2.1   Articles 2 and 3 ECHR

A person will not be expelled from the UK to a country where there are substantial reasons for believing that he faces a real risk of:

(a)   being unlawfully killed either by the State, or through the State being unable or unwilling to protect him contrary to Article 2 ECHR; or

(b)   suffering serious harm or other treatment contrary to Article 3 ECHR. This includes torture, as well as treatment or punishment that is degrading because it arouses in the victim feelings of fear, anguish or inferiority capable of humiliating and debasing him, and possibly breaking his physical and moral resistance. Severe discrimination based on race, sex or other grounds is also capable of constituting degrading treatment.

Home Office guidance is that in order for a claimant to establish that there would be a breach of Article 3 ECHR on medical grounds if they were removed from or required to leave the UK, the claimant must show that there are substantial grounds for believing that:

(a)   they would face a real risk of being exposed to either:

(i)   a serious, rapid and irreversible decline in their state of health resulting in intense suffering, or

(ii)   a significant (meaning substantial) reduction in life expectancy; and

(b)   the serious, rapid and irreversible decline in health leading to intense suffering and/or the significant reduction in life expectancy must be as a result of either:

(i)   the absence of appropriate treatment in the receiving country, or

(ii)   the lack of access to such treatment.

Whether a claimant's reduction in life expectancy is substantial will depend on the facts. The Home Office guidance gives the following example. Claimants aged 74 and 24 both have a normal life expectancy for their respective ages in their country of origin. If their life expectancies were to be reduced to just two years it might be considered as a substantial reduction for the 24-year-old but not the 74-year-old.

A claimant must produce evidence to show that on the face of it there is an infringement of their rights which, if unchallenged, would establish a breach of Article 3 ECHR on medical grounds. Home Office guidance is that the claimant should produce evidence of their medical condition, their current treatment for that condition, the likely suitability of any alternate treatment for their condition and the effect that an inability to obtain effective treatment would have on their health. Once a claimant has established their prima facie case, it is for the decision maker to investigate any serious doubts about whether the claimant can be safely removed from the UK, taking into account the availability and accessibility of treatment in the receiving state to determine whether the care and treatment which is generally available in the receiving state is in practice sufficient to prevent a breach of Article 3 ECHR and whether the care and treatment is accessible, taking into consideration the cost, the existence of any family or support network and geographical location. If serious doubts persist after the investigation has been concluded, the UK Government will need to obtain individual assurances from the receiving state that appropriate treatment will be available and accessible to the claimant.

Also see **9.9.2** and **9.9.3**.

10.2.2 Articles 5 and 6 ECHR

In resisting expulsion on the ground that his Article 5 ECHR right will be threatened in the country to which he is sent, a person must establish that there are substantial grounds for believing that, if removed, he will face a real risk of a flagrant breach of that Article. In this context, a flagrant breach is a breach the consequences of which are so severe that they override the right of a State to expel an alien from its territory. In describing such a breach of Article 5 in R (Ullah) v Special Adjudicator [2004] UKHL 26, Lord Steyn (at [43]) gave by way of example the case of intended expulsion to a country in which the rule of law is flagrantly flouted, *habeas corpus* is unavailable and there is a real risk that the individual may face arbitrary detention for many years.

Before the expulsion of a person will be capable of violating Article 6 ECHR, there must be substantial grounds for believing that there is a real risk:

(a)   that there will be a fundamental breach of the principles of a fair trial guaranteed by Article 6 ('[w]hat is required is that the deficiency or deficiencies in the trial process should be such as fundamentally to destroy the fairness of the prospective trial', per Lord Phillips in RB (Algeria) v Secretary of State for the Home Department [2009] UKHL 10 at [136]); and

(b)   that this failure will lead to a miscarriage of justice that itself constitutes a flagrant violation of the victim's fundamental rights. This was the situation in RB (Algeria), where the appellant had already been tried in his absence and sentenced to life imprisonment. There were substantial grounds for believing that he would not be able to obtain a retrial and would be imprisoned to serve the sentence imposed in his absence.

What is required is a breach of the principles of fair trial guaranteed by Article 6 ECHR which is so fundamental as to amount to a nullification of, or destruction of the very essence of, the right guaranteed by that Article: see Othman (Abu Qatada) v UK [2012] ECHR 56. Note that in this case the ECtHR held that the applicant's deportation to Jordan would be in violation of Article 6 on account of the real risk that evidence obtained by torturing third persons would be admitted when the applicant was (re-)tried in Jordan.

Article 6 ECHR might also be engaged where the person has an outstanding civil claim in the UK for private law damages, eg a personal injury claim, or is a prospective party to such a civil claim which he actively is pursuing. Home Office guidance is that it may be relevant if the person:

(a)   does not have access to communication facilities in the country of return;

(b)   needs to undertake a medical examination;

(c)   will not have access to funding to pursue his civil claim;

(d)   will not be able to have access to interpreters;

(e)   wants to represent himself in court;

(f)   is required to give evidence in court; and

(g)   needs direct personal contact in order to instruct his UK legal representatives.

Other factors may include the complexity of the case; access to telephone and conferencing facilities in the country to which the individual is to be returned; the reliability of postal, email and fax facilities in that country; and whether or not liability has been admitted.

10.3   ARTICLE 8 ECHR CHALLENGES TO DEPORTATION

10.3.1   Article 8: private life

For the purposes of Article 8 ECHR, what is a person's private life in the UK? The answer is found by establishing the strength of his ties to the UK, which he has established here in terms of friends, education, work and leisure activities.

Can a person's contribution to society whilst in the UK, such as voluntary work for a charity, be taken into account as a factor in the balancing exercise necessary to decide whether his expulsion from the UK will breach this right? The Court of Appeal answered this question in the affirmative in *UE (Nigeria) v Secretary of State for the Home Department* [2010] EWCA Civ 975. The Court held that a person's contributions to the community in which he lived would reduce the need to maintain effective immigration control for administrative removal (see **10.4**) purposes, but they would be unlikely to make much difference in a deportation case. However, the greater the person's contribution, the more weight the factor might be given, especially if the person is an essential worker in a company engaged in a successful export business, or a social worker upon whom a local community depends or a scientific research worker engaged on research of public importance.

The fact that a foreign criminal's prospects for rehabilitation are better in the UK than in his country of origin is not a factor which should be taken into account in an appeal against deportation based on Article 8 ECHR. An offender cannot rely on his own partially unreformed criminality as a factor relevant to his private (or family) life: *SE (Zimbabwe) v Secretary of State for the Home Department* [2014] EWCA Civ 256.

> [T]he weight which [rehabilitation] will bear will vary from case to case, but it will rarely be of great weight bearing in mind that ... the public interest in the deportation of criminals is not based only on the need to protect the public from further offending by the foreign criminal in question but also on wider policy considerations of deterrence and public concern. (per Underhill LJ in *HA (Iraq) v Secretary of State for the Home Department* [2020] EWCA Civ 1176 at [141])

10.3.2   Article 8: family life

Article 8 ECHR may also be engaged where the person claims that to expel him from the UK will separate him from his family here and would therefore constitute a breach of his right to respect for family life in the UK. Who might form part of a family? Partners in a lawful and genuine marriage or civil partnership, or a relationship akin to such, will normally constitute family life. Home Office guidance is that a relationship between unmarried and same-sex partners of sufficient substance or stability will qualify even if the couple do not meet the usual two years' cohabitation requirement in Appendix FM to the Immigration Rules (see **8.3**). In any event, such relationships would fall within a person's private life. A new relationship, or that between people who are not regular or established partners, will not suffice.

In the case of natural parents and their minor children, there is a general presumption of family life. Further, the relationship between an adoptive parent and an adopted person is in principle the same. The Home Office accepts that family life may exist between a child and his natural parent even if at the time of birth the relationship between the two parents has ended, and even if the child does not live with his parent. However, the fact that a parent has only infrequent contact with his child may be relevant to the question of whether removal would disproportionately interfere with their family life.

Family life may continue between parent and child after the child has attained his majority because it does not suddenly stop when the child reaches 18: see *Secretary of State for the Home Department v HK (Turkey)* [2010] EWCA Civ 583, where Sir Scott Baker said, at [16]:

> [I]t is apparent that the respondent had lived in the same house as his parents since 1994. He reached his majority in September 2005 but continued to live at home. Undoubtedly he had family life while he was growing up and I would not regard it as suddenly cut off when he reached his majority.

Also note that in *AP (India) v Secretary of State for the Home Department* [2015] EWCA Civ 89, McCombe LJ said at [45]:

> It seems to me that adult children (male or female) who are young students, from most backgrounds, usually continue to form an important part of the family in which they have grown up. They attend their courses and gravitate to their homes during the holidays, and upon graduation, while (as the FTT put it) they seek to 'make their own way' in the world. Such a child is very much part of the on-going family unit and, until such a child does fly the nest, his or her belonging to the family is as strong as ever. The proportionality of interference with the family rights of the various family members should receive, I think, careful consideration in individual cases where this type of issue arises.

Relationships of grandparents and grandchildren, uncles and aunts, nephews and nieces, may fall within the scope of family life, depending upon the strength of the emotional ties. It is rare for relationships between adult siblings or adult children and their parents to count (*Odawey v Entry Clearance Officer* [2011] EWCA Civ 840), unless there are special elements of dependency beyond normal emotional ties (*Kugathas v Secretary of State for the Home Department* [2003] EWCA Civ 31), for example the support of an elder brother for his very sick younger brother in *R (Ahmadi) v Secretary of State for the Home Department* [2005] EWCA Civ 1721.

> [T]he case law establishes clearly that love and affection between family members are not of themselves sufficient. There has to be something more. Normal emotional ties will not usually be enough; further elements of emotional and/or financial dependency are necessary, albeit that there is no requirement to prove exceptional dependency. The formal relationship(s) between the relevant parties will be relevant, although ultimately it is the substance and not the form of the relationship(s) that matters. The existence of effective, real or committed support is an indicator of family life. Co-habitation is generally a strong pointer towards the existence of family life. The extent and nature of any support from other family members will be relevant, as will the existence of any relevant cultural or social traditions. Indeed, in a case where the focus is on the parent, the issue is the extent of the dependency of the older relative on the younger ones in the UK and whether or not that dependency creates something more than the normal emotional ties. (per Carr DBE LJ in *Mobeen v Secretary of State for the Home Department* [2021] EWCA Civ 886 at [46])

10.3.3   The traditional five questions

As Article 8 ECHR is a qualified right, traditionally five questions have been posed in determining its role in a person's expulsion:

Question 1: Does the person have a private and/or family life in the UK? See **10.3.1** and **10.3.2** above.

Question 2: If a private and/or family life exists, will removal interfere with that?

As to family life, the answer depends to some extent on whose family life is being considered – only that of the person being removed, or that of all members of his family unit? The House of Lords, in *Beoku-Betts v Secretary of State for the Home Department* [2008] UKHL 39, held that the effect of expulsion on all members of the person's family unit should be taken into account. Together these members enjoy a single family life, and whether or not the removal would interfere with it has to be looked at by reference to the family unit as a whole and the impact of removal upon each member.

In *Huang v Secretary of State for the Home Department* [2007] UKHL 11, the House of Lords held that the expulsion of the person must prejudice his family life in a manner sufficiently serious to amount to a breach of Article 8 ECHR. However, as Sedley LJ indicated in *AG (Eritrea) v Secretary of State for the Home Department* [2007] EWCA Civ 801, at [28], the threshold of engagement is not a specifically high one. So, for example, in *A (Afghanistan) v Secretary of State for the Home Department* [2009] EWCA Civ 825, the Court held that the interference with family life which would result from not allowing a husband and his heavily pregnant wife in a genuine and subsisting marriage to cohabit, engaged the operation of Article 8 ECHR.

The burden is on an applicant to establish positive answers to questions 1 and 2 (see *PG (USA) v Secretary of State for the Home Department* [2015] EWCA Civ 118).

Question 3: If there is interference with a private and/or family life, is it in accordance with the law?

The answer will be yes, provided the decision is in accordance with the relevant statutory provisions, Immigration Rules and the published policies of the Home Office.

Question 4: Is the interference in pursuit of one or more of the permissible aims set out under Article 8(2)?

This may include the maintenance of effective immigration controls by administrative removal (see **10.4**) and public safety, the prevention of crime and disorder, and national security by deportation (see **10.1.4**).

The answer will be yes, provided the decision is in accordance with the stated Government policy.

Question 5: Is the interference proportionate to the permissible aim or aims?

This is normally the key question, and often a difficult one to answer as the assessment of proportionality is a balancing exercise between the individual's private interests and the Government's permissible aims. It is this question that the Immigration Rules seek to address.

10.3.4 Immigration policy

10.3.4.1 Criminality thresholds

When is it a proportionate step to deport a person for the purposes of Article 8 ECHR? Current government policy, reflected in the Immigration Act 2014 and the Immigration Rules, is that:

(a)   the more serious the offence committed by a foreign criminal, the greater the public interest in deportation;

(b)   the more criminal convictions a foreign criminal has, the greater the public interest in deportation;

(c)   it is in the public interest to deport a foreign criminal even where there is evidence of remorse or rehabilitation or that he presents a low risk of reoffending;

(d)   the need to deter other non-British nationals from committing crimes – by leading them to understand that, whatever the other circumstances, one consequence may well be deportation – is a very important facet of the public interest in deporting a foreign criminal;

(e)   the role of deportation as an expression of society's revulsion at serious crimes, and in building public confidence in the treatment of non-British nationals who have committed serious crimes, is a very important facet of the public interest in deporting a foreign criminal; and

(f)   where a foreign criminal has also been convicted of an offence outside the UK, the overseas conviction will usually add to the public interest in deportation. An example of an exception to this general rule might be where there is evidence that prosecution was pursued solely for political reasons.

Home Office guidance also indicates that the following factors are capable of adding weight to the public interest in deportation, namely, where a foreign criminal:

(a)   is considered to have a high risk of reoffending;

(b)   does not accept responsibility for his offending or express remorse;

(c)   has an adverse immigration history or precarious immigration status;

(d)   has a history of immigration-related non-compliance (eg failing to co-operate fully and in good faith with the travel document process) or frustrating the removal process in other ways;

(e)   has previously obtained or attempted to obtain limited or indefinite leave to enter or remain by means of deception;

(f)   has used deception in any other circumstances (eg to secure employment, benefits or free NHS healthcare to which he was not entitled); and

(g)   has entered the UK in breach of a deportation order.

> The correct approach to be taken to the 'public interest' in the balance to be undertaken by a tribunal is to recognise that the public interest in the deportation of foreign criminals has a moveable rather than fixed quality. It is necessary to approach the public interest flexibly, recognising that there will be cases where the person's circumstances in the individual case reduce the legitimate and strong public interest in removal. (per Sir Ernest Ryder, Senior President in *Akinyemi v Secretary of State for the Home Department (No 2)* [2019] EWCA Civ 2098, at [39])

In particular, s 117C of the NIAA 2002 and para 398 of the Immigration Rules address the situation where a person claims that his deportation would be contrary to the UK's obligations under Article 8 ECHR.

By sub-para (b) of para 398, if the person has been convicted of an offence for which he has been sentenced to a period of imprisonment of less than four years but at least 12 months, or under sub-para (c) if, in the view of the Secretary of State, his offending has caused serious harm (see **10.3.5**) or he is a persistent offender who shows a particular disregard for the law (see **10.3.6**), then the Secretary of State may decide not to deport that person but grant him limited leave to remain (see **10.3.10**) should he meet the requirements of paras 399 (see **10.3.7** and **10.3.8**) or 399A (see **10.3.9**); otherwise, the public interest in deportation will only be outweighed by other factors where there are very compelling circumstances over and above those described in paras 399 and 399A (see **10.3.7**, **10.3.8** and **10.3.11**).

By sub-para (a) of para 398, if the person has been convicted of an offence for which he has been sentenced to a period of imprisonment of at least four years, it will be only in very compelling circumstances (see **10.3.11**) that the public interest in deportation will be outweighed by other factors.

What does 'sentenced to a period of imprisonment' mean? Home Office guidance is that the determinative factor is the sentence imposed and not the actual time spent in prison. However, this does not include a suspended sentence, unless that sentence is subsequently activated, nor convictions which are subsequently quashed on appeal. Where sentences are subsequently increased or reduced on appeal but the person nevertheless remains convicted of the offence, the revised sentence length applies.

It is important not to confuse consecutive and concurrent sentences of imprisonment in this context. For a consecutive sentence, the period of imprisonment equals the sum of all the sentences. But for a concurrent sentence, the period of imprisonment equals the length of the longest sentence.

Does it matter when the conviction leading to the period of imprisonment occurred? No, held the Court of Appeal in *OH (Algeria) v Secretary of State for the Home Department* [2019] EWCA Civ 1763.

10.3.4.2 Other public policy considerations

Section 117A of the NIAA 2002 (inserted by s 19 of the Immigration Act 2014) provides that whenever a court or tribunal is required to determine whether a decision made under the Immigration Acts breaches a person's right to respect for private and family life under Article 8 ECHR, in considering whether an interference with the person's right to respect for private and family life is justified under Article 8(2) ECHR, the court or tribunal must (in particular) have regard to the following:

(a) The maintenance of effective immigration controls is in the public interest.

(b) It is in the public interest, and in particular in the interests of the economic well-being of the UK, that persons who seek to enter or remain in the UK (i) are able to speak English, and (ii) are financially independent, because such persons are less of a burden on taxpayers and better able to integrate into society. However, it does not follow that because a person is able to speak English and/or is financially independent, it is in the public interest that they should be given leave to enter or remain. Moreover, financially independent means not being financially dependent upon the State; any evidence of support from third parties must be credible and the support reliable (*Rhuppiah v Secretary of State for the Home Department* [2018] UKSC 58).

(c) Little weight should be given to (i) a private life, or (ii) a relationship formed with a qualifying partner (see **10.3.8**), that is established by a person at a time when the person is in the UK unlawfully. What does unlawfully mean in this context? It means that the person's presence in the UK is in breach of UK law (*Akinyemi v Secretary of State for the Home Department* [2017] EWCA Civ 236).

(d) Little weight should be given to a private life established by a person at a time when the person's immigration status is precarious (see **10.3.8**).

What does 'little weight' in (c) and (d) above mean?

> Although a court or tribunal should have regard to the consideration that little weight should be given to private life established in [the specified] circumstances, it is possible without violence to the language to say that such generalised normative guidance may be overridden in an exceptional case by particularly strong features of the private life in question. (per Sales LJ in *Rhuppiah v Secretary of State for the Home Department* [2016] EWCA Civ 803 at [53] and approved in the subsequent Supreme Court decision [2018] UKSC 58 at [49])

10.3.5 Paragraph 398(c): what is meant by 'serious harm'?

Home Office guidance is that references to an 'offence which has caused serious harm' includes, but is not limited to, causing death or serious injury to an individual or group of individuals. A person does not need to be convicted of specifically causing a death or serious injury. Examples might include, but are not limited to, manslaughter; dangerous driving; driving whilst under the influence of drink and/or drugs; and arson.

The provision was considered by Simon LJ giving the judgment of the Court of Appeal in *Mahmood v Upper Tribunal (Immigration & Asylum Chamber)* [2020] EWCA Civ 717:

> 39. So far as the word 'caused' is concerned, the harm must plainly be causatively linked to the offence. In the case of an offence of violence, injury will be caused to the immediate victim and possibly others. However, what matters is the harm caused by the particular offence. The prevalence of (even minor)

offending may cause serious harm to society, but that does not mean that an individual offence considered in isolation has done so. Shoplifting, for example, may be a significant social problem, causing serious economic harm and distress to the owner of a modest corner shop; and a thief who steals a single item of low value may contribute to that harm, but it cannot realistically be said that such a thief caused serious harm himself, either to the owner or to society in general. Beyond this, we are doubtful that a more general analysis of how the law approaches causation in other fields is helpful.

40. As to 'harm', often it will be clear from the nature of the offence that harm has been caused. Assault Occasioning Actual Bodily Harm under s.47 of the Offences Against the Person Act 1861 is an obvious example.

41. Mr Biggs argued on behalf of Mahmood that the harm must be physical or psychological harm to an identifiable individual that is identifiable and quantifiable. We see no good reason for interpreting the provision in this way. The criminal law is designed to prevent harm that may include psychological, emotional or economic harm. Nor is there good reason to suppose a statutory intent to limit the harm to an individual. Some crimes, for example, supplying class A drugs, money laundering, possession of firearms, cybercrimes, perjury and perverting the course of public justice may cause societal harm. In most cases the nature of the harm will be apparent from the nature of the offence itself, the sentencing remarks or from victim statements. However, we agree with Mr Biggs, at least to this extent: harm in this context does not include the potential for harm or an intention to do harm. Where there is a conviction for a serious attempt offence, it is likely that the sentence will be more than 12 months.

42. The adjective 'serious' qualifies the extent of the harm; but provides no precise criteria. It is implicit that an evaluative judgment has to be made in the light of the facts and circumstances of the offending. There can be no general and all-embracing test of seriousness. In some cases, it will be a straightforward evaluation and will not need specific evidence of the extent of the harm; but in every case, it will be for the tribunal to evaluate the extent of the harm on the basis of the evidence that is available and drawing common sense conclusions.

10.3.6 Paragraph 398(c): who is a persistent offender?

Home Office guidance is that references to a 'persistent offender who, in the view of the Secretary of State, has shown a disregard for the law' involve a case-specific assessment of the nature, extent, seriousness and impact of the person's offending, taking into account the following non-exhaustive list of factors:

(a) *The number of offences committed.* The decision maker must look at how many offences have been committed by the individual. There is no numerical value or limit at which deportation begins to outweigh the person's right to family or private life. But this should be borne in mind when looking at the factors at (b), (c), (d) and (e) below in reaching a decision about persistence and whether the public interest is served by that person's deportation.

(b) *The seriousness of those offences.* The sentence or disposal should be the primary indicator of the seriousness of the offence, but the decision maker should nevertheless consider the nature of any offence(s) of which the person has been convicted and whether there are offences which give rise to the public interest being met.

(c) *Any escalation in seriousness of the offences.* The decision maker must consider whether the pattern of offending gives particular cause to believe that the public interest would be served by the person's deportation and that it would outweigh that person's right to family or private life. The aim for the decision maker is to identify a pattern of escalating offending and intervene before a very serious offence is committed.

(d) *The timescale over which the offences were committed.* The decision maker must consider over what timescale the offending has taken place and how recently the last of the offending took place. Less weight might be placed on a series of offences committed over a very short period of time which has long since ceased, particularly if this could be attributed to a particular incident or issue in the person's life which would make deportation now a disproportionate response. But repeated criminality over a lengthy period of time would weigh in favour of deportation. The length of time the person has spent in the UK will be an appropriate consideration. For example, a person who has committed four offences in the 10 years he has spent in the UK might not be viewed as a persistent offender; a person who commits three offences in the course of just six months' residence might be so viewed.

(e) *The frequency within which they were committed.* Again, the length of time the person has spent in the UK will be an appropriate consideration. The less time a person has spent in the UK relative to the number of offences and level of offending, the more deportation begins to outweigh that person's right to family or private life.

(f) *Any action taken to address the cause of the offending.* The decision maker should consider any programs or activities aimed at addressing the cause of the offending. Examples might include courses aimed at reduction of alcohol dependency or drug dependency, and anger management. These must demonstrate that they are having the necessary impact, such that the person's offending can be seen to have significantly reduced to the extent that his right to family or private life outweighs the public interest in deporting him.

In *Chege* ('*is a persistent offender*') [2016] UKUT 187 (IAC), the Upper Tribunal held that a 'persistent offender' is someone who keeps on breaking the law. That does not mean, however, that he has to keep on offending until the date of the relevant decision or that the continuity of the offending cannot be broken. A 'persistent offender' is not a permanent status that can never be lost once it is acquired, but an individual can be regarded as a 'persistent offender' for the purpose of the Immigration Rules even though he may not have offended for some time. The question whether he fits that description will depend on the overall picture and pattern of his offending over his entire offending history up to that date. Each case will turn on its own facts. This was approved by the Court of Appeal in *SC (Zimbabwe) v Secretary of State for the Home Department* [2018] EWCA Civ 929 and *Binbuga (Turkey) v Secretary of State for the Home Department* [2019] EWCA Civ 551.

10.3.7 Paragraph 399: exception based on relationship with a child

What weight should be given to the best interests of children who are affected by the decision to remove one or both of their parents from the UK? The Supreme Court addressed this question in *H (Tanzania) v Secretary of State for the Home Department* [2011] UKSC 4. The Court held that the best interests of the child must be a primary consideration. A decision maker must identify what the best interests of the child require, and then assess whether the strength of any other consideration, or the cumulative effect of other considerations, outweighs the consideration of the best interests of the child.

Home Office guidance is that where a person asserts that he has a family life with a child or children in the UK, the decision maker must ensure that the person can satisfy all of the following requirements of para 399 (emphasis added):

(a) the person has a genuine and subsisting parental relationship with a child under the age of 18 years who is in the UK [see **8.5.1.1**], *and*

   (i) the child is a British Citizen [see **2.2**]; *or*

   (ii) the child has lived in the UK continuously for at least the 7 years immediately preceding the date of the immigration decision [see **8.5.1.2**]; *and in either case*

      (a) it would be unduly harsh for the child to live in the country to which the person is to be deported, and

      (b) it would be unduly harsh for the child to remain in the UK without the person who is to be deported.

In what circumstances is it proportionate to remove a parent where the effect will be that a child who is a British citizen will also have to leave? The Supreme Court also addressed this question in *H (Tanzania) v Secretary of State for the Home Department*. The Court stated that whilst nationality is not a 'trump card', it is of particular importance in assessing the best interests of any child. The intrinsic importance of British citizenship should not be played down. As a British citizen, a child has rights which he will not be able to exercise if he moves to another country. He will lose the advantages of growing up and being educated in his own country, his own culture and his own language.

What does 'unduly harsh' mean in para 399(a)(ii)(a) and (b)? The Supreme Court in *KO (Nigeria) v Secretary of State for the Home Department* [2018] UKSC 53 indicated at [23] that the word 'unduly' implies an element of comparison. It assumes that there is a 'due' level of 'harshness', namely a level which may be acceptable or justifiable in the relevant context. 'Unduly' implies something going beyond that level. The relevant context is that set by s 117C(1) of the NIAA 2002, that is the public interest in the deportation of foreign criminals. A decision maker is therefore looking for a degree of harshness going beyond what would necessarily be involved for any child faced with the deportation of a parent:

> It is therefore now clear that a tribunal or court must focus not on the comparative seriousness of the offence or offences committed by the foreign criminal who faces deportation, but rather, on whether the effects of their deportation on a child or partner would go beyond the degree of harshness which would necessarily be involved for any child or partner of a foreign criminal faced with deportation. Pursuant to Rule 399, the tribunal or court must consider both whether it would be unduly harsh for the child to live in the country to which the foreign criminal parent is to be deported and whether it would be unduly harsh for the child to remain in the UK without him. (per Holroyde LJ in *Secretary of State for the Home Department v PG (Jamaica)* [2019] EWCA Civ 1213 at [34])

In *HA (Iraq) v Secretary of State for the Home Department* [2020] EWCA Civ 1176, the Court of Appeal said that the Supreme Court's decision should not be read entirely literally since it is hard to define the level of harshness that would 'necessarily' be suffered by 'any' child. The Court observed that there could be unusual cases where the deportation of a parent would not be 'harsh' for the child at all, even where there was a genuine and subsisting relationship:

> The essential point is that the criterion of undue harshness sets a bar which is 'elevated' and carries a 'much stronger emphasis' than mere undesirability .... The reason why some degree of harshness is acceptable is that there is a strong public interest in the deportation of foreign criminals .... The underlying question for tribunals is whether the harshness which the deportation will cause for the partner and/or child is of a sufficiently elevated degree to outweigh that public interest.

> However, while recognising the 'elevated' nature of the statutory test, it is important not to lose sight of the fact that the hurdle which it sets is not as high as that set by the test of 'very compelling circumstances' in section 117C (6) .... It follows that the observations in the case-law to the effect that it will be rare for the test of 'very compelling circumstances' to be satisfied have no application in this context .... The statutory intention is evidently that the hurdle representing the unacceptable impact on a partner or child should be set somewhere between the (low) level applying in the case of persons who are liable to ordinary immigration removal ... and the (very high) level applying to serious offenders. (per   Underhill LJ at [51] and [52])

10.3.7.1   Would it be unduly harsh for the child to live in the country to which the person is to be deported?

Home Office guidance is that although a child's nationality and length of residence in the UK are both important factors to be considered, it is not inherently unduly harsh to expect a child who is a British citizen and/or has lived in the UK for at least seven years to leave the UK. That is why the rules expressly provide for a child's nationality and length of residence to be considered separately from the unduly harsh question. It will depend on the circumstances of the case. The Home Office takes the view that many people around the world reasonably and legitimately take their children to live in another country either temporarily or permanently, and where this complies with the law, the state does not interfere with those decisions. It is the responsibility of the foreign criminal to consider the impact on his family of the consequences of his criminal activity.

In the same vein, the Home Office asserts that, although children are innocent of any wrongdoing, sometimes they will be affected by the consequences of a foreign criminal's offending. In a deportation context, that can mean the child will go and live in another country, usually because the parents decide that the child should go with the foreign criminal (and perhaps the other parent) to that country, or in a smaller number of cases because the child cannot remain in the UK without the presence of the foreign criminal. Just as there is no automatic bar to sentencing a parent to a period of imprisonment despite the adverse impact on a child (and imprisoning a parent does not mean the child is being punished), there is no automatic bar to deporting a parent and the consequences of deportation are not a punishment for the child. However, Parliament accepts that where a foreign criminal has not been sentenced to a period of imprisonment of four years or more and the effect of deportation on a child would be unduly harsh, the child's best interests outweigh the public interest in deporting the parent.

The following is a non-exhaustive list of relevant factors that the Home Office provides to its decision makers when assessing whether it would be unduly harsh for a child to live in the country to which the foreign criminal will be deported:

(a)   the age and nationality of the child;

(b)   whether the child could obtain citizenship or a visa to reside in the country of return;

(c)   whether the child would be able to adapt to life in the country of return or whether there would be very significant obstacles to his integration there, and, if so, the nature and extent of those obstacles;

(d)   whether the child could be raised by both parents in the country of return (including, if the other parent lives in the UK, whether it is open to him or her to choose to go with the foreign criminal and the child to the country of return);

(e)   the prevailing conditions in the country of return and whether they are such that it would be unduly harsh for the child to live there (this is likely to be rare, and the onus is on the foreign criminal to particularise the impact country conditions will have on the child; decision makers should assess claims on the basis of country conditions with reference to the country guidance used in asylum cases);

(f)   whether the child has formed any family or private life in the UK outside of the home and the strength of those ties.

The Home Office anticipates that families or children may highlight the differences in quality of education, health and wider public services and economic or social opportunities between the UK and the country of return and argue that these work against the best interests of the child. The Home Office states that, other than in exceptional circumstances, this would not normally mean it is unduly harsh for the child to live in the country of return, particularly if one or both parents or wider family have the means or resources to support the child on return or the skills, education and training to provide for their family on return, or if facilitated return scheme support is available.

The Home Office accepts that consideration must also be given to the extent of a child's private life in the UK, taking into account factors such as the child's age, length of residence, dependence on wider family in the UK and any other ties to the community, to determine whether it would be unduly harsh to expect the child to live in a country other than the UK.

10.3.7.2   Would it be unduly harsh for the child to remain in the UK without the person who is to be deported?

To answer this question, it is first necessary to establish whether the child would be able to remain in the UK when the foreign criminal is deported. The following is a non-exhaustive list of relevant factors the Home Office takes into account:

(a)   whether the child has a legal guardian, a family member who has a legal obligation to care for the child (for example, responsibility or a residence order) or an existing relationship with a family member;

(b) whether someone other than the foreign criminal is the child's primary or joint-primary carer and whether that person normally has day-to-day care and wider welfare and developmental responsibility for the child;

(c) whether the person who cared for the child while the foreign criminal was in prison would be able to care for the child when the foreign criminal is deported;

(d) whether it is reasonable to expect the other person to fulfil the role of primary carer (eg whether he or she has fulfilled that role in the past, whether he or she is able to care for the child, whether he or she cares for any other children or has done so before);

(e) whether there are any factors which undermine the ability of that person to act as the primary carer of the child or would suggest that he or she is unsuitable (eg criminal convictions, concerns expressed by social services, etc).

Is it relevant, when answering this question, that another person would have to make a choice about working full time or part time or not at all and might need to arrange suitable childcare? The Home Office states that this is not likely to be a determinative factor in his or her ability to care for the child, particularly in the case of someone with a legal responsibility towards the child, and particularly where family life was formed in full knowledge that the foreign criminal may not be able to remain in the UK (because his immigration status was unlawful or precarious, or because he was liable to deportation). The Home Office view is that all parents and guardians have to make difficult choices about how to balance their working lives and their parental responsibilities.

What if the only way a child could remain in the UK if a foreign criminal is deported would be in the care of social services or foster care that is not already in place (excluding care provided by a family member or a private fostering arrangement)? The Home Office accepts that this would usually be unduly harsh, unless there is evidence that the child's best interests would be better served in such care than in the care of the foreign criminal. However, consideration must be given to the age of the child and how long he is likely to remain in care.

Is it appropriate for a decision maker to conclude that a child can remain in the UK in the care of another person who is him- of herself liable to removal or deportation? No. Home Office guidance is that if there is someone who would be able to care for the child in the UK but for having no immigration status then that person's status should be resolved before it can be determined whether it would be unduly harsh for the child to remain in the UK without the foreign criminal. Decision makers must check whether the person has an outstanding application for leave to remain in his or her own right. If he or she does, decision makers should liaise with the other caseworking unit to ensure that the application is decided before the foreign criminal's claim is considered. If the person is granted leave to remain then this will factor into the consideration of the unduly harsh question.

If it is established that the child is able to remain in the UK when the foreign criminal is deported, the following is a non-exhaustive list of relevant factors used by the Home Office when assessing whether it would be unduly harsh for the child to continue living in the UK without the presence of the foreign criminal:

(a) whether there are any reasons (related to the foreign criminal's offending history, or other reasons) why it would be in the child's best interests to be separated from the foreign criminal;

(b) the age of the child;

(c) how in practice the child would be affected by the foreign criminal's absence;

(d) whether there is credible evidence that the foreign criminal's presence is needed to prevent the child from being ill-treated, his health or development being significantly impaired, or his care being other than safe and effective;

(e) the extent of any practical difficulties the remaining parent or guardian would face in caring for the child alone (if he or she is not already effectively caring for the child alone);

(f)   whether there is credible evidence that the child would lose all contact with the foreign criminal, eg because telephone and internet contact would not be possible and there would be no possibility of visits either to the country of return or a third country. If so, whether this is unduly harsh will depend on the severity of the foreign criminal's conduct, the nature of the relationship the foreign criminal has with the child, and the impact on the child of the loss of contact.

Where a child's parents or guardians have a choice about whether the child leaves or remains in the UK, it will not be appropriate for the decision to deport to prescribe any particular outcome for the child. According to the Home Office, it is the responsibility of the family to decide for themselves whether the child will accompany the foreign criminal overseas or whether to make suitable arrangements for the child to remain in the UK based on where they think the child's best interests lie. The decision to deport requires the child's parents or guardians to make this decision.

10.3.7.3   Seeking the views of children

In deportation cases where the consequence of the decision may be to separate a child from a parent, the decision maker, when assessing the best interests of the child, must be prepared to discover the views of any affected children. These may already be available or known from information and representations supplied. If not available, and there are no reasons for their non-availability, consideration should be given to obtaining them by means of a request in writing to a parent, legal adviser or other suitable adult (eg social worker or other family member). The decision maker should be prepared to consider hearing the views of the child directly, if requested or deemed necessary.

If there are ongoing proceedings in the UK family courts concerning the child, should the decision to deport be delayed? No, stated the Court of Appeal in *Mohan v Secretary of State for the Home Department* [2012] EWCA Civ 1363, if the material in favour of the applicant lacks substance and the public interest in deportation is overwhelming. But, otherwise, the judgment of the family court, with all the tools at its disposal (including the assistance of the Children and Family Court Advisory and Support Service (CAFCASS) and the opportunity to assess all the adults), can and should inform the decision maker on the issue of the proportionality of deportation in relation to the best interests of the child. See further *RS (immigration/family court liaison: outcome) India* [2013] UKUT 82 (IAC) where the family court held that the child's best interests did not lie with her parents but by being placed in long-term foster care in the UK. The family court regarded it as acceptable for the child to have contact with his parents face-to-face annually by visiting them in India and monthly by means of Skype. On that basis, the deportation of the child's father did not interfere with the child's best interests.

The fact that, in law, the Secretary of State is not bound by an order of the Family Court (as it now is), or of the Family Division, does not, of course, mean that she can simply ignore it. As Hoffmann LJ said in *R v Secretary of State for Home Department, ex p T* [1995] 1 FLR 293 at [297]:

> Clearly, any order made or views expressed by the [Family Court] would be a matter to be taken into account by the Secretary of State in the exercise of his powers. If he simply paid no attention to such an order, he would run the risk of his decision being reviewed on the ground that he had failed to take all relevant matters into consideration.
>
> Be that as it may, the fact is – the law is – that the Secretary of State when exercising her powers of removal or deportation is not bound by any order of the Family Court or of the Family Division and that the Secretary of State, if she wishes to remove or deport a child or the child's parent, does not have to apply for the discharge or variation of any order of the Family Court of Family Division which provides for the child or parent to remain here. (per the President of the Family Division in *GD (Ghana) v Secretary of State for Home Department* [2017] EWCA Civ 1126 at [51])

10.3.8 Paragraph 399: exception based on relationship with a partner

Home Office guidance is that where a person asserts that he has a family life with a qualifying partner in the UK, the decision maker must ensure that the person can satisfy all of the following requirements of para 399 (emphasis added):

(b)   the person has a genuine and subsisting relationship [see **8.3.5.5**] with a partner who is in the UK and is a British Citizen [see **2.2**] or settled in the UK [see **3.8**], *and*

   (i)   the relationship was formed at a time when the person (deportee) was in the UK lawfully and their immigration status was not precarious; and

   (ii)   it would be unduly harsh for that partner to live in the country to which the person is to be deported, because of compelling circumstances over and above those described in paragraph EX.2. of Appendix FM [see **8.5.2.1**]; and

   (iii) it would be unduly harsh for that partner to remain in the UK without the person who is to be deported.

10.3.8.1 The immigration status of the deportee

The starting point here is s 117B(4) of the NIAA 2002, which provides that little weight should be given to a relationship formed by a deportee at a time when he is in the UK unlawfully, that is when he required leave to enter or remain but did not have it. Likewise, s 117B(5) provides that a relationship formed at a time when the foreign criminal had a precarious immigration status will be less capable of outweighing the public interest. For these purposes, Home Office guidance is that a person's immigration status is precarious if he is in the UK with limited leave to enter or remain, or he has settled status which was obtained fraudulently. Is the former correct? Yes – 'everyone who, not being a UK citizen, is present in the UK and who has leave to reside here other than to do so indefinitely has a precarious immigration status' (per Lord Wilson in *Rhuppiah v Secretary of State for the Home Department* [2018] UKSC 58 at [44]).

The onus is on the foreign criminal to provide evidence that the relationship with his partner was formed when he was in the UK lawfully with indefinite leave to enter or remain and before the criminality which he should have been aware would make him liable to removal or deportation.

10.3.8.2 Unduly harsh for partner to live in the country to which the person is to be deported

Here, unduly harsh means compelling circumstances over and above the very serious hardship described in para EX.2 of Appendix FM, as follows: 'the very significant difficulties which would be faced by the applicant or their partner in continuing their family life together outside the UK and which could not be overcome or would entail very serious hardship for the applicant or their partner.' But note that it is only the impact on a foreign criminal's partner which will be considered by the Home Office, not the impact on the foreign criminal.

In determining whether the unduly harsh threshold is met, decision makers should consider the difficulties which the partner would face and whether they entail something that could not (or could not be expected to) be overcome, other than with a very severe degree of hardship for the partner. According to the Home Office, lack of knowledge of a language spoken in the country in which the foreign criminal and his partner would be required to live would not reach the unduly harsh threshold. Why? Because it is reasonable to conclude that the couple must have been communicating whilst in the UK. Therefore, it is reasonable for that to continue outside the UK, whether or not the partner chooses to learn the (or a) language spoken in the country to which the foreign criminal is to be deported.

According to the Home Office, being separated from extended family members would also be unlikely to reach the unduly harsh threshold, such as might happen where a partner's parents and siblings live in the UK, unless there were particular very compelling factors in the case.

Home Office guidance is that the factors which might be relevant to the consideration of whether it would be unduly harsh for a partner to live in the country to which the foreign criminal is to be deported include, but are not limited to, the following:

(a) *The ability of the partner lawfully to enter and stay in the country to which the foreign criminal is to be deported.* The onus is on the foreign criminal to show that this is not possible in order for the unduly harsh threshold to be met. A mere wish/desire/preference to live in the UK would not meet the threshold.

(b) *Cultural barriers.* This might be relevant in situations where the partner would be so disadvantaged that he or she could not be expected to go and live in that country. It must be a barrier which either cannot be overcome or would present very severe hardship such that it would be unduly harsh.

(c) *The impact of a mental or physical disability.* Whether or not a partner has a mental or physical disability, a move to another country may involve a period of hardship as the person adjusts to new surroundings (just as there may have been when a foreign national first comes to live in the UK). But a mental or physical disability could be such that in some cases it could lead to very severe hardship such that it would be unduly harsh.

10.3.8.3 Unduly harsh for partner to remain in the UK without the deportee

When assessing whether it would be unduly harsh for a partner who could not accompany the foreign criminal to the country of return to be separated from the foreign criminal, consideration must be given to the practical impact of separation on the partner and whether that impact is unduly harsh. The onus is on the foreign criminal to submit evidence demonstrating that the effect would be unduly harsh, not on the Secretary of State to demonstrate that it would not be.

Home Office guidance gives as an example of what might be considered unduly harsh, depending on the facts in an individual case, where there is credible evidence that the foreign criminal's presence is essential to prevent the partner's health from being severely impaired because it would not be possible to receive adequate care from other family members, medical professionals, social services, etc.

10.3.9 Paragraph 399A private life exceptions

Home Office guidance is that where a person asserts that he has a private life in the UK, the decision maker must ensure that the person can satisfy the following set of requirements of para 399A (emphasis added):

(a) the person has been lawfully resident in the UK for most of his life; *and*

(b) he is socially and culturally integrated in the UK; *and*

(c) there would be very significant obstacles to his integration into the country to which it is proposed he is deported.

10.3.9.1 The deportee has been lawfully resident in the UK for most of his life

Lawful residence for the purposes of this requirement means that the deportee had limited or indefinite leave to enter or remain, or was in the UK while exempt from immigration control. A person granted immigration bail (see **3.5.5**) is not lawfully resident in the UK for these purposes, but is there any reason to treat the fact that such a person has made an application for leave to remain which is subsequently granted as bringing them within the scope of the provision?

> In general, it seems to me that there is not. The grant of leave to enter or remain to someone who does not currently have it is not ordinarily a matter of entitlement. By the same token, the Secretary of State is not ordinarily under a legal obligation to grant an application for leave to enter or remain. It is a matter of administrative discretion. A foreign national whose presence in the UK is in breach of immigration law but is tolerated while such an application is pending and who develops a private or

family life during this period cannot claim to do so with a legitimate expectation of being allowed to stay, even if the application is subsequently granted. (per Leggatt LJ in *CI (Nigeria) v Secretary of State for the Home Department* [2019] EWCA Civ 2027 at [42]–[43])

In assessing a foreign criminal's residence in the UK, the Home Office states that 'most of his life' means more than half of his life.

10.3.9.2 The deportee is socially and culturally integrated in the UK

Home Office guidance is that positive and negative factors need to be balanced against each other to form an overall assessment of whether a foreign criminal meets this requirement.

The Home Office places reliance here on s 117B(2) of the NIAA 2002, which provides that it is in the public interest that persons who seek to remain in the UK are able to speak English. So if a foreign criminal cannot speak English, the Home Office will take this as an indication that he is not integrated in the UK because he is unable to communicate with the majority of the population. However, if a foreign criminal can speak English, this alone will not be sufficient to demonstrate integration, although it will count in the foreign criminal's favour when balancing all the evidence for and against integration.

There is no prescribed standard of English which must be met for this requirement and no prescribed evidence which must be submitted. However, the Home Office may accept the following:

(a)   evidence of citizenship (eg a passport) of a country where English is the (or a) main or official language;

(b)   evidence of an academic qualification that was taught in English;

(c)   evidence of passing an English language test;

(d)   evidence that he has been interviewed (eg in connection with an asylum claim) or given evidence at an appeal hearing in English.

In this context, the Home Office also places reliance on s 117B(3) of the NIAA 2002, which provides that it is in the public interest that persons who seek to remain in the UK are financially independent. If a foreign criminal cannot demonstrate that he is financially independent, this will indicate to the Home Office that he is not integrated in the UK because he may be reliant on public funds, wider family members or charities, rather than contributing to the economic wellbeing of the country. However, if a foreign criminal can demonstrate that he is financially independent, this alone will not be sufficient to demonstrate to the Home Office his integration, but it will count in the foreign criminal's favour when balancing all the evidence for and against integration.

Home Office guidance is that financial independence means not being a burden on the taxpayer. It includes not having access to income-related benefits or tax credits, on the basis of the foreign criminal's income or savings or those of his partner, but not those of a third party. There is no prescribed financial threshold which must be met and no prescribed evidence which must be submitted. Decision makers should consider all available information, though less weight will be given to claims unsubstantiated by original, independent and verifiable documentary evidence, eg from an employer or regulated financial institution.

The Home Office also treats the foreign criminal's immigration status as important in this context. Why? Because the Home Office takes the view that a person who has been in the UK with limited leave to enter or remain is less likely to be integrated because of the temporary nature of his immigration status. A person who is in the UK unlawfully will have even less of a claim to be integrated. Criminal offending will also often be an indication of lack of integration. The nature of offending, such as anti-social behaviour against a local community or offending that may have caused a serious and/or long-term impact on a victim or victims (eg sexual assault, burglary), may be further evidence of non-integration.

According to the Home Office, it will usually be more difficult for a foreign criminal who has been sentenced more than once to a period of imprisonment of at least 12 months but less than four years to demonstrate that he is socially and culturally integrated. Why? Because he will have spent more time excluded from society, than for a foreign criminal who has been convicted of a single offence.

> Criminal offending and time spent in prison are also in principle relevant in so far as they indicate that the person concerned lacks (legitimate) social and cultural ties in the UK. Thus, a person who leads a criminal lifestyle, has no lawful employment and consorts with criminals or pro-criminal groups can be expected, by reason of those circumstances, to have fewer social relationships and areas of activity that are capable of attracting the protection of 'private life'. Periods of imprisonment represent time spent excluded from society during which the prisoner has little opportunity to develop social and cultural ties and which may weaken or sever previously established ties and make it harder to re-establish them or develop new ties (for example, by finding employment) upon release. In such ways criminal offending and consequent imprisonment may affect whether a person is socially and culturally integrated in the UK. (per Leggatt LJ in CI (Nigeria) v Secretary of State for the Home Department [2019] EWCA Civ 2027 at [61] and approved in KM v Secretary of State for the Home Department [2021] EWCA Civ 693)

EXAMPLE

The foreign criminal, AM, has lived in the UK since the age of 11 and is now 43. He attended secondary school, worked, married and had three daughters. AM's marriage broke down about 14 years ago and he separated from his wife, leaving the family home to live in a hostel. At that time his eldest daughter was no more than eight years old. The youngest was only three. He has had no contact with his wife or daughters since that time. The breakdown of AM's marriage led him to turn to drink which in turn resulted in a long history of persistent drink-related offending, with 27 criminal convictions for 45 offences over the 14-year period. He was both homeless and jobless during this time. There was no evidence of any ties of friendship or other indications of any private life. He knew very few people here. He had a brother but had no contact with him or with any other member of his family. It appears that some of his offences involved taking money from other family members.

AM's offences could be said to be 'low-level criminal convictions' but it is notable that they included racially aggravated offences, as well as an assault on a police officer. Those features of his offending are significant in that they indicate an alienation from important values of society which has at least some bearing on the issue of social and cultural integration.

AM was dealt with for his offending by a series of community orders, offering him the chance to reform, but he proved unable to do so. Eventually he committed a more serious offence, a street robbery involving the snatching of a mobile phone from a young woman late at night. For this he was sentenced to two years imprisonment. He was sent to prison three years ago and since his release has been in immigration detention.

In these circumstances, AM is not socially and culturally integrated in the UK. That is not merely because of his conviction for a serious offence and the time which he has spent in prison as a result, but also because of the long period of anti-social criminal behaviour leading up to that conviction, the complete absence of any family life in the UK for the last 14 years, and the absence of any evidence of social or other connections here other than the mere fact of his lawful presence in this country.

See AM (Somalia) v Secretary of State for the Home Department [2019] EWCA Civ 774.

To outweigh any evidence of a lack of integration, the foreign criminal will need to demonstrate to the Home Office strong evidence of integration. Home Office guidance is that mere presence in the UK is not an indication of integration. Positive contributions to society may be evidence of integration, eg an exceptional contribution to a local community or to wider society, which has not been undertaken at a time that suggests an attempt to avoid deportation. If such a claim is made, decision makers will expect to see credible evidence of significant voluntary work of real practical benefit.

According to the Court of Appeal in *Binbuga (Turkey) v Secretary of State for the Home Department* [2019] EWCA Civ 551:

> In this context, social integration refers to the extent to which a foreign criminal has become incorporated within the lawful social structure of the UK. This includes various incidents of society such as clubs, societies, workplaces or places of study, but not association with pro-criminal peers.
>
> Similarly, cultural integration refers to the acceptance and assumption by the foreign criminal of the culture of the UK, its core values, ideas, customs and social behaviour. This includes acceptance of the principle of the rule of law. Membership of a pro-criminal gang shows a lack of such acceptance. It demonstrates disdain for the rule of law and indeed undermines it.
>
> Social and cultural integration in the UK connotes integration as a law-abiding citizen. That is why it is recognised that breaking the law may involve discontinuity in integration. (per Hamblen LJ at [56]–[58])

10.3.9.3   There would be very significant obstacles to the deportee's integration into the country to which it is proposed he is deported

Home Office guidance is that the starting point for this requirement is to assume that the applicant will be able to integrate into his country of return, unless he can demonstrate why that is not the case. The onus is on the applicant to show that there are very significant obstacles to that integration.

> [T]he concept of a foreign criminal's 'integration' into the country to which it is proposed that he be deported, as set out in section 117C(4)(c) and paragraph 399A, is a broad one. It is not confined to the mere ability to find a job or to sustain life while living in the other country. It is not appropriate to treat the statutory language as subject to some gloss and it will usually be sufficient for a court or tribunal simply to direct itself in the terms that Parliament has chosen to use. The idea of 'integration' calls for a broad evaluative judgment to be made as to whether the individual will be enough of an insider in terms of understanding how life in the society in that other country is carried on and a capacity to participate in it, so as to have a reasonable opportunity to be accepted there, to be able to operate on a day-to-day basis in that society and to build up within a reasonable time a variety of human relationships to give substance to the individual's private or family life. (per Sales LJ in *Kamara v Secretary of State for Home Department* [2016] EWCA Civ 813 at [14] and approved in *Sanambar v Secretary of State for the Home Department* [2021] UKSC 30)

Decision makers expect to see original, independent and verifiable documentary evidence of any claims made in this regard, and will place less weight on assertions which are unsubstantiated. Where it is not reasonable to expect corroborating evidence to be provided, consideration is given to the credibility of the applicant's claims.

A very significant obstacle to integration means something which would prevent or seriously inhibit the applicant from integrating into the country of return. The decision maker is looking for more than obstacles. They are looking to see whether there are 'very significant' obstacles, which is a high threshold. Very significant obstacles will exist where the applicant demonstrates that he would be unable to establish a private life in the country of return, or where establishing a private life in the country of return would entail very serious hardship for the applicant.

The decision maker must consider all the reasons put forward by the applicant as to why there would be obstacles to his integration in the country of return. These reasons must be considered individually and cumulatively. The question is whether the applicant has the ability to form an adequate private life by the standards of the country of return – not by UK standards. The decision maker will take into account whether the applicant will be able to establish a private life in respect of all its essential elements, even if, for example, his job, or his ability to find work, or his network of friends and relationships may be differently constituted in the country of return.

> '[V]ery significant obstacles', erects a self-evidently elevated threshold, such that mere hardship, mere difficulty, mere hurdles and mere upheaval or inconvenience, even where multiplied, will generally be insufficient in this context. (per McCloskey J in *Treebhawon (NIAA 2002 Part 5A - compelling circumstances test)* [2017] UKUT 00013 (IAC) at [37])

The decision maker will need to consider the specific obstacles raised by the applicant. They will also need to set these against other factors in order to make an assessment in the individual case. Relevant considerations include:

(a)   *Cultural background by way of the applicant's exposure to and level of understanding of the cultural norms in the country of return.* Where the person has spent his time in the UK living mainly amongst a diaspora community from that country, then it may be reasonable to conclude that he has cultural ties with that country even if he has never lived there or has been absent from that country for a lengthy period. If the applicant has cultural ties with the country of return, then it is likely that it would be possible for him to establish a private life there. Even if there are no cultural ties, the cultural norms of that country may be such that there are no barriers to integration.

(b)   *Length of time spent in the country of return.* Where the applicant has spent a significant period of time in the country of return, it will be difficult for them to demonstrate that there would be very significant obstacles to integration into that country. The decision maker must consider the proportion of the person's life spent in that country and the stage of life the person was at when in that country.

What if the applicant has never lived in the country of return, or only spent his early years there? Home Office guidance is that this will not necessarily mean that there are very significant obstacles preventing him from integrating, particularly if he can speak a language of that country, eg if the country of return is one where English is spoken or if a language of the country was spoken at home when he was growing up. For these purposes, fluency is not required – conversational level language skills or a basic level of language which could be improved on return would be sufficient. The cultural norms of the country and how easy it is for the person to adapt to them will also be relevant.

What if there is credible evidence that an applicant cannot speak any language which is spoken in the country of return? The Home Office states that this will not in itself be a very significant obstacle to integration unless he can also show that he would be unable to learn a language of that country, for example because of a mental or physical disability.

(c)   *Family, friends and social network.* An applicant who has family or friends in the country of return should be able to turn to them for support to help them to integrate into that country. The decision maker must consider whether the applicant or his family have sponsored or hosted visits in the UK by family or friends from the country of return, or the applicant has visited family or friends in the country of return. The decision maker must consider the quality of any relationships with family or friends in the country of return, but they do not have to be strong familial ties and can include ties that could be strengthened if the person were to return.

Where there are no family, friends or social networks in the country of return, that is not in itself a very significant obstacle to integration. Why? The Home Office states that many people successfully migrate to countries where they have no ties.

Home Office policy is that the degree of private life an individual has established in the UK is not relevant to the consideration of whether there are very serious obstacles to integration into the country of return. However, it is relevant to the consideration of whether, where the applicant falls for refusal under the Immigration Rules, there are exceptional circumstances which would make refusal unjustifiably harsh for the applicant.

10.3.10   Grant of limited leave under paras 399 or 399A

By para 399B, where para 399 (see **10.3.7** and **10.3.8**) or 399A (see **10.3.9**) applies, the person may be granted limited leave for a period not exceeding 30 months. Can further periods of limited leave be granted? Yes, the requirements for further leave are that the applicant continues to meet the criteria set out in paras 399 or 399A.

10.3.11   Very compelling circumstances

If a person falls within para 398(a) (he has been convicted of an offence and sentenced to a period of imprisonment of at least four years (see **10.3.4**)), or otherwise does not fall within any of the para 399 (see **10.3.7** and **10.3.8**) or para 399A (see **10.3.9**) exceptions, the person's deportation will be the proper course in all but very exceptional cases.

Home Office guidance is that in determining whether there are very compelling circumstances, decision makers must consider all relevant factors that weigh in favour of and against deportation.

Decision makers should be mindful that whilst all cases are to an extent unique, those unique factors do not generally render them exceptional. For these purposes, exceptional cases should be numerically rare. Furthermore, a case is not exceptional just because the exceptions to deportation in paras 399 or 399A have been missed by a small margin. Rather, the Immigration Rules establish those thresholds as determining when deportation would be appropriate bar other factors. However, in assessing if there are very compelling circumstances, the matters identified in paras 399 and 399A need to be considered along with all other aspects of the case. The decision maker then needs to determine whether removal would have such severe consequences for the individual or his family that very exceptionally deportation is not appropriate despite the clear articulation of the public interest in para 398 (see **10.3.4**). Home Office guidance is that that is likely to be the case only very rarely indeed.

In *Secretary of State for the Home Department v CT (Vietnam)* [2016] EWCA Civ 488, Rafferty LJ held at [34]–[36]:

> The FTT whilst it reminded itself of the legitimate public interest in the removal of foreign criminals as a deterrence and an expression of condemnation, and that only in exceptional circumstances will that public interest be outweighed by other factors, did not go on to direct itself as to the very great weight to be given to that public interest, the scales heavily weighted in favour of deportation and something very compelling required to swing the outcome in favour of a foreign criminal. The starting point is not neutral.

> The FTT concluded that there was ample evidence of the deleterious effect on the children of the Respondent's removal. Coupled with a low risk of reoffending that tipped the balance in his favour.

> The effect on the children was, on the evidence, to leave them unhappy at the prospect of their father being on another continent. I readily accept that description. Experience teaches that most children would so react. I cannot accept the conclusion that, added to a low risk of reoffending, the effect on them tips the balance. These children will not be bereft of both loving parents. Nor was there evidence of a striking condition in either (I ignore the stepchildren by virtue of their age) which his presence in the UK would dispositively resolve. He is said to have 'a particular tie' with the Respondent. The son was said to have spoken less confidently when his father was in prison and to have returned to confidence upon his release. That is not exceptional.

> The 'very compelling circumstances' test in section 117C(3) and (6) provides a safety valve, with an appropriately high threshold of application, for those exceptional cases involving foreign criminals in which the private and family life considerations are so strong that it would be disproportionate and in violation of Article 8 to remove them. If, after working through the decision-making framework in section 117C, a court or tribunal concludes that it is a case in which section 117C(3) or (6) says that the public interest 'requires' deportation, it is not open to the court or tribunal to deny this and to hold that

the public interest does not require deportation. (per Sales LJ in *Rhuppiah v Secretary of State for the Home Department* [2016] EWCA Civ 803 at [50])

In *R (on the application of Kiarie) v Secretary of State for the Home Department* [2017] UKSC 42, the Supreme Court at [55] indicated that the following factors may be relevant here:

(a) the depth of the appellant's integration in UK society in terms of family, employment and otherwise;

(b) the quality of his relationship with any child, partner or other family member in the UK;

(c) the extent to which any relationship with family members might reasonably be sustained even after deportation, whether by their joining him abroad or otherwise;

(d) the impact of his deportation on the need to safeguard and promote the welfare of any child in the UK;

(e) the likely strength of the obstacles to his integration in the society of the country of his nationality; and, surely in every case,

(f) any significant risk of his re-offending in the UK, judged, no doubt with difficulty, in the light of his criminal record set against the credibility of his probable assertions of remorse and reform.

Also see *Secretary of State for the Home Department v JZ (Zambia)* [2016] EWCA Civ 116, *NA (Pakistan) v Secretary of State for the Home Department* [2016] EWCA Civ 662 and *Secretary of State for the Home Department v JG (Jamaica)* [2019] EWCA Civ 982.

10.3.12   Decision maker's approach

The Immigration Rules constitute a complete code for the application of Article 8 ECHR in this context (*MA (Somalia) v Secretary of State for the Home Department* [2015] EWCA Civ 48):

42.   ... [In] approaching the question of whether removal is a proportionate interference with an individual's article 8 rights, the scales are heavily weighted in favour of deportation and something very compelling (which will be 'exceptional') is required to outweigh the public interest in removal. In our view, it is no coincidence that the phrase 'exceptional circumstances' is used in the new rules in the context of weighing the competing factors for and against deportation of foreign criminals.

43.   The word 'exceptional' is often used to denote a departure from a general rule. The general rule in the present context is that, in the case of a foreign [criminal] to whom paragraphs 399 and 399A do not apply, very compelling reasons will be required to outweigh the public interest in deportation. These compelling reasons are the 'exceptional circumstances'.

44.   We would, therefore, hold that the new rules are a complete code and that the exceptional circumstances to be considered in the balancing exercise involve the application of a proportionality test as required by the Strasbourg jurisprudence ... (per Lord Dyson MR in *MF (Nigeria) v Secretary of State for the Home Department* [2013] EWCA Civ 1192).

The reasons why it is important to assess the matter within the Immigration Rules rather than outside them were spelled out by Sales LJ in *Secretary of State for the Home Department v AJ (Angola)* [2014] EWCA Civ 1636:

39.   The fact that the new rules are intended to operate as a comprehensive code is significant, because it means that an official or a tribunal should seek to take account of any Convention rights of an appellant through the lens of the new rules themselves, rather than looking to apply Convention rights for themselves in a free-standing way outside the new rules ...

40.   The requirement that claims by appellants who are foreign criminals for leave to remain, based on the Convention rights of themselves or their partners, relations or children, should be assessed under the new rules and through their lens is important, as the Court of Appeal in *MF (Nigeria)* has emphasised. It seeks to ensure uniformity of approach between different officials, tribunals and courts who have to assess such claims, in the interests of fair and equal treatment of different appellants with similar cases on the facts. In this regard, the new rules also serve as a safeguard in relation to rights of appellants under Article 14 to equal treatment within the scope of Article 8. The requirement of assessment through the lens of the new rules also seeks

> to ensure that decisions are made in a way that is properly informed by the considerable weight to be given to the public interest in deportation of foreign criminals ...

In *AS v Secretary of State for the Home Department* [2019] EWCA Civ 417, the Court of Appeal stated that in cases which call for an assessment by reference to the test whether deportation would be 'unduly harsh' or whether there are 'very compelling circumstances' which trump the public interest in deportation, a balance sheet approach should be taken by the decision maker. The Court approved the following suggestion of Lord Thomas of Cwmgiedd in *Ali v Secretary of State for the Home Department* [2016] UKSC 60:

> 83   One way of structuring such a judgment would be to follow what has become known as the 'balance sheet' approach. After the judge has found the facts, the judge would set out each of the 'pros' and 'cons' in what has been described as a 'balance sheet' and then set out reasoned conclusions as to whether the countervailing factors outweigh the importance attached to the public interest in the deportation of foreign offenders.

10.4   ADMINISTRATIVE REMOVAL

10.4.1   Grounds for removal

Removal from the UK is often described as 'administrative removal', as that is what it is in reality, namely, an administrative step. Under s 10 of the Immigration and Asylum Act 1999 (IAA 1999) a person may be removed from the UK under the authority of the Secretary of State or an immigration officer if the person requires leave to enter or remain in the UK but does not have it. This means that the following people may be administratively removed from the UK:

(a)   anyone who has failed to observe the conditions attached to his leave (see **3.3**);

(b)   overstayers (see **3.6.6**);

(c)   anyone who has obtained leave to remain by deception, or who sought to obtain such leave by deception;

(d)   the family members (partner or child) of such people (see the Immigration (Removal of Family Members) Regulations 2014 (SI 2014/2816)).

The most common grounds for administrative removal are that a person has remained beyond the period specified in his limited leave, or has broken a condition attached to it. For example, a person's leave to enter or remain will often either prohibit or restrict his freedom to take employment, and the person is liable to administrative removal procedures if he is found to be working without authority. Home Office guidance is that there must be firm and recent (within six months) evidence of working in breach. The immigration officer will look for at least an admission by the offender under caution of working in breach; or a statement by the employer; or pay slips or the offender's details on the payroll; or visual observation, by the immigration officer, of the applicant working.

As explained in **3.6.2**, a person who wishes to extend his stay should apply for a variation before his leave expires. He commits a criminal offence under s 24(1)(b) of the IA 1971 if he knowingly overstays or fails to observe a condition of the leave. Note that it is not usual practice for a prosecution to occur. Removal does not require a knowing breach, and so normally the person is removed and not prosecuted.

In addition, illegal entrants (see **10.4.2**) may be removed from the UK in the same way.

10.4.2   Definition of illegal entrant

An illegal entrant is a person who unlawfully enters or seeks to enter in breach of a deportation order or of the immigration laws. This includes a person who has so entered.

Typically, a person might enter the UK without leave clandestinely, eg concealed in a vehicle such as a lorry. Or he might present a forged or false British passport to an immigration officer.

A person who, contrary to the IA 1971, knowingly enters the UK in breach of a deportation order or without leave commits a criminal offence under s 24(1)(a). However, it is possible to be an illegal entrant without having committed any criminal offence, for instance where a person obtains leave by producing false documents, without knowing them to be false (R v *Immigration Officer, ex p Chan* [1992] 1 WLR 541).

A person will be an illegal entrant if he obtains leave to enter by deception, although mere non-disclosure of material facts will not amount to deception, as the entrant has no positive duty to reveal facts if a relevant question is not asked. It is for the Home Office to prove the deception (R v *Secretary of State for the Home Department, ex p Khawaja* [1984] AC 74).

10.4.3 Procedure

If the Home Office decides not to remove the person, he is normally granted indefinite to leave to remain.

If, after consideration of all the relevant facts, the Home Office decides that administrative removal is the correct course of action, a notice of liability to administrative removal is served. The immigration officer normally serves the notice in person. It still remains open to the person who is subject to enforcement action to leave the UK voluntarily. Otherwise the immigration officer will set removal directions. The costs of complying with removal directions (so far as reasonably incurred) are met by the Secretary of State.

10.4.4 Effect of administrative removal

Unlike someone who has been deported, a person who is subject to administrative removal does not need to have the decision to remove him rescinded before he may return to the UK, provided that he otherwise qualifies for admission under the Immigration Rules.

10.4.5 Government policy: deportation and administrative removal

It is important to remember that deportation may be automatic (see **10.1.5**), or otherwise there is a presumption of deportation (see **10.1.11**). But administrative removal is never automatic, neither is there a presumption of administrative removal. Why the difference? It is because different government policies are pursued by the use of deportation and administrative removal, as methods to expel a person from the UK.

As we saw at **10.1.4**, there are three important features of the public interest in deportation, namely:

(a)   the risk of re-offending by the person concerned;

(b)   the need to deter foreign nationals from committing serious crimes by leading them to understand that, whatever the other circumstances, one consequence for them may well be their deportation; and

(c)   the role of deportation as an expression of society's revulsion at serious crimes and in building public confidence in the criminal justice system's treatment of foreign citizens who have committed serious crimes.

In *UE (Nigeria) v Secretary of State for the Home Department* [2010] EWCA Civ 975, the Court identified that the main element of public interest in administrative removal is the need for the Government to maintain a firm policy of immigration control.

The difference in aims is important, because it explains why the factors in favour of expulsion are capable of carrying greater weight in a deportation case than in a case of administrative removal. This led Richards LJ, in *JO (Uganda) v Secretary of State for the Home Department* [2010] EWCA Civ 10, to observe (at [29]):

> The maintenance of effective immigration control is an important matter, but the protection of society against serious crime is even more important and can properly be given correspondingly greater weight in the balancing exercise. Thus I think it perfectly possible in principle for a given set of considerations

of family life and/or private life to be sufficiently weighty to render expulsion disproportionate in an ordinary removal case, yet insufficient to render expulsion disproportionate in a deportation case because of the additional weight to be given to the criminal offending on which the deportation decision was based.

10.4.6   Human rights challenges to removal

See **10.2** as to challenges based on provisions other than Article 8 ECHR.

As to Article 8 ECHR, see **10.3**, but note that para 400 of the Immigration Rules provides that where a person claims that his removal would be contrary to the UK's obligations under Article 8, the Secretary of State may require an application under para 276ADE (private life) or Appendix FM (family life) of the Rules. Where an application is not required, in assessing that claim the Secretary of State or an immigration officer will, subject to para 353 (see **9.14**), consider that claim against the requirements to be met under para 276ADE or Appendix FM, and if appropriate the removal decision will be cancelled.

10.4.6.1   Paragraph 276ADE

A person who has lived in the UK for at least 20 years continuously, lawfully or unlawfully, can apply to the Home Office for leave to remain in the UK on the basis of the Article 8 ECHR right to respect for private life. Alternative provisions allow an applicant to be granted limited leave to remain in the UK on the basis of private life after seven years' continuous residence if he is under the age of 18; or if he has spent at least half of his life in the UK if he is aged between 18 and 24; or if the applicant has less than 20 years' continuous residence in the UK but there would be very significant obstacles to the applicant's integration into his country of origin.

Full details are given at **8.13**.

10.4.6.2   Appendix FM (family life)

Under para EX.1 of Appendix FM to the Immigration Rules, an applicant may be allowed to remain in the UK on the basis of his family life with a child and/or a partner if it would breach Article 8 ECHR to remove him.

Paragraph EX.1 applies if the applicant has a genuine and subsisting parental relationship with a child (under the age of 18 years) who is in the UK, who is a British citizen or who has lived in the UK continuously for at least the seven years immediately preceding the date of application, and it would not be reasonable to expect that child to leave the UK. See **8.5.1**.

Paragraph EX.1 additionally, or alternatively, applies if the applicant has a genuine and subsisting relationship with a partner who is in the UK and who is a British citizen, settled in the UK, or in the UK with refugee leave or humanitarian protection, and there are insurmountable obstacles to family life with that partner continuing outside the UK. See **8.5.2**.

10.5   REMOVAL TO REQUIRE ENTRY CLEARANCE

In *Chikwamba v Secretary of State for the Home Department* [2008] UKHL 40, the House of Lords had to answer this question: When determining an appeal under s 82 of the NIAA 2002 (see **Chapter 11**) on the ground that to remove the appellant would interfere disproportionately with his Article 8 right to respect for his family life, when, if ever, is it appropriate to dismiss the appeal on the basis that the appellant should be required to leave the country and seek leave to enter from an ECO abroad?

The answer was 'comparatively rarely, certainly in family cases involving children, should an Article 8 appeal be dismissed on the basis that it would be proportionate and more appropriate for the appellant to apply for leave from abroad' (per Lord Brown of Eaton-under-Heywood, at [44]).

For an example of an exceptional case justifying removal for an application to be made, see R *(Kotecha) v Secretary of State for the Home Department* [2011] EWHC 2070.

CHAPTER 11

APPEALS AND REVIEWS

11.1 APPEALS: THE GENERAL RULE

The NIAA 2002 (as amended) sets out a system of appeals, including a system for a 'one stop' comprehensive appeal. It replaces all rights of appeal established in earlier legislation. The Act establishes the principle that there is one right of appeal against a limited number of decisions made by the Secretary of State (see **11.2**). Where multiple decisions would result in multiple rights of appeal, these are subsumed into one appeal. All appealable grounds can and should be raised in an appeal (see **11.5**). Only some appeal rights can be exercised by the appellant in the UK (see **11.4**).

11.2 DECISIONS AGAINST WHICH THERE IS A RIGHT OF APPEAL

By s 82(1) of the NIAA 2002, an appeal can be made against the decision of the Secretary of State to:

(a) refuse a protection claim;

(b) refuse a human rights claim; or

(c) revoke protection status.

Where a person has already had a protection claim or a human rights claim refused and there is no pending appeal, do further submissions which rely on protection or human rights grounds have to be accepted by the Secretary of State as a fresh claim in accordance with para 353 of the Immigration Rules (see **9.14**) if a decision in response to those representations is to attract a right of appeal under s 82 of the 2002 Act? Yes, answered the Supreme Court in *Robinson v Secretary of State for the Home Department* [2019] UKSC 11.

As to the grounds of appeal, see **11.3**.

What if there is no right of appeal? It may be possible to apply for administrative review of the refusal of an application, provided it is an eligible decision and on the basis that a case working error has occurred (see **11.16**).

11.2.1 Protection claim and status

A protection claim is a claim for asylum or humanitarian protection.

A person has protection status when granted leave (permission) to remain as a refugee, or humanitarian protection.

What if an asylum claim is refused but humanitarian protection is granted? There is a right of appeal against the refusal of asylum on the basis that the person ought to have been granted refugee status. Why? Because refugee status provides benefits to the applicant that are additional to those conferred by the grant of humanitarian protection.

See **Chapter 9**.

11.2.2 Human rights claim

A human rights claim includes the following applications made under the Immigration Rules:

(a)   long residence under para 276B (see **3.8.8**);

(b)   private life under paras 276ADE(1) or 276DE (see **8.13**);

(c)   asylum under Part 11 (see **Chapter 9**);

(d)   family member under Appendix FM, but not BPILR (bereavement) or DVILR (domestic violence) (see **Chapter 8**).

11.2.3 Deprivation of citizenship

Under s 40A of the BNA 1981, there is a right of appeal against a decision to make an order depriving a person of a British citizenship status (see **2.2.9** and **11.9**).

11.3 GROUNDS OF APPEAL

An appeal under s 82(1)(a) of the NIAA 2002 (refusal of protection claim – see **11.2.1**) must be brought on one or more of the following grounds:

(a)   that removal of the appellant from the UK would breach the UK's obligations under the Refugee Convention;

(b)   that removal of the appellant from the UK would breach the UK's obligations in relation to persons eligible for a grant of humanitarian protection;

(c)   that removal of the appellant from the UK would be unlawful under s 6 of the HRA 1998 (public authority not to act contrary to the ECHR).

An appeal under s 82(1)(b) (refusal of human rights claim – see **11.2.2**) must be brought on the ground that the decision is unlawful under s 6 of the HRA 1998.

An appeal under s 82(1)(c) (revocation of protection status – see **11.2.1**) must be brought on one or more of the following grounds:

(a)   that the decision to revoke the appellant's protection status breaches the UK's obligations under the Refugee Convention;

(b)   that the decision to revoke the appellant's protection status breaches the UK's obligations in relation to persons eligible for a grant of humanitarian protection.

11.4 WHERE APPEAL RIGHTS ARE EXERCISABLE

Section 92 of the NIAA 2002 determines whether an appeal right is exercisable whilst the appellant is in the UK, or if it can be made only from abroad. The general rule is that where the appellant was outside the UK when he made the claim, he must appeal from outside the UK. When the appellant was inside the UK when he made the claim, he may appeal from within the UK unless the claim has been certified under s 94 (see **11.11**) or s 94B (see **11.12**).

An appeal made from outside the UK is compatible with the requirements of the ECHR if the appellant has access to facilities abroad which enable him to assemble evidence and prepare and present his case and give live evidence to the tribunal and otherwise to participate in the hearing: *Kiarie and Byndloss v Secretary of State for the Home Department* [2017] UKSC 42. But, if the only way in which an appellant can have a fair and effective appeal is to be permitted to come to the UK to pursue their appeal, can that be ordered? Yes, held the Court of Appeal in *Begum v Special Immigration Appeals Commission* [2020] EWCA Civ 918. No, held the Supreme Court, overturning that decision in *R (Begum) v Special Immigration Appeals Commission* [2021] UKSC 7:

> the Court of Appeal mistakenly believed that, when an individual's right to have a fair hearing of an appeal came into conflict with the requirements of national security, her right to a fair hearing must prevail. As I have explained, if a vital public interest - in this case, the safety of the public - makes it impossible for a case to be fairly heard, then the courts cannot ordinarily hear it. The appropriate response to the problem in the present case is for the appeal to be stayed until Ms Begum is in a position to play an effective part in it without the safety of the public being compromised. That is not a perfect solution, as it is not known how long it may be before that is possible. But there is no perfect solution to a dilemma of the present kind. (per Lord Reed at [135])

Does hearing a human rights appeal from abroad via video link breach Regulation (EU) 2016/679 (the General Data Protection Regulation)? No, held the Court of Appeal in *Johnson v Secretary of State for the Home Department* [2020] EWCA Civ 1032.

11.5 THE 'ONE STOP' PROCESS

11.5.1 Notice of appealable decision

The Immigration (Notices) Regulations 2003 (SI 2003/658) provide that a decision maker (eg ECO, immigration officer, Secretary of State) must give written notice to a person of any appealable decision. The notice must include, or be accompanied by, a statement of the reasons for the decision to which it relates.

The notice must also include, or be accompanied by, a statement advising the person of his right of appeal and the statutory provision on which his right of appeal is based; whether or not such an appeal may be brought while in the UK; the grounds on which such an appeal may be brought; and the facilities available for advice and assistance in connection with such an appeal.

Further, by s 120 of the NIAA 2002, the notice will set a deadline for the appellant to provide, where appropriate:

(a)   his reasons for wishing to enter or remain in the UK;

(b)   any grounds on which he should be permitted to enter or remain in the UK; and

(c)   any grounds on which he should not be removed from or required to leave the UK.

After being served with a s 120 notice, the appellant has an on-going duty, so that a further statement should be made if a new reason or ground for remaining in the UK arises. Any reasons or grounds should be raised as soon as reasonably practicable. There is no requirement to reiterate the same grounds or reasons of which the Secretary of State is already aware, or any that have been considered.

11.5.2 Consequences of failing to disclose all grounds of appeal

What if a s 120 notice is not answered? Any attempt to raise such grounds later on may lead to certification under s 96 of the NIAA 2002, with the effect that there can be no appeal against the decision, or that those grounds cannot be raised in connection with a further appeal.

Before the Secretary of State can lawfully decide to certify, four steps must be taken:

(Step 1)   The Secretary of State must be satisfied that the person was notified of a right of appeal under s 82 of the Act against another immigration decision (s 96(1)), or that the person received a notice under s 120 by virtue of an application other than that to which the new decision relates or by virtue of a decision other than the new decision (s 96(2)).

(Step 2)   The Secretary of State must conclude that the claim or application to which the new decision relates relies on a matter that could have been raised in an appeal against the old decision (s 96(1)(b)), or that the new decision relates to an application or claim that relies on a matter that should have been but has not been raised in a statement made in response to that notice (s 96(2)(b)).

(Step 3)   The Secretary of State must form the opinion that there is no satisfactory reason for that matter's not having been raised in an appeal against the old decision (s 96(1)(c)), or that there is no satisfactory reason for that matter's not having been raised in a statement made in response to that notice (s 96(2)(c)).

(Step 4)   The Secretary of State must consider whether, having regard to all relevant factors, he should exercise his discretion to certify, and must conclude that it is appropriate to exercise the discretion in favour of certification.

As to the interpretation of the word 'matter' in Steps 2 and 3, see *Khan v Secretary of State for the Home Department* [2014] EWCA Civ 88.

11.5.3   Other certificates under s 96

Certificates can be issued under s 96 of the NIAA 2002 otherwise than in relation to s 120 notices (see **11.5.2**).

Note that no appeal can be brought on any ground against an otherwise appealable decision if the Secretary of State or immigration officer certifies that the person was notified of a right of appeal against another decision (whether or not any appeal was lodged or completed) *and* that in his opinion the person made the claim or application in order to delay removal, or the removal of a family member, *and* that in his opinion the person had no other legitimate purpose for making the claim or application. If an appeal has already been brought, the appeal may not be continued if a certificate is issued.

Further, s 96 prevents an appeal being brought if the Secretary of State or immigration officer certifies that a new decision relates to a ground that was raised on an earlier appeal, or which could have been raised at an appeal had the applicant chosen to exercise a right of appeal. If an appeal has already been brought, the appeal may not be continued if a certificate is issued. See, for example, *Khan v Secretary of State for the Home Department* [2014] EWCA Civ 88.

Lastly, where a further appeal right does arise, the Secretary of State or immigration officer may certify that certain grounds of appeal were already considered in an earlier appeal. The appellant is not then allowed to rely on those grounds.

The certificate may be challenged by way of an application for judicial review: see *R (Adebisi) v Secretary of State for the Home Department* [2011] LTL 5 May; *R (J) v Secretary of State for the Home Department* [2009] EWHC 705; and **Chapter 12**.

11.6   THE APPEALS SYSTEM

11.6.1   The First-tier Tribunal (Immigration and Asylum Chamber)

A right of appeal against an appealable decision lies to the Immigration and Asylum Chamber (IAC) under s 82 of the NIAA 2002 (see **11.2**).

The title of the legally-qualified member of the IAC is an Immigration Judge. All IAC appeals are heard in various appeal centres across the UK.

An appeal to the IAC may only be started by giving notice of appeal on a prescribed form in accordance with the Tribunal Procedure (First-tier Tribunal) (Immigration and Asylum

Chamber) Rules 2014 (SI 2014/2604). Practitioners should be familiar with the Rules. Normally there is an initial case management review hearing. This will determine the issues in dispute and the evidence necessary to deal with them. Directions are usually given as to the filing of evidence, etc.

At the appeal hearing, the Immigration Judge determines whether or not to uphold the original decision. If it is upheld, appeal lies on a point of law to the Upper Tribunal (Immigration and Asylum Chamber). Permission to appeal is required from the IAC or, failing that, the Upper Tribunal. If both the IAC and the Upper Tribunal refuse permission to appeal, that decision can be judicially reviewed, but limited to the grounds that either:

(a) the proposed appeal would raise some important point of principle or practice; or

(b) there is some other compelling reason for the court to hear the appeal: see R (*Cart*) *v The Upper Tribunal* [2011] UKSC 28.

As to ground (b), note that in PR (*Sri Lanka*) *v Secretary of State for the Home Department* [2011] EWCA Civ 988, the Court of Appeal (per Carnwath LJ at [35]) stated that 'compelling means *legally* compelling, rather than compelling, perhaps, from a political or emotional point of view, although such considerations may exceptionally add weight to the legal arguments'. See also **Chapter 12**.

The right of appeal to the Upper Tribunal is on any point of law arising from a decision made by the First-tier Tribunal (other than an excluded decision under the Tribunals, Courts and Enforcement Act 2007, s 11(1) and (2)). If the Upper Tribunal finds an error of law, it may set aside and remake the decision. Although 'error of law' is widely defined, it is not the case that the Upper Tribunal is entitled to remake the decision simply because it does not agree with it, or because it thinks it can produce a better one (see UT (*Sri Lanka*) *v Secretary of State for the Home Department* [2019] EWCA Civ 1095).

Appeal on a point of law from the Upper Tribunal lies to the Court of Appeal (see **11.6.2**). It is necessary to obtain that Court's permission first.

11.6.2 Appeals to the Court of Appeal

The Court of Appeal has the power to give any decision that might have been given by the IAC. It can also remit the matter for rehearing and determination by the IAC, and then may offer the IAC its opinion and make directions with which the IAC must comply.

11.7 PENDING AND ABANDONED APPEALS

Section 104 of the NIAA 2002 sets out when an appeal is pending and when it ends: it clarifies that an appeal ceases to be pending when it is 'abandoned'. An appeal may be treated as abandoned because the appellant leaves the UK, is granted leave to enter or remain, or a deportation order is made against him. However, an appeal continues to be pending so long as a further appeal may be brought, and until such further appeal is finally determined.

As a general rule, while an appeal is pending, the leave to which the appeal relates and any conditions subject to which it was granted continue to have effect. Hence, the person has a right to remain in the UK whilst pursuing the appeal. But what does 'the leave to which the appeal relates' mean? It is referring to the leave the appellant had when he made the application that has been refused. It does not mean the leave for which the appellant applied.

By s 77 of the 2002 Act, while a person's claim for asylum is pending he may not be removed from or required to leave the UK in accordance with a provision of the Immigration Acts. However, this does not prevent the giving of a direction for the claimant's removal from the UK, the making of a deportation order in respect of the claimant, or the taking of any other interim or preparatory action.

By s 78, while a person's appeal under s 82 is pending he may not be removed from or required to leave the UK in accordance with a provision of the Immigration Acts. However, this does not prevent the giving of a direction for the appellant's removal from the UK, the making of a deportation order in respect of the appellant (subject to s 79 – see below), or the taking of any other interim or preparatory action.

Section 78 only applies to an appeal brought while the appellant is in the UK in accordance with s 92 (see **11.4**).

By s 79, a deportation order may not be made in respect of a person while an appeal under s 82 against the decision to make the order could be brought (ignoring any possibility of an appeal out of time with permission) or is pending.

Note that s 99 provides that where a certificate is issued under s 97 (see **11.8**) in respect of a pending appeal, that appeal lapses.

11.8 NATIONAL SECURITY AND SIMILAR MATTERS

Section 97 of the NIAA 2002 provides that an appeal under s 82 cannot be made or continued where the Secretary of State certifies that a decision was taken to exclude or remove a person from the UK:

(a)   in the interests of national security;

(b)   in the interests of the relationship between the UK and another country; or

(c)   otherwise in the public interest.

However, under the Special Immigration Appeals Commission Act 1997, an appeal can be made to the Special Immigration Appeals Commission (SIAC). This body was set up specifically to deal with appeals where national security and other sensitive matters are a consideration. The proceedings of the SIAC are governed by the Special Immigration Appeals Commission (Procedure) Rules 2003 (SI 2003/1034).

11.9 DEPORTATION ORDER MADE ON NATIONAL SECURITY GROUNDS

Section 97 of the NIAA 2002 (see **11.8**) does not apply where the Secretary of State certifies that the decision to make a deportation order (see **10.1**) in respect of a person was taken on the grounds that his removal from the UK would be in the interests of national security. In those circumstances s 97A applies instead, and an appeal can be made only from outside the UK. If the appellant makes a human rights claim the appeal can be brought in country, unless the Secretary of State certifies that removal would not breach the ECHR. Provision is made for an appeal against such a certificate to the SIAC.

11.10 EU SETTLEMENT SCHEME

Section 3 of the Immigration (Citizens' Rights Appeals) (EU Exit) Regulations 2020 (SI 2020/61) provides for a right of appeal to EEA nationals and their family members against decisions affecting their entitlement to enter and remain in the UK under the EU Settlement Scheme (see **Chapter 4**).

Where a person has made a valid application for entry clearance or leave under the EU Settlement Scheme, they have a right of appeal against its refusal. In addition, a person granted pre-settled status may appeal on the ground that they should have been granted settled status. Moreover, where a person has been granted status under the Scheme, they have a right of appeal against a decision which varies their leave to enter or remain so that they have no leave, or revokes or cancels their entry clearance or indefinite leave to enter or remain.

Such a decision can be appealed on the grounds that it breaches any rights the person has under the European Union (Withdrawal Agreement) Act 2020 or was not in accordance with the relevant Immigration Rule or legislation under which it was made.

Appeals can be brought from either inside or outside the UK and are heard by the IAC or, where appropriate, the SIAC, with an onward right of appeal to the Upper Tribunal with permission and on a point of law (see **11.6.1**).

11.11 UNFOUNDED CLAIMS

By s 94(1) of the NIAA 2002, the Secretary of State may certify that a protection claim (see **11.2.1**) or a human rights claim (see **11.2.2**) is clearly unfounded.

Note that if the Secretary of State is satisfied that a claimant is entitled to reside in a State listed in s 94(4), he *must* certify the claim unless he is satisfied that it is not clearly unfounded. The s 94(4) States considered to be generally safe in the context of protection and human rights claims are:

(a)   the Republic of Albania;

(b)   Bosnia-Hertzegovina;

(c)   South Korea;

(d)   Macedonia;

(e)   the Republic of Moldova;

(f)   India;

(g)   Bolivia;

(h)   Brazil;

(i)   Ecuador;

(j)   South Africa;

(k)   Ukraine;

(l)   Mongolia;

(m)   Ghana (in respect of men);

(n)   Nigeria (in respect of men);

(o)   Gambia (in respect of men);

(p)   Kenya (in respect of men);

(q)   Liberia (in respect of men);

(r)   Malawi (in respect of men);

(s)   Mali (in respect of men);

(t)   Mauritius;

(u)   Montenegro;

(v)   Peru;

(w)   Serbia;

(x)   Sierra Leone (in respect of men);

(y)   Kosovo.

A case can be certified under s 94(1) where the claimant is not entitled to reside in one of the designated states. It can also be used where the claimant is entitled to reside in a designated state but falls within a category not covered by the designation, as long as the claim is clearly unfounded on its facts. The Home Office gives the following example:

> State A is designated for men only. The claimant is a woman entitled to reside in state A. Her claim is clearly unfounded. It should not be certified under section 94(3), but it should be certified under section 94(1).

The Home Office gives the following as examples of clearly unfounded claims:

(a)   A claim which raises nothing that could be construed as amounting to an expression of a fear of mistreatment upon return. For example, a person says he is seeking asylum but gives as his reason that he is fleeing poverty or unemployment.

(b)   The claimant expresses a fear of mistreatment, but from the objective evidence it is not arguable that the mistreatment, even if it occurred, would amount to persecution or treatment contrary to Article 3 ECHR.

(c)   The claimant expresses a fear of persecution or Article 3 treatment by non-State actors, but the State provides a sufficiency of protection against such actions.

Further, a person may not bring an appeal if the Secretary of State certifies that it is proposed to remove the person to a country of which he is not a national or citizen, and there is no reason to believe that the person's rights under the ECHR will be breached in that country. In determining whether a person in relation to whom such a certificate has been issued may be removed from the UK, the country specified in the certificate is to be regarded as a place where a person's life and liberty is not threatened by reason of his race, religion, nationality, membership of a particular social group, or political opinion, and a place from which a person will not be sent to another country otherwise than in accordance with the Refugee Convention.

Home Office guidance is that claims should be assessed at their highest and are certified only when they are bound to fail (following R (Yogathas) v Secretary of State for the Home Department [2002] UKHL 36). See also TT (Vietnam) v Secretary of State for the Home Department [2019] EWCA Civ 248 and SP (Albania) v Secretary of State for the Home Department [2019] EWCA Civ 951.

A certificate may be challenged by way of judicial review:

> It follows that a challenge to the Secretary of State's conclusion that a claim is clearly unfounded is a rationality challenge. There is no way that a court can consider whether her conclusion was rational other than by asking itself the same question that she has considered. If the court concludes that a claim has a realistic prospect of success when the Secretary of State has reached a contrary view, the court will necessarily conclude that the Secretary of State's view was irrational. (per Lord Phillips in ZT (Kosovo) v Secretary of State for the Home Department [2009] UKHL 6 at [23])

How should the Secretary of State set about making the decision? His Lordship explained (at [22]) that five steps need to be taken, namely, that the Secretary of State should:

(i)   consider the factual substance and detail of the claim,

(ii)   consider how it stands with the known background data,

(iii)   consider whether in the round it is capable of belief,

(iv)   if not, consider whether some part of it is capable of belief,

(v)   consider whether, if eventually believed in whole or in part, it is capable of coming within the Convention.

If the answers are such that the claim cannot on any legitimate view succeed, then the claim is clearly unfounded; if not, not.

See further **Chapter 12**.

Where a certificate is issued concerning a national of a country listed in s 94(4) of the NIAA 2002, the first challenge may be as to whether the country in question has been properly listed. To succeed, the claimant will have to demonstrate that the evidence clearly establishes that there is a serious risk of persecution in that country that affects a significant number of people: see R (MD (Gambia)) v Secretary of State for the Home Department [2011] EWCA Civ 121. It follows that if the listing is lawful, the next question is whether the Secretary of State was obliged to certify the claim on the basis that it was clearly unfounded.

Note that in R (on the application of Brown (Jamaica)) v Secretary of State for the Home Department [2015] UKSC 8, the Supreme Court held that the inclusion of Jamaica on the list was unlawful.

11.12   HUMAN RIGHTS CLAIMS

By s 94B of the NIAA 2002, if a human rights claim is made, the Secretary of State may certify that claim if he considers that, despite the appeals process' not having been begun or not having been exhausted, refusing the appellant entry to, removing him from or requiring him to leave the UK, pending the outcome of an appeal in relation to the claim, would not be unlawful under s 6 of the HRA 1998.

The grounds on which the Secretary of State may certify a claim include in particular that the appellant would not, before the appeals process is exhausted, face a real risk of serious irreversible harm if refused entry to, removed from or required to leave the UK.

A decision to certify a claim under this section can be challenged by way of judicial review (see **Chapter 12**) but there is no right of appeal against the certification itself: see R (*on the application of Kiarie and Byndloss*) *v Secretary of State for the Home Department* [2015] EWCA Civ 1020.

11.13   PERSONS EXCLUDED FROM ASYLUM

Where the Home Office decides that a claimant is excluded from asylum (see **9.5**), the Secretary of State will issue a certificate to that effect. As a result, any appeal made to the IAC or SIAC must start by considering the statements made in the Secretary of State's certificate. By s 55(4) of the IANA 2006, if the Tribunal or Commission agrees with those statements, it must dismiss such part of the appeal as amounts to an asylum claim before considering any other aspect of the case.

11.14   IMMIGRATION STATUS DURING AN APPEAL

What if an appellant's leave expires before their appeal is determined? Section 3C of the IA 1971 provides that an appellant's leave is extended until their appeal is finally determined (withdrawn or abandoned) provided they had leave when they made the appeal. The purpose of s 3C leave is to prevent an appellant who makes an in-time appeal from becoming an overstayer as their leave continues during any period when an in-country appeal could be brought (ignoring any possibility of appeal out of time with permission) and the appeal is pending (see **11.7**).

EXAMPLE

Annabel makes an in-time application which is refused but can be appealed in country within 14 days. Annabel's s 3C leave will end 14 days after the appealable decision is sent to her unless she lodges an appeal within the time limit. If she makes an in-time appeal, her s 3C leave will continue until her appeal is finally determined (withdrawn or abandoned).

Section 3C leave ends when a person does not appeal or seek permission to appeal within the relevant time limit. Does an appeal made out of time extend s 3C leave? No, but if the Tribunal grants permission for the appeal to proceed, s 3C leave will run from when the Tribunal grants that permission.

A person who has s 3C leave remains subject to the conditions attached to their still existing leave (unless those conditions are varied by the Secretary of State). For example, a person subject to a condition allowing employment may continue to work as before. Any restrictions on the type of employment allowed or the number of hours they can work will still apply (see further **3.3.1**).

The conditions attached to a person's leave may be varied while they are on s 3C leave, for example, by imposing a residence requirement and/or reporting conditions (see **3.3.4**).

As to cancelling s 3C leave, see **3.4.5.7** and **3.4.5.8**.

Where the right of appeal is exercised from within the UK, s 78 of the NIAA 2002 provides that the appellant will not be removed while the appeal is pending.

11.15 DEPRIVATION OF CITIZENSHIP ORDERS

By s 40A of the BNA 1981, a person given notice of a decision to make an order depriving him of his British citizenship (see **2.2.9**) has a right of appeal to the IAC. Where, however, the Secretary of State has certified that the decision to deprive was based wholly or partly in reliance on information which he believes should not be made public, the appeal at first instance will instead be heard by the SIAC.

11.16 ADMINISTRATIVE REVIEW

As we saw at **11.2**, there are very few decisions against which an appeal can be made. In those circumstances it will often be possible to apply for an administrative review of a refusal of an application, provided it is an 'eligible decision' and on the basis that a 'case working error' has occurred. The detail is set out in Appendix AR of the Immigration Rules and summarised below.

11.16.1 What decisions can be reviewed?

Only an 'eligible' decision can be reviewed. This is either the refusal of an application or its approval, but a review is sought of the period and/or conditions of leave granted. The decision must concern:

(a)   permission to stay as a Student, Child Student or their dependant (see **Chapter 6**);

(b)   the employment, business and investment categories addressed in **Chapter 7**; or

(c)   in-country applications for leave to remain, unless the applicant applied as a visitor (see **Chapter 5**) or made a protection claim (see **11.2.1**) or human rights claim (see **11.2.2**).

For applicants at the UK border, eligible decisions are those cancelling leave to enter or remain that were in force with the result that the applicant has no leave to enter or remain, due either to a change of circumstances, or to false representations or failure to disclose material facts. The applicant will be granted temporary admission if he is allowed to enter the UK to make an administrative review application.

A person who receives an eligible decision on an entry clearance application may apply for administrative review. For applicants overseas, an eligible decision is a decision to refuse an application for entry clearance, unless it was made in the category of short-term student or visitor (see **Chapter 5**), or as a human rights claim (see **11.2.2**).

11.16.2 What is a case working error?

If an eligible decision has been made, only the following case working errors can be reviewed:

(a)   That the original decision maker's decision was incorrect in relation to either:

   (i)   refusing an application on the basis of para 9.7.1, 9.7.2, 9.8.1 or 9.8.2 of Part 9 of the Immigration Rules (see **Chapter 3**), or

   (ii)   cancelling leave to enter or remain which is in force under para 9.7.3 of Part 9 of the Immigration Rules (see **Chapter 3**).

(b)   That the original decision maker's decision to refuse an application, on the basis that the date of application was beyond any time limit in the Immigration Rules, was incorrect.

(c)   That the original decision maker's decision not to request specified documents (see **3.11**) was incorrect.

(d)   That the original decision maker otherwise applied the Immigration Rules incorrectly.

(e)   That the original decision maker failed to apply the Secretary of State's relevant published policy and guidance in relation to the application.

(f)   That there has been an error in calculating the correct period or conditions of immigration leave either held or to be granted.

The following examples are taken from Home Office guidance.

Examples

Case working error	Facts
Where the original decision maker's decision to refuse an application under para 9.7.1 of Part 9 of the Immigration Rules on the basis that the supporting documents were not genuine, was incorrect.	The migrant has submitted Internet bank statements that appear to have been stamped in a branch to authenticate them. The statements were verified and the issuing bank stated that they were false. The migrant has evidence from the bank stating that the verification was done incorrectly and the statements are genuine.
Where the original decision maker has incorrectly refused an application on the basis that it was made more than 28 days after leave expired.	The original decision maker uses the date on which the application was input as the date of application, rather than the date the application was posted. The 28-day period has therefore been calculated incorrectly.
Where the original decision maker applied the wrong Immigration Rules.	The caseworker applies the rules for Students rather than Child Students
Where the original decision maker applied the Immigration Rules incorrectly.	The caseworker refuses the application because a resident labour market test has not been carried out, but the applicant's occupation is exempt from this requirement.
Where the original decision maker has considered some or all of the evidence submitted incorrectly, as evidenced in the eligible decision.	Where the migrant has submitted multiple sets of bank statements and the amounts have been added up incorrectly by the original decision maker, resulting in a decision to refuse on the grounds of insufficient funds.
Where the original decision maker failed to apply the Secretary of State's relevant published policy and guidance.	The migrant's original sponsor loses his licence while the application is under consideration. The original decision maker fails to correctly apply the policy to allow the migrant 60 days to find a new sponsor and vary his application.

11.16.3   Applying for an administrative review

The requirements for an administrative review application are set out in paras 34M to 34Y in Part 1 of the Immigration Rules. A valid application can only be made either by completing the relevant online application, or by using the specified application form.

What is the deadline? An in country request must be made within 14 calendar days after the date on which the applicant received the decision, but that will be only seven calendar days if the applicant is in immigration detention. If the request is about a decision made overseas, the deadline is 28 calendar days.

What if the deadline is missed? The Secretary of State may waive the time limit if it is just to do so and the application was made as soon as reasonably practicable. The applicant will normally have to provide evidence to persuade the Secretary of State that it would be unjust not to accept the late application. Home Office guidance gives the example of an applicant who is prevented from making the application before the deadline because he is admitted to hospital as an emergency admission for immediate treatment and a period of recuperation. Here, a letter from the consultant should be produced, confirming the dates of admission and discharge and the nature of the emergency treatment. The applicant must make the application as soon as he is well enough to do so. See further R (Hasan) v Secretary of State for the Home Department [2019] EWCA Civ 389.

As a general rule an applicant is allowed one valid administrative review for each eligible decision. The exception to this is where, following an administrative review, the Home Office maintains its refusal of leave decision but on additional or different grounds. Only in these circumstances is the applicant entitled to a further administrative review, but that is limited to the new grounds.

11.16.4 How an administrative review is conducted

The Home Office case worker, immigration officer or ECO conducting the administrative review is known as the 'reviewer'. Will the reviewer be the same person who made the initial decision? No: Home Office guidance is that an administrative review is carried out by a different person on an independent team.

Home Office instructions to the reviewer are that he must:

(a)   normally only consider the specific aspects of the decision the applicant is challenging. However, if it becomes clear during the review that the original decision contained errors that have not been identified, those errors must also be corrected;

(b)   carefully consider all the claimed errors raised in the application and address each of them in the review decision;

(c)   request additional information if the applicant is allowed to provide it (see **11.18.1**) and it is needed to conduct the review;

(d)   not consider any new evidence or information unless it impacts on the decision and the applicant is allowed to provide new evidence (see **11.18.1**);

(e)   consider if correcting the case work error would change the outcome of the original decision (whether or not the outcome of the review is that the original decision is overturned).

11.16.5 Evidence

The reviewer will not consider any evidence that was not before the original decision maker, except where such evidence is submitted to demonstrate that a case working error has occurred in the following circumstances:

(a)   the original decision maker did not consider all the evidence submitted with the original application;

(b)   the original decision maker reached an unreasonable decision as to the credibility of the applicant, where the Immigration Rules allow the original decision maker to consider credibility;

(c)   documents provided with the original application were genuine; or

(d)   the original decision maker incorrectly refused the application on the basis that it was made more than 28 days after leave expired.

As to (b), what test is applied by the reviewer? Home Office guidance is that the reviewer must determine whether it is more likely than not, based on the evidence and facts available, that the original decision maker made the right decision that the applicant is not credible. The following example is based on Home Office guidance.

> **EXAMPLE**
>
> Angela applies for a Student visa (see **Chapter 6**). Her application is refused on the basis that she is not a genuine student. Angela applies for the decision to be reviewed.
>
> The reviewer must check whether the original caseworker made an error. He must decide whether any errors were made in respect of the relevant Immigration Rules and Home Office guidance based on the information supplied by Angela with her application, any interview with her and the caseworker's reasoning in the case notes and decision notice. The reviewer must then consider whether, based on those factors and that information, it is more likely than not that the original caseworker made the right decision.

11.16.6 Outcomes of a review

The review may conclude in any of the following ways:

(a) it is successful and the decision is withdrawn;

(b) it fails and the decision remains in force, and all of the reasons given for the decision are maintained;

(c) it fails and the decision remains in force, but one or more of the reasons given for the decision is or are withdrawn; or

(d) it fails and the decision remains in force, but with reasons different from or additional to those specified in the decision under review.

If the outcome of the administrative review is that the decision on the original application is withdrawn and leave is granted, the Home Office will refund the fee. This includes reviews of granted cases where the outcome of the review is that the original grant of leave was issued for the wrong period or subject to the wrong conditions.

CHAPTER 12

JUDICIAL REVIEW PROCEEDINGS

12.1 WHAT IS JUDICIAL REVIEW?

Judicial review involves a challenge to the legal validity of the decision. It does not allow the court of review to examine the evidence with a view to forming its own view about the substantial merits of the case. It may be that the tribunal whose decision is being challenged has done something which it had no lawful authority to do. It may have abused or misused the authority which it had. It may have departed from the procedures which either by statute or at common law as matter of fairness it ought to have observed. As regards the decision itself it may be found to be perverse, or irrational, or grossly disproportionate to what was required. Or the decision may be found to be erroneous in respect of a legal deficiency, as for example, through the absence of evidence, or of sufficient evidence, to support it, or through account being taken of irrelevant matter, or through a failure for any reason to take account of a relevant matter, or through some misconstruction of the terms of the statutory provision which the decision-maker is required to apply. But while the evidence may have to be explored in order to see if the decision is vitiated by such legal deficiencies it is perfectly clear that in a case of review, as distinct from an ordinary appeal, the court may not set about forming its own preferred view of the evidence. (per Lord Clyde in *Reid v Secretary of State for Scotland* [1998] UKHL 43)

12.1.1 Use of judicial review in immigration cases

As we saw at **11.2**, the NIAA 2002 sets out those immigration decisions against which there is a right of appeal. But what about those decisions where there is no right of appeal? Or where all appeal rights have been exhausted? This is where judicial review proceedings may be an appropriate step for the client to take.

Judicial review will be refused if an alternative remedy is more appropriate, such as where an applicant has failed to use a right of appeal, unless he can show that the circumstances are exceptional: see *R v Secretary of State for the Home Department, ex p Swati* [1986] 1 All ER 717. It is not enough to show that the right of appeal is a less convenient remedy, for instance because it must be conducted from abroad: see *Soon Ok Ryoo v Secretary of State for the Home Department* [1992] Imm AR 59. However, if it would be practically impossible to conduct the appeal from abroad, permission may be given: see *R v Chief Immigration Officer, Gatwick Airport, ex p Kharrazi* [1980] 1 WLR 1396 and *R v Secretary of State for the Home Department and Immigration Officer, Waterloo International Station, ex p Canbolat* [1997] INLR 198.

The vast majority of judicial review proceedings concern aspects of asylum and human rights claims, eg when the Secretary of State does not accept that a fresh claim was made (**9.14**), or certifies a claim as no longer appealable (**11.5.2** and **11.5.3**) or unfounded (**11.11**); deportation and removal cases (particularly human rights-based challenges: **Chapter 10**); as well as cases where the Secretary of State refuses to register or naturalise a person as a British citizen (**Chapter 2**).

12.1.2 Grounds for judicial review

The most common grounds for judicial review are set out in the extract from *Reid* at **12.1**.

The usual starting point is to consider if the decision-maker made an error of law, eg did the Secretary of State ask the right question? Otherwise, in many cases the client will be arguing that the decision made was irrational or unreasonable. The test for this was originally laid down by Lord Greene MR in the landmark Court of Appeal case of *Associated Provincial Picture Houses Ltd v Wednesbury Corporation* [1948] 1 KB 223, namely, having regard to relevant considerations only, did the decision-maker come to a conclusion that was so unreasonable that no reasonable authority could ever have come to it? Note that here consideration needs to be given as to whether the Secretary of State took into account factors that were irrelevant and/or omitted to take relevant matters into account. Equally, it should be asked whether the Secretary of State gave undue weight to one or more factors over other relevant factors.

Subsequently, the test of irrationality has been refined. In *CCSU v Minister for Civil Service* [1984] 3 All ER 935, Lord Diplock stated that, to be irrational, a decision needs to be so outrageous in its defiance of logic, or of accepted moral standards, that no sensible person could have arrived at it. In the later case of *R v Ministry of Defence, ex p Smith* [1996] 1 All ER 257, the Court of Appeal found that, to establish irrationality, the decision or policy should be beyond the range of reasonable responses open to the decision-maker.

When making a decision, the Secretary of State or a court must take all relevant considerations into account. This is often known as the 'anxious scrutiny' requirement. In *WM (DRC) v Secretary of State for the Home Department* [2006] EWCA Civ 1495, Buxton LJ stated, at [7], that in an asylum case, for example, 'the consideration of all the decision-makers, the Secretary of State, the [Immigration Judge] and the court, must be informed by the anxious scrutiny of the material that is axiomatic in decisions that if made incorrectly may lead to the Applicant's exposure to persecution.' As Carnwath LJ later explained in R (YH) v *Secretary of State for the Home Department* [2010] EWCA Civ 116, at [24], the requirement has 'by usage acquired special significance as underlining the very special human context in which such cases are brought, and the need for decisions to show by their reasoning that every factor which might tell in favour of an Applicant has been properly taken into account'.

12.1.3 Remedies

The most common remedy sought in an immigration case is for the decision to be quashed, ie declared void. The court may, in addition, remit the case to the Secretary of State for the Home Department, or relevant tribunal, with a direction to reconsider it according to the findings of the court. See further **12.3.6**.

12.2 MAKING A CLAIM: PRE-ACTION STEPS

Before an application is made to the court, the Pre-Action Protocol for Judicial Review should be consulted (there is a copy at **Appendix 14**). The Protocol sets out a code of best practice and contains the steps which parties should normally follow before starting court proceedings. The Protocol will not be appropriate where judicial review is required of a tribunal decision or in urgent cases, for example when directions have been set, or are in force, for the client's removal from the UK.

When following the Protocol, a claimant must always have in mind the fact that any application for judicial review must be filed promptly, and in any event, not later than three months after the grounds to make the claim first arose.

12.2.1 Letter before claim

Where the Protocol applies, the claimant should send a letter before claim to the Secretary of State for the Home Department who will act as the defendant. The prescribed Home Office email address and/or postal address can be found in Appendix A of the Protocol. The letter should clearly, succinctly and accurately identify the issues in dispute and seek to establish whether litigation can be avoided. Normally, the suggested standard format for the letter outlined at Annex A should be used, but in addition you should include, where known and appropriate, the client's Home Office, Port, Tribunal and National Asylum Support Service reference numbers. Otherwise, ensure the client's full name, nationality and date of birth are set out.

There is a specimen letter before claim at **12.5**.

12.2.2 Home Office response

Home Office guidance is that if the caseworker decides the representations in the letter before claim have merit then they should try to rectify the problem without the need for court proceedings. If the representations are without merit, the letter of response should fully explain the reasons for that decision and answer any queries the claimant has made. If the caseworker decides that some of the claim has merit but other points do not, the response should comprehensively set out the reasons for this decision, with a full explanation of what is agreed and what steps will be taken to rectify this, and why the other points are not accepted.

12.3 COURT PROCEEDINGS

Judicial review proceedings must be started in the High Court (see the Senior Courts Act 1981, s 31). Claims are dealt with by the Administrative Court (save a challenge to the Secretary of State's refusal to treat submissions as a fresh asylum or human rights claim (**9.14**) as these reviews are normally transferred to the Upper Tribunal under the Senior Courts Act 1981, s 31A).

The judicial review procedure is governed by Part 54 of the Civil Procedure Rules 1998 (SI 1998/3132) (CPR 1998). By r 54.1(2)(a), a 'claim for judicial review' is defined as 'a claim to review the lawfulness of an enactment; or a decision, action or failure to act in relation to the exercise of a public function'.

12.3.1 The two stages of an application

The judicial review procedure has the unusual feature of two separate stages. First, the claimant must start the proceedings by filing a CPR 1998, Part 8 claim form and obtain the court's permission to proceed with it. If permission is granted then, secondly, after the parties have filed various documents, a full judicial review hearing takes place.

12.3.2 The need for a prompt application

An application for permission to apply for judicial review must be made promptly, and in any event within three months from the date when grounds for the application first arose. The time limit cannot be extended by agreement between the parties. The court may extend the period if there is good reason for the delay, but delay may still result in refusal of a remedy at the final hearing (R (*Lichfield Securities Ltd*) *v Lichfield District Council* (2001) *The Times*, 30 March).

12.3.3 Applying for permission

The claim form and other documents prescribed by CPR 1998, Practice Direction 54A (such as a detailed statement of the grounds for bringing the claim, a statement of the facts relied on, any written evidence relied on and a copy of any order sought to have quashed) must be filed and served on the defendant and any interested party. Where the review is sought of a tribunal decision, the Secretary of State will be an interested party. Rule 6.10 of the CPR 1998 provides that service on a government department must be effected on the solicitor acting for that department, which in the case of the Home Office is the Treasury Solicitor. The address for the Treasury Solicitor can be found in the Annex to Part 66 of the CPR 1998.

The defendant and any interested party have 21 days to acknowledge service of the claim form. Where a party filing an acknowledgment intends to contest the claim, a summary of the grounds on which it will be contested must be included.

12.3.4 Permission hearing

Normally the court determines whether or not to grant permission to proceed without an oral hearing. Permission is granted if the claimant can show on the materials filed a case which is 'arguable' and so requires a full investigation of the substantive merits (see R v Inland Revenue Commissioners, ex p National Federation of Self-Employed and Small Businesses Ltd [1982] AC 617).

If permission to proceed is refused or granted subject to conditions and/or on certain grounds only, the claimant may within seven days request an oral hearing for that decision to be reconsidered. But note that a judge who refuses permission on the papers may certify that it is totally without merit and thereby prevent the applicant from seeking an oral hearing. In these circumstances there is a right of appeal to the Court of Appeal but with no right to an oral hearing: see further Wasif v The Secretary of State for the Home Department [2016] EWCA Civ 82.

12.3.5 Next steps if permission granted

If permission to proceed is granted, the court will normally give case management directions as to how the parties are to prepare for the final hearing. This normally includes the the filing and service of a detailed response by the defendant and any interested parties, along with their written evidence. The claimant will prepare the trial bundle and each party should file a skeleton argument.

12.3.6 The hearing

The hearing usually takes place before a single judge nominated to hear cases in the Administrative Court. The parties' advocates make their respective submissions on the evidence filed. Only in exceptional cases will any witnesses be called and cross-examined.

What if the key factual evidence submitted to the court is disputed? The court's approach to this issue was summarised by Silber J in R (McVey) v Secretary of State for Health [2010] EWHC 437 as follows (at [35]):

(i)   The basic rule is that where there is a dispute on evidence in a judicial review application, then in the absence of cross-examination, the facts in the defendants' evidence must be assumed to be correct;

(ii)   An exception to this rule arises where the documents show that the defendants' evidence cannot be correct; and that

(iii) The proper course for a claimant who wishes to challenge the correctness of an important aspect of the defendant's evidence relating to a factual matter on which the judge will have to make a critical factual finding is to apply to cross-examine the maker of the witness statement on which the defendant relies.

What are the court's powers when making a quashing order? The court will usually remit the matter to the decision-maker, direct it to reconsider the case and reach a decision in accordance with the judgment of the court.

When can the court substitute its own decision? Only if that decision was made by a court or tribunal, the decision is quashed on the ground that there was an error of law, and without that error there would have been only one decision which the court or tribunal could have reached.

12.4 APPEALS FROM JUDICIAL REVIEW DECISIONS

What if permission to proceed is refused at an oral hearing or on reconsideration? The claimant can apply within seven days to the Court of Appeal for permission to appeal that decision. Note that the Court of Appeal is not limited to granting permission to appeal but may grant permission for the judicial review. What if the Court of Appeal refuses permission to appeal? That is the end of the matter. Only if permission to appeal is granted but permission to proceed with the judicial review claim is refused can an appeal be made to the Supreme Court.

What if a party does not agree with the outcome of a judicial review? Permission to appeal can be sought from the court or the Court of Appeal. Any further appeal will be to the Supreme Court.

12.5 SPECIMEN LETTER BEFORE CLAIM

To
The Secretary of State for the Home Department
UKVIPAP@homeoffice.gsi.gov.uk
Litigation Allocation Unit
6, New Square
Bedfont Lakes
Feltham, Middlesex
TW14 8HA

The claimant
Christopher Katongo

Reference details
Home Office reference number [   ].

The details of the matter being challenged
The decision made by the Secretary of State under Section 94 of the Nationality Immigration and Asylum Act 2002 (NIAA 2002) to certify as clearly unfounded the claimant's claim that his removal from the UK would be a disproportionate interference with his right to a family and private life under Article 8 of the European Convention on Human Rights (ECHR).

The issue

1. *Date of decision:* [   ]

2. *Relevant law*

A case which is clearly unfounded is one which has no real prospect of success if an appeal was made to the First Tier Tribunal, Immigration and Asylum Chamber.

The Secretary of State was required to give the claim anxious scrutiny. In determining whether the test was met, the Secretary of State had to consider, amongst other matters, the factual substance and detail of the claim; how it stands with the known background data; whether in the round it is capable of belief; if not, whether some part of it is capable of belief; and whether if eventually believed, in whole or in part, it is capable of coming within the ECHR. Only if the answers are such that the claim cannot on any legitimate view succeed is the claim clearly unfounded (*ZT (Kosovo) v Secretary of State for the Home Department* [2009] UKHL 6).

The Secretary of State had to approach the matter by addressing the questions set out by Lord Bingham in paragraph 17 of R *(Razgar) v Secretary of State for the Home Department* [2004] 2 AC 368, as further explained by the subsequent case of R *(Huang) v Secretary of State for the Home Department* [2007] UKHL 11, namely:

(a) Will the proposed removal be an interference by a public authority with the exercise of the applicant's rights to respect for his private or, as the case may be, family life?

(b) If so, will such interference have consequences of such gravity as potentially to engage the operation of Article 8?

(c) If so, is such interference in accordance with law?

(d) If so, is such interference necessary in a democratic society in a number of legitimate interests including, on the established case law, the maintenance of effective immigration control?

(e) If so, is such interference proportionate to the legitimate public ends sought to be achieved?

The relationship of a nephew and his aunt as adults falls within the scope of family life as it started when the nephew was a child and continued after he reached 18 (*Secretary of State for the Home Department v HK (Turkey)* [2010] EWCA Civ 583), and there are special elements of dependency beyond normal emotional ties (*Kugathas v Secretary of State for the Home Department* [2003] EWCA Civ 31 and *Odawey v Entry Clearance Officer* [2011] EWCA Civ 840).

By paragraph 276ADE of the Immigration Rules the Secretary of State had to consider granting the claimant leave to remain on the grounds of his private life in the UK as he is over 18, he has lived continuously in the UK for less than 20 years and has no ties (including social, cultural or family) with the country to which he would have to go if required to leave the UK, namely, Zambia.

As to proportionality, the Supreme Court (then the House of Lords) in *Huang* stated at paragraph 20 that the ultimate question for the appellate authority is whether the refusal of leave to enter or remain, in circumstances where the life of the family cannot reasonably be expected to be enjoyed elsewhere, taking full account of all considerations weighing in favour of the refusal, prejudices the family life of the applicant in a manner that is sufficiently serious to amount to a breach of the fundamental right protected by Article 8.

3. Relevant facts

The claimant is a national of Zambia, aged 22. He was born in Zambia and lived there until he was 15. When he was 5 years old, his mother died. Shortly afterwards his father was diagnosed with a terminal illness. The claimant was an only child. He was cared for, together with his father, by his paternal grandmother. His father died when he was 10. The claimant's grandmother died when he was 15. It was at this point that the claimant was invited by his aunt, Mrs Francis, to visit her and her family in Huddersfield, England. Mrs Francis is a British citizen and the claimant's only living relative.

The claimant entered the UK as a minor. His passport was stamped with a 6-month visitor's visa but he stayed on in the UK when that period expired. His case, supported by Mrs Francis, is that Mrs Francis decided the claimant should stay with her family in the UK permanently but she overlooked applying for the appropriate permissions for the claimant from the immigration authorities.

The claimant had no formal education in Zambia. He can speak little English. He cannot speak Bemba which is spoken nationwide in Zambia. He has no understanding of the cultural norms in Zambia. Mrs Francis describes him as very slow in his learning. She says that he is not capable of looking after himself as an adult. The claimant is dependent on her both financially and emotionally. This is supported by a doctor's report. The report also confirms that the claimant has suffered from time to time with depression and that he has mentioned on occasions that he was thinking of committing suicide because he is very lonely and, in particular, because he misses his father.

4. Why the decision is wrong

The claimant has established a family and private life in the UK. He entered as a child and has been here for approximately 7 years. During that time he has been staying with and has been both financially and emotionally dependent on his aunt, Mrs Francis. The Secretary of State failed to give sufficient weight to the significant relationship that the claimant has with, and his dependency on, Mrs Francis. He is dependent upon her for his day to day health and wellbeing. He has no family, friends or social network to turn to for support in Zambia.

To remove the claimant from the UK is a disproportionate interference with that established family life. The Secretary of State's conclusion that the claimant entered the UK by deception is erroneous. It is the claimant's case that when he arrived in the UK he told the Immigration Officer that he was coming to stay with his aunt in Huddersfield and his visa was stamped. It is Mrs Francis' evidence that she had given the claimant a letter to hand to the immigration authorities confirming this. It was only after the claimant had lived with the family in Huddersfield for several months that it was decided the claimant should remain here permanently with them. This is not a case where the claimant chose to enter or remain in the UK unlawfully. Nor is it a case where the claimant has developed a private and family life in flagrant disregard of orders requiring him to leave the UK.

The claimant is a depressed young man who is suffering from the loss of all of his immediate family members. He was brought up in a family environment and this has continued for the last 7 years in the UK. To separate him from Mrs Francis' family unit, will, as the medical report states, significantly contribute to his state of alienation and depression.

In all these circumstances the Secretary of State's conclusion that the claimant would be able to establish and maintain a private life in his own right on his return to Zambia is irrational.

The claimant has a realistic prospect of persuading an appeal tribunal that to remove him from the UK would be a disproportionate interference with the family life that he has established here.

The details of the action that the defendant is expected to take
The Secretary of State is asked to review the decision and revoke the certificate.

The details of the legal advisers dealing with this claim and the claimant's address for reply and service of court documents
The details of the claimant's legal advisers and his address for service are as follows:

XYZ Lawyers LLP
1 The Avenue
Nowhere
Mythshire
MY11 1AB
Tel: 012345678
Ref: 123/ABC/CK

The details of any interested parties
n/a

Information sought and documents that are considered relevant and necessary
If the Secretary of State intends to rely on additional information and/or documents, please ensure that full details and copies are enclosed with the reply to this letter.

Proposed reply date
Please ensure that a reply is given within 14 days.

APPENDICES

APPENDIX 1

Immigration Rules

Contents (selected Parts and Appendices: statements of changes to HC 617, 10 September 2021)

Immigration Rules: introduction

This contains an explanation of who's covered by the Immigration Rules, dates of effect and definitions/interpretations of the terms used.

1. The Home Secretary has made changes in the Rules laid down by him as to the practice to be followed in the administration of the Immigration Acts for regulating entry into and the stay of persons in the United Kingdom and contained in the statement laid before Parliament on 23 March 1990 (HC 251) (as amended). This statement contains the Rules as changed and replaces the provisions of HC 251 (as amended).

2. Immigration Officers, Entry Clearance Officers and all staff of the Home Office will carry out their duties without regard to the race, colour or religion of persons seeking to enter or remain in the United Kingdom.

3. In these Rules words importing the masculine gender include the feminine unless the contrary intention appears.

Implementation and transitional provisions

4. These Rules come into effect on 1 October 1994 and will apply to all decisions taken on or after that date save that any application made before 1 October 1994 for entry clearance, leave to enter or remain or variation of leave to enter or remain other than an application for leave by a person seeking asylum shall be decided under the provisions of HC 251, as amended, as if these Rules had not been made.

    Rider 294

Provision for Irish citizens

5.   DELETED

5A. DELETED

5B. DELETED

5C. Save where expressly indicated throughout these rules, these rules do not apply to an Irish citizen who as a result of section 3ZA of the Immigration Act 1971 does not require leave to enter or remain, but an Irish citizen who does require leave to enter or remain is covered by these rules.

5D. Paragraph 5C does not apply to paragraph 11, Appendix EU, Appendix S2 Healthcare Visitor, Appendix Service Providers from Switzerland, Appendix EU (Family Permit), Appendix AR (EU), Part 11 (asylum) or Part 13 (deportation).

5E. An Irish citizen who as a result of section 3ZA of the Immigration Act 1971 does not require leave to enter or remain is considered settled for the purposes of these rules.

Interpretation

6.1. In these rules, unless the contrary intention appears, references to paragraphs are to paragraphs of the Immigration Rules (HC 395 as amended) made under section 3(2) of the Immigration Act 1971, and references to Appendices are to Appendices to those rules.

6.2. In these rules:

   (a)   references to primary and secondary legislation refers to that legislation as amended from time to time; and

   (b)   unless the contrary intention appears, the following definitions apply:

   "Accompanying Person" in Appendix S2 Healthcare Visitor is a person with a healthcare right of entry and who is accompanying a patient (P) to the UK at the same time as P's entry into the UK, or who is joining P in the UK on a date after P's entry into the UK, for the purpose of providing P with care or support during their course of planned healthcare treatment.

   "Accredited Institution" means an institution which is:

   (a)   the holder of a student sponsor licence; or

   (b)   the holder of valid accreditation from Accreditation UK, the Accreditation Body for Language Services (ABLS), the British Accreditation Council (BAC), or the Accreditation Service for International Colleges (ASIC); or

   (c)   the holder of a valid and satisfactory full institutional inspection, review or audit by Estyn, Education Scotland, the Independent Schools Inspectorate, Office for Standards in Education, the Office for Students, the Quality Assurance Agency for Higher Education or the Education and Training Inspectorate Northern Ireland; or

   (d)   an overseas higher education institution offering only part of its programmes in the UK.

"**Adequate**" and "**adequately**" in relation to a maintenance and accommodation requirement means that, after income tax, national insurance contributions and housing costs have been deducted, there must be available to the person or family the level of income or funds that would be available to them if the person or family was in receipt of income support.

"**Administrative review**" means a review conducted in accordance with Appendix AR, or where applicable Appendix AR (EU).

"**Adoption**" includes a de facto adoption in accordance with the requirements of paragraph 309A, and "adopted" and "adoptive parent" shall be construed accordingly.

"**Agreement on the Free Movement of Persons**" in Appendix Service Providers from Switzerland means the agreement between the Swiss Confederation and the European Union and its member states, which was signed in 1999 and came into force in 2002.

"**Amateur**" means a person who engages in a sport or creative activity solely for personal enjoyment and who is not seeking to derive a living from the activity.

"**Applicant**" means a person who is making an application for entry clearance, permission to enter or permission to stay (and a person seeking entry at the UK Border is to be regarded as making an application for permission to enter).

"**Application for asylum**" has the meaning given in paragraph 327 of these rules.

"**Application for leave to remain**" and "**application for permission to stay**" includes an application for variation of leave to enter or remain of a person in the UK.

"**Application Centre**" in the context of an application for entry clearance, means a commercial partner, a British Diplomatic Mission or Consular Post overseas, or designated government office overseas, authorised by the Secretary of State to take biometrics and receive documents from applicants for entry clearance.

"**Approved Destination Status Agreement with China**" means the Memorandum of Understanding on visa and related issues concerning tourist groups from the People's Republic of China to the United Kingdom as an approved destination, signed on 21 January 2005.

"**Approved qualification**" means a qualification which meets the Approved qualification requirements in Appendix Student.

"**Approved sponsor**" means a sponsor which is listed in the register of licensed sponsors: workers or register of licensed sponsors: students on the gov.uk website as being licensed for the relevant route of these rules and found at: https://www.gov.uk/government/publications/register-of-licensed-sponsors-workers https://www.gov.uk/government/publications/register-of-licensed-sponsors-students.

"**Biometrics**" has the same meaning as "biometric information" in section 15 of the UK Borders Act 2007 and means, in particular, a record of a person's fingerprints and a photograph of a person's face.

"**Biometric immigration document**" means a document recording biometric information issued in accordance with regulations made under section 5 of the UK Borders Act 2007.

"**Bona fide private education institution**" is a private education institution which:

(a)   maintains satisfactory records of enrolment and attendance of students, and supplies these to the Home Office when requested; and

(b)   provides courses which involve a minimum of 15 hours' organised daytime study per week; and

(c)   ensures a suitably qualified tutor is present during the hours of study to offer teaching and instruction to the students; and

(d)   offers courses leading to qualifications recognised by the appropriate accreditation bodies; and

(e)   employs suitably qualified staff to provide teaching, guidance and support to the students; and

(f)   provides adequate accommodation, facilities, staffing levels and equipment to support the numbers of students enrolled at the institution; and

(g)   if it offers tuition support to external students at degree level, ensures that such students are registered with the UK degree awarding body.

"**Born in the UK or Islands**" in Appendix UK Ancestry means born:

(a)   in the UK; or

(b)   in the Channel Islands (Bailiwick of Guernsey, Bailiwick of Jersey); or

(c)   in the Isle of Man; or

(d)   before 31 March 1922, in Ireland; or

(e)   on a British-owned or registered ship or aircraft if the requirements of either section 50(7)(a) of the British Nationality Act 1981, or section 32(5) of the British Nationality Act 1948, as applicable, are met.

"BN(O) Adult Dependent Relative" means a person granted permission as a BN(O) Adult Dependent Relative under Appendix Hong Kong British National (Overseas).

"BN(O) Household Child" means a person falling within HK 15.1. and who is granted permission as a BN(O) Household Child under Appendix Hong Kong British National (Overseas).

"BN(O) Household Member" means a person granted permission as a BN(O) Household Member under Appendix Hong Kong British National (Overseas).

"BN(O) Status Holder" means a person granted permission as a BN(O) Status Holder under Appendix Hong Kong British National (Overseas).

"Breach of immigration laws">{:#breachimmlaws} - a person is in breach of immigration laws for the purpose of these rules where the person is an overstayer; is an illegal entrant; is in breach of a condition of their permission; or used deception in relation to their most recent application for entry clearance or permission; and **"previously breached immigration laws"** – a person previously breached immigration laws if they overstayed or used deception in relation to a previous application for entry clearance or permission.

"Business day" means any day other than Saturday or Sunday, a day which is a bank holiday under the Banking and Financial Dealings Act 1971 in the part of the UK to which the notice is sent, Christmas Day or Good Friday.

"Cabotage operations" in Appendix Visitor: Permitted Activities means

(a)   in relation to goods, national carriage for hire or reward carried out on a temporary basis in the UK; or

(b)   in relation to passengers either:

    i.   national road passenger services for hire and reward carried out on a temporary basis by a carrier in the UK, or

    ii.   the picking up and setting down of passengers within the UK, in the course of a regular international service, provided that it is not the principal purpose of the service.

"Calendar year" means a year beginning on 1 January and ending on 31 December.

"Cancellation" in Part 9, Appendix S2 Healthcare Visitor and Appendix Service Providers from Switzerland means cancellation, variation in duration, or curtailment, of entry clearance or permission, which can take effect immediately or at a specified future date and whether the person is in the UK or overseas.

"Certificate of Sponsorship" means an electronic document with a unique reference number issued by a sponsor via the Sponsor Management System. The document confirms the details of the job for which the sponsor is sponsoring the applicant.

"Charity Worker" means a person who has, or had, permission under any of the following:

(i)   Appendix Temporary Work – Charity Worker; or

(ii)   Appendix T5 (Temporary Worker) Charity Worker under the rules in force between 1 December 2020 and 10 October 2021 (inclusive); or

(iii)   as a Tier 5 (Temporary Worker) migrant in the Charity Worker sub-category under part 6A of the rules in force before 1 December 2020.

"Child" means a person who is aged under 18 years.

"Child Student" means a person who has, or had, permission under Appendix Child Student, Appendix CS: Child Student under the rules in force before 1 December 2020, or as a Tier 4 (Child) Student under the rules in force before 5 October 2020.

"Civil partnership" means a civil partnership under or by virtue of the Civil Partnership Act 2004.

"Close relative" means a grandparent, brother, sister, step-parent, uncle (brother or half-brother of a child's parent) or aunt (sister or half-sister of a child's parent) who is aged 18 or over.

"Common Travel Area" is as defined in section 1(3) of the Immigration Act 1971.

"Commonwealth citizen" means:

(a)   a British Overseas Territories citizen, a British National (Overseas), a British Overseas citizen or a British subject; or

(b)   a citizen of a country listed in Schedule 3 to the British Nationality Act 1981.

"Condition" means a condition of leave to enter or leave to remain under section 3(1)(c) of the Immigration Act 1971, such as a prohibition on employment or study.

"**Confirmation of Acceptance for Studies reference number**" means a number which links to a single Confirmation of Acceptance for Studies that was assigned to a Student or Child Student by their student sponsor.

"**Consecutive engagements**" means where:

(a)   the applicant is being sponsored for more than one engagement in the UK as a Creative or Sporting Worker regardless of whether the applicant has engagements outside the UK that take place between those engagements in the UK; and

(b)   the applicant will be sponsored by more than one sponsor for those engagements,

(c)   each sponsor has issued a Certificate of Sponsorship on the Creative or Sporting Worker route for the relevant engagement, or engagements; and

(d)   there is no more than 14 days between each individual engagement in the UK, and for the purposes of calculating that 14-day period, time spent by the applicant outside the UK (including the dates of their departure from and return to the UK) will not be counted towards this period.

"**Contact point meeting**" means for the purpose of Appendix Start-up and Appendix Innovator a meeting between the applicant and their Endorsing body to assess progress against the applicant's business plan. For Start-up contact point meetings must be held at least after 6 months and 12 months from the date the application was granted. For Innovator contact point meetings must be held at least after 6 months, 12 months and 24 months from the date the application was granted.

"**Control Zone**" is as defined by article 2(1) of, and Schedule 1 to, the Channel Tunnel (International Arrangements) Order 1993 (SI 1993/1813) and article 2 of the Nationality, Immigration and Asylum Act 2002 (Juxtaposed Controls) Order 2003 (SI 2003/2818) (as amended from time to time).

"**Course of study**" means the course for which a Confirmation of Acceptance for Studies was assigned, or a new course with the person's current student sponsor which they were permitted to study without applying for further permission on the Student route.

"**Confirmation of Acceptance for Studies**" means an electronic document with a unique reference number electronically issued by a student sponsor via the Sponsor Management System, to a person who the student sponsor has agreed to sponsor, for use in an application as a Student or Child Student, in accordance with these rules.

"**Conviction**" means conviction for a criminal offence in the UK or any other country.

"**Creative Worker**" means a person who has, or had, permission under any of the following:

(i)   Appendix Temporary Work – Creative Worker; or

(ii)   Appendix T5 (Temporary Worker) Creative or Sporting Worker, working in the creative sector under the rules in force between 1 December 2020 and 10 October 2021 (inclusive); or

(iii)   as a Tier 5 (Temporary Worker) migrant in the Creative and Sporting sub-category working in the creative sector under part 6A of the rules in force before 1 December 2020 (inclusive).

"**Crew member**" has the same meaning as in the Immigration Act 1971.

"**Curtailment**", in relation to the curtailment of a person's leave to enter or leave to remain, means cancelling or curtailing their leave such that they will have a shorter period of, or no, leave remaining.

"**Custodial sentence**" means a period of imprisonment, not including a suspended sentence.

"**Customs breach**" means a breach of any provision of the Customs and Excise Acts or any other breach relating to an assigned matter (which is any matter in relation to which the Commissioners or officers of Her Majesty's Revenue and Customs have a power or duty which the Home Office may exercise at the border).

"**Date of application**" means: If applying for entry clearance either:

(a)   the date of payment of the relevant fee; or

(b)   where a fee is not required, the date on which the application is submitted online; or

(c)   where a fee is not required and an online application is not available, the date on which the paper application form is received by the Home Office.

If applying for permission to enter, the date the person seeks entry.

If applying for permission to stay:

(a)   where the paper application form is sent by post by Royal Mail, whether or not accompanied by a fee waiver request form, the date of posting as shown on the tracking information provided by Royal Mail or, if not tracked, by the postmark date on the envelope; or

(b)   where the paper application form is sent by courier, or other postal services provider, the date on which it is delivered to the Home Office; or

(c)   where the application is made via the online application process, and there is no request for a fee waiver, the date on which the online application is submitted, and the relevant fee is paid; or

(d)   where the application is made via the online application process, and includes a request for a fee waiver, the date on which the online request for a fee waiver is submitted, as long as the completed application is submitted within 10 days of the receipt of the decision on the request for a fee waiver.

"Decision maker" means an entry clearance officer, immigration officer or the Secretary of State, as the case may be.

"Deemed sponsorship status" means that the country or territory is not required to issue its nationals or passport holders with a Certificate of Sponsorship in order to enable a successful application under either of the following:

(i)   Appendix Youth Mobility; or

(ii)   Appendix T5 (Temporary Worker) Youth Mobility Scheme under the rules in force between 1 December 2020 and 10 October 2012,

and is a status held by a country or territory listed as such at Appendix Youth Mobility Scheme eligible nationals.

"Degree level study" means a course which leads to a recognised UK bachelor's degree, or an equivalent qualification at level 6 of the Regulated Qualifications Framework, or at level 9 or 10 of the Scottish Credit and Qualifications Framework.

"Deportation order" means an order made under section 5(1) of the Immigration Act 1971.

"Distance learning course" means a course being undertaken at a UK Accredited Institution by a person who is overseas, and which does not require the person to be physically present in the UK for the majority of the course.

"Doctorate extension scheme" means a sponsored scheme which enables successful applicants to remain in the UK for 12 months from the expected end date of a course leading to the award of a PhD as in Appendix Student, or under the rules in force before 1 December 2020.

"Domestic Worker in a Private Household" means a person who has, or had, permission under Appendix Domestic Worker in a Private Household, or as a domestic worker in a private household under paragraph 159EA of the rules in force before 6 May 2021.

"Domestic Worker who is a Victim of Modern Slavery" means a person who has, or had, permission under Appendix Domestic Worker Victim of Modern Slavery, or as a domestic worker who is a victim of slavery or human trafficking under paragraph 159J of the rules in force before 6 May 2021.

"ECAA route" means Appendix ECAA Extension of Stay or under the ECAA rules in force on 30 December 2020.

"Ecctis" is a service which provides information, advice and opinion on academic, vocational and professional qualifications and skills from all over the world, set out at: https://ecctis.com/.

"EEA citizen" and **"EEA national"** means a person who is a national of: Austria, Belgium, Bulgaria, Croatia, Republic of Cyprus, Czech Republic, Denmark, Estonia, Finland, France, Germany, Greece, Hungary, Iceland, Ireland, Italy, Latvia, Liechtenstein, Lithuania, Luxembourg, Malta, Netherlands, Norway, Poland, Portugal, Romania, Slovakia, Slovenia, Spain, Sweden or Switzerland; and who is not also a British citizen.

"EEA EFTA separation agreement" means (as modified from time to time in accordance with any provision of it) the Agreement on arrangements between Iceland, the Principality of Liechtenstein, the Kingdom of Norway and the United Kingdom of Great Britain and Northern Ireland following the withdrawal of the United Kingdom from the European Union, the EEA Agreement and other agreements applicable between the United Kingdom and the EEA EFTA States by virtue of the United Kingdom's membership of the European Union.

"EEA Regulations" means:

(a)   (where relevant to something done before 11pm on 31 December 2020) the Immigration (European Economic Area) Regulations 2016 (as they have effect immediately before that date or, in the case of an application made under these rules where the date of decision is before 11pm on 31 December 2020, as they have effect at the date of application); or

(b)   (where relevant to something done after 11pm on 31 December 2020) the Immigration (European Economic Area) Regulations 2016 (as, despite the revocation of those Regulations, they continue to have effect, with specified modifications, by virtue of regulations made under section 7, 9 or 11 of the European Union (Withdrawal Agreement) Act 2020).

"Employment" includes paid and unpaid employment, paid and unpaid work placements undertaken as part of a course or period of study, self-employment and engaging in business or any professional activity.

"Employment as a doctor or dentist in training" means employment in a medical post or training programme which has been approved by the General Medical Council, or employment in a postgraduate training programme in dentistry.

"Endorsed funder" means an organisation accepted by UKRI, and on a list published by them, as prestigious funders of research and innovation who have an excellent track record of awarding funding to researchers with critical skills, following a rigorous peer review process.

"Endorsing body" means an organisation which has been approved by the Home Office to endorse an application under one or more of the following routes:

(a)   Start-up;

(b)   Innovator;

(c)   Global Talent.

"Endorsement letter" means an official letter issued by an endorsing body, confirming that the endorsing body has endorsed the applicant in the relevant category.

"English language course" means a course that solely consists of English language study.

"Evidence of P's permission to enter or remain" under Appendix S2 Healthcare Visitor means:

(a)   a valid document which is either a biometric immigration document, stamp or endorsement in a passport (whether or not the passport has expired), or other document or electronic document issued by the Home Office, confirming that the patient (P) has permission to enter or remain in the UK as an S2 Healthcare Visitor, which has not been cancelled; or

(b)   the decision maker is otherwise satisfied from the information available that P has permission as an S2 Healthcare Visitor, which has not been cancelled.

"Exclusion decision" means a decision made personally by the Secretary of State that a person be excluded from the UK.

"Exclusion order" means an order made under regulation 23(5) of the EEA Regulations that the exclusion of an EEA national or the family member of an EEA national is justified on the grounds of public policy, public security or public health.

"Expected end date of a course leading to the award of a PhD" means the date the PhD is expected to be formally confirmed, by the student sponsor, as completed to the standard required for the award of a PhD and recorded on the Confirmation of Acceptance for Studies which applies to the application on the doctorate extension scheme.

"External student" means a student studying for a degree from a UK degree awarding body without any requirement to attend the UK degree awarding body's premises or a UK listed body's premises for lectures and tutorials.

"False document" includes:

(a)   a document which has been altered or tampered with; and

(b)   a counterfeit document; and

(c)   a document which is being used by an imposter; and

(d)   a document which has been fraudulently obtained or issued; and

(e)   a document which contains a falsified or counterfeit entry clearance, visa or endorsement.

"Fee" means the amount the applicant must pay to the Secretary of State as specified in regulations made in exercise of the powers in sections 68, 69 and 74 of the Immigration Act 2014.

"Foundation degree" means a programme of study which leads to a qualification awarded by an English higher education provider with degree awarding powers which is at a minimum of level 5 on the Regulated Qualifications Framework, or awarded on a directly equivalent basis in the devolved administrations.

"Full-time course" means a course which is:

(a)   a full-time course of course of study at UK bachelor's degree level or above; or

(b)   an overseas higher education course that a Student is studying in the UK and leads to a qualification from an overseas higher education institution that is recognised as being equivalent to a UK higher education qualification; or

(c)   a course of study below UK degree level that involves a minimum of 15 hours a week of classroom-based, daytime study (08:00 – 18:00, Monday to Friday), but scheduled breaks do not count towards the 15 hours.

"Global Talent" means the route, or a person with permission as a lead applicant on the route, under Appendix Global Talent or as a Global Talent migrant under Appendix W of the rules in force before 1 December 2020, or as a Tier 1 (Exceptional Talent) Migrant.

"Government Authorised Exchange Scheme" means a scheme under the T5 (Temporary Worker) Government Authorised Exchange Worker route which is endorsed by a Government Department in support of Government objectives and provides temporary work in an occupation which appears in Table 1 or Table 2 of Appendix Skilled Occupations and where the migrant will be supernumerary.

"Government Authorised Exchange route" means any of the following:

(i)   the route in Appendix Temporary Work – Government Authorised Exchange; or

(ii)   the route in Appendix T5 (Temporary Worker) Government Authorised Exchange Worker, under the rules in force between 1 December 2020 and 10 October 2021 (inclusive); or

(iii)   the Government Authorised Exchange sub-category in the Tier 5 (Temporary Worker) route under part 6A of the rules in force before 1 December 2020.

"Graduate" means a person who has, or had, permission as a Graduate under Appendix Graduate of these Rules.

"Grandparent" in Appendix UK Ancestry includes the applicant's blood grandparent or grandparent by reason of an adoption recognised by the laws of the UK relating to adoption.

"High earner" under Appendix Intra-Company routes is a person who is sponsored in a job with a gross annual salary of £73,900 or more (based on working a maximum of 48 hours per week) as confirmed by their sponsor.

"Higher education provider" means a student sponsor which:

(a)   in England, is an institution that is required to register with the Office for Students, because it is an "English Higher Education Provider", as defined in the Office for Students Regulations and section 83 of the Higher Education and Research Act 2017; or

(b)   in Northern Ireland, is a higher education institution as set out in the Education and Libraries (Northern Ireland) Order 1993, or a body that provides higher education, and is recognised under the Further Education (Northern Ireland) Order 1997, with "in developmental" or "established provider" status; or

(c)   in Scotland, is an institution that provides higher education within the meaning of section 38 of the Further and Higher Education (Scotland) Act 1992 and which is a post-16 education body within the meaning of section 35(1) of the Further and Higher Education (Scotland) Act 2005; or

(d)   in Wales, is an institution that offers higher education provision and is a "regulated institution", as defined in the Higher Education (Wales) Act 2015 (for the purpose of the 2015 Act, higher education is defined as education provided by means of a course of any description mentioned in Schedule 6 to the Education Reform Act 1988).

"Human Rights Convention" means the Convention for the Protection of Human Rights and Fundamental Freedoms, agreed by the Council of Europe at Rome on 4th November 1950, as it has effect for the time being in relation to the UK.

"Humanitarian protection" means leave granted pursuant to paragraph 339C and which has not been revoked pursuant to paragraph 339G to 339H.

"Illegal entrant" has the same meaning as in section 33(1) of the Immigration Act 1971.

"Immigration Acts" has the same meaning as in section 61(2) of the UK Borders Act 2007.

"Immigration employment document" means a work permit or any other document which relates to employment and is issued for the purpose of these rules or in connection with leave to enter or remain in the UK.

"Immigration Health Charge" means a charge under section 38 of the Immigration Act 2014 and the Immigration (Health Charge) Order 2015.

"Immigration Officer" includes a Customs Officer acting as an Immigration Officer.

"Immigration Skills Charge" means a charge payable under regulations made under section 70A of the Immigration Act 2014.

"**Independent School**" means:

(a) a school in England or Wales (which is not an Academy, a school maintained by a local authority, or a non-maintained special school), at which full-time education is provided for:

(i) five or more pupils of compulsory school age (whether or not such education is also provided at it for pupils under or over that age); or

(ii) for at least one pupil of compulsory school age (whether or not such education is also provided at it for pupils under or over that age) for whom an education, health and care (EHC) plan or a statement of special educational needs is maintained, or who is looked after by a local authority (within the meaning of section 22 of the Children Act 1989); or

(b) a school in Scotland (which is not a public school or a grant-aided school), at which full-time education is provided for pupils of school age (whether or not such education is also provided for pupils under or over that age); or

(c) a school in Northern Ireland (which is not grant-aided), which has been registered with the Department of Education.

"**Innovator**" means a person who has, or had, permission as an Innovator under Appendix Innovator or as an Innovator migrant under Appendix W of the rules in force before 1 December 2020.

"**Intention to live permanently with the other in the UK**" or "**intend to live together permanently in the UK**" means an intention to live together, evidenced by a clear commitment from both parties that they will live together permanently in the UK immediately following the outcome of the application in question or as soon as circumstances permit thereafter. However, where an application is made under Appendix Armed Forces the words "in the UK" in this definition do not apply. Where an application is made under Appendix FM and the sponsor is a permanent member of HM Diplomatic Service, or a comparable UK-based staff member of the British Council, the Foreign, Commonwealth and Development Office or the Home Office on a tour of duty outside the UK, the words "in the UK" in this definition do not apply.

"**International Agreement route**" means any of the following:

(i) the route in Appendix Temporary Work – International Agreement; or

(ii) the route in Appendix T5 (Temporary Worker) International Agreement Worker under the rules in force between 1 December 2020 and 10 October 2021 (inclusive); or

(iii) the International Agreement sub-category in the Tier 5 (Temporary Worker) route under part 6A of the rules in force before 1 December 2020.

"**International Operator Licence**" in Appendix Visitor: Permitted Activities means:

(a) a licence issued by the competent authority of a country other than the United Kingdom authorising an operator to undertake international carriage of goods or passengers by road in accordance with an international agreement to which the United Kingdom is a party; or

(b) a community licence issued by a Member State of the Union in accordance with Regulation (EC) No 1072/2009 or Regulation (EC) No 1073/2009.

"**International scholarship agency**" means an international institution or organisation which provides funding to students studying in the UK.

"**International Sportsperson**" means a person who has, or had, permission under any of the following:

(i) Appendix International Sportsperson; or

(ii) Appendix T2 Sportsperson under the rules in force between 1 December 2020 and 10 October 2021 (inclusive); or

(iii) as a sporting worker under Appendix T5 (Temporary Worker) Creative or Sporting Worker under the rules in force between 1 December 2020 and 10 October 2021 (inclusive); or

(iv) as a Tier 5 (Temporary Worker) migrant in the Creative and Sporting sub-category as a sporting worker under part 6A of the rules in force before 1 December 2020, and/or (v) as a Tier 2 (Sportsperson) Migrant under part 6A of the rules in force before 1 December 2020.

"**Intra-Company Graduate Trainee**" means a person who has, or last had, permission as an Intra-Company Graduate Trainee route under Appendix Intra-Company Routes or as a Tier 2 (Intra-Company Transfer) migrant in the Graduate Trainee sub-category under the rules in force before 1 December 2020.

"**Intra-Company Transfer**" means permission on the Intra-Company Transfer route under Appendix Intra-Company Routes or as a Tier 2 (Intra-Company Transfer) migrant in the Long-Term Staff sub-category under the rules in force before 1 December 2020.

"**Intra-Company routes**" means the Intra-Company Transfer route and Intra-Company Graduate Trainee route under Appendix Intra-Company routes, or the Tier 2 (Intra-Company Transfer) route under the rules in force before 1 December 2020.

"**Islands**" means any of the Channel Islands or the Isle of Man.

"**Lead applicant**", under Appendix KOLL, Appendix KOL UK and Appendix English Language, means the applicant on whose status, or previous status, a dependent partner or dependent child is relying as the basis of their application.

"**Legal guardian**" is a person appointed according to local laws to take care of a child.

"**Letter of authority**" means a written authorisation from a person that they wish to appoint or change their immigration adviser (who must be a qualified person as required by section 84 of the Immigration and Asylum Act 1999 or regulated by the Office of the Immigration Services Commissioner).

"**Marriage/Civil Partnership Visitor**" means a person who has, or had, entry clearance under Appendix V: Visitor to marry or form a civil partnership, or give notice of marriage or civil partnership, in the UK.

"**Media representative**" means a person who has, or had, permission on the Representative of an Overseas Business route having met the requirement at ROB 4.4.(b) of Appendix Representative of an Overseas Business, or as a Representative of an Overseas Business having met the requirement of paragraph 144(ii)(b) of Part 5 of the rules in force before 1 December 2020.

"**Medical inspector**" means a medical inspector appointed under Schedule 2 to the Immigration Act 1971.

"**Must not be leading an independent life**" or "**is not leading an independent life**" means that the person:

(a)   does not have a partner; and

(b)   is living with their parent (except where they are at boarding school, college or university as part of their full-time education); and

(c)   is not in full-time employment (unless aged 18 or over); and

(d)   is wholly or mainly dependent upon their parent for financial support (unless aged 18 or over); and

(e)   is wholly or mainly dependent upon their parent for emotional support.

Where under these rules a relative other than a parent may act as the sponsor or carer of the person, references in this definition to "parent" shall be read as applying to that other relative.

"**National minimum wage**" means as defined in the National Minimum Wage Act 1998.

"**National Referral Mechanism**" means the arrangements administered by the Competent Authorities as set out in the guidance found at: https://www.gov.uk/government/publications/victims-of-trafficking-guidance-for-competent-bodies.

"**Notice of liability for removal**" means a notice given that a person is or will be liable for removal under section 10 of the Immigration and Asylum Act 1999, and for notices that pre-date the Immigration Act 2014 coming into force, refers to a decision to remove in accordance with section 10 of the Immigration and Asylum Act 1999, a decision to remove an illegal entrant by way of directions under paragraphs 8 to 10 of Schedule 2 to the Immigration Act 1971, or a decision to remove in accordance with section 47 of the Immigration, Asylum and Nationality Act 2006.

"**Occupation code**" means the relevant 4-digit code in the Standard Occupational Classification (SOC) 2010 system, published by the Office for National Statistics at: https://www.ons.gov.uk/methodology/classificationsandstandards/standardoccupationalclassificationsoc/soc2010.

"**Occupy exclusively**" in relation to accommodation means that part of the accommodation must be for the exclusive use of the person or family.

"**Occupy exclusively**" in relation to accommodation means that part of the accommodation must be for the exclusive use of the person or family.

"**Overcrowded**" means overcrowded within the meaning of the Housing Act 1985, the Housing (Scotland) Act 1987 or the Housing (Northern Ireland) Order 1988 (as appropriate).

"**Overseas Business**" is a business which has it main place of operation outside of the UK.

"**Overseas Domestic Worker**" means a person who has, or had, permission under Appendix Overseas Domestic Worker, or as a domestic worker in a private household under paragraph 159A of the rules in force before 6 May 2021.

"**Overseas Government Language Programme**" means an overseas Government sponsored professional language development programme under the Government Authorised Exchange Scheme where the person concerned delivers language training and participates in a cultural exchange programme that is fully or partially paid for by the overseas government or an organisation affiliated to an overseas government.

"**Overseas higher education institution**" means an institution which holds overseas accreditation confirmed by Ecctis as offering degree programmes which are equivalent to UK degree level qualifications, and which teaches no more than half of a degree programme in the UK as a study abroad programme.

"**Overstayed**" or "**overstaying**" means the person has stayed in the UK beyond the latest of:

(a)   the time limit attached to the last permission granted; or

(b)   the period that the permission was extended under section 3C or 3D of the Immigration Act 1971.

"**Own Account**" in Appendix Visitor: Permitted Activities means the transport of goods by a business where the following conditions are fulfilled:

(a)   the goods carried are the property of the business or have been sold, bought, let out on hire or hired, produced, extracted, processed or repaired by the business; and

(b)   the purpose of the journey is to carry the goods to or from the premises of the business or to move them, either inside or outside the business for its own requirements; and

(c)   the vehicles used for such transport are driven by personnel employed by, or put at the disposal of, the business under a contractual obligation; and

(d)   the vehicles carrying the goods are owned by the business, have been bought by it on deferred terms or have been hired; and

(e)   such transport is no more than ancillary to the overall activities of the business.

"**Parent**" includes:

(a)   the stepfather of a child whose father is dead, and reference to stepfather includes a relationship arising through civil partnership; and

(b)   the stepmother of a child whose mother is dead, and reference to stepmother includes a relationship arising through civil partnership; and

(c)   the father, as well as the mother, of an illegitimate child where the person is proved to be the father; and

(d)   an adoptive parent, where a child was adopted in accordance with a decision taken by the competent administrative authority or court in a country whose adoption orders are recognised by the UK or where a child is the subject of a de facto adoption in accordance with the requirements of paragraph 309A (except that an adopted child or a child who is the subject of a de facto adoption may not make an application for leave to enter or remain in order to accompany, join or remain with an adoptive parent under paragraphs 297 to 303); and

(e)   in the case of a child born in the UK who is not a British citizen, a person to whom there has been a genuine transfer of parental responsibility on the ground of the original parents' inability to care for the child.

"**Parent of a Child Student**" means a person who has, or had, permission under Appendix Parent of a Child Student or as a Parent of a Tier 4 (Child) Student under the rules in force before 5 October 2020.

"**Partner**" means a person's:

(a)   spouse; or

(b)   civil partner; or

(c)   unmarried partner, where the couple have been living together in a relationship similar to marriage or a civil partnership for at least two years.

"**Partner Institution**" means an institution which has a partnership agreement with a student sponsor, which has been approved by the Home Office in accordance with the requirements set out in the student sponsor guidance published on the gov.uk website. Teaching partnerships allow a student sponsor's students to undertake study of a specified type at a partner institution's site.

"**Passport**" means a document which:

(a)   is issued by or on behalf of the government of any country recognised by the UK, or dealt with as a government by the UK, and which complies with international passport practice; and

(b)   shows both the identity and nationality of the holder; and

(c)   gives the holder the right to enter the country of the government which issued the document; and

(d)   is authentic and not unofficially altered or tampered with; and

(e)   is not damaged in a way that compromises the integrity of the document; and

(f)   is used by the rightful holder; and

(g)   has not expired.

"**Pathway Course**" means a course which prepares a student for progression to another course at a specific UK recognised body or a body in receipt of public funding as a higher education institution from the Department for the Economy in Northern Ireland, the Office for Students, the Higher Education Funding Council for Wales, the Scottish Funding Council or any other provider registered with the Office for Students. It does not include a pre-sessional course.

"**Patient**", in Appendix S2 Healthcare Visitor, means a person who is undergoing or plans to undergo a course of planned healthcare treatment in the UK.

"**PAYE**" means HM Revenue and Customs' Pay As You Earn system for collecting Income Tax and National Insurance from employee earnings.

"**Peer reviewed research fellowship or award**" means a specific fellowship or award which appears on the list of peer reviewed research fellowships or awards published by The Royal Society, The Royal Academy of Engineering or The British Academy.

"**Pending appeal**" has the same meaning as in section 104 of the Nationality, Immigration and Asylum Act 2002.

"**Period of imprisonment**" has the same meaning as in section 38(2) of the UK Borders Act 2007.

"**Permission to enter**" has the same meaning as leave to enter under the Immigration Act 1971.

"**Permission to stay**" has the same meaning as leave to remain under the Immigration Act 1971 (and includes a variation of leave to enter or remain and an extension of leave to enter or remain).

And references in these rules to a person having, having had or being granted "**Permission**" means either permission to enter or permission to stay.

"**Permitted Paid Engagement Visitor**" means a person who has, or had, permission under Appendix V: Visitor to undertake specific paid engagements for up to one month.

"**Postgraduate doctor or dentist**" in Appendix Student means a student undertaking a recognised Foundation Programme with Health Education England following completion of a recognised degree in medicine or dentistry in the UK.

"**Postgraduate level study**" means a course at level 7 or above of the Regulated Qualifications Framework, or level 11 or above of the Scottish Credit and Qualifications Framework, which leads to a recognised UK postgraduate degree at master's level or above, or an equivalent qualification at the same level.

"**Premium Sponsor**" means a sponsor which is recorded as holding Premium status on the register of licensed sponsors maintained by the Home Office.

"**Present and settled**" means that the person concerned is settled in the UK and, at the date of application, is physically present in the UK.

Where the person concerned is a British Citizen or settled in the UK and is:

(a)   a member of HM Forces serving overseas; or

(b)   a permanent member of HM Diplomatic Service, or a comparable UK-based staff member of the British Council, the Foreign, Commonwealth and Development Office or the Home Office on a tour of duty outside the UK, and the applicant has provided the evidence specified in paragraph 26A of Appendix FM-SE, then for the purposes of Appendix FM the person is to be regarded as present and settled in the UK, and in paragraphs R-LTRP.1.1.(a) and RILRP.1.1.(a) of Appendix FM the words "and their partner must be in the UK" are to be disregarded.

For the purposes of an application under Appendix FM, or as a child under Part 8, an EEA or non-EEA national with a permanent right to reside in the UK under EU law must hold either a valid residence permit or document issued under the Immigration (European Economic Area) Regulations 2000 which has been endorsed under the Immigration Rules to show permission to remain in the UK indefinitely, or a valid document certifying permanent residence or permanent residence card issued under the Immigration (European Economic Area) Regulations 2016, 2006 or predecessor instruments in order to be regarded as present and settled in the UK. This does not, however, apply if the EEA or non-EEA national in question holds valid indefinite leave to enter or remain granted under Appendix EU to these Rules or, in the case of an Irish citizen, would hold such leave if they made (or, where the date of application under Appendix FM is on or after 1 July 2021, if they had made) a valid application under that Appendix before 1 July 2021.

"**Primary degree**" means a qualification obtained from a course of degree level study, which did not feature as an entry requirement a previous qualification obtained from degree level study, for example an undergraduate degree is a primary degree, but a master's degree that has a bachelor's degree as an entry requirement is not a primary degree.

"Private foster care arrangement" means an arrangement in which a child aged under 16, or aged under 18 if disabled, is cared for, on a full-time basis for a period of 28 days or more, by a person aged 18 or over who is not the child's parent or a close relative.

"Private medical insurance" means insurance to cover treatment provided by a private health provider, or a reciprocal arrangement in place with another country by which certain nationals may receive NHS treatment.

"Private medical treatment" means treatment provided by a private health provider, or by the NHS where there is a reciprocal arrangement in place with another country by which certain nationals may receive NHS treatment.

"Probationary Sponsor" means a student sponsor which is recorded as having "Probationary Sponsor status" on the register of licensed student sponsors maintained by the Home Office.

"Professional Sportsperson" means a person who is one or more of the following:

(a)   currently providing services as a sportsperson, or is playing or coaching in any capacity, at a professional or semi-professional level of sport (whether paid or unpaid); or

(b)   currently receiving payment, including payment in kind, for playing or coaching, and that payment covers all, or the majority of, their costs for travelling to, and living in, the UK, or has received such payment within the previous 4 years; or

(c)   currently registered to a professional or semi-professional sports team or has been so registered within the previous 4 years (this includes all academy and development team age groups); or

(d)   has represented their nation or national team within the previous two years, including all youth and development age groups from under 17s upwards; or

(e)   has represented their state or regional team within the previous two years, including all youth and development age groups from under 17s upwards; or

(f)   has an established international reputation in their chosen field of sport; or

(g)   engages an agent or representative, with the aim of finding opportunities as a sportsperson, and/or developing a current or future career as a sportsperson, or has engaged such an agent in the last 12 months; or

(h)   is providing services as a sportsperson or coach, unless they are doing so as an "Amateur" in a charity event; or

(i)   is providing services as a sportsperson or coach, unless they are doing so as a Student who is studying a course at degree level or above at a higher education provider and playing or coaching sport as an Amateur or as part of a work placement that is undertaken as an integral and assessed part of their course.

"Prohibited degree of relationship" has the same meaning as in the Marriage Act 1949, the Marriage (Prohibited Degrees of Relationship) Act 1986 and the Civil Partnership Act 2004.

"Protection claim" has the same meaning as in section 82(2)(a) of the Nationality, Immigration and Asylum Act 2002.

"Public funds" means:

(a)   housing under Part VI or VII of the Housing Act 1996 and under Part II of the Housing Act 1985, Part I or II of the Housing (Scotland) Act 1987, Part II of the Housing (Northern Ireland) Order 1981 or Part II of the Housing (Northern Ireland) Order 1988; and

(b)   attendance allowance, severe disablement allowance, carer's allowance and disability living allowance under Part III of the Social Security Contribution and Benefits Act 1992; income support, council tax benefit and housing benefit under Part VII of that Act; a social fund payment under Part VIII of that Act; child benefit under Part IX of that Act; income based jobseeker's allowance under the Jobseekers Act 1995, income related allowance under Part 1 of the Welfare Reform Act 2007 (employment and support allowance) state pension credit under the State Pension Credit Act 2002; or child tax credit and working tax credit under Part 1 of the Tax Credits Act 2002; and

(c)   attendance allowance, severe disablement allowance, carer's allowance and disability living allowance under Part III of the Social Security Contribution and Benefits (Northern Ireland) Act 1992; income support, council tax benefit and, housing benefit under Part VII of that Act; a social fund payment under Part VIII of that Act; child benefit under Part IX of that Act; income based jobseeker's allowance under the Jobseekers (Northern Ireland) Order 1995 or income related allowance under Part 1 of the Welfare Reform Act (Northern Ireland) 2007; and

(d) Universal Credit under Part 1 of the Welfare Reform Act 2012 or Personal Independence Payment under Part 4 of that Act; and

(e) Universal Credit, Personal Independence Payment or any domestic rate relief under the Welfare Reform (Northern Ireland) Order 2015; and

(f) a council tax reduction under a council tax reduction scheme made under section 13A of the Local Government Finance Act 1992 in relation to England or Wales or a council tax reduction pursuant to the Council Tax Reduction (Scotland) Regulations 2012 or the Council Tax Reduction (State Pension Credit) (Scotland) Regulations 2012; and

(g) a payment made from a welfare fund under the Welfare Funds (Scotland) Act 2015; and

(h) a discretionary support payment made in accordance with any regulations made under article 135 of the Welfare Reform (Northern Ireland) Order 2015; and

(i) a discretionary payment made by a local authority under section 1 of the Localism Act 2011.

For the purpose of these rules,

(i) a person (P) is not to be regarded as having (or potentially having) recourse to public funds merely because P is (or will be) reliant in whole or in part on public funds provided to P's family sponsor unless, as a result of P's presence in the UK, the family sponsor is (or would be) entitled to increased or additional public funds (save where such entitlement to increased or additional public funds is by virtue of P and the family sponsor's joint entitlement to benefits under the regulations referred to in subparagraph (ii) below; and

(ii) subject to subparagraph (iii) below, a person (P) shall not be regarded as having recourse to public funds if P is entitled to benefits specified under section 115 of the Immigration and Asylum Act 1999 by virtue of regulations made under sub-sections (3) and (4) of that section or section 42 of the Tax Credits Act 2002; and

(iii) a person (P) making an application from outside the UK will be regarded as having recourse to public funds where P relies upon the future entitlement to any public funds that would be payable to P or to P's family sponsor as a result of P's presence in the UK (including those benefits to which P or the family sponsor would be entitled as a result of P's presence in the UK under the regulations referred to in subparagraph (ii) above).

"**Recreational Course**" means a course undertaken purely for leisure purposes, other than English Language training, that does not lead to a formal qualification, for example, a leisure course in pottery or horse riding.

"**Refugee**" has the same meaning as in regulation 2 of the Refugee or Person in Need of International Protection (Qualification) Regulations 2006.

"**Refugee Convention**" means the 1951 United Nations Convention and its 1967 Protocol relating to the Status of Refugees.

"**Refugee status**" is the recognition by the UK that a person meets the criteria in paragraph 334.

"**Refugee leave**" means limited leave granted pursuant to paragraph 334 or 335, which has not been revoked pursuant to paragraph 339A to 339AC or 339B.

"**Relevant NHS body**" in Part 9, and in paragraphs S-EC.2.3., S-LTR.2.3. and S-ILR.2.3. of Appendix FM, means:

(a) in relation to England-

(i) a National Health Service Trust established under section 25 of the National Health Service Act 2006; or

(ii) a National Health Service foundation trust; and

(b) in relation to Wales-

(i) a Local Health Board established under section 11 of the National Health Service (Wales) Act 2006; or

(ii) a National Health Service Trust established under section 18 of the National Health Service (Wales) Act 2006; or

(iii) a Special Health Authority established under 22 of the National Health Service (Wales) Act 2006; and

(c) in relation to Scotland-

(i) a Health Board or Special Health Board established under section 2 of the National Health Service (Scotland) Act 1978 (c. 29); or

(ii) the Common Services Agency for the Scottish Health Service established under section 10 of that Act; or

(iii) Healthcare Improvement Scotland established under section 10A of that Act; and

(d) in relation to Northern Ireland-

(i) the Regional Health and Social Care Board established under the Health and Social Care (Reform) Act (Northern Ireland) 2009; or

(ii) a Health and Social Care trust established under the Health and Personal Social Services (Northern Ireland) Order 1991 (S.I. 1991/194 (N.I. 1)) and renamed under the Health and Social Care (Reform) Act (Northern Ireland) 2009.

"Relevant NHS regulations" means:

(a) in Wales, the National Health Service (Charges to Overseas Visitors) Regulations 1989 (1989 No 306); and

(b) in Scotland, the National Health Service (Charges to Overseas Visitors) (Scotland) Regulations 1989 as amended (1989 No 364); and

(c) in Northern Ireland, the Provision of Health Services to Persons Not Ordinarily Resident Regulations (Northern Ireland) 2015 (2015 No 227); and

(d) in England, the National Health Service (Charges to Overseas Visitors) Regulations 2015 (2015 No 238).

"Religious Worker" means a person who has, or had, permission under any of the following:

(i) Appendix Temporary Work – Religious Worker; or

(ii) Appendix T5 (Temporary Worker) Religious Worker under the rules in force between 1 December 2020 and 10 October 2021 (inclusive); or

(iii) as a Tier 5 (Temporary Worker) migrant in the Religious Worker subcategory under part 6A of the rules in force before 1 December 2020.

"Representative of an Overseas Business" means a person who has, or had, permission under Appendix Representative of an Overseas Business or as a Representative of an Overseas Business under Part 5 of the rules in force before 1 December 2020.

"Research Programme" means research programmes and fellowships under a Government Authorised Exchange Scheme where the person is working on a scientific, academic, medical, or government research project at either a UK higher education institution or another research institution operating under the authority and/or financial sponsorship of a relevant Government Department.

"Rough sleeping" means sleeping, or bedding down, in the open air (for example on the street or in doorways) or in buildings or other places not designed for habitation (for example sheds, car parks or stations).

"S2 certificate of entitlement to scheduled treatment" has the same meaning as a portable document S2 issued under Regulation (EC) No 883/2004.

"S2 Healthcare Visitor" means a patient (P) or an accompanying person (AP) who meets the requirements of Appendix S2 Healthcare Visitor.

"Seasonal work" is work which fluctuates or is restricted according to the season or time of the year.

"Seasonal Worker" means a person who has, or had, permission under any of the following:

(i) Appendix Temporary Work – Seasonal Worker; or

(ii) Appendix T5 (Temporary Worker) Seasonal Worker under the rules in force between 1 December 2020 and 10 October 2021 (inclusive); or

(iii) as a Tier 5 (Temporary Worker) migrant in the Seasonal Worker subcategory under part 6A of the rules in force before 1 December 2020.

"Seeking entry" refers to a person applying for entry clearance or permission to enter the UK.

"Self-employed" means a person who is registered as self-employed with HM Revenue & Customs, or an overseas equivalent, or is employed by a company of which the person is a controlling shareholder.

"Self-employed Lawyer" means a person granted permission outside the rules under the concession for self-employed lawyers that formerly appeared in Chapter 6, Section 1 Annex D of the Immigration Directorate Instructions.

"Series of events" in relation to sport is two or more linked events, such as a tour, or rounds of a competition, which do not add up to a league or a season.

"Settled" has the same meaning as in section 33(1) of the Immigration Act 1971.

"**Settled worker**" means:

(a)   a British citizen; or

(b)   a person who is resident in the UK in accordance with the EEA Regulations or who holds a permanent right of residence in the UK in accordance with regulation 15 of the EEA Regulations; or

(c)   a person with leave to remain or indefinite leave to remain granted under Appendix EU; or

(d)   a British Overseas Territories citizen, except those from the Sovereign Base Areas in Cyprus; or

(e)   a Commonwealth citizen who has been granted permission on the UK Ancestry route on the basis that they have a grandparent born in the UK and Islands; or

(f)   a person who is otherwise settled within the meaning of section 33(2A) of the Immigration Act 1971.

"**Settlement**" means indefinite leave to enter or remain.

"**Sham marriage**" and "**sham civil partnership**" has the same meaning as in section 62 of the Immigration Act 2014 and "**involvement in a sham marriage or sham civil partnership**" means a person who is a party to a sham marriage or sham civil partnership, or who has enabled the marriage or civil partnership to take place.

"**Short-term Student**" means a person who has, or had, permission under Appendix Short Term Student, or paragraph A57E of the rules in force before 1 December 2020.

"**Skilled Worker**" means a person who has, or had, permission under Appendix Skilled Worker, or as a Tier 2 (General) migrant under the rules in force before 1 December 2020.

"**Sole Representative**" means a person who has, or had, permission on the Representative of an Overseas Business route having met the requirement at ROB 4.4.(a) of Appendix Representative of an Overseas Business, or as a Representative of an Overseas Business having met the requirement of paragraph 144(ii)(a) of Part 5 of the rules in force before 1 December 2020.

"**Sponsor**" and "**family sponsor**", in relation to a family member, means the person in relation to whom an applicant is seeking leave to enter or remain as their spouse, fiancé(e), civil partner, proposed civil partner, unmarried partner, same-sex partner or dependent relative, as the case may be, under paragraphs 277 to 295O or 317 to 319 or the person in relation to whom an applicant is seeking entry clearance or leave as their partner or dependent relative under Appendix FM.

"**Sponsor**", in relation to study or work, means the person or organisation licensed by the Home Office that the Certificate of Sponsorship or Confirmation of Acceptance for Studies records as being the sponsor for a person.

"**Sponsor group**", under Appendix Intra-Company routes, means the sponsor and any business or organisation that is linked to the sponsor by common ownership or control, or by a joint venture on which the applicant is sponsored to work.

"**Sponsor licence**" means a licence granted by the Home Office to a person who, by virtue of such a grant, is licensed as a sponsor in relation to applications to study or work in the UK.

"**Standard Visitor**" means a person who has, or had, permission under Appendix V: Visitor to undertake the activities of a standard visitor set out in Appendix Visitor: Permitted Activities.

"**Start-up route**" means Appendix Start-up, and also includes a person who has, or had, permission as a Start-Up migrant under Appendix W of the rules in force before 1 December 2020.

"**State-funded school or academy**" means:

(a)   in England, an "Academy" as defined by and established under the Academies Act 2010, including academy schools, 16-19 academies and alternative provision academies; and

(b)   in England and Wales, a "school maintained by a local authority" being an institution defined in the School Standards and Framework Act 1998 or the Education Act 1996, including community schools, foundation schools, voluntary aided schools, voluntary controlled schools, community special schools, foundation special schools, pupil referral units and maintained nursery schools; and

(c)   in Northern Ireland, a "grant-aided school" being a school to which grants are paid under the Education Orders as defined in the Education and Libraries (Northern Ireland) Order 1986, including controlled, maintained, grant-maintained integrated schools and voluntary grammar schools; and

(d)   in Scotland, a "public school" and a "grant-aided school", defined in section 135 of the Education (Scotland) Act 1980 (for the avoidance of doubt, these definitions include any such nursery schools and special schools) and "Special school" has the meaning given in section 29(1) of the Education (Additional Support for Learning) (Scotland) Act 2004.

"**Student**" means a person who has, or had, permission under Appendix Student, or Appendix ST: Student of the rules in force immediately before 1 December 2020, or as a Tier 4 (General) Student under the rules in force before 5 October 2020.

"**Student sponsor**" means a sponsor which listed on the register of licensed sponsors maintained by the Home Office: https://www.gov.uk/government/publications/register-of-licensed-sponsors-students.

"**Student Union Sabbatical Officer**" means a person who has, or had, permission under Appendix Student, Appendix ST: Student of the rules in force immediately before 1 December 2020, or under paragraph 245ZV or paragraph 245ZX of the rules in force before 5 October 2020, and has been elected to a full-time, salaried, executive union position in the student union of the person's sponsor institution or with the National Union of Students of the UK.

"**Studying in London**" means the applicant's Confirmation of Acceptance for Studies confirms they will be studying at an institution wholly within the Greater London Area. If the applicant will be studying at more than one site, one or more of which is in Greater London Area and one or more outside, then the applicant will be considered to be studying in London if the applicant's Confirmation of Acceptance for Studies states that the applicant will be spending the majority of time studying at a site or sites situated within the Greater London Area.

"**Studying outside London**" means the applicant's Confirmation of Acceptance for Studies confirms they will be studying in the UK but the site of study does not meet the definition of Studying in London.

"**Successfully completed**" means the Student or Child Student has completed their course and been assessed by their sponsor, and has been or will be awarded, a qualification that is:

(a)   for the course of study for which their Confirmation of Acceptance for Studies was assigned; or

(b)   a degree at either UK Bachelor's degree level or UK postgraduate degree level, as part of an integrated programme for which their Confirmation of Acceptance for Studies was assigned; or

(c)   for the course of study with their student sponsor to which they were allowed to change without applying for further permission on the Student route.

"**Supplementary employment**" means employment in a job (other than the job for which the person is being sponsored) which appears on the Shortage Occupation Lists in Appendix Shortage Occupation Lists, or in the same profession and at the same professional level as the job for which the person is being sponsored, provided that:

(a)   the person remains working for the sponsor in the job for which the Certificate of Sponsorship records the person is being sponsored; and

(b)   the other employment does not exceed 20 hours per week and takes place outside of the hours when the person is contracted to work for the sponsor in the job for which the person is being sponsored.

"**Swiss citizens' rights agreement**" means (as modified from time to time in accordance with any provision of it) the Agreement signed at Bern on 25 February 2019 between the United Kingdom of Great Britain and Northern Ireland and the Swiss Confederation on citizens' rights following the withdrawal of the United Kingdom from:

(a)   the European Union; and

(b)   the Agreement on the Free Movement of Persons.

"**Tier 1 (Entrepreneur) Migrant**" means a person who has, or had leave under paragraphs 245D to 245DF.

"**Tier 1 (Exceptional Talent) Migrant**" means a person who was granted leave under paragraphs 245B to 245BF of the rules in force before 1 December 2020.

"**Tier 1 (General) Migrant**" means a person who was granted leave under paragraphs 245C to 245CE of the rules in force before 6 April 2018.

"**Tier 1 (Graduate Entrepreneur) Migrant**" means a person who was granted leave under paragraphs 245F to 245FB of the rules in force on or after 6 April 2012 and before 29 March 2019.

"**Tier 1 (Investor) Migrant**" means a person who has, or had, leave under paragraphs 245E to 245EF.

"**Tier 2 (General) Migrant**" means a person granted leave under paragraphs 245H to 245HF and who obtained points under paragraphs 76 to 84A of Appendix A of the rules in force before 1 December 2020.

"**Tier 2 (Intra-Company Transfer) Migrant**" means a person granted leave under paragraphs 245G to 245GF of the rules in force before 1 December 2020.

"**Tier 2 Migrant**" means a person granted leave as a Tier 2 (Intra-Company Transfer) Migrant, a Tier 2 (General) Migrant, a Tier 2 (Minister of Religion) Migrant or a Tier 2 (Sportsperson) Migrant under the rules in force before 1 December 2020.

"Tier 2 (Minister of Religion) Migrant" means a person granted leave under the Tier 2 Minister of Religion route as a missionary or a member of a religious order under paragraphs 245H to 245HF of the rules in force before 1 December 2020.

"T2 Minister of Religion" means a person who has, or had, permission under Appendix T2 Minister of Religion, or as a Tier 2 (Minister of Religion) migrant under the rules in force before 1 December 2020.

"Tier 2 (Sportsperson) Migrant" means a person granted leave under paragraphs 245H to 245HF (and who obtained points under paragraphs 93 to 100 of Appendix A) of the rules in force before 1 December 2020.

"Tier 4 (Child) Student" means a person granted leave under paragraphs 245ZZ to 245ZZD of the rules in force before 5 October 2020.

"Tier 4 (General) Student" means a person granted leave under paragraphs 245ZT to 245ZY of the rules in force before 5 October 2020.

"Tier 4 Migrant" means a Tier 4 (General) Student or a Tier 4 (Child) Student.

"Tier 5 Migrant" means a person granted leave as either a Tier 5 (Temporary Worker) Migrant or a Tier 5 (Youth Mobility Scheme) Temporary Migrant under the rules in force before 1 December 2020.

"Temporary Worker" means a person who has, or had, permission as a Charity Worker, Creative Worker, Religious Worker, Seasonal Worker, on the International Agreement route, Youth Mobility Scheme or Government Authorised Exchange route.

"Tier 5 (Temporary Worker) Migrant" means a person granted leave under paragraphs 245ZM to 245ZS of the rules in force before 1 December 2020.

"Track record of compliance" means a 4-year track record of immigration compliance and Educational Oversight, established by a student sponsor in accordance with the requirements set out in the student sponsor guidance which is published on the visa and immigration pages of the gov.uk website.

"Training Programme" means a training programme under a Government Authorised Exchange Scheme where the person concerned either receives formal, practical training in the fields of science and / or medicine or will be trained by HM Forces or by UK emergency services.

"Transit Visitor" means a person who has, or had, permission under Appendix V: Visitor, or Appendix Visitor: Transit Without Visa Scheme, to transit the UK on route to another country outside the Common Travel Area.

"UK" means the United Kingdom.

"UK Ancestry route" means the route in Appendix UK Ancestry, or paragraphs 186 to 199B in Part 5 of the Rules in force before 1 December 2020, and "person with UK Ancestry" means a person applying for, or granted, permission on the basis that they have a grandparent born in the UK and Islands and meet the requirements in Appendix UK Ancestry, or under paragraphs 186 to 193 in Part 5 of the Rules in force before 1 December 2020.

"UK bachelor's degree" means:

(a)   a programme of study or research which leads to the award by or on behalf of a university, college or other body which is authorised by Royal Charter, an Act of Parliament, the Privy Council or the Office for Students to grant degrees, of a qualification designated by the awarding institution to be of bachelor's degree level; or

(b)   a programme of study or research, which leads to a recognised award for the purposes of section 214(2)(c) of the Education Reform Act 1988, of a qualification designated by the awarding institution to be of bachelor's degree level.

"UK Border" means immigration control at a UK port and a control zone in France or Belgium or a supplementary control zone in France as defined by Article 2(1) and Schedule 1 to the Channel Tunnel (International Arrangements) Order 1993 (SI 1993/1813) and Article 2 of the Nationality, Immigration and Asylum Act 2002 (Juxtaposed Controls) Order 2003 (SI 2003/2818).

"UK listed body" is an institution which is not a UK recognised body but which provides full courses that lead to the award of a degree by a UK recognised body.

"UK postgraduate degree" means:

(a)   a programme of study or research which leads to an award, by or on behalf of a university, college or another body which is authorised by a Royal Charter, an Act of Parliament, the Privy Council or the Office for Students to grant degrees, of a qualification designated by the awarding institution to be of master's degree level or above; or

(b)   a programme of study or research, which leads to a recognised award for the purposes of section 214(2)(c) of the Education Reform Act 1988, of a qualification designated by the awarding institution to be of master's degree level or above.

"UK recognised body" means a higher learning institution that has been granted degree awarding powers by Royal Charter, an Act of Parliament, the Privy Council or the Office for Students, and for the purposes of these rules, Health Education South London and Health Education England are equivalent to UK recognised bodies, as set out at: https://www.gov.uk/check-a-university-is-officially-recognised.

"UK Regulated Profession" means a profession regulated by UK law which is listed at: https://cpq.ecctis.com/Individuals/Inbound/Regulated%20Professions.

"UKRI" means UK Research and Innovation.

"United Kingdom passport" has the same meaning as in the Immigration Act 1971.

"Unmarried partner", under Appendix ECAA Extension of Stay or Appendix ECAA Settlement, means a person who is:

(a)   resident with the ECAA worker or ECAA business person unless applying for entry clearance; and

(b)   intends to live, or continue living, with the ECAA worker or ECAA business person; and

(c)   is in a relationship with the ECAA worker or ECAA business person that is genuine and subsisting.

"Valid application" means an application made in accordance with the requirements of Part 1, or the validity requirements of the route in question, whichever is applicable.

"Visa nationals" means persons specified in Appendix Visitor: Visa National list as needing a visa, or entry clearance, for the UK for a visit or for any other purposes where seeking entry for 6 months or less and **"Non-visa nationals"** are persons who are not so specified in that Appendix.

"Visitor" means a person granted permission under paragraphs 40-56Z, 75A-M or 82-87 of the rules in force before 24 April 2015 or Appendix V on or after 24 April 2015 or Appendix V: Visitor after 9am on 1 December 2020.

"Voluntary fieldwork" means activities which would not normally be offered at a waged or salaried rate and which contribute directly to the achievement or advancement of the sponsor's charitable purpose. It does not include work ancillary to the sponsor's charitable purpose including, for example, routine back office administrative roles, retail or other sales roles, fund-raising roles and roles involved in the maintenance of the sponsor's offices and other assets.

"Voluntary work" has the same meaning as applies to a voluntary worker in the National Minimum Wage Act 1998.

"Week" means a period of 7 days beginning with a Monday.

"Withdrawal Agreement" means the agreement between the United Kingdom and the EU under Article 50(2) of the Treaty on European Union which sets out the arrangements for the United Kingdom's withdrawal from the EU (as that agreement is modified from time to time in accordance with any provision of it).

"Work" has the same meaning as **"Employment"**, except that work does not include being party to an employment contract but not working.

"Work Experience Programme" means work experience including volunteering and job-shadowing, internships and work exchange programmes under a Government Authorised Exchange Scheme.

"Work placement" means a placement that forms an integral and assessed part of the course of study which meets the requirements in Appendix Student or Appendix Child Student.

"Working day" means a business day in the part of the UK in which the applicant resides or (as the case may be) is detained.

"Working illegally" means working in breach of a condition of leave or working in the UK without valid leave where such leave is required.

"Youth Mobility Scheme" means a person who has, or had, permission under any of the following:

(i)   Appendix Youth Mobility Scheme; or

(ii)   Appendix T5 (Temporary Worker) Youth Mobility Scheme under the rules in force between 1 December 2020 and 10 October 2021(inclusive); or

(iii)   as a Tier 5 Youth Mobility Scheme migrant under part 6A of the rules in force before 1 December 2020.

Part 1: leave to enter or stay in the UK

General provisions regarding entry clearance, leave to enter or remain in the United Kingdom (paragraphs 7 to 39E).

Leave to enter the United Kingdom

7. A person who is neither a British citizen nor a Commonwealth citizen with the right of abode nor a person who is entitled to enter or remain in the United Kingdom by virtue of section 3ZA of the Immigration Act 1971 requires leave to enter the United Kingdom.

8. Under Sections 3 and 4 of the Immigration Act 1971 an Immigration Officer when admitting to the United Kingdom a person subject to immigration control under that Act may give leave to enter for a limited period and, if he does, may impose all or any of the following conditions:

    (i)   a condition restricting employment or occupation in the United Kingdom;

    (ii)   a condition requiring the person to maintain and accommodate himself, and any dependants of his, without recourse to public funds;

    (iii)   a condition requiring the person to register with the police; and

    (iv)   a condition restricting his studies in the United Kingdom

He may also require him to report to the appropriate Medical Officer of Environmental Health. Under Section 24 of the 1971 Act it is an offence knowingly to remain beyond the time limit or fail to comply with such a condition or requirement.

9. The time limit and any conditions attached will be made known to the person concerned either:

    (i)   by written notice given to him or endorsed by the Immigration Officer in his passport or travel document; or

    (ii)   in any other manner permitted by the Immigration (Leave to Enter and Remain) Order 2000.

Exercise of the power to refuse leave to enter the United Kingdom or to cancel leave to enter or remain which is in force

10. The power to refuse leave to enter the United Kingdom or to cancel leave to enter or remain which is already in force is not to be exercised by an Immigration Officer acting on his own. The authority of a Chief Immigration Officer or of an Immigration Inspector must always be obtained.

Suspension of leave to enter or remain in the United Kingdom

10A. Where a person has arrived in the United Kingdom with leave to enter or remain which is in force but which was given to him before his arrival he may be examined by an Immigration Officer under paragraph 2A of Schedule 2 to the Immigration Act 1971. An Immigration Officer examining a person under paragraph 2A may suspend that person's leave to enter or remain in the United Kingdom until the examination is completed.

Cancellation of leave to enter or remain in the United Kingdom

10.B Where a person arrives in the United Kingdom with leave to enter or remain in the United Kingdom which is already in force, an Immigration Officer may cancel that leave.

Requirement for persons arriving in the United Kingdom or seeking entry through the Channel Tunnel to produce evidence of identity and nationality

11. A person must, on arrival in the United Kingdom or when seeking entry through the Channel Tunnel, produce on request by an Immigration Officer:

    (i)   a valid national passport or, subject to paragraph 11A, other document satisfactorily establishing their identity and nationality; and

    (ii)   such information as may be required to establish whether they require leave to enter the United Kingdom and, if so, whether and on what terms leave to enter should be given.

11A. A national identity card is not valid for the purposes of paragraph 11(i), except where the holder is one of the following:

    (a)   ~~a British citizen of Gibraltar; or~~

    (b)   a national of Switzerland with a valid entry clearance granted under Appendix Service Providers from Switzerland to these Rules; or

(c)   a national of one of the countries listed in paragraph 11B with valid indefinite or limited leave to enter or remain granted under Appendix EU to these Rules, or who has made a valid application under that Appendix (other than as a joining family member of a relevant sponsor, as defined in Annex 1 to that Appendix) which has not yet been finally determined; or

(d)   a national of one of the countries listed at paragraph 11B with a valid entry clearance in the form of an EU Settlement Scheme Family Permit; or

(e)   a national of one of the countries listed at paragraph 11B with a frontier worker permit; or

(f)   a national of one of the countries listed at paragraph 11B seeking to come to the UK as an S2 Healthcare Visitor; or

(g)   a national of one of the countries listed at paragraph 11B who has been granted immigration permission equivalent to that set out in subparagraphs (b) to (f) above by the Islands, or who has made a valid application under the equivalent in the Islands of Appendix EU to these rules (other than as the equivalent of a joining family member of a relevant sponsor, as defined in Annex 1 to that Appendix) which has not yet been finally determined.

11B.   For the purposes of subparagraphs (c) to (g) of paragraph 11A, the holder must be a national of one of the following countries:

Austria

Belgium

Bulgaria

Croatia

Cyprus

Czech Republic

Denmark

Estonia

Finland

France

Germany

Greece

Hungary

Iceland

Italy

Latvia

Liechtenstein

Lithuania

Luxembourg

Malta

Netherlands

Norway

Poland

Portugal

Romania

Slovakia

Slovenia

Spain

Sweden

Switzerland.

Requirement for a person not requiring leave to enter the United Kingdom to prove that he has the right of abode

12.   A person claiming to be a British citizen must prove that he has the right of abode in the United Kingdom by producing either:

(i)   a United Kingdom passport describing him as a British citizen or as a citizen of the United Kingdom and Colonies having the right of abode in the United Kingdom; or

(ii)   a certificate of entitlement duly issued by or on behalf of the Government of the United Kingdom certifying that he has the right of abode.

13. A person claiming to be a Commonwealth citizen with the right of abode in the United Kingdom must prove that he has the right of abode by producing a certificate of entitlement duly issued to him by or on behalf of the Government of the United Kingdom certifying that he has the right of abode.

14. A Commonwealth citizen who has been given limited leave to enter the United Kingdom may later claim to have the right of abode. The time limit on his stay may be removed if he is able to establish a claim to the right of abode, for example by showing that:

(i)   immediately before the commencement of the British Nationality Act 1981 he was a Commonwealth citizen born to or legally adopted by a parent who at the time of the birth had citizenship of the United Kingdom and Colonies by his birth in the United Kingdom or any of the Islands; and

(ii)   he has not ceased to be a Commonwealth citizen in the meanwhile.

Common Travel Area

15. The United Kingdom, the Channel Islands, the Isle of Man and the Republic of Ireland collectively form a common travel area. A person who has been examined for the purpose of immigration control at the point at which he entered the area does not normally require leave to enter any other part of it. However certain persons subject to the Immigration (Control of Entry through the Republic of Ireland) Order 1972 (as amended) who enter the United Kingdom through the Republic of Ireland do require leave to enter. This includes:

(i)   those who merely passed through the Republic of Ireland;

(ii)   persons requiring visas;

(iii) persons who entered the Republic of Ireland unlawfully;

(iv)   persons who are subject to directions given by the Secretary of State for their exclusion from the United Kingdom on the ground that their exclusion is conducive to the public good;

(v)   persons who entered the Republic from the United Kingdom and Islands after entering there unlawfully or overstaying their leave.

Admission of certain British passport holders

16. A person in any of the following categories may be admitted freely to the United Kingdom on production of a United Kingdom passport issued in the United Kingdom and Islands or the Republic of Ireland prior to 1 January 1973, unless his passport has been endorsed to show that he was subject to immigration control:

(i)   a British Dependent Territories citizen;

(ii)   a British National (Overseas);

(iii) a British Overseas citizen;

(iv)   a British protected person;

(v)   a British subject by virtue of Section 30(a) of the British Nationality Act 1981, (who, immediately before the commencement of the 1981 Act would have been a British subject not possessing citizenship of the United Kingdom and Colonies or the citizenship of any other Commonwealth country or territory).

17. British Overseas citizens who hold United Kingdom passports wherever issued and who satisfy the Immigration Officer that they have, since 1 March 1968, been given indefinite leave to enter or remain in the United Kingdom may be given indefinite leave to enter.

Persons outside the United Kingdom

17A. Where a person is outside the United Kingdom but wishes to travel to the United Kingdom an Immigration Officer may give or refuse him leave to enter. An Immigration Officer may exercise these powers whether or not he is, himself, in the United Kingdom. However, an Immigration Officer is not obliged to consider an application for leave to enter from a person outside the United Kingdom.

17B. Where a person having left the common travel area, has leave to enter the United Kingdom which remains in force under article 13 of the Immigration (Leave to Enter and Remain) Order 2000, an Immigration Officer may cancel that leave. An Immigration Officer may exercise these powers whether or not he is, himself, in the United Kingdom. If a person outside the United Kingdom has leave to remain in the United Kingdom which is in force in this way, the Secretary of State may cancel that leave.

Returning Residents

18. A person may resume their residence in the UK provided the Immigration Officer is satisfied that the person concerned:

    (i)   had indefinite leave to enter or remain in the United Kingdom when he last left; and

    (ii)   has not been away from the United Kingdom for more than 2 years; and

    (iii)   did not receive assistance from public funds towards the cost of leaving the United Kingdom; and

    (iv)   now seeks admission for the purpose of settlement.

18A. Those who qualify to resume their residence in accordance with paragraph 18 do not need a visa to enter the UK.

19. A person who does not benefit from the preceding paragraph by reason only of having been absent from the United Kingdom for more than two consecutive years, must have applied for, and been granted indefinite leave to enter by way of entry clearance if, he can demonstrate he has strong ties to the United Kingdom and intends to make the United Kingdom his permanent home.

19A. Sub paragraphs (ii) and (iii) of paragraph 18 shall not apply where a person who has indefinite leave to enter or remain in the United Kingdom accompanies on an overseas posting a partner, parent, a spouse, civil partner, unmarried partner or same-sex partner who is:

    (a)   a member of HM Forces serving overseas; or

    (b)   a British citizen or is settled in the UK and

            (i)   a permanent member of HM Diplomatic Service;

            (ii)   a comparable United Kingdom based permanent staff member of the British Council;

            (iii)   a permanent staff member of the Department for International Development; or

            (iv)   a permanent Home Office employee.

20. The leave of a person whose stay in the United Kingdom is subject to a time limit lapses on his going to a country or territory outside the common travel area if the leave was given for a period of six months or less or conferred by a visit visa. In other cases, leave lapses on the holder remaining outside the United Kingdom for a continuous period of more than two years. A person whose leave has lapsed and who returns after a temporary absence abroad within the period of this earlier leave has no claim to admission as a returning resident. His application to re-enter the United Kingdom should be considered in the light of all the relevant circumstances. The same time limit and any conditions attached will normally be reimposed if he meets the requirements of these Rules, unless he is seeking admission in a different capacity from the one in which he was last given leave to enter or remain.

Non-lapsing leave

20A. Leave to enter or remain in the United Kingdom will usually lapse on the holder going to a country or territory outside the common travel area. However, under article 13 of the Immigration (Leave to Enter and Remain) Order 2000 such leave will not lapse where it was given for a period exceeding six months or where it was conferred by means of an entry clearance (other than a visit visa).

20B. Those who seek leave to enter the United Kingdom within the period of their earlier leave and for the same purpose as that for which that leave was granted, unless it

    (i)   was for a period of six months or less; or

    (ii)   was extended by statutory instrument or by section 3C of the Immigration Act 1971 (inserted by section 3 of the Immigration and Asylum Act 1999); do not need a visa to enter the UK.

Holders of restricted travel documents and passports

21. The leave to enter or remain in the United Kingdom of the holder of a passport or travel document whose permission to enter another country has to be exercised before a given date may be restricted so as to terminate at least 2 months before that date.

22. If his passport or travel document is endorsed with a restriction on the period for which he may remain outside his country of normal residence, his leave to enter or remain in the United Kingdom may be limited so as not to extend beyond the period of authorised absence.

23. The holder of a travel document issued by the Home Office should not be given leave to enter or remain for a period extending beyond the validity of that document. This paragraph and paragraphs 21-22 do not apply to a person who is eligible for admission for settlement or to a spouse or civil partner who is eligible for admission under paragraph 282 or to a person who qualifies for the removal of the time limit on his stay.

Leave to enter granted on arrival in the United Kingdom

23A.   A person who is not a visa national and who is seeking leave to enter on arrival in the United Kingdom for a period not exceeding 6 months for a purpose for which prior entry clearance is not required under these Rules may be granted such leave, for a period not exceeding 6 months. This paragraph does not apply where the person is a British National (Overseas), a British overseas territories citizen, a British Overseas citizen, a British protected person, or a person who under the British Nationality Act 1981 is a British subject.

23B.   A person who is a British National (Overseas), a British overseas territories citizen, a British Overseas citizen, a British protected person, or a person who under the British Nationality Act 1981 is a British subject, and who is seeking leave to enter on arrival in the United Kingdom for a purpose for which prior entry clearance is not required under these Rules may be granted such leave, irrespective of the period of time for which he seeks entry, for a period not exceeding 6 months.

Entry clearance

24.   The following:

(i)   a visa national;

(ii)   a non visa national not a British national and is seeking entry for a period exceeding six months, or for a purpose for which prior entry clearance is required under these Rules;

(iii)   a British national without the right of abode who is seeking entry for a purpose for which prior entry clearance is required under these Rules.

must either:

(i)   produce to the Immigration Officer a valid passport or other identity document endorsed with a United Kingdom entry clearance, issued to him for the purpose for which he seeks entry, which is still in force,

or:

(ii)   where he has been granted a United Kingdom entry clearance which was issued to him in electronic form for the purpose for which he seeks entry and which is still in force, produce to the Immigration Officer a valid passport or other identity document.

Such a person will be refused leave to enter if he has no such current entry clearance. Any other person who wishes to ascertain in advance whether he is eligible for admission to the United Kingdom may apply for the issue of an entry clearance.

25.   Entry clearance takes the form of a visa (for visa nationals) or an entry certificate (for non visa nationals). A visa or an entry certificate may be issued in electronic form. These documents are to be taken as evidence of the holder's eligibility for entry into the United Kingdom, and accordingly accepted as "entry clearances" within the meaning of the Immigration Act 1971.

25A.   An entry clearance which satisfies the requirements set out in article 3 of the Immigration (Leave to Enter and Remain) Order 2000 will have effect as leave to enter the United Kingdom. The requirements are that the entry clearance must specify the purpose for which the holder wishes to enter the United Kingdom and should be endorsed with the conditions to which it is subject or wish a statement that it has effect as indefinite leave to enter the United Kingdom. The holder of such an entry clearance will not require leave to enter on arrival in the United Kingdom and, for the purposes of these Rules, will be treated as a person who has arrived in the United Kingdom with leave to enter the United Kingdom which is in force but which was given to him before his arrival.

26.   An application for entry clearance will be considered in accordance with the provisions in these Rules governing the grant or refusal of leave to enter. Where appropriate, the term "Entry Clearance Officer" should be substituted for "Immigration Officer".

27.   An application for entry clearance is to be decided in the light of the circumstances existing at the time of the decision, except that an applicant will not be refused an entry clearance where entry is sought in one of the categories contained in paragraphs 296-316 or paragraph EC-C of Appendix FM solely on account of his attaining the age of 18 years between receipt of his application and the date of the decision on it.

28.   An applicant for an entry clearance must be outside the United Kingdom and Islands at the time of the application. An application for an entry clearance as a visitor or as a short-term student must be made to any post designated by the Secretary of State to accept such applications. Subject to paragraph 28A, any other application must be made to a post in the country or territory where the applicant is living which has been designated by the Secretary of State to accept applications for entry clearance for that purpose and from that category of applicant. Where there is no such post the applicant must apply to the appropriate designated post outside the country or territory where he is living.

28A. (a) An application for entry clearance under Appendix T5 (Temporary Worker) Creative or Sporting Worker may also be made at the post in the country or territory where the applicant is situated at the time of the application, provided that:

    (i) the post has been designated by the Secretary of State to accept applications for entry clearance for that purpose and from that category of applicant,

    (ii) the applicant is in that country or territory for a similar purpose to the activity he proposes to undertake in the UK, and

    (iii) the applicant is able to demonstrate to the Entry Clearance Officer that he has authority to be living in that country or territory in accordance with its immigration laws. Those applicants who are known to the authorities of that country or territory but who have not been given permission to live in that country or territory will not be eligible to make an application.

(b) An application for entry clearance as a Global Talent migrant or as a under Appendix T5 (Temporary Worker) Youth Mobility Scheme may also be made at the post in the country or territory where the applicant is situated at the time of the application, provided that:

    (i) the post has been designated by the Secretary of State to accept applications for entry clearance for that purpose and from that category of applicant, and

    (ii) the applicant is able to demonstrate to the Entry Clearance Officer that he has authority to be living in that country or territory in accordance with its immigration laws and that when he was given authority to live in that country or territory he was given authority to live in that country or territory for a period of more than 6 months. Those applicants who are known to the authorities of that country or territory but who have not been given permission to live in that country or territory will not be eligible to make an application.

29. For the purposes of paragraph 28 "post" means a British Diplomatic Mission, British Consular post or the office of any person outside the United Kingdom and Islands who has been authorised by the Secretary of State to accept applications for entry clearance. A list of designated posts is published by the Foreign and Commonwealth Office.

30. An application for an entry clearance is not made until any fee required to be paid under the regulations made under sections 68 and 69 of the Immigration Act 2014 has been paid.

30A. DELETED

30B. An entry clearance shall cease to have effect where the entry clearance has effect as leave to enter and an Immigration Officer cancels that leave in accordance with paragraph 2A(8) of Schedule 2 to the Immigration Act 1971.

30C. An Immigration Officer may cancel an entry clearance which is capable of having effect as leave to enter if the holder arrives in the United Kingdom before the day on which the entry clearance becomes effective or if the holder seeks to enter the United Kingdom for a purpose other than the purpose specified in the entry clearance.

Variation of leave to enter or remain in the United Kingdom

31. Under Section 3(3) of the 1971 Act a limited leave to enter or remain in the United Kingdom may be varied by extending or restricting its duration, by adding, varying or revoking conditions or by removing the time limit (where upon any condition attached to the leave ceases to apply). When leave to enter or remain is varied an entry is to be made in the applicant's passport or travel document (and his registration certificate where appropriate) or the decision may be made known in writing in some other appropriate way.

31A. Where a person has arrived in the United Kingdom with leave to enter or remain in the United Kingdom which is in force but was given to him before his arrival, he may apply, on arrival at the port of entry in the United Kingdom, for variation of that leave. An Immigration Officer acting on behalf of the Secretary of State may vary the leave at the port of entry but is not obliged to consider an application for variation made at the port of entry. If an Immigration Officer acting on behalf of the Secretary of State has declined to consider an application for variation of leave at a port of entry but the leave has not been cancelled under paragraph 2A(8) of Schedule 2 to the Immigration Act 1971, the person seeking variation should apply to the Home Office under paragraph 32.

32. DELETED

33. DELETED

33A. Where a person having left the common travel area, has leave to enter or remain in the United Kingdom which remains in force under article 13 of the Immigration (Leave to Enter and Remain) Order 2000., his leave may be varied (including any condition to which it is subject in such form and manner as permitted for the giving of leave to enter. However, the Secretary of State is not obliged to consider an application for variation of leave to enter or remain from a person outside the United Kingdom.

33B-33G.   DELETED

A34.   DELETED

A34.   Paragraphs 34 and 34A do not apply to an application made under the following:

Appendix Settlement Protection: settlement for people on a protection route

Appendix V: Visitor

Appendix S2 Healthcare Visitor

Appendix Student

Appendix Short-term Student

Appendix Graduate

Appendix Child Student

Appendix Parent of a Child Student

Appendix Skilled Worker

Appendix Intra-Company routes

Appendix T2 Minister of Religion

Appendix International Sportsperson

Appendix Representative of an Overseas Business

Appendix UK Ancestry

Appendix Global Talent

Appendix Start-up

Appendix Innovator

Appendix Temporary Work - Seasonal Worker

Appendix Youth Mobility Scheme

Appendix Temporary Work - Creative Worker

Appendix Temporary Work - Religious Worker

Appendix Temporary Work - Charity Worker

Appendix Temporary Worker - International Agreement

Appendix Temporary Work - Government Authorised Exchange

Appendix Service Providers from Switzerland

Appendix Hong Kong British National (Overseas)

Appendix EU.

How to make a valid application for leave to remain in the UK

34.   (1)   an application for leave to remain must be made in accordance with sub-paragraphs (1) to (9) below.

(a)   Subject to paragraph 34(1)(c), the application must be made on an application form which is specified for the immigration category under which the applicant is applying on the date on which the application is made.

(b)   An application form is specified when it is posted on the visa and immigration pages of the GOV.UK website.

(c)   An application can be made on a previous version of a specified paper application form (and shall be treated as made on a specified form) as long as it is no more than 21 days out of date.

(2)   All mandatory sections of the application form must be completed.

(3)   Where the applicant is required to pay a fee, this fee must be paid in full in accordance with the process set out in the application form.

(4)   Where the applicant is required to pay the Immigration Health Surcharge, this must be paid in accordance with the process set out on the visa and immigration pages of the GOV.UK website.

(5)   (a)   Subject to paragraph 34(5)(c), the applicant must provide proof of identity as described in 34(5)(b) below and in accordance with the process set out in the application form.

(b)   Proof of identity for the purpose of this paragraph means:

(i)   a valid passport or, if an applicant (except a PBS applicant) does not have a valid passport, a valid national identity card; or

(ii)   if the applicant does not have a valid passport or national identity card, their most recent passport or (except a PBS applicant) their most recent national identity card; or

(iii)   if the applicant does not have any of the above, a valid travel document.

(c)   Proof of identity need not be provided where:

    (i)   the applicant's passport, national identity card or travel document is held by the Home Office at the date of application; or

    (ii)   the applicant's passport, nationality identity card or travel document has been permanently lost or stolen and there is no functioning national government to issue a replacement; or

    (iii)   the applicant's passport, nationality identity card or travel document has been retained by an employer or other person in circumstances which have led to the applicant being the subject of a positive conclusive grounds decision made by a competent authority under the National Referral Mechanism; or

    (iv)   the application is for limited leave to enable access to public funds pending an application under paragraph 289A of, or under Part 6 of Appendix Armed Forces or section DVILR of Appendix FM to these Rules; or

    (v)   the application is made under Part 14 of these Rules for leave as a stateless person or as the family member of a stateless person; or

    (vi)   the application was made by a person in the UK with refugee leave or humanitarian protection; or

    (vii) the applicant provides a good reason beyond their control why they cannot provide proof of their identity.

(6)   Where any of paragraph 34(5)(c)(ii)-(vii) applies, the Secretary of State may ask the applicant to provide alternative satisfactory evidence of their identity and nationality.

(7)   Where the main applicant is under the age of eighteen, their parent or legal guardian must provide written consent to the application.

(8)   Where the application is made on a paper application form, it must be sent by pre-paid post or courier to the address on the application form.

(9)   An applicant must comply with the application process set out on the visa and immigration pages on GOV.UK and in the invitation to enrol biometrics which is provided as part of the application process in relation to –

    (a)   making an appointment to provide biometrics, and

    (b)   providing any evidence requested by the Secretary of State in support of their application.

Invalid applications

34A.   Subject to paragraph 34B, where an application for leave to remain does not meet the requirements of paragraph 34, it is invalid and will not be considered.

34B.   (1)   Where an application for permission to stay does not meet the requirements of paragraph 34(1) to (9), or the validity requirements for the route under which they are applying, the Secretary of State may notify the applicant and give them one opportunity to correct the error(s) or omission(s) identified by the Secretary of State within the timescale specified in the notification.

    (2)   Where an applicant does not comply with the notification in paragraph 34B(1), or with the requirements in paragraph 34G(4), the application is invalid and will not be considered unless the Secretary of State exercises discretion to treat an invalid application as valid and the requirements of paragraph 34(3) and (5), or a requirement to pay a fee and provide biometrics has been met

    (3)   Notice of invalidity will be given in writing and served in accordance with Appendix SN of these Rules.

Multiple Applications

34BB.   (1)   An applicant may only have one outstanding application for leave to remain at a time.

    (2)   If an application for leave to remain is submitted in circumstances where a previous application for leave to remain has not been decided, it will be treated as a variation of the previous application.

(3)   Where more than one application for leave to remain is submitted on the same day then subject to sub-paragraph (4), each application will be invalid and will not be considered.

(4)   The Secretary of State may give the applicant a single opportunity to withdraw all but one of the applications within 10 working days of the date on which the notification was sent. If all but one of the applications are not withdrawn by the specified date each application will be invalid and will not be considered.

(5)   Notice of invalidity will be given in writing and served in accordance with Appendix SN of these Rules.

Dependent applicants applying at the same time as the main applicant

34C.   A dependent applicant can be included on a main applicant's application form where the application form allows the dependant to be included. Otherwise, a dependent must make a separate application.

34D.   DELETED

Variation of application for permission to stay

34E.   If a person wishes to vary the purpose of an application for permission to stay, the variation must comply with the requirements of paragraph 34, or the validity requirements for the route now applied for (if different), as if the variation were a new application. If it does not, subject to paragraph 34B, the variation will be invalid and will not be considered.

34F.   Any valid variation of an application for permission to stay will be decided in accordance with the immigration rules in force at the date the variation is made.

Date of application (or variation of application) for permission to stay

34G.   For the purposes of these rules, and subject to paragraph 34GB, the date on which an application is made is:

(1)   where the paper application form is sent by post by Royal Mail, whether or not accompanied by a fee waiver request form, the date of posting as shown on the tracking information provided by Royal Mail or, if not tracked, by the postmark date on the envelope; or

(2)   where the paper application form is sent by courier, or other postal services provider, the date on which it is delivered to the Home Office; or

(3)   where the application is made via the online application process, and there is no request for a fee waiver, the date on which the online application is submitted; or

(4)   where the online application includes a request for a fee waiver, the date on which the online request for a fee waiver is submitted, as long as the completed application for permission to stay is submitted within 10 days of the receipt of the decision on the fee waiver application.

34GA.   Where an application is rejected as invalid that decision will be served in accordance with Appendix SN.

34GB.   Where a variation application is made in accordance with paragraph 34E, the date the variation application (the new application) is made is deemed to be the date the application was made prior to it being varied (the old application).

34GC.   Where a partner, child or other dependent is included in the variation application (the new application) and was not included in the application which has been varied (the old application) the date of application for the dependant's application is the date the variation application (the new application) was made.

Withdrawal of an application for entry clearance, permission to enter and permission to stay in the United Kingdom

34H.   An applicant may ask to withdraw their application for entry clearance, permission to enter or permission to stay at any time before a decision is made on the application by making a request in writing or by completing the withdrawal process at www.gov.uk/cancel-visa. If the request to withdraw the application is accepted the date of withdrawal is the date on which the request was received by the Home Office.

34I.   There is no requirement to agree to the withdrawal of an application for entry clearance, permission to enter or permission to stay and the decision maker may instead decide the application.

34J.   The proof of identity provided under paragraph 34(5), or any other application for permission to stay, will be returned to the applicant whilst their application is being considered, unless the Secretary of State considers it necessary to retain it.

34K.   Where a decision on an application for permission to stay has not been made and the applicant travels outside the common travel area their application will be treated as withdrawn on the date the applicant left the common travel area.

Specified forms and procedures in connection with applications for administrative review

Notice of an eligible decision

34L. (1) Unless sub-paragraph (2) applies, written notice must be given to a person of any eligible decision. The notice given must:

    (a) include or be accompanied by a statement of reasons for the decision to which it relates, and

    (b) include information on how to apply for an administrative review and the time limit for making an application.

    (2) Sub-paragraph (1) does not apply where the eligible decision is a grant of leave to remain.

Making an application

34M. An application for administrative review must be made in accordance with the requirements set out in paragraphs 34N to 34S. If it is not it will be invalid and will not be considered.

34N. (1) Unless sub-paragraph (2) or (2A) applies only one valid application for administrative review may be made in respect of an eligible decision.

    (2) A further application for administrative review in respect of an eligible decision as set out in Appendix AR may be made where the outcome of the administrative review is as set out in paragraph AR2.2(d) of Appendix AR of these Rules.

    (2A) A further application for administrative review in respect of an eligible decision under Appendix AR (EU) may be made where a decision is withdrawn and a new decision made in accordance with paragraph AR(EU)2.2. of Appendix AR (EU).

    (3) An application for administrative review of an eligible decision under Appendix AR may not be made if the applicant has previously signed an administrative review waiver form in respect of the eligible decision, in accordance with paragraph AR2.10 of Appendix AR of these Rules.

    (4) If, after receiving notice of the eligible decision, an application for entry clearance, leave to enter or leave to remain is made during the time within which an application for administrative review under Appendix AR may be brought within paragraph 34R (including any possibility of an administrative review out-of-time under paragraph 34R(3)), an application for administrative review of the eligible decision may not be made under Appendix AR.

34O. An application for administrative review under Appendix AR or Appendix AR (EU) must be made online in accordance with paragraph 34U, unless the eligible decision relates to an application that was a valid paper application, in which case it can be made:

    (a) in accordance with paragraph 34U;

    (b) in relation to a leave to enter or remain application, in accordance with paragraph 34V; or

    (c) in relation to an entry clearance application, in accordance with paragraph 34VA.

34P. The application must be made in relation to an eligible decision.

34Q. An application under Appendix AR must be made:

    (a) when the administrative review is in relation to an eligible decision on an in country application, as defined in paragraph AR3.2 of Appendix AR, while the applicant is in the UK;

    (b) when the administrative review is in relation to an eligible decision made on arrival at the United Kingdom, as defined in paragraph AR4.2 of Appendix AR, while the applicant is in the UK, unless the eligible decision is made in the Control Zone (as defined in Appendix AR of these Rules), in which case administrative review may not be applied for and will not be considered until after the applicant has left or been removed from the Control Zone;

    (c) when the administrative review is in relation to an eligible decision on an application for entry clearance, as defined in paragraph AR5.2 of Appendix AR, while the applicant is outside the UK.

34QA. An application under Appendix AR (EU) of these Rules may be made from either inside or outside the UK.

34R. (1) An application under Appendix AR must be made:

    (a) where the applicant is in the UK and not detained, no more than 14 calendar days after receipt by the applicant of the notice of the eligible decision;

    (b) where the applicant is in detention in the UK under the Immigration Acts, no more than 7 calendar days after receipt by the applicant of the notice of the eligible decision;

(c)   where the applicant is overseas, no more than 28 calendar days after receipt by the applicant of the notice of the eligible decision; or

(d)   where the eligible decision is a grant of leave to remain, no more than 14 calendar days after receipt by the applicant of the biometric immigration document which states the length and conditions of leave granted.

34R.   (1A)   An application under Appendix AR (EU) must be made:

(a)   where the applicant is in the UK and not detained, no more than 28 calendar days after receipt by the applicant of the notice of the eligible decision;

(b)   where the applicant is in detention in the UK under the Immigration Acts, no more than 7 calendar days after receipt by the applicant of the notice of the eligible decision;

(c)   where the applicant is overseas, no more than 28 calendar days after receipt by the applicant of the notice of the eligible decision.

(2)   An application which is permitted under paragraph 34N(2) or 34N(2A) of these Rules must be made within the relevant time limit stated in paragraph 34R(1) as if it was an initial application, and the notice of the outcome of the previous administrative review will be treated as the notice of the eligible decision.

(3)   But the application may be accepted out of time if the Secretary of State is satisfied that it would be unjust not to waive the time limit and that the application was made as soon as reasonably practicable.

(4)   DELETED

(5)   For provision about when an application is made see paragraph 34W.

34S.   An applicant may only include an application on behalf of a dependant of the applicant if that dependant:

(a)   was a dependant on the application which resulted in the eligible decision; or

(b)   was previously granted leave to enter or remain as a dependant of the applicant and that leave is being cancelled at the same time as that of the applicant

Notice of invalidity

34T.   A notice of invalidity will be given in writing and served in accordance with Appendix SN of these Rules.

Online applications for administrative review

34U.   (1)   In this paragraph:

"the relevant online application process" means the application process accessible via the gov.uk website and identified there as relevant for applications for administrative review; and

"specified" in relation to the relevant online application process means specified in the online guidance accompanying that process.

(2)   An application may be made online by completing the relevant online application process.

(3)   Where an application is made online:

(a)   any specified fee in connection with the application must be paid in accordance with the method specified;

(b)   any section of the online application which is designated as mandatory must be completed as specified; and

(c)   documents specified as mandatory on the online application or in the related guidance must be submitted either electronically with the online application and in the specified manner, where this is permitted, or received by post and in the specified manner no more than seven working days after the day on which the online application is submitted.

Postal applications for administrative review

34V.   (1)   Subject to paragraph 34O, an application may be made by post or courier in accordance with this paragraph.

(2)   here an application is made by post or courier:

(a)   it must be made on the application form as specified within the meaning of paragraph 34 (but see paragraph 34Y);

(b)   any specified fee in connection with the application must be paid in accordance with the method specified in the application form, separate payment form or related guidance notes (as applicable);

(c)   any section of the application form which is designated as mandatory in the form itself or related guidance notes must be completed;

(d)   the form must be signed by the applicant or their representative;

(e)   the application must be accompanied by any documents specified as mandatory in the application form or related guidance notes; and

(f)   the application must be sent to the address specified on the form.

Applications for administrative review of entry clearance decisions

34VA.   (1)   Subject to paragraph 34O, an application may be made by post, courier, hand, fax or email in accordance with this paragraph.

(2)   Where an application is made by post, courier, hand, fax or email:

(a)   it must be made on the application form as specified within the meaning of paragraph 34 (but see paragraph 34Y);

(b)   any section of the application form which is designated as mandatory in the form itself or related guidance notes must be completed;

(c)   the form must be signed by the applicant or their representative;

(d)   the application must be accompanied by any documents specified as mandatory in the application form or related guidance notes;

(e)   the application must be delivered to the postal address, email address or fax number specified on the form; and

(f)   any specified fee in connection with the application must be paid in accordance with the method specified in the application form, separate payment form or related guidance notes (as applicable).

Determining the date of an application

34W.   (1)   An application for administrative review is made:

(a)   where it is made by post in accordance with paragraph 34V, on the marked date of posting;

(b)   where it is made by courier in accordance with paragraph 34V, on the date on which it is delivered; and

(c)   where it is made online in accordance with paragraph 34U, on the date on which it is submitted.

(2)   Accepting an application has been made does not mean that it is accepted as being valid.

Withdrawal of applications

34X.   (1)   An application which may only be brought from within the UK and has not been determined will be treated as withdrawn if the applicant requests the return of their passport for the purpose of travel outside the UK.

(2)   An application which may only be brought from within the UK and which has not been determined will be treated as withdrawn if the applicant leaves the UK.

(3)   The application for administrative review may be withdrawn by the applicant. A request to withdraw an application must be made in writing to the Home Office at the address provided for that purpose on the visas and immigration pages of the gov.uk website. The application will be treated as withdrawn on the date on which the request is received.

(4)   An application for administrative review which has not been determined will be treated as withdrawn if the applicant makes an application for entry clearance, leave to enter or leave to remain.

(5)   Sub-paragraphs (1) and (2) above do not apply to an application for administrative review made under Appendix AR (EU).

Transitional arrangements for specified forms used in postal and courier applications

34Y.   Where an application is made no more than 21 days after the date on which a form is specified (within the meaning of paragraph 34 or the validity requirements for the route applied for) and on a form that was specified immediately prior to the date of the new specification, the application is deemed to have been made on the specified form (and is therefore not to be treated as invalid by reason only of being made on the "wrong" form).

Undertakings

35.   A sponsor of a person seeking leave to enter or remain in the United Kingdom may be asked to give an undertaking in writing to be responsible for that person's maintenance, accommodation and (as appropriate) personal care for the period of any leave granted, including any further variation or for a period of 5 years from date of grant where indefinite leave to enter or remain is granted. Under the Social Security Administration Act 1992 and the Social Security Administration (Northern Ireland) Act 1992, the Department of Social Security or, as the case may be, the Department of Health and Social Services in Northern Ireland, may seek to recover from the person giving such an undertaking any income support paid to meet the needs of the person in respect of whom the undertaking has been given. Under the Immigration and Asylum Act 1999 the Home Office may seek to recover from the person giving such an undertaking amounts attributable to any support provided under section 95 of the Immigration and Asylum Act 1999 (support for asylum seekers) to, or in respect of, the person in respect of whom the undertaking has been given. Failure by the sponsor to maintain that person in accordance with the undertaking, may also be an offence under section 105 of the Social Security Administration Act 1992 and/or under section 108 of the Immigration and Asylum Act 1999 if, as a consequence, asylum support and/or income support is provided to, or in respect of, that person.

Medical

36.   A person who intends to remain in the United Kingdom for more than 6 months should normally be referred to the Medical Inspector for examination. If he produces a medical certificate he should be advised to hand it to the Medical Inspector. Any person seeking entry who mentions health or medical treatment as a reason for his visit, or who appears not to be in good mental or physical health, should also be referred to the Medical Inspector; and the Immigration Officer has discretion, which should be exercised sparingly, to refer for examination in any other case.

37.   Where the Medical Inspector advises that a person seeking entry is suffering from a specified disease or condition which may interfere with his ability to support himself or his dependants, the Immigration Officer should take account of this, in conjunction with other factors, in deciding whether to admit that person. The Immigration Officer should also take account of the Medical Inspector's assessment of the likely course of treatment in deciding whether a person seeking entry for private medical treatment has sufficient means at his disposal.

38.   A returning resident should not be refused leave to enter or have existing leave to enter or remain cancelled on medical grounds. But where a person would be refused leave to enter or have existing leave to enter or remain cancelled on medical grounds if he were not a returning resident or in any case where it is decided on compassionate grounds not to exercise the power to refuse leave to enter or to cancel existing leave to enter or remain, or in any other case where the Medical Inspector so recommends, the Immigration Officer should give the person concerned a notice requiring him to report to the Medical Officer of Environmental Health designated by the Medical Inspector with a view to further examination and any necessary treatment.

A39. Any person making an application for entry clearance to come to the UK for more than six months or as a fiancé(e) or proposed civil partner applying for leave to enter under Section EC-P:Entry clearance as a partner under Appendix FM, having been present in a country listed in Appendix T for more than six months immediately prior to their application, must present, at the time of application, a valid medical certificate issued by a medical practitioner approved by the Secretary of State for these purposes, as listed on the Gov.uk website, confirming that they have undergone screening for active pulmonary tuberculosis and that this tuberculosis is not present in the applicant.

B39. Applicants seeking leave to enter as a returning resident under paragraph 19 of these rules, having been absent from the United Kingdom for more than two years are also subject to the requirements in paragraph A39.

C39. Where a person has lawfully been present in a country not mentioned in Appendix T for more than six months and they are applying for entry clearance as in A39 in a country in Appendix T but have not been in that country or any other country mentioned in Appendix T for more than six months immediately before making their application, they will not be required to produce a medical certificate showing they are free from active pulmonary TB. This does not alter the discretionary powers as in paragraph 39 below.

39.   The Entry Clearance Officer has the same discretion as an Immigration Officer to refer applicants for entry clearance for medical examination and the same principles will apply to the decision whether or not to issue an entry clearance.

Students

39A. DELETED

Specified documents

39B. (a) Where these Rules state that specified documents must be provided, that means documents specified in these Rules as being specified documents for the route under which the applicant is applying. If the specified documents are not provided, the applicant will not meet the requirement for which the specified documents are required as evidence.

(b) Where these Rules specify documents that are to be provided, those documents are considered to be specified documents, whether or not they are named as such, and as such are subject to the requirements in (c) to (f) below.

(c) If the Entry Clearance Officer or Secretary of State has reasonable cause to doubt the genuineness of any document submitted by an applicant which is, or which purports to be, a specified document under these Rules, and having taken reasonable steps to verify the document is unable to verify that it is genuine, the document will be discounted for the purposes of this application.

(d) Specified documents may be originals or copies.

(e) Specified documents must contain, or the applicant must provide, full contact details to allow each document to be verified.

(f) Where any specified documents provided are not in English or Welsh, the applicant must provide the version in the original language and a full translation that can be independently verified by the Entry Clearance Officer, Immigration Officer or the Secretary of State.

The translation must be dated and include:

(i) confirmation that it is an accurate translation of the original document;

(ii) the full name and signature of the translator or an authorised official of the translation company;

(iii) the translator or translation company's contact details; and

(iv) if the applicant is applying for leave to remain or indefinite leave to remain, certification by a qualified translator and details of the translator or translation company's credentials.

Indefinite leave to enter or remain

39C. (a) An applicant for indefinite leave to enter or remain must, unless the applicant provides a reasonable explanation, comply with any request made by the Secretary of State to attend an interview.

(b) If the decision-maker has reasonable cause to doubt (on examination or interview or on any other basis) that any evidence submitted by or on behalf of an applicant for the purposes of satisfying the requirements of Appendix KoLL of these Rules was genuinely obtained, that evidence may be discounted for the purposes of the application.

(c) Where sub-paragraph (b) applies, the decision-maker may give the applicant a further opportunity to demonstrate sufficient knowledge of the English language and about life in the United Kingdom in accordance with paragraph 3.2 or 3.3 of Appendix KoLL.

(d) A decision-maker may decide not to give the applicant a further opportunity under sub-paragraph (c) where the decision-maker does not anticipate that the supply of further evidence will lead to a grant of leave to enter or remain in the United Kingdom because the application may be refused for other reasons.

Power to interview a person with limited leave to enter or remain

39D. For the purpose of assessing whether any of the grounds of cancellation of entry clearance or permission under Part 9 apply the Secretary of State may request a person to:

(a) provide additional information to the Home Office at the address specified in the request within 28 calendar days of the date the request is sent; and

(b) attend an interview.

Exceptions for overstayers

39E. This paragraph applies where:

(1) the application was made within 14 days of the applicant's leave expiring and the Secretary of State considers that there was a good reason beyond the control of the applicant or their representative, provided in or with the application, why the application could not be made in-time; or

   (2)   the application was made:

       (a)   following the refusal of a previous application for leave which was made in-time; and

       (b)   within 14 days of:

           (i)   the refusal of the previous application for leave; or

           (ii)   the expiry of any leave extended by section 3C of the Immigration Act 1971; or

           (iii)   the expiry of the time-limit for making an in-time application for administrative review or appeal (where applicable); or

           (iv)   any administrative review or appeal being concluded, withdrawn, abandoned or lapsing; or

   (3)   the period of overstaying was between 24 January and 31 August 2020; or

   (4)   where the applicant has, or had, permission on the Hong Kong BN(O) route, and the period of overstaying was between 1 July 2020 and 31 January 2021.

Part 9: grounds for refusal

Grounds for the refusal

Suitability requirements apply to all routes and must be met in addition to validity and eligibility requirements.

Where this Part applies a person will not meet the suitability requirements if they fall for refusal under this Part.

A person may also have their entry clearance or permission cancelled on suitability grounds.

More than one grounds for refusal or cancellation may apply, for example, the presence of a foreign criminal in the UK may not be conducive to the public good.

The Immigration Act 1971, section 76 of the Nationality, Immigration and Asylum Act 2002 (revocation of indefinite leave), the Immigration (Leave to Enter and Remain) Order 2000 and Schedule 2 of the Immigration Act 1971 set out the powers to cancel entry clearance or permission. These rules set out how those powers are to be exercised.

Decisions on suitability are either mandatory (must) or discretionary (may) and must be compatible with the UK obligations under the Refugee Convention and the European Convention on Human Rights, which are mainly provided for under other provisions in these Rules.

Some routes have their own, or additional, suitability requirements.

This Part is in 5 sections.

1. Application of this Part;
2. Grounds for refusal, or cancellation of, entry clearance, permission to enter and permission to stay;
3. Additional grounds for refusal of entry, or cancellation of entry clearance or permission, on arrival in the UK;
4. Additional grounds for refusal, or cancellation, of permission to stay;
5. Additional grounds for cancellation of entry clearance, permission to enter and permission to stay which apply to specified routes.

Section 1: Application of this Part

9.1.1.   Part 9 does not apply to the following:

(a)   Appendix FM, except paragraphs 9.2.2, 9.3.2, 9.4.5, 9.9.2, 9.15.1, 9.15.2, 9.15.3, 9.16.2, 9.19.2, 9.20.1, 9.23.1 and 9.24.1. apply, and paragraph 9.7.3 applies to permission to stay; and paragraph 9.8.2 (a) and (c). applies where the application is for entry clearance; and

(b)   an application on grounds of private life under paragraphs 276ADE to 276DH, except paragraph 9.13.1; and

(c)   Appendix Armed Forces, except paragraphs 9.2.2, 9.3.2, 9.4.5, 9.7.3, 9.8.1. to 9.8.8, 9.9.2, 9.15.1. to 9.15.3, 9.16.2, 9.19.2, 9.20.1, 9.23.1. and 9.24.1. apply; and paragraph 9.10.2. applies where the application is under Part 9, 9A or 10 of Appendix Armed Forces; and

(d)   Appendix EU; and

(e)   Appendix EU (Family Permit); and

(f)   Paragraph DWMS 2.1, except paragraphs 9.2.1(c), 9.2.2, 9.3.1, 9.3.2, 9.4.1(b), 9.4.1(c), 9.4.2, 9.4.5, 9.7.1, 9.7.2, 9.7.3, 9.9.1, 9.9.2. 9.16.2, 9.20.1, 9.23.1, 9.24.1; and

(g)   Part 11 (Asylum), except Part 9 does apply to paragraphs 352ZH to 352ZS, and 352I to 352X and 352A to 352FJ; and

(h)   applications for entry clearance or permission to stay granted by virtue of the ECAA Association Agreement, except that in relation to permission granted under the Agreement paragraphs 9.2.2, 9.3.2, 9.4.2, 9.4.5, 9.6.2, 9.7.3 and 9.21.2 apply where the criminal offence or adverse conduct occurred after 11pm on 31 December 2020; and

(i)   applications for permission to stay under Appendix ECAA Extension of Stay, except paragraphs 9.2.1, 9.3.1, 9.4.1, 9.4.3, 9.6.1, 9.7.1, 9.7.2, 9.11.1, 9.12.1 and 9.21.1, and in relation to such permission paragraphs 9.2.2, 9.3.2, 9.4.2, 9.4.5, 9.6.2, 9.7.3 and 9.21.2 apply where the criminal offence or adverse conduct occurred after 11pm on 31 December 2020; and

(j)   Appendix S2 Healthcare Visitor; and

(k)   Appendix Service Providers from Switzerland.

Section 2: Grounds for refusal, or cancellation, of entry clearance, permission to enter and permission to stay

Exclusion or deportation order grounds

9.2.1.   An application for entry clearance, permission to enter or permission to stay must be refused where:

(a)   the Secretary of State has personally directed that the applicant be excluded from the UK; or

(b)   the applicant is the subject of an exclusion order; or.

(c)   the applicant is the subject of a deportation order, or a decision to make a deportation order.

9.2.2.   Entry clearance or permission held by a person must be cancelled where the Secretary of State has personally directed that the person be excluded from the UK.

Non-conducive grounds

9.3.1.   An application for entry clearance, permission to enter or permission to stay must be refused where the applicant's presence in the UK is not conducive to the public good because of their conduct, character, associations or other reasons (including convictions which do not fall within the criminality grounds).

9.3.2.   Entry clearance or permission held by a person must be cancelled where the person's presence in the UK is not conducive to the public good.

Criminality grounds

9.4.1.   An application for entry clearance, permission to enter or permission to stay must be refused where the applicant:

(a)   has been convicted of a criminal offence in the UK or overseas for which they have received a custodial sentence of 12 months or more; or

(b)   is a persistent offender who shows a particular disregard for the law; or

(c)   has committed a criminal offence, or offences, which caused serious harm.

9.4.2.   Entry clearance or permission held by a person must be cancelled where the person:

(a)   has been convicted of a criminal offence in the UK or overseas for which they have received a custodial sentence of 12 months or more; or

(b)   is a persistent offender who shows a particular disregard for the law; or

(c)   has committed a criminal offence, or offences, which caused serious harm.

9.4.3.   An application for entry clearance, permission to enter or permission to stay may be refused (where paragraph 9.4.2. and 9.4.4. do not apply) where the applicant:

(a)   has been convicted of a criminal offence in the UK or overseas for which they have received a custodial sentence of less than 12 months; or

(b)   has been convicted of a criminal offence in the UK or overseas for which they have received a non-custodial sentence, or received an out-of-court disposal that is recorded on their criminal record.

9.4.4.   An application for entry clearance or permission to enter under Appendix V: Visitor, or where a person is seeking entry on arrival in the UK for a stay for less than 6 months, must be refused where the applicant:

(a)   has been convicted of a criminal offence in the UK or overseas for which they have received a custodial sentence of less than 12 months, unless more than 12 months have passed since the end of the custodial sentence; or

(b)   has been convicted of a criminal offence in the UK or overseas for which they have received a non-custodial sentence, or received an out-of-court disposal that is recorded on their criminal record, unless more than 12 months have passed since the date of conviction.

9.4.5.   Entry clearance or permission held by a person may be cancelled (where paragraph 9.4.2. does not apply) where the person:

(a)   has been convicted of a criminal offence in the UK or overseas for which they have received a custodial sentence of less than 12 months; or

(b)   has been convicted of a criminal offence in the UK or overseas for which they have received a non-custodial sentence, or received an out-of-court disposal that is recorded on their criminal record.

Exclusion from asylum or humanitarian protection grounds

9.5.1.   An application for entry clearance, permission to enter or permission to stay may be refused where the Secretary of State:

(a) has at any time decided that paragraph 339AA (exclusion from Refugee Convention), 339AC (danger to the UK), 339D (exclusion from a grant of humanitarian protection) or 339GB (revocation of humanitarian protection on grounds of exclusion) of these rules applies to the applicant; or

(b) has decided that paragraph 339AA, 339AC, 339D or 339GB of these rules would apply, but for the fact that the person has not made a protection claim in the UK, or that the person has made a protection claim which was finally determined without reference to any of the relevant matters described in paragraphs 339AA, 339AC, 339D or 339GB.

9.5.2. Entry clearance or permission held by a person may be cancelled where the Secretary of State:

(a) has at any time decided that paragraph 339AA (exclusion from Refugee Convention), 339AC (danger to the UK), 339D (exclusion from a grant of humanitarian protection) or 339GB (revocation of humanitarian protection on grounds of exclusion) of these rules applies to the applicant; or

(b) has decided that paragraph 339AA, 339AC, 339D or 339GB of these rules would apply, but for the fact that the person has not made a protection claim in the UK, or that the person has made a protection claim which was finally determined without reference to any of the relevant matters described in paragraphs 339AA, 339AC, 339D or 339GB.

Involvement in a sham marriage or sham civil partnership grounds

9.6.1. An application for entry clearance, permission to enter or permission to stay may be refused where the decision maker is satisfied that it is more likely than not that the applicant is, or has been, involved in a sham marriage or sham civil partnership.

9.6.2. Entry clearance or permission held by a person may be cancelled where the decision maker is satisfied that it is more likely than not the person is, or has been, involved in a sham marriage or sham civil partnership.

False representations, etc. grounds

9.7.1. An application for entry clearance, permission to enter or permission to stay may be refused where, in relation to the application, or in order to obtain documents from the Secretary of State or a third party provided in support of the application:

(a) false representations are made, or false documents or false information submitted (whether or not relevant to the application, and whether or not to the applicant's knowledge); or

(b) relevant facts are not disclosed.

9.7.2. An application for entry clearance, permission to enter or permission to stay must be refused where the decision maker can prove that it is more likely than not the applicant used deception in the application.

9.7.3. Entry clearance or permission held by a person may be cancelled where, in relation to an application, or in order to obtain documents from the Secretary of State or a third party provided in support of the application:

(a) false representations were made, or false documents or false information submitted (whether or not relevant to the application, and whether or not to the applicant's knowledge); or

(b) relevant facts were not disclosed.

9.7.4. Permission extended under section 3C of the Immigration Act 1971 may be cancelled where the decision maker can prove that it is more likely than not the applicant used deception in the application for permission to stay.

Previous breach of immigration laws grounds

9.8.1. An application for entry clearance or permission to enter must be refused if:

(a) the applicant has previously breached immigration laws; and

(b) the application is for entry clearance or permission to enter and it was made within the relevant time period in paragraph 9.8.7.

9.8.2. An application for entry clearance or permission to enter may be refused where:

(a) the applicant has previously breached immigration laws; and

(b) the application was made outside the relevant time period in paragraph 9.8.7; and

(c) the applicant has previously contrived in a significant way to frustrate the intention of the rules, or there are other aggravating circumstances (in addition to the immigration breach), such as a failure to cooperate with the redocumentation process, such as using a false identity, or a failure to comply with enforcement processes, such as failing to report, or absconding.

9.8.3. An application for permission to stay may be refused where a person has previously failed to comply with the conditions of their permission, unless permission has been granted in the knowledge of the previous breach.

9.8.3A.   An application for permission to stay may be refused where a person used deception in relation to a previous application (whether or not successfully).

9.8.4.   In paragraphs 9.8.1. and 9.8.2, a person will only be treated as having previously breached immigration laws if, when they were aged 18 or over, they:

(a)   overstayed their permission and neither paragraph 9.8.5. nor paragraph 9.8.6. apply; or

(b)   breached a condition attached to their permission and entry clearance or further permission was not subsequently granted in the knowledge of the breach; or

(c)   were (or still are) an illegal entrant; or

(d)   used deception in relation to an application (whether or not successfully).

9.8.5.   A period of overstaying will be disregarded for the purpose of paragraph 9.8.4. (a) where the person left the UK voluntarily, not at the expense (directly or indirectly) of the Secretary of State, and:

(a)   the person overstayed for 90 days or less, where the overstaying began before 6 April 2017; or

(b)   the person overstayed for 30 days or less, where the overstaying began on or after 6 April 2017; or

(c)   paragraph 39E applied to the period of overstaying.

9.8.6.   A period of overstaying will be disregarded for the purpose of paragraph 9.8.4.(a) where the overstaying arose from a decision to refuse an application, or cancellation of permission, which was subsequently withdrawn, or quashed, or reconsidered by direction of a court or tribunal, unless the legal challenge which led to the reconsideration was brought more than 3 months after the date of the decision to refuse or cancel.

9.8.7.   The relevant time period under paragraphs 9.8.1. and 9.8.2. is as set out in the following table (and where the person previously breached more than one immigration law, only the breach which leads to the longest period of absence from the UK will be taken into account):

Time from date the person left the UK (or date of refusal of the application under row (f))	This applies where the applicant	And the applicant left the UK	And the applicant left the UK
(a) 12 months	left voluntarily	at their own expense	N/A
(b) 2 years	left voluntarily	at public expense	Within 6 months of being given notice of liability for removal or when they no longer had a pending appeal or administrative review, whichever is later.
(c) 5 years	left voluntarily	at public expense	more than 6 months after being given notice of liability for removal or when they no longer had a pending appeal or administrative review, whichever is later.
(d) 5 years	left or was removed from the UK	as a condition of a caution issued in accordance with section 22 of the Criminal Justice Act 2003 (and providing that any condition prohibiting their return to the UK has itself expired)	-
(e) 10 years	was deported or removed from the UK	at public expense	-

(f) 10 years	Used deception in an application (for visits this applies to applications for entry clearance only).	-	-

9.8.8.   Permission (including permission extended under section 3C of the Immigration Act 1971) may be cancelled where the person has failed to comply with the conditions of their permission.

Failure to provide required information, etc grounds

9.9.1.   An application for entry clearance, permission to enter or permission to stay may be refused where a person fails without reasonable excuse to comply with a reasonable requirement to:

(a)   attend an interview; or

(b)   provide information; or

(c)   provide biometrics (whether or not requested as part of an application); or

(d)   undergo a medical examination; or

(e)   provide a medical report.

9.9.2.   Any entry clearance or permission held by a person may be cancelled where the person fails without reasonable excuse to comply with a reasonable requirement to:

(a)   attend an interview; or

(b)   provide information; or

(c)   provide biometrics; or

(d)   undergo a medical examination; or

(e)   provide a medical report.

Admissibility to the Common Travel Area or other countries grounds

9.10.1.   An application for entry clearance or permission to enter must be refused where a person is seeking entry to the UK with the intention of entering another part of the Common Travel Area and fails to satisfy the decision maker that they are acceptable to the immigration authorities there.

9.10.2.   An application for entry clearance, permission to enter or permission to stay may be refused where a person seeking entry fails to satisfy the decision maker that they will be admitted to another country after a stay in the UK.

Debt to the NHS grounds

9.11.1.   An application for entry clearance, permission to enter or permission to stay may be refused where a relevant NHS body has notified the Secretary of State that the applicant has failed to pay charges under relevant NHS regulations on charges to overseas visitors and the outstanding charges have a total value of at least £500.

Unpaid litigation costs grounds

9.12.1.   An application for entry clearance, permission to enter or permission to stay may be refused where a person has failed to pay litigation costs awarded to the Home Office.

Purpose not covered by the Immigration Rules grounds

9.13.1.   An application for entry clearance, permission to enter or permission to stay may be refused where a person is seeking to come to or stay in the UK for a purpose not covered by these rules.

Section 3: Additional grounds for refusal of entry on arrival in the UK

No entry clearance grounds

9.14.1.   Permission to enter must be refused if the person seeking entry is required under these rules to hold on arrival entry clearance for the purpose for which entry is sought, or the person is a visa national, and the person does not hold the required entry clearance.

Failure to produce recognised passport or travel document grounds

9.15.1.   Permission to enter must be refused if the person seeking entry fails to produce a passport or other travel document that satisfies the decision maker as to their identity and nationality, unless the person holds a travel document issued by the national authority of a state of which the person is not a national and the person's statelessness or other status prevents the person from obtaining a document satisfactorily establishing their identity and nationality.

9.15.2.   Permission to enter may be refused if the person seeking entry produces a passport or other travel document which:

(a)   was issued by a territorial entity or authority which is not recognised by Her Majesty's Government as a state, or is not dealt with as a government by them; or

(b)   was issued by a territorial entity or authority which does not accept valid UK passports for the purpose of its own immigration controls; or

(c)   does not comply with international passport practice.

9.15.3.   Entry clearance or permission held by a person may be cancelled where on arrival a person fails to produce a passport or other travel document that meets the requirements in paragraph 9.15.1. or 9.15.2.

Medical grounds

9.16.1.   Permission to enter must be refused where a medical inspector advises that for medical reasons it is undesirable to grant entry to the person, unless the decision maker is satisfied that there are strong compassionate reasons justifying admission.

9.16.2.   Entry clearance or permission held by a person may be cancelled where a medical inspector advises that for medical reasons it is undesirable to grant entry to the person.

Consent for a child to travel grounds

9.17.1.   A child may be refused permission to enter if they are not travelling with their parent or legal guardian and, if required to do so, the child's parent or legal guardian fails to provide the decision maker with written consent to the child seeking entry to the UK.

Returning residents grounds

9.18.1.   A person seeking entry as a returning resident under paragraph 18 of these rules may be refused permission to enter if they fail to satisfy the decision maker that they meet the requirements of that paragraph, or that they are seeking entry for the same purpose as that for which their previous permission was granted.

Customs breaches grounds

9.19.1.   Permission to enter may be refused where the decision maker is satisfied that a person has committed a customs breach, whether or not a criminal prosecution is pursued.

9.19.2.   Where the decision maker is satisfied that a person has committed a customs breach, whether or not a criminal prosecution is pursued, any entry clearance or permission held by the person may be cancelled.

Change of circumstances or purpose grounds

9.20.1.   Entry clearance or permission held by a person may be cancelled where there has been such a change in circumstances since the entry clearance or permission was granted that it should be cancelled.

9.20.2.   Entry clearance or permission to enter held by a person on arrival in the UK may be cancelled where the person's purpose in seeking entry is different from the purpose specified in their entry clearance. 9.20.3.

Section 4: Additional grounds for refusal of permission to stay

Rough sleeping in the UK

9.21.1.   Permission to stay may be refused where the decision maker is satisfied that a person has been rough sleeping in the UK and has repeatedly refused offers of suitable support and has engaged in persistent anti-social behaviour.

9.21.2.   Where the decision maker is satisfied that a person has been rough sleeping in the UK and has repeatedly refused offers of suitable support, and has engaged in persistent anti-social behaviour, any permission held by the person may be cancelled.

Crew members

9.22.1. Where a person has permission to enter as a crew member an application for permission to stay may be refused, unless permission to stay is granted to fulfil the purpose for which the person has permission to enter.

Section 5: Additional grounds for cancellation of entry clearance, permission to enter and permission to stay

Ceasing to meet requirement of rules

9.23.1. A person's entry clearance or permission may be cancelled if they cease to meet the requirements of the rules under which the entry clearance or permission was granted.

Dependent grounds

9.24.1. A person's entry clearance or permission may be cancelled where they are the dependent of another person whose permission is, or has been, cancelled.

Withdrawal of sponsorship or endorsement grounds

9.25.1. A person's entry clearance or permission may be cancelled where their sponsorship or endorsement has been withdrawn and they have entry clearance or permission on one of the following routes:

(a)   Student; or

(b)   Child Student; or

(c)   Skilled Worker; or

(d)   Intra-Company Transfer; or

(e)   Intra-Company Graduate Trainee; or

(f)   Representative of an Overseas Business; or

(g)   T2 Minister of Religion; or

(h)   International Sportsperson: or

(i)   Temporary Worker; or

(j)   Start-up; or

(k)   Innovator; or

(l)   Global Talent.

9.25.2. A Student's permission may be cancelled where the sponsor withdraws their sponsorship of the Student because, having completed a pre-sessional course, the student does not have a knowledge of English equivalent to level B2 or above of the Council of Europe's Common European Framework for Language Learning in all four components (reading, writing, speaking and listening).

9.25.3. Entry clearance or permission held under the Global Talent route may be cancelled where the prize named in Appendix Global Talent: Prestigious Prizes which they used to qualify, has been withdrawn.

Student does not start course or ceases to study

9.26.1. The entry clearance or permission of a Student or Child Student may be cancelled if:

(a)   they do not start their studies with their sponsor; or

(b)   they or their sponsor confirm that their course of study has ceased, or will cease before the end date recorded on the Certificate of Acceptance for Studies; or

(c)   the start date for the course is delayed for more than 28 days; or

(d)   they cease to study with their sponsor.

Worker does not start work or ceases their employment

9.27.1. The entry clearance or permission of a Skilled Worker, person on the Intra-Company routes, Representative of an Overseas Business, T2 Minister of Religion, International Sportsperson or Temporary Worker, may be cancelled if:

(a)   they do not start working for their sponsor; or

(b)   they or their sponsor confirm that their employment, volunteering, training or job shadowing has ceased or will cease before the end date recorded on the Certificate of Sponsorship; or

(c)   the start date for the job, as recorded in the Certificate of Sponsorship, is delayed by more than 28 days; or

(d)   they cease to work for their sponsor.

Sponsor loses licence or transfers business

9.28.1.   Where a person has entry clearance or permission as a Student, Child Student, Skilled Worker, person on the Intra-Company Routes, T2 Minister of Religion, International Sportsperson or Temporary Worker, their entry clearance or permission may be cancelled if:

(a)   their sponsor does not have a sponsor licence; or

(b)   their sponsor transfers the business for which the person works, or at which they study, to another business or institution, and that business or institution:

(i)   fails to apply for a sponsor licence; or

(ii)   fails to apply for a sponsor licence within 28 days of the date of a transfer of their business or institution; or

(iii)   applies for a sponsor licence but is refused; or

(iv)   makes a successful application for a sponsor licence, but the sponsor licence granted is not in a category that would allow the sponsor to issue a Certificate of Sponsorship or Confirmation of Acceptance for Studies to the person.

Change of employer

9.29.1.   Where a person has permission as a Skilled Worker, person on the Intra-Company routes, T2 Minister of Religion, International Sportsperson or Temporary Worker, their permission may be cancelled where they have changed their employer, unless any of the following exceptions apply:

(a)   they are a person on the Government Authorised Exchange route or a Seasonal Worker and the change of employer is authorised by the sponsor; or

(b)   they are working for a different sponsor unless the change of sponsor does not result in a change of employer, or the change in employer is covered by the Transfer of Undertakings (Protection of Employment) Regulations 2006, equivalent statutory transfer schemes, or the Cabinet Office Statement of Practice on Staff Transfers in the Public Sector; or

(c)   they have permission as an International Sportsperson, and all of the following apply:

(i)   they are sponsored by a sports club; and

(ii)   they are sponsored as a player and are being temporarily loaned to another sports club; and

(iii)   player loans are specifically permitted in rules set down by the relevant sports governing body; and

(iv)   their sponsor has made arrangements with the loan club to enable to the sponsor to continue to meet its sponsor duties; and

(v)   the player will return to working for the sponsor at the end of the loan.

Absence from employment

9.30.1.   A person on the Skilled Worker, Intra-Company, Representative of an Overseas Business, T2 Minister of Religion, International Sportsperson or Temporary Worker routes who has been absent from work without pay, or on reduced pay, for more than 4 weeks during any calendar year may have their permission cancelled unless the reason for absence is one of the following:

(a)   statutory maternity leave, paternity leave, parental leave, or shared parental leave; or

(b)   statutory adoption leave; or

(c)   sick leave; or

(d)   assisting with a national or international humanitarian or environmental crisis, providing their sponsor agreed to the absence for that purpose; or

(e)   taking part in legally organised industrial action.

Change of job or lower salary rate

9.31.1.   A person on the Skilled Worker, Intra-Company, Representative of an Overseas Business, T2 Minister of Religion or Temporary Worker routes may have their permission cancelled where they have changed jobs or they receive a lower salary rate (unless any of paragraphs 9.31.2. to 9.31.3. apply) if:

(a) they are on an Intra-Company route or are a Skilled Worker and have changed to a different job in the same occupation code but the salary rate for the new job is lower than the salary rate for the old job as set out in the Appendix Skilled Occupations.

(b) they are a Skilled Worker and scored points for a job in a Shortage Occupation and the new job does not appear in Appendix Shortage Occupation List.

(c) they have changed jobs and the new job has a different occupation code to that recorded by the Certificate of Sponsorship (unless paragraph 9.31.2. applies); or

(d) the person no longer meets the salary requirement or going rate requirement for the job.

9.31.2. The following exception applies to paragraph 9.31.1.(c):

(a) the person is sponsored to undertake a graduate training programme covering multiple roles within the organisation; and

(b) the person is changing to a job with a different occupation code either as a part of that programme or when appointed to a permanent role with the sponsor at the end of that programme; and

(c) their sponsor has notified the Home Office of the change of job and any change in salary.

9.31.3. The following exceptions apply to reduction in salary under paragraph 9.31.1:

(a) a reduction in salary coincides with an absence from employment permitted under paragraph 9.30.1; or

(b) the person is on an Intra-Company route and a reduction in salary coincides with working for the sponsor group while the person is not physically present in the UK; or

(c) the person is a Skilled Worker and:

(i) if the person has permission under Appendix Skilled Worker, they would, after the change to the job, score 20 tradeable points in either the same option in the table in paragraph SW 4.2, or under paragraph SW 14.5(b), whichever they had scored points under when obtaining their most recent grant of permission; or

(ii) if the person has permission as a Tier 2 (General) Migrant, they would, after the change to the job, score 20 tradeable points under option A or F in the table in paragraph SW 4.2, or under paragraph SW 14.5(b), if they were to apply under Appendix Skilled Worker; or

(iii) if the person has permission as a Tier 2 (General) Migrant who was considered a new entrant in their application for that Tier 2 (General) permission, they would, after the change to the job, score 20 tradeable points under option E in the table in paragraph SW 4.2, if they were to apply under Appendix Skilled Worker.

Endorsing body no longer approved

9.32.1. Where a person has entry clearance or permission on the Global Talent, Start-up or Innovator route their entry clearance or permission may be cancelled if their endorsing body ceases to hold that status for the route in which they were endorsed.

Part 10: registering with the police

Registration with the police (paragraphs 325 to 326).

325.   For the purposes of paragraph 326, a "relevant foreign national" is a person aged 16 or over who is:

   (i)   a national or citizen of a country or territory listed in Appendix 2 to these Rules;

   (ii)   a stateless person; or

   (iii)   a person holding a non-national travel document.

326.   (1)   Subject to sub-paragraph (2) below, a condition requiring registration with the police should normally be imposed on any relevant foreign national who is:

   (i)   given limited leave to enter the United Kingdom for longer than six months; or

   (ii)   given limited leave to remain which has the effect of allowing him to remain in the United Kingdom for longer than six months, reckoned from the date of his arrival (whether or not such a condition was imposed when he arrived).

   (2)   Such a condition should not normally be imposed where the leave is given:

   (i)   as a seasonal agricultural worker;

   (ii)   as a Tier 5 (Temporary Worker) Migrant, provided the Certificate of Sponsorship Checking System reference for which points were awarded records that the applicant is being sponsored as an overseas government employee or a private servant is a diplomatic household;

   (iii)   as a Tier 2 (Minister of Religion) Migrant;

   (iv)   on the basis of marriage to or civil partnership with a person settled in the United Kingdom or as the unmarried or same-sex partner of a person settled in the United Kingdom

   (v)   as a person exercising access rights to a child resident in the United Kingdom;

   (vi)   as the Parent of a **Child Student**; or

   (vii)   following the grant of asylum.

   (3)   Such a condition should also be imposed on any foreign national given limited leave to enter the United Kingdom where, exceptionally, the Immigration Officer considers it necessary to ensure that he complies with the terms of the leave.

Part 11: asylum

Asylum (paragraphs 326A to 352H).

Procedure

326A. The procedures set out in these Rules shall apply to the consideration of admissible applications for asylum and humanitarian protection.

326B. Where the Secretary of State is considering a claim for asylum or humanitarian protection under this Part, she will consider any Article 8 elements of that claim in line with the provisions of Appendix FM (family life) and in line with paragraphs 276ADE(1) to 276DH (private life) of these Rules which are relevant to those elements unless the person is someone to whom Part 13 of these Rules applies.

Definition of EU asylum applicant

326C. Under this Part an EU asylum applicant is a national of a Member State of the European Union who either;

(a) makes a request to be recognised a refugee under the Refugee Convention on the basis that it would be contrary to the United Kingdom's obligations under the Refugee Convention for them to be removed from or required to leave the United Kingdom, or

(b) otherwise makes a request for international protection. "EU asylum application" shall be construed accordingly.

326D. 'Member State' has the same meaning as in Schedule 1 to the European Communities Act 1972".

Inadmissibility of EU asylum applications

326E. An EU asylum application will be declared inadmissible and will not be considered unless the requirement in paragraph 326F is met.

326F. An EU asylum application will only be admissible if the applicant satisfies the Secretary of State that there are exceptional circumstances which require the application to be admitted for full consideration. Exceptional circumstances may include in particular:

(a) the Member State of which the applicant is a national has derogated from the European Convention on Human Rights in accordance with Article 15 of that Convention;

(b) the procedure detailed in Article 7(1) of the Treaty on European Union has been initiated, and the Council or, where appropriate, the European Council, has yet to make a decision as required in respect of the Member State of which the applicant is a national; or

(c) the Council has adopted a decision in accordance with Article 7(1) of the Treaty on European Union in respect of the Member State of which the applicant is a national, or the European Council has adopted a decision in accordance with Article 7(2) of that Treaty in respect of the Member State of which the applicant is a national.

Definition of asylum applicant

327. Under the Rules, an asylum applicant is a person who, in person and at a designated place of asylum claim, either:

(a) makes a request to be recognised as a refugee under the Refugee Convention on the basis that it would be contrary to the United Kingdom's obligations under the Refugee Convention for them to be removed from or required to leave the United Kingdom, or

(b) otherwise makes a request for international protection. "Application for asylum" shall be construed accordingly.

327A. Every person has the right to make an application for asylum on their own behalf.

Applications for asylum

327B. A designated place of asylum claim is:

(i) an asylum intake unit;

(ii) an immigration removal centre;

(iii) a port or airport;

(iv) a location to which the person has been directed by the Secretary of State to make a claim for asylum; or

(v) any other location where an officer authorised to accept an asylum application is present and capable of receiving the claim.

327C.   If the officer is not capable of receiving the claim, they will direct the applicant to a designated place of asylum claim.

327D.   An officer is not capable of receiving the claim in the territorial waters of the United Kingdom.

328.   All asylum applications will be determined by the Secretary of State in accordance with the Refugee Convention. Every asylum application made by a person at a port or airport in the United Kingdom will be referred by the Immigration Officer for determination by the Secretary of State in accordance with these Rules.

328A.   The Secretary of State shall ensure that authorities which are likely to be addressed by someone who wishes to make an application for asylum are able to advise that person how and where such an application may be made.

329.   Until an asylum application has been determined by the Secretary of State or the Secretary of State has issued a certificate under Part 2, 3, 4 or 5 of Schedule 3 to the Asylum and Immigration (Treatment of Claimants, etc.) Act 2004 no action will be taken to require the departure of the asylum applicant or their dependants from the United Kingdom.

330.   If the Secretary of State decides to grant refugee status and the person has not yet been given leave to enter, the Immigration Officer will grant limited leave to enter.

331.   If a person seeking leave to enter is refused asylum or their application for asylum is withdrawn or treated as withdrawn under paragraph 333C of these Rules, the Immigration Officer will consider whether or not they are in a position to decide to give or refuse leave to enter without interviewing the person further. If the Immigration Officer decides that a further interview is not required they may serve the notice giving or refusing leave to enter by post. If the Immigration Officer decides that a further interview is required, they will then resume their examination to determine whether or not to grant the person leave to enter under any other provision of these Rules. If the person fails at any time to comply with a requirement to report to an Immigration Officer for examination, the Immigration Officer may direct that the person's examination shall be treated as concluded at that time. The Immigration Officer will then consider any outstanding applications for entry on the basis of any evidence before them.

332.   If a person who has been refused leave to enter makes an application for asylum and that application is refused or withdrawn or treated as withdrawn under paragraph 333C of these Rules, leave to enter will again be refused unless the applicant qualifies for admission under any other provision of these Rules.

333.   Written notice of decisions on applications for asylum shall be given in reasonable time. Where the applicant is legally represented, notice may instead be given to the representative. Where the applicant has no legal representative and free legal assistance is not available, they shall be informed of the decision on the application for asylum and, if the application is rejected, how to challenge the decision, in a language that they may reasonably be supposed to understand.

333A.   The Secretary of State shall ensure that a decision is taken on each application for asylum as soon as possible, without prejudice to an adequate and complete examination.

   Where a decision on an application for asylum cannot be taken within six months of the date it was recorded, the Secretary of State shall either:

   (a)   inform the applicant of the delay; or

   (b)   if the applicant has made a specific written request for it, provide information on the timeframe within which the decision on their application is to be expected. The provision of such information shall not oblige the Secretary of State to take a decision within the stipulated time-frame.

333B.   Applicants for asylum shall be allowed an effective opportunity to consult, at their own expense or at public expense in accordance with provision made for this by the Legal Aid Agency or otherwise, a person who is authorised under Part V of the Immigration and Asylum Act 1999 to give immigration advice. This paragraph shall also apply where the Secretary of State is considering revoking a person's refugee status in accordance with these Rules.

Withdrawal of applications

333C.   If an application for asylum is withdrawn either explicitly or implicitly, consideration of it may be discontinued. An application will be treated as explicitly withdrawn if the applicant signs the relevant form provided by the Secretary of State. An application may be treated as impliedly withdrawn if an applicant leaves the United Kingdom without authorisation at any time prior to the conclusion of their asylum claim, or fails to complete an asylum questionnaire as requested by the Secretary of State, or fails to attend the personal interview as provided in paragraph 339NA of these Rules unless the applicant demonstrates within a reasonable time that that failure was due to circumstances beyond their control. The Secretary of State will indicate on the applicant's asylum file that the application for asylum has been withdrawn and consideration of it has been discontinued.

Grant of refugee status

334.   An asylum applicant will be granted refugee status in the United Kingdom if the Secretary of State is satisfied that:

(i)   they are in the United Kingdom or have arrived at a port of entry in the United Kingdom;

(ii)   they are a refugee, as defined in regulation 2 of The Refugee or Person in Need of International Protection (Qualification) Regulations 2006;

(iii)   there are no reasonable grounds for regarding them as a danger to the security of the United Kingdom;

(iv)   having been convicted by a final judgment of a particularly serious crime, they do not constitute a danger to the community of the United Kingdom; and

(v)   refusing their application would result in them being required to go (whether immediately or after the time limited by any existing leave to enter or remain) in breach of the Refugee Convention, to a country in which their life or freedom would be threatened on account of their race, religion, nationality, political opinion or membership of a particular social group.

335.   If the Secretary of State decides to grant refugee status to a person who has previously been given leave to enter (whether or not the leave has expired) or to a person who has entered without leave, the Secretary of State will vary the existing leave or grant limited leave to remain.

Refusal of asylum

336.   An application which does not meet the criteria set out in paragraph 334 will be refused. Where an application for asylum is refused, the reasons in fact and law shall be stated in the decision and information provided in writing on how to challenge the decision.

337.   DELETED

338.   DELETED

339.   DELETED

Revocation or refusal to renew a grant of refugee status

338A. A person's grant of refugee status under paragraph 334 shall be revoked or not renewed if any of paragraphs 339A to 339AB apply. A person's grant of refugee status under paragraph 334 may be revoked or not renewed if paragraph 339AC applies.

Refugee Convention ceases to apply (cessation)

339A. This paragraph applies when the Secretary of State is satisfied that one or more of the following applies:

(i)   they have voluntarily re-availed themselves of the protection of the country of nationality;

(ii)   having lost their nationality, they have voluntarily re-acquired it;

(iii)   they have acquired a new nationality, and enjoy the protection of the country of their new nationality;

(iv)   they have voluntarily re-established themselves in the country which they left or outside which they remained owing to a fear of persecution;

(v)   they can no longer, because the circumstances in connection with which they have been recognised as a refugee have ceased to exist, continue to refuse to avail themselves of the protection of the country of nationality; or

(vi)   being a stateless person with no nationality, they are able, because the circumstances in connection with which they have been recognised as a refugee have ceased to exist, to return to the country of former habitual residence

In considering (v) and (vi), the Secretary of State shall have regard to whether the change of circumstances is of such a significant and non-temporary nature that the refugee's fear of persecution can no longer be regarded as well-founded.

Exclusion from the Refugee Convention

339AA. This paragraph applies where the Secretary of State is satisfied that the person should have been or is excluded from being a refugee in accordance with regulation 7 of The Refugee or Person in Need of International Protection (Qualification) Regulations 2006.

As regards the application of Article 1F of the Refugee Convention, this paragraph also applies where the Secretary of State is satisfied that the person has instigated or otherwise participated in the crimes or acts mentioned therein.

Misrepresentation

339AB.   This paragraph applies where the Secretary of State is satisfied that the person's misrepresentation or omission of facts, including the use of false documents, were decisive for the grant of refugee status.

Danger to the United Kingdom

339AC.   This paragraph applies where the Secretary of State is satisfied that:

(i)   there are reasonable grounds for regarding the person as a danger to the security of the United Kingdom; or

(ii)   having been convicted by a final judgment of a particularly serious crime, the person constitutes a danger to the community of the United Kingdom.

339B.   When a person's refugee status is revoked or not renewed any limited or indefinite leave which they have may be curtailed or cancelled.

339BA.   Where the Secretary of State is considering revoking refugee status in accordance with these Rules, the following procedure will apply. The person concerned shall be informed in writing that the Secretary of State is reconsidering their qualification for refugee status and the reasons for the reconsideration. That person shall be given the opportunity to submit, in a personal interview or in a written statement, reasons as to why their refugee status should not be revoked. If there is a personal interview, it shall be subject to the safeguards set out in these Rules.

339BB.   The procedure in paragraph 339BA is subject to the following exceptions:

(i)   where a person acquires British citizenship status, their refugee status is automatically revoked in accordance with paragraph 339A (iii) upon acquisition of that status without the need to follow the procedure.

(ii)   where refugee status is revoked under paragraph 339A, or if the person has unequivocally renounced their recognition as a refugee, refugee status may be considered to have lapsed by law without the need to follow the procedure.

339BC.   If the person leaves the United Kingdom, the procedure set out in paragraph 339BA may be initiated, and completed, while the person is outside the United Kingdom.

Grant of humanitarian protection

339C.   A person will be granted humanitarian protection in the United Kingdom if the Secretary of State is satisfied that:

(i)   they are in the United Kingdom or have arrived at a port of entry in the United Kingdom;

(ii)   they do not qualify as a refugee as defined in regulation 2 of The Refugee or Person in Need of International Protection (Qualification) Regulations 2006;

(iii)   substantial grounds have been shown for believing that the person concerned, if returned to the country of return, would face a real risk of suffering serious harm and is unable, or, owing to such risk, unwilling to avail themselves of the protection of that country; and

(iv)   they are not excluded from a grant of humanitarian protection.

339CA.   For the purposes of paragraph 339C, serious harm consists of:

(i)   the death penalty or execution;

(ii)   unlawful killing;

(iii)   torture or inhuman or degrading treatment or punishment of a person in the country of return; or

(iv)   serious and individual threat to a civilian's life or person by reason of indiscriminate violence in situations of international or internal armed conflict.

Exclusion from humanitarian protection

339D.   A person is excluded from a grant of humanitarian protection for the purposes of paragraph 339C (iv) where the Secretary of State is satisfied that:

(i)   there are serious reasons for considering that they have committed a crime against peace, a war crime, a crime against humanity, or any other serious crime or instigated or otherwise participated in such crimes;

(ii) there are serious reasons for considering that they have guilty of acts contrary to the purposes and principles of the United Nations or have committed, prepared or instigated such acts or encouraged or induced others to commit, prepare or instigate such acts;

(iii) there are serious reasons for considering that they constitute a danger to the community or to the security of the United Kingdom; or

(iv) there are serious reasons for considering that they have committed a serious crime; or

(v) prior to their admission to the United Kingdom the person committed a crime outside the scope of (i) and (iv) that would be punishable by imprisonment were it committed in the United Kingdom and the person left their country of origin solely in order to avoid sanctions resulting from the crime.

339E. If the Secretary of State decides to grant humanitarian protection and the person has not yet been given leave to enter, the Secretary of State or an Immigration Officer will grant limited leave to enter. If the Secretary of State decides to grant humanitarian protection to a person who has been given limited leave to enter (whether or not that leave has expired) or a person who has entered without leave, the Secretary of State will vary the existing leave or grant limited leave to remain.

Refusal of humanitarian protection

339F. Where the criteria set out in paragraph 339C is not met humanitarian protection will be refused.

Revocation of, ending of or refusal to renew humanitarian protection

339G. A person's humanitarian protection granted under paragraph 339C will be revoked or not renewed if any of paragraphs 339GA to 339GB apply. A person's humanitarian protection granted under paragraph 339C may be revoked or not renewed if any of paragraphs 339GC to paragraph 339GD apply.

Humanitarian protection ceases to apply

339GA. This paragraph applies where the Secretary of State is satisfied that the circumstances which led to the grant of humanitarian protection have ceased to exist or have changed to such a degree that such protection is no longer required.

In applying this paragraph the Secretary of State shall have regard to whether the change of circumstances is of such a significant and non-temporary nature that the person no longer faces a real risk of serious harm.

Revocation of humanitarian protection on the grounds of exclusion

339GB. This paragraph applies where the Secretary of State is satisfied that:

(i) the person granted humanitarian protection should have been or is excluded from humanitarian protection because there are serious reasons for considering that they have committed a crime against peace, a war crime, a crime against humanity, or any other serious crime or instigated or otherwise participated in such crimes;

(ii) the person granted humanitarian protection should have been or is excluded from humanitarian protection because there are serious reasons for considering that they are guilty of acts contrary to the purposes and principles of the United Nations or have committed, prepared or instigated such acts or encouraged or induced others to commit, prepare or instigate such acts;

(iii) the person granted humanitarian protection should have been or is excluded from humanitarian protection because there are serious reasons for considering that they constitute a danger to the community or to the security of the United Kingdom;

(iv) the person granted humanitarian protection should have been or is excluded from humanitarian protection because there are serious reasons for considering that they have committed a serious crime; or

(v) the person granted humanitarian protection should have been or is excluded from humanitarian protection because prior to their admission to the United Kingdom the person committed a crime outside the scope of paragraph 339GB (i) and (iv) that would be punishable by imprisonment had it been committed in the United Kingdom and the person left their country of origin solely in order to avoid sanctions resulting from the crime.

339GC. DELETED

Revocation of humanitarian protection on the basis of misrepresentation

339GD. This paragraph shall apply where the Secretary of State is satisfied that the person granted humanitarian protection misrepresented or omitted facts, including the use of false documents, which were decisive to the grant of humanitarian protection.

339H.   When a person's humanitarian protection is revoked or not renewed any limited or indefinite leave which they have may be curtailed or cancelled.

Consideration of applications

339HA. The Secretary of State shall ensure that the personnel examining applications for asylum and taking decisions on the Secretary of State's behalf have the knowledge with respect to relevant standards applicable in the field of asylum and refugee law.

339I.   When the Secretary of State considers a person's asylum claim, eligibility for a grant of humanitarian protection or human rights claim it is the duty of the person to submit to the Secretary of State as soon as possible all material factors needed to substantiate the asylum claim or establish that they are a person eligible for humanitarian protection or substantiate the human rights claim, which the Secretary of State shall assess in cooperation with the person.

The material factors include:

(i)   the person's statement on the reasons for making an asylum claim or on eligibility for a grant of humanitarian protection or for making a human rights claim;

(ii)   all documentation at the person's disposal regarding the person's age, background (including background details of relevant relatives), identity, nationality(ies), country(ies) and place(s) of previous residence, previous asylum applications, travel routes; and

(iii)   identity and travel documents.

339IA. For the purposes of examining individual applications for asylum

(i)   information provided in support of an application and the fact that an application has been made shall not be disclosed to the alleged actor(s) of persecution of the applicant, and

(ii)   information shall not be obtained from the alleged actor(s) of persecution that would result in their being directly informed that an application for asylum has been made by the applicant in question and would jeopardise the physical integrity of the applicant and their dependants, or the liberty and security of their family members still living in the country of origin.

This paragraph shall also apply where the Secretary of State is considering revoking a person's refugee status in accordance with these Rules.

339J.   The assessment by the Secretary of State of an asylum claim, eligibility for a grant of humanitarian protection or a human rights claim will be carried out on an individual, objective and impartial basis. This will include taking into account in particular:

(i)   all relevant facts as they relate to the country of origin or country of return at the time of taking a decision on the grant; including laws and regulations of the country of origin or country of return and the manner in which they are applied;

(ii)   relevant statements and documentation presented by the person including information on whether the person has been or may be subject to persecution or serious harm;

(iii)   the individual position and personal circumstances of the person, including factors such as background, gender and age, so as to assess whether, on the basis of the person's personal circumstances, the acts to which the person has been or could be exposed would amount to persecution or serious harm;

(iv)   whether the person's activities since leaving the country of origin or country of return were engaged in for the sole or main purpose of creating the necessary conditions for making an asylum claim or establishing that they are a person eligible for humanitarian protection or a human rights claim, so as to assess whether these activities will expose the person to persecution or serious harm if returned to that country; and

(v)   whether the person could reasonably be expected to avail themselves of the protection of another country where they could assert citizenship.

339JA. Reliable and up-to-date information shall be obtained from various sources as to the general situation prevailing in the countries of origin of applicants for asylum and, where necessary, in countries through which they have transited. Such information shall be made available to the personnel responsible for examining applications and taking decisions and may be provided to them in the form of a consolidated country information report.

This paragraph shall also apply where the Secretary of State is considering revoking a person's refugee status in accordance with these Rules.

339K.   The fact that a person has already been subject to persecution or serious harm, or to direct threats of such persecution or such harm, will be regarded as a serious indication of the person's well-founded fear of persecution or real risk of suffering serious harm, unless there are good reasons to consider that such persecution or serious harm will not be repeated.

339L.   It is the duty of the person to substantiate the asylum claim or establish that they are a person eligible for humanitarian protection or substantiate their human rights claim. Where aspects of the person's statements are not supported by documentary or other evidence, those aspects will not need confirmation when all of the following conditions are met:

(i)   the person has made a genuine effort to substantiate their asylum claim or establish that they are a person eligible for humanitarian protection or substantiate their human rights claim;

(ii)   all material factors at the person's disposal have been submitted, and a satisfactory explanation regarding any lack of other relevant material has been given;

(iii)   the person's statements are found to be coherent and plausible and do not run counter to available specific and general information relevant to the person's case;

(iv)   the person has made an asylum claim or sought to establish that they are a person eligible for humanitarian protection or made a human rights claim at the earliest possible time, unless the person can demonstrate good reason for not having done so; and

(v)   the general credibility of the person has been established.

339M.   The Secretary of State may consider that a person has not substantiated their asylum claim or established that they are a person eligible for humanitarian protection or substantiated their human rights claim, and thereby reject their application for asylum, determine that they are not eligible for humanitarian protection or reject their human rights claim, if they fail, without reasonable explanation, to make a prompt and full disclosure of material facts, either orally or in writing, or otherwise to assist the Secretary of State in establishing the facts of the case; this includes, for example, failure to report to a designated place to be fingerprinted, failure to complete an asylum questionnaire or failure to comply with a requirement to report to an immigration officer for examination.

339MA.   Applications for asylum shall be neither rejected nor excluded from examination on the sole ground that they have not been made as soon as possible.

339N.   In determining whether the general credibility of the person has been established the Secretary of State will apply the provisions in s.8 of the Asylum and Immigration (Treatment of Claimants, etc.) Act 2004.

Personal interview

339NA.   Before a decision is taken on the application for asylum, the applicant shall be given the opportunity of a personal interview on their application for asylum with a representative of the Secretary of State who is legally competent to conduct such an interview.

The personal interview may be omitted where:

(i)   the Secretary of State is able to take a positive decision on the basis of evidence available;

(ii)   the Secretary of State has already had a meeting with the applicant for the purpose of assisting them with completing their application and submitting the essential information regarding the application;

(iii)   the applicant, in submitting their application and presenting the facts, has only raised issues that are not relevant or of minimal relevance to the examination of whether they are a refugee, as defined in regulation 2 of the Refugee or Person in Need of International Protection (Qualification) Regulations 2006;

(iv)   the applicant has made inconsistent, contradictory, improbable or insufficient representations which make their claim clearly unconvincing in relation to having been the object of persecution;

(v)   the applicant has submitted a subsequent application which does not raise any relevant new elements with respect to their particular circumstances or to the situation in their country of origin;

(vi)   the applicant is making an application merely in order to delay or frustrate the enforcement of an earlier or imminent decision which would result in their removal;

(vii)   it is not reasonably practicable, in particular where the Secretary of State is of the opinion that the applicant is unfit or unable to be interviewed owing to enduring circumstances beyond their control; or

(viii)   the applicant is an EU national whose claim the Secretary of State has nevertheless decided to consider substantively in accordance with paragraph 326F above.

The omission of a personal interview shall not prevent the Secretary of State from taking a decision on the application.

Where the personal interview is omitted, the applicant and dependants shall be given a reasonable opportunity to submit further information.

339NB.   (i)   The personal interview mentioned in paragraph 339NA above shall normally take place without the presence of the applicant's family members unless the Secretary of State considers it necessary for an appropriate examination to have other family members present.

(ii)   The personal interview shall take place under conditions which ensure appropriate confidentiality.

339NC.   (i)   A written report shall be made of every personal interview containing at least the essential information regarding the asylum application as presented by the applicant in accordance with paragraph 339I of these Rules.

(ii)   The Secretary of State shall ensure that the applicant has timely access to the report of the personal interview and that access is possible as soon as necessary for allowing an appeal to be prepared and lodged in due time.

339ND.   The Secretary of State shall provide at public expense an interpreter for the purpose of allowing the applicant to submit their case, wherever necessary. The Secretary of State shall select an interpreter who can ensure appropriate communication between the applicant and the representative of the Secretary of State who conducts the interview.

339NE.   The Secretary of State may require an audio recording to be made of the personal interview referred to in paragraph 339NA. Where an audio recording is considered necessary for the processing of a claim for asylum, the Secretary of State shall inform the applicant in advance that the interview will be recorded.

Internal relocation

339O.   (i)   The Secretary of State will not make:

(a)   a grant of refugee status if in part of the country of origin a person would not have a well founded fear of being persecuted, and the person can reasonably be expected to stay in that part of the country; or

(b)   a grant of humanitarian protection if in part of the country of return a person would not face a real risk of suffering serious harm, and the person can reasonably be expected to stay in that part of the country.

(ii)   In examining whether a part of the country of origin or country of return meets the requirements in (i) the Secretary of State, when making a decision on whether to grant asylum or humanitarian protection, will have regard to the general circumstances prevailing in that part of the country and to the personal circumstances of the person.

(iii)   (i) applies notwithstanding technical obstacles to return to the country of origin or country of return

Sur place claims

339P.   A person may have a well-founded fear of being persecuted or a real risk of suffering serious harm based on events which have taken place since the person left the country of origin or country of return and/or activities which have been engaged in by a person since they left the country of origin or country of return, in particular where it is established that the activities relied upon constitute the expression and continuation of convictions or orientations held in the country of origin or country of return.

Residence Permits

339Q   (i)   The Secretary of State will issue to a person granted refugee status in the United Kingdom a residence permit as soon as possible after the grant of refugee status. The residence permit may be valid for five years and renewable, unless compelling reasons of national security or public order otherwise require or where there are reasonable grounds for considering that the applicant is a danger to the security of the United Kingdom or having been convicted by a final judgment of a particularly serious crime, the applicant constitutes a danger to the community of the United Kingdom or the person's character, conduct or associations otherwise require.

(ii) The Secretary of State will issue to a person granted humanitarian protection in the United Kingdom a residence permit as soon as possible after the grant of humanitarian protection. The residence permit may be valid for five years and renewable, unless compelling reasons of national security or public order otherwise require or where there are reasonable grounds for considering that the person granted humanitarian protection is a danger to the security of the United Kingdom or having been convicted by a final judgment of a serious crime, this person constitutes a danger to the community of the United Kingdom or the person's character, conduct or associations otherwise require.

(iii) The Secretary of State will issue a residence permit to a family member of a person granted refugee status or humanitarian protection where the family member does not qualify for such status. A residence permit may be granted for a period of five years. The residence permit is renewable on the terms set out in (i) and (ii) respectively. "Family member" for the purposes of this sub-paragraph refers only to those who are treated as dependants for the purposes of paragraph 349.

(iv) The Secretary of State may revoke or refuse to renew a person's residence permit where their grant of refugee status or humanitarian protection is revoked under the provisions in the immigration rules.

Requirements for indefinite leave to remain for persons granted refugee status or humanitarian protection

339R. DELETED

Indefinite leave to remain for a person granted refugee status or humanitarian protection

339S. DELETED

Refusal of indefinite leave to remain for a person granted refugee status or humanitarian protection

339T. DELETED

Consideration of asylum applications and human rights claims

340. DELETED
341. DELETED
342. DELETED
343. DELETED
344. DELETED

Travel documents

344A. (i) After having received a complete application for a travel document, the Secretary of State will issue to a person granted refugee status in the United Kingdom and their family members travel documents, in the form set out in the Schedule to the Refugee Convention, for the purpose of travel outside the United Kingdom, unless compelling reasons of national security or public order otherwise require.

(ii) After having received a complete application for a travel document, the Secretary of State will issue to a person granted humanitarian protection in the United Kingdom and their family members a travel document where that person is unable to obtain a national passport or other identity documents which enable that person to travel, unless compelling reasons of national security or public order otherwise require.

(iii) Where the person referred to in (ii) can obtain a national passport or identity documents but has not done so, the Secretary of State will issue that person with a travel document where that person can show that they have made reasonable attempts to obtain a national passport or identity document and there are serious humanitarian reasons for travel.

(iv) For the purposes of paragraph 344A, a 'family member' refers only to a person who has been treated as a dependant under paragraph 349 of these Rules or a person who has been granted leave to enter or remain in accordance with paragraphs 352A-352FJ of these Rules.

Access to Employment

344B. The Secretary of State will not impose conditions restricting the employment or occupation in the United Kingdom of a person granted refugee status or humanitarian protection.

Information

344C.   A person who is granted refugee status or humanitarian protection will be provided with access to information in a language that they may reasonably be supposed to understand which sets out the rights and obligations relating to that status. The Secretary of State will provide the information as soon as possible after the grant of refugee status or humanitarian protection.

345.   DELETED

345(2A).   DELETED

Inadmissibility of non-EU applications for asylum

345A.   An asylum application may be treated as inadmissible and not substantively considered if the Secretary of State determines that:

(i)   the applicant has been recognised as a refugee in a safe third country and they can still avail themselves of that protection; or

(ii)   the applicant otherwise enjoys sufficient protection in a safe third country, including benefiting from the principle of non-refoulement; or

(iii)   the applicant could enjoy sufficient protection in a safe third country, including benefiting from the principle of non-refoulement because:

(a)   they have already made an application for protection to that country; or

(b)   they could have made an application for protection to that country but did not do so and there were no exceptional circumstances preventing such an application being made, or

(c)   they have a connection to that country, such that it would be reasonable for them to go there to obtain protection.

Safe Third Country of Asylum

345B.   A country is a safe third country for a particular applicant, if:

(i)   the applicant's life and liberty will not be threatened on account of race, religion, nationality, membership of a particular social group or political opinion in that country;

(ii)   the principle of non-refoulement will be respected in that country in accordance with the Refugee Convention;

(iii)   the prohibition of removal, in violation of the right to freedom from torture and cruel, inhuman or degrading treatment as laid down in international law, is respected in that country; and

(iv)   the possibility exists to request refugee status and, if found to be a refugee, to receive protection in accordance with the Refugee Convention in that country.

345C.   When an application is treated as inadmissible, the Secretary of State will attempt to remove the applicant to the safe third country in which they were previously present or to which they have a connection, or to any other safe third country which may agree to their entry.

Exceptions for admission of inadmissible claims to UK asylum process

345D.   When an application has been treated as inadmissible and either

(i)   removal to a safe third country within a reasonable period of time is unlikely; or

(ii)   upon consideration of a claimant's particular circumstances the Secretary of State determines that removal to a safe third country is inappropriate

the Secretary of State will admit the applicant for consideration of the claim in the UK.

Dublin Transfers

345E.   DELETED

Previously rejected applications

346.   DELETED

347.   DELETED

Rights of appeal

348.   DELETED

Dependants

349. A spouse, civil partner, unmarried partner, or minor child accompanying a principal applicant may be included in the application for asylum as a dependant, provided, in the case of an adult dependant with legal capacity, the dependant consents to being treated as such at the time the application is lodged. A spouse, civil partner, unmarried partner or minor child may also claim asylum in their own right. If the principal applicant is granted refugee status or humanitarian protection and leave to enter or remain any spouse, civil partner, unmarried partner or minor child will be granted leave to enter or remain for the same duration. The case of any dependant who claims asylum in their own right will be also considered individually in accordance with paragraph 334 above. An applicant under this paragraph, including an accompanied child, may be interviewed where they make a claim as a dependant or in their own right.

If the spouse, civil partner, unmarried partner, or minor child in question has a claim in their own right, that claim should be made at the earliest opportunity. Any failure to do so will be taken into account and may damage credibility if no reasonable explanation for it is given. Where an asylum or humanitarian protection application is unsuccessful, at the same time that asylum or humanitarian protection is refused the applicant may be notified of removal directions or served with a notice of the Secretary of State's intention to deport them, as appropriate. In this paragraph and paragraphs 350-352 a child means a person who is under 18 years of age or who, in the absence of documentary evidence establishing age, appears to be under that age. An unmarried partner for the purposes of this paragraph, is a person who has been living together with the principal applicant in a subsisting relationship akin to marriage or a civil partnership for two years or more.

Unaccompanied children

350. Unaccompanied children may also apply for asylum and, in view of their potential vulnerability, particular priority and care is to be given to the handling of their cases.

351. A person of any age may qualify for refugee status under the Convention and the criteria in paragraph 334 apply to all cases. However, account should be taken of the applicant's maturity and in assessing the claim of a child more weight should be given to objective indications of risk than to the child's state of mind and understanding of their situation. An asylum application made on behalf of a child should not be refused solely because the child is too young to understand their situation or to have formed a well founded fear of persecution. Close attention should be given to the welfare of the child at all times.

352. Any child over the age of 12 who has claimed asylum in their own right shall be interviewed about the substance of their claim unless the child is unfit or unable to be interviewed. When an interview takes place it shall be conducted in the presence of a parent, guardian, representative or another adult independent of the Secretary of State who has responsibility for the child. The interviewer shall have specialist training in the interviewing of children and have particular regard to the possibility that a child will feel inhibited or alarmed. The child shall be allowed to express themselves in their own way and at their own speed. If they appear tired or distressed, the interview will be suspended. The interviewer should then consider whether it would be appropriate for the interview to be resumed the same day or on another day.

352ZA. The Secretary of State shall as soon as possible after an unaccompanied child makes an application for asylum take measures to ensure that a representative represents and/or assists the unaccompanied child with respect to the examination of the application and ensure that the representative is given the opportunity to inform the unaccompanied child about the meaning and possible consequences of the interview and, where appropriate, how to prepare themselves for the interview. The representative shall have the right to be present at the interview and ask questions and make comments in the interview, within the framework set by the interviewer.

352ZB. The decision on the application for asylum shall be taken by a person who is trained to deal with asylum claims from children.

Requirements for limited leave to remain as an unaccompanied asylum seeking child.

352ZC. The requirements to be met in order for a grant of limited leave to remain to be made in relation to an unaccompanied asylum seeking child under paragraph 352ZE are:

a) the applicant is an unaccompanied asylum seeking child under the age of 17½ years throughout the duration of leave to be granted in this capacity;

b) the applicant must have applied for asylum and been granted neither refugee status nor Humanitarian Protection;

c) there are no adequate reception arrangements in the country to which they would be returned if leave to remain was not granted;

d) the applicant must not be excluded from being a refugee under Regulation 7 of the Refugee or Person in Need of International Protection (Qualification) Regulations 2006 or excluded from a grant of Humanitarian Protection under paragraph 339D or both;

e) there are no reasonable grounds for regarding the applicant as a danger to the security of the United Kingdom;

f) the applicant has not been convicted by a final judgment of a particularly serious crime, and the applicant does not constitute a danger to the community of the United Kingdom; and

g) the applicant is not, at the date of their application, the subject of a deportation order or a decision to make a deportation order.

352ZD. An unaccompanied asylum seeking child is a person who:

a) is under 18 years of age when the asylum application is submitted.

b) is applying for asylum in their own right; and

c) is separated from both parents and is not being cared for by an adult who in law or by custom has responsibility to do so.

352ZE. Limited leave to remain should be granted for a period of 30 months or until the child is 17½ years of age whichever is shorter, provided that the Secretary of State is satisfied that the requirements in paragraph 352ZC are met.

352ZF. Limited leave granted under this provision will cease if

a) any one or more of the requirements listed in paragraph 352ZC cease to be met, or

b) a misrepresentation or omission of facts, including the use of false documents, were decisive for the grant of leave under 352ZE.

Section 67 of the Immigration Act 2016 leave

352ZG. Paragraphs 352ZH to 352ZS only apply where a person has been transferred to the United Kingdom under Section 67 of the Immigration Act 2016.

Grant of Section 67 of the Immigration Act 2016 leave

352ZH. The person described in paragraph 352ZG will be granted Section 67 of the Immigration Act 2016 leave to remain in the United Kingdom ("Section 67 leave") if the Secretary of State is satisfied that:

(i) the person is not excluded from being a refugee under regulation 7 of the Refugee or Person in Need of International Protection (Qualification) Regulations 2006 or excluded from a grant of humanitarian protection under paragraph 339D of these Rules;

(ii) where the person has made an application for refugee status or humanitarian protection, that application has been refused;

(iii) there are no reasonable grounds for regarding the person as a danger to the security of the United Kingdom;

(iv) the person has not been convicted by a final judgment of a particularly serious crime, and does not constitute a danger to the community of the United Kingdom; and

(v) must not fall for refusal under paragraphs 9.2.1 (c), 9.3.1, 9.4.1, 9.4.3, 9.5.1, 9.7.1, 9.7.2, 9.8.1. to 9.8.4, 9.9.1, 9.11.1, 9.12.1 or 9.13.1 of Part 9 Grounds for refusal.

352ZHA. For persons arriving in the United Kingdom after 1 October 2019, the grant of Section 67 leave will be made upon their arrival in the United Kingdom.

Residence Permits

352ZI. The Secretary of State will issue to a person granted Section 67 leave a residence permit as soon as possible after the grant of Section 67 leave. The residence permit will be valid for five years.

352ZJ. The Secretary of State will issue a residence permit to a dependant of a person granted Section 67 leave in accordance with paragraph 352ZO.

352ZK. The Secretary of State may revoke a person's residence permit where their grant of Section 67 leave is revoked under the provisions in these Rules.

Requirements for indefinite leave to remain for a person granted Section 67 leave

352ZL.   A person may apply for indefinite leave to remain under paragraph 352ZN where:

(i)   they have been granted Section 67 leave; or

(ii)   they transferred to the UK under Section 67 of the Immigration Act 2016 and, having been granted refugee status or humanitarian protection, that person has had their status ended or refused under either paragraph 339A or paragraph 339G of the Immigration Rules following a review.

352ZM.   The requirements for indefinite leave to remain for a person described in paragraph 352ZL are that:

(i)   each of the requirements of paragraph 352ZH continue to be met;

(ii)   the person has held a residence permit issued under paragraph 352ZI, 352ZJ or 339Q for a continuous period of five years in the UK;

(iii) the person's residence permit has not been revoked; and

(iv)   the person has not in the view of the Secretary of State, at the date on which the application has been decided, demonstrated the undesirability of granting settlement in the United Kingdom in light of his or her conduct (including convictions which do not fall within paragraphs 339R(iii)(a-e)), character or associations or the fact that he or she represents a threat to national security.

Indefinite leave to remain for a person granted Section 67 leave

352ZN.   Indefinite leave to remain will, on application, be granted to a person described in paragraph 352ZL where each of the requirements in paragraph 352ZM is met.

Dependants of a person transferred to the UK under Section 67 of the Immigration Act 2016

352ZO.   The dependent child of a person granted leave to remain under paragraph 352ZH or 352ZN, will be granted leave to enter or remain for the same duration as that person ("leave in line") provided that the requirements of paragraph 352ZH (except for (ii)); and 352ZM (iv) are met. For the purposes of this paragraph, a dependent child means a child who is under 18 years of age and for whom the person has parental responsibility.

Curtailment and Revocation of Section 67 leave

352ZP.   A person's grant of leave under paragraph 352ZH or 352ZN may be curtailed or revoked if any of the grounds in paragraph 9.3.2, 9.4.2 (b), 9.4.2(c), 9.4.5, 9.7.3, 9.8.8 and 9.9.2 of Part 9 Grounds for refusal apply.

352ZQ.   Any curtailment or revocation of a person's leave under paragraph 352ZP shall also apply to any leave in line granted to a dependent child of that person.

Travel documents

352ZR.   Following receipt of a completed application for a travel document, the Secretary of State will issue to a person granted Section 67 leave, unless compelling reasons of national security or public order otherwise require, a travel document if that person can demonstrate they are unable to obtain a national passport or other identity documents which enable that person to travel.

352ZS.   Where the person referred to in paragraph 352ZR can obtain a national passport or identity documents but has not done so, the Secretary of State will issue that person with a travel document if that person can show that they have made reasonable attempts to obtain a national passport or identity document and there are compelling reasons for travel.

Family Reunion Requirements for leave to enter or remain as the partner of a refugee

352A.   The requirements to be met by a person seeking leave to enter or remain in the United Kingdom as the partner of a person granted refugee status are that:

(i)   the applicant is the partner of a person who currently has refugee status granted under the Immigration Rules in the United Kingdom; and

(ii)   the marriage or civil partnership did not take place after the person granted refugee status left the country of their former habitual residence in order to seek asylum or the parties have been living together in a relationship akin to marriage or a civil partnership which has subsisted for two years or more before the person granted refugee status left the country of their former habitual residence in order to seek asylum; and

(iii) the relationship existed before the person granted refugee status left the country of their former habitual residence in order to seek asylum; and

(iv)   the applicant would not be excluded from protection by virtue of paragraph 334(iii) or (iv) of these Rules or Article 1F of the Refugee Convention if they were to seek asylum in their own right; and

(v)   each of the parties intends to live permanently with the other as their partner and the relationship is genuine and subsisting

(vi)   the applicant and their partner must not be within the prohibited degree of relationship; and

(vii) if seeking leave to enter, the applicant holds a valid United Kingdom entry clearance for entry in this capacity.

352AA.   DELETED

Granting family reunion to the partner of a refugee

352B.   Limited leave to enter the United Kingdom as the partner of a person who currently has refugee status may be granted provided on arrival, a valid passport or other identity document is produced to the Immigration Officer and the applicant has entry clearance for entry in this capacity. Limited leave to remain in the United Kingdom as the partner of a person who currently has refugee status may be granted provided the Secretary of State is satisfied that each of the requirements of paragraph 352A (i) to (vi) are met.

352BA Limited leave to enter the United Kingdom as the unmarried or same-sex partner of a person who currently has refugee status may be granted provided on arrival, a valid passport or other identity document is produced to the Immigration Officer and the applicant has entry clearance for entry in this capacity. Limited leave to remain in the United Kingdom as the unmarried or same sex partner of a person who currently has refugee status may be granted provided the Secretary of State is satisfied that each of the requirements of paragraph 352AA (i) - (vii) are met.

Refusing family reunion to the partner of a refugee

352C.   Limited leave to enter the United Kingdom as the partner of a person who currently has refugee status is to be refused if on arrival, a valid passport or other identity document is not produced to the Immigration Officer and the applicant does not have entry clearance for entry in this capacity. Limited leave to remain as the partner of a person who currently has refugee status is to be refused if the Secretary of State is not satisfied that each of the requirements of paragraph 352A (i) to (vi) are met.

352CA.   DELETED

Requirements for leave to enter or remain as the child of a refugee

352D.   The requirements to be met by a person seeking leave to enter or remain in the United Kingdom in order to join or remain with the parent who currently has refugee status are that the applicant:

(i)   is the child of a parent who currently has refugee status granted under the Immigration Rules in the United Kingdom; and

(ii)   is under the age of 18; and

(iii) is not leading an independent life, is unmarried and is not a civil partner, and has not formed an independent family unit; and

(iv)   was part of the family unit of the person granted asylum at the time that the person granted asylum left the country of their habitual residence in order to seek asylum; and

(v)   the applicant would not be excluded from protection by virtue of paragraph 334(iii) or (iv) of these Rules or Article 1F of the Refugee Convention if they were to seek asylum in their own right; and

(vi)   if seeking leave to enter, holds a valid United Kingdom entry clearance for entry in this capacity.

Granting family reunion to the child of a refugee

352E.   Limited leave to enter the United Kingdom as the child of a person who currently has refugee status may be granted provided, on arrival, a valid passport or other identity document is produced to the Immigration Officer and the applicant has entry clearance for entry in this capacity. Limited leave to remain in the United Kingdom as the child of a person who currently has refugee status may be granted provided the Secretary of State is satisfied that each of the requirements of paragraph 352D (i) to (v) are met.

Refusing family reunion to the child of a refugee

352F.   Limited leave to enter the United Kingdom as the child of a person who currently has refugee status is to be refused if on arrival, a valid passport or other identity document is not produced to the Immigration Officer and the applicant does not have entry clearance for entry in this capacity. Limited leave to remain as the child of a person who currently has refugee status is to be refused if the Secretary of State is not satisfied that each of the requirements of paragraph 352D (i) to (v) are met.

Requirements for leave to enter or remain as the partner of a person with humanitarian protection

352FA.　The requirements to be met by a person seeking leave to enter or remain in the United Kingdom as the partner of a person who currently has humanitarian protection and was granted that status on or after 30 August 2005 are that:

(i)　the applicant is the partner of a person who currently has humanitarian protection granted under the Immigration Rules in the United Kingdom and was granted that status on or after 30 August 2005; and

(ii)　the marriage or civil partnership did not take place after the person granted humanitarian protection left the country of their former habitual residence in order to seek asylum in the United Kingdom or the parties have been living together in a relationship akin to marriage or a civil partnership which has subsisted for two years or more before the person granted humanitarian protection left the country of their former habitual residence in order to seek asylum; and

(iii)　the relationship existed before the person granted humanitarian protection left the country of their former habitual residence in order to seek asylum; and

(iv)　the applicant would not be excluded from a grant of humanitarian protection for any of the reasons in paragraph 339D; and

(v)　each of the parties intends to live permanently with the other as their partner and the relationship is genuine and subsisting

(vi)　the applicant and their partner must not be within the prohibited degree of relationship; and

(vii)　if seeking leave to enter, the applicant holds a valid United Kingdom entry clearance for entry in this capacity.

Granting family reunion to the partner of a person with humanitarian protection

352FB.　Limited leave to enter the United Kingdom as the partner of a person who currently has humanitarian protection may be granted provided, on arrival, a valid passport or other identity document is produced to the Immigration Officer and the applicant has entry clearance for entry in this capacity. Limited leave to remain in the United Kingdom as the partner of a person who currently has humanitarian protection may be granted provided the Secretary of State is satisfied that each of the requirements in sub paragraphs 352FA(i) to (vi) are met.

Refusing family reunion to the partner of a person with humanitarian protection

352FC.　Limited leave to enter the United Kingdom as the partner of a person who currently has humanitarian protection is to be refused if on arrival, a valid passport or other identity document is not produced to the Immigration Officer and the applicant does not have entry clearance for entry in this capacity. Limited leave to remain as the partner of a person who currently has humanitarian protection is to be refused if the Secretary of State is not satisfied that each of the requirements in sub paragraphs 352FA (i) to (vi) are met.

352FD.　DELETED

352FE.　DELETED

352FF.　DELETED

Requirements for leave to enter or remain as the child of a person with humanitarian protection

352FG.　The requirements to be met by a person seeking leave to enter or remain in the United Kingdom in order to join or remain with their parent who currently has humanitarian protection and was granted that status on or after 30 August 2005 are that the applicant:

(i)　is the child of a parent currently who has humanitarian protection and was granted that status on or after 30 August 2005 under the Immigration Rules in the United Kingdom; and

(ii)　is under the age of 18, and

(iii)　is not leading an independent life, is unmarried or is not in a civil partnership, and has not formed an independent family unit; and

(iv)　was part of the family unit of the person granted humanitarian protection at the time that the person granted humanitarian protection left the country of their habitual residence in order to seek asylum in the United Kingdom; and

(v)   would not be excluded from a grant of humanitarian protection for any of the reasons in paragraph 339D; and

(vi)   if seeking leave to enter, holds a valid United Kingdom entry clearance for entry in this capacity.

Granting family reunion to the child of a person with humanitarian protection

352FH.   Limited leave to enter the United Kingdom as the child of a person who currently has humanitarian protection may be granted provided on arrival, a valid passport or other identity document is produced to the Immigration Officer and the applicant has entry clearance for entry in this capacity. Limited leave to remain in the United Kingdom as the child of a person who currently has humanitarian protection may be granted provided the Secretary of State is satisfied that each of the requirements in sub paragraphs 352FG (i) to (v) are met.

Refusing family reunion to the child of a person with humanitarian protection

352FI.   Limited leave to enter the United Kingdom as the child of a person who currently has humanitarian protection is to be refused if on arrival, a valid passport or other identity document is not produced to the Immigration Officer and the applicant does not have entry clearance for entry in this capacity. Limited leave to remain as the child of a person who currently has humanitarian protection is to be refused if the Secretary of State is not satisfied that each of the requirements in sub paragraphs 352FG (i) to (v) are met.

Refusing family reunion where the sponsor is a British Citizen

352FJ.   Nothing in paragraphs 352A to 352FI shall allow a person to be granted leave to enter or remain in the United Kingdom as the partner or child of a person who has been granted refugee status, or granted humanitarian protection under the immigration rules in the United Kingdom on or after 30 August 2005, if the person granted refugee status or person granted humanitarian protection, is a British Citizen.

Interpretation

352G.   For the purposes of this Part:

(a)   DELETED

(b)   "Country of return" means a country or territory listed in paragraph 8(c) of Schedule 2 of the Immigration Act 1971;

(c)   "Country of origin" means the country or countries of nationality or, for a stateless person, or former habitual residence.

(d)   "Partner" means the applicant's spouse, civil partner, or a person who has been living together with the applicant in a relationship akin to a marriage or civil partnership for at least two years prior to the date of application;

(e)   "Dublin Regulation" means Regulation (EU) No. 604/2013 establishing the criteria and mechanisms for determining the Member State responsible for examining an application for international protection lodged in one of the Member States by a third-country national or a stateless person

Restriction on study

352H.   Where a person is granted leave in accordance with the provisions set out in Part 11 of the Immigration Rules that leave will, in addition to any other conditions which may apply, be granted subject to the condition in Appendix ATAS of these Rules.

Calais leave to remain in the United Kingdom

352I.   Paragraphs 352I to 352X only apply to a person who was transferred to the United Kingdom:

(i)   from 17 October 2016 to 13 July 2017 inclusive; and

(ii)   in connection with the clearing of the Calais migrant camp; and

(iii) for the purpose of being reunited with family in the United Kingdom,

and either:

(a)   as part of the expedited process operated by the Secretary of State;

(b)   pursuant to an order of the Tribunal; or

(c)   under the Dublin III Regulation.

Grant of Calais leave

352J.   The person described in paragraph 325I will be granted Calais leave to remain in the United Kingdom ("Calais leave") for a period of five years if the Secretary of State is satisfied that:

(i)   the person is not excluded from being a refugee under regulation 7 of the Refugee or Person in Need of International Protection (Qualification) Regulations 2006 or excluded from a grant of humanitarian protection under paragraph 339D of these Rules;

(ii)   the person's application for refugee status or humanitarian protection has been refused;

(iii) there are no reasonable grounds for regarding the person as a danger to the security of the United Kingdom;

(iv)   the person has not been convicted by a final judgment of a particularly serious crime, and does not constitute a danger to the community of the United Kingdom; and

(v)   must not fall for refusal under paragraphs 9.2.1 (c), 9.3.1, 9.4.1, 9.4.3, 9.5.1, 9.7.1, 9.7.2, 9.8.1 to 9.8.4, 9.9.1, 9.11.1, 9.12.1 or 9.13.1 of Part 9: grounds for refusal.

352K.   At the end of the five-year period, if each of the requirements of paragraph 352J continue to be met, the person will be granted Calais leave for a further period of five years.

Persons previously granted a form of protection

352L.   Where a person was transferred to the UK in accordance with paragraph 352I and, having been granted refugee status or humanitarian protection, that person has had their status ended or refused under either paragraph 339A or paragraph 339G of the Immigration Rules following a review, that person will be entitled to a grant of Calais leave providing that the requirements of paragraph 352J (except sub-paragraph (ii)) are met.

Residence Permits

352M.   The Secretary of State will issue to a person granted Calais leave a residence permit as soon as possible after the grant of Calais leave. The residence permit will be valid for five years.

352N.   The Secretary of State will issue a residence permit to a dependant of a person granted Calais leave in accordance with paragraph 352T.

352O.   The Secretary of State may revoke or refuse to renew a person's residence permit where their grant of Calais leave is revoked under the provisions in these Rules.

352P.   At the end of the five-year period, if the person's Calais leave has been renewed, they will be issued with another residence permit, valid for a further period of five years.

Requirements for indefinite leave to remain for a person granted Calais leave

352Q.   A person may apply for indefinite leave to remain under paragraph 352S where:

(i)   they have been granted Calais leave for a continuous period of ten years; or

(ii)   having been granted Calais leave under paragraph 352L, they have been granted leave to remain in the UK for a continuous period of ten years.

352R.   The requirements for indefinite leave to remain for a person described in paragraph 352Q are that:

(i)   each of the requirements of paragraph 352J continue to be met;

(ii)   the person has held residence permits issued under paragraph 352M, 352N or 352P, and, in the case of a person to whom paragraph 352L applies, paragraph 339Q(i)-(iii), for a continuous period of ten years in the UK;

(iii) the person's residence permit has not been revoked; and

(iv)   the person has not in the view of the Secretary of State, at the date on which the application has been decided, demonstrated the undesirability of granting settlement in the United Kingdom in light of his or her conduct (including convictions which do not fall within paragraphs 339R(iii)(a-e)), character or associations or the fact that he or she represents a threat to national security.

Indefinite leave to remain for a person granted Calais leave

352S.   Indefinite leave to remain will, on application, be granted to a person described in paragraph 352Q where each of the requirements in paragraph 352R is met.

Dependants of a person granted Calais leave

352T.   The dependent child of a person granted leave to remain under paragraph 352J or 352S, will be granted leave to enter or remain for the same duration as that person ("leave in line") provided that the requirements of paragraph 352J (except for (ii)); and 352R (iv) are met. For the purposes of this paragraph, a dependent child means a child who is under 18 years of age and for whom the person has parental responsibility.

Curtailment and Revocation of Calais leave

352U.   A person's grant of leave under paragraph 352J or 352S may be curtailed or revoked if any of the grounds in paragraph 9.3.2, 9.4.2 (b), 9.4.2(c), 9.4.5, 9.7.3, 9.8.8. and 9.9.2. of Part 9 Grounds for refusal apply.

352V.   Any curtailment or revocation of a person's leave under paragraph 352U shall also apply to any leave in line granted to a dependent child of that person.

Travel documents

352W.   Following receipt of a completed application for a travel document, the Secretary of State will issue to a person granted Calais leave, unless compelling reasons of national security or public order otherwise require, a travel document if that person can demonstrate they are unable to obtain a national passport or other identity documents which enable that person to travel.

352X.6.   Where the person referred to in paragraph 352W can obtain a national passport or identity documents but has not done so, the Secretary of State will issue that person with a travel document if that person can show that they have made reasonable attempts to obtain a national passport or identity document and there are compelling reasons for travel.

Part 13: deportation

Deportation (paragraphs A362 to 400).

A deportation order

A362. Where Article 8 is raised in the context of deportation under Part 13 of these Rules, the claim under Article 8 will only succeed where the requirements of these rules as at 28 July 2014 are met, regardless of when the notice of intention to deport or the deportation order, as appropriate, was served.

362. A deportation order requires the subject to leave the United Kingdom and authorises his detention until he is removed. It also prohibits him from re-entering the country for as long as it is in force and invalidates any leave to enter or remain in the United Kingdom given him before the Order is made or while it is in force.

363. The circumstances in which a person is liable to deportation include:

(i)   where the Secretary of State deems the person's deportation to be conducive to the public good;

(ii)   where the person is the spouse or civil partner or child under 18 of a person ordered to be deported; and

(iii) where a court recommends deportation in the case of a person over the age of 17 who has been convicted of an offence punishable with imprisonment.

363A. Prior to 2 October 2000, a person would have been liable to deportation in certain circumstances in which he is now liable to administrative removal. However, such a person remains liable to deportation, rather than administrative removal where:

(i)   a decision to make a deportation order against him was taken before 2 October 2000; or

(ii)   the person has made a valid application under the Immigration (Regularisation Period for Overstayers) Regulations 2000.

Deportation of family members

364. DELETED

364A. DELETED

365. Section 5 of the Immigration Act 1971 gives the Secretary of State power in certain circumstances to make a deportation order against the spouse, civil partner or child of a person against whom a deportation order has been made. The Secretary of State will not normally decide to deport the spouse or civil partner of a deportee under section 5 of the Immigration Act 1971 where:

(i)   he has qualified for settlement in his own right; or

(ii)   he has been living apart from the deportee.

366. The Secretary of State will not normally decide to deport the child of a deportee "under section 5 of the Immigration Act 1971 where:

(i)   he and his mother or father are living apart from the deportee; or

(ii)   he has left home and established himself on an independent basis; or

(iii) he married or formed a civil partnership before deportation came into prospect.

367. DELETED

368. DELETED

Right of appeal against destination

369. DELETED

Restricted right of appeal against deportation in cases of breach of limited leave

370. DELETED

Exemption to the restricted right of appeal

371. DELETED

372. DELETED

A deportation order made on the recommendation of a Court

373. DELETED

Where deportation is deemed to be conducive to the public good

374. DELETED
375. DELETED

Hearing of appeals

376. DELETED
377. DELETED
378. DELETED

Persons who have claimed asylum

379. DELETED
379A. DELETED
380. DELETED

Procedure

381. When a decision to make a deportation order has been taken (otherwise than on the recommendation of a court) a notice will be given to the person concerned informing him of the decision.

382. Following the issue of such a notice the Secretary of State may authorise detention or make an order restricting a person as to residence, employment or occupation and requiring him to report to the police, pending the making of a deportation order.

383. DELETED
384. DELETED

Arrangements for removal

385. A person against whom a deportation order has been made will normally be removed from the United Kingdom. The power is to be exercised so as to secure the person's return to the country of which he is a national, or which has most recently provided him with a travel document, unless he can show that another country will receive him. In considering any departure from the normal arrangements, regard will be had to the public interest generally, and to any additional expense that may fall on public funds.

386. DELETED

Supervised departure

387. DELETED

Returned deportees

388. Where a person returns to the UK when a deportation order is in force against him, he may be deported under the original order. The Secretary of State will consider every such case in the light of all the relevant circumstances before deciding whether to enforce the order.

Returned family members

389. Persons deported in the circumstances set out in paragraphs 365-368 above (deportation of family members) may be able to seek re-admission to the United Kingdom under the Immigration Rules where:

    (i)   a child reaches 18 (when he ceases to be subject to the deportation order); or

    (ii)   in the case of a spouse or civil partner, the marriage or civil partnership comes to an end.

Revocation of deportation order

390. An application for revocation of a deportation order will be considered in the light of all the circumstances including the following:

    (i)   the grounds on which the order was made;

    (ii)   any representations made in support of revocation;

    (iii) the interests of the community, including the maintenance of an effective immigration control;

    (iv)   the interests of the applicant, including any compassionate circumstances.

390A. Where paragraph 398 applies the Secretary of State will consider whether paragraph 399 or 399A applies and, if it does not, it will only be in exceptional circumstances that the public interest in maintaining the deportation order will be outweighed by other factors.

391.   In the case of a person who has been deported following conviction for a criminal offence, the continuation of a deportation order against that person will be the proper course:

   (a)   in the case of a conviction for an offence for which the person was sentenced to a period of imprisonment of less than 4 years, unless 10 years have elapsed since the making of the deportation order when, if an application for revocation is received, consideration will be given on a case by case basis to whether the deportation order should be maintained, or

   (b)   in the case of a conviction for an offence for which the person was sentenced to a period of imprisonment of at least 4 years, at any time,

   Unless, in either case, the continuation would be contrary to the Human Rights Convention or the Convention and Protocol Relating to the Status of Refugees, or there are other exceptional circumstances that mean the continuation is outweighed by compelling factors.

391A. In other cases, revocation of the order will not normally be authorised unless the situation has been materially altered, either by a change of circumstances since the order was made, or by fresh information coming to light which was not before the appellate authorities or the Secretary of State. The passage of time since the person was deported may also in itself amount to such a change of circumstances as to warrant revocation of the order.

392.   Revocation of a deportation order does not entitle the person concerned to re-enter the United Kingdom; it renders him eligible to apply for admission under the Immigration Rules. Application for revocation of the order may be made to the Entry Clearance Officer or direct to the Home Office.

Rights of appeal in relation to a decision not to revoke a deportation order

393.   DELETED

394.   DELETED

395.   DELETED

396.   Where a person is liable to deportation the presumption shall be that the public interest requires deportation. It is in the public interest to deport where the Secretary of State must make a deportation order in accordance with section 32 of the UK Borders Act 2007.

397.   A deportation order will not be made if the person's removal pursuant to the order would be contrary to the UK's obligations under the Refugee Convention or the Human Rights Convention. Where deportation would not be contrary to these obligations, it will only be in exceptional circumstances that the public interest in deportation is outweighed.

Deportation and Article 8

A398. These rules apply where:

   (a)   a foreign criminal liable to deportation claims that his deportation would be contrary to the United Kingdom's obligations under Article 8 of the Human Rights Convention;

   (b)   a foreign criminal applies for a deportation order made against him to be revoked.

398.   Where a person claims that their deportation would be contrary to the UK's obligations under Article 8 of the Human Rights Convention, and

   (a)   the deportation of the person from the UK is conducive to the public good and in the public interest because they have been convicted of an offence for which they have been sentenced to a period of imprisonment of at least 4 years;

   (b)   the deportation of the person from the UK is conducive to the public good and in the public interest because they have been convicted of an offence for which they have been sentenced to a period of imprisonment of less than 4 years but at least 12 months; or

   (c)   the deportation of the person from the UK is conducive to the public good and in the public interest because, in the view of the Secretary of State, their offending has caused serious harm or they are a persistent offender who shows a particular disregard for the law, the Secretary of State in assessing that claim will consider whether paragraph 399 or 399A applies and, if it does not, the public interest in deportation will only be outweighed by other factors where there are very compelling circumstances over and above those described in paragraphs 399 and 399A.

399.   This paragraph applies where paragraph 398 (b) or (c) applies if –

   (a)   the person has a genuine and subsisting parental relationship with a child under the age of 18 years who is in the UK, and

      (i)   the child is a British Citizen; or

(ii)   the child has lived in the UK continuously for at least the 7 years immediately preceding the date of the immigration decision; and in either case

    (a)   it would be unduly harsh for the child to live in the country to which the person is to be deported; and

    (b)   it would be unduly harsh for the child to remain in the UK without the person who is to be deported; or

(b)   the person has a genuine and subsisting relationship with a partner who is in the UK and is a British Citizen or settled in the UK, and

    (i)   the relationship was formed at a time when the person (deportee) was in the UK lawfully and their immigration status was not precarious; and

    (ii)   it would be unduly harsh for that partner to live in the country to which the person is to be deported, because of compelling circumstances over and above those described in paragraph EX.2. of Appendix FM; and

    (iii)   it would be unduly harsh for that partner to remain in the UK without the person who is to be deported.

399A.   This paragraph applies where paragraph 398(b) or (c) applies if –

(a)   the person has been lawfully resident in the UK for most of his life; and

(b)   he is socially and culturally integrated in the UK; and

(c)   there would be very significant obstacles to his integration into the country to which it is proposed he is deported.

399B.   Where an Article 8 claim from a foreign criminal is successful:

(a)   in the case of a person who is in the UK unlawfully or whose leave to enter or remain has been cancelled by a deportation order, limited leave may be granted for periods not exceeding 30 months and subject to such conditions as the Secretary of State considers appropriate;

(b)   in the case of a person who has not been served with a deportation order, any limited leave to enter or remain may be curtailed to a period not exceeding 30 months and conditions may be varied to such conditions as the Secretary of State considers appropriate;

(c)   indefinite leave to enter or remain may be revoked under section 76 of the 2002 Act and limited leave to enter or remain granted for a period not exceeding 30 months subject to such conditions as the Secretary of State considers appropriate;

(d)   revocation of a deportation order does not confer entry clearance or leave to enter or remain or re-instate any previous leave.

399C.   Where a foreign criminal who has previously been granted a period of limited leave under this Part applies for further limited leave or indefinite leave to remain his deportation remains conducive to the public good and in the public interest notwithstanding the previous grant of leave.

399D.   Where a foreign criminal has been deported and enters the United Kingdom in breach of a deportation order enforcement of the deportation order is in the public interest and will be implemented unless there are very exceptional circumstances.

400.   Where a person claims that their removal under paragraphs 8 to 10 of Schedule 2 to the Immigration Act 1971, section 10 of the Immigration and Asylum Act 1999 or section 47 of the Immigration, Asylum and Nationality Act 2006 would be contrary to the UK's obligations under Article 8 of the Human Rights Convention, the Secretary of State may require an application under paragraph 276ADE(1) (private life) or under paragraphs R-LTRP.1.1.(a), (b) and (d), R-LTRPT.1.1.(a), (b) and (d) and EX.1. of Appendix FM (family life as a partner or parent) of these rules. Where an application is not required, in assessing that claim the Secretary of State or an immigration officer will, subject to paragraph 353, consider that claim against the requirements to be met (except the requirement to make a valid application) under paragraph 276ADE(1) (private life) or paragraphs R-LTRP.1.1.(a), (b) and (d), R-LTRPT.1.1.(a), (b) and (d) and EX.1. of Appendix FM (family life as a partner or parent) of these rules as appropriate and if appropriate the removal decision will be cancelled.

Appendix 2: police registration

Countries or territories whose nationals or citizens are relevant foreign nationals for the purposes of Part 10 of these Rules

Registration with the police

Afghanistan
Algeria
Argentina
Armenia
Azerbaijan
Bahrain
Belarus
Bolivia
Brazil
China
Colombia
Cuba
Egypt
Georgia
Iran
Iraq
Israel
Jordan
Kazakhstan
Kuwait
Kyrgyzstan
Lebanon
Libya
Moldova
Morocco
North Korea
Oman
Palestine
Peru
Qatar
Russia
Saudi Arabia
Sudan
Syria
Tajikistan
Tunisia
Turkey
Turkmenistan
United Arab Emirates
Ukraine
Uzbekistan
Yemen

Appendix ATAS: Academic Technology Approval Scheme (ATAS)

Immigration Rules Appendix ATAS: Academic Technology Approval Scheme (ATAS)

ATAS seeks to prevent the transfer of information, knowledge or technology which could develop, advance or support an Advanced Conventional Military Technology (ACMT) and Weapons of Mass Destruction (WMD) programme or their means of delivery.

The ATAS requirement means the applicant must obtain a valid ATAS certificate, issued by the Counter-Proliferation and Arms Control Centre, and to provide it with an application on Student, Skilled Worker, ICT, T5 International Agreement and Government Authorised Exchange routes to study or work as a researcher in any of the specified subjects listed in this Appendix.

The ATAS condition means that someone must obtain a valid ATAS certificate prior to commencing study or research in any of the specified subjects or fields of research.

A person is subject to the ATAS condition if they have been granted permission which allows study or work subject to the ATAS condition.

A person is exempt from the ATAS requirement and ATAS condition if they are a national of one of the countries listed in this Appendix.

ATAS requirement

ATAS 1.1.   An applicant (who is not a national of a country listed at ATAS 3.1.) requires a valid ATAS certificate if the course of study for which the Confirmation of Acceptance for Studies was assigned is a subject set out at ATAS 4.1. which:

(a)   leads to a master's degree; or

(b)   leads to a PhD; or

(c)   leads to another postgraduate qualification; or

(d)   is a period of study or research which is part of an overseas postgraduate qualification.

ATAS 1.2.   An applicant (who is not a national of a country listed at ATAS 3.1.) requires a valid ATAS certificate if they are applying in a work route which requires a Certificate of Sponsorship, that Certificate of Sponsorship is issued by a work sponsor that is also a licensed student sponsor, and the role set out in the Certificate of Sponsorship:

(a)   is in one of the following occupation codes:

- 2111 Chemical scientists
- 2112 Biological scientists and biochemists
- 2113 Physical scientists
- 2114 Social and humanities scientists
- 2119 Natural and social science professionals not elsewhere classified
- 2150 Research and development managers
- 2122 Mechanical engineers
- 2123 Electrical engineers
- 2124 Electronics engineers
- 2127 Production and process engineers
- 2129 Engineering professionals not elsewhere classified
- 2311 Higher education teaching professionals;
- 3111 Laboratory technicians
- 3112 Electrical and electronics technicians
- 3113 Engineering technicians
- 3114 Building and civil engineering technicians
- 5235 Aircraft maintenance and related trades

(b)   includes an element of research at PhD level or above; and

(c)   that field of research is a subject set out at ATAS 4.1

ATAS 1.3.   The applicant must provide a print-out of the valid ATAS certificate for the course of study or research role to show that the ATAS requirement is met.

ATAS condition

ATAS 2.1. The ATAS condition means the person (who is not a national of a country listed at ATAS 3.1), must have a valid ATAS certificate before commencing study (unless they are a student continuing a course of study and they have made, or intend to make within the required time period, an application required by ATAS 2.2) or research in a subject listed at ATAS 4.1 which:

(a)   leads to a UK postgraduate degree; or

(b)   leads to another postgraduate qualification; or

(c)   is a period of study which is part of an overseas postgraduate qualification; or

(d)   is research as part of a course of postgraduate study, employment or academic activity at a licensed student sponsor.

ATAS 2.2. A Student who intends to continue study on a course of study which is subject to the ATAS requirement must apply for a new ATAS certificate where:

(a)   the completion date of the course of study has changed and will be delayed by more than 3 months; or

(b)   the course contents or research proposal of the course of study change,

and the application for a new certificate must be made within 28 days of the change in (a) or (b) above being known to the Student.

Nationals who are exempt from the ATAS requirement and condition

ATAS 3.1. A person does not need to meet the ATAS requirement, and will not be subject to the ATAS condition, if they are a national of any of the following countries:

Australia

Austria

Belgium

Bulgaria

Canada

Croatia

Republic of Cyprus

Czech Republic

Denmark

Estonia

Finland

France

Germany

Greece

Hungary

Iceland

Ireland

Italy

Japan

Latvia

Liechtenstein

Lithuania

Luxembourg

Malta

Netherlands

New Zealand

Norway

Poland

Portugal

Republic of Korea

Romania

Singapore

Slovakia

Slovenia

Spain

Sweden

Switzerland

United States of America

Academic Subjects relevant to ATAS

ATAS 4.1.   The ATAS requirement and ATAS condition apply to the following subjects:

(a)   research, or doctorates or master's by research in:

Subjects allied to Medicine:

CAH codes:

CAH02-02-01 - Pharmacology

CAH02-02-02 - Toxicology

CAH02-02-03 - Pharmacy

CAH10-01-06 - Bioengineering, Medical and Biomedical Engineering

CAH02-05-03 - Others in subjects allied to Medicine

Biological Sciences:

CAH codes:

CAH03-01-02 - Biology (non-specific)

CAH03-01-03 - Ecology and Environmental Biology

CAH03-01-06 - Zoology

CAH03-01-04 - Microbiology and Cell Science

CAH03-01-05 - Plant Sciences

CAH10-03-05 - Biotechnology

CAH03-01-07 - Genetics

CAH02-05-03 - Biomedical Sciences (non-specific)

CAH03-01-08 - Molecular Biology, Biophysics and Biochemistry

CAH03-01-01 - Biosciences (non-specific)

CAH03-01-10 - Others in Biological Sciences

Veterinary Sciences, Agriculture and related subjects:

CAH codes:

CAH05-01-02 - Others in Veterinary Sciences

CAH06-01-02 - Agricultural sciences

Physical Sciences:

CAH codes:

CAH07-02-01 - Chemistry

CAH10-03-07 - Materials Science

CAH07-01-01 - Physics

CAH07-01-02 - Astronomy

CAH26-01-05 - Others in Geographical Studies

CAH07-04-01 - Physical Sciences (non-specific)

CAH07-04-03 - Sciences (non-specific)

CAH07-04-04 - Natural Sciences (non-specific)

Mathematical and Computer Sciences:

CAH codes:

CAH09-01-01 - Mathematics

CAH09-01-02 - Operational Research

CAH11-01-01 - Computer Science

CAH11-01-02 - Information Technology

CAH11-01-03 - Information Systems

CAH11-01-04 - Software Engineering

CAH11-01-05 - Artificial Intelligence

Engineering:

CAH codes:

CAH10-01-01 - Engineering (non-specific)

CAH10-01-07 - Civil Engineering

CAH10-01-02 - Mechanical Engineering

CAH10-01-04 - Aeronautical and Aerospace Engineering

CAH10-01-05 - Naval Architecture

CAH10-01-08 - Electrical and Electronic Engineering

CAH10-01-09 - Chemical, Process and Energy Engineering

Technologies:

CAH codes:

CAH10-03-03 - Polymers and Textiles

CAH10-03-01 - Minerals Technology

CAH10-03-02 - Materials Technology

CAH10-03-04 - Maritime Technology

(b)   taught master's in:

CAH codes:

CAH10-03-07 - Materials Science

CAH07-01-01 - Physics (including Nuclear Physics)

CAH10-01-02 - Mechanical Engineering

CAH10-01-04 - Aeronautical and Aerospace Engineering

CAH10-01-09 - Chemical, Process and Energy Engineering

CAH10-03-01 - Minerals Technology

CAH10-03-02 - Materials Technology

Appendix English Language

This Appendix sets out how the English language requirement is met.

It applies only to applications under Appendix Student, Appendix Skilled Worker, Appendix Representative of an Overseas Business, Appendix T2 Minister of Religion, Appendix International Sportsperson, Appendix UK Ancestry, Appendix Global Talent, Appendix Start-up, Appendix Innovator, Appendix Temporary Work - International Agreement, Appendix Domestic Worker in a Private Household and Appendix Hong Kong British National (Overseas).

The route sets out whether the English language requirement must be met and at what level.

Exemption

EL 1.1.   An applicant for settlement is exempt from the English language requirement if at the date of application:

    (a)   they are aged 65 or over; or

    (b)   they are aged under 18; or

    (c)   they have a disability (physical or mental condition) which prevents them from meeting the requirement.

How the requirement is met

EL 2.1.   The English language requirement is met if any of the requirements in EL 3 to EL 6 are met.

EL 2.2.   The English language requirement is also met by a person applying for entry clearance or permission to stay as a Student if any of the requirements in EL 7.1. to EL 8.4. are met.

EL 2.3.   The English language requirement is also met by a person applying for entry clearance or permission to stay as a Skilled Worker route if:

    (a)   the requirements in EL 7.1. and EL 7.2. are met: or

    (b)   the requirement in EL 9.1. is met.

EL 2.4.   The English language requirement is also met by a person applying for entry clearance or permission to stay on the Start-up route, or for entry clearance, permission to stay or settlement on the Innovator route if the requirements in EL 7.1 and EL 7.2. are met.

EL 2.5.   The English language requirement is also met by a dependent partner or dependent child applying for settlement if they meet the requirements in paragraph 3.2. of Appendix KOLL.

Met in a previous application

EL 3.1.   An applicant will meet the English language requirement if they have already shown they met the requirement, at the level required for their current application, in a previous successful application for entry clearance or permission to stay.

Majority English speaking country

EL 4.1.   An applicant will meet the English language requirement if they are a national of any of the following majority-English-speaking countries:

Antigua and Barbuda

Australia

The Bahamas

Barbados

Belize

Canada

Dominica

Grenada

Guyana

Jamaica

Malta

New Zealand

St Kitts and Nevis

St Lucia

St Vincent and the Grenadines

Trinidad and Tobago

United States of America

Academic qualification

EL 5.1. An applicant will meet the English language requirement if they have an academic qualification which meets one of the requirements at EL 5.2. and is proven by the required evidence under EL 5.3. or EL 5.4.

EL 5.2. The requirements are that the applicant has:

(a)   a bachelor's degree, master's degree or doctorate awarded in the UK; or

(b)   a degree or degree-level qualification taught in a university or college in a majority- English-speaking country listed in EL 4.1. (except Canada), or Ireland, which meets or exceeds the recognised standard of a bachelor's degree, master's degree or doctorate awarded in the UK; or

(c)   a degree or degree level qualification which meets, or exceeds, the recognised standard of a UK bachelor's degree; master's degree or doctorate and was taught or researched in English.

EL 5.3. The requirement at EL 5.2. must be proven by one of:

(a)   a certificate from the awarding body: or

(b)   a transcript issued by the university or college that awarded the qualification; or

(c)   an official letter from the university or college that awarded the qualification containing information equivalent to a degree certificate.

EL 5.4. If the qualification was awarded by a body from outside the UK, the requirement at EL 5.2. must, in addition to the requirement at EL 5.3, be proven by confirmation from Ecctis that the qualification meets the requirements at EL 5.2(b) or EL 5.2(c).

English language test

EL 6.1. An applicant will meet the English language requirement if they have provided a valid digital reference number from an approved provider showing they have passed an approved English language test to the required level in the two years before the date of application.

The list of approved tests and providers, updated from time to time, can be found at https://www.gov.uk/ uidance/prove-your-english-language-abilitieswith-a-secure-english-language-test-selt#approved-test-providers-andapproved-tests.

GCSE or A Level English

EL 7.1. An applicant applying for entry clearance or permission to stay under Appendix Student, Appendix Skilled Worker, Appendix Start-up or Appendix Innovator will meet the English language requirement if they have a GCSE, A level, Scottish National Qualification at level 4 or 5 or, Scottish Higher or Advanced Higher, in English (language or literature), that was awarded:

(a)   by an Ofqual (or SQA, Qualifications Wales or CCEA) regulated awarding body; and

(b)   following education undertaken in a UK based school which began while they were aged under 18.

EL 7.2. The requirement at EL 7.1. must be proven by either:

(a)   a certificate from the awarding body: or

(b)   an official transcript issued by the awarding body

Additional ways Students can meet the English language requirement

EL 8.1. An applicant under Appendix Student will meet the English language requirement if they are applying for a course of study at degree level or above and are sponsored by a higher education provider with a track record of compliance who states on the Confirmation of Acceptance for Studies that they have assessed the applicant's English language ability and how they have assessed it.

EL 8.2. Where an assessment under EL 8.1. has been carried out the Confirmation of Acceptance for Studies entry must confirm that the applicant has a knowledge of English equivalent to level B2, or above, of the Council of Europe's Common European Framework for Language Learning in all 4 components (reading, writing, speaking and listening) or that the requirement at ST 15.3. is met.

EL 8.3. An applicant under Appendix Student will meet the English language requirement if they have taken an approved English test and been exempted from a component of that test by the test provider due to a disability, and the student sponsor has confirmed that they are satisfied the English language ability of the applicant is sufficient to undertake the course of study.

EL 8.4.   An applicant under Appendix Student will meet the English language requirement if they are applying for a short-term study abroad programme of up to six months and both:

(a)   the study abroad programme is part of a course of study at degree level or above at an overseas higher education institution in the United States of America; and

(b)   Ecctis confirm that the course of study overseas will lead to an academic (not a professional or vocational) qualification at UK bachelor's degree level or above.

Professional regulation for Skilled Workers

EL 9.1.   An applicant applying for entry clearance or permission to stay under Appendix Skilled Worker will meet the English language requirement if they are being sponsored to work as a doctor, dentist, nurse, midwife or veterinarian, and have passed an English Language assessment which is accepted by the relevant regulated professional body as a requirement for registration.

Appendix FM: family members

Family members

General

Section GEN: General

Purpose

GEN.1.1. This route is for those seeking to enter or remain in the UK on the basis of their family life with a person who is a British Citizen, is settled in the UK, is in the UK with limited leave as a refugee or person granted humanitarian protection (and the applicant cannot seek leave to enter or remain in the UK as their family member under Part 11 of these rules), is in the UK with limited leave under Appendix EU, or is in the UK with limited leave as a worker or business person by virtue of either Appendix ECAA Extension of Stay or under the provisions of the relevant 1973 Immigration Rules (or Decision 1/80) that underpinned the European Community Association Agreement (ECAA) with Turkey prior to 1 January 2021. It sets out the requirements to be met and, in considering applications under this route, it reflects how, under Article 8 of the Human Rights Convention, the balance will be struck between the right to respect for private and family life and the legitimate aims of protecting national security, public safety and the economic well-being of the UK; the prevention of disorder and crime; the protection of health or morals; and the protection of the rights and freedoms of others (and in doing so also reflects the relevant public interest considerations as set out in Part 5A of the Nationality, Immigration and Asylum Act 2002). It also takes into account the need to safeguard and promote the welfare of children in the UK, in line with the Secretary of State's duty under section 55 of the Borders, Citizenship and Immigration Act 2009.

Definitions

GEN.1.2. For the purposes of this Appendix "partner" means-

(i) the applicant's spouse;

(ii) the applicant's civil partner;

(iii) the applicant's fiancé(e) or proposed civil partner; or

(iv) a person who has been living together with the applicant in a relationship akin to a marriage or civil partnership for at least two years prior to the date of application, unless a different meaning of partner applies elsewhere in this Appendix.

GEN.1.3. For the purposes of this Appendix

(a) "application for leave to remain" also includes an application for variation of leave to enter or remain by a person in the UK;

(b) references to a person being present and settled in the UK also include a person who is being admitted for settlement on the same occasion as the applicant;

(c) references to a British Citizen in the UK also include a British Citizen who is coming to the UK with the applicant as their partner or parent;

(d) references to a person being "in the UK with limited leave under Appendix EU" mean an EEA national in the UK who holds valid limited leave to enter or remain granted under paragraph EU3 of Appendix EU to these Rules on the basis of meeting condition 1 in paragraph EU14 of that Appendix; and

(e) references to a person being "in the UK with limited leave as a worker or business person under Appendix ECAA Extension of Stay" mean a person granted such leave by virtue of either Appendix ECAA Extension of Stay or under the provisions of the relevant 1973 Immigration Rules (or Decision 1/80) that underpinned the European Community Association Agreement (ECAA) with Turkey prior to 1 January 2021.

GEN.1.4. In this Appendix "specified" means specified in Appendix FM-SE, unless otherwise stated.

GEN.1.5. If the Entry Clearance Officer, or Secretary of State, has reasonable cause to doubt the genuineness of any document submitted in support of an application, and having taken reasonable steps to verify the document, is unable to verify that it is genuine, the document will be discounted for the purposes of the application.

GEN.1.6. For the purposes of paragraph E-ECP.4.1.(a); E-LTRP.4.1.(a); E-LTRP.4.1A.(a); E-ECPT. 4.1(a); E-LTRPT.5.1.(a); and E-LTRPT.5.1A.(a) the applicant must be a national of Antigua and Barbuda; Australia; the Bahamas; Barbados; Belize; Canada; Dominica; Grenada; Guyana; Jamaica; Malta; New Zealand; St Kitts and Nevis; St Lucia; St Vincent and the Grenadines; Trinidad and Tobago; or the United States of America.

GEN.1.7.   In this Appendix references to paragraphs are to paragraphs of this Appendix unless the context otherwise requires.

GEN.1.8.   Paragraphs 277-280, 289AA, 295AA and 296 of Part 8 of these Rules shall apply to this Appendix.

GEN.1.9.   In this Appendix:

    (a)   the requirement to make a valid application will not apply when the Article 8 claim is raised:

        (i)   as part of an asylum claim, or as part of a further submission in person after an asylum claim has been refused;

        (ii)   where a migrant is in immigration detention. A migrant in immigration detention or their representative must submit any application or claim raising Article 8 to a prison officer, a prisoner custody officer, a detainee custody officer or a member of Home Office staff at the migrant's place of detention; or

        (iii)   in an appeal (subject to the consent of the Secretary of State where applicable); and

    (b)   where an application or claim raising Article 8 is made in any of the circumstances specified in paragraph GEN.1.9.(a), or is considered by the Secretary of State under paragraph A277C of these rules, the requirements of paragraphs R-LTRP.1.1.(c) and R-LTRPT.1.1.(c) are not met.

GEN.1.10.   Where paragraph GEN.3.1.(2) or GEN.3.2.(3) applies, and the applicant is granted entry clearance or leave to enter or remain under, as appropriate, paragraph D-ECP.1.2., D-LTRP.1.2., D-ECC.1.1., D-LTRC.1.1., D-ECPT.1.2. or D-LTRPT.1.2., that grant of entry clearance or leave to enter or remain will be subject to a condition of no recourse to public funds unless the decision-maker considers, with reference to paragraph GEN.1.11A., that the applicant should not be subject to such a condition.

GEN.1.11.   Where entry clearance or leave to enter or remain is granted under this Appendix (and without prejudice to the specific provision that is made in this Appendix in respect of a no recourse to public funds condition), that leave may be subject to such conditions as the decision-maker considers appropriate in a particular case.

GEN.1.11A   Where entry clearance or leave to remain as a partner, child or parent is granted under paragraph D-ECP.1.2.,
.   D-LTRP.1.2., D-ECC.1.1., D-LTRC.1.1., D-ECPT.1.2. or D-LTRPT.1.2., it will normally be granted subject to a condition of no recourse to public funds, unless the applicant has provided the decision-maker with:

    (a)   satisfactory evidence that the applicant is destitute as defined in section 95 of the Immigration and Asylum Act 1999; or

    (b)   satisfactory evidence that there are particularly compelling reasons relating to the welfare of a child of a parent in receipt of a very low income.

GEN.1.12.   In this Appendix, "decision-maker" refers, as the case may be, to the Secretary of State, an Immigration Officer or an Entry Clearance Officer.

GEN.1.13.   For the purposes of paragraphs D-LTRP.1.1., D-LTRP.1.2., DILRP.1.2., D-LTRPT.1.1., D-LTRPT.1.2. and D-ILRPT.1.2. (excluding a grant of limited leave to remain as a fiancé(e) or proposed civil partner), where at the date of application the applicant has extant leave as a partner or parent (as applicable) granted under this Appendix, the remaining period of that extant leave up to a maximum of 28 days will be added to the period of limited leave to remain granted under that paragraph (which may therefore exceed 30 months).

GEN.1.14.   Where a person aged 18 or over is granted entry clearance or limited leave to enter or remain under this Appendix, or where a person granted such entry clearance or limited leave to enter or remain will be aged 18 before that period of entry clearance or limited leave expires, the entry clearance or leave will, in addition to any other conditions which may apply, be granted subject to the conditions in Appendix ATAS of these rules.

GEN.1.15.   Where, pursuant to paragraph D-ILRP.1.2., D-ILRP.1.3., D-ILRPT.1.2. or D-ILRPT.1.3., a person who has made an application for indefinite leave to remain under this Appendix does not meet the requirements for indefinite leave to remain but falls to be granted limited leave to remain under those provisions or paragraphs 276ADE(1) to 276DH:

    (a)   The Secretary of State will treat that application for indefinite leave to remain as an application for limited leave to remain;

    (b)   The Secretary of State will notify the applicant in writing of any requirement to pay an immigration health charge under the Immigration (Health Charge) Order 2015; and

    (c)   If there is such a requirement and that requirement is not met, the application for limited leave to remain will be invalid and the Secretary of State will not refund any application fee paid in respect of the application for indefinite leave to remain.

GEN.1.16.   Where an application or claim raising Article 8 is considered under Appendix FM and EX.1. applies, the requirements of paragraphs R-LTRP.1.1.(c) and R-LTRPT.1.1.(c) are not met.

Leave to enter

GEN.2.1.   Subject to paragraph GEN.2.3., the requirements to be met by a person seeking leave to enter the UK under this route are that the person-

(a)   must have a valid entry clearance for entry under this route; and

(b)   must produce to the Immigration Officer on arrival a valid national passport or other document satisfactorily establishing their identity and nationality.

GEN.2.2.   If a person does not meet the requirements of paragraph GEN.2.1. entry will be refused.

GEN.2.3.   (1)   Where an applicant for leave to enter the UK remains in the UK on immigration bail and the requirements of sub-paragraph (2) are met, paragraph GEN.1.10., D-LTRP.1.2., D-LTRC.1.1. or D-LTRPT.1.2. (as appropriate) will apply, as if paragraph D-LTRP.1.2., D-LTRC.1.1. or D-LTRPT.1.2. (where relevant) provided for the granting of leave to enter not leave to remain (and except that the references to leave to remain and limited leave to remain are to be read as leave to enter).

(2)   The requirements of this sub-paragraph are met where:

(a)   the applicant satisfies the requirements in paragraph R-LTRP.1.1.(a), (b) and (d), paragraph R-LTRC.1.1.(a), (b) and (d) or paragraph R-LTRPT.1.1.(a), (b) and (d), as if those were requirements for leave to enter not leave to remain (and except that the references to leave to remain and indefinite leave to remain are to be read as leave to enter); or

(b)   a parent of the applicant has been granted leave to enter in accordance with this paragraph and the applicant satisfies the requirements in paragraph R-LTRC.1.1.(a), (b) and (d), as if those were requirements for leave to enter not leave to remain and as if paragraph R-LTRC.1.1.(d)(iii) referred to a parent of the applicant being or having been granted leave to enter in accordance with this paragraph (and except that the references to leave to remain are to be read as leave to enter).

Exceptional circumstances

GEN.3.1.   (1)   Where:

(a)   the financial requirement in paragraph E-ECP.3.1., E-LTRP.3.1. (in the context of an application for limited leave to remain as a partner), E-ECC.2.1. or E-LTRC.2.1. applies, and is not met from the specified sources referred to in the relevant paragraph; and

(b)   it is evident from the information provided by the applicant that there are exceptional circumstances which could render refusal of entry clearance or leave to remain a breach of Article 8 of the European Convention on Human Rights, because such refusal could result in unjustifiably harsh consequences for the applicant, their partner or a relevant child; then

the decision-maker must consider whether such financial requirement is met through taking into account the sources of income, financial support or funds set out in paragraph 21A(2) of Appendix FM-SE (subject to the considerations in sub-paragraphs (3) to (8) of that paragraph).

(2)   Where the financial requirement in paragraph E-ECP.3.1., E-LTRP.3.1. (in the context of an application for limited leave to remain as a partner), E-ECC.2.1. or E-LTRC.2.1. is met following consideration under sub-paragraph (1) (and provided that the other relevant requirements of the Immigration Rules are also met), the applicant will be granted entry clearance or leave to remain under, as appropriate, paragraph D-ECP.1.2., D-LTRP.1.2., D-ECC.1.1. or D-LTRC.1.1. or paragraph 315 or 316B of the Immigration Rules.

GEN.3.2.   (1)   Subject to sub-paragraph (4), where an application for entry clearance or leave to enter or remain made under this Appendix, or an application for leave to remain which has otherwise been considered under this Appendix, does not otherwise meet the requirements of this Appendix or Part 9 of the Rules, the decision-maker must consider whether the circumstances in sub-paragraph (2) apply.

(2)   Where sub-paragraph (1) above applies, the decision-maker must consider, on the basis of the information provided by the applicant, whether there are exceptional circumstances which would render refusal of entry clearance, or leave to enter or remain, a breach of Article 8 of the European Convention on Human Rights, because such refusal would result in unjustifiably harsh consequences for the applicant, their partner, a relevant child or another family member whose Article 8 rights it is evident from that information would be affected by a decision to refuse the application.

(3)   Where the exceptional circumstances referred to in sub-paragraph (2) above apply, the applicant will be granted entry clearance or leave to enter or remain under, as appropriate, paragraph D-ECP.1.2., D-LTRP.1.2., D-ECC.1.1., D-LTRC.1.1., D-ECPT.1.2., D-LTRPT.1.2., D-ECDR.1.1. or D-ECDR.1.2.

(4)   This paragraph does not apply in the context of applications made under section BPILR or DVILR.

GEN.3.3.   (1)   In considering an application for entry clearance or leave to enter or remain where paragraph GEN.3.1. or GEN.3.2. applies, the decision-maker must take into account, as a primary consideration, the best interests of any relevant child.

(2)   In paragraphs GEN.3.1. and GEN.3.2., and this paragraph, "relevant child" means a person who:

(a)   is under the age of 18 years at the date of the application; and

(b)   it is evident from the information provided by the applicant would be affected by a decision to refuse the application.

Family life with a partner

Section EC-P: Entry clearance as a partner

EC-P.1.1.   The requirements to be met for entry clearance as a partner are that-

(a)   the applicant must be outside the UK;

(b)   the applicant must have made a valid application for entry clearance as a partner;

(c)   the applicant must not fall for refusal under any of the grounds in Section S-EC: Suitability–entry clearance; and

(d)   the applicant must meet all of the requirements of Section E-ECP: Eligibility for entry clearance as a partner.

Section S-EC: Suitability-entry clearance

S-EC.1.1.   The applicant will be refused entry clearance on grounds of suitability if any of paragraphs S-EC.1.2. to 1.9. apply.

S-EC.1.2.   The Secretary of State has personally directed that the exclusion of the applicant from the UK is conducive to the public good.

S-EC.1.3.   The applicant is currently the subject of a deportation order.

S-EC.1.4.   The exclusion of the applicant from the UK is conducive to the public good because they have:

(a) been convicted of an offence for which they have been sentenced to a period of imprisonment of at least 4 years; or

(b)   been convicted of an offence for which they have been sentenced to a period of imprisonment of at least 12 months but less than 4 years, unless a period of 10 years has passed since the end of the sentence; or

(c)   been convicted of an offence for which they have been sentenced to a period of imprisonment of less than 12 months, unless a period of 5 years has passed since the end of the sentence.

S-EC.1.5.   The exclusion of the applicant from the UK is conducive to the public good because, for example, the applicant's conduct (including convictions which do not fall within paragraph S-EC.1.4.), character, associations, or other reasons, make it undesirable to grant them entry clearance.

S-EC.1.6.   The applicant has failed without reasonable excuse to comply with a requirement to-

(a)   attend an interview;

(b)   provide information;

(c)   provide physical data; or

(d)   undergo a medical examination or provide a medical report.

S-EC.1.7.   It is undesirable to grant entry clearance to the applicant for medical reasons.

S-EC.1.8.   The applicant left or was removed from the UK as a condition of a caution issued in accordance with section 22 of the Criminal Justice Act 2003 less than 5 years prior to the date on which the application is decided.

S-EC.1.9.   The Secretary of State considers that the applicant's parent or parent's partner poses a risk to the applicant. That person may be considered to pose a risk to the applicant if, for example, they - –

(a)   have a conviction as an adult, whether in the UK or overseas, for an offence against a child;

(b)   are a registered sex offender and have failed to comply with any notification requirements; or

(c)   are required to comply with a sexual risk order made under the Anti-Social Behaviour, Crime and Policing Act 2014 and have failed to do so.

S-EC.2.1.   The applicant will normally be refused on grounds of suitability if any of paragraphs S-EC.2.2. to 2.5. apply.

S-EC.2.2.   Whether or not to the applicant's knowledge-

(a)   false information, representations or documents have been submitted in relation to the application (including false information submitted to any person to obtain a document used in support of the application); or

(b)   there has been a failure to disclose material facts in relation to the application.

S-EC.2.3.   DELETED.

S-EC.2.4.   A maintenance and accommodation undertaking has been requested or required under paragraph 35 of these Rules or otherwise and has not been provided.

S-EC.2.5.   The exclusion of the applicant from the UK is conducive to the public good because:

(a)   within the 12 months prior to the date on which the application is decided, the person has been convicted of or admitted an offence for which they received a non-custodial sentence or other out of court disposal that is recorded on their criminal record; or

(b)   in the view of the Secretary of State:

(i)   the person's offending has caused serious harm; or

(ii)   the person is a persistent offender who shows a particular disregard for the law.

S-EC.3.1.   The applicant may be refused on grounds of suitability if the applicant has failed to pay litigation costs awarded to the Home Office.

S-EC.3.2.   The applicant may be refused on grounds of suitability if one or more relevant NHS bodies has notified the Secretary of State that the applicant has failed to pay charges in accordance with the relevant NHS regulations on charges to overseas visitors and the outstanding charges have a total value of at least £500.

Section E-ECP: Eligibility for entry clearance as a partner

E-ECP.1.1.   To meet the eligibility requirements for entry clearance as a partner all of the requirements in paragraphs E-ECP.2.1. to 4.2. must be met.

Relationship requirements

E-ECP.2.1.   The applicant's partner must be-

(a)   a British Citizen in the UK, subject to paragraph GEN.1.3.(c); or

(b)   present and settled in the UK, subject to paragraph GEN.1.3.(b); or

(c)   in the UK with refugee leave or with humanitarian protection; or

(d)   in the UK with limited leave under Appendix EU, in accordance with paragraph GEN 1.3.(d); or

(e)   in the UK with limited leave as a worker or business person under Appendix ECAA Extension of Stay, in accordance with paragraph GEN.1.3.(e).

E-ECP.2.2.   The applicant must be aged 18 or over at the date of application.

E-ECP.2.3.   The partner must be aged 18 or over at the date of application.

E-ECP.2.4.   The applicant and their partner must not be within the prohibited degree of relationship.

E-ECP.2.5.   The applicant and their partner must have met in person.

E-ECP.2.6.   The relationship between the applicant and their partner must be genuine and subsisting.

E-ECP.2.7.   If the applicant and partner are married or in a civil partnership it must be a valid marriage or civil partnership, as specified.

E-ECP.2.8.   If the applicant is a fiancé(e) or proposed civil partner they must be seeking entry to the UK to enable their marriage or civil partnership to take place in the United Kingdom.

E-ECP.2.9.   (i)   Any previous relationship of the applicant or their partner must have broken down permanently, unless it is a relationship which falls within paragraph 278(i) of these Rules; and

(ii)   If the applicant is a fiancé(e) or proposed civil partner, neither the applicant nor their partner can be married to, or in a civil partnership with, another person at the date of application.

E-ECP.2.10.   The applicant and partner must intend to live together permanently in the UK.

Financial requirements

E-ECP.3.1.   The applicant must provide specified evidence, from the sources listed in paragraph E-ECP.3.2., of-

(a)   a specified gross annual income of at least-

(i)   £18,600;

(ii)   an additional £3,800 for the first child; and

(iii)   an additional £2,400 for each additional child; alone or in combination with

(b)   specified savings of-

    (i)   £16,000; and

    (ii)   additional savings of an amount equivalent to 2.5 times the amount which is the difference between the gross annual income from the sources listed in paragraph E-ECP.3.2.(a)-(d) and the total amount required under paragraph E-ECP.3.1.(a); or

(c)   the requirements in paragraph E-ECP.3.3. being met.

In this paragraph "child" means a dependent child of the applicant or the applicant's partner who is-

(a)   under the age of 18 years, or who was under the age of 18 years when they were first granted entry under this route;

(b)   applying for entry clearance as a dependant of the applicant or the applicant's partner, or is in the UK with leave as their dependant;

(c)   not a British Citizen, settled in the UK, or in the UK with valid limited leave to enter or remain granted under paragraph EU3 or EU3A of Appendix EU to these Rules; and

(d)   not an EEA national with a right to be admitted to or reside in the UK under the Immigration (European Economic Area) Regulations 2016.

E-ECP.3.2.   When determining whether the financial requirement in paragraph E-ECP. 3.1. is met only the following sources will be taken into account-

(a)   income of the partner from specified employment or self-employment, which, in respect of a partner returning to the UK with the applicant, can include specified employment or self-employment overseas and in the UK;

(b)   specified pension income of the applicant and partner;

(c)   any specified maternity allowance or bereavement benefit received by the partner in the UK or any specified payment relating to service in HM Forces received by the applicant or partner;

(d)   other specified income of the applicant and partner; and

(e)   specified savings of the applicant and partner.

E-ECP.3.3.   The requirements to be met under this paragraph are-

(a)   the applicant's partner must be receiving one or more of the following -

    (i)   disability living allowance;

    (ii)   severe disablement allowance;

    (iii)   industrial injury disablement benefit;

    (iv)   attendance allowance;

    (v)   carer's allowance;

    (vi)   personal independence payment;

    (vii)   Armed Forces Independence Payment or Guaranteed Income Payment under the Armed Forces Compensation Scheme;

    (viii)   Constant Attendance Allowance, Mobility Supplement or War Disablement Pension under the War Pensions Scheme; or

    (ix)   Police Injury Pension; and

(b)   the applicant must provide evidence that their partner is able to maintain and accommodate themselves, the applicant and any dependants adequately in the UK without recourse to public funds.

E-ECP.3.4.   The applicant must provide evidence that there will be adequate accommodation, without recourse to public funds, for the family, including other family members who are not included in the application but who live in the same household, which the family own or occupy exclusively: accommodation will not be regarded as adequate if-

(a)   it is, or will be, overcrowded; or

(b)   it contravenes public health regulations.

English language requirement

E-ECP.4.1.   The applicant must provide specified evidence that they-

(a)   are a national of a majority English speaking country listed in paragraph GEN.1.6.;

(b)   have passed an English language test in speaking and listening at a minimum of level A1 of the Common European Framework of Reference for Languages with a provider approved by the Secretary of State;

(c) have an academic qualification which is either a Bachelor's or Master's degree or PhD awarded by an educational establishment in the UK; or, if awarded by an educational establishment outside the UK, is deemed by Ecctis to meet or exceed the recognised standard of a Bachelor's or Master's degree or PhD in the UK, and Ecctis has confirmed that the degree was taught or researched in English to level A1 of the Common European Framework of Reference for Languages or above; or

(d) are exempt from the English language requirement under paragraph E-ECP.4.2.

E-ECP.4.2. The applicant is exempt from the English language requirement if at the date of application-

(a) the applicant is aged 65 or over;

(b) the applicant has a disability (physical or mental condition) which prevents the applicant from meeting the requirement; or

(c) there are exceptional circumstances which prevent the applicant from being able to meet the requirement prior to entry to the UK.

Section D-ECP: Decision on application for entry clearance as a partner

D-ECP.1.1. Except where paragraph GEN.3.1.(2) or GEN.3.2.(3) of this Appendix applies, an applicant who meets the requirements for entry clearance as a partner (other than as a fiancé(e) or proposed civil partner) will be granted entry clearance for an initial period not exceeding 33 months, and subject to a condition of no recourse to public funds, and they will be eligible to apply for settlement after a continuous period of at least 60 months in the UK with leave to enter granted on the basis of such entry clearance or with limited leave to remain as a partner granted under paragraph D-LTRP.1.1. (excluding in all cases any period of leave to enter or limited leave to remain as a fiancé(e) or proposed civil partner); or, where the applicant is a fiancé(e) or proposed civil partner, the applicant will be granted entry clearance for a period not exceeding 6 months, and subject to a prohibition on employment and a condition of no recourse to public funds.

D-ECP.1.2. Where paragraph GEN.3.1.(2) or GEN.3.2.(3) of this Appendix applies, an applicant who meets the requirements for entry clearance as a partner (other than as a fiancé(e) or proposed civil partner) will be granted entry clearance for an initial period not exceeding 33 months, and subject to a condition of no recourse to public funds unless the decision-maker considers, with reference to paragraph GEN.1.11A., that the applicant should not be subject to such a condition, and they will be eligible to apply for settlement after a continuous period of at least 120 months in the UK with leave to enter granted on the basis of such entry clearance or of entry clearance granted under paragraph D-ECP.1.1. or with limited leave to remain as a partner granted under paragraph D-LTRP.1.1. or D-LTRP.1.2. (excluding in all cases any period of leave to enter or limited leave to remain as a fiancé(e) or proposed civil partner); or, where the applicant is a fiancé(e) or proposed civil partner, the applicant will be granted entry clearance for a period not exceeding 6 months, and subject to a prohibition on employment and a condition of no recourse to public funds.

D-ECP.1.3. If the applicant does not meet the requirements for entry clearance as a partner, the application will be refused.

Section R-LTRP: Requirements for limited leave to remain as a partner

R-LTRP.1.1. The requirements to be met for limited leave to remain as a partner are-

(a) the applicant and their partner must be in the UK;

(b) the applicant must have made a valid application for limited or indefinite leave to remain as a partner; and either

(c) (i) the applicant must not fall for refusal under Section S-LTR: Suitability leave to remain; and

(ii) the applicant meets all of the requirements of Section E-LTRP: Eligibility for leave to remain as a partner; or

(d) (i) the applicant must not fall for refusal under Section S-LTR: Suitability leave to remain; and

(ii) the applicant meets the requirements of paragraphs E-LTRP.1.2-1.12. and E-LTRP.2.1-2.2.; and

(iii) paragraph EX.1. applies.

Section S-LTR: Suitability-leave to remain

S-LTR.1.1. The applicant will be refused limited leave to remain on grounds of suitability if any of paragraphs S-LTR.1.2. to 1.8. apply.

S-LTR.1.2.   The applicant is currently the subject of a deportation order.

S-LTR.1.3.   The presence of the applicant in the UK is not conducive to the public good because they have been convicted of an offence for which they have been sentenced to imprisonment for at least 4 years.

S-LTR.1.4.   The presence of the applicant in the UK is not conducive to the public good because they have been convicted of an offence for which they have been sentenced to imprisonment for less than 4 years but at least 12 months, unless a period of 10 years has passed since the end of the sentence; or

S-LTR.1.5.   The presence of the applicant in the UK is not conducive to the public good because, in the view of the Secretary of State, their offending has caused serious harm or they are a persistent offender who shows a particular disregard for the law.

S-LTR.1.6.   The presence of the applicant in the UK is not conducive to the public good because their conduct (including convictions which do not fall within paragraphs S-LTR.1.3. to 1.5.), character, associations, or other reasons, make it undesirable to allow them to remain in the UK.

S-LTR.1.7.   The applicant has failed without reasonable excuse to comply with a requirement to-

    (a)   attend an interview;

    (b)   provide information;

    (c)   provide physical data; or

    (d)   undergo a medical examination or provide a medical report.

S-LTR.1.8.   The presence of the applicant in the UK is not conducive to the public good because the Secretary of State:

    (a)   has made a decision under Article 1F of the Refugee Convention to exclude the person from the Refugee Convention or under paragraph 339D of these Rules to exclude them from humanitarian protection; or

    (b)   has previously made a decision that they are a person to whom Article 33(2) of the Refugee Convention applies because there are reasonable grounds for regarding them as a danger to the security of the UK; or

    (c)   considers that they are a person to whom sub-paragraph (a) or (b) would apply except that (i) the person has not made a protection claim, or (ii) the person made a protection claim which has already been finally determined without reference to Article 1F of the Refugee Convention or paragraph 339D of these Rules; or

    (d)   has previously made a decision that they are a person to whom Article 33(2) of the Refugee Convention applies because, having been convicted by a final judgment of a particularly serious crime, they constitute a danger to the community of the UK.

S-LTR.2.1.   The applicant will normally be refused on grounds of suitability if any of paragraphs S-LTR.2.2. to 2.5. apply.

S-LTR.2.2.   Whether or not to the applicant's knowledge –

    (a)   false information, representations or documents have been submitted in relation to the application (including false information submitted to any person to obtain a document used in support of the application); or

    (b)   there has been a failure to disclose material facts in relation to the application.

S-LTR.2.3.   DELETED.

S-LTR.2.4.   A maintenance and accommodation undertaking has been requested under paragraph 35 of these Rules and has not been provided.

S-LTR.2.5.   The Secretary of State has given notice to the applicant and their partner under section 50(7)(b) of the Immigration Act 2014 that one or both of them have not complied with the investigation of their proposed marriage or civil partnership.

S-LTR.3.1.   When considering whether the presence of the applicant in the UK is not conducive to the public good any legal or practical reasons why the applicant cannot presently be removed from the UK must be ignored.

S-LTR.4.1.   The applicant may be refused on grounds of suitability if any of paragraphs S-LTR.4.2. to S-LTR.4.5. apply.

S-LTR.4.2.   The applicant has made false representations or failed to disclose any material fact in a previous application for entry clearance, leave to enter, leave to remain or a variation of leave, or in a previous human rights claim; or did so in order to obtain from the Secretary of State or a third party a document required to support such an application or claim (whether or not the application or claim was successful).

S-LTR.4.3.   The applicant has previously made false representations or failed to disclose material facts for the purpose of obtaining a document from the Secretary of State that indicates that he or she has a right to reside in the United Kingdom.

S-LTR.4.4.   The applicant has failed to pay litigation costs awarded to the Home Office.

S-LTR.4.5.   One or more relevant NHS bodies has notified the Secretary of State that the applicant has failed to pay charges in accordance with the relevant NHS regulations on charges to overseas visitors and the outstanding charges have a total value of at least £500.

Section E-LTRP: Eligibility for limited leave to remain as a partner

E-LTRP.1.1.   To qualify for limited leave to remain as a partner all of the requirements of paragraphs E-LTRP.1.2. to 4.2. must be met.

Relationship requirements

E-LTRP.1.2.   The applicant's partner must be-

    (a)   a British Citizen in the UK;

    (b)   present and settled in the UK;

    (c)   in the UK with refugee leave or with humanitarian protection;

    (d)   in the UK with limited leave under Appendix EU, in accordance with paragraph GEN.1.3.(d);or

    (e)   in the UK with limited leave as a worker or business person under Appendix ECAA Extension of Stay, in accordance with paragraph GEN.1.3.(e).

E-LTRP.1.3.   The applicant must be aged 18 or over at the date of application.

E-LTRP.1.4.   The partner must be aged 18 or over at the date of application.

E-LTRP.1.5.   The applicant and their partner must not be within the prohibited degree of relationship.

E-LTRP.1.6.   The applicant and their partner must have met in person.

E-LTRP.1.7.   The relationship between the applicant and their partner must be genuine and subsisting.

E-LTRP.1.8.   If the applicant and partner are married or in a civil partnership it must be a valid marriage or civil partnership, as specified.

E-LTRP.1.9.   Any previous relationship of the applicant or their partner must have broken down permanently, unless it is a relationship which falls within paragraph 278(i) of these Rules.

E-LTRP.1.10.   The applicant and their partner must intend to live together permanently in the UK and, in any application for further leave to remain as a partner (except where the applicant is in the UK as a fiancé(e) or proposed civil partner) and in any application for indefinite leave to remain as a partner, the applicant must provide evidence that, since entry clearance as a partner was granted under paragraph D-ECP1.1. or since the last grant of limited leave to remain as a partner, the applicant and their partner have lived together in the UK or there is good reason, consistent with a continuing intention to live together permanently in the UK, for any period in which they have not done so.

E-LTRP.1.11.   If the applicant is in the UK with leave as a fiancé(e) or proposed civil partner and the marriage or civil partnership did not take place during that period of leave, there must be good reason why and evidence that it will take place within the next 6 months.

E-LTRP.1.12.   The applicant's partner cannot be the applicant's fiancé(e) or proposed civil partner, unless the applicant was granted entry clearance as that person's fiancé(e) or proposed civil partner.

Immigration status requirements

E-LTRP.2.1.   The applicant must not be in the UK-

    (a)   as a visitor; or

    (b)   with valid leave granted for a period of 6 months or less, unless that leave is as a fiancé(e) or proposed civil partner, or was granted pending the outcome of family court or divorce proceedings

E-LTRP.2.2.   The applicant must not be in the UK –

    (a)   on immigration bail, unless:

       (i)   the Secretary of State is satisfied that the applicant arrived in the UK more than 6 months prior to the date of application; and

       (ii)   paragraph EX.1. applies; or

    (b)   in breach of immigration laws (except that, where paragraph 39E of these Rules applies, any current period of overstaying will be disregarded), unless paragraph EX.1. applies.

Financial requirements

E-LTRP.3.1.   The applicant must provide specified evidence, from the sources listed in paragraph E-LTRP.3.2., of-

    (a)   a specified gross annual income of at least-

        (i)   £18,600;

        (ii)   an additional £3,800 for the first child; and

        (iii)   an additional £2,400 for each additional child; alone or in combination with

    (b)   specified savings of-

        (i)   £16,000; and

        (ii)   additional savings of an amount equivalent to 2.5 times the amount which is the difference between the gross annual income from the sources listed in paragraph E-LTRP.3.2.(a)-(f) and the total amount required under paragraph E-LTRP.3.1.(a); or

    (c)   the requirements in paragraph E-LTRP.3.3.being met, unless paragraph EX.1. applies.

In this paragraph "child" means a dependent child of the applicant or the applicant's partner who is-

    (a)   under the age of 18 years, or who was under the age of 18 years when they were first granted entry under this route;

    (b)   applying for entry clearance or leave to remain as a dependant of the applicant or the applicant's partner, or is in the UK with leave as their dependant;

    (c)   not a British Citizen, settled in the UK, or in the UK with valid limited leave to enter or remain granted under paragraph EU3 or EU3A of Appendix EU to these Rules; and

    (d)   not an EEA national with a right to be admitted to or reside in the UK under the Immigration (European Economic Area) Regulations 2016.

E-LTRP.3.2.   When determining whether the financial requirement in paragraph E-LTRP. 3.1. is met only the following sources may be taken into account-

    (a)   income of the partner from specified employment or self-employment;

    (b)   income of the applicant from specified employment or self-employment unless they are working illegally;

    (c)   specified pension income of the applicant and partner;

    (d)   any specified maternity allowance or bereavement benefit received by the applicant and partner in the UK or any specified payment relating to service in HM Forces received by the applicant or partner;

    (e)   other specified income of the applicant and partner;

    (f)   income from the sources at (b), (d) or (e) of a dependent child of the applicant or of the applicant's partner under paragraph E-LTRP.3.1. who is aged 18 years or over; and

    (g)   specified savings of the applicant, partner and a dependent child of the applicant or of the applicant's partner under paragraph E-LTRP.3.1. who is aged 18 years or over.

E-LTRP.3.3.   The requirements to meet this paragraph are-

    (a)   the applicant's partner must be receiving one or more of the following -

        (i)   disability living allowance;

        (ii)   severe disablement allowance;

        (iii)   industrial injury disablement benefit;

        (iv)   attendance allowance;

        (v)   carer's allowance;

        (vi)   personal independence payment;

        (vii)   Armed Forces Independence Payment or Guaranteed Income Payment under the Armed Forces Compensation Scheme;

        (viii)   Constant Attendance Allowance, Mobility Supplement or War Disablement Pension under the War Pensions Scheme; or

        (ix)   Police Injury Pension; and

    (b)   the applicant must provide evidence that their partner is able to maintain and accommodate themselves, the applicant and any dependants adequately in the UK without recourse to public funds.

E-LTRP.3.4.   The applicant must provide evidence that there will be adequate accommodation, without recourse to public funds, for the family, including other family members who are not included in the application but who live in the same household, which the family own or occupy exclusively, unless paragraph EX.1. applies: accommodation will not be regarded as adequate if-

    (a)   it is, or will be, overcrowded; or

(b)   it contravenes public health regulations.

English language requirement

E-LTRP.4.1.   If the applicant has not met the requirement in a previous application for entry clearance or leave to remain as a partner or parent, the applicant must provide specified evidence that they-

(a)   are a national of a majority English speaking country listed in paragraph GEN.1.6.;

(b)   have passed an English language test in speaking and listening at a minimum of level A1 of the Common European Framework of Reference for Languages with a provider approved by the Secretary of State;

(c)   have an academic qualification which is either a Bachelor's or Master's degree or PhD awarded by an educational establishment in the UK; or, if awarded by an educational establishment outside the UK, is deemed by Ecctis to meet or exceed the recognised standard of a Bachelor's or Master's degree or PhD in the UK, and Ecctis has confirmed that the degree was taught or researched in English to level A1 of the Common European Framework of Reference for Languages or above; or

(d)   are exempt from the English language requirement under paragraph E-LTRP.4.2.;

unless paragraph EX.1. applies.

E-LTRP.4.1A.   Where the applicant:

(i)   in a previous application for entry clearance or leave to remain as a partner or parent, met the English language requirement in paragraph E-ECP.4.1.(b), E-LTRP.4.1.(b), E-ECPT.4.1.(b) or E-LTRPT.5.1.(b) on the basis that they had passed an English language test in speaking and listening at level A1 of the Common European Framework of Reference for Languages;

(ii)   was granted entry clearance or leave to remain as a partner or parent; and

(iii)   now seeks further leave to remain as a partner after 30 months in the UK with leave as a partner; then, the applicant must provide specified evidence that they:

(a)   are a national of a majority English speaking country listed in paragraph GEN.1.6.;

(b)   have passed an English language test in speaking and listening at a minimum of level A2 of the Common European Framework of Reference for Languages with a provider approved by the Secretary of State;

(c)   have an academic qualification which is either a Bachelor's or Master's degree or PhD awarded by an educational establishment in the UK; or, if awarded by an educational establishment outside the UK, is deemed by Ecctis to meet or exceed the recognised standard of a Bachelor's or Master's degree or PhD in the UK, and Ecctis has confirmed that the degree was taught or researched in English to level A2 of the Common European Framework of Reference for Languages or above; or

(d)   are exempt from the English language requirement under paragraph E-LTRP.4.2.;

unless paragraph EX.1. applies.

E-LTRP.4.2.   The applicant is exempt from the English language requirement in paragraph E-LTRP.4.1. or E-LTRP.4.1A. if at the date of application-

(a)   the applicant is aged 65 or over;

(b)   the applicant has a disability (physical or mental condition) which prevents the applicant from meeting the requirement; or

(c)   there are exceptional circumstances which prevent the applicant from being able to meet the requirement.

Section D-LTRP: Decision on application for limited leave to remain as a partner

D-LTRP.1.1.   If the applicant meets the requirements in paragraph R-LTRP.1.1.(a) to (c) for limited leave to remain as a partner the applicant will be granted limited leave to remain for a period not exceeding 30 months, and subject to a condition of no recourse to public funds, and they will be eligible to apply for settlement after a continuous period of at least 60 months with such leave or in the UK with leave to enter granted on the basis of entry clearance granted under paragraph D-ECP.1.1. (excluding in all cases any period of leave to enter or limited leave to remain as a fiancé(e) or proposed civil partner); or, if paragraph E-LTRP.1.11. applies, the applicant will be granted limited leave for a period not exceeding 6 months and subject to a condition of no recourse to public funds and a prohibition on employment.

D-LTRP.1.2.   If the applicant meets the requirements in paragraph R-LTRP.1.1.(a), (b) and (d) for limited leave to remain as a partner, or paragraph GEN.3.1.(2) or GEN.3.2.(3) applies to an applicant for leave to remain as a partner, the applicant will be granted leave to remain for a period not exceeding 30 months and subject to a condition of no recourse to public funds unless the decision-maker considers, with reference to paragraph GEN.1.11A., that the applicant should not be subject to such a condition, and they will be eligible to apply for settlement after a continuous period of at least 120 months in the UK with such leave, with limited leave to remain as a partner granted under paragraph D-LTRP.1.1., or in the UK with leave to enter granted on the basis of entry clearance as a partner granted under paragraph D-ECP1.1. or D-ECP.1.2. (excluding in all cases any period of leave to enter or limited leave to remain as a fiancé(e) or proposed civil partner); or, if paragraph E-LTRP.1.11.

applies, the applicant will be granted limited leave for a period not exceeding 6 months and subject to a condition of no recourse to public funds and a prohibition on employment.

D-LTRP.1.3.   If the applicant does not meet the requirements for limited leave to remain as a partner the application will be refused.

Section R-ILRP: Requirements for indefinite leave to remain (settlement) as a partner

R-ILRP.1.1.   The requirements to be met for indefinite leave to remain as a partner are that-

    (a)   the applicant and their partner must be in the UK;

    (b)   the applicant must have made a valid application for indefinite leave to remain as a partner;

    (c)   the applicant must not fall for refusal under any of the grounds in Section S-ILR: Suitability for indefinite leave to remain; and

    (d)   deleted

    (e)   the applicant must meet all of the requirements of Section E-ILRP: Eligibility for indefinite leave to remain as a partner.

Section S-ILR: Suitability for indefinite leave to remain

S-ILR.1.1.   The applicant will be refused indefinite leave to remain on grounds of suitability if any of paragraphs S-ILR.1.2. to 1.10. apply.

S-ILR.1.2.   The applicant is currently the subject of a deportation order.

S-ILR.1.3.   The presence of the applicant in the UK is not conducive to the public good because they have been convicted of an offence for which they have been sentenced to imprisonment for at least 4 years.

S-ILR.1.4.   The presence of the applicant in the UK is not conducive to the public good because they have been convicted of an offence for which they have been sentenced to imprisonment for less than 4 years but at least 12 months, unless a period of 15 years has passed since the end of the sentence.

S-ILR.1.5.   The presence of the applicant in the UK is not conducive to the public good because they have been convicted of an offence for which they have been sentenced to imprisonment for less than 12 months, unless a period of 7 years has passed since the end of the sentence.

S-ILR.1.6.   The applicant has, within the 24 months prior to the date on which the application is decided, been convicted of or admitted an offence for which they received a non-custodial sentence or other out of court disposal that is recorded on their criminal record.

S-ILR.1.7.   The presence of the applicant in the UK is not conducive to the public good because, in the view of the Secretary of State, their offending has caused serious harm or they are a persistent offender who shows a particular disregard for the law.

S-ILR.1.8.   The presence of the applicant in the UK is not conducive to the public good because their conduct (including convictions which do not fall within paragraphs S-ILR.1.3. to 1.6.), character, associations, or other reasons, make it undesirable to allow them to remain in the UK.

S-ILR.1.9.   The applicant has failed without reasonable excuse to comply with a requirement to-

    (a)   attend an interview;

    (b)   provide information;

    (c)   provide physical data; or

    (d)   undergo a medical examination or provide a medical report.

S-ILR.1.10.   The presence of the applicant in the UK is not conducive to the public good because the Secretary of State:

    (a)   has made a decision under Article 1F of the Refugee Convention to exclude the person from the Refugee Convention or under paragraph 339D of these Rules to exclude them from humanitarian protection; or

(b) has previously made a decision that they are a person to whom Article 33(2) of the Refugee Convention applies because there are reasonable grounds for regarding them as a danger to the security of the UK; or

(c) considers that they are a person to whom sub-paragraph (a) or (b) would apply except that (i) the person has not made a protection claim, or (ii) the person made a protection claim which has already been finally determined without reference to Article 1F of the Refugee Convention or paragraph 339D of these Rules; or

(d) has previously made a decision that they are a person to whom Article 33(2) of the Refugee Convention applies because, having been convicted by a final judgment of a particularly serious crime, they constitute a danger to the community of the UK.

S-ILR.2.1. The applicant will normally be refused on grounds of suitability if any of paragraphs S-ILR.2.2. to 2.4. apply.

S-ILR.2.2. Whether or not to the applicant's knowledge –

(a) false information, representations or documents have been submitted in relation to the application (including false information submitted to any person to obtain a document used in support of the application); or

(b) there has been a failure to disclose material facts in relation to the application.

S-ILR.2.3. DELETED.

S-ILR.2.4. A maintenance and accommodation undertaking has been requested under paragraph 35 of these Rules and has not been provided.

S-ILR.3.1. When considering whether the presence of the applicant in the UK is not conducive to the public good, any legal or practical reasons why the applicant cannot presently be removed from the UK must be ignored.

S-ILR.4.1. The applicant may be refused on grounds of suitability if any of paragraphs S-ILR.4.2. to S-ILR.4.5. apply.

S-ILR.4.2. The applicant has made false representations or failed to disclose any material fact in a previous application for entry clearance, leave to enter, leave to remain or a variation of leave, or in a previous human rights claim; or did so in order to obtain from the Secretary of State or a third party a document required to support such an application or claim (whether or not the application or claim was successful).

S-ILR.4.3. The applicant has previously made false representations or failed to disclose material facts for the purpose of obtaining a document from the Secretary of State that indicates that he or she has a right to reside in the United Kingdom.

S-ILR.4.4. The applicant has failed to pay litigation costs awarded to the Home Office.

S-ILR.4.5. One or more relevant NHS bodies has notified the Secretary of State that the applicant has failed to pay charges in accordance with the relevant NHS regulations on charges to overseas visitors and the outstanding charges have a total value of at least £500.

Section E-ILRP: Eligibility for indefinite leave to remain as a partner

E-ILRP.1.1. To meet the eligibility requirements for indefinite leave to remain as a partner all of the requirements of paragraphs E-ILRP.1.2. to 1.6. must be met.

E-ILRP.1.2. The applicant must be in the UK with valid leave to remain as a partner under this Appendix (except that, where paragraph 39E of these Rules applies, any current period of overstaying will be disregarded).

E-ILRP.1.3. (1) Subject to sub-paragraph (2), the applicant must, at the date of application, have completed a continuous period of either:

(a) at least 60 months in the UK with:

(i) leave to enter granted on the basis of entry clearance as a partner granted under paragraph D-ECP.1.1.; or

(ii) limited leave to remain as a partner granted under paragraph D-LTRP.1.1.; or

(iii) a combination of (i) and (ii);

or

(b) at least 120 months in the UK with:

(i) leave to enter granted on the basis of entry clearance as a partner granted under paragraph D-ECP.1.1. or D-ECP.1.2.; or

(ii) limited leave to remain as a partner granted under paragraph D-LTRP.1.1. or D-LTRP.1.2.; or

(iii) a combination of (i) and (ii).

(1A)   In respect of an application falling within sub-paragraph (1)(a) above, the applicant must meet all of the requirements of Section E-LTRP: Eligibility for leave to remain as a partner (except that paragraph E-LTRP.1.2. cannot be met on the basis set out in sub-paragraph (c), (d), or (e) of that paragraph, and in applying paragraph E-LTRP.3.1.(b)(ii) delete the words "2.5 times").

(1B)   In respect of an application falling within sub-paragraph (1)(b) above:

(a)   the applicant must meet all of the requirements of paragraphs E-LTRP.1.2.-1.12. (except that paragraph E-LTRP.1.2. cannot be met on the basis set out in sub-paragraph (c), (d) or (e) of that paragraph) and E-LTRP.2.1. - 2.2.; and

(b)   paragraph EX.1. must apply.

(2)   In calculating periods of leave for the purposes of sub-paragraph (1) above, any period of leave to enter or limited leave to remain as a fiancé(e) or proposed civil partner will be excluded.

E-ILRP.1.4.   In calculating the periods under paragraph E-ILRP.1.3. only the periods when the applicant's partner is the same person as the applicant's partner for the previous period of limited leave shall be taken into account.

E-ILRP.1.5.   In calculating the periods under paragraph E-ILRP.1.3. the words "in the UK" in that paragraph shall not apply to any period(s) to which the evidence in paragraph 26A of Appendix FM-SE applies.

E-ILRP.1.5A.   In calculating the periods under paragraph E-ILRP.1.3., any current period of overstaying will be disregarded where paragraph 39E of these Rules applies. Any previous period of overstaying between periods of leave will also be disregarded where: the further application was made before 24 November 2016 and within 28 days of the expiry of leave; or the further application was made on or after 24 November 2016 and paragraph 39E of these Rules applied.

E-ILRP.1.6.   The applicant must have demonstrated sufficient knowledge of the English language and sufficient knowledge about life in the United Kingdom in accordance with the requirements of Appendix KoLL of these Rules.

Section D-ILRP: Decision on application for indefinite leave to remain as a partner

D-ILRP.1.1.   If the applicant meets all of the requirements for indefinite leave to remain as a partner the applicant will be granted indefinite leave to remain.

D-ILRP.1.2.   If the applicant does not meet the requirements for indefinite leave to remain as a partner only for one or both of the following reasons-

(a)   paragraph S-ILR.1.5. or S-ILR.1.6. applies;

(b)   the applicant has not demonstrated sufficient knowledge of the English language or about life in the United Kingdom in accordance with Appendix KoLL,

subject to compliance with any requirement notified under paragraph GEN.1.15.(b), the applicant will be granted further limited leave to remain as a partner for a period not exceeding 30 months, and subject to a condition of no recourse to public funds.

D-ILRP.1.3.   If the applicant does not meet all the eligibility requirements for indefinite leave to remain as a partner, and does not qualify for further limited leave to remain as a partner under paragraph DILRP. 1.2., the application will be refused, unless the applicant meets the requirements in paragraph R-LTRP.1.1.(a), (b) and (d) for limited leave to remain as a partner. Where they do, and subject to compliance with any requirement notified under paragraph GEN.1.15.(b), the applicant will be granted further limited leave to remain as a partner for a period not exceeding 30 months under paragraph D-LTRP.1.2. and subject to a condition of no recourse to public funds unless the Secretary of State considers that the person should not be subject to such a condition.

Section EX: Exceptions to certain eligibility requirements for leave to remain as a partner or parent

EX.1.   This paragraph applies if

(a)   (i)   the applicant has a genuine and subsisting parental relationship with a child who-

(aa)   is under the age of 18 years, or was under the age of 18 years when the applicant was first granted leave on the basis that this paragraph applied;

(bb)   is in the UK;

(cc)   is a British Citizen or has lived in the UK continuously for at least the 7 years immediately preceding the date of application; and

(ii)   taking into account their best interests as a primary consideration, it would not be reasonable to expect the child to leave the UK; or

(b) the applicant has a genuine and subsisting relationship with a partner who is in the UK and is a British Citizen, settled in the UK, or in the UK with refugee leave, or humanitarian protection, in the UK with limited leave under Appendix EU in accordance with paragraph GEN.1.3.(d), or in the UK with limited leave as a worker or business person under Appendix ECAA Extension of Stay in accordance with paragraph GEN.1.3.(e), and there are insurmountable obstacles to family life with that partner continuing outside the UK.

EX.2. For the purposes of paragraph EX.1.(b) "insurmountable obstacles" means the very significant difficulties which would be faced by the applicant or their partner in continuing their family life together outside the UK and which could not be overcome or would entail very serious hardship for the applicant or their partner.

Bereaved partner

Section BPILR: Indefinite leave to remain (settlement) as a bereaved partner

BPILR.1.1. The requirements to be met for indefinite leave to remain in the UK as a bereaved partner are that-

(a) the applicant must be in the UK;

(b) the applicant must have made a valid application for indefinite leave to remain as a bereaved partner;

(c) the applicant must not fall for refusal under any of the grounds in Section S-ILR: Suitability-indefinite leave to remain; and

(d) the applicant must meet all of the requirements of Section E-BPILR:

Eligibility for indefinite leave to remain as a bereaved partner.

Section E-BPILR: Eligibility for indefinite leave to remain as a bereaved partner

E-BPILR.1.1. To meet the eligibility requirements for indefinite leave to remain as a bereaved partner all of the requirements of paragraphs E-BPILR1.2. to 1.4. must be met.

E-BPILR.1.2. The applicant's last grant of limited leave must have been granted under this Appendix as-

(a) a partner (other than a fiancé(e) or proposed civil partner) of a British Citizen, a person settled in the UK, or a person in the UK with limited leave under Appendix EU in accordance with paragraph GEN.1.3.(d); or

(b) a bereaved partner.

E-BPILR.1.3. The person who was the applicant's partner at the time of the last grant of limited leave as a partner must have died.

E-BPILR.1.4. At the time of the partner's death the relationship between the applicant and the partner must have been genuine and subsisting and each of the parties must have intended to live permanently with the other in the UK.

Section D-BPILR: Decision on application for indefinite leave to remain as a bereaved partner

D-BPILR.1.1. If the applicant meets all of the requirements for indefinite leave to remain as a bereaved partner the applicant will be granted indefinite leave to remain.

D-BPILR.1.2. If the applicant does not meet the requirements for indefinite leave to remain as a bereaved partner only because paragraph S-ILR.1.5. or S-ILR.1.6. applies, the applicant will be granted further limited leave to remain for a period not exceeding 30 months, and subject to a condition of no recourse to public funds.

D-BPILR.1.3. If the applicant does not meet the requirements for indefinite leave to remain as a bereaved partner, or limited leave to remain as a bereaved partner under paragraph D-BPILR.1.2., the application will be refused.

Victim of domestic abuse

Section DVILR: Indefinite leave to remain (settlement) as a victim of domestic abuse

DVILR.1.1. The requirements to be met for indefinite leave to remain in the UK as a victim of domestic abuse are that-

(a) the applicant must be in the UK;

(b) the applicant must have made a valid application for indefinite leave to remain as a victim of domestic abuse;

(c) the applicant must not fall for refusal under any of the grounds in Section S-ILR: Suitability-indefinite leave to remain; and

(d) the applicant must meet all of the requirements of Section E-DVILR: Eligibility for indefinite leave to remain as a victim of domestic abuse.

Section E-DVILR: Eligibility for indefinite leave to remain as a victim of domestic abuse

E-DVILR.1.1.   To meet the eligibility requirements for indefinite leave to remain as a victim of domestic abuse all of the requirements of paragraphs E-DVILR.1.2. and 1.3. must be met.

E-DVILR.1.2.   The applicant's first grant of limited leave under this Appendix must have been as a partner (other than a fiancé(e) or proposed civil partner) of a British Citizen, a person present and settled in the UK, a person with refugee leave, or a person in the UK with limited leave under Appendix EU in accordance with paragraph GEN.1.3.(d), under paragraph D-ECP.1.1., D-LTRP.1.1., or D-LTRP.1.2. of this Appendix, or as a partner of a refugee granted under paragraph 352A, and any subsequent grant of limited leave must have been:

  (a)   granted as a partner (other than a fiancé(e) or proposed civil partner) of a British Citizen, a person present and settled in the UK, a person with refugee leave, or a person in the UK with limited leave under Appendix EU in accordance with paragraph GEN.1.3.(d), under paragraph D-ECP.1.1., D-LTRP.1.1. or D-LTRP.1.2. of this Appendix; or

  (b)   granted to enable access to public funds pending an application under DVILR and the preceding grant of leave was granted as a partner (other than a fiancé(e) or proposed civil partner) of a British Citizen, a person present and settled in the UK, a person with refugee leave, or a person in the UK with limited leave under Appendix EU in accordance with paragraph GEN.1.3.(d), under paragraph D-ECP.1.1., DLTRP.1.1. or D-LTRP.1.2. of this Appendix; or

  (c)   granted under paragraph D-DVILR.1.2.

E-DVILR.1.3.   The applicant must provide evidence that during the last period of limited leave as a partner of a British Citizen, a person present and settled in the UK, a person with refugee leave, or a person in the UK with limited leave under Appendix EU in accordance with paragraph GEN.1.3.(d), under paragraph D-ECP.1.1., DLTRP.1.1 or D-LTRP.1.2 of this Appendix, or during their only period of leave under paragraph 352A, the applicant's relationship with their partner broke down permanently as a result of domestic abuse.

Section D-DVILR: Decision on application for indefinite leave to remain as a victim of domestic abuse

D-DVILR.1.1.   If the applicant meets all of the requirements for indefinite leave to remain as a victim of domestic abuse the applicant will be granted indefinite leave to remain.

D-DVILR.1.2.   If the applicant does not meet the requirements for indefinite leave to remain as a victim of domestic abuse only because paragraph S-ILR.1.5. or S-ILR.1.6. applies, the applicant will be granted further limited leave to remain for a period not exceeding 30 months.

D-DVILR.1.3.   If the applicant does not meet the requirements for indefinite leave to remain as a victim of domestic abuse, or further limited leave to remain under paragraph D-DVILR.1.2. the application will be refused.

Family life as a child of a person with limited leave as a partner or parent

This route is for a child whose parent is applying under this Appendix for entry clearance or leave, or who has limited leave, as a partner or parent. For further provision on a child seeking to enter or remain in the UK for the purpose of their family life see Part 8 of these Rules.

Section EC-C: Entry clearance as a child

EC-C.1.1.   The requirements to be met for entry clearance as a child are that-

  (a)   the applicant must be outside the UK;

  (b)   the applicant must have made a valid application for entry clearance as a child;

  (c)   the applicant must not fall for refusal under any of the grounds in Section S-EC: Suitability for entry clearance; and

  (d)   the applicant must meet all of the requirements of Section E-ECC: Eligibility for entry clearance as a child.

Section E-ECC: Eligibility for entry clearance as a child

E-ECC.1.1.   To meet the eligibility requirements for entry clearance as a child all of the requirements of paragraphs E-ECC.1.2. to 2.4. must be met.

Relationship requirements

E-ECC.1.2.   The applicant must be under the age of 18 at the date of application.

E-ECC.1.3.   The applicant must not be married or in a civil partnership.

E-ECC.1.4.   The applicant must not have formed an independent family unit.

E-ECC.1.5.   The applicant must not be leading an independent life.

E-ECC.1.6.   One of the applicant's parents must be in the UK with limited leave to enter or remain, or be being granted, or have been granted, entry clearance, as a partner or a parent under this Appendix (referred to in this section as the "applicant's parent"), and

(a)   the applicant's parent's partner under Appendix FM is also a parent of the applicant; or

(b)   the applicant's parent has had and continues to have sole responsibility for the child's upbringing; or

(c)   there are serious and compelling family or other considerations which make exclusion of the child undesirable and suitable arrangements have been made for the child's care.

Financial requirement

E-ECC.2.1.   Where a parent of the applicant has, or is applying or has applied for, entry clearance or limited leave to enter or remain as a partner under this Appendix, the applicant must provide specified evidence, from the sources listed in paragraph E-ECC.2.2., of-

(a)   a specified gross annual income of at least-

(i)   £18,600;

(ii)   an additional £3,800 for the first child; and

(iii)   an additional £2,400 for each additional child; alone or in combination with

(b)   specified savings of

(i)   £16,000; and

(ii)   additional savings of an amount equivalent to 2.5 times the amount which is the difference between the gross annual income from the sources listed in paragraph E-ECC.2.2.(a)-(f) and the total amount required under paragraph E-ECC.2.1.(a); or

(c)   the requirements in paragraph E-ECC.2.3. being met.

In this paragraph "child" means the applicant and any other dependent child of the applicant's parent or the applicant's parent's partner who is-

(a)   under the age of 18 years, or who was under the age of 18 years when they were first granted entry under this route;

(b)   applying for entry clearance as a dependant of the applicant's parent or of the applicant's parent's partner, or is in the UK with leave as their dependant;

(c)   not a British Citizen, settled in the UK, or in the UK with valid limited leave to enter or remain granted under paragraph EU3 or EU3A of Appendix EU to these Rules; and

(d)   not an EEA national with a right to be admitted to or reside in the UK under the Immigration (European Economic Area) Regulations 2016.

E-ECC.2.2.   When determining whether the financial requirement in paragraph E-ECC.2.1. is met only the following sources may be taken into account-

(a)   income of the applicant's parent's partner from specified employment or self-employment, which, in respect of an applicant's parent's partner returning to the UK with the applicant, can include specified employment or self-employment overseas and in the UK;

(b)   income of the applicant's parent from specified employment or self employment if they are in the UK unless they are working illegally;

(c)   specified pension income of the applicant's parent and that parent's partner;

(d)   any specified maternity allowance or bereavement benefit received by the applicant's parent and that parent's partner in the UK or any specified payment relating to service in HM Forces received by the applicant's parent and that parent's partner;

(e)   other specified income of the applicant's parent and that parent's partner;

(f)   income from the sources at (b), (d) or (e) of a dependent child of the applicant's parent under paragraph E-ECC.2.1. who is aged 18 years or over; and

(g)   specified savings of the applicant's parent, that parent's partner and a dependent child of the applicant's parent under paragraph E-ECC.2.1. who is aged 18 years or over.

E-ECC.2.3.   The requirements to be met under this paragraph are-

(a)   the applicant's parent's partner must be receiving one or more of the following-

(i)   disability living allowance;

      (ii)   severe disablement allowance;

      (iii)   industrial injury disablement benefit;

      (iv)   attendance allowance;

      (v)   carer's allowance;

      (vi)   personal independence payment;

      (vii) Armed Forces Independence Payment or Guaranteed Income Payment under the Armed Forces Compensation Scheme;

      (viii) Constant Attendance Allowance, Mobility Supplement or War Disablement Pension under the War Pensions Scheme; or

      (ix)   Police Injury Pension; and

(b)   the applicant must provide evidence that their parent's partner is able to maintain and accommodate themselves, the applicant's parent, the applicant and any dependants adequately in the UK without recourse to public funds.

E-ECC.2.3A.   Where a parent of the applicant has, or is applying or has applied for, entry clearance or limited leave to enter or remain as a parent under this Appendix, the applicant must provide evidence that that parent is able to maintain and accommodate themselves, the applicant and any other dependants adequately in the UK without recourse to public funds.

E-ECC.2.4.   The applicant must provide evidence that there will be adequate accommodation, without recourse to public funds, for the family, including other family members who are not included in the application but who live in the same household, which the family own or occupy exclusively: accommodation will not be regarded as adequate if-

(a)   it is, or will be, overcrowded; or

(b)   it contravenes public health regulations.

Section D-ECC: Decision on application for entry clearance as a child

D-ECC.1.1.   If the applicant meets the requirements for entry clearance as a child they will be granted entry clearance of a duration which will expire at the same time as the leave granted to the applicant's parent, and will be subject to the same conditions in respect of recourse to public funds as that parent.

D-ECC.1.2.   If the applicant does not meet the requirements for entry clearance as a child the application will be refused.

Section R-LTRC: Requirements for leave to remain as a child

R-LTRC.1.1. The requirements to be met for leave to remain as a child are that-

(a)   the applicant must be in the UK;

(b)   the applicant must have made a valid application for leave to remain as a child; and either

(c)   (i)   the applicant must not fall for refusal under any of the grounds in Section S- LTR: Suitability-leave to remain; and

      (ii)   the applicant meets all of the requirements of Section E-LTRC: Eligibility for leave to remain as a child; and

      (iii) a parent of the applicant has been or is at the same time being granted leave to remain under paragraph D-LTRP.1.1. or D-LTRPT.1.1. or indefinite leave to remain under this Appendix (except as an adult dependent relative); or

(d)   (i)   the applicant must not fall for refusal under any of the grounds in Section S- LTR: Suitability-leave to remain; and

      (ii)   the applicant meets the requirements of paragraphs E-LTRC.1.2.-1.6.; and

      (iii) a parent of the applicant has been or is at the same time being granted leave to remain under paragraph D-LTRP.1.2., D-ILRP.1.2., D-LTRPT.1.2. or D-ILRPT.1.2. or indefinite leave to remain under this Appendix (except as an adult dependent relative).

Section E-LTRC: Eligibility for leave to remain as a child

E-LTRC.1.1.   To qualify for limited leave to remain as a child all of the requirements of paragraphs E-LTRC.1.2. to 2.4. must be met (except where paragraph R-LTRC.1.1.(d)(ii) applies).

Relationship requirements

E-LTRC.1.2.   The applicant must be under the age of 18 at the date of application or when first granted leave as a child under this route.

E-LTRC.1.3.   The applicant must not be married or in a civil partnership.

E-LTRC.1.4.   The applicant must not have formed an independent family unit.

E-LTRC.1.5.   The applicant must not be leading an independent life.

E-LTRC.1.6.   One of the applicant's parents (referred to in this section as the "applicant's parent") must be in the UK and have leave to enter or remain or indefinite leave to remain, or is at the same time being granted leave to remain or indefinite leave to remain, under this Appendix (except as an adult dependent relative), and

(a)   the applicant's parent's partner under Appendix FM is also a parent of the applicant; or

(b)   the applicant's parent has had and continues to have sole responsibility for the child's upbringing or the applicant normally lives with this parent and not their other parent; or

(c)   there are serious and compelling family or other considerations which make exclusion of the child undesirable and suitable arrangements have been made for the child's care.

Financial requirements

E-LTRC.2.1.   Where a parent of the applicant has, or is applying or has applied for, limited leave to remain as a partner under this Appendix, the applicant must provide specified evidence, from the sources listed in paragraph E-LTRC.2.2., of -

(a)   a specified gross annual income of at least-

(i)   £18,600;

(ii)   an additional £3,800 for the first child; and

(iii)   an additional £2,400 for each additional child; alone or in combination with

(b)   specified savings of-

(i)   £16,000; and

(ii)   additional savings of an amount equivalent to 2.5 times (or if the parent is applying for indefinite leave to remain 1 times) the amount which is the difference between the gross annual income from the sources listed in paragraph E-LTRC.2.2.(a)-(f) and the total amount required under paragraph E-LTRC.2.1.(a); or

(c)   the requirements in paragraph E-LTRC.2.3. being met.

In this paragraph "child" means the applicant and any other dependent child of the applicant's parent or the applicant's parent's partner who is-

(a)   under the age of 18 years, or who was under the age of 18 years when they were first granted entry under this route;

(b)   applying for entry clearance as a dependant of the applicant's parent or of the applicant's parent's partner, or is in the UK with leave as their dependant;

(c)   not a British Citizen, settled in the UK, or in the UK with valid limited leave to enter or remain granted under paragraph EU3 or EU3A of Appendix EU to these Rules; and

(d)   not an EEA national with a right to be admitted to or reside in the UK under the Immigration (European Economic Area) Regulations 2016.

E-LTRC.2.2.   When determining whether the financial requirement in paragraph E-LTRC.2.1. is met only the following sources may be taken into account-

(a)   income of the applicant's parent's partner from specified employment or self-employment;

(b)   income of the applicant's parent from specified employment or self employment;

(c)   specified pension income of the applicant's parent and that parent's partner;

(d)   any specified maternity allowance or bereavement benefit received by the applicant's parent and that parent's partner in the UK or any specified payment relating to service in HM Forces received by the applicant's parent and that parent's partner;

(e)   other specified income of the applicant's parent and that parent's partner;

(f)   income from the sources at (b), (d) or (e) of a dependent child of the applicant's parent under paragraph E-LTRC.2.1. who is aged 18 years or over; and

(g)   specified savings of the applicant's parent, that parent's partner and a dependent child of the applicant's parent under paragraph E-ECC.2.1. who is aged 18 years or over.

E-LTRC.2.3.   The requirements to be met under this paragraph are-

(a)   the applicant's parent's partner must be receiving one or more of the following -

(i)   disability living allowance;

(ii)   severe disablement allowance;

(iii)   industrial injury disablement benefit;

(iv)   attendance allowance;

(v)   carer's allowance;

(vi)   personal independence payment;

(vii)   Armed Forces Independence Payment or Guaranteed Income Payment under the Armed Forces Compensation Scheme;

(viii) Constant Attendance Allowance, Mobility Supplement or War Disablement Pension under the War Pensions Scheme; or

(ix)   Police Injury Pension; and

(b)   the applicant must provide evidence that their parent's partner is able to maintain and accommodate themselves, the applicant's parent, the applicant and any dependants adequately in the UK without recourse to public funds.

E-LTRC.2.3A. Where a parent of the applicant has, or is applying or has applied for, limited leave to remain as a parent under this Appendix, the applicant must provide evidence that that parent is able to maintain and accommodate themselves, the applicant and any other dependants adequately in the UK without recourse to public funds.

E-LTRC.2.4.   The applicant must provide evidence that there will be adequate accommodation in the UK, without recourse to public funds, for the family, including other family members who are not included in the application but who live in the same household, which the family own or occupy exclusively: accommodation will not be regarded as adequate if-

(a)   it is, or will be, overcrowded; or

(b)   it contravenes public health regulations.

Section D-LTRC: Decision on application for leave to remain as a child

D-LTRC.1.1.   If the applicant meets the requirements for leave to remain as a child the applicant will be granted leave to remain of a duration which will expire at the same time as the leave granted to the applicant's parent, and will be subject to the same conditions in respect of recourse to public funds as that parent. To qualify for indefinite leave to remain as a child of a person with indefinite leave to remain as a partner or parent, the applicant must meet the requirements of paragraph 298 of these rules.

D-LTRC.1.2.   If the applicant does not meet the requirements for leave to remain as a child the application will be refused.

Family life as a parent of a child in the UK

Section EC-PT: Entry clearance as a parent of a child in the UK

EC-PT.1.1.   The requirements to be met for entry clearance as a parent are that-

(a)   the applicant must be outside the UK;

(b)   the applicant must have made a valid application for entry clearance as a parent;

(c)   the applicant must not fall for refusal under any of the grounds in Section S-EC: Suitability–entry clearance; and

(d)   the applicant must meet all of the requirements of Section E-ECPT: Eligibility for entry clearance as a parent.

Section E-ECPT: Eligibility for entry clearance as a parent

E-ECPT.1.1.   To meet the eligibility requirements for entry clearance as a parent all of the requirements in paragraphs E-ECPT.2.1. to 4.2. must be met.

Relationship requirements

E-ECPT.2.1.   The applicant must be aged 18 years or over.

E-ECPT.2.2.   The child of the applicant must be-

(a)   under the age of 18 years at the date of application;

(b)   living in the UK; and

(c)   a British Citizen, settled in the UK, or in the UK with limited leave under Appendix EU in accordance with paragraph GEN.1.3.(d).

E-ECPT.2.3.   Either -
    (a)   the applicant must have sole parental responsibility for the child; or
    (b)   the parent or carer with whom the child normally lives must be-
        (i)   a British Citizen in the UK, settled in the UK, or in the UK with limited leave under Appendix EU in accordance with paragraph GEN.1.3.(d);
        (ii)   not the partner of the applicant; and
        (iii)   the applicant must not be eligible to apply for entry clearance as a partner under this Appendix.
E-ECPT.2.4.   (a)   The applicant must provide evidence that they have either-
        (i)   sole parental responsibility for the child; or
        (ii)   direct access (in person) to the child, as agreed with the parent or carer with whom the child normally lives or as ordered by a court in the UK; and
    (b)   The applicant must provide evidence that they are taking, and intend to continue to take, an active role in the child's upbringing.

Financial requirements

E-ECPT.3.1.   The applicant must provide evidence that they will be able to adequately maintain and accommodate themselves and any dependants in the UK without recourse to public funds
E-ECPT.3.2.   The applicant must provide evidence that there will be adequate accommodation in the UK, without recourse to public funds, for the family, including other family members who are not included in the application but who live in the same household, which the family own or occupy exclusively: accommodation will not be regarded as adequate if-
    (a)   it is, or will be, overcrowded; or
    (b)   it contravenes public health regulations.

English language requirement

E-ECPT.4.1.   The applicant must provide specified evidence that they-
    (a)   are a national of a majority English speaking country listed in paragraph GEN.1.6.;
    (b)   have passed an English language test in speaking and listening at a minimum of level A1 of the Common European Framework of Reference for Languages with a provider approved by the Secretary of State;
    (c)   have an academic qualification which is either a Bachelor's or Master's degree or PhD awarded by an educational establishment in the UK; or, if awarded by an educational establishment outside the UK, is deemed by Ecctis to meet or exceed the recognised standard of a Bachelor's or Master's degree or PhD in the UK, and Ecctis has confirmed that the degree was taught or researched in English to level A1 of the Common European Framework of Reference for Languages or above; or
    (d)   are exempt from the English language requirement under paragraph E-ECPT.4.2.
E-ECPT.4.2.   The applicant is exempt from the English language requirement if at the date of application-
    (a)   the applicant is aged 65 or over;
    (b)   the applicant has a disability (physical or mental condition) which prevents the applicant from meeting the requirement; or
    (c)   there are exceptional circumstances which prevent the applicant from being able to meet the requirement prior to entry to the UK.

Section D-ECPT: Decision on application for entry clearance as a parent

D-ECPT.1.1.   If the applicant meets the requirements for entry clearance as a parent (except where paragraph GEN.3.2.(3) applies), the applicant will be granted entry clearance for an initial period not exceeding 33 months, and subject to a condition of no recourse to public funds, and they will be eligible to apply for settlement after a continuous period of at least 60 months in the UK with leave to enter granted on the basis of such entry clearance or with limited leave to remain as a parent granted under paragraph D-LTRPT.1.1.
D-ECPT.1.2.   If paragraph GEN.3.2.(3) applies to an applicant for entry clearance as a parent, the applicant will be granted entry clearance for an initial period not exceeding 33 months, and subject to a condition of no recourse to public funds unless the decision-maker considers, with reference to paragraph GEN.1.11A., that the person should not be subject to such a condition, and they will be eligible to apply for settlement after a continuous period of at least 120 months in the UK with leave to enter granted on the basis of such entry clearance or of

entry clearance granted under paragraph D-ECPT.1.1. or with limited leave to remain as a parent granted under paragraph D-LTRPT.1.1. or D-LTRPT.1.2.

D-ECPT.1.3.   If the applicant does not meet the requirements for entry clearance as a parent, the application will be refused.

Section R-LTRPT: Requirements for limited leave to remain as a parent

R-LTRPT.1.1.   The requirements to be met for limited leave to remain as a parent are-

    (a)   the applicant and the child must be in the UK;

    (b)   the applicant must have made a valid application for limited or indefinite leave to remain as a parent or partner; and either

    (c)   (i)   the applicant must not fall for refusal under Section S-LTR: Suitability leave to remain; and

        (ii)   the applicant meets all of the requirements of Section E-LTRPT: Eligibility for leave to remain as a parent, or

    (d)   (i)   the applicant must not fall for refusal under S-LTR: Suitability leave to remain; and

        (ii)   the applicant meets the requirements of paragraphs E-LTRPT.2.2-2.4. and E-LTRPT.3.1-3.2.; and

        (iii)   paragraph EX.1. applies.

Section E-LTRPT: Eligibility for limited leave to remain as a parent

E-LTRPT.1.1.   To qualify for limited leave to remain as a parent all of the requirements of paragraphs E-LTRPT.2.2. to 5.2. must be met.

Relationship requirements

E-LTRPT.2.2.   The child of the applicant must be-

    (a)   under the age of 18 years at the date of application, or where the child has turned 18 years of age since the applicant was first granted entry clearance or leave to remain as a parent under this Appendix, must not have formed an independent family unit or be leading an independent life;

    (b)   living in the UK; and

    (c)   a British Citizen, settled in the UK, or in the UK with limited leave under Appendix EU in accordance with paragraph GEN.1.3.(d); or

    (d)   has lived in the UK continuously for at least the 7 years immediately preceding the date of application and paragraph EX.1. applies.

E-LTRPT.2.3.   Either-

    (a)   the applicant must have sole parental responsibility for the child or the child normally lives with the applicant and not their other parent (who is a British Citizen, settled in the UK, or in the UK with limited leave under Appendix EU in accordance with paragraph GEN.1.3.(d)), and the applicant must not be eligible to apply for leave to remain as a partner under this Appendix; or

    (b)   the parent or carer with whom the child normally lives must be-

        (i)   a British Citizen in the UK, settled in the UK, or in the UK with limited leave under Appendix EU in accordance with paragraph GEN.1.3.(d);

        (ii)   not the partner of the applicant (which here includes a person who has been in a relationship with the applicant for less than two years prior to the date of application); and

        (iii)   the applicant must not be eligible to apply for leave to remain as a partner under this Appendix.

E-LTRPT.2.4.   (a)   The applicant must provide evidence that they have either-

        (i)   sole parental responsibility for the child, or that the child normally lives with them; or

        (ii)   direct access (in person) to the child, as agreed with the parent or carer with whom the child normally lives or as ordered by a court in the UK; and

    (b)   The applicant must provide evidence that they are taking, and intend to continue to take, an active role in the child's upbringing.

Immigration status requirement

E-LTRPT.3.1.   The applicant must not be in the UK-

    (a)   as a visitor; or

(b)   with valid leave granted for a period of 6 months or less, unless that leave was granted pending the outcome of family court or divorce proceedings;

E-LTRPT.3.2.   The applicant must not be in the UK –

(a)   on immigration bail, unless:

(i)   the Secretary of State is satisfied that the applicant arrived in the UK more than 6 months prior to the date of application; and

(ii)   paragraph EX.1. applies; or

(b)   in breach of immigration laws (except that, where paragraph 39E of these Rules applies, any current period of overstaying will be disregarded), unless paragraph EX.1. applies.

Financial requirements

E-LTRPT.4.1.   The applicant must provide evidence that they will be able to adequately maintain and accommodate themselves and any dependants in the UK without recourse to public funds, unless paragraph EX.1. applies.

E-LTRPT.4.2.   The applicant must provide evidence that there will be adequate accommodation in the UK, without recourse to public funds, for the family, including other family members who are not included in the application but who live in the same household, which the family own or occupy exclusively, unless paragraph EX.1. applies: accommodation will not be regarded as adequate if-

(a)   it is, or will be, overcrowded; or

(b)   it contravenes public health regulations.

English language requirement

E-LTRPT.5.1.   If the applicant has not met the requirement in a previous application for entry clearance or leave to remain as a parent or partner, the applicant must provide specified evidence that they-

(a)   are a national of a majority English speaking country listed in paragraph GEN.1.6.;

(b)   have passed an English language test in speaking and listening at a minimum of level A1 of the Common European Framework of Reference for Languages with a provider approved by the Secretary of State;

(c)   have an academic qualification which is either a Bachelor's or Master's degree or PhD awarded by an educational establishment in the UK; or, if awarded by an educational establishment outside the UK, is deemed by Ecctis to meet or exceed the recognised standard of a Bachelor's or Master's degree or PhD in the UK, and Ecctis has confirmed that the degree was taught or researched in English to level A1 of the Common European Framework of Reference for Languages or above; or

(d)   are exempt from the English language requirement under paragraph E-LTRPT.5.2.;

unless paragraph EX.1. applies.

E-LTRPT.5.1A.   Where the applicant:

(i)   in a previous application for entry clearance or leave to remain as a parent or partner, met the English language requirement in paragraph E-ECP.4.1.(b), E-LTRP.4.1.(b), E-ECPT.4.1.(b) or E-LTRPT.5.1.(b) on the basis that they had passed an English language test in speaking and listening at level A1 of the Common European Framework of Reference for Languages; and

(ii)   was granted entry clearance or leave to remain as a parent or partner; and

(iii)   now seeks further leave to remain as a parent after 30 months in the UK with leave as a parent; then, the applicant must provide specified evidence that they:

(a)   are a national of a majority English speaking country listed in paragraph GEN.1.6.;

(b)   have passed an English language test in speaking and listening at a minimum of level A2 of the Common European Framework of Reference for Languages with a provider approved by the Secretary of State;

(c)   have an academic qualification which is either a Bachelor's or Master's degree or PhD awarded by an educational establishment in the UK; or, if awarded by an educational establishment outside the UK, is deemed by Ecctis to be equivalent to the standard of a Bachelor's or Master's degree or PhD in the UK, and Ecctis has confirmed that the degree was taught or researched in English to level A2 of the Common European Framework of Reference for Languages or above; or

(d)   are exempt from the English language requirement under paragraph E-LTRPT.5.2.;

unless paragraph EX.1. applies.

E-LTRPT.5.2.   The applicant is exempt from the English language requirement in paragraph E-LTRPT.5.1. or E-LTRPT.5.1A. if at the date of application-

(a)   the applicant is aged 65 or over;

(b)   the applicant has a disability (physical or mental condition) which prevents the applicant from meeting the requirement; or

(c)   there are exceptional circumstances which prevent the applicant from being able to meet the requirement.

Section D-LTRPT: Decision on application for limited leave to remain as a parent

D-LTRPT.1.1.   If the applicant meets the requirements in paragraph R-LTRPT.1.1.(a) to (c) for limited leave to remain as a parent the applicant will be granted limited leave to remain for a period not exceeding 30 months, and subject to a condition of no recourse to public funds, and they will be eligible to apply for settlement after a continuous period of at least 60 months with such leave or in the UK with leave to enter granted on the basis of entry clearance as a parent granted under paragraph D-ECPT.1.1.

D-LTRPT.1.2.   If the applicant meets the requirements in paragraph R-LTRPT.1.1.(a), (b) and (d) for limited leave to remain as a parent, or paragraph GEN.3.2.(3) applies to an applicant for leave to remain as a parent, the applicant will be granted leave to remain for a period not exceeding 30 months and subject to a condition of no recourse to public funds unless the decision-maker considers, with reference to paragraph GEN.1.11A., that the applicant should not be subject to such a condition, and they will be eligible to apply for settlement after a continuous period of at least 120 months in the UK with such leave, with limited leave to remain as a parent granted under paragraph D-LTRPT.1.1., or in the UK with leave to enter granted on the basis of entry clearance as a parent granted under paragraph D-ECPT.1.1. or D-ECPT.1.2.

D-LTRPT.1.3.   If the applicant does not meet the requirements for limited leave to remain as a parent the application will be refused.

Section R-ILRPT: Requirements for indefinite leave to remain (settlement) as a parent

R-ILRPT.1.1.   The requirements to be met for indefinite leave to remain as a parent are that-

(a)   the applicant must be in the UK;

(b)   the applicant must have made a valid application for indefinite leave to remain as a parent;

(c)   the applicant must not fall for refusal under any of the grounds in Section S-ILR: Suitability-indefinite leave to remain; and

(d)   deleted

(e)   the applicant must meet all of the requirements of Section E-ILRPT: Eligibility for indefinite leave to remain as a parent.

Section E-ILRPT: Eligibility for indefinite leave to remain as a parent

E-ILRPT.1.1.   To meet the eligibility requirements for indefinite leave to remain as a parent all of the requirements of paragraphs E-ILRPT.1.2. to 1.5. must be met.

E-ILRPT.1.2.   The applicant must be in the UK with valid leave to remain as a parent under this Appendix (except that, where paragraph 39E of these Rules applies, any current period of overstaying will be disregarded).

E-ILRPT.1.3.   (1)   The applicant must, at the date of application, have completed a continuous period of either:

(a)   at least 60 months in the UK with:

(i)   leave to enter granted on the basis of entry clearance as a parent granted under paragraph D-ECPT.1.1.; or

(ii)   limited leave to remain as a parent granted under paragraph D-LTRPT.1.1.; or

(iii)   a combination of (i) and (ii);

or

(b)   at least 120 months in the UK with:

(i)   leave to enter granted on the basis of entry clearance as a parent granted under paragraph D-ECPT.1.1. or D-ECPT.1.2.;

or

(ii)   limited leave to remain as a parent granted under paragraph D-LTRPT.1.1. or D-LTRPT.1.2.; or

(iii)   a combination of (i) and (ii).

(1A)   In respect of an application falling within sub-paragraph (1)(a) above, the applicant must meet all of the requirements of Section E-LTRPT: Eligibility for leave to remain as a parent (except that paragraph E-LTRPT.2.2.(c) cannot be met on the basis of a person being in the UK with limited leave under Appendix EU in accordance with paragraph GEN.1.3.(d)).

(1B)   In respect of an application falling within sub-paragraph (1)(b) above:

(a)   the applicant must meet all of the requirements of paragraphs E-LTRPT.2.2.- 2.4. (except that paragraph E-LTRPT.2.2.(c) cannot be met on the basis of a person being in the UK with limited leave under Appendix EU in accordance with paragraph GEN.1.3.(d)) and E-LTRPT.3.1.- 3.2.; and

(b)   paragraph EX.1. must apply.

E-ILRPT.1.4.   DELETED.

E-ILRPT.1.5.   The applicant must have demonstrated sufficient knowledge of the English language and sufficient knowledge about life in the United Kingdom in accordance with the requirements of Appendix KoLL of these Rules.

E-ILRPT.1.5A.   In calculating the periods under paragraph E-ILRPT.1.3., any current period of overstaying will be disregarded where paragraph 39E of these Rules applies. Any previous period of overstaying between periods of leave will also be disregarded where: the further application was made before 24 November 2016 and within 28 days of the expiry of leave; or the further application was made on or after 24 November 2016 and paragraph 39E of these Rules applied.

Section D-ILRPT: Decision on application for indefinite leave to remain as a parent

D-ILRPT.1.1.   If the applicant meets all of the requirements for indefinite leave to remain as a parent the applicant will be granted indefinite leave to remain.

D-ILRPT.1.2.   If the applicant does not meet the requirements for indefinite leave to remain as a parent only for one or both of the following reasons-

(a)   paragraph S-ILR.1.5. or S-ILR.1.6. applies; or

(b)   the applicant has not demonstrated sufficient knowledge of the English language or about life in the United Kingdom in accordance with Appendix KoLL,

subject to compliance with any requirement notified under paragraph GEN.1.15.(b), the applicant will be granted further limited leave to remain as a parent for a period not exceeding 30 months, and subject to a condition of no recourse to public funds.

D-ILRPT.1.3.   If the applicant does not meet all the eligibility requirements for indefinite leave to remain as a parent, and does not qualify for further limited leave to remain under paragraph D-ILRPT.1.2., the application will be refused, unless the applicant meets the requirements in paragraph R-LTRPT.1.1.(a), (b) and (d) for limited leave to remain as a parent. Where they do, and subject to compliance with any requirement notified under paragraph GEN.1.15.(b), the applicant will be granted further limited leave to remain as a parent for a period not exceeding 30 months under paragraph D-LTRPT.1.2. and subject to a condition of no recourse to public funds unless the Secretary of State considers that the person should not be subject to such a condition.

Adult dependent relative

Section EC-DR: Entry clearance as an adult dependent relative

EC-DR.1.1.   The requirements to be met for entry clearance as an adult dependent relative are that-

(a)   the applicant must be outside the UK;

(b)   the applicant must have made a valid application for entry clearance as an adult dependent relative;

(c)   the applicant must not fall for refusal under any of the grounds in Section S-EC: Suitability for entry clearance; and

(d)   the applicant must meet all of the requirements of Section E-ECDR: Eligibility for entry clearance as an adult dependent relative.

Section E-ECDR: Eligibility for entry clearance as an adult dependent relative

E-ECDR.1.1.   To meet the eligibility requirements for entry clearance as an adult dependent relative all of the requirements in paragraphs E-ECDR.2.1. to 3.2. must be met.

Relationship requirements

E-ECDR.2.1.   The applicant must be the-

(a)   parent aged 18 years or over;

(b)   grandparent;

(c)   brother or sister aged 18 years or over; or

(d)   son or daughter aged 18 years or over of a person ("the sponsor") who is in the UK.

E-ECDR.2.2.   If the applicant is the sponsor's parent or grandparent they must not be in a subsisting relationship with a partner unless that partner is also the sponsor's parent or grandparent and is applying for entry clearance at the same time as the applicant.

E-ECDR.2.3.   The sponsor must at the date of application be-

(a)   aged 18 years or over; and

(b)   (i)   a British Citizen in the UK; or

(ii)   present and settled in the UK; or

(iii)   in the UK with refugee leave or humanitarian protection; or

(iv)   in the UK with limited leave under Appendix EU, in accordance with paragraph GEN.1.3.(d).

E-ECDR.2.4.   The applicant or, if the applicant and their partner are the sponsor's parents or grandparents, the applicant's partner, must as a result of age, illness or disability require long-term personal care to perform everyday tasks.

E-ECDR.2.5.   The applicant or, if the applicant and their partner are the sponsor's parents or grandparents, the applicant's partner, must be unable, even with the practical and financial help of the sponsor, to obtain the required level of care in the country where they are living, because-

(a)   it is not available and there is no person in that country who can reasonably provide it; or

(b)   it is not affordable.

Financial requirements

E-ECDR.3.1.   The applicant must provide evidence that they can be adequately maintained, accommodated and cared for in the UK by the sponsor without recourse to public funds.

E-ECDR.3.2.   If the applicant's sponsor is a British Citizen or settled in the UK, the applicant must provide an undertaking signed by the sponsor confirming that the applicant will have no recourse to public funds, and that the sponsor will be responsible for their maintenance, accommodation and care, for a period of 5 years from the date the applicant enters the UK if they are granted indefinite leave to enter.

Section D-ECDR: Decision on application for entry clearance as an adult dependent relative

D-ECDR.1.1.   If the applicant meets the requirements for entry clearance as an adult dependent relative of a British Citizen or person settled in the UK they will be granted indefinite leave to enter.

D-ECDR.1.2.   If the applicant meets the requirements for entry clearance as an adult dependent relative and the sponsor has limited leave the applicant will be granted limited leave of a duration which will expire at the same time as the sponsor's limited leave, and subject to a condition of no recourse to public funds. If the sponsor applies for further limited leave, the applicant may apply for further limited leave of the same duration, if the requirements in EC-DR.1.1. (c) and (d) continue to be met, and subject to no recourse to public funds.

D-ECDR.1.3.   If the applicant does not meet the requirements for entry clearance as an adult dependent relative the application will be refused.

Section R-ILRDR: Requirements for indefinite leave to remain as an adult dependent relative

R-ILRDR.1.1.   The requirements to be met for indefinite leave to remain as an adult dependent relative are that-

(a)   the applicant is in the UK;

(b)   the applicant must have made a valid application for indefinite leave to remain as an adult dependent relative;

(c)   the applicant must not fall for refusal under any of the grounds in Section S-ILR: Suitability-indefinite leave to remain; and

(d)   the applicant must meet all of the requirements of Section E-ILRDR: Eligibility for indefinite leave to remain as an adult dependent relative.

Section E-ILRDR: Eligibility for indefinite leave to remain as an adult dependent relative

E-ILRDR.1.1.   To qualify for indefinite leave to remain as an adult dependent relative all of the requirements of paragraphs E-ILRDR.1.2. to 1.5. must be met.

E-ILRDR.1.2.   The applicant must be in the UK with valid leave to remain as an adult dependent relative (except that, where paragraph 39E of these Rules applies, any current period of overstaying will be disregarded).

E-ILRDR.1.3.   The applicant's sponsor must at the date of application be:

(a)   present and settled in the UK; or

(b)   in the UK with refugee leave or as a person with humanitarian protection, or in the UK with limited leave under Appendix EU in accordance with paragraph GEN.1.3.(d), and have made an application for indefinite leave to remain.

E-ILRDR.1.4.   The applicant must provide evidence that they can be adequately maintained, accommodated and cared for in the UK by the sponsor without recourse to public funds.

E-ILRDR.1.5.   The applicant must provide an undertaking signed by the sponsor confirming that the applicant will have no recourse to public funds, and that the sponsor will be responsible for their maintenance, accommodation and care, for a period ending 5 years from the date the applicant entered the UK with limited leave as an adult dependent relative.

Section D-ILRDR: Decision on application for indefinite leave to remain as an adult dependent relative

D-ILRDR.1.1.   If the applicant meets the requirements for indefinite leave to remain as an adult dependent relative and the applicant's sponsor is settled in the UK, the applicant will be granted indefinite leave to remain as an adult dependent relative.

D-ILRDR.1.2.   If the applicant does not meet the requirements for indefinite leave to remain as an adult dependent relative because paragraph S-ILR.1.5. or S-ILR.1.6. applies, the applicant will be granted further limited leave to remain as an adult dependent relative for a period not exceeding 30 months, and subject to a condition of no recourse to public funds.

D-ILRDR.1.3.   If the applicant's sponsor has made an application for indefinite leave to remain and that application is refused, the applicant's application for indefinite leave to remain will be refused. If the sponsor is granted limited leave, the applicant will be granted further limited leave as an adult dependent relative of a duration which will expire at the same time as the sponsor's further limited leave, and subject to a condition of no recourse to public funds.

D-ILRDR.1.4.   Where an applicant does not meet the requirements for indefinite leave to remain, or further limited leave to remain under paragraphs D-ILRDR.1.2. or 1.3., the application will be refused.

Deportation and removal

Where the Secretary of State or an immigration officer is considering deportation or removal of a person who claims that their deportation or removal from the UK would be a breach of the right to respect for private and family life under Article 8 of the Human Rights Convention that person may be required to make an application under this Appendix or paragraph 276ADE(1), but if they are not required to make an application Part 13 of these Rules will apply.

Appendix FM-SE: family members specified evidence

Family members - specified evidence

A.   This Appendix sets out the specified evidence applicants need to provide to meet the requirements of rules contained in Appendix FM and, where those requirements are also contained in other rules, including Appendix Armed Forces, and unless otherwise stated, the specified evidence applicants need to provide to meet the requirements of those rules.

B.   Where evidence is not specified by Appendix FM, but is of a type covered by this Appendix, the requirements of this Appendix shall apply.

C.   In this Appendix references to paragraphs are to paragraphs of this Appendix unless the context otherwise requires.

D.   (a)   In deciding an application in relation to which this Appendix states that specified documents must be provided, the Entry Clearance Officer or Secretary of State ("the decision-maker") will consider documents that have been submitted with the application, and will only consider documents submitted after the application where sub-paragraph (b), (e) or (f) applies.

    (b)   If the applicant:

        (i)   Has submitted:

            (aa)   A sequence of documents and some of the documents in the sequence have been omitted (e.g. if one bank statement from a series is missing);

            (bb)   A document in the wrong format (for example, if a letter is not on letterhead paper as specified); or

            (cc)   DELETED

            (dd)   A document which does not contain all of the specified information; or

        (ii)   Has not submitted a specified document, the decision-maker may contact the applicant or his representative in writing or otherwise, and request the document(s) or the correct version(s). The material requested must be received at the address specified in the request within a reasonable timescale specified in the request.

    (c)   The decision-maker will not request documents where he or she does not anticipate that addressing the error or omission referred to in sub-paragraph (b) will lead to a grant because the application will be refused for other reasons.

    (d)   If the applicant has submitted:

        (i)   A document in the wrong format; or

        (ii)   DELETED

        (iii)   A document that does not contain all of the specified information, but the missing information is verifiable from:

            (1)   other documents submitted with the application,

            (2)   the website of the organisation which issued the document, or

            (3)   the website of the appropriate regulatory body,

    the application may be granted exceptionally, providing the decision-maker is satisfied that the document(s) is genuine and that the applicant meets the requirement to which the document relates.

    (e)   Where the decision-maker is satisfied that there is a valid reason why a specified document(s) cannot be supplied, e.g. because it is not issued in a particular country or has been permanently lost, he or she may exercise discretion not to apply the requirement for the document(s) or to request alternative or additional information or document(s) be submitted by the applicant.

    (f)   Before making a decision under Appendix FM or this Appendix, the decision-maker may contact the applicant or their representative in writing or otherwise to request further information or documents. The material requested must be received at the address specified in the request within a reasonable timescale specified in the request.

E.   A reference in this Appendix to the provision of evidence from a UK government department includes evidence from a body performing an equivalent function to such a department.

Evidence of Financial Requirements under Appendix FM

A1.   To meet the financial requirement under paragraphs E-ECP.3.1., E-LTRP.3.1., E-ECC.2.1. and E-LTRC.2.1. of Appendix FM, the applicant must meet:

(a)   The level of financial requirement applicable to the application under Appendix FM; and

(b)   The requirements specified in Appendix FM and this Appendix as to:

    (i)   The permitted sources of income and savings;

    (ii)   The time periods and permitted combinations of sources applicable to each permitted source relied upon; and

    (iii)   The evidence required for each permitted source relied upon.

1.   In relation to evidencing the financial requirements in Appendix FM the following general provisions shall apply:

(a)   Bank statements must:

    (i)   be from a financial institution to which Appendix Finance applies.

    (ii)   DELETED

    (iii)   in relation to personal bank statements be only in the name of:

        (1)   the applicant's partner, the applicant or both as appropriate; or

        (2)   if the applicant is a child the applicant parent's partner, the applicant's parent or both as appropriate; or

        (3)   if the applicant is an adult dependent relative, the applicant's sponsor or the applicant, unless otherwise stated.

    (iv)   cover the period(s) specified.

    (v)   be:

        (1)   on official bank stationery; or

        (2)   electronic bank statements which are either accompanied by a letter from the bank on its headed stationery confirming that the documents are authentic or which bear the official stamp of the issuing bank on every page.

(aa)   Where a bank statement is specified in this Appendix, a building society statement, a building society pass book, a letter from the applicant's bank or building society, or a letter from a financial institution regulated by the Financial Conduct Authority and the Prudential Regulation Authority or, for overseas accounts, the appropriate regulatory body for the country in which the institution operates and the funds are located, may be submitted as an alternative to a bank statement(s) provided that:

    (1)   the requirements in paragraph 1(a)(i)-(iv) are met as if the document were a bank statement; and

    (2)   a building society pass book must clearly show:

        (i)   the account number;

        (ii)   the building society's name and logo; and

        (iii)   the information required on transactions, funds held and time period(s) or as otherwise specified in this Appendix in relation to bank statements; and/or

    (3)   a letter must be on the headed stationery of the bank, building society or other financial institution and must clearly show:

        (i)   the account number,

        (ii)   the date of the letter;

        (iii)   the financial institution's name and logo; and

        (iv)   the information required on transactions, funds held and time period(s) or as otherwise specified in this Appendix in relation to bank statements.

(b)   Promises of third party support will not be accepted, except in the limited circumstances set out in paragraph 21A (and to the extent permitted by that paragraph). Existing sources of third party support will be accepted in the form of:

    (i)   payments from a former partner of the applicant for the maintenance of the applicant or any children of the applicant and the former partner, and payments from a former partner of the applicant's partner for the maintenance of that partner;

    (ii)   income from a dependent child who has turned 18, remains in the same UK household as the applicant and continues to be counted towards the financial requirement under Appendix FM;

    (iii)   gift of cash savings (whose source must be declared) evidenced at paragraph 1(a)(iii), provided that the cash savings have been held by the person or persons at paragraph 1(a)(iii) for at least 6 months prior to the date of application and are under their control; and

      (iv)   a maintenance grant or stipend associated with undergraduate study or postgraduate study or research.

(bb)   Payslips must be:

      (i)   formal payslips issued by the employer and showing the employer's name; or

      (ii)   accompanied by a letter from the employer, on the employer's headed paper and signed by a senior official, confirming the payslips are authentic;

(c)   The employment or self employment income of an applicant will be taken into account if they are in the UK, aged 18 years or over and working legally, and prospective employment income will not be taken into account (except that of an applicant's partner or parent's partner who is returning to employment or self-employment in the UK at paragraphs E-ECP.3.2.(a) and E-ECC.2.2.(a) of Appendix FM, or where paragraph 21A of this Appendix so permits).

(cc)   The income of an applicant or sponsor working in the UK in salaried or non-salaried employment or in self-employment can include income from work undertaken overseas, provided paragraph E-LTRP.1.10 of Appendix FM and the other requirements of this Appendix are met.

(d)   All income and savings must be lawfully derived.

(e)   Savings must be held in cash.

(f)   Income or cash savings in a foreign currency will be converted to pounds sterling using the closing spot exchange rate which appears on www.oanda.com* on the date of application.

(g)   Where there is income or cash savings in different foreign currencies, each will be converted into pounds sterling before being added together, and then added to any UK income or savings to give a total amount.

(h)   DELETED

(i)   Evidence of profit from the sale of a business, property, investment, bond, stocks, shares or other asset will:

      (i)   not be accepted as evidence of income, but

      (ii)   the associated funds will be accepted as cash savings subject to the requirements of this Appendix and Appendix FM.

(j)   Where any specified documents provided are not in English or Welsh, the applicant must provide document in the original language and a full translation that can be independently verified by the Entry Clearance Officer, Immigration Officer or the Secretary of State. The translation must be dated and include:

      (i)   confirmation that it is an accurate translation of the document;

      (ii)   the full name and signature of the translator or an authorised official of the translation company;

      (iii)   the translator or translation company's contact details; and

      (iv)   if the applicant is applying for leave to remain or indefinite leave to remain, certification by a qualified translator and details of the translator or translation company's credentials.

(k)   Where the gross (pre-tax) amount of any income cannot be properly evidenced, the net (post-tax) amount will be counted, including towards a gross income requirement.

(l)   Where this Appendix requires the applicant to provide specified evidence relating to a period which ends with the date of application, that evidence, or the most recently dated part of it, must be dated no earlier than 28 days before the date of application.

(m)   Cash income on which the correct tax has been paid may be counted as income under this Appendix, subject to the relevant evidential requirements of this Appendix.

(n)   The gross amount of any cash income may be counted where the person's specified bank statements show the net amount which relates to the gross amount shown on their payslips (or in the relevant specified evidence provided in addition to the specified bank statements in relation to non-employment income). Otherwise, only the net amount shown on the specified bank statements may be counted.

(o)   In this Appendix, a reference to the "average" is a reference to the mean average.

2.   In respect of salaried employment in the UK (except where paragraph 9 applies), all of the following evidence must be provided:

    (a)   Payslips covering:

       (i)   a period of 6 months prior to the date of application if the person has been employed by their current employer for at least 6 months (and where paragraph 13(b) of this Appendix does not apply); or

       (ii)   any period of salaried employment in the period of 12 months prior to the date of application if the person has been employed by their current employer for less than 6 months (or at least 6 months but the person does not rely on paragraph 13(a) of this Appendix), or in the financial year(s) relied upon by a self-employed person.

    (b)   A letter from the employer(s) who issued the payslips at paragraph 2(a) confirming:

       (i)   the person's employment and gross annual salary;

       (ii)   the length of their employment;

       (iii)   the period over which they have been or were paid the level of salary relied upon in the application; and

       (iv)   the type of employment (permanent, fixed-term contract or agency).

    (c)   Personal bank statements corresponding to the same period(s) as the payslips at paragraph 2(a), showing that the salary has been paid into an account in the name of the person or in the name of the person and their partner jointly.

    (d)   Where the person is a director of a limited company based in the UK, evidence that the company is not of a type specified in paragraph 9(a). This can include the latest Annual Return filed at Companies House.

    (e)   Where a person appointed as a non-executive director of a limited company based in the UK, which is not a company of the type specified in paragraph 9(a), is paid a fee instead of a salary, this income may be treated and evidenced as though it were income received for employment in that capacity.

2A.   (i)   In respect of salaried employment in the UK (paragraph 2 of this Appendix), statutory or contractual maternity, paternity, adoption or sick pay in the UK (paragraph 5 or 6 of this Appendix), or a director's salary paid to a self-employed person (paragraph 9 of this Appendix), the applicant may, in addition to the payslips and personal bank statements required under that paragraph, submit the P60 for the relevant period(s) of employment relied upon (if issued). If they do not, the Entry Clearance Officer or Secretary of State may grant the application if otherwise satisfied that the requirements of this Appendix relating to that employment are met. The Entry Clearance Officer or Secretary of State may request that the applicant submit the document(s) in accordance with paragraph D of this Appendix.

       (ii)   In respect of salaried employment in the UK (paragraph 2 of this Appendix), or statutory or contractual maternity, paternity, adoption or sick pay in the UK (paragraph 5 or 6 of this Appendix), the applicant may, in addition to the letter from the employer(s) required under that paragraph, submit a signed contract of employment. If they do not, the Entry Clearance Officer or Secretary of State may grant the application if otherwise satisfied that the requirements of this Appendix relating to that employment are met. The Entry Clearance Officer or Secretary of State may request that the applicant submit the document(s) in accordance with paragraph D of this Appendix.

3.   In respect of salaried employment outside of the UK, evidence should be a reasonable equivalent to that set out in paragraph 2 and (where relevant) paragraph 2A. In respect of an equity partner whose income from the partnership is treated as salaried employment under paragraph 17, the payslips and employer's letter referred to in paragraph 2 may be replaced by other evidence providing the relevant information in paragraph 2 (which may include, but is not confined to, a letter on official stationery from an accountant, solicitor or business manager acting for the partnership).

4.   In respect of a job offer in the UK (for an applicant's partner or parent's partner returning to salaried employment in the UK at paragraphs E-ECP.3.2.(a) and E-ECC.2.2.(a) of Appendix FM) a letter from the employer must be provided:

    (a)   confirming the job offer, the gross annual salary and the starting date of the employment which must be within 3 months of the applicant's partner's return to the UK; or

    (b)   enclosing a signed contract of employment, which must have a starting date within 3 months of the applicant's partner's return to the UK.

5.   In respect of statutory or contractual maternity, paternity or adoption pay all of the following, and in respect of parental leave in the UK only the evidence at paragraph 5(c), must be provided:

    (a)   Personal bank statements corresponding to the same period(s) as the payslips at paragraph 5(b), showing that the salary has been paid into an account in the name of the person or in the name of the person and their partner jointly.

(b)   Payslips covering:

    (i)   a period of 6 months prior to the date of application or to the commencement of the maternity, paternity or adoption leave, if the applicant has been employed by their current employer for at least 6 months (and where paragraph 13(b) does not apply); or

    (ii)   any period of salaried employment in the period of 12 months prior to the date of application or to the commencement of the maternity, paternity or adoption leave, if the applicant has been employed by their current employer for less than 6 months (or at least 6 months but the person does not rely on paragraph 13(a)).

(c)   A letter from the employer confirming:

    (i)   the length of the person's employment;

    (ii)   the gross annual salary and the period over which it has been paid at this level;

    (iii)   the entitlement to maternity, paternity, parental or adoption leave; and

    (iv)   the date of commencement and the end-date of the maternity, paternity, parental or adoption leave.

6.   In respect of statutory or contractual sick pay in the UK all of the following must be provided:

(a)   Personal bank statements corresponding to the same period(s) as the payslips at paragraph 6(b), showing that the salary has been paid into an account in the name of the person or in the name of the person and their partner jointly.

(b)   Payslips covering:

    (i)   a period of 6 months prior to the date of application or to the commencement of the sick leave, if the applicant has been employed by their current employer for at least 6 months (and where paragraph 13(b) does not apply); or,

    (ii)   any period of salaried employment in the period of 12 months prior to the date of application or to the commencement of the sick leave, if the applicant has been employed by their current employer for less than 6 months (or at least 6 months but the person does not rely on paragraph 13(a)).

(c)   A letter from employer confirming:

    (i)   the length of the person's employment;

    (ii)   the gross annual salary and the period over which it has been paid at this level;

    (iii)   that the person is in receipt of statutory or contractual sick pay; and

    (iv)   the date of commencement of the sick leave.

7.   In respect of self-employment in the UK as a partner, as a sole trader or in a franchise all of the following must be provided:

(a)   Evidence of the amount of tax payable, paid and unpaid for the last full financial year.

(b)   The following documents for the last full financial year, or for the last two such years (where those documents show the necessary level of gross profit as an average of those two years):

    (i)   annual self-assessment tax return to HMRC (a copy or print-out); and

    (ii)   Statement of Account (SA300 or SA302).

(c)   Proof of registration with HMRC as self-employed if available.

(d)   Each partner's Unique Tax Reference Number (UTR) and/or the UTR of the partnership or business.

(e)   Where the person holds or held a separate business bank account(s), bank statements for the same 12-month period as the tax return(s).

(f)   personal bank statements for the same 12-month period as the tax return(s) showing that the income from self-employment has been paid into an account in the name of the person or in the name of the person and their partner jointly.

(g)   Evidence of ongoing self-employment through the provision of at least one of the following: a bank statement dated no more than three months earlier than the date of application showing transactions relating to ongoing trading, or evidence dated no more than three months earlier than the date of application of the renewal of a licence to trade or of ongoing payment of business rates, business-related insurance premiums, employer National Insurance contributions or franchise payments to the parent company.

(h)   One of the following documents must also be submitted:

        (i)   (aa)   If the business is required to produce annual audited accounts, such accounts for the last full financial year; or

                (bb)   If the business is not required to produce annual audited accounts, unaudited accounts for the last full financial year and an accountant's certificate of confirmation, from an accountant who is a member of a UK Recognised Supervisory Body (as defined in the Companies Act 2006) or who is a member of the Institute of Financial Accountants, The Association of Authorised Public Accountants, The Chartered Institute of Public Finance and Accountancy, The Chartered Institute of Management Accountants, the Association of International Accountants and The Association of Accounting Technicians;

        (ii)   A certificate of VAT registration and the VAT return for the last full financial year (a copy or print-out) confirming the VAT registration number, if turnover is in excess of £79,000 or was in excess of the threshold which applied during the last full financial year;

        (iii)   Evidence to show appropriate planning permission or local planning authority consent is held to operate the type/class of business at the trading address (where this is a local authority requirement); or

        (iv)   A franchise agreement signed by both parties.

    (i)   The document referred to in paragraph 7(h)(iv) must be provided if the organisation is a franchise.

8.   In respect of self-employment outside of the UK, evidence should be a reasonable equivalent to that set out in paragraph 7.

8A.   In respect of prospective self-employment in the UK (for an applicant's partner or parent's partner who, in respect of paragraph E-ECP.3.2.(a) or E-ECC.2.2.(a) of Appendix FM, is in self-employment outside the UK at the date of application and is returning to the UK to continue that self-employment), one of the following must be provided, with a starting date within three months of the person's return to the UK:

    (a)   An application to the appropriate authority for a licence to trade;

    (b)   Details of the purchase or rental of business premises;

    (c)   A signed employment contract or a signed contract for the provision of services; or

    (d)   A partnership or franchise agreement signed by the relevant parties to the agreement.

9.   In respect of income from employment and/or shares in a limited company based in the UK of a type specified in paragraph 9(a), the requirements of paragraph 9(b)-(e) shall apply in place of the requirements of paragraphs 2 and 10(b).

    (a)   The specified type of limited company is one in which:

        (i)   the person is either a director or employee of the company, or both, or of another company within the same group; and

        (ii)   shares are held (directly or indirectly) by the person, their partner or the following family members of the person or their partner: parent, grandparent, child, stepchild, grandchild, brother, sister, uncle, aunt, nephew, niece or first cousin; and

        (iii)   any remaining shares are held (directly or indirectly) by fewer than five other persons.

    (b)   All of the following must be provided:

        (i)   Company Tax Return CT600 (a copy or print-out) for the last full financial year and evidence this has been filed with HMRC, such as electronic or written acknowledgment from HMRC.

        (ii)   Evidence of registration with the Registrar of Companies at Companies House.

        (iii)   If the company is required to produce annual audited accounts, such accounts for the last full financial year.

        (iv)   If the company is not required to produce annual audited accounts, unaudited accounts for the last full financial year and an accountant's certificate of confirmation, from an accountant who is a member of a UK Recognized Supervisory Body (as defined in the Companies Act 2006) or who is a member of the Institute of Financial Accountants, The Association of Authorised Public Accountants, The Chartered Institute of Public Finance and Accountancy, The Chartered Institute of Management Accountants, the Association of International Accountants and The Association of Accounting Technicians.

        (v)   Corporate/business bank statements covering the same 12-month period as the Company Tax Return CT600.

        (vi)   A current Appointment Report from Companies House.

        (vii)   One of the following documents must also be provided:

(1)   A certificate of VAT registration and the VAT return for the last full financial year (a copy or print-out) confirming the VAT registration number, if turnover is in excess of £79,000 or was in excess of the threshold which applied during the last full financial year.

(2)   Proof of ownership or lease of business premises.

(3)   Proof of registration with HMRC as an employer for the purposes of PAYE and National Insurance, proof of PAYE reference number and Accounts Office reference number. This evidence may be in the form of a certified copy of the documentation issued by HMRC.

(c)   Where the person is either listed as a director of the company, or is an employee of the company, or both, and receives a salary from the company, all of the following documents must also be provided:

(i)   Payslips and P60 (if issued) covering the same period as the Company Tax Return CT600.

(ii)   Personal bank statements covering the same 12-month period as the Company Tax Return CT600 showing that the salary as a director or employee of the company (or both) was paid into an account in the name of the person or in the name of the person and their partner jointly.

(d)   Where the person receives dividends from the company, all of the following documents must also be provided:

(i)   Dividend vouchers for all dividends declared in favour of the person during or in respect of the period covered by the Company Tax Return CT600 showing the company's and the person's details with the person's net dividend amount.

(ii)   Personal bank statement(s) showing that those dividends were paid into an account in the name of the person or in the name of the person and their partner jointly.

(e)   For the purposes of paragraph 19(a), evidence of ongoing employment as a director or other employee of the company or of ongoing receipt of dividend income from the company must be provided. This evidence may include payslips (or dividend vouchers) and personal bank statements showing that, in the period since the latest 12-month period covered by the Company Tax Return CT600, the person's salary as a director or employee of the company (or both) (or dividend income from the company) was paid into an account in the name of the person or in the name of the person and their partner jointly. Alternative evidence may include evidence of ongoing payment of business rates, business-related insurance premiums or employer National Insurance contributions in relation to the company.

10.   In respect of non-employment income all the following evidence, in relation to the form of income relied upon, must be provided:

(a)   To evidence property rental income:

(i)   Confirmation that the person or the person and their partner jointly own the property for which the rental income is received, through:

(1)   A copy of the title deeds of the property or of the title register from the Land Registry (or overseas equivalent); or

(2)   A mortgage statement.

(ii)   personal bank statements for or from the 12-month period prior to the date of application showing the income relied upon was paid into an account in the name of the person or of the person and their partner jointly.

(iii)   A rental agreement or contract.

(b)   To evidence dividends (except where paragraph 9 applies) or other income from investments, stocks, shares, bonds or trust funds:

(i)   A certificate showing proof of ownership and the amount(s) of any investment(s).

(ii)   A portfolio report (for a financial institution regulated by the Financial Conduct Authority (and the Prudential Regulation Authority where applicable) in the UK) or a dividend voucher showing the company and person's details with the person's net dividend amount.

(iii)   personal bank statements for or from the 12-month period prior to the date of application showing that the income relied upon was paid into an account in the name of the person or of the person and their partner jointly.

(iv)   Where the person is a director of a limited company based in the UK, evidence that the company is not of a type specified in paragraph 9(a). This can include the latest Annual Return filed at Companies House.

(c)   To evidence interest from savings:

(i) personal bank statements for or from the 12-month period prior to the date of application showing the amount of the savings held and that the interest was paid into an account in the name of the person or of the person and their partner jointly.

(d) To evidence maintenance payments (from a former partner of the applicant to maintain their and the applicant's child or children or the applicant, or from a former partner of the applicant's partner to maintain the applicant's partner):

    (i) Evidence of a maintenance agreement through any of the following:

        (1) A court order;

        (2) Written voluntary agreement; or

        (3) Child Support Agency documentation.

    (ii) personal bank statements for or from the 12-month period prior to the date of application showing the income relied upon was paid into an account in the name of the person or the person and their partner jointly.

(e) To evidence a pension:

    (i) Official documentation from:

        (1) The Department for Work and Pensions (in respect of the Basic State Pension and the Additional or Second State Pension) or other government department or agency, including the Veterans Agency;

        (2) An overseas pension authority; or

        (3) A pension company,

    confirming pension entitlement and amount (and, where applicable, reflecting any funds withdrawn from the pension account or fund).

    (ii) At least one personal bank statement in the 12-month period prior to the date of application showing payment of the pension into the person's account.

    (iii) For the purposes of sub-paragraph (i), War Disablement Pension, War Widow's/Widower's Pension and any other pension or equivalent payment for life made under the War Pensions Scheme, the Armed Forces Compensation Scheme or the Armed Forces Attributable Benefits Scheme may be treated as a pension, unless excluded under paragraph 21 of this Appendix.

(f) To evidence UK Maternity Allowance, Bereavement Allowance, Bereavement Payment and Widowed Parent's Allowance:

    (i) Department for Work and Pensions documentation confirming the person or their partner is or was in receipt of the benefit in the 12-month period prior to the date of application.

    (ii) personal bank statements for or from the 12-month period prior to the date of application showing the income was paid into the person's account.

(ff) Subject to paragraph 12, to evidence payments under the War Pensions Scheme, the Armed Forces Compensation Scheme or the Armed Forces Attributable Benefits Scheme which are not treated as a pension for the purposes of paragraph 10(e)(i):

    (i) Veterans Agency or Department for Work and Pensions documentation in the form of an award notification letter confirming the person or their partner is or was in receipt of the payment at the date of application.

    (ii) personal bank statements for or from the 12-month period prior to the date of application showing the income was paid into the person's account.

(g) To evidence a maintenance grant or stipend (not a loan) associated with undergraduate study or postgraduate study or research:

    (i) Documentation from the body or company awarding the grant or stipend confirming that the person is currently in receipt of the grant or stipend or will be within 3 months of the date of application, confirming that the grant or stipend will be paid for a period of at least 12 months or for at least one full academic year from the date of application or from the date on which payment of the grant or stipend will commence, and confirming the annual amount of the grant or stipend. Where the grant or stipend is or will be paid on a tax-free basis, the amount of the gross equivalent may be counted as income under this Appendix.

    (ii) personal bank statements for any part of the 12-month period prior to the date of the application during which the person has been in receipt of the grant or stipend showing the income was paid into the person's account.

(h)   To evidence ongoing insurance payments (such as, but not exclusively, payments received under an income protection policy):

    (i)   documentation from the insurance company confirming:

        (a)   that in the 12 months prior to the date of application the person has been in receipt of insurance payments and the amount and frequency of the payments.

        (b)   the reason for the payments and their expected duration.

        (c)   that, provided any relevant terms and conditions continue to be met, the payment(s) will continue for at least the 12 months following the date of application.

    (ii)   personal bank statements for or from the 12-month period prior to the date of application showing the insurance payments were paid into the person's account.

(i)   To evidence ongoing payments (other than maintenance payments under paragraph 10(d)) arising from a structured legal settlement (such as, but not exclusively, one arising from settlement of a personal injury claim):

    (i)   documentation from a court or the person's legal representative confirming:

        (a)   that in the 12 months prior to the date of application the person has been in receipt of structured legal settlement payments and the amount and frequency of those payments.

        (b)   the reason for the payments and their expected duration.

        (c)   that the payment(s) will continue for at least the 12 months following the date of application.

    (ii)   personal bank statements for or from the 12-month period prior to the date of application showing the payments were paid into the person's account, either directly or via the person's legal representative.

11.   In respect of cash savings the following must be provided:

(a)   personal bank statements showing that at least the level of cash savings relied upon in the application has been held in an account(s) in the name of the person or of the person and their partner jointly throughout the period of 6 months prior to the date of application.

(b)   A declaration by the account holder(s) of the source(s) of the cash savings.

11A.   In respect of cash savings:

(a)   The savings may be held in any form of bank/savings account (whether a current, deposit or investment account, provided by a financial institution regulated by the appropriate regulatory body for the country in which that institution is operating), provided that the account allows the savings to be accessed immediately (with or without a penalty for withdrawing funds without notice). This can include savings held in a pension savings account which can be immediately withdrawn.

(b)   Paid out competition winnings or a legacy which has been paid can contribute to cash savings.

(c)   Funds held as cash savings by the applicant, their partner or both jointly at the date of application can have been transferred from investments, stocks, shares, bonds or trust funds within the period of 6 months prior to the date of application, provided that:

    (i)   The funds have been in the ownership and under the control of the applicant, their partner or both jointly for at least the period of 6 months prior to the date of application.

    (ii)   The ownership of the funds in the form of investments, stocks, shares, bonds or trust funds; the cash value of the funds in that form at or before the beginning of the period of 6 months prior to the date of application; and the transfer of the funds into cash, are evidenced by a portfolio report or other relevant documentation from a financial institution regulated by the appropriate regulatory body for the country in which that institution is operating.

    (iii)   The requirements of this Appendix in respect of the cash savings held at the date of application are met, except that the period of 6 months prior to the date of application in paragraph 11(a) will be reduced by the amount of that period in which the relevant funds were held in the form of investments, stocks, shares, bonds or trust funds.

    (iv)   For the purposes of sub-paragraph 11A(c), "investments" includes funds held in an investment account or pension account or fund which does not meet the requirements of paragraphs 11 and 11A(a).

(d)   Funds held as cash savings by the applicant, their partner or both jointly at the date of application can be from the proceeds of the sale of property, in the form only of a dwelling, other building or land, which took place within the period of 6 months prior to the date of application, provided that:

(i)   The property (or relevant share of the property) was owned at the beginning of the period of 6 months prior to the date of application and at the date of sale by the applicant, their partner or both jointly.

(ii)   Where ownership of the property was shared with a third party, only the proceeds of the sale of the share of the property owned by the applicant, their partner or both jointly may be counted.

(iii)   The funds deposited as cash savings are the net proceeds of the sale, once any mortgage or loan secured on the property (or relevant share of the property) has been repaid and once any taxes and professional fees associated with the sale have been paid.

(iv)   The decision-maker is satisfied that the requirements in sub-paragraphs (i)-(iii) are met on the basis of information and documents submitted in support of the application. These may include for example:

    (1)   Registration information or documentation (or a copy of this) from the Land Registry (or overseas equivalent).

    (2)   A letter from a solicitor (or other relevant professional, if the sale takes place overseas) instructed in the sale of the property confirming the sale price and other relevant information.

    (3)   A letter from a lender (a bank or building society) on its headed stationery regarding the repayment of a mortgage or loan secured on the property.

    (4)   Confirmation of payment of taxes or professional fees associated with the sale.

    (5)   Any other relevant evidence that the requirements in subparagraphs (i)-(iii) are met.

(v)   The requirements of this Appendix in respect of the cash savings held at the date of application are met, except that the period of 6 months mentioned in paragraph 11(a) will be reduced by the amount of time which passed between the start of that 6-month period and the deposit of the proceeds of the sale in an account mentioned in paragraph 11(a).

12. Where a person is in receipt of Carer's Allowance, Disability Living Allowance, Severe Disablement Allowance, Industrial Injuries Disablement Benefit, Attendance Allowance or Personal Independence Payment or Armed Forces Independence Payment or Guaranteed Income Payment under the Armed Forces Compensation Scheme or Constant Attendance Allowance, Mobility Supplement or War Disablement Pension under the War Pensions Scheme, or a Police Injury Pension, all the following must be provided:

(a)   Official documentation from the Department for Work and Pensions, Veterans Agency or Police Pension Authority confirming the current entitlement and the amount currently received.

(b)   At least one personal bank statement in the 12-month period prior to the date of application showing payment of the amount of the benefit or allowance to which the person is currently entitled into their account.

12A. Where the financial requirement the applicant must meet under Appendix FM relates to adequate maintenance, paragraphs 2 to 12 apply only to the extent and in the manner specified by this paragraph. Where such a financial requirement applies, the applicant must provide the following evidence:

(a)   Where the current salaried employment in the UK of the applicant or their partner, parent, parent's partner or sponsor is relied upon:

(i)   A letter from the employer confirming the employment, the gross annual salary and the annual salary after income tax and National Insurance contributions have been paid, how long the employment has been held, and the type of employment (permanent, fixed-term contract or agency).

(ii)   Payslips covering the period of 6 months prior to the date of application or such shorter period as the current employment has been held.

(iii)   personal bank statement covering the same period as the payslips, showing that the salary has been paid into an account in the name of the person or in the name of the person and their partner jointly.

(b)   Where statutory or contractual maternity, paternity, adoption or sick pay in the UK of the applicant or their partner, parent, parent's partner or sponsor are relied upon, paragraph 5(b)(i) and (c) or paragraph 6(b)(i) and (c) apply as appropriate.

(c)   Where self-employment in the UK of the applicant or their partner, parent, parent's partner or sponsor, or income from employment and/or shares in a limited company based in the UK of a type to which paragraph 9 applies, is relied upon, paragraph 7 or 9 applies as appropriate.

(d)   Where the non-employment income of the applicant or their partner, parent, parent's partner or sponsor is relied upon, paragraph 10 applies and paragraph 10(f) shall apply as if it referred to any UK welfare benefit or tax credit relied upon and to HMRC as well as Department for Work and Pensions or other official documentation.

(e)   Where the cash savings of the applicant or their partner, parent, parent's partner or sponsor are relied upon, paragraphs 11 and 11A apply.

(f)   The monthly housing and Council Tax costs for the accommodation in the UK in which the applicant (and any other family members who are or will be part of the same household) lives or will live if the application is granted.

(g)   Where the applicant is an adult dependent relative applying for entry clearance, the applicant must in addition provide details of the care arrangements in the UK planned for them by their sponsor (which can involve other family members in the UK), of the cost of these arrangements and of how that cost will be met by the sponsor.

12B.   Where the financial requirement an applicant must meet under Part 8 (excluding an applicant who is a family member of a Relevant Points Based System Migrant) or under Appendix FM relates to adequate maintenance and where cash savings are relied upon to meet the requirement in full or in part, the decision-maker will:

(a)   Establish the total cash savings which meet the requirements of paragraphs 11 and 11A;

(b)   Divide this figure by the number of weeks of limited leave which would be issued if the application were granted, or by 52 if the application is for indefinite leave to enter or remain;

(c)   Add the figure in sub-paragraph 12B(b) to the weekly net income (before the deduction of housing costs) available to meet the requirement.

Calculating Gross Annual Income under Appendix FM

13.   Based on evidence that meets the requirements of this Appendix, and can be taken into account with reference to the applicable provisions of Appendix FM, gross annual income under paragraphs E-ECP.3.1., E-LTRP.3.1., E-ECC.2.1. and E-LTRC.2.1. will, subject to paragraph 21A of this Appendix, be calculated in the following ways:

(a)   Where the person is in salaried employment in the UK at the date of application, has been employed by their current employer for at least 6 months and has been paid throughout the period of 6 months prior to the date of application at a level of gross annual salary which equals or exceeds the level relied upon in paragraph 13(a)(i), their gross annual income will be (where paragraph 13(b) does not apply) the total of:

(i)   The level of gross annual salary relied upon in the application;

(ii)   The gross amount of any specified non-employment income (other than pension income) received by them or their partner in the 12 months prior to the date of application; and

(iii)   The gross annual income from a UK or foreign State pension or a private pension received by them or their partner.

(b)   Where the person is in salaried employment in the UK at the date of application and has been employed by their current employer for less than 6 months (or at least 6 months but the person does not rely on paragraph 13(a)), their gross annual income will be the total of:

(i)   The gross annual salary from employment as it was at the date of application;

(ii)   The gross amount of any specified non-employment income (other than pension income) received by them or their partner in the 12 months prior to the date of application; and

(iii)   The gross annual income from a UK or foreign State pension or a private pension received by them or their partner. In addition, the requirements of paragraph 15 must be met.

(c)   Where the person is the applicant's partner, is in salaried employment outside of the UK at the date of application, has been employed by their current employer for at least 6 months, and is returning to the UK to take up salaried employment in the UK starting within 3 months of their return, the person's gross annual income will be calculated:

(i)   On the basis set out in paragraph 13(a); and also

(ii)   On that basis but substituting for the gross annual salary at paragraph 13(a)(i) the gross annual salary in the salaried employment in the UK to which they are returning.

(d)   Where the person is the applicant's partner, has been in salaried employment outside of the UK within 12 months of the date of application, and is returning to the UK to take up salaried employment in the UK starting within 3 months of their return, the person's gross annual income will be calculated:

(i) On the basis set out in paragraph 13(a) but substituting for the gross annual salary at paragraph 13(a)(i) the gross annual salary in the salaried employment in the UK to which they are returning; and also

(ii) On the basis set out in paragraph 15(b).

(e) Where the person is self-employed, their gross annual income will be the total of their gross income from their self-employment (and that of their partner if that person is in the UK with permission to work), from any salaried or non-salaried employment they have had or their partner has had (if their partner is in the UK with permission to work), from specified non-employment income received by them or their partner, and from income from a UK or foreign State pension or a private pension received by them or their partner, in the last full financial year or as an average of the last two full financial years. The requirements of this Appendix for specified evidence relating to these forms of income shall apply as if references to the date of application were references to the end of the relevant financial year(s). The relevant financial year(s) cannot be combined with any financial year(s) to which paragraph 9 applies and vice versa.

(f) Where the person is self-employed, they cannot combine their gross annual income at paragraph 13(e) with specified savings in order to meet the level of income required under Appendix FM.

(g) Where the person is not relying on income from salaried employment or self-employment, their gross annual income will be the total of:

(i) The gross amount of any specified non-employment income (other than pension income) received by them or their partner in the 12 months prior to the date of application; and

(ii) The gross annual income from a UK or foreign State pension or a private pension received by them or their partner.

(h) Where the person is the applicant's partner and is in self-employment outside the UK at the date of application and is returning to the UK to take up salaried employment in the UK starting within 3 months of their return, the person's gross annual income will be calculated:

(i) On the basis set out in paragraph 13(a) but substituting for the gross annual salary at paragraph 13(a)(i) the gross annual salary in the salaried employment in the UK to which they are returning; and also

(ii) On the basis set out in paragraph 13(e).

(i) Any period of unpaid maternity, paternity, adoption, parental or sick leave in the 12 months prior to the date of application will not be counted towards any period relating to employment, or any period relating to income from employment, for which this Appendix provides.

(j) The provisions of paragraph 13 which apply to self-employment and to a person who is self-employed also apply to income from employment and/or shares in a limited company based in the UK of a type to which paragraph 9 applies and to a person in receipt of such income.

(k) Where the application relies on the employment income of the applicant and the sponsor, all of that income must be calculated either under subparagraph 13(a) or under sub-paragraph 13(b) and paragraph 15, and not under a combination of these methods.

14. Where the requirements of this Appendix and Appendix FM are met by the combined income or cash savings of more than one person, the income or the cash savings must only be counted once unless stated otherwise.

15. In respect of paragraph 13(b) and paragraph 13(d), the provisions in this paragraph also apply:

(a) In order to evidence the level of gross annual income required by Appendix FM, the person must meet the requirements in paragraph 13(b) or paragraph 13(d)(i); and

(b) The person must also meet the level of gross annual income required by Appendix FM on the basis that their income is the total of:

(i) The gross income from salaried employment in the UK or overseas earned by the person in the 12 months prior to the date of application;

(ii) The gross amount of any specified non-employment income (other than pension income) received by the person or their partner in the 12 months prior to the date of application;

(iii) The gross amount received from a UK or foreign State pension or a private pension by the person or their partner in the 12 months prior to the date of application; and

(iv) The person cannot combine the gross annual income at paragraph 15(b)(i)-(iii) with specified savings in order to meet the level of income required.

16. Where a person is in receipt of maternity, paternity, adoption or sick pay or has been so in the 6 months prior to the date of application, this paragraph applies:

   (a) the relevant date for considering the length of employment with their current employer will be the date that the maternity, paternity, adoption or sick leave commenced or the date of application; and

   (b) the relevant period for calculating income from their salaried employment will be the period prior to the commencement of the maternity, paternity, adoption or sick pay or to the date of application.

17. If a person is an equity partner, for example in a law firm, the income they draw from the partnership (including where this is in the form of a profit share) will be treated as salaried employment for the purposes of this Appendix and Appendix FM.

17A. Where a person is a subcontractor under the Construction Industry Scheme administered by HMRC and does not rely on paragraph 13(e), the income they receive as a subcontractor under the Construction Industry Scheme may be treated as income from salaried employment for the purposes of this Appendix and Appendix FM. In that case, the requirements for specified evidence in paragraph 2 must be met, subject to applying those requirements so as to reflect the person's status as a subcontractor under the Construction Industry Scheme.

18. When calculating income from salaried employment under paragraphs 12A and 13 to 16, this paragraph applies:

   (a) Basic pay, skills-based allowances, and UK location-based allowances will be counted as income provided that:

      (i) They are contractual; and

      (ii) Where these allowances make up more than 30% of the total salary, only the amount up to 30% is counted.

   (b) Overtime, payments to cover travel time, commission-based pay and bonuses (which can include tips and gratuities paid via a tronc scheme registered with HMRC) will be counted as income, where they have been received in the relevant period(s) of employment or self-employment relied upon in the application.

   (bb) In respect of a person in salaried employment at the date of application, the amount of income in sub-paragraph (b) which may be added to their gross annual salary, and counted as part of that figure for the purposes of paragraph 13(a)(i) or 13(b)(i), is the annual equivalent of the person's average gross monthly income from that income in their current employment in the 6 months prior to the date of application.

   (c) Payments relating to the costs of UK or overseas travel, including (for example) travelling or relocation expenses and subsistence or accommodation allowances, and payments made towards the costs of living overseas, will not be counted as income.

   (d) Gross income from non-salaried employment will be calculated on the same basis as income from salaried employment, except as provided in paragraph 18(e) and 18(f), and the requirements of this Appendix for specified evidence relating to salaried employment shall apply as if references to salary were references to income from non-salaried employment. Non-salaried employment includes that paid at an hourly or other rate (and the number and/or pattern of hours required to be worked may vary), or paid an amount which varies according to the work undertaken, whereas salaried employment includes that paid at a minimum fixed rate (usually annual) and is subject usually to a contractual minimum number of hours to be worked.

   (e) For the purpose of paragraph 13(a)(i), in respect of a person in non-salaried employment at the date of application "the level of gross annual salary relied upon in the application" shall be no greater than the annual equivalent of the person's average gross monthly income from non-salaried employment in the 6 months prior to the date of application, where that employment was held throughout that period.

   (f) For the purpose of paragraph 13(b)(i), "the gross annual salary from employment as it was at the date of application" of a person in non-salaried employment at the date of application shall be considered to be the annual equivalent of:

      (aa) the person's gross income from non-salaried employment in the period immediately prior to the date of application, where the employment has been held for a period of no more than one month at the date of application; or

      (bb) the person's average gross monthly income from non-salaried employment, where the employment has been held for a period of more than one month at the date of application.

(g)   For the purpose of paragraphs 13(c)(ii) and 13(d)(i), "the gross annual salary in the salaried employment in the UK to which they are returning" of a person who is returning to the UK to take up non-salaried employment in the UK starting within 3 months of their return is the gross annual income from that employment, based on the rate or amount of pay, and the standard or core hours of work, set out in the document(s) from the employer provided under paragraph 4. Notwithstanding paragraph 18(b), this may include the gross "on-target" earnings which may be expected from satisfactory performance in the standard or core hours of work.

19.   When calculating income from self-employment under paragraphs 12A and 13(e), and in relation to income from employment and/or shares in a limited company based in the UK of a type to which paragraph 9 applies, this paragraph applies:

(a)   There must be evidence of ongoing self-employment, and (where income from salaried employment is also relied upon or where paragraph 9(c) applies) ongoing employment, at the date of application.

(b)   Where the self-employed person is a sole trader or is in a partnership or franchise agreement, the income will be the gross taxable profits from their share of the business in the relevant financial year(s), not including any deductible allowances, expenses or liabilities which may be applied to the gross taxable profits to establish the final tax liability.

(c)   Where income to which paragraph 19 applies is being used to meet the financial requirement for an initial application for leave to remain as a partner under Appendix FM by an applicant who used such income to meet that requirement in an application for entry clearance as a fiancé(e) or proposed civil partner under that Appendix in the last 12 months, the Secretary of State may continue to accept the same level and evidence of income to which paragraph 19 applies that was accepted in granting the application for entry clearance, provided that there is evidence of ongoing self-employment, and (where income from salaried employment is also relied upon or where paragraph 9(c) applies) ongoing employment, at the date of the application for leave to remain.

(d)   The financial year(s) to which paragraph 7 refers is the period of the last full financial year(s) to which the required Statement(s) of Account (SA300 or SA302) relates.

(e)   The financial year(s) to which paragraph 9 refers is the period of the last full financial year(s) to which the required Company Tax Return(s) CT600 relates.

20.   When calculating income from specified non-employment sources under paragraphs 12A and 13 to 15, this paragraph applies:

(a)   Assets or savings must be in the name of the person, or jointly with their partner.

(b)   Any asset or savings on which income is based must be held or owned by the person at the date of application.

(c)   Any rental income from property, in the UK or overseas, must be from a property that is:

(i)   owned by the person;

(ii)   not their main residence and will not be so if the application is granted, except in the circumstances specified in paragraph 20(e); and

(iii)   if ownership of the property is shared with a third party, only income received from their share of the property can be counted.

(cc)   The amount of rental income from property received before any management fee was deducted may be counted.

(d)   Equity in a property cannot be used to meet the financial requirement.

(e)   Where the applicant and their partner are resident outside the UK at the date of application, rental income from a property in the UK that will become their main residence if the application is granted may only be counted under paragraph 13(c)(i) and paragraph 13(d)(ii).

(f)   Any future entitlement to a maintenance grant or stipend of the type specified in paragraph 10(g) may be counted as though the person had received the annual amount of that grant or stipend in the 12 months prior to the date of application.

20A. When calculating the gross annual income from pension under paragraph 13, the gross annual amount of any pension received may be counted where the pension has become a source of income at least 28 days prior to the date of application.

21.   When calculating income under paragraphs 13 to 16, the following sources will not be counted:

(a)   Loans and credit facilities.

(b)   Income-related benefits: Income Support, income-related Employment and Support Allowance, Pension Credit, Housing Benefit, Council Tax Benefit or Support (or any equivalent) and income-based Jobseeker's Allowance.

(c)   The following contributory benefits: contribution-based Jobseeker's Allowance, contribution-based Employment and Support Allowance and Incapacity Benefit.

(cc)   Unemployability Allowance, Allowance for a Lowered Standard of Occupation and Invalidity Allowance under the War Pension Scheme.

(d)   Child Benefit.

(e)   Working Tax Credit.

(f)   Child Tax Credit.

(ff)   Universal Credit.

(g)   Any other source of income not specified in this appendix.

Other sources of income, financial support or funds in exceptional circumstances

21A. (1)   Where paragraph GEN.3.1.(1) of Appendix FM applies, the decision-maker is required to take into account the sources of income, financial support or funds specified in sub-paragraph (2).

(2)   Subject to sub-paragraphs (3) to (8), the following sources of income, financial support or funds will be taken into account (in addition to those set out in, as appropriate, paragraph E-ECP.3.2., E-LTRP.3.2., E-ECC.2.2. or E-LTRC.2.2. of Appendix FM):

(a)   a credible guarantee of sustainable financial support to the applicant or their partner from a third party;

(b)   credible prospective earnings from the sustainable employment or self-employment of the applicant or their partner; or

(c)   any other credible and reliable source of income or funds for the applicant or their partner, which is available to them at the date of application or which will become available to them during the period of limited leave applied for.

(3)   Where the applicant is a child:

(a)   other references in this paragraph to "applicant" mean the "applicant's parent" under paragraph E-ECC.1.6. or E-LTRC.1.6. of Appendix FM; and

(b)   references in this paragraph to "partner" refer to the "applicant's parent's partner" under those paragraphs.

(4)   The onus is on the applicant to satisfy the decision-maker of the genuineness, credibility and reliability of the source of income, financial support or funds relied upon, on the basis of the information and evidence provided, having regard (in particular, but without limitation) to the factors set out below.

(5)   The source of income, financial support or funds must not be a loan, unless evidence submitted with the application shows that:

(a)   the source is a mortgage on a residential or commercial property in the UK or overseas which at the date of application is owned by the applicant, their partner or both, or by the third party to whom sub-paragraph (2)(a) refers;

(b)   the mortgage is provided by a financial institution regulated by the appropriate regulatory body for the country in which that institution is operating; and

(c)   the mortgage payments are reasonably affordable by the person(s) responsible for them and are likely to remain so for the period of limited leave applied for.

(6)   Any cash savings or any current financial investment or product relied upon by the applicant under sub-paragraph (2)(c) must at the date of application be in the name(s), and under the control, of the applicant, their partner or both.

(7)   Any cash savings relied upon by the applicant must enable the financial requirement in paragraph E-ECP.3.1.(b), E-LTRP.3.1.(b), E-ECC.2.1.(b) or E-LTRC.2.1.(b) of Appendix FM (as applicable) to be met, except that the criteria in sub-paragraph (8)(c) apply in place of the requirements in paragraphs 11 and 11A of this Appendix.

(8)   In determining the genuineness, credibility and reliability of the source of income, financial support or funds relied upon under sub-paragraph (2), the decision-maker will take into account all the information and evidence provided, and will consider (in particular):

(a)   in respect of a guarantee of sustainable financial support from a third party:

(i)   whether the applicant has provided verifiable documentary evidence from the third party in question of their guarantee of financial support;

(ii)   whether that evidence is signed, dated and witnessed or otherwise independently verified;

(iii)   whether the third party has provided sufficient evidence of their general financial situation to enable the decision-maker to assess the likelihood of the guaranteed financial support continuing for the period of limited leave applied for;

(iv)   whether the third party has provided verifiable documentary evidence of the nature, extent and duration of any current or previous financial support which they have provided to the applicant or their partner;

(v)   the extent to which this source of financial support is relied upon by the applicant to meet the financial requirement in paragraph E-ECP.3.1., E-LTRP.3.1., E-ECC.2.1. or E-LTRC.2.1. of Appendix FM (as applicable); and

(vi)   the likelihood of a change in the third party's financial situation or in their relationship with the applicant or the applicant's partner during the period of limited leave applied for.

(b)   in respect of prospective earnings from sustainable employment or self-employment of the applicant or their partner:

(i)   whether, at the date of application, a specific offer of employment has been made, or a clear basis for self-employment exists. In either case, such employment or self-employment must be expected to commence within three months of the applicant's arrival in the UK (if the applicant is applying for entry clearance) or within three months of the date of application (if the applicant is applying for leave to remain);

(ii)   whether the applicant has provided verifiable documentary evidence of the offer of employment or the basis for self-employment, and, if so, whether that evidence:

    (aa)   is on the headed notepaper of the company or other organisation offering the employment, or of a company or other organisation which has agreed to purchase the goods or services of the applicant or their partner as a self-employed person;

    (bb)   is signed, dated and witnessed or otherwise independently verified;

    (cc)   includes (in respect of an offer of employment) a signed or draft contract of employment;

    (dd)   includes (in respect of self-employment) any of a signed or draft contract for the provision of goods or services; a signed or draft partnership or franchise agreement; an application to the appropriate authority for a licence to trade; or details of the agreed or proposed purchase or rental of business premises;

(iii)   whether, in respect of an offer of employment in the UK, the applicant has provided verifiable documentary evidence:

    (aa)   of a relevant employment advertisement and employment application;

    (bb)   of the hours to be worked and the rate of gross pay, which that evidence must establish equals or exceeds the National Living Wage or the National Minimum Wage (as applicable, given the age of the person to be employed) and equals or exceeds the going rate for such work in that part of the UK; and

    (cc)   which enables the decision-maker to assess the reliability of the offer of employment, including in light of the total size of the workforce and the turnover (annual gross income or sales) of the relevant company or other organisation;

(iv)   whether the applicant has provided verifiable documentary evidence that at the date of application, the person to be employed or self-employed is in, or has recently been in, sustained employment or self-employment of the same or a similar type, of the same or a similar level of complexity and at the same or a similar level of responsibility;

(v)   whether the applicant has provided verifiable documentary evidence that the person to be employed or self-employed has relevant professional, occupational or educational qualifications and that these are recognised in the UK;

(vi)   whether the applicant has provided verifiable documentary evidence that the person to be employed or self-employed has the level of English language skills such prospective employment or self-employment is likely to require;

(vii) the extent to which this source of income is relied upon by the applicant to meet the financial requirement in paragraph E-ECP.3.1., E-LTRP.3.1., E-ECC.2.1. or E-LTRC.2.1. of Appendix FM (as applicable); and

(viii) where an offer of employment is relied upon, and where the proposed employer is a family member or friend of the applicant or their partner, the likelihood of a relevant change in that relationship during the period of limited leave applied for.

(c) in respect of any other credible and reliable source of income or funds for the applicant or their partner:

(i) whether the applicant has provided verifiable documentary evidence of the source;

(ii) whether that evidence is provided by a financial institution regulated by the appropriate regulatory body for the country in which that institution is operating, and is signed, dated and witnessed or otherwise independently verified;

(iii) where the income is or the funds are based on, or derived from, ownership of an asset, whether the applicant has provided verifiable documentary evidence of its current or previous ownership by the applicant, their partner or both;

(iv) whether the applicant has provided sufficient evidence to enable the decision-maker to assess the likelihood of the source of income or funds being available to them during the period of limited leave applied for; and

(v) the extent to which this source of income or funds is relied upon by the applicant to meet the financial requirement in paragraph E-ECP.3.1., E-LTRP.3.1., E-ECC.2.1. or E-LTRC.2.1. of Appendix FM (as applicable).

Evidence of Marriage or Civil Partnerships

22. A marriage in the United Kingdom must be evidenced by a valid marriage certificate recognised under the laws of England and Wales, Scotland or Northern Ireland.

23. A divorce in the United Kingdom must be evidenced by a decree absolute from a civil court.

24. A civil partnership in the United Kingdom must be evidenced by a civil partnership certificate.

25. The dissolution of a civil partnership in the UK must be evidenced by a final order of civil partnership dissolution from a civil court.

26. Marriages, civil partnerships or evidence of divorce or dissolution from outside the UK must be evidenced by a reasonable equivalent to the evidence detailed in paragraphs 22 to 25, valid under the law in force in the relevant country.

Evidence of the Applicant Living Overseas with a Crown Servant

26A. Where

(a) An applicant for entry clearance, limited leave to enter or remain or indefinite leave to remain as a partner under Appendix FM (except as a fiancé(e) or proposed civil partner) intends to enter or remain in the UK to begin their probationary period (or has done so) and then to live outside the UK for the time being with their sponsor (or is doing so or has done so) before the couple live together permanently in the UK; and

(b) The sponsor, who is a British Citizen or settled in the UK, is a permanent member of HM Diplomatic Service or a comparable UK-based staff member of the British Council, the Foreign, Commonwealth and Development Office or the Home Office on a tour of duty outside the UK, the applicant must provide a letter on official stationery from the sponsor's head of mission confirming the information at (a) and (b) and confirming the start date and expected end date of the sponsor's tour of duty outside the UK.

Evidence of English Language Requirements

27. The evidence required of passing an English language test in speaking and listening (at a minimum of level A1 or A2 (as the case may be) of the Common European Framework of Reference for Languages) with a provider approved by the Secretary of State, where the applicant relies on that pass to meet an English language requirement, is confirmation on the on-line verification system operated by an approved English language test provider and at an approved Secure English Language Test centre that:

(i) the applicant has passed such a test; and

(ii) that test was an English language test in speaking and listening which is approved by the Secretary of State and was taken no more than two years before the date of application and at a test centre approved by the Secretary of State as a Secure English Language Test Centre or if they have already shown they met the requirement in this manner at the level required for their current application, in a previous successful application for entry clearance or permission to stay.

28. The evidence required to show that a person is a citizen or national of a majority English speaking country is a valid passport or travel document, unless paragraphs 29 and 30 apply. A dual national may invoke either of their nationalities.

29. If the applicant has not provided their passport or travel document other evidence of nationality can be supplied in the following circumstances only (as indicated by the applicant on their application form):

    (a) where the passport or travel document has been lost or stolen;

    (b) where the passport or travel document has expired and been returned to the relevant authorities; or

    (c) where the passport or travel document is with another part of the Home Office.

30. Alternative evidence as proof of nationality, if acceptable, must be either:

    (a) A current national identity document; or

    (b) A letter from the applicant's national government, Embassy or High Commission confirming the applicant's full name, date of birth and nationality.

31. Evidence of an academic qualification under paragraphs 284(ix)(c), (d) and (e), 290(vii)(c), (d) and (e) and 295D(xi)(c), (d) and (e) of Part 8, paragraph 68(c) of Appendix Armed Forces, and paragraphs E-ECP.4.1.(c), E-LTRP.4.1.(c), E-LTRP.4.1A.(c), E-ECPT.4.1.(c), E-LTRPT.5.1.(c) and E-LTRPT.5.1A.(c) of Appendix FM must be:

    (a) a certificate issued by the relevant institution confirming the award of the academic qualification showing:

        (i) the applicant's name;

        (ii) the title of award;

        (iii) the date of award; and

        (iv) the name of the awarding institution; or

    (b) if the applicant is awaiting graduation or no longer has the certificate and cannot obtain a new one, either:

        (i) an academic reference from the institution awarding the academic qualification that:

            (1) is on official letter headed paper;

            (2) shows the applicant's name;

            (3) shows the title of award;

            (4) explains when the academic qualification has been, or will be, awarded; and

            (5) confirms either the date that the certificate will be issued (if the applicant has not yet graduated) or that the institution is unable to re-issue the certificate of award; or

        (ii) an academic transcript that:

            (1) is on official letter headed paper;

            (2) shows the applicant's name;

            (3) shows the name of the academic institution;

            (4) shows the course title; and

            (5) confirms either the date that the certificate will be issued (if the applicant has not yet graduated) or that the institution is unable to re-issue the certificate of award; and

    (c) if the qualification was awarded by an educational establishment outside the UK, a document from Ecctis which confirms that the qualification meets or exceeds the recognised standard of a Bachelor's or Master's degree or PhD in the UK and was taught or researched in English to level A1 or A2 (as the case may be) of the Common Framework of Reference for Languages or above.

32. If the qualification was taken in one of the following countries, it will be assumed for the purpose of paragraph 31 that it was taught or researched in English: Antigua and Barbuda, Australia, the Bahamas, Barbados, Belize, Dominica, Grenada, Guyana, Ireland, Jamaica, New Zealand, St Kitts and Nevis, St Lucia, St Vincent and the Grenadines, Trinidad and Tobago, the UK, the USA, Malta.

32A. For the avoidance of doubt paragraphs 27 to 32D of this Appendix apply to fiancé(e), proposed civil partner, spouse, civil partner, unmarried partner and same sex partner applications for limited leave to enter or remain made under Part 8 of these Rules where English language requirements apply, regardless of the date of application. Paragraphs 27 to 32D of this Appendix also apply to spouse, civil partner, unmarried partner and same sex partner applications which do not meet the requirements of Part 8 of these Rules for indefinite leave to remain (where the application is for indefinite leave to remain) and are being considered for a grant of limited leave to remain where paragraph A277A(b) of these Rules applies. Any references in paragraphs 27 to 32D of this Appendix to "limited leave to enter or remain" shall therefore be read as referring to all applicants referred to in this paragraph.

32B. Where the decision-maker has:

(a) reasonable cause to doubt that an English language test in speaking and listening at a minimum of level A1 or A2 (as the case may be) of the Common Framework of Reference for Languages relied on at any time to meet a requirement for limited leave to enter or remain in Part 8 or Appendix FM was genuinely obtained; or

(b) information that the test certificate or result awarded to the applicant has been withdrawn by the test provider for any reason,

the decision-maker may discount the test certificate or result and require the applicant to provide a new test certificate or result from an approved provider which shows that they meet the requirement, if they are not exempt from it.

32C. If an applicant applying for limited leave to enter or remain under Part 8 or Appendix FM submits an English language test certificate or result which has ceased by the date of application to be:

(a) from an approved test provider, or

(b) in respect of an approved test, or

(c) from an approved test centre, the decision-maker will not accept that certificate or result as valid, unless the decision-maker does so in accordance with paragraph 32D of this Appendix and subject to any transitional arrangements made in respect of the test provider, test or test centre in question.

32D. If an applicant applying for limited leave to enter or remain under Part 8 or Appendix FM submits an English language test certificate or result and the Home Office has already accepted it as part of a successful previous partner or parent application (but not where the application was refused, even if on grounds other than the English language requirement), the decision-maker will accept that certificate or result as valid if it is:

(a) from a provider which is no longer approved, or

(b) from a provider who remains approved but the test the applicant has taken with that provider is no longer approved, or

(c) from a test centre which is no longer approved, or

(d) past its validity date (if a validity date is required), provided that it is at or above the requisite level of the Common European Framework of Reference for Languages and when the subsequent application is made the award to the applicant does not fall within the circumstances set out in paragraph 32B of this Appendix.

Adult dependent relatives

33. Evidence of the family relationship between the applicant(s) and the sponsor should take the form of birth or adoption certificates, or other documentary evidence.

34. Evidence that, as a result of age, illness or disability, the applicant requires long-term personal care should take the form of:

(a) Independent medical evidence that the applicant's physical or mental condition means that they cannot perform everyday tasks; and

(b) This must be from a doctor or other health professional.

35. Independent evidence that the applicant is unable, even with the practical and financial help of the sponsor in the UK, to obtain the required level of care in the country where they are living should be from:

(a) a central or local health authority;

(b) a local authority; or

(c) a doctor or other health professional.

36. If the applicant's required care has previously been provided through a private arrangement, the applicant must provide details of that arrangement and why it is no longer available.

37. If the applicant's required level of care is not, or is no longer, affordable because payment previously made for arranging this care is no longer being made, the applicant must provide records of that payment and an explanation of why that payment cannot continue. If financial support has been provided by the sponsor or other close family in the UK, the applicant must provide an explanation of why this cannot continue or is no longer sufficient to enable the required level of care to be provided.

Appendix Innovator

The Innovator route is for a person seeking to establish a business in the UK based on an innovative, viable and scalable business idea they have generated, or to which they have significantly contributed.

The application must be supported by an endorsing body.

An applicant will normally be expected to have funds of at least £50,000 to invest in their business and they must have a key role in the day to day management and development of the business.

A dependent partner and dependent children can apply on this route.

The Innovator route is a route to settlement.

Validity requirements for an Innovator

INN 1.1.   A person applying for entry clearance or permission to stay as an Innovator must apply online on the gov.uk website on the specified form as follows:

Applicant	Specified form
EEA national with a chipped passport	Either: • Start-up or Innovator using the UK Immigration: ID Check app (when available); or • the forms listed below for applicants outside or inside the UK (as relevant)
Applicants outside the UK	Start-up or Innovator visa
Applicants inside the UK	Start-up or Innovator permission to stay

INN 1.2.   An application for entry clearance or permission to stay on the Innovator route must meet all the following requirements:

(a)   any fee and Immigration Health Charge must have been paid; and

(b)   the applicant must have provided any required biometrics; and

(c)   the applicant must have provided a passport or other travel document which satisfactorily establishes their identity and nationality; and

(d)   the applicant must have been issued with an endorsement letter by an endorsing body no more than 3 months before the date of application and that endorsement must not have been withdrawn.

INN 1.3.   The applicant must be aged 18 or over on the date of application.

INN 1.4.   If the applicant has in the 12 months before the date of application received an award from a Government or international scholarship agency covering both fees and living costs for study in the UK, they must have provided written consent to the application from that Government or agency.

INN 1.5.   A person applying for permission to stay must be in the UK and must not have, or have last been granted, permission:

(a)   as a Visitor; or

(b)   as a Short-term Student; or

(c)   as a Parent of a Child Student; or

(d)   as a Seasonal Worker; or

(e)   as a domestic worker in a private household; or

(f)   outside the Immigration Rules.

INN 1.6.   An application which does not meet all the validity requirements for the Innovator route is invalid and may be rejected and not considered.

Suitability requirements for an Innovator

INN 2.1.   The applicant must not fall for refusal under Part 9: grounds for refusal.

INN 2.2.   If applying for permission to stay the applicant must not be:

(a)   in breach of immigration laws, except that where paragraph 39E applies, that period of overstaying will be disregarded; or

(b)   on immigration bail.

Eligibility requirements for an Innovator

Entry requirements for an Innovator

INN 3.1.   A person seeking to come to the UK as an Innovator must apply for and obtain entry clearance on the Innovator route before they arrive in the UK.

INN 3.2.   A person applying for entry clearance as an Innovator must, if paragraph A39 and Appendix T of these rules apply, provide a valid medical certificate confirming that they have undergone screening for active pulmonary tuberculosis and that this tuberculosis is not present in them.

Genuine Innovator requirement

INN 4.1.   The applicant must be a genuine Innovator applicant.

Points requirement for the Innovator route

INN 5.1.   The applicant must be awarded 70 points from the table below; of which 50 must either be under the new business criteria or under the same business criteria, but not both.

Requirement	New or same business	Points available
Business plan	New Business	10
Business venture is innovative, viable and scalable.	New Business	20
£50,000 available funds to invest or having been invested	New Business	20
Applicant's previous permission was as in the Innovator, Start-up or Tier 1 (Graduate Entrepreneur) route and they are pursuing a business assessed by a Home Office approved endorsing body either for the previous endorsement or at a contact point.	Same Business	10
Business is active, trading and sustainable and demonstrates significant achievements against the business plan	Same Business	20
Applicant is active in day-to-day management and development of business	Same Business	20
English Language requirement at level B2	Mandatory for all applicants	10
Financial requirement	Mandatory for all applicants	10
Total number of points required		70

Requirements for Innovator route where it is a new business

Business Plan requirement for an Innovator

INN 6.1.   The applicant must have an endorsement letter from an endorsing body which confirms that:

(a)   the applicant has either generated, or made a significant contribution to, the ideas in their business plan; and

(b)   the applicant will have a day-to-day role in carrying out the business plan,

(c)   the applicant is either the sole founder or an instrumental member of the founding team.

Innovative, viable and scalable business requirements for an Innovator

INN 7.1.   The applicant must have an innovative, viable and scalable business venture and they must meet all the following requirements:

(a)   the applicant must have a genuine, original business plan that meets new or existing market needs and/or creates a competitive advantage; and

(b)   the applicant's business plan must be realistic and achievable based on the applicant's available resources; and

(c) the applicant must have, or be actively developing, the necessary skills, knowledge, experience and market awareness to successfully run the business; and

(d) there must be evidence of structured planning and of potential for job creation and growth into national and international markets.

INN 7.2. The applicant must be supported by an endorsing body for this route which confirms in their endorsement letter that they consider that the applicant meets the above requirements.

Investment funds requirement for an Innovator

INN 8.1. The applicant must show that they have at least £50,000 of funds available to invest, or which have been invested, in their business by one of the following:

(a) providing confirmation from the endorsing body that it is providing the funds of at least £50,000; or

(b) providing confirmation from the endorsing body that it has verified the funds are available from other sources (which can include the applicant); or

(c) providing confirmation from the endorsing body that it has verified that at least £50,000 has already been invested in the applicant's business; or

(d) providing evidence that the £50,000 of funds are available from another source.

INN 8.2. Where the business has one or more other team members who are applying for, or have been granted, permission on the Innovator route, there must be at least £50,000 available to, or which has been invested by, each team member.

INN 8.3. Where the requirement is being met under INN 8.1 (a), (b) or (c) the applicant must be supported by an endorsing body which confirms as part of their endorsement letter that they consider that the applicant meets those requirements.

INN 8.4. Where the requirement is being met under INN 8.1 (d) and any of the funds are being provided by a UK organisation which employs at least 10 people, the applicant must provide a letter from that organisation confirming this and which must include:

(a) how they know the applicant; and

(b) the amount of funding they are making available in pounds sterling (£); and

(c) confirmation that this funding has not been promised to any other person or business for another purpose; and

(d) the name and contact details (telephone number, email and workplace address) of an individual at the organisation who will verify the contents of the letter to the Home Office if requested.

INN 8.5. Where the requirement is being met under INN 8.1 (d) and any of the funds are being provided by an overseas organisation, a UK organisation which employs less than 10 people, or an individual, the applicant must provide all of the following:

(a) a signed declaration from the funding provider, dated no more than 3 months before the date of application, setting out all of the following:

(i) how they know the applicant; and

(ii) the amount of funding they are making available in pounds sterling (£); and confirmation that this funding has not been promised to any other person or business for another purpose; and

(iii) the name and contact details (telephone number, email and workplace address) of an individual at the organisation who will verify the contents of the letter to the Home Office if requested; and

(b) a letter from a legal representative (who is registered to practise legally in the country where the third party or the money is), confirming that the declaration and signature in (a) above is genuine; and

(c) a bank letter, dated no earlier than 1 month before the date of application, confirming that the funds are held in a regulated financial institution(s) and if the institution is outside the UK, the letter must also confirm that the funds are transferable to the UK.

INN 8.6. If any of the funds are held by the applicant, they must provide either of the following:

(a) bank statements, showing the funds are held in the UK in an institution regulated by the Financial Conduct Authority. The statements must cover a consecutive 3 months, ending no earlier than 1 month before the date of application; or

(b) a bank letter, dated no earlier than 1 month before the date of application, confirming that the funds are held in a regulated financial institution(s) and, if the institution is outside the UK, the letter must also confirm that the funds are transferable to the UK.

INN 8.7.   If the documents in INN 8.6. do not show that the applicant has held the funds for at least 3 months, the applicant must also provide the signed declaration and letter from a legal representative set out in INN 8.5 (a) and (b) in relation to the organisation or person who provided the funds to the applicant.

INN 8.8.   If any of the funds have already been invested in the applicant's business, the applicant must provide either of the following, showing the amount that has been invested:

(a)   business accounts, showing the name of the accountant and the date they were produced; or

(b)   business bank statements.

INN 8.9.   If any of the evidence in INN 8.4 to INN 8.8. show that the funds are available to the applicant's business rather than to the applicant, or have been invested in the business, the applicant must provide a Companies House document showing their connection to the business. This document is not needed if the endorsement letter confirms the applicant's connection to the business.

INN 8.10.   Any funds in a foreign currency will be converted to pounds sterling (£) using the spot exchange rate which appeared on www.oanda.com on the date of application.

INN 8.11.   Funds will not be accepted if they are held in a financial institution not permitted in Appendix Finance.

Requirements for Innovator where it is the same business as the business in a previous endorsement under the Innovator, Start-up route or Tier 1 (Graduate Entrepreneur) route.

Business previously assessed by an endorsing body requirement

INN 9.1.   The applicant must be supported by an endorsing body which confirms that they are endorsing the application on the basis of a business they or another endorsing body have previously assessed while the applicant had permission on the Innovator Start-up route or Tier 1 (Graduate Entrepreneur).

INN 9.2.   The endorsing body must confirm that they are satisfied that the applicant meets the new business requirements in INN 6.1 to INN 8.3., with the exception that applicants previously endorsed in the Start-up or Tier 1 (Graduate Entrepreneur) routes do not need to meet the investment funds requirement at INN 8.1 to INN 8.11.

Business is active, trading and sustainable requirement for an Innovator

INN 10.1.   The applicant's business must be active, trading and sustainable and the applicant must have made significant progress against their business plan.

INN 10.2.   The applicant's business must be registered with Companies House and the applicant must be listed as a director or member of that business.

INN 10.3.   The applicant must be supported by an endorsing body which has assessed the applicant's business and confirmed that it meets the requirements set out in INN10.1. and INN 10.2.

Day to day management requirement for an Innovator

INN 11.1.   The applicant must be involved in the day to day management and development of their business and provide a letter confirming this from an endorsing body.

English Language requirement for an Innovator

INN 12.1.   The applicant must show English language ability on the Common European Framework of Reference for Languages in all 4 components (reading, writing, speaking and listening) of at least level B2.

INN 12.2.   The applicant must show they meet the English language requirement as specified in Appendix English Language.

Financial requirement for an Innovator

INN 13.1.   If the applicant is applying for permission to stay and has been in the UK with permission for 12 months or longer on the date of application, they will meet the financial requirement and do not need to show funds.

INN 13.2.   An applicant who is applying for entry clearance, or who is applying for permission to stay and has been in the UK for less than 12 months at the date of application, must have funds of at least £1,270.

INN 13.3.   The applicant must show that they have held the required level of funds for a 28- day period and as set out in Appendix Finance.

Decision on application as an Innovator

INN 14.1.   If the decision maker is satisfied that all the suitability and the relevant eligibility requirements for an Innovator are met, the application will be granted, otherwise the application will be refused.

INN 14.2.   If the application is refused the person can apply for an Administrative Review under Appendix AR: Administrative Review.

Period and conditions of grant as an Innovator

INN 15.1.   The applicant will be granted permission for a maximum period of 3 years.

INN 15.2.   The grant will be subject to the following conditions:

(a)   no access to public funds; and

(b)   no work, other than working for the business(es) the applicant has established and

(c)   study is permitted, subject to the ATAS condition in Appendix ATAS; and

(d)   if Part 10 applies the applicant will be required to register with the police.

INN 15.3.   In INN 15.2.(b), working for the business(es) does not include any apprenticeship or any work pursuant to a contract of service, whether express or implied and whether oral or written, with another business, (which means successful applicants cannot fill a position or hire their labour to another business, even if the work is undertaken through contracting with the applicant's own business or through a recruitment or employment agency).

Settlement by a person on the Innovator route

Validity requirements for settlement by an Innovator

INN 16.1.   A person on the Innovator route who is applying for settlement must apply online on the gov.uk website on the specified form 'Settlement Innovator'.

INN 16.2.   An application for settlement must meet all the following requirements:

(a)   any fee must have been paid; and

(b)   the applicant must have provided any required biometrics; and

(c)   the applicant must have provided a passport or other travel document which satisfactorily establishes their identity and nationality; and

(d)   the applicant must be in the UK; and

(e)   the applicant must have been issued with an endorsement letter by an endorsing body no more than 3 months before the date of application and that endorsement must not have been withdrawn.

INN 16.3.   The applicant must have, or have last been granted, permission on the Innovator route.

INN 16.4.   An application which does not meet all the validity requirements for settlement for a person on the Innovator route is invalid and may be rejected and not considered.

Suitability Requirements for settlement by an Innovator

INN 17.1.   The applicant must not fall for refusal under Part 9: grounds for refusal.

INN 17.2.   The applicant must not be:

(a)   in breach of immigration laws, except that where paragraph 39E applies, that period of overstaying will be disregarded; or

(b)   on immigration bail.

Eligibility requirements for settlement by an Innovator

Endorsement requirements for settlement by an Innovator

INN 18.1.   The applicant must provide an endorsement letter issued by an endorsing body, which includes all of the following information:

(a)   the name of the endorsing body; and

(b)   the endorsement reference number; and

(c)   the date of issue, which must be no earlier than 3 months before the date of application; and

(d)   the applicant's name, date of birth, nationality and passport number; and

(e)   a short description of the applicant's business venture and the main products or services it has provided; and

(f)   the name and contact details (telephone number, email and workplace address) of an individual at the endorsing body who will verify the contents of the letter to the Home Office if requested; and

(g)   confirmation that the applicant has shown significant achievements, judged against the business plan assessed in their previous endorsement; and

(h)   confirmation that the applicant's business is registered with Companies House and the applicant is listed as a director or member of that business; and

(i)   confirmation the business is active and trading; and

(j)   confirmation that the business appears to be sustainable for at least the following 12 months, based on its assets and expected income, weighed against its current and planned expenses; and

(k)   confirmation the applicant has demonstrated an active key role in the day-to-day management and development of the business; and

(l)   confirmation the applicant's business venture has met at least two of the following requirements:

    (i)   at least £50,000 has been invested into the business and actively spent furthering the business; or

    (ii)   the number of the business's customers has at least doubled within the most recent three years and is currently higher than the mean number of customers for other UK businesses offering comparable main products or services; or

    (iii)   the business has engaged in significant research and development activity and has applied for intellectual property protection in the UK; or

    (iv)   the business has generated a minimum annual gross revenue of £1 million in the last full year covered by its accounts; or

    (v)   the business is generating a minimum annual gross revenue of £500,000 in the last full year covered by its accounts, with at least £100,000 from exporting overseas; or

    (vi)   the business has created the equivalent of at least 10 full-time jobs for settled workers; or

    (vii)   the business has created the equivalent of at least 5 full-time jobs for settled workers, each of which has a mean salary of at least £25,000 a year (gross pay, excluding any allowances).

INN 18.2.   An applicant cannot meet the requirement at INN 18.1. by relying on the same criterion twice (for example, an applicant who has invested £100,000 (2 x £50,000) in their business venture will be considered to have met one criterion, not two).

INN 18.3.   If the business venture has one or more other team members who are applying for, or have been granted, settlement on the Innovator route, they cannot share the same means of meeting these criteria (for example, if two applicants are relying on the requirement to have created 10 jobs, 20 jobs must have been created in total).

INN 18.4.   If the applicant is relying on the criteria for creating jobs in INN 18.1.(l)(vi) or (vii) the following requirements must be met:

(a)   each job must have existed for at least 12 months and comply with all relevant UK legislation, including (but not limited to) the National Minimum Wage Act 1998 and the Working Time Regulations 1998; and

(b)   each job must involve an average of at least 30 hours of paid work per week, but two or more part time jobs held by different employees that when combined add up to 30 hours per week will represent the equivalent of a single full-time job, as long as each of the jobs has existed for at least 12 months; and

(c)   a job will be considered one for settled worker if the worker met the definition of settled worker in the rules in force at the time they started the job, and they remained employed for the whole claimed 12-month period, even if they ceased to be a settled worker at a later date.

Qualifying period requirement for settlement by an Innovator

INN 19.1.   The applicant must have spent at least 3 years in the UK with permission on the Innovator route.

Continuous requirement for settlement by an Innovator

INN 20.1.   The applicant must prove that they have met the continuous residence requirement as set out in Appendix Continuous Residence for the qualifying period in INN 19.1.

Knowledge of life in the UK requirement for settlement by an Innovator

INN 21.1.   The applicant must meet the Knowledge of Life in the UK requirement as set out in Appendix KOL UK.

Decision on an application for settlement by an Innovator

INN 22.1.   If the decision maker is satisfied all the suitability and eligibility requirements are met the application will be granted settlement, otherwise the application will be refused.

INN 22.2.   If the application is refused the person may apply for an Administrative Review under Appendix AR: Administrative Review.

Dependants of an Innovator

Validity requirements for a dependent partner or dependent child on the Innovator route

INN 23.1.   An application as a dependent partner or dependent child on the Innovator route must be made online on the gov.uk website on the specified form as follows:

Applicant	Specified form
EEA national with a chipped passport	Either (as applicable): • Dependant partner or dependant child using the UK Immigration: ID Check app; or • the forms listed below for dependant applicants outside or inside the UK as relevant.
Applicants outside the UK	Dependant partner visa Dependant child visa
Applicants inside the UK	If the dependant is applying at the same time as the Innovator, they can be included in the form "Start-Up or Innovator permission to stay" where the form allows dependants to be added. Otherwise: - Dependant partner - Dependant child

INN 23.2.   An application for entry clearance or permission to stay as a partner or child on the Innovator route must meet all the following requirements:

(a)   any fee and Immigration Health Charge must have been paid; and

(b)   the applicant must have provided any required biometrics; and

(c)   the applicant must have provided a passport or other travel document which satisfactorily establishes their identity and nationality.

INN 23.3.   A person applying as a dependent partner must be aged 18 or over on the date of application.

INN 23.4.   A person applying for permission to stay must be in the UK and must not have, or have last been granted, permission:

(a)as a Visitor; or

(b)   as a Short-term Student; or

(c)   as a Parent of a Child Student; or

(d)   as a Seasonal Worker; or

(e)   as a domestic worker in a private household; or

(f)   outside the Immigration Rules.

INN 23.5.   An application which does not meet all the validity requirements for the Innovator route is invalid and may be rejected and not considered.

Suitability requirements for dependent partner and dependent child on the Innovator route

INN 24.1.   The applicant must not fall for refusal under Part 9: grounds for refusal.

INN 24.2.   If applying for permission to stay the applicant must not be:

(a)   in breach of immigration laws, except that where paragraph 39E applies, that period of overstaying will be disregarded; or

(b)   on immigration bail.

Eligibility requirements for a dependent partner and dependent child on the Innovator route

Entry requirement for a dependent partner and dependent child on the Innovator route

INN 25.1.   A person seeking to come to the UK as a partner or child must apply for and obtain entry clearance as a partner or child before they arrive in the UK.

INN 25.2.   A person applying for entry clearance as the partner or child of an Innovator must, if paragraph A39 and Appendix T of these rules apply, provide a valid medical certificate confirming that they have undergone screening for active pulmonary tuberculosis and that this tuberculosis is not present in them.

Relationship requirements for a dependent partner on the Innovator route

INN 26.1.   The applicant must be the partner of a person (P) and one of the following must apply:

(a)   P has permission on the Innovator route; or

(b)   P is, at the same time, applying for (and is granted) permission on the Innovator route.

INN 26.2.   If the applicant and their Innovator partner are not married or in a civil partnership, all of the following requirements must be met:

(a)   they must have been living together in a relationship similar to marriage or civil partnership for at least the two years before the date of application; and

(b)   any previous relationship of the applicant or their Innovator partner with another person must have permanently broken down; and

(c)   the applicant and their Innovator partner must not be so closely related that they would not be allowed to marry or form a civil partnership in the UK.

INN 26.3.   The relationship between the applicant and their Innovator partner must be genuine and subsisting.

INN 26.4.   The applicant and their Innovator partner must intend to live together throughout the applicant's stay in the UK.

Relationship requirement for a dependent child on the Innovator route

INN 27.1.   The applicant must be the child of a person (P) or of P's partner and one of the following must apply:

(a)   P has permission on the Innovator route; or

(b)   P is, at the same time, applying for (and is granted) permission on the Innovator route.

INN 27.2.   The applicant's parents must each be either applying at the same time as the applicant, or have permission to be in the UK (other than as a visitor) unless:

(a)   the parent applying for or with entry clearance or permission to stay as an Innovator is the sole surviving parent; or

(b)   the parent applying for or with entry clearance or permission to stay as an Innovator has sole responsibility for the child's upbringing; or

(c)   the parent who does not have permission as an Innovator –

(i)   is a British citizen or a person who has a right to enter or stay in the UK without restriction; and

(ii)   is or will be ordinarily resident in the UK; or

(d)   the decision maker is satisfied that there are serious and compelling reasons to grant the child entry clearance or permission to stay with the parent who is applying for or has entry clearance or permission on the Innovator route.

Care requirement for a dependent child on the Innovator route

INN 28.1.   If the applicant is aged under 18 on the date of application there must be suitable arrangements for the child's care and accommodation in the UK, which must comply with relevant UK legislation and regulations.

Age requirement for a dependent child on the Innovator route

INN 29.1.   The applicant must be under the age of 18 at the date of application, unless they were last granted permission as the dependent child of their parent or parents.

INN 29.2.   If the applicant is aged 16 or over at the date of application, they must not be leading an independent life.

Financial requirement for a dependent partner or dependent child on the Innovator route

INN 30.1.   If the applicant is applying for permission to stay and has been living in the UK with permission for 12 months or longer on the date of application, they will meet the financial requirement and do not need to show funds.

INN 30.2.   If the applicant is applying for entry clearance, or has been in the UK for less than 12 months on the date of application, funds of at least the amount required in INN 30.2A must be held collectively by one or more of the following:

(a)   the applicant; and

(b)   the Innovator (P); and

(c)   if the applicant is applying as a dependent child, their parent who is lawfully present in the UK or being granted entry clearance, or permission to stay, at the same time.

INN 30.2A.   The funds required are:

(a)   £285 for a dependent partner in the UK, or applying for entry clearance; and

(b)   £315 for the first dependent child in the UK, or applying for entry clearance; and

(c)   £200 for any other dependent child in the UK, or applying for entry clearance.

INN 30.3.   The funds held must be in addition to any funds required by the Innovator to meet the financial requirement or any dependants in the UK or applying at the same time.

INN 30.4.   If INN 30.2. applies, the required level of funds must have been held for a 28-day period and as specified in Appendix Finance.

Decision on application for a dependent partner and dependent child on the Innovator route

INN 31.1.   If the decision maker is satisfied that all the suitability and eligibility requirements are met for a dependent partner or dependent child on the Innovator route the application will be granted, otherwise the application will be refused.

INN 31.2.   If the application is refused the person can apply for an Administrative Review under Appendix AR: Administrative Review.

Period and conditions of grant for a dependent partner and dependent child on the Innovator route

INN 32.1.   A partner will be granted permission which either:

(a)   ends on the same date as their partner's permission on the Innovator route; or

(b)   for 3 years' if the partner was (or is being) granted settlement on the Innovator route.

INN 32.2.   A child will be granted permission which ends on the same date as whichever of their parents' permission ends first unless both parents have (or are being granted) settlement or British Citizenship, in which case the child will be granted permission for 3 years.

INN 32.3.   The grant will be subject to all the following conditions:

(a)   no access to public funds; and

(b)   work (including self-employment and voluntary work) permitted; except for employment as a professional sportsperson (including as a sports coach); and

(c)   study is permitted, subject to the ATAS condition in Appendix ATAS; and

(d)   if Part 10 applies the applicant will be required to register with the police.

Settlement for dependent partner and dependent child on the Innovator route

Validity requirements for settlement for dependent partner and dependent child on the Innovator route

INN 33.1.   A partner and child on the Innovator route who is applying for settlement must apply online on the GOV.UK website on the specified form as follows:

Applicant	Form
Partner	'Settlement as the partner of an Innovator or a person with protection status'
Child	'Settlement as the child of an Innovator or partner of an Innovator or a person with protection status'

INN 33.2.   An application for settlement must meet all the following requirements:

(a)   any fee must have been paid; and

(b)   the applicant must have provided any required biometrics; and

(c)   the applicant must have provided a passport or other travel document which satisfactorily establishes their identity and nationality; and

(d)   the applicant must be in the UK.

INN 33.3.   DELETED

INN 33.4.   An application which does not meet all the validity requirements for settlement as a partner and child on the Innovator route is invalid and may be rejected and not considered.

Suitability Requirements for settlement by a dependent partner and dependent child on the Innovator route

INN 34.1.   The applicant must not fall for refusal under Part 9: grounds for refusal.

INN 34.2.   The applicant must not be:

    (a)   in breach of immigration laws, except that where paragraph 39E applies, that period of overstaying will be disregarded; or

    (b)   on immigration bail.

Eligibility requirements for settlement by a dependent partner and dependent child on the Innovator route

Relationship requirement for settlement for a dependent partner or dependent child on the Innovator route

INN 35.1.   The applicant must be the partner or child of a person (P) where one of the following applies:

    (a)   P is, at the same time, being granted settlement as an Innovator; or

    (b)   P is settled or has become a British citizen, providing P had permission as an Innovator when they settled and the applicant either:

        i)   had permission as P's partner or child at that time; or

        ii)   is applying as a child of P, and was born in the UK before P settled.

INN 35.2.   The applicant must either:

    (a)   have last been granted permission as a dependent partner or dependent child of the person (P) in INN 35.1; or

    (b)   have been born in the UK and be applying as a child of the person (P) in INN 35.1.

INN 35.3.   If applying as a child, the applicant's other parent must be being granted settlement at the same time, or be settled or a British citizen, unless:

    (a)   the person (P) in INN 35.1. or applying as the dependent partner of the person (P) in INN 35.1 is the applicant's sole surviving parent; or

    (b)   the person (P) in INN 35.1. or the person applying as the dependent partner of person (P) in INN 35.1 has sole responsibility for the applicant's upbringing; or

    (c)   the decision maker is satisfied that there are serious and compelling reasons to grant the applicant settlement.

Care requirement for settlement as a dependent child on the Innovator route

INN 36.1.   If the applicant is under the age of 18 on the date of application there must be suitable arrangements for the child's care and accommodation in the UK, which must comply with relevant UK legislation and regulations.

Age requirement for settlement as a dependent child on the Innovator route

INN 37.1.   The child must be under the age of 18 at the date of application, unless they were last granted permission as the dependent child of their parent or parents.

INN 37.2.   If the applicant is aged 16 or over on the date of application they must not be leading an independent life.

Qualifying period requirement for settlement as a dependent partner on the Innovator route

INN 38.1.   The applicant must have spent a continuous period of 5 years in the UK with permission as a dependent partner of the person (P) in INN 35.1.

Continuous residence requirement for settlement as a dependent partner of on the Innovator route

INN 39.1.   The applicant must meet the continuous residence requirement as set out in Appendix Continuous Residence during the period in INN 38.1.

English language requirement for a dependent partner or dependent child on the Innovator route

INN 40.1.   Unless an exemption applies, the applicant must show English language ability on the Common European Framework of Reference for Languages in speaking and listening to at least level B1.

INN 40.2. The applicant must show they meet the English language requirement as specified in Appendix English Language.

Knowledge of life in the UK requirement for settlement as a dependent partner or dependent child on the Innovator route

INN 41.1. If the applicant is aged 18 or over at the date of application, they must meet the Knowledge of Life in the UK requirement as set out in Appendix KOL UK.

Decision on an application for settlement as a dependent partner or dependent child on the Innovator route

INN 42.1. If the decision maker is satisfied all the suitability and eligibility requirements are met for settlement as a dependent partner or child on the Innovator route, the application will be granted settlement, otherwise the application will be refused.

INN 42.2. If the application is refused the person can apply for an Administrative Review under Appendix AR: Administrative Review.

Appendix KOL UK

This Appendix sets out how the Knowledge of Life in the UK requirement is met by a person applying for settlement.

It applies only to applications under Appendix Student, Appendix Skilled Worker, Appendix Representatives of an Overseas Business, Appendix T2 Minister of Religion, Appendix T2 Sportsperson, Appendix UK Ancestry, Appendix Global Talent, Appendix Innovator, Appendix T5 (Temporary Worker) International Agreement Worker, Appendix Domestic Worker in a Private Household, and Appendix Hong Kong British National (Overseas).

Exemption

KOL 1.1.   An applicant is exempt from the Knowledge of Life in the UK requirement if at the date of application they:

    (a)   are aged 65 or over; or

    (b)   are aged under 18; or

    (c)   have a disability (physical or mental condition) which prevents them from meeting the requirement.

Knowledge of Life in the UK requirement

KOL 2.1.   An applicant will meet the Knowledge of Life in the UK requirement if they:

    (a)   provide a valid digital reference number from an educational institution or other person approved for this purpose by the Secretary of State showing they have passed the Life in the UK test; or

    (b)   are resident in the Isle of Man, and provide a valid digital reference number from an educational institution or other person approved for this purpose by the Lieutenant Governor showing they have passed the Isle of Man's Life in the UK test; or

    (c)   are resident in the Bailiwick of Guernsey or in the Bailiwick of Jersey, and provide a valid digital reference number from an educational institution or other person approved for that purpose by the Lieutenant Governor of Guernsey or Jersey showing they have passed the "Citizenship Test".

Appendix Representative of an Overseas Business

Immigration Rules for Representative of an Overseas Business

The Representative of an Overseas Business route is for an employee of an overseas business which does not have a presence in the UK.

A person applying as a Representative of an Overseas Business must either be a Sole Representative or a Media Representative.

A Sole Representative is a senior employee of an overseas business who is assigned to the United Kingdom for the purpose of establishing a branch or subsidiary.

A Media Representative is an employee of an overseas media organisation posted to the United Kingdom on a long-term assignment.

A dependent partner and dependent children can apply under this route.

Representative of an Overseas Business is a route to settlement.

Validity requirements for a Representative of an Overseas Business

ROB 1.1. A person applying for entry clearance or permission to stay as a Representative of an Overseas Business must apply online on gov.uk on the specified form as follows:

(a)   for entry clearance, form "Other work" on the "Find and apply for other visas from outside the UK" form; or

(b)   for permission to stay, form "Application to extend stay in the UK: FLR(IR)".

ROB 1.2. An application for entry clearance or permission to stay as the Representative of an Overseas Business must meet all the following requirements:

(a)   any fee and Immigration Health Charge must have been paid; and

(b)   the applicant must have provided any required biometrics; and

(c)   the applicant must have provided a passport or other travel document which satisfactorily establishes their identity and nationality.

ROB 1.3. The applicant must be aged 18 or over on the date of application.

ROB 1.4. If the applicant has, in the last 12 months before the date of application, received an award from a Government or international scholarship agency covering both fees and living costs for study in the UK, they must provide written consent to the application from that Government or agency.

ROB 1.5. An applicant who is applying for permission to stay must be in the UK on the date of application and must not have, or have last been granted, permission:

(a)   as a Visitor; or

(b)   as a Short-term Student; or

(c)   as a Parent of a Child Student; or

(d)   as a Seasonal Worker; or

(e)   as a Domestic Worker in a Private Household; or

(f)   outside the Immigration Rules.

ROB 1.6. An application which does not meet all the validity requirements for a Representative of an Overseas Business is invalid and may be rejected and not considered.

Suitability requirements for a Representative of an Overseas Business

ROB 2.1. The applicant must not fall for refusal under Part 9: grounds for refusal.

ROB 2.2. If applying for permission to stay the applicant must not be:

(a)   in breach of immigration laws, except that where paragraph 39E applies, that period of overstaying will be disregarded; or

(b)   on immigration bail.

Eligibility requirements for Representative of an Overseas Business

Entry requirements for Representative of an Overseas Business

ROB 3.1. A person seeking to come to the UK as a Representative of an Overseas Business must have applied for and obtained entry clearance as a Representative of an Overseas Business before their arrival in the UK.

ROB 3.2.   A person applying for entry clearance as a Representative of an Overseas Business must, if paragraph A39 and Appendix T of these rules apply, provide a valid medical certificate confirming that they have undergone screening for active pulmonary tuberculosis and that this tuberculosis is not present in them.

Work requirement for Representative of an Overseas Business

ROB 4.1.   The overseas business or media organisation that the applicant represents must be active and trading outside the UK, with its headquarters and principle place of business remaining outside the UK.

ROB 4.2.   The applicant must have been recruited and taken on as an employee outside the UK by the business they will represent.

ROB 4.3.   The applicant must intend to work full-time as the representative of the overseas business or media organisation and must not intend to undertake work for any other business or engage in business of their own.

ROB 4.4.   An applicant must be either:

(a)   a Sole Representative who is a senior employee of an overseas business, who is assigned to the UK to establish and supervise a branch or subsidiary of an overseas business, where that branch or subsidiary will actively trade in the same type of business as the overseas business; or

(b)   a Media Representative who is posted on a long-term assignment to the UK on behalf of a newspaper, news agency or broadcasting organisation.

Genuineness requirement for the Representative of an Overseas Business

ROB 5.1.   The decision maker must be satisfied that the applicant is a genuine Representative of an Overseas Business.

ROB 5.2.   The decision maker must not have reasonable grounds to believe the business is being established in the UK by the overseas business, or the applicant has been appointed as a representative of the overseas business or media organisation, mainly so the applicant can apply for entry clearance or permission to stay.

English language requirement for a Representative of an Overseas Business

ROB 6.1.   The applicant must show English language ability on the Common European Framework of Reference for Languages in speaking and listening of at least level A1.

ROB 6.2.   The applicant must show they meet the English language requirement as specified in Appendix English Language.

Financial requirement for a Representative of an Overseas Business

ROB 7.1.   The decision maker must be satisfied that the applicant can, and will, adequately maintain and accommodate themselves, and any dependants in the UK, without access to public funds.

ROB 7.2.   Funds must be shown as specified in Appendix Finance.

Additional business requirements for a Sole Representative on the Representative of an Overseas Business route

ROB 8.1.   Where the applicant is applying as a Sole Representative on the Representative of an Overseas Business route, the applicant must meet the additional business requirements set out in ROB 8.2. to ROB 8.6.

ROB 8.2.   The applicant must be a senior employee of the overseas business with the skills, experience and knowledge of the business necessary to undertake the role, with full authority to negotiate and take operational decisions on behalf of the overseas business.

ROB 8.3.   The applicant must not have a majority stake in, or otherwise own or control a majority of the overseas business they represent, whether that ownership or control is by means of a shareholding, partnership agreement, sole proprietorship or any other arrangement.

ROB 8.4.   Where the applicant does not have, or was not last granted, permission as a Sole Representative, the applicant must represent an overseas business that does not have any other active branch, subsidiary or representative in the UK.

ROB 8.5.   Where the applicant does not have, or was not last granted, permission as a Sole Representative, the applicant must provide all of the following from their employer:

(a)   a full description of the overseas business's activities, including details of assets and accounts and the share distribution or ownership for the previous year; and

(b)   a letter which confirms the overseas business will establish a registered branch or wholly-owned subsidiary in the UK in the same business activity as the overseas business; and

(c)   a job description, salary details and contract of employment for the applicant; and

(d)   a letter confirming the applicant has the relevant skills, experience, knowledge and authority required at ROB 8.2; and

(e)   a notarised statement which confirms the applicant will be their sole representative in the UK, that the company has no other active branch, subsidiary or representative in the UK and, that its operations will remain centred overseas.

ROB 8.6.   Where the applicant is applying for permission to stay and has, or was last granted permission as a Sole Representative, the applicant must meet all the following requirements:

(a)   the applicant must have established the registered branch or wholly-owned subsidiary of the overseas business for which they were last granted permission under this route; and

(b)   the applicant must be engaged in full time employment and must supervise the registered branch or wholly-owned subsidiary that they have established, and must be required by their employer to continue in that role; and

(c)   the applicant must provide all of the following:

(i)   evidence of business that has been generated, principally with firms in the UK, on behalf of their employer since their last permission, in the form of accounts, copies of invoices or letters from businesses with whom the applicant has done business, including the value of transactions; and

(ii)   a Companies House certificate of registration as a UK establishment (for a branch), or a certificate of incorporation (for a subsidiary), together with either a copy of the share register or a letter from the overseas business's accountant confirming that the UK business is wholly owned by the overseas business; and

(iii)   a letter from the applicant's employer confirming that the applicant supervises the UK branch or subsidiary and is required to continue in that employment; and

(iv)   evidence of salary paid by the employer in the 12 months immediately before the date of application and details of the renumeration package the employee receives.

Additional business requirements for a Media Representative on the Representative of an Overseas Business route

ROB 9.1.   Where the applicant is applying as a Media Representative on the Representative of Overseas Business route, the applicant must meet the additional business requirements in ROB 9.2. and ROB 9.3.

ROB 9.2.   The applicant must be an employee of an overseas newspaper, news agency or broadcasting organisation undertaking a long-term assignment as a representative of their overseas employer.

ROB 9.3.   Where the applicant is applying for permission to stay and has, or was last granted, permission as a Media Representative, the applicant must meet all the following:

(a)   the applicant must be engaged in full time employment for which their last period of permission was granted and be required by their employer to continue in that role; and

(b)   the applicant must provide the following:

(i)   a letter from the applicant's employer confirming that the applicant is required to continue in their employment; and

(ii)   evidence of the applicant's salary paid in the 12 months immediately before the date of application and details of the remuneration package the employee receives.

Decision on application as Representative of an Overseas Business

ROB 10.1.   If the decision maker is satisfied that all the suitability and relevant eligibility requirements are met as a Representative of an Overseas Business the application will be granted, otherwise the application will be refused.

ROB 10.2.   If the application is refused, a person can apply for an Administrative Review under Appendix AR: Administrative Review.

Period and conditions of grant.

ROB 11.1.   If the applicant is applying for entry clearance under the Representative of an Overseas Business routes or is applying for permission to stay and does not have, or did not last have, permission on the Representative of an Overseas Business route they will be granted permission for a period not exceeding 3 years.

ROB 11.2.   If the applicant has or last had, permission under the Representative of an Overseas Business route, they will be granted permission for a period not exceeding 2 years.

ROB 11.3.   The grant will be subject to all the following conditions:

    (a)   no access to public funds; and

    (b)   no work permitted other than working for the overseas business which the applicant represents; and

    (c)   study is permitted, subject to the ATAS condition in Appendix ATAS; and

    (d)   if Part 10 applies the applicant will be required to register with the police.

Settlement as a Representative of an Overseas Business Route

Validity requirements for Settlement by a Representative of an Overseas Business

ROB 12.1.   A person applying for settlement as a Representative of an Overseas Business must apply online on the gov.uk website on the specified form, "Settle in the UK in various immigration categories: form SET(O)".

ROB 12.2.   An application for settlement as a Representative of an Overseas Business must meet all the following requirements:

    (a)   any fee must have been paid; and

    (b)   the applicant must have provided any required biometrics; and

    (c)   the applicant must have provided a valid passport or other travel document which satisfactorily establishes their identity and nationality.

ROB 12.3.   The applicant must be in the UK and have, or have last been granted, permission as a Representative of an Overseas Business.

ROB 12.4.   An application which does not meet the validity requirements for settlement as a Representative of an Overseas Business is invalid and may be rejected and not considered.

Suitability requirements for settlement by a Representative of an Overseas Business

ROB 13.1.   The applicant must not fall for refusal under Part 9: grounds for refusal.

ROB 13.2.   The applicant must not be:

    (a)   in breach of immigration laws, except that where paragraph 39E applies, that period of overstaying will be disregarded; or

    (b)   on immigration bail.

Eligibility requirements for settlement by a Representative of an Overseas Business

Qualifying period requirement for settlement by a Representative of an Overseas Business

ROB 14.1.   The applicant must have spent the last 5 years before the date of application in the UK with permission as a Representative of an Overseas Business.

Continuous residence requirement for settlement by a Representative of an Overseas Business

ROB 15.1.   The applicant must meet the continuous resident requirement in Appendix Continuous Residence during the period in ROB 14.1.

Work requirement for settlement by a Representative of an Overseas Business

ROB 16.1.   Throughout the period in ROB 14.1:

    (a)   the overseas business or media organisation that the applicant represents must have been active and trading with its headquarters and principle place of business remaining outside the UK; and

    (b)   the applicant must have been employed and working fulltime for the overseas business or media organisation they represent, or for that business's UK branch or subsidiary, and

    (c)   the applicant must not have undertaken work for any other business or engaged in business of their own.

ROB 16.2.   The applicant must provide:

    (a)   evidence of salary paid by their employer in the 12 months immediately before the date of application and details of the renumeration package the employee receives; and

    (b)   a letter from their employer confirming that they still require the applicant to work for them, and that the applicant will be required for the foreseeable future.

ROB 16.3.   The applicant must be required by their employer to continue in the role for which their last period of permission was granted.

Additional business requirements for settlement by a Sole Representative on the Representative of an Overseas Business route

ROB 16A.1. Where the applicant has, or was last granted permission as a Sole Representative, the applicant must meet the additional business requirements set out in ROB 16A.2. and ROB 16A.3.

ROB 16A.2. Throughout the period in ROB 14.1, the applicant must have met the following requirements:

(a) they must not have had a majority stake in, or otherwise owned or controlled a majority of the overseas business they represent, whether that ownership or control was by means of a shareholding, partnership agreement, sole proprietorship or any other arrangement; and

(b) the applicant must have established and then supervised the registered a branch or wholly owned subsidiary of the overseas business they represent in the UK, where that branch or subsidiary was actively trading in the same type of business as the overseas business.

ROB 16A.3. The applicant must provide all of the following:

(a) evidence of business that has been generated, principally with firms in the UK, on behalf of their employer since their last grant of permission, in the form of accounts, copies of invoices or letters from businesses with whom the applicant has done business, including the value of transactions; and

(b) either a copy of the share register or a letter from the overseas business's accountant confirming that the UK business is wholly owned by the overseas business; and

(c) a letter from the applicant's employer confirming that the applicant has supervised the UK branch or subsidiary since the last grant of permission.

Additional business requirements for settlement by a Media Representative on the Representative of an Overseas Business route

ROB 16B.1. Where the applicant has, or was last granted, permission as a Media Representative, the applicant must meet the additional business requirements set out in ROB 16B.2.

ROB 16B.2. Throughout the period in ROB 14.1, the applicant must have met the following requirements:

(a) they must have been an employee of an overseas newspaper, news agency or broadcasting organisation undertaking a longterm assignment as a representative of their overseas employer; and

(b) the applicant must have been engaged in the employment for which their last period of permission was granted.

English language requirement for settlement by a Representative of an Overseas Business

ROB 17.1. Unless an exemption applies, the applicant must show English language ability on the Common European Framework of Reference for Languages in speaking and listening to at least level B1.

ROB 17.2. The applicant must show they meet the English language requirement as specified in Appendix English Language.

Knowledge of life in the UK requirement for settlement by a Representative of an Overseas Business

ROB 18.1. The applicant must meet the Knowledge of Life in the UK requirement as specified in Appendix KOL UK.

Decision on an application for settlement as a Representative of an Overseas Business Route

ROB 19.1. If the decision maker is satisfied all the suitability and relevant eligibility requirements are met for settlement by a Representative of an Overseas Business, the applicant will be granted settlement, otherwise the application will be refused.

ROB 19.2. If the application is refused, a person can apply for an Administrative Review under Appendix AR: Administrative Review.

Dependants of Representatives of Overseas Businesses

Validity requirements for a dependent partner or dependent child of a Representative of an Overseas Business

ROB.20.1. A person applying for entry clearance or permission to stay as a partner or child on the Representative of an Overseas Business route must apply online on the gov.uk website on the specified form as follows:

(a)   for entry clearance, "Join or accompany a family member" on the "Find and apply for other visas from outside the UK" form; or

(b)   for permission to stay, "Application to extend stay in the UK: FLR(IR)".

ROB 20.2.   An application for entry clearance or permission to stay as a partner or child on the Representative of an Overseas Business route must meet all the following requirements:

(a)   any fee and Immigration Health Charge must have been paid; and

(b)   the applicant must have provided any required biometrics; and

(c)   the applicant must have provided a passport or other travel document which satisfactorily establishes their identity and nationality.

ROB 20.3.   A person applying as a dependent partner must be aged 18 or over on the date of application.

ROB 20.4.   A person applying for permission to stay must be in the UK on the date of application and must not have, or have last been granted, permission:

(a)   as a Visitor; or

(b)   as a Short-term student; or

(c)   as a Parent of a Child Student; or

(d)   as a Seasonal worker; or

(e)   as a Domestic worker in a private household: or

(f)   outside the Immigration Rules.

ROB 20.5.   An application which does not meet all the validity requirements for a partner or child on the Representative of an Overseas Business route is invalid and may be rejected and not considered.

Suitability requirements for a partner or child on the Representative of an Overseas Business route

ROB 21.1.   The applicant must not fall for refusal under Part 9: grounds for refusal.

ROB 21.2.   If applying for permission to stay the applicant must not be:

(a)   in breach of immigration laws, except that where paragraph 39E applies, that period of overstaying will be disregarded; or

(b)   on immigration bail.

Eligibility requirements for a partner or child on the Representative of an Overseas Business route

Entry requirement for a partner or child on the Representative of an Overseas Business route

ROB 22.1.   A person seeking to come to the UK as a partner or child must apply for and obtain an entry clearance as a partner or child before they arrive in the UK.

ROB 22.2.   A person applying for entry clearance as a partner of child on the Representative of an Overseas Business route must, if paragraph A39 and Appendix T of these rules apply, provide a valid medical certificate confirming that they have undergone screening for active pulmonary tuberculosis and that this tuberculosis is not present in them.

Relationship requirements for a partner of a Representative of an Overseas Business route

ROB 23.1.   The applicant must be the partner of a person (P) and one of the following must apply:

(a)   P has permission on the Representative of an Overseas Business route; or

(b)   P is, at the same time, applying for (and is granted) permission on the Representative of an Overseas Business route; or

(c)   P is settled or has become a British citizen, providing they had permission on a Representative of an Overseas Business route when they settled and the applicant had permission as their partner at that time.

ROB 23.2.   If the applicant and the Representative of an Overseas Business are not married or in a civil partnership, all of the following requirements must be met:

(a)   they must have been living together in a relationship similar to marriage or civil partnership for at least the two years before the date of application; and

(b)   any previous relationship of the applicant or the Representative of an Overseas Business with another person must have permanently broken down; and

(c)   the applicant and the Representative of an Overseas Business must not be so closely related that they would not be allowed to marry or form a civil partnership in the UK.

ROB 23.3.   The relationship between the applicant and the Representative of an Overseas Business must be genuine and subsisting.

ROB 23.4.   The applicant and the Representative of an Overseas Business must intend to live together throughout the applicant's stay in the UK.

Relationship requirement for a dependent child on the Representative of an Overseas Business route

ROB 24.1.   The applicant must be the child of a person (P) and one of the following must apply:

(a)   P has permission on the Representative of an Overseas Business route; or

(b)   P is, at the same time, applying for (and is granted) permission on the Representative of an Overseas Business route; or

(c)   P is settled or has become a British citizen, providing P previously had permission on the Representative of an Overseas Business route and the applicant had permission as P's child at that time.

ROB 24.2.   The applicant's parents must each be either applying at the same time as the applicant or have permission to be in the UK (other than as a Visitor) unless:

(a)   the parent applying for or with entry clearance or permission to stay on the Representative of an Overseas Business route is the sole surviving parent; or

(b)   the parent applying for or with entry clearance or permission to stay on the Representative of an Overseas Business route has sole responsibility for the child's upbringing; or

(c)   the parent who does not have permission on the Representative of an Overseas Business route –

(i)   is a British citizen or a person who has a right to enter or stay in the UK without restriction; and

(ii)   is or will be ordinarily resident in the UK; or

(d)   the decision maker is satisfied that there are serious and compelling reasons to grant the child entry clearance or permission to stay with the parent who is applying for or has entry clearance or permission on the Representative of an Overseas Business route.

Care requirement for a dependent child on the Representative of an Overseas Business route

ROB 25.1.   If the child is under the age of 18 on the date of application, there must be suitable arrangements for the child's care and accommodation in the UK, which must comply with relevant UK legislation and regulations.

Age requirement for a dependent child on the Representative of an Overseas Business route

ROB 26.1.   The child must be under the age of 18 on the date of application, unless they were last granted permission as the dependent child of their parent or parents.

ROB 26.2.   If the child is aged 16 or over on the date of application, they must not be leading an independent life.

Financial requirement for a partner or child on the Representative of an Overseas Business route

ROB 27.1.   The decision maker must be satisfied that the applicant or the Representative of an Overseas Business can and will adequately maintain and accommodate the applicant, and any other dependants in the UK, or applying for entry clearance, without access to public funds.

ROB 27.2.   Funds must be shown as specified in Appendix Finance.

Overseas business requirement for a partner or child on the Representative of an Overseas Business route

ROB 28.1.   If the person (P) in ROB 23.1. is a Sole Representative, the applicant must not have a majority stake in, or otherwise own or control a majority of the overseas business P represents, whether that ownership or control is by means of a shareholding, partnership agreement, sole proprietorship or any other arrangement.

Decision on application for a dependent partner and dependent child on the Representative of an Overseas Business route

ROB 29.1.   If the decision maker is satisfied that all the suitability and eligibility requirements are met for a dependent partner or dependent child on the Representative of an Overseas Business route the application will be granted, otherwise the application will be refused.

ROB 29.2.   If the application is refused the person can apply for an Administrative Review under Appendix AR: Administrative Review.

Period and conditions of grant for a dependent partner and dependent child on the Representative of an Overseas Business route

ROB 30.1.   A partner will be granted:

   (a)   permission which ends on the same date as the permission as the Representative of an Overseas Business; or

   (b)   2 years' permission if the Representative of an Overseas Business was (or is being) granted settlement as a Representative of an Overseas Business.

ROB 30.2.   A dependent child will be granted permission which ends on the same date as whichever of their parents' permission ends first, unless both parents have (or are being granted) settlement or British Citizenship, in which case the child will be granted permission for 30 months.

ROB 30.3.   The grant will be subject to all the following conditions:

   (a)   no access to public funds; and

   (b)   work (including self-employment and voluntary work) permitted; except for employment as a professional sportsperson (including as a sports coach); and

   (c)   study is permitted, subject to the ATAS condition in Appendix ATAS; and

   (d)   if Part 10 applies the applicant will be required to register with the police.

Settlement by dependent partner and dependent child on the Representative of an Overseas Business route

Validity requirements for settlement by a dependent partner or dependent child on the Representative of an Overseas Business route

ROB 31.1.   A partner or child on the Representative of an Overseas Business route who is applying for settlement must apply online on the gov.uk website on the specified form "Settle in the UK in various immigration categories: form SET(O)".

ROB 31.2.   An application for settlement must meet all the following requirements:

   (a)   any fee must have been paid; and

   (b)   the applicant must have provided any required biometrics; and

   (c)   the applicant must have provided a passport or other travel document which satisfactorily establishes their identity and nationality; and

   (d)   the applicant must be in the UK.

ROB 31.3.   DELETED

ROB 31.4.   An application which does not meet all the validity requirements for settlement as a partner or child on the Representative of an Overseas Business route is invalid and may be rejected and not considered.

Suitability Requirements for settlement by a dependent partner and dependent child on the Representative of an Overseas Business route

ROB 32.1.   The applicant must not fall for refusal under Part 9: grounds for refusal.

ROB 32.2.   The applicant must not be:

   (a)   in breach of immigration laws, except that where paragraph 39E applies, that period of overstaying will be disregarded; or

   (b)   on immigration bail.

Eligibility requirements for settlement by a dependent partner or dependent child on the Representative of an Overseas Business route

Relationship requirement for settlement by a partner or child on the Representative of an Overseas Business route

ROB 33.1.   The applicant must be the partner or child of a person (P) where one of the following applies:

(a)   P is, at the same time, being granted settlement as a Representative of an Overseas Business; or

(b)   P is settled in the UK or has become a British citizen, providing P had permission as a Representative of an Overseas Business when they settled and the applicant either:

i)   had permission as P's partner or child at that time; or

ii)   is applying as a child of P, and was born in the UK before P settled.

ROB 33.1A.   The applicant must either:

(a)   have last been granted permission as a dependent partner or dependent child of the person (P) in ROB 33.1; or

(b)   have been born in the UK and be applying as a child of the person (P) in ROB 33.1.

ROB 33.2.   If applying as a child, the applicant's other parent must be being granted settlement at the same time, or be settled or a British citizen, unless:

(a)   the person (P) in ROB 33.1. is the applicant's sole surviving parent; or

(b)   the person (P) in ROB 33.1. has sole responsibility for the applicant's upbringing; or

(c)   the decision maker is satisfied that there are serious and compelling reasons to grant the applicant settlement.

Care requirement for settlement by a child on the Representative of an Overseas Business route

ROB 34.1.   If the applicant is under the age of 18 on the date of application, there must be suitable arrangements for the child's care and accommodation in the UK, which must comply with relevant UK legislation and regulations.

Age requirement for settlement by a child on the Representative of an Overseas Business route

ROB 35.1.   The child must be under the age of 18 on the date of application, unless they were last granted permission as the dependent child of their parent or parents.

ROB 35.2.   If the child is aged 16 or over on the date of application, they must not be leading an independent life.

English language requirement for settlement by a partner or child on the Representative of an Overseas Business route

ROB 36.1.   Unless an exemption applies, the applicant must show English language ability on the Common European Framework of Reference for Languages in speaking and listening to at least level B1.

ROB 36.2.   The applicant must show they meet the English language requirement as specified in Appendix English Language.

Knowledge of life in the UK requirement for settlement by a partner or child on the Representative of an Overseas Business route

ROB 37.1.   If the applicant is aged 18 or over at the date of application, they must meet the Knowledge of Life in the UK requirement as set out in Appendix KOL UK.

Decision on an application for settlement by a partner or child on the Representative of an Overseas Business route

ROB 38.1.   If the decision maker is satisfied all the suitability and eligibility requirements are met for settlement as a dependent partner or dependent child on the Representative of an Overseas Business route, the applicant will be granted settlement, otherwise the application will be refused.

ROB 38.2.   If the application is refused the person can apply for an Administrative Review under Appendix AR: Administrative Review.

Appendix Shortage Occupation List

Shortage Occupations for the Skilled Worker route

Table 1: Shortage occupations where applicants for entry clearance or permission to stay may be paid 80% of the going rate for the occupation code

Occupation code and any further criteria	Shortage occupation in			
	England	Scotland	Wales	Northern Ireland
1181 Health services and public health managers and directors – all jobs	Yes	Yes	Yes	Yes
1242 Residential, day and domiciliary care managers and proprietors – all jobs	Yes	Yes	Yes	Yes
2111 Chemical scientists – only jobs in the nuclear industry	-	Yes	-	-
2112 Biological scientists and biochemists – all jobs	Yes	Yes	Yes	Yes
2113 Physical scientists – only the following jobs in the oil and gas industry:				
• geophysicist				
• geoscientist				
• geologist				
• geochemist				
• technical services manager in the decommissioning and waste areas of the nuclear industry				
• senior resource geologist and staff geologist in the mining sector	Yes	Yes	Yes	Yes
2114 Social and humanities scientists – only archaeologists	Yes	Yes	Yes	Yes
2121 Civil engineers – all jobs	Yes	Yes	Yes	Yes
2122 Mechanical engineers – all jobs	Yes	Yes	Yes	Yes
2123 Electrical engineers – all jobs	Yes	Yes	Yes	Yes
2124 Electronics engineers – all jobs	Yes	Yes	Yes	Yes
2126 Design and development engineers – all jobs	Yes	Yes	Yes	Yes
2127 Production and process engineers – all jobs	Yes	Yes	Yes	Yes
2129 Engineering professionals not elsewhere classified – all jobs	Yes	Yes	Yes	Yes
2135 IT business analysts, architects and systems designers – all jobs	Yes	Yes	Yes	Yes
2136 Programmers and software development professionals – all jobs	Yes	Yes	Yes	Yes
2137 Web design and development professionals – all jobs	Yes	Yes	Yes	Yes
2139 Information technology and communications professionals not elsewhere classified – only cyber security specialists	Yes	Yes	Yes	Yes
2216 Veterinarians – all jobs	Yes	Yes	Yes	Yes
2425 Actuaries, economists and statisticians – only bio-informaticians and informaticians	Yes	Yes	Yes	Yes
2431 Architects – all jobs	Yes	Yes	Yes	Yes
2461 Quality control and planning engineers – all jobs	Yes	Yes	Yes	Yes
3111 Laboratory technicians – all jobs	Yes	Yes	Yes	Yes
3411 Artists – all jobs	Yes	Yes	Yes	Yes

Occupation code and any further criteria	Shortage occupation in			
3414 Dancers and choreographers – only skilled classical ballet dancers or skilled contemporary dancers who meet the standard required by internationally recognised UK ballet or contemporary dance companies. The company must be endorsed as being internationally recognised by a UK industry body such as the Arts Councils (of England, Scotland or Wales).	Yes	Yes	Yes	Yes
3415 Musicians – only skilled orchestral musicians who are leaders, principals, sub-principals or numbered string positions, and who meet the standard required by internationally recognised UK orchestras. The orchestra must be a full member of the Association of British Orchestras.	Yes	Yes	Yes	Yes
3416 Arts officers, producers and directors – all jobs	Yes	Yes	Yes	Yes
3421 Graphic designers – all jobs	Yes	Yes	Yes	Yes
5215 Welding trades – only high integrity pipe welders, where the job requires 3 or more years' related on-the-job experience. This experience must not have been gained through working illegally.	Yes	Yes	Yes	Yes
6146 Senior care workers – all jobs	Yes	Yes	Yes	Yes

Table 2: Shortage occupations in eligible health and education occupation codes where going rates are based on national pay scales

Occupation code and any further criteria	Shortage occupation in			
	England	Scotland	Wales	Northern Ireland
2211 Medical practitioners – all jobs	-	Yes	-	-
2212 Psychologists – all jobs	Yes	Yes	Yes	Yes
2213 Pharmacists – all jobs	Yes	Yes	Yes	Yes
2217 Medical radiographers – all jobs (including radiotherapy practitioners / technologists)	Yes	Yes	Yes	Yes
2219 Health professionals not elsewhere classified – all jobs	Yes	Yes	Yes	Yes
2221 Physiotherapists – all jobs	Yes	Yes	Yes	Yes
2222 Occupational therapists – all jobs	Yes	Yes	Yes	Yes
2223 Speech and language therapists – all jobs	Yes	Yes	Yes	Yes
2231 Nurses – all jobs	Yes	Yes	Yes	Yes
2314 Secondary education teaching professionals – only teachers in maths, physics, science (where an element of physics will be taught), computer science and modern foreign languages	Yes	Yes	Yes	Yes
2314 Secondary education teaching professionals – only teachers in Gaelic	-	Yes	-	-
2315 Primary and nursery education teaching professionals – only Gaelic medium teachers	-	Yes	-	-
2442 Social workers – all jobs	Yes	Yes	Yes	Yes
3213 Paramedics – all jobs	Yes	Yes	Yes	Yes
6141 Nursing auxiliaries and assistants – all jobs	Yes	Yes	Yes	Yes

Appendix Skilled Occupations

Eligible occupation codes and going rates for Skilled Workers and Intra-Company Transfers

In this appendix, "SW" refers to the Skilled Worker route, "ICT" refers to the Intra-Company Transfer route and "ICGT" refers to the Intra-Company Graduate Trainee route.

Table 1: Eligible occupation codes where going rates are based on Annual Survey of Hours and Earnings (ASHE) data

Going rates in Table 1 are per year and based on a 39-hour working week. They must be pro-rated for other working patterns, based on the weekly working hours stated by the applicant's sponsor. Options A to F refer to the tradeable points options set out in Appendix Skilled Worker.

Occupation Code	Related job titles	Going rate (SW – option A, ICT minimum rate)	90% of going rate (SW - option B)	80% of going rate (SW - options C and D)	70% of going rate (SW - option E, ICGT - minimum rate)	Eligible for PhD points (SW)	Eligible for ICT and ICGT
1115 Chief executives and senior officials	• Chief executive • Chief medical officer • Civil servant (grade 5 and above) • Vice president	£67,300 (£33.19 per hour)	£60,570 (£29.87 per hour)	£53,840 (£26.55 per hour)	£47,110 (£23.23 per hour)	Yes	Yes
1121 Production managers and directors in manufacturing	• Engineering manager • Managing director (engineering) • Operations manager (manufacturing) • Production manager	£33,000 (£16.27 per hour)	£29,700 (£14.64 per hour)	£26,400 (£13.02 per hour)	£23,100 (£11.39 per hour)	Yes	Yes
1122 Production managers and directors in construction	• Building Services manager • Construction manager • Director (building construction) • Owner (electrical contracting)	£34,900 (£17.21 per hour)	£31,410 (£15.49 per hour)	£27,920 (£13.77 per hour)	£24,430 (£12.05 per hour)	Yes	Yes
1123 Production managers and directors in mining and energy	• Operations manager (mining, water & energy) • Quarry manager	£37,500 (£18.49 per hour)	£33,750 (£16.64 per hour)	£30,000 (£14.79 per hour)	£26,250 (£12.94 per hour)	Yes	Yes
1131 Financial managers and directors	• Investment banker • Treasury manager	£43,600 (£21.50 per hour)	£39,240 (£19.35 per hour)	£34,880 (£17.20 per hour)	£30,520 (£15.05 per hour)	Yes	Yes
1132 Marketing and sales directors	• Marketing director • Sales director	£54,900 (£27.07 per hour)	£49,410 (£24.36 per hour)	£43,920 (£21.66 per hour)	£38,430 (£18.95 per hour)	Yes	Yes
1133 Purchasing managers and directors	• Bid manager • Purchasing manager	£39,300 (£19.38 per hour)	£35,370 (£17.44 per hour)	£31,440 ((15.50 per hour)	£27,510 (£13.57 per hour)	Yes	Yes
1134 Advertising and public relations directors	• Account director (advertising) • Head of public relations	£45,400 (£22.39 per hour)	£40,860 (£20.15 per hour)	£36,320 (£17.91 per hour)	£31,780 (£15.67 per hour)	Yes	Yes
1135 Human resource managers and directors	• Human resources manager • Personnel manager • Recruitment manager	£36,400 (£17.95 per hour)	£32,760 (£16.15 per hour)	£29,120 (£14.36 per hour)	£25,480 (£12.56 per hour)	Yes	Yes
1136 Information technology and telecommunications directors	• IT Director • Technical director (computer services) • Telecommunications director	£56,100 (£27.66 per hour)	£50,490 (£24.90 per hour)	£44,880 (£22.13 per hour)	£39,270 (£19.36 per hour)	Yes	Yes
1139 Functional managers and directors not elsewhere classified	• Manager (charitable organisation) • Research director	£40,600 (£20.02 per hour)	£36,540 (£18.02 per hour)	£32,480 (£16.02 per hour)	£28,420 (£14.01 per hour)	Yes	Yes
1150 Financial institution managers and directors	• Bank manager • Insurance manager	£36,600 (£18.05 per hour)	£32,940 (£16.24 per hour)	£29,280 (£14.44 per hour)	£25,620 (£12.63 per hour)	Yes	Yes
1161 Managers and directors in transport and distribution	• Fleet manager • Transport manager	£30,900 (£15.24 per hour)	£27,810 (£13.71 per hour)	£24,720 (£12.19 per hour)	£21,630 (£10.67 per hour)	Yes	Yes

Occupation Code	Related job titles	Going rate (SW – option A, ICT minimum rate)	90% of going rate (SW - option B)	80% of going rate (SW - options C and D)	70% of going rate (SW - option E, ICGT - minimum rate)	Eligible for PhD points (SW)	Eligible for ICT and ICGT
1162 Managers and directors in storage and warehousing	• Logistics manager • Warehouse manager	£24,300 (£11.98 per hour)	£21,870 (£10.78 per hour)	£19,440 (£9.59 per hour)	£17,010 (£8.39 per hour)	Yes	No
1172 Senior police officers	• Chief superintendent (police service) • Detective inspector • Police inspector	£52,000 (£25.64 per hour)	£46,800 (£23.08 per hour)	£41,600 (£20.51 per hour)	£36,400 (£17.95 per hour)	Yes	Yes
1173 Senior officers in fire, ambulance, prison and related services	• Fire service officer (government) • Prison governor • Station officer (ambulance service)	£36,300 (£17.90 per hour)	£32,670 (£16.11 per hour)	£29,040 (£14.32 per hour)	£25,410 (£12.53 per hour)	Yes	Yes
1181 Health services and public health managers and directors	• Director of nursing • Health Service manager • Information manager (health authority: hospital service)	£38,400 (£18.93 per hour)	£34,560 (£17.04 per hour)	£30,720 (£15.15 per hour)	£26,880 (£13.25 per hour)	Yes	Yes
1184 Social services managers and directors	• Care manager (local government: social services) • Service manager (welfare services)	£29,400 (£14.50 per hour)	£26,460 (£13.05 per hour)	£23,520 (£11.60 per hour)	£20,580 (£10.15 per hour)	Yes	Yes
1190 Managers and directors in retail and wholesale	• Managing director (retail trade) • Retail manager • Shop manager (charitable organisation) • Wholesale manager	£21,900 (£10.80 per hour)	£19,710 (£9.72 per hour)	£17,520 (£8.64 per hour)	£15,330 (£7.56 per hour)	Yes	No
1211 Managers and proprietors in agriculture and horticulture	• Farm manager • Farm owner • Nursery manager (horticulture)	£25,200 (£12.43 per hour)	£22,680 (£11.18 per hour)	£20,160 (£9.94 per hour)	£17,640 (£8.70 per hour)	No	No
1213 Managers and proprietors in forestry, fishing and related services	• Cattery owner • Forest manager • Racehorse trainer	£21,200 (£10.45 per hour)	£19,080 (£9.41 per hour)	£16,960 (£8.36 per hour)	£14,840 (£7.32 per hour)	No	No
1221 Hotel and accommodation managers and proprietors	• Caravan park owner • Hotel manager • Landlady (boarding, guest, lodging house)	£21,800 (£10.75 per hour)	£19,620 (£9.67 per hour)	£17,440 (£8.60 per hour)	£15,260 (£7.52 per hour)	No	No
1223 Restaurant and catering establishment managers and proprietors	• Café owner • Fish & chip shopkeeper • Operations manager (catering) • Restaurant manager • Shop manager (take-away food shop)	£21,000 (£10.36 per hour)	£18,900 (£9.32 per hour)	£16,800 (£8.28 per hour)	£14,700 (£7.25 per hour)	No	No
1224 Publicans and managers of licensed premises	• Landlady (public house) • Licensee • Manager (wine bar) • Publican	£20,700 (£10.21 per hour)	£18,630 (£9.19 per hour)	£16,560 (£8.17 per hour)	£14,490 (£7.14 per hour)	No	No
1225 Leisure and sports managers	• Amusement arcade owner • Leisure centre manager • Social club manager • Theatre manager	£24,200 (£11.93 per hour)	£21,780 (£10.74 per hour)	£19,360 (£9.55 per hour)	£16,940 (£8.35 per hour)	No	No
1226 Travel agency managers and proprietors	• Tourist information manager • Travel agency owner • Travel manager	£24,800 (£12.23 per hour)	£22,320 (£11.01 per hour)	£19,840 (£9.78 per hour)	£17,360 (£8.56 per hour)	No	No
1241 Health care practice managers	• Clinic manager • GP practice manager • Veterinary practice manager	£25,500 (£12.57 per hour)	£22,950 (£11.32 per hour)	£20,400 (£10.06 per hour)	£17,850 (£8.80 per hour)	No	No

Occupation Code	Related job titles	Going rate (SW – option A, ICT minimum rate)	90% of going rate (SW - option B)	80% of going rate (SW - options C and D)	70% of going rate (SW - option E, ICGT - minimum rate)	Eligible for PhD points (SW)	Eligible for ICT and ICGT
1242 Residential, day and domiciliary care managers and proprietors	• Care manager • Day centre manager • Nursing home owner • Residential manager (residential home)	£26,700 (£13.17 per hour)	£24,030 (£11.85 per hour)	£21,360 (£10.53 per hour)	£18,690 (£9.22 per hour)	No	No
1251 Property, housing and estate managers	• Estate manager • Facilities manager • Landlord (property management) • Property manager	£26,300 (£12.97 per hour)	£23,670 (£11.67 per hour)	£21,040 (£10.37 per hour)	£18,410 (£9.08 per hour)	No	No
1252 Garage managers and proprietors	• Garage director • Garage owner • Manager (repairing: motor vehicles)	£30,200 (£14.89 per hour)	£27,180 (£13.40 per hour)	£24,160 (£11.91 per hour)	£21,140 (£10.42 per hour)	No	No
1253 Hairdressing and beauty salon managers and proprietors	• Hairdressing salon owner • Health and fitness manager • Manager (beauty salon)	£19,300 (£9.52 per hour)	£17,370 (£8.57 per hour)	£15,440 (£7.61 per hour)	£13,510 (£6.66 per hour)	No	No
1254 Shopkeepers and proprietors - wholesale and retail	• Antiques dealer • Fashion retailer • Newsagent • Shopkeeper	£24,600 (£12.13 per hour)	£22,140 (£10.92 per hour)	£19,680 (£9.70 per hour)	£17,220 (£8.49 per hour)	No	No
1255 Waste disposal and environmental services managers	• Environmental manager (refuse disposal) • Manager (local government: cleansing dept.) • Recycling plant manager • Scrap metal dealer	£32,900 (£16.22 per hour)	£29,610 (£14.60 per hour)	£26,320 (£12.98 per hour)	£23,030 (£11.36 per hour)	No	No
1259 Managers and proprietors in other services not elsewhere classified	• Betting shop manager • Graphic design classified manager • Library manager • Plant hire manager • Production manager (entertainment)	£22,700 (£11.19 per hour)	£20,430 (£10.07 per hour)	£18,160 (£8.95 per hour)	£15,890 (£7.84 per hour)	No	No
2111 Chemical Scientists	• Analytical chemist • Chemist • Development chemist • Industrial chemist • Research chemist	£26,700 (£13.17 per hour)	£24,030 (£11.85 per hour)	£21,360 (£10.53 per hour)	£18,690 (£9.22 per hour)	Yes	Yes
2112 Biological scientists and biochemists	• Biomedical scientist • Forensic scientist • Horticulturist • Microbiologist • Pathologist	£29,700 (£14.64 per hour)	£26,730 (£13.18 per hour)	£23,760 (£11.72 per hour)	£20,790 (£10.25 per hour)	Yes	Yes
2113 Physical scientists	• Geologist • Geophysicist • Medical physicist • Meteorologist • Oceanographer • Physicist • Seismologist	£36,500 (£18.00 per hour)	£32,850 (£16.20 per hour)	£29,200 (£14.40 per hour)	£25,550 (£12.60 per hour)	Yes	Yes
2114 Social and humanities scientists	• Anthropologist • Archaeologist • Criminologist • Epidemiologist • Geographer • Historian • Political scientist • Social scientist	£25,900 (£12.77 per hour)	£23,310 (£11.49 per hour)	£20,720 (£10.22 per hour)	£18,130 (£8.94 per hour)	Yes	Yes

Occupation Code	Related job titles	Going rate (SW – option A, ICT minimum rate)	90% of going rate (SW - option B)	80% of going rate (SW - options C and D)	70% of going rate (SW - option E, ICGT - minimum rate)	Eligible for PhD points (SW)	Eligible for ICT and ICGT
2119 Natural and social science professionals not elsewhere classified For Skilled Worker purposes, occupation code 2119 includes researchers in research organisations other than universities.	• Operational research scientist • Research associate (medical) • Research fellow • Researcher • Scientific officer • Scientist • Sports scientist • University researcher	£33,000 (£16.27 per hour)	£29,700 (£14.64 per hour)	£26,400 (£13.02 per hour)	£23,100 (£11.39 per hour)	Yes	Yes
2121 Civil engineers	• Building engineer • Civil engineer (professional) • Highways engineer • Petroleum engineer • Public health engineer • Site engineer • Structural engineer	£35,000 (£17.26 per hour)	£31,500 (£15.53 per hour)	£28,000 (£13.81 per hour)	£24,500 (£12.08 per hour)	Yes	Yes
2122 Mechanical engineers	• Aeronautical engineer (professional) • Aerospace engineer • Automotive engineer (professional • Marine engineer (professional) • Mechanical engineer (professional)	£33,400 (£16.47 per hour)	£30,060 (£14.82 per hour)	£26,720 (£13.18 per hour)	£23,380 (£11.53 per hour)	Yes	Yes
2123 Electrical engineers	• Electrical engineer (professional) • Electrical surveyor • Equipment engineer • Power engineer • Signal engineer (railways)	£37,000 (£18.24 per hour)	£33,300 (£16.42 per hour)	£29,600 (£14.60 per hour)	£25,900 (£12.77 per hour)	Yes	Yes
2124 Electronics engineers	• Avionics engineer • Broadcasting engineer (professional) • Electronics engineer (professional) • Microwave engineer • Telecommunications engineer (professional)	£34,700 (£17.11 per hour)	£31,230 (£15.40 per hour)	£27,760 (£13.69 per hour)	£24,290 (£11.98 per hour)	Yes	Yes
2126 Design and development engineers	• Clinical engineer • Design engineer • Development engineer • Ergonomist • Research and development engineer	£34,100 (£16.81 per hour)	£30,690 (£15.13 per hour)	£27,280 (£13.45 per hour)	£23,870 (£11.77 per hour)	Yes	Yes
2127 Production and process engineers	• Chemical engineer • Industrial engineer • Process engineer • Production consultant • Production engineer	£33,100 (£16.32 per hour)	£29,790 (£14.69 per hour)	£26,480 (£13.06 per hour)	£23,170 (£11.43 per hour)	Yes	Yes

Occupation Code	Related job titles	Going rate (SW – option A, ICT minimum rate)	90% of going rate (SW - option B)	80% of going rate (SW - options C and D)	70% of going rate (SW - option E, ICGT - minimum rate)	Eligible for PhD points (SW)	Eligible for ICT and ICGT
2129 Engineering professionals not elsewhere classified	• Acoustician (professional) • Ceramicist • Food technologist • Metallurgist • Patent agent • Project engineer • Scientific consultant • Technical engineer • Technologist • Traffic engineer	£32,700 (£16.12 per hour)	£29,430 (£14.51 per hour)	£26,160 (£12.90 per hour)	£22,890 (£11.29 per hour)	Yes	Yes
2133 IT specialist managers	• Data centre manager • IT manager • IT support manager • Network operations manager (computer services) • Service delivery manager	£38,000 (£18.74 per hour)	£34,200 (£16.86 per hour)	£30,400 (£14.99 per hour)	£26,600 (£13.12 per hour)	Yes	Yes
2134 IT project and programme managers	• Implementation manager (computing) • IT project manager • Programme manager (computing) • Project leader (software design)	£40,000 (£19.72 per hour)	£36,000 (£17.75 per hour)	£32,000 (£15.78 per hour)	£28,000 (£13.81 per hour)	Yes	Yes
2135 IT business analysts, architects and systems designers	• Business analyst (computing) • Data communications analyst • Systems analyst • Systems consultant • Technical analyst (computing) • Technical architect	£36,600 (£18.05 per hour)	£32,940 (£16.24 per hour)	£29,280 (£14.44 per hour)	£25,620 (£12.63 per hour)	Yes	Yes
2136 Programmers and software development professionals	• Analyst-programmer • Database developer • Games programmer • Programmer • Software engineer	£33,300 (£16.42 per hour)	£29,970 (£14.78 per hour)	£26,640 (£13.14 per hour)	£23,310 (£11.49 per hour)	Yes	Yes
2137 Web design and development professionals	• Internet developer • Multimedia developer • Web design consultant • Web designer	£26,000 (£12.82 per hour)	£23,400 (£11.54 per hour)	£20,800 (£10.26 per hour)	£18,200 (£8.97 per hour)	Yes	Yes
2139 Information technology and telecommunications professionals not elsewhere classified	• IT consultant • Quality analyst (computing) • Software tester • Systems tester (computing) • Telecommunications planner	£31,800 (£15.68 per hour)	£28,620 (£14.11 per hour)	£25,440 (£12.54 per hour)	£22,260 (£10.98 per hour)	Yes	Yes
2141 Conservation professionals	• Conservation officer • Ecologist • Energy conservation officer • Heritage manager • Marine conservationist	£23,600 (£11.64 per hour)	£21,240 (£10.47 per hour)	£18,880 (£9.31 per hour)	£16,520 (£8.15 per hour)	Yes	Yes
2142 Environment professionals	• Energy manager • Environmental consultant • Environmental engineer • Environmental protection officer • Environmental scientist • Landfill engineer	£27,900 (£13.76 per hour)	£25,110 (£12.38 per hour)	£22,320 (£11.01 per hour)	£19,530 (£9.63 per hour)	Yes	Yes
2150 Research and development managers	• Creative manager (research and development) • Design manager • Market research manager • Research manager (broadcasting)	£38,200 (£18.84 per hour)	£34,380 (£16.95 per hour)	£30,560 (£15.07 per hour)	£26,740 (£13.19 per hour)	Yes	Yes

Occupation Code	Related job titles	Going rate (SW – option A, ICT minimum rate)	90% of going rate (SW - option B)	80% of going rate (SW - options C and D)	70% of going rate (SW - option E, ICGT - minimum rate)	Eligible for PhD points (SW)	Eligible for ICT and ICGT
2216 Veterinarians	• Veterinarian • Veterinary practitioner • Veterinary surgeon	£32,500 (£16.03 per hour)	£29,250 (£14.42 per hour)	£26,000 (£12.82 per hour)	£22,750 (£11.22 per hour)	Yes	Yes
2311 Higher education teaching professionals	• Fellow (university) • Lecturer (higher education, university) • Professor (higher education, university) • Tutor (higher education, university) • University lecturer	£40,700 (£20.07 per hour)	£36,630 (£18.06 per hour)	£32,560 (£16.06 per hour)	£28,490 (£14.05 per hour)	Yes	Yes
2317 Senior professionals of educational establishments	• Administrator (higher education, university) • Bursar • Head teacher (primary school) • Principal (further education) • Registrar (educational establishments)	£39,000 (£19.23 per hour)	£35,100 (£17.31 per hour)	£31,200 (£15.38 per hour)	£27,300 (£13.46 per hour)	Yes	Yes
2318 Education advisers and school inspectors	• Curriculum adviser • Education adviser • Education officer • School inspector	£25,500 (£12.57 per hour)	£22,950 (£11.32 per hour)	£20,400 (£10.06 per hour)	£17,850 (£8.80 per hour)	Yes	Yes
2319 Teaching and other educational professionals not elsewhere classified	• Adult education tutor • Education consultant • Music teacher • Nursery manager (day nursery) • Owner (nursery: children's) • Private tutor • TEFL	£21,300 (£10.50 per hour)	£19,170 (£9.45 per hour)	£17,040 (£8.40 per hour)	£14,910 (£7.35 per hour)	Yes	Yes
2412 Barristers and judges	• Advocate • Barrister • Chairman (appeals tribunal, inquiry) • Coroner • Crown prosecutor • District judge	£29,600 (£14.60 per hour)	£26,640 (£13.14 per hour)	£23,680 (£11.68 per hour)	£20,720 (£10.22 per hour)	Yes	Yes
2413 Solicitors	• Managing clerk (qualified solicitor) • Solicitor • Solicitor-partner • Solicitor to the council	£34,300 (£16.91 per hour)	£30,870 (£15.22 per hour)	£27,440 (£13.53 per hour)	£24,010 (£11.84 per hour)	Yes	Yes
2419 Legal professionals not elsewhere classified	• Attorney • Justice's clerk • Lawyer • Legal adviser • Legal consultant • Legal counsel • Solicitor's clerk (articled)	£49,700 (£24.51 per hour)	£44,730 (£22.06 per hour)	£39,760 (£19.61 per hour)	£34,790 (£17.15 per hour)	Yes	Yes
2421 Chartered and certified accountants	• Accountant (qualified) • Auditor (qualified) • Chartered accountant • Company accountant • Cost accountant (qualified) • Financial controller (qualified) • Management accountant (qualified)	£30,000 (£14.79 per hour)	£27,000 (£13.31 per hour)	£24,000 (£11.83 per hour)	£21,000 (£10.36 per hour)	Yes	Yes

Occupation Code	Related job titles	Going rate (SW – option A, ICT minimum rate)	90% of going rate (SW - option B)	80% of going rate (SW - options C and D)	70% of going rate (SW - option E, ICGT - minimum rate)	Eligible for PhD points (SW)	Eligible for ICT and ICGT
2423 Management consultants and business analysts	• Business adviser • Business consultant • Business continuity manager • Financial risk analyst • Management consultant	£30,900 (£15.24 per hour)	£27,810 (£13.71 per hour)	£24,720 (£12.19 per hour)	£21,630 (£10.67 per hour)	Yes	Yes
2424 Business and financial project management professionals	• Chief knowledge officer • Contracts manager (security services) • Project manager • Research support officer	£37,300 (£18.39 per hour)	£33,570 (£16.55 per hour)	£29,840 (£14.71 per hour)	£26,110 (£12.87 per hour)	Yes	Yes
2425 Actuaries, economists and statisticians	• Actuarial consultant • Actuary • Economist • Statistician • Statistical analyst	£32,800 (£16.17 per hour)	£29,520 (£14.56 per hour)	£26,240 (£12.94 per hour)	£22,960 (£11.32 per hour)	Yes	Yes
2426 Business and related research professionals	• Crime analyst (police force) • Fellow (research) • Games researcher (broadcasting) • Inventor	£29,700 (£14.64 per hour)	£26,730 (£13.18 per hour)	£23,760 (£11.72 per hour)	£20,790 (£10.25 per hour)	Yes	Yes
2429 Business, research and administrative professionals not elsewhere classified	• Civil servant (grade 6, 7) • Company secretary (qualified) • Policy adviser (government) • Registrar (government)	£33,700 (£16.62 per hour)	£30,330 (£14.96 per hour)	£26,960 (£13.29 per hour)	£23,590 (£11.63 per hour)	Yes	Yes
2431 Architects	• Architect • Architectural consultant • Chartered architect • Landscape architect	£35,000 (£17.26 per hour)	£31,500 (£15.53 per hour)	£28,000 (£13.81 per hour)	£24,500 (£12.08 per hour)	Yes	Yes
2432 Town planning officers	• Planning officer (local government: building and contracting) • Town planner • Town planning consultant	£28,500 (£14.05 per hour)	£25,650 (£12.65 per hour)	£22,800 (£11.24 per hour)	£19,950 (£9.84 per hour)	Yes	Yes
2433 Quantity surveyors	• Quantity surveyor • Surveyor (quantity surveying)	£30,600 (£15.09 per hour)	£27,540 (£13.58 per hour)	£24,480 (£12.07 per hour)	£21,420 (£10.56 per hour)	Yes	Yes
2434 Chartered surveyors	• Building surveyor • Chartered surveyor • Hydrographic surveyor • Land surveyor	£30,200 (£14.89 per hour)	£27,180 (£13.40 per hour)	£24,160 (£11.91 per hour)	£21,140 (£10.42 per hour)	Yes	Yes
2435 Chartered architectural technologists	• Architectural technologist	£27,900 (£13.76 per hour)	£25,110 (£12.38 per hour)	£22,320 (£11.01 per hour)	£19,530 (£9.63 per hour)	Yes	Yes
2436 Construction project managers and related professionals	• Contract manager (building construction) • Project manager (building construction) • Transport planner	£28,700 (£14.15 per hour)	£25,830 (£12.74 per hour)	£22,960 (£11.32 per hour)	£20,090 (£9.91 per hour)	Yes	Yes
2443 Probation officers	• Inspector (National Probation Service) • Probation officer • Youth justice officer	£28,700 (£14.15 per hour)	£25,830 (£12.74 per hour)	£22,960 (£11.32 per hour)	£20,090 (£9.91 per hour)	Yes	Yes
2449 Welfare professionals not elsewhere classified	• Children's guardian • Rehabilitation officer • Social services officer • Youth worker (professional)	£24,000 (£11.83 per hour)	£21,600 (£10.65 per hour)	£19,200 (£9.47 per hour)	£16,800 (£8.28 per hour)	Yes	Yes

Occupation Code	Related job titles	Going rate (SW – option A, ICT minimum rate)	90% of going rate (SW - option B)	80% of going rate (SW - options C and D)	70% of going rate (SW - option E, ICGT - minimum rate)	Eligible for PhD points (SW)	Eligible for ICT and ICGT
2451 Librarians	• Chartered librarian • Librarian • Technical librarian • University librarian	£21,800 (£10.75 per hour)	£19,620 (£9.67 per hour)	£17,440 (£8.60 per hour)	£15,260 (£7.52 per hour)	Yes	Yes
2452 Archivists and curators	• Archivist • Conservator • Curator • Keeper (art gallery) • Museum officer	£23,600 (£11.64 per hour)	£21,240 (£10.47 per hour)	£18,880 (£9.31 per hour)	£16,520 (£8.15 per hour)	Yes	Yes
2461 Quality control and planning engineers	• Planning engineer • Quality assurance engineer • Quality control officer (professional) • Quality engineer	£30,500 (£15.04 per hour)	£27,450 (£13.54 per hour)	£24,400 (£12.03 per hour)	£21,350 (£10.53 per hour)	Yes	Yes
2462 Quality assurance and regulatory professionals	• Compliance manager • Financial regulator • Patent attorney • Quality assurance manager • Quality manager	£33,200 (£16.37 per hour)	£29,880 (£14.73 per hour)	£26,560 (£13.10 per hour)	£23,240 (£11.46 per hour)	Yes	Yes
2463 Environmental health professionals	• Air pollution inspector • Environmental health officer • Food inspector • Public health inspector • Technical officer (environmental health)	£29,600 (£14.60 per hour)	£26,640 (£13.14 per hour)	£23,680 (£11.68 per hour)	£20,720 (£10.22 per hour)	Yes	Yes
2471 Journalists, newspaper and periodical editors	• Broadcast journalist • Editor • Journalist • Radio journalist • Reporter	£26,500 (£13.07 per hour)	£23,850 (£11.76 per hour)	£21,200 (£10.45 per hour)	£18,550 (£9.15 per hour)	Yes	Yes
2472 Public relations professionals	• Account manager (public relations) • Information officer (public relations) • PR consultant • Press officer • Public relations officer	£25,700 (£12.67 per hour)	£23,130 (£11.41 per hour)	£20,560 (£10.14 per hour)	£17,990 (£8.87 per hour)	Yes	Yes
2473 Advertising accounts managers and creative directors	• Account manager (advertising) • Advertising Manager • Campaign Manager • Creative Director • Projects Manager (advertising)	£31,900 (£15.73 per hour)	£28,710 (£14.16 per hour)	£25,520 (£12.58 per hour)	£22,330 (£11.01 per hour)	Yes	Yes
3111 Laboratory technicians	• Laboratory analyst • Laboratory technician • Medical laboratory assistant • Scientific technician • Water tester	£18,200 (£8.97 per hour)	£16,380 (£8.08 per hour)	£14,560 (£7.18 per hour)	£12,740 (£6.28 per hour)	Yes	No
3112 Electrical and electronics technicians	• Avionics technician • Electrical technician • Electronics technician • Installation engineer (Electricity Supplier)	£28,100 (£13.86 per hour)	£25,290 (£12.47 per hour)	£22,480 (£11.08 per hour)	£19,670 (£9.70 per hour)	Yes	No
3113 Engineering technicians	• Aircraft technician • Commissioning engineer • Engineering technician • Manufacturing engineer • Mechanical technician	£27,300 (£13.46 per hour)	£24,570 (£12.12 per hour)	£21,840 (£10.77 per hour)	£19,110 (£9.42 per hour)	Yes	No

Occupation Code	Related job titles	Going rate (SW – option A, ICT minimum rate)	90% of going rate (SW - option B)	80% of going rate (SW - options C and D)	70% of going rate (SW - option E, ICGT - minimum rate)	Eligible for PhD points (SW)	Eligible for ICT and ICGT
3114 Building and civil engineering technicians	• Building services consultant • Civil engineering technician • Survey technician • Technical assistant (civil engineering)	£23,400 (£11.54 per hour)	£21,060 (£10.38 per hour)	£18,720 (£9.23 per hour)	£16,380 (£8.08 per hour)	Yes	No
3115 Quality assurance technicians	• Quality assurance technician • Quality control technician • Quality officer • Quality technician • Test technician	£23,600 (£11.64 per hour)	£21,240 (£10.47 per hour)	£18,880 (£9.31 per hour)	£16,520 (£8.15 per hour)	Yes	No
3116 Planning, process and production technicians	• Process technician • Production controller • Production planner • Production technician	£25,200 (£12.43 per hour)	£22,680 (£11.18 per hour)	£20,160 (£9.94 per hour)	£17,640 (£8.70 per hour)	Yes	No
3119 Science, engineering and production technicians not elsewhere classified	• School technician • Technical assistant • Technician • Textile consultant • Workshop technician	£22,000 (£10.85 per hour)	£19,800 (£9.76 per hour)	£17,600 (£8.68 per hour)	£15,400 (£7.59 per hour)	Yes	No
3121 Architectural and town planning technicians	• Architectural assistant • Architectural technician • Construction planner • Planning enforcement officer	£23,800 (£11.74 per hour)	£21,420 (£10.56 per hour)	£19,040 (£9.39 per hour)	£16,660 (£8.21 per hour)	Yes	No
3122 Draughtspersons	• CAD operator • Cartographer • Design technician • Draughtsman	£25,800 (£12.72 per hour)	£23,220 (£11.45 per hour)	£20,640 (£10.18 per hour)	£18,060 (£8.91 per hour)	Yes	No
3131 IT operations technicians	• Computer games tester • Database administrator • IT technician • Network administrator • Systems administrator	£24,500 (£12.08 per hour)	£22,050 (£10.87 per hour)	£19,600 (£9.66 per hour)	£17,150 (£8.46 per hour)	Yes	No
3132 IT user support technicians	• Customer support analyst • Help desk operator • IT support technician • Systems support officer	£24,400 (£12.03 per hour)	£21,960 (£10.83 per hour)	£19,520 (£9.63 per hour)	£17,080 (£8.42 per hour)	Yes	No
3216 Dispensing opticians	• Dispensing optician • Optical dispenser	£18,900 (£9.32 per hour)	£17,010 (£8.39 per hour)	£15,120 (£7.46 per hour)	£13,230 (£6.52 per hour)	No	No
3217 Pharmaceutical technicians	• Dispensing technician • Pharmaceutical technician • Pharmacy technician	£20,300 (£10.01 per hour)	£18,270 (£9.01 per hour)	£16,240 (£8.01 per hour)	£14,210 (£7.01 per hour)	No	No
3231 Youth and community workers	• Community development officer • Youth and community worker • Youth project coordinator • Youth worker	£22,200 (£10.95 per hour)	£19,980 (£9.85 per hour)	£17,760 (£8.76 per hour)	£15,540 (£7.66 per hour)	No	No
3234 Housing officers	• Housing adviser • Housing officer • Homeless prevention officer • Housing support officer	£24,200 (£11.93 per hour)	£21,780 (£10.74 per hour)	£19,360 (£9.55 per hour)	£16,940 (£8.35 per hour)	No	No
3235 Counsellors	• Counsellor (welfare services) • Debt adviser • Drugs and alcohol counsellor • Student counsellor	£20,800 (£10.26 per hour)	£18,720 (£9.23 per hour)	£16,640 (£8.21 per hour)	£14,560 (£7.18 per hour)	No	No

Occupation Code	Related job titles	Going rate (SW – option A, ICT minimum rate)	90% of going rate (SW - option B)	80% of going rate (SW - options C and D)	70% of going rate (SW - option E, ICGT - minimum rate)	Eligible for PhD points (SW)	Eligible for ICT and ICGT
3239 Welfare and housing associate professionals not elsewhere classified	• Day centre officer • Health coordinator • Key worker (welfare services) • Outreach worker (welfare services) • Probation services officer • Project worker (welfare services)	£20,900 (£10.31 per hour)	£18,810 (£9.28 per hour)	£16,720 (£8.24 per hour)	£14,630 (£7.21 per hour)	No	No
3312 Police officers (sergeant and below)	• Detective (police service) • Police constable • Police officer • Sergeant • Transport police officer	£35,400 (£17.46 per hour)	£31,860 (£15.71 per hour)	£28,320 (£13.96 per hour)	£24,780 (£12.22 per hour)	No	No
3313 Fire service officers (watch manager and below)	• Fire engineer • Fire safety officer • Firefighter • Watch manager (fire service)	£32,200 (£15.88 per hour)	£28,980 (£14.29 per hour)	£25,760 (£12.70 per hour)	£22,540 (£11.11 per hour)	No	No
3319 Protective service associate professionals not elsewhere classified	• Customs officer • Immigration officer • Operations manager (security services) • Scenes of crime officer • Security manager	£29,900 (£14.74 per hour)	£26,910 (£13.27 per hour)	£23,920 (£11.79 per hour)	£20,930 (£10.32 per hour)	No	No
3411 Artists	• Artist • Illustrator • Portrait painter • Sculptor	£21,000 (£10.36 per hour)	£18,900 (£9.32 per hour)	£16,800 (£8.28 per hour)	£14,700 (£7.25 per hour)	No	Yes
3412 Authors, writers and translators	• Copywriter • Editor (books) • Interpreter • Technical author • Translator • Writer	£25,600 (£12.62 per hour)	£23,040 (£11.36 per hour)	£20,480 (£10.10 per hour)	£17,920 (£8.84 per hour)	No	Yes
3413 Actors, entertainers and presenters	• Actor • Disc jockey • Entertainer • Presenter (broadcasting) • Singer	£32,200 (£15.88 per hour)	£28,980 (£14.29 per hour)	£25,760 (£12.70 per hour)	£22,540 (£11.11 per hour)	No	Yes
3414 Dancers and choreographers	• Ballet dancer • Choreographer • Dancer • Dance teacher	£29,800 (£14.69 per hour)	£26,820 (£13.22 per hour)	£23,840 (£11.76 per hour)	£20,860 (£10.29 per hour)	No	Yes
3415 Musicians	• Composer • Musician • Organist • Pianist • Song writer • Violinist	£27,500 (£13.56 per hour)	£24,750 (£12.20 per hour)	£22,000 (£10.85 per hour)	£19,250 (£9.49 per hour)	No	Yes
3416 Arts officers, producers and directors	• Film editor • Production assistant (broadcasting) • Studio manager • Television producer • Theatrical agent	£30,000 (£14.79 per hour)	£27,000 (£13.31 per hour)	£24,000 (£11.83 per hour)	£21,000 (£10.36 per hour)	No	Yes
3417 Photographers, audio-visual and broadcasting equipment operators	• Audio visual technician • Cameraman • Photographer • Projectionist • Sound engineer • Theatre technician (entertainment)	£21,100 (£10.40 per hour)	£18,990 (£9.36 per hour)	£16,880 (£8.32 per hour)	£14,770 (£7.28 per hour)	No	No

Occupation Code	Related job titles	Going rate (SW – option A, ICT minimum rate)	90% of going rate (SW - option B)	80% of going rate (SW - options C and D)	70% of going rate (SW - option E, ICGT - minimum rate)	Eligible for PhD points (SW)	Eligible for ICT and ICGT
3421 Graphic designers	• Commercial artist • Designer (advertising) • Graphic artist • Graphic designer • MAC operator	£23,500 (£11.59 per hour)	£21,150 (£10.43 per hour)	£18,800 (£9.27 per hour)	£16,450 (£8.11 per hour)	No	No
3422 Product, clothing and related designers	• Design consultant • Fashion designer • Furniture designer • Interior designer • Kitchen designer • Textile designer	£25,400 (£12.52 per hour)	£22,860 (£11.27 per hour)	£20,320 (£10.02 per hour)	£17,780 (£8.77 per hour)	No	Yes
3443 Fitness instructors	• Aerobics instructor • Fitness instructor • Gym instructor • Lifestyle consultant • Personal trainer • Pilates instructor	£15,600 (£7.69 per hour)	£14,040 (£6.92 per hour)	£12,480 (£6.15 per hour)	£10,920 (£5.38 per hour)	No	No
3511 Air traffic controllers	• Air traffic control officer • Air traffic controller • Air traffic services assistant • Flight planner	£82,400 (£40.63 per hour)	£74,160 (£36.57 per hour)	£65,920 (£32.50 per hour)	£57,680 (£28.44 per hour)	No	No
3512 Aircraft pilots and flight engineers	• Airline pilot • First officer (airlines) • Flight engineer • Flying instructor • Helicopter pilot	£60,800 (£29.98 per hour)	£54,720 (£26.98 per hour)	£48,640 (£23.98 per hour)	£42,560 (£20.99 per hour)	No	Yes
3513 Ship and hovercraft officers	• Chief engineer (shipping) • Marine engineer (shipping) • Merchant navy officer • Petty officer • Tug master • Yacht skipper	£32,900 (£16.22 per hour)	£29,610 (£14.60 per hour)	£26,320 (£12.98 per hour)	£23,030 (£11.36 per hour)	No	No
3520 Legal associate professionals	• Barrister's clerk • Compliance officer • Conveyancer • Legal executive • Litigator • Paralegal	£21,900 (£10.80 per hour)	£19,710 (£9.72 per hour)	£17,520 (£8.64 per hour)	£15,330 (£7.56 per hour)	No	No
3531 Estimators, valuers and assessors	• Claims assessor • Claims investigator • Engineering surveyor • Estimator • Loss adjuster • Valuer	£25,800 (£12.72 per hour)	£23,220 (£11.45 per hour)	£20,640 (£10.18 per hour)	£18,060 (£8.91 per hour)	No	No
3532 Brokers	• Foreign exchange dealer • Insurance broker • Investment administrator • Stockbroker • Trader (stock exchange)	£46,900 (£23.13 per hour)	£42,210 (£20.81 per hour)	£37,520 (£18.50 per hour)	£32,830 (£16.19 per hour)	No	Yes
3533 Insurance underwriters	• Account handler (insurance) • Commercial underwriter • Insurance inspector • Mortgage underwriter • Underwriter	£27,100 (£13.36 per hour)	£24,390 (£12.03 per hour)	£21,680 (£10.69 per hour)	£18,970 (£9.35 per hour)	No	No
3534 Finance and investment analysts and advisers	• Financial adviser • Financial analyst • Financial consultant • Mortgage adviser • Pensions consultant	£29,400 (£14.50 per hour)	£26,460 (£13.05 per hour)	£23,520 (£11.60 per hour)	£20,580 (£10.15 per hour)	No	Yes

Occupation Code	Related job titles	Going rate (SW – option A, ICT minimum rate)	90% of going rate (SW - option B)	80% of going rate (SW - options C and D)	70% of going rate (SW - option E, ICGT - minimum rate)	Eligible for PhD points (SW)	Eligible for ICT and ICGT
3535 Taxation experts	• Tax adviser • Tax consultant • Tax inspector • Taxation specialist	£38,000 (£18.74 per hour)	£34,200 (£16.86 per hour)	£30,400 (£14.99 per hour)	£26,600 (£13.12 per hour)	No	Yes
3536 Importers and exporters	• Export controller • Export coordinator • Exporter • Import agent • Importer	£22,300 (£11.00 per hour)	£20,070 (£9.90 per hour)	£17,840 (£8.80 per hour)	£15,610 (£7.70 per hour)	No	No
3537 Financial and accounting technicians	• Accounting technician • Business associate (banking) • Financial controller • Insolvency administrator • Managing clerk (accountancy)	£32,500 (£16.03 per hour)	£29,250 (£14.42 per hour)	£26,000 (£12.82 per hour)	£22,750 (£11.22 per hour)	No	No
3538 Financial accounts managers	• Accounts manager • Audit manager • Credit manager • Fund manager • Relationship manager (bank)	£29,100 (£14.35 per hour)	£26,190 (£12.91 per hour)	£23,280 (£11.48 per hour)	£20,370 (£10.04 per hour)	No	Yes
3539 Business and related associate professionals not elsewhere classified	• Business systems analyst • Data analyst • Marine consultant • Planning assistant • Project administrator • Project coordinator	£23,300 (£11.49 per hour)	£20,970 (£10.34 per hour)	£18,640 (£9.19 per hour)	£16,310 (£8.04 per hour)	No	No
3541 Buyers and procurement officers	• Buyer • Procurement officer • Purchasing consultant	£25,500 (£12.57 per hour)	£22,950 (£11.32 per hour)	£20,400 (£10.06 per hour)	£17,850 (£8.80 per hour)	No	No
3542 Business sales executives	• Corporate account executive • Sales agent • Sales consultant • Sales executive • Technical representative	£25,800 (£12.72 per hour)	£23,220 (£11.45 per hour)	£20,640 (£10.18 per hour)	£18,060 (£8.91 per hour)	No	No
3543 Marketing associate professionals	• Business development executive • Fundraiser • Market research analyst • Marketing consultant • Marketing executive	£24,400 (£12.03 per hour)	£21,960 (£10.83 per hour)	£19,520 (£9.63 per hour)	£17,080 (£8.42 per hour)	No	No
3544 Estate agents and auctioneers	• Auctioneer • Auctioneer and valuer • Estate agent • Letting agent • Property consultant	£20,700 (£10.21 per hour)	£18,630 (£9.19 per hour)	£16,560 (£8.17 per hour)	£14,490 (£7.14 per hour)	No	No
3545 Sales accounts and business development managers	• Account manager (sales) • Area sales manager • Business development manager • Product development manager • Sales manager	£35,400 (£17.46 per hour)	£31,860 (£15.71 per hour)	£28,320 (£13.96 per hour)	£24,780 (£12.22 per hour)	No	Yes
3546 Conference and exhibition managers and organisers	• Conference coordinator • Event organiser • Events manager • Exhibition organiser • Hospitality manager	£22,900 (£11.29 per hour)	£20,610 (£10.16 per hour)	£18,320 (£9.03 per hour)	£16,030 (£7.90 per hour)	No	No
3550 Conservation and environmental associate professionals	• Conservation worker • Countryside ranger • National park warden • Park ranger	£20,900 (£10.31 per hour)	£18,810 (£9.28 per hour)	£16,720 (£8.24 per hour)	£14,630 (£7.21 per hour)	No	No

Occupation Code	Related job titles	Going rate (SW – option A, ICT minimum rate)	90% of going rate (SW - option B)	80% of going rate (SW - options C and D)	70% of going rate (SW - option E, ICGT - minimum rate)	Eligible for PhD points (SW)	Eligible for ICT and ICGT
3561 Public services associate professionals	• Higher executive officer (government) • Principle revenue officer (local government) • Senior executive officer (government)	£29,800 (£14.69 per hour)	£26,820 (£13.22 per hour)	£23,840 (£11.76 per hour)	£20,860 (£10.29 per hour)	No	No
3562 Human resources and industrial relations officers	• Employment adviser • Human resources officer • Personnel officer • Recruitment consultant	£23,500 (£11.59 per hour)	£21,150 (£10.43 per hour)	£18,800 (£9.27 per hour)	£16,450 (£8.11 per hour)	No	No
3563 Vocational and industrial trainers and instructors	• IT trainer • NVQ assessor • Technical instructor • Training consultant • Training manager	£23,400 (£11.54 per hour)	£21,060 (£10.38 per hour)	£18,720 (£9.23 per hour)	£16,380 (£8.08 per hour)	No	No
3564 Careers advisers and vocational guidance specialists	• Careers adviser • Careers consultant • Careers teacher • Placement officer	£24,500 (£12.08 per hour)	£22,050 (£10.87 per hour)	£19,600 (£9.66 per hour)	£17,150 (£8.46 per hour)	No	No
3565 Inspectors of standards and regulations	• Building inspector • Driving examiner • Housing inspector • Meat hygiene inspector • Trading standards officer	£26,600 (£13.12 per hour)	£23,940 (£11.80 per hour)	£21,280 (£10.49 per hour)	£18,620 (£9.18 per hour)	No	No
3567 Health and safety officers	• Fire protection engineer (professional) • Health and safety officer • Occupational hygienist • Safety consultant • Safety officer	£29,500 (£14.55 per hour)	£26,550 (£13.09 per hour)	£23,600 (£11.64 per hour)	£20,650 (£10.18 per hour)	No	No
4112 National government administrative occupations	• Administrative assistant (courts of justice) • Administrative officer (government) • Civil servant (EO) • Clerk (government) • Revenue officer (government)	£22,400 (£11.05 per hour)	£20,160 (£9.94 per hour)	£17,920 (£8.84 per hour)	£15,680 (£7.73 per hour)	No	No
4114 Officers of nongovernmental organisations	• Administrator (charitable organisation) • Organiser (trade union) • Secretary (research association) • Trade union official	£22,900 (£11.29 per hour)	£20,610 (£10.16 per hour)	£18,320 (£9.03 per hour)	£16,030 (£7.90 per hour)	No	No
4134 Transport and distribution clerks and assistants	• Export clerk • Logistics controller • Shipping clerk • Transport administrator • Transport clerk • Transport coordinator	£20,600 (£10.16 per hour)	£18,540 (£9.14 per hour)	£16,480 (£8.13 per hour)	£14,420 (£7.11 per hour)	No	No
4151 Sales administrators	• Marketing administrator • Sales administrator • Sales clerk • Sales coordinator	£18,700 (£9.22 per hour)	£16,830 (£8.30 per hour)	£14,960 (£7.38 per hour)	£13,090 (£6.45 per hour)	No	No
4161 Office managers	• Business support manager • Delivery office manager • Office manager • Practice manager • Sales administration manager • Sales office manager	£25,000 (£12.33 per hour)	£22,500 (£11.09 per hour)	£20,000 (£9.86 per hour)	£17,500 (£8.63 per hour)	No	No

Occupation Code	Related job titles	Going rate (SW – option A, ICT minimum rate)	90% of going rate (SW - option B)	80% of going rate (SW - options C and D)	70% of going rate (SW - option E, ICGT - minimum rate)	Eligible for PhD points (SW)	Eligible for ICT and ICGT
4214 Company secretaries	• Assistant secretary • Club secretary • Company secretary	£19,500 (£9.62 per hour)	£17,550 (£8.65 per hour)	£15,600 (£7.69 per hour)	£13,650 (£6.73 per hour)	No	No
4215 Personal assistants and other secretaries	• Executive assistant • PA-secretary • Personal assistant • Personal secretary • Secretary	£22,000 (£10.85 per hour)	£19,800 (£9.76 per hour)	£17,600 (£8.68 per hour)	£15,400 (£7.59 per hour)	No	No
5111 Farmers	• Agricultural contractor • Agricultural technician • Crofter (farming) • Farmer • Herd manager	£20,100 (£9.91 per hour)	£18,090 (£8.92 per hour)	£16,080 (£7.93 per hour)	£14,070 (£6.94 per hour)	No	No
5112 Horticultural trades	• Grower • Horticulturalist (market gardening) • Market Gardener • Nursery Assistant (agriculture) • Nurseryman	£17,000 (£8.38 per hour)	£15,300 (£7.54 per hour)	£13,600 (£6.71 per hour)	£11,900 (£5.87 per hour)	No	No
5113 Gardeners and landscape gardeners	• Garden designer • Gardener • Gardener-handyman • Landscape gardener	£18,600 (£9.17 per hour)	£16,740 (£8.25 per hour)	£14,880 (£7.34 per hour)	£13,020 (£6.42 per hour)	No	No
5114 Grounds-men and greenkeepers	• Greenkeeper • Groundsman • Groundsperson	£17,700 (£8.73 per hour)	£15,930 (£7.86 per hour)	£14,160 (£6.98 per hour)	£12,390 (£6.11 per hour)	No	No
5119 Agricultural and fishing trades not elsewhere classified	• Aboricultural consultant • Bee farmer • Gamekeeper • Share fisherman • Trawler skipper • Tree surgeon	£18,800 (£9.27 per hour)	£16,920 (£8.34 per hour)	£15,040 (£7.42 per hour)	£13,160 (£6.49 per hour)	No	No
5211 Smiths and forge workers	• Blacksmith • Chain repairer • Farrier • Pewtersmith • Steel presser	£20,400 (£10.06 per hour)	£18,360 (£9.05 per hour)	£16,320 (£8.05 per hour)	£14,280 (£7.04 per hour)	No	No
5212 Moulders, core makers and die casters	• Core Maker (metal trades) • Die Caster • Moulder (metal trades) • Pipe Maker (foundry)	£17,300 (£8.53 per hour)	£15,570 (£7.68 per hour)	£13,840 (£6.82 per hour)	£12,110 (£5.97 per hour)	No	No
5213 Sheet metal workers	• Coppersmith • Panel beater (metal trades) • Sheet metal fabricator • Sheet metal worker	£21,800 (£10.75 per hour)	£19,620 (£9.67 per hour)	£17,440 (£8.60 per hour)	£15,260 (£7.52 per hour)	No	No
5214 Metal plate workers, and riveters	• Boiler maker • Metal plate worker • Plater • Plater-welder	£25,300 (£12.48 per hour)	£22,770 (£11.23 per hour)	£20,240 (£9.98 per hour)	£17,710 (£8.73 per hour)	No	No
5215 Welding trades	• Fabricator-welder • Fitter-welder • Spot welder (metal) • Welder • Welding technician	£22,800 (£11.24 per hour)	£20,520 (£10.12 per hour)	£18,240 (£8.99 per hour)	£15,960 (£7.87 per hour)	No	No
5216 Pipe fitters	• Pipe engineer • Pipe fitter • Pipe welder-fitter	£32,300 (£15.93 per hour)	£29,070 (£14.33 per hour)	£25,840 (£12.74 per hour)	£22,610 (£11.15 per hour)	No	No

Occupation Code	Related job titles	Going rate (SW – option A, ICT minimum rate)	90% of going rate (SW - option B)	80% of going rate (SW - options C and D)	70% of going rate (SW - option E, ICGT - minimum rate)	Eligible for PhD points (SW)	Eligible for ICT and ICGT
5221 Metal machining	• CNC machinist • CNC programmer • Centre lathe turner • Miller (metal trades) • Tool setter • Turner	£22,000 (£10.85 per hour)	£19,800 (£9.76 per hour)	£17,600 (£8.68 per hour)	£15,400 (£7.59 per hour)	No	No
5222 Tool makers, tool fitters and markers-out	• Die maker • Engineer-toolmaker • Jig maker • Marker-out (engineering) • Tool fitter • Tool maker	£24,700 (£12.18 per hour)	£22,230 (£10.96 per hour)	£19,760 (£9.74 per hour)	£17,290 (£8.53 per hour)	No	No
5223 Metal working production and maintenance fitters	• Agricultural engineer • Bench fitter • Engineering machinist • Fabricator • Installation engineer • Maintenance fitter • Mechanical engineer	£25,300 (£12.48 per hour)	£22,770 (£11.23 per hour)	£20,240 (£9.98 per hour)	£17,710 (£8.73 per hour)	No	No
5224 Precision instrument makers and repairers	• Calibration engineer • Horologist • Instrument maker • Instrument mechanic • Instrument technician • Optical technician • Precision engineer • Watchmaker	£21,000 (£10.36 per hour)	£18,900 (£9.32 per hour)	£16,800 (£8.28 per hour)	£14,700 (£7.25 per hour)	No	No
5225 Airconditioning and refrigeration engineers	• Air conditioning engineer • Air conditioning fitter • Refrigeration engineer • Refrigeration technician • Service engineer (refrigeration)	£26,800 (£13.21 per hour)	£24,120 (£11.89 per hour)	£21,440 (£10.57 per hour)	£18,760 (£9.25 per hour)	No	No
5231 Vehicle technicians, mechanics and electricians	• Auto electrician • Car mechanic • HGV mechanic • Mechanic (garage) • MOT tester • Motor mechanic • Motor vehicle technician • Technician (motor vehicles) • Vehicle technician	£21,900 (£10.80 per hour)	£19,710 (£9.72 per hour)	£17,520 (£8.64 per hour)	£15,330 (£7.56 per hour)	No	No
5232 Vehicle body builders and repairers	• Bodyshop technician • Car body repairer • Coach builder • Panel beater • Restoration technician (motor vehicles) • Vehicle builder	£20,700 (£10.21 per hour)	£18,630 (£9.19 per hour)	£16,560 (£8.17 per hour)	£14,490 (£7.14 per hour)	No	No
5234 Vehicle paint technicians	• Car paint sprayer • Coach painter • Paint technician (motor vehicles) • Vehicle refinisher	£23,000 (£11.34 per hour)	£20,700 (£10.21 per hour)	£18,400 (£9.07 per hour)	£16,100 (£7.94 per hour)	No	No
5235 Aircraft maintenance and related trades	• Aeronautical engineer • Aircraft electrician • Aircraft engineer • Aircraft fitter • Aircraft mechanic • Maintenance engineer (aircraft)	£31,700 (£15.63 per hour)	£28,530 (£14.07 per hour)	£25,360 (£12.50 per hour)	£22,190 (£10.94 per hour)	No	No

Occupation Code	Related job titles	Going rate (SW – option A, ICT minimum rate)	90% of going rate (SW - option B)	80% of going rate (SW - options C and D)	70% of going rate (SW - option E, ICGT - minimum rate)	Eligible for PhD points (SW)	Eligible for ICT and ICGT
5236 Boat and ship builders and repairers	• Boat builder • Fitter (boat building) • Frame turner (ship building) • Marine engineer • Ship's joiner • Shipwright	£25,000 (£12.33 per hour)	£22,500 (£11.09 per hour)	£20,000 (£9.86 per hour)	£17,500 (£8.63 per hour)	No	No
5237 Rail and rolling stock builders and repairers	• Coach repairer (railways) • Mechanical fitter (railway and rolling stock) • Railway engineer • Rolling stock technician	£37,200 (£18.34 per hour)	£33,480 (£16.51 per hour)	£29,760 (£14.67 per hour)	£26,040 (£12.84 per hour)	No	No
5241 Electricians and electrical fitters	• Electrical contractor • Electrical engineer • Electrical fitter • Electrician	£27,200 (£13.41 per hour)	£24,480 (£12.07 per hour)	£21,760 (£10.73 per hour)	£19,040 (£9.39 per hour)	No	No
5242 Telecommunications engineers	• Cable jointer • Customer service engineer (telecommunications) • Installation engineer (telecommunications) • Network officer (telecommunications) • Telecommunications engineer • Telephone engineer	£30,300 (£14.94 per hour)	£27,270 (£13.45 per hour)	£24,240 (£11.95 per hour)	£21,210 (£10.46 per hour)	No	No
5244 TV, video and audio engineers	• Installation engineer (radio, television and video) • Satellite engineer • Service engineer (radio, television and video) • Technician (radio, television and video) • Television engineer	£28,300 (£13.95 per hour)	£25,470 (£12.56 per hour)	£22,640 (£11.16 per hour)	£19,810 (£9.77 per hour)	No	No
5245 IT engineers	• Computer repairer • Computer service engineer • Hardware engineer (computer) • Maintenance engineer (computer servicing)	£24,400 (£12.03 per hour)	£21,960 (£10.83 per hour)	£19,520 (£9.63 per hour)	£17,080 (£8.42 per hour)	No	No
5249 Electrical and electronic trades not elsewhere classified	• Alarm engineer • Electronics engineer • Field engineer • Linesman • Service engineer	£28,000 (£13.81 per hour)	£25,200 (£12.43 per hour)	£22,400 (£11.05 per hour)	£19,600 (£9.66 per hour)	No	No
5250 Skilled metal, electrical and electronic trades supervisors	• Electrical supervisor • Maintenance supervisor (manufacturing) • Workshop manager	£30,300 (£14.94 per hour)	£27,270 (£13.45 per hour)	£24,240 (£11.95 per hour)	£21,210 (£10.46 per hour)	No	No
5311 Steel erectors	• Steel erector • Steel fabricator • Steel worker (structural engineering)	£23,700 (£11.69 per hour)	£21,330 (£10.52 per hour)	£18,960 (£9.35 per hour)	£16,590 (£8.18 per hour)	No	No
5312 Bricklayers and masons	• Bricklayer • Dry stone waller • Stone mason	£23,000 (£11.34 per hour)	£20,700 (£10.21 per hour)	£18,400 (£9.07 per hour)	£16,100 (£7.94 per hour)	No	No
5313 Roofers, roof tilers and slaters	• Mastic asphalt spreader • Roof tiler • Roofer • Roofing contractor • Slater • Thatcher	£21,400 (£10.55 per hour)	£19,260 (£9.50 per hour)	£17,120 (£8.44 per hour)	£14,980 (£7.39 per hour)	No	No

Occupation Code	Related job titles	Going rate (SW – option A, ICT minimum rate)	90% of going rate (SW - option B)	80% of going rate (SW - options C and D)	70% of going rate (SW - option E, ICGT - minimum rate)	Eligible for PhD points (SW)	Eligible for ICT and ICGT
5314 Plumbers and heating and ventilating engineers	• Gas engineer • Gas service engineer • Heating and ventilating engineer • Heating engineer • Plumber • Plumbing and heating engineer	£25,800 (£12.72 per hour)	£23,220 (£11.45 per hour)	£20,640 (£10.18 per hour)	£18,060 (£8.91 per hour)	No	No
5315 Carpenters and joiners	• Carpenter • Carpenter and joiner • Joiner • Kitchen fitter • Shop fitter	£22,300 (£11.00 per hour)	£20,070 (£9.90 per hour)	£17,840 (£8.80 per hour)	£15,610 (£7.70 per hour)	No	No
5316 Glaziers, window fabricators and fitters	• Glass Cutter • Glazier • Installer (double glazing) • Window fabricator • Window fitter	£19,100 (£9.42 per hour)	£17,190 (£8.48 per hour)	£15,280 (£7.53 per hour)	£13,370 (£6.59 per hour)	No	No
5319 Construction and building trades not elsewhere classified	• Acoustician • Builder • Building contractor • Fencer • Maintenance manager (buildings and other structures) • Property developer (building construction)	£23,000 (£11.34 per hour)	£20,700 (£10.21 per hour)	£18,400 (£9.07 per hour)	£16,100 (£7.94 per hour)	No	No
5321 Plasterers	• Fibrous plasterer • Plasterer • Plastering contractor	£24,300 (£11.98 per hour)	£21,870 (£10.78 per hour)	£19,440 (£9.59 per hour)	£17,010 (£8.39 per hour)	No	No
5322 Floorers and wall tilers	• Carpet fitter • Ceramic tiler • Flooring contractor • Mosaic floor layer	£21,800 (£10.75 per hour)	£19,620 (£9.67 per hour)	£17,440 (£8.60 per hour)	£15,260 (£7.52 per hour)	No	No
5323 Painters and decorators	• Artexer • French polisher • Paper hanger • Ship sprayer • Wood stainer	£21,400 (£10.55 per hour)	£19,260 (£9.50 per hour)	£17,120 (£8.44 per hour)	£14,980 (£7.39 per hour)	No	No
5330 Construction and building trades supervisors	• Builder's foreman • Construction foreman • Construction supervisor • Maintenance supervisor • Site foreman	£31,400 (£15.48 per hour)	£28,260 (£13.93 per hour)	£25,120 (£12.39 per hour)	£21,980 (£10.84 per hour)	No	No
5411 Weavers and knitters	• Carpet weaver • Knitter • Knitwear manufacturer • Weaver	£19,300 (£9.52 per hour)	£17,370 (£8.57 per hour)	£15,440 (£7.61 per hour)	£13,510 (£6.66 per hour)	No	No
5412 Upholsterers	• Curtain fitter • Curtain maker • Soft furnisher • Trimmer (furniture mfr) • Upholsterer	£18,500 (£9.12 per hour)	£16,650 (£8.21 per hour)	£14,800 (£7.30 per hour)	£12,950 (£6.39 per hour)	No	No
5413 Footwear and leather working trades	• Cobbler • Leather worker (leather goods mfr • Machinist (leather goods mfr) • Shoe machinist • Shoe repairer	£17,300 (£8.53 per hour)	£15,570 (£7.68 per hour)	£13,840 (£6.82 per hour)	£12,110 (£5.97 per hour)	No	No

Occupation Code	Related job titles	Going rate (SW – option A, ICT minimum rate)	90% of going rate (SW - option B)	80% of going rate (SW - options C and D)	70% of going rate (SW - option E, ICGT - minimum rate)	Eligible for PhD points (SW)	Eligible for ICT and ICGT
5414 Tailors and dressmakers	• Cutter (hosiery, knitwear mfr) • Dressmaker • Fabric cutter • Tailor • Tailoress	£16,200 (£7.99 per hour)	£14,580 (£7.19 per hour)	£12,960 (£6.39 per hour)	£11,340 (£5.59 per hour)	No	No
5419 Textiles, garments and related trades not elsewhere classified	• Clothing manufacturer • Embroiderer • Hand sewer • Sail maker • Upholstery cutter	£18,300 (£9.02 per hour)	£16,470 (£8.12 per hour)	£14,640 (£7.22 per hour)	£12,810 (£6.32 per hour)	No	No
5421 Pre-press technicians	• Compositor • Plate maker • Pre-press manager • Pre-press technician • Type setter	£19,900 (£9.81 per hour)	£17,910 (£8.83 per hour)	£15,920 (£7.85 per hour)	£13,930 (£6.87 per hour)	No	No
5422 Printers	• Lithographic printer • Machine minder (printing) • Print manager • Screen printer • Wallpaper printer	£20,800 (£10.26 per hour)	£18,720 (£9.23 per hour)	£16,640 (£8.21 per hour)	£14,560 (£7.18 per hour)	No	No
5423 Print finishing and binding workers	• Binder's assistant • Book binder • Finishing supervisor (printing) • Print finisher	£19,800 (£9.76 per hour)	£17,820 (£8.79 per hour)	£15,840 (£7.81 per hour)	£13,860 (£6.83 per hour)	No	No
5431 Butchers	• Butcher • Butcher's assistant • Butchery manager • Master butcher • Slaughterman	£19,300 (£9.52 per hour)	£17,370 (£8.57 per hour)	£15,440 (£7.61 per hour)	£13,510 (£6.66 per hour)	No	No
5432 Bakers and flour confectioners	• Baker • Baker's assistant • Bakery manager • Cake decorator • Confectioner	£17,300 (£8.53 per hour)	£15,570 (£7.68 per hour)	£13,840 (£6.82 per hour)	£12,110 (£5.97 per hour)	No	No
5433 Fishmongers and poultry dressers	• Butcher (fish, poultry) • Filleter (fish) • Fish processor • Fishmonger • Poultry processor	£17,100 (£8.43 per hour)	£15,390 (£7.59 per hour)	£13,680 (£6.75 per hour)	£11,970 (£5.90 per hour)	No	No
5434 Chefs	• Chef • Chef-manager • Head chef • Pastry chef	£18,900 (£9.32 per hour)	£17,010 (£8.39 per hour)	£15,120 (£7.46 per hour)	£13,230 (£6.52 per hour)	No	No
5436 Catering and bar managers	• Bar manager • Catering manager • Floor manager (restaurant) • Kitchen manager • Steward (club)	£18,400 (£9.07 per hour)	£16,560 (£8.17 per hour)	£14,720 (£7.26 per hour)	£12,880 (£6.35 per hour)	No	No
5441 Glass and ceramics makers, decorators and finishers	• Ceramic artist • Glass blower • Potter (ceramics mfr) • Pottery worker • Sprayer (ceramics mfr) • Stained glass artist	£17,800 (£8.78 per hour)	£16,020 (£7.90 per hour)	£14,240 (£7.02 per hour)	£12,460 (£6.14 per hour)	No	No

Occupation Code	Related job titles	Going rate (SW – option A, ICT minimum rate)	90% of going rate (SW - option B)	80% of going rate (SW - options C and D)	70% of going rate (SW - option E, ICGT - minimum rate)	Eligible for PhD points (SW)	Eligible for ICT and ICGT
5442 Furniture makers and other craft woodworkers	• Antiques restorer • Cabinet maker • Coffin maker • Furniture restorer • Picture framer • Sprayer (furniture mfr)	£18,900 (£9.32 per hour)	£17,010 (£8.39 per hour)	£15,120 (£7.46 per hour)	£13,230 (£6.52 per hour)	No	No
5443 Florists	• Floral assistant • Floral designer • Florist • Flower arranger	£14,000 (£6.90 per hour)	£12,600 (£6.21 per hour)	£11,200 (£5.52 per hour)	£9,800 (£4.83 per hour)	No	No
5449 Other skilled trades not elsewhere classified	• Diamond mounter • Engraver • Goldsmith • Paint sprayer • Piano tuner • Sign maker • Silversmith • Wig maker	£22,300 (£11.00 per hour)	£20,070 (£9.90 per hour)	£17,840 (£8.80 per hour)	£15,610 (£7.70 per hour)	No	No
6121 Nursery nurses and assistants	• Crèche assistant • Crèche worker • Nursery assistant • Nursery nurse	£14,700 (£7.25 per hour)	£13,230 (£6.52 per hour)	£11,760 (£5.80 per hour)	£10,290 (£5.07 per hour)	No	No
6122 Childminders and related occupations	• Au pair • Child care assistant • Child minder • Nanny	£17,600 (£8.68 per hour)	£15,840 (£7.81 per hour)	£14,080 (£6.94 per hour)	£12,320 (£6.07 per hour)	No	No
6123 Playworkers	• Playgroup assistant • Playgroup leader • Playgroup supervisor • Playworker	£12,700 (£6.26 per hour)	£11,430 (£5.64 per hour)	£10,160 (£5.01 per hour)	£8,890 (£4.38 per hour)	No	No
6125 Teaching assistants	• Classroom assistant • School assistant • Teaching assistant	£14,400 (£7.10 per hour)	£12,960 (£6.39 per hour)	£11,520 (£5.68 per hour)	£10,080 (£4.97 per hour)	No	No
6126 Educational support assistants	• Education support assistant • Learning support assistant • Non-teaching assistant (schools) • Special needs assistant (educational establishments) • Support assistant (educational establishments)	£13,800 (£6.80 per hour)	£12,420 (£6.12 per hour)	£11,040 (£5.44 per hour)	£9,660 (£4.76 per hour)	No	No
6131 Veterinary nurses	• Animal nurse • Veterinary nurse	£16,900 (£8.33 per hour)	£15,210 (£7.50 per hour)	£13,520 (£6.67 per hour)	£11,830 (£5.83 per hour)	No	No
6139 Animal care services occupations not elsewhere classified	• Animal technician • Canine beautician • Groom • Kennel assistant • Kennel maid • Stable hand	£16,100 (£7.94 per hour)	£14,490 (£7.14 per hour)	£12,880 (£6.35 per hour)	£11,270 (£5.56 per hour)	No	No
6144 Houseparents and residential wardens	• Foster carer • Matron (residential home) • Resident warden • Team leader (residential care home) • Warden (sheltered housing)	£19,700 (£9.71 per hour)	£17,730 (£8.74 per hour)	£15,760 (£7.77 per hour)	£13,790 (£6.80 per hour)	No	No

Occupation Code	Related job titles	Going rate (SW – option A, ICT minimum rate)	90% of going rate (SW - option B)	80% of going rate (SW - options C and D)	70% of going rate (SW - option E, ICGT - minimum rate)	Eligible for PhD points (SW)	Eligible for ICT and ICGT
6146 Senior care workers	• Senior care assistant • Senior carer • Senior support worker (Local government: welfare services) • Team leader (nursing home)	£16,900 (£8.33 per hour)	£15,210 (£7.50 per hour)	£13,520 (£6.67 per hour)	£11,830 (£5.83 per hour)	No	No
6214 Air travel assistants	• Air hostess • Cabin crew • Customer service agent (travel) • Flight attendant • Passenger service agent	£17,600 (£8.68 per hour)	£15,840 (£7.81 per hour)	£14,080 (£6.94 per hour)	£12,320 (£6.07 per hour)	No	No
6215 Rail travel assistants	• Retail service manager (railways) • Station assistant (underground railway) • Ticket inspector (railways) • Train conductor • Train manager	£31,400 (£15.48 per hour)	£28,260 (£13.93 per hour)	£25,120 (£12.39 per hour)	£21,980 (£10.84 per hour)	No	No
7125 Merchandisers and window dressers	• Merchandiser • Sales merchandiser • Visual merchandising manager • Window dresser	£19,100 (£9.42 per hour)	£17,190 (£8.48 per hour)	£15,280 (£7.53 per hour)	£13,370 (£6.59 per hour)	No	No
7130 Sales supervisors	• Sales supervisor (retail trade: delivery round) • Section manager (retail trade) • Shop supervisor (retail trade) • Supervisor (retail, wholesale trade) • Team leader (retail trade)	£18,900 (£9.32 per hour)	£17,010 (£8.39 per hour)	£15,120 (£7.46 per hour)	£13,230 (£6.52 per hour)	No	No
7215 Market research interviewers	• Interviewer (market research) • Market researcher (interviewing) • Telephone interviewer • Telephone researcher • Traffic enumerator	£9,800 (£4.83 per hour)	£8,820 (£4.35 per hour)	£7,840 (£3.87 per hour)	£6,860 (£3.38 per hour)	No	No
7220 Customer service managers and supervisors	• After sales manager • Call centre supervisor • Customer service manager • Customer service supervisor • Team leader (customer care)	£22,900 (£11.29 per hour)	£20,610 (£10.16 per hour)	£18,320 (£9.03 per hour)	£16,030 (£7.90 per hour)	No	No
8124 Energy plant operatives	• Boilerman • Control room operator(electric) • Hydraulic engineman • Plant operator (electricity supplier) • Power station operator	£23,900 (£11.79 per hour)	£21,510 (£10.61 per hour)	£19,120 (£9.43 per hour)	£16,730 (£8.25 per hour)	No	No
8126 Water and sewerage plant operatives	• Controller (water treatment) • Plant operator (sewage works) • Pump attendant • Water treatment engineer • Water treatment operator	£25,000 (£12.33 per hour)	£22,500 (£11.09 per hour)	£20,000 (£9.86 per hour)	£17,500 (£8.63 per hour)	No	No
8215 Driving instructors	• Driving instructor • HGV instructor • Instructor (driving school) • Motorcycle instructor	£22,800 (£11.24 per hour)	£20,520 (£10.12 per hour)	£18,240 (£8.99 per hour)	£15,960 (£7.87 per hour)	No	No
8232 Marine and waterways transport operatives	• Engine room attendant (shipping) • Engineer, nos (boat, barge) • Ferryman • Merchant seaman • Seaman (shipping)	£30,200 (£14.89 per hour)	£27,180 (£13.40 per hour)	£24,160 (£11.91 per hour)	£21,140 (£10.42 per hour)	No	No

Occupation Code	Related job titles	Going rate (SW – option A, ICT minimum rate)	90% of going rate (SW - option B)	80% of going rate (SW - options C and D)	70% of going rate (SW - option E, ICGT - minimum rate)	Eligible for PhD points (SW)	Eligible for ICT and ICGT
9119 Fishing and other elementary agriculture occupations not elsewhere classified – ONLY the listed job titles are eligible in this occupation code and ONLY where the job requires the worker to have at least 3 years' full-time experience in using their skills. This experience must not have been gained through working illegally	• Vent chick sexer • Deckhand on large fishing vessel (9 metres and above)	£17,100 (£8.43 per hour)	£15,390 (£7.59 per hour)	£13,680 (£6.75 per hour)	£11,970 (£5.90 per hour)	No	No

Table 2: Eligible health and education occupation codes where going rates are based on national pay scales

Occupation codes in Table 2 are eligible for the Intra-Company Routes unless otherwise stated.

Occupation Code	Related job titles	Going rate (annual)	National pay scale source
2211 Medical practitioners	• Anaesthetist • Consultant (Hospital Service) • Doctor •General practitioner • Medical practitioner • Paediatrician • Psychiatrist • Radiologist • Surgeon	Medical professionals on the NHS junior doctor contract: • Foundation year 1 (F1) and equivalent: £28,243 • Foundation year 2 (F2) and equivalent: £32,691 • Specialty registrar (StR) at ST/CT1-2 and equivalent: £38,693 • Specialty registrar (StR) at CT/ST3 and above £49,036 Other medical professionals including those on contract with health services of devolved administrations: • Foundation year 1 (F1) and equivalent: £24,504 • Foundation year 2 (F2) and equivalent: £30,393 • Specialty registrar (StR) and equivalent: £32,478 • Specialty doctor and equivalent: £40,037 • Salaried General practitioner (GP) and equivalent: £58,808 • Consultant and equivalent: £79,860 These going rates are per year and based on a 40-hour working week. They must be pro-rated for other working patterns, based on the weekly working hours stated by the applicant's sponsor.	The relevant rate in the current NHS Employers Pay and Conditions Circular (M&D)

Occupation Code	Related job titles	Going rate (annual)	National pay scale source
2212 Psychologists	• Clinical psychologist • Educational psychologist • Forensic psychologist • Occupational psychologist • Psychologist • Psychometrist	See relevant pay band in Table 3	NHS Agenda for Change 2020/21
2213 Pharmacists	• Chemist (pharmaceutical) • Dispensary manager • Pharmaceutical chemist • Pharmacist • Pharmacy manager	See relevant pay band in Table 3	NHS Agenda for Change 2020/21
2214 Ophthalmic opticians	• Ophthalmic optician • Optician • Optologist • Optometrist	See relevant pay band in Table 3	NHS Agenda for Change 2020/21
2215 Dental practitioners	• Dental surgeon • Dentist • Orthodontist • Periodontist	See relevant pay band in Table 3	The relevant rate in the current NHS Employers Pay and Conditions Circular (M&D)
2217 Medical radiographers	• Medical radiographer • Radiographer • Sonographer • Therapeutic radiographer • Vascular technologist	See relevant pay band in Table 3	NHS Agenda for Change 2020/21
2218 Podiatrists	• Chiropodist • Chiropodist-podiatrist • Podiatrist	See relevant pay band in Table 3	NHS Agenda for Change 2020/21
2219 Health professionals not elsewhere classified	• Audiologist • Dental hygiene therapist • Dietician-nutritionist • Family planner • Occupational health adviser • Paramedical practitioner	See relevant pay band in Table 3	NHS Agenda for Change 2020/21
2221 Physiotherapists	• Electro-therapist • Physiotherapist • Physiotherapy practitioner	See relevant pay band in Table 3	NHS Agenda for Change 2020/21
2222 Occupational therapists	• Occupational therapist	See relevant pay band in Table 3	NHS Agenda for Change 2020/21
2223 Speech and language therapists	• Language therapist • Speech and language therapist • Speech therapist	See relevant pay band in Table 3	NHS Agenda for Change 2020/21
2229 Therapy professionals not elsewhere classified	• Art therapist • Chiropractor • Cognitive behavioural therapist • Dance movement therapist • Family therapist • Nutritionist • Osteopath • Psychotherapist	See relevant pay band in Table 3	NHS Agenda for Change 2020/21
2231 Nurses	• District nurse • Health visitor • Mental health practitioner • Nurse • Practice nurse • Psychiatric nurse • Staff nurse • Student nurse	See relevant pay band in Table 3	NHS Agenda for Change 2020/21
2232 Midwives	• Midwife • Midwifery sister	See relevant pay band in Table 3	NHS Agenda for Change 2020/21

Occupation Code	Related job titles	Going rate (annual)	National pay scale source
2312 Further education teaching professionals	• FE College lecturer • Lecturer (further education) • Teacher (further education) • Tutor (further education)	• Lecturer or equivalent (new entrant): £22,609 • Senior lecturer / advanced teacher and equivalent: £37,258 • Further education management / principal lecturer and equivalent: £43,734 These going rates are per year and based on the definition of a full-time teaching professional used when determining these pay scales. They must be prorated for other working patterns, based on the weekly working hours stated by the applicant's sponsor.	Teachers' national pay scales from each devolved authority, lowest value selected
2314 Secondary education teaching professionals	• Deputy head teacher (secondary school) • Secondary school teacher • Sixth form teacher • Teacher (secondary school)	See relevant pay rate in Table 4	Teachers' national pay scales
2315 Primary and nursery education teaching professionals	• Deputy head teacher (primary school) • Infant teacher • Nursery school teacher • Primary school teacher	See relevant pay rate in Table 4	Teachers' national pay scales
2316 Special needs education teaching professionals	• Deputy head teacher (special school) • Learning support teacher • Special needs coordinator • Special needs teacher	See relevant pay rate in Table 4	Teachers' national pay scales
2442 Social workers	• Psychiatric social worker • Senior practitioner (local government: social services) • Social worker	See relevant pay band in Table 3	NHS Agenda for Change 2020/21
3213 Paramedics	• Ambulance paramedic • Emergency care practitioner • Paramedic • Paramedic-ECP	See relevant pay band in Table 3	NHS Agenda for Change 2020/21
3218 Medical and dental technicians (not eligible for ICT or ICGT)	• Cardiographer • Dental hygienist • Dental technician • Medical technical officer • Orthopaedic technician	See relevant pay band in Table 3	NHS Agenda for Change 2020/21
3219 Health associate professionals not elsewhere classified (not eligible for ICT or ICGT)	• Acupuncturist • Homeopath • Hypnotherapist • Massage therapist • Reflexologist • Sports therapist	See relevant pay band in Table 3	NHS Agenda for Change 2020/21
6141 Nursing auxiliaries and assistants (not eligible for ICT or ICGT)	• Auxiliary nurse • Health care assistant (hospital service) • Health care support worker • Nursing assistant • Nursing auxiliary	See relevant pay band in Table 3	NHS Agenda for Change 2020/21
6143 Dental nurses (not eligible for ICT or ICGT)	• Dental assistant • Dental nurse • Dental nurse-receptionist • Dental surgery assistant	See relevant pay band in Table 3	NHS Agenda for Change 2020/21

Table 3: Going rates for listed healthcare occupation codes by administration and band

Going rates in Table 3 are per year and based on a 37.5-hour week. They must be pro-rated for other working patterns, based on the weekly working hours stated by the applicant's sponsor.

Band or equivalent	England	Scotland	Wales	Northern Ireland
Band 3	£19,737	£20,700	£19,737	£19,737

Band 4	£21,892	£22,700	£21,892	£21,892
Band 5	£24,907	£25,100	£24,907	£24,907
Band 6	£31,365	£31,800	£31,365	£31,365
Band 7	£38,890	£39,300	£38,890	£38,890
Band 8a	£45,753	£49,480	£45,753	£45,753
Band 8b	£53,168	£59,539	£53,168	£53,168
Band 8c	£63,751	£71,365	£63,751	£63,751
Band 8d	£75,914	£85,811	£75,914	£75,914
Band 9	£91,004	£102,558	£91,004	£91,004

Table 4: Going rates for listed education occupation codes by administration and role

Going rates in Table 4 are per year and based on the definition of a full-time teacher used when determining these pay scales. They must be pro-rated for other working patterns, based on the weekly working hours stated by the applicant's sponsor.

Band or equivalent	England (excluding London/ Fringe)	London Fringe	Outer London	Inner London	Scotland	Wales	Northern Ireland
Unqualified teachers / Probationers	£17,682	£18,844	£21,004	£22,237	£27,498	£17,682	£14,760
Qualified teachers	£24,373	£25,543	£28,355	£30,480	£32,994	£24,906	£23,199
Chartered teachers	-	-	-	-	£42,696	-	-
Principal teachers	-	-	-	-	£45,150	-	-
Leadership group	£41,065	£42,195	£44,323	£48,824	-	£41,065	£40,256
Lead practitioners	£41,267	£42,403	£44,541	£49,065	-	**£41,267**	-

Table 5: Occupation codes which are not eligible for the Skilled Worker, Intra-Company Transfer and Intra-Company Graduate Trainee routes

These occupations are ineligible because:

• they do not meet the required skill level; or

• applicants must be sponsored in other routes for jobs in these occupations; or

• those subject to immigration control cannot apply for jobs in these occupations.

Where indicated, some occupations codes in Tables 1 and 2 are also not eligible for the Intra- Company Transfer and Intra-Company Graduate Trainee routes.

Occupation code	Related job titles
1116 Elected officers and representatives	• Councillor (local government) • Member of Parliament
1171 Officers in armed forces	• Army officer • Flight-lieutenant • Squadron-leader
2444 Clergy	• Chaplain Minister (religious organisation) • Pastor • Priest • Vicar
3311 NCOs and other ranks	• Aircraftman • Aircraft technician (armed forces) • Lance-corporal • Sergeant (armed forces) • Soldier • Weapons engineer (armed forces)
3314 Prison service officers (below principal officer)	• Prison custodial officer • Prison escort officer • Prison officer • Prison warden
3441 Sports players	• Cricketer • Footballer • Golfer
3442 Sports coaches, instructors and officials	• Referee • Riding instructor • Sports development officer • Swimming teacher

Occupation code	Related job titles
3233 Child and early years officers	• Child protection officer • Education welfare officer • Portage worker (educational establishments)
3315 Police community support officers	• Civilian support officer (police service) • Community support officer (police service) • Police community support officer
4113 Local government administrative occupations	• Administrative assistant (local government) • Administrative officer (police service) • Benefits assistant (local government) • Clerical officer (local government) • Local government officer nos
4121 Credit controllers	• Credit control clerk • Credit controller • Debt management associate • Loans administrator
4122 Book-keepers, payroll managers and wages clerks	• Accounts administrator • Accounts assistant • Accounts clerk • Auditor • Bookkeeper • Payroll clerk
4123 Bank and post office clerks	• Bank clerk • Cashier (bank) • Customer adviser (building society) • Customer service officer (bank) • Post office clerk
4124 Finance officers	• Deputy finance officer • Finance officer • Regional finance officer (PO)
4129 Financial administrative occupations not elsewhere classified	• Cashier • Finance administrator • Finance assistant • Finance clerk • Tax assistant • Treasurer • Valuation assistant
4131 Records clerks and assistants	• Admissions officer • Clerical officer (hospital service) • Filing clerk • Records clerk • Ward clerk
4132 Pensions and insurance clerks and assistants	• Administrator (insurance) • Claims handler • Clerical assistant (insurance) • Insurance clerk • Pensions administrator
4133 Stock control clerks and assistants	• Despatch clerk • Material controller • Stock control clerk • Stock controller • Stores administrator
4135 Library clerks and assistants	• Information assistant (library) • Learning resource assistant • Library assistant • Library clerk • Library supervisor
4138 Human resources administrative occupations	• Course administrator • Human resources administrator • Personnel administrator • Personnel clerk

Occupation code	Related job titles
4159 Other administrative occupations not elsewhere classified	• Administrative assistant • Clerical assistant • Clerical officer • Clerk Office administrator
4162 Office supervisors	• Administration supervisor • Clerical supervisor • Facilities supervisor • Office supervisor
4211 Medical secretaries	• Clinic coordinator • Clinic administrator • Medical administrator • Medical secretary • Secretary (medical practice)
4212 Legal secretaries	• Legal administrator • Legal clerk • Legal secretary • Secretary (legal services)
4213 School secretaries	• Clerical assistant (schools) • School administrator • School secretary • Secretary (schools)
4216 Receptionists	• Dental receptionist • Doctor's receptionist • Medical receptionist • Receptionist • Receptionist-secretary
4217 Typists and related keyboard occupations	• Audio typist • Computer operator • Typist • Typist-clerk • Word processor
5435 Cooks	• Cook • Cook-supervisor • Head cook
6132 Pest control officers	• Fumigator • Pest control officer • Pest control technician • Pest controller
6142 Ambulance staff (excluding paramedics)	• Ambulance care assistant • Ambulance driver • Ambulance technician • Emergency medical technician
6145 Care workers and home carers	• Care assistant • Care worker • Carer • Home care assistant • Home carer • Support worker (nursing home)
6147 Care escorts	• Bus escort • Escort • Escort-driver • School escort
6148 Undertakers, mortuary and crematorium assistants	• Crematorium technician • Funeral director • Pall bearer • Undertaker
6211 Sports and leisure assistants	• Croupier • Leisure attendant • Lifeguard • Sports assistant

Occupation code	Related job titles
6212 Travel agents	• Reservations clerk (travel) • Sales consultant (travel agents) • Travel adviser • Travel agent • Travel consultant
6219 Leisure and travel service occupations not elsewhere classified	• Bus conductor • Holiday representative • Information assistant (tourism) • Steward (shipping) • Tour guide
6221 Hairdressers and barbers	• Barber • Colourist (hairdressing) • Hair stylist • Hairdresser
6222 Beauticians and related occupations	• Beautician Beauty therapist • Nail technician • Tattooist
6231 Housekeepers and related occupations	• Cook-housekeeper • House keeper • Lifestyle manager
6232 Caretakers	• Caretaker • Janitor • Porter (college) • Site manager (educational establishments)
6240 Cleaning and housekeeping managers and supervisors	• Butler • Cleaner-in-charge • Cleaning supervisor • Domestic supervisor • Head house keeper • Supervisor (cleaning)
7111 Sales and retail assistants	• Retail assistant • Sales adviser • Sales assistant • Sales consultant (retail trade) • Shop assistant
7112 Retail cashiers and check-out operators	• Check-out operator • Forecourt attendant • General assistant (retail trade: check-out) • Till operator
7113 Telephone salespersons	• Sales adviser (telephone sales) • Telesales executive • Telesales operator
7114 Pharmacy and other dispensing assistants	• Dispenser • Health care assistant (retail chemist) • Optical assistant • Pharmacy assistant
7115 Vehicle and parts salespersons and advisers	• Car sales executive • Car salesman • Parts adviser (retail trade) • Parts salesman (motor vehicle repair)
7121 Collector salespersons and credit agents	• Agent (insurance) • Canvasser • Collector (insurance) • Distributor (door-to-door sales) • Insurance agent
7122 Debt, rent and other cash collectors	• Collecting agent • Collector (gas supplier) • Debt collector • Meter reader • Vending operator

Occupation code	Related job titles
7123 Roundspersons and van salespersons	• Dairyman (retail trade: delivery round) • Ice-cream salesman • Milkman (milk retailing) • Roundsman • Van salesman
7124 Market and street traders and assistants	• Market assistant • Market trader • Owner (market stall) • Stall holder • Street trader
7129 Sales related occupations not elsewhere classified	• Demonstrator • Hire controller • Sales representative (retail trade)
7211 Call and contact centre occupations	• Call centre agent • Call centre operator • Customer service adviser (call centre) • Customer service operator
7213 Telephonists	• Call handler (motoring organisation) • Operator (telephone) • Switchboard operator (telephone) • Telephonist • Telephonist-receptionist
7214 Communication operators	• Call handler (emergency services) • Communications operator • Control room operator (emergency services) • Controller (taxi service)
7219 Customer service occupations not elsewhere classified	• Customer adviser • Customer service administrator • Customer service adviser • Customer service assistant • Customer services representative
8111 Food, drink and tobacco process operatives	• Baker (food products mfr) • Bakery assistant • Factory worker (food products mfr) • Meat processor • Process worker (brewery) • Process worker (dairy)
8112 Glass and ceramics process operatives	• Glass worker • Kiln man (glass mfr) • Process worker (fibre glass mfr)
8113 Textile process operatives	• Hosiery worker • Machinist (rope, twine mfr) • Process worker (textile mfr) • Spinner (paper twine mfr)
8114 Chemical and related process operatives	• Gas producer operator • Process technician (chemical mfr) • Process worker (cement mfr) • Process worker (nuclear fuel production)
8115 Rubber process operatives	• Disc cutter (rubber mfr) • Moulder (rubber goods mfr) • Process worker (rubber reclamation) • Tyre builder
8116 Plastics process operatives	• Extrusion operator (plastics mfr) • Fabricator (plastics mfr) • Injection moulder • Laminator (fibreglass) • Process worker (plastic goods mfr)

Occupation code	Related job titles
8117 Metal making and treating process operatives	• Degreaser (metal trades)
	• Foreman (metal refining)
	• Furnaceman (metal trades)
	• Process worker (nickel mfr)
	• Wire drawer
8118 Electroplaters	• Electroplater
	• Galvaniser
	• Metal sprayer
	• Powder coater
8119 Process operatives not elsewhere classified	• Melting pot assistant (electric cable)
	• Mixing plant foreman (asphalt mfr)
	• Process worker (electrical engineering)
	• Stone finisher (cast concrete products mfr)
8121 Paper and wood machine operatives	• Box maker (cardboard)
	• Guillotine operator (printing)
	• Machinist (paper goods mfr)
	• Sawyer
	• Wood machinist
8122 Coal mine operatives	• Coal miner
	• Colliery worker
	• Driller (coal mine)
8123 Quarry workers and related operatives	• Derrickman (oil wells)
	• Diamond driller (well sinking)
	• Plant operator (quarry)
	• Quarry operative
8125 Metal working machine operatives	• Engineer, nos
	• Machinist (metal trades)
	• Metal polisher • Process worker (metal trades)
8127 Printing machine assistants	• Finishing operative (printing)
	• Lithographer (printing)
	• Machinist (printing)
	• Print operator
	• Printer's assistant
8129 Plant and machine operatives not elsewhere classified	• Bench hand (metal trades)
	• Cable maker (spring mfr)
	• Laser operator
	• Manufacturer (metal goods mfr)
	• Saw doctor
8131 Assemblers (electrical and electronic products)	• Assembler (electrical, electronic equipment mfr)
	• Line operator (electrical)
	• Solderer
	• Team leader (electrical, electronic equipment mfr: assembly)
	• Technical operator (circuit board mfr)
8132 Assemblers (vehicles and metal goods)	• Assembler (metal trades)
	• Lineworker (vehicle mfr)
	• Manufacturing operator (metal trades)
	• Process worker (metal trades: assembly)
	• Team leader (motor vehicle mfr: assembly)
8133 Routine inspectors and testers	• Quality assurance inspector
	• Quality auditor
	• Quality controller
	• Quality inspector
	• Test engineer
8134 Weighers, graders and sorters	• Grader (food products mfr)
	• Metal sorter
	• Selector (ceramics mfr)
	• Weighbridge clerk
	• Weighbridge operator

Occupation code	Related job titles
8135 Tyre, exhaust and windscreen fitters	• Tyre and exhaust fitter • Tyre fitter • Tyre technician • Windscreen fitter
8137 Sewing machinists	• Overlocker • Seamstress • Sewing machinist • Stitcher • Upholstery machinist
8139 Assemblers and routine operatives not elsewhere classified	• Assembler • Gluer (furniture mfr) • Paint line operator • Production assistant • Riveter (soft toy mfr)
8141 Scaffolders, stagers and riggers	• Bell hanger (church bells) • Stage rigger (shipbuilding) • Tackleman (steelworks)
8142 Road construction operatives	• Asphalter • Concrete finisher (building construction) • Highways maintenance hand • Paver • Road worker
8143 Rail construction and maintenance operatives	• Line Inspector (railways) • Maintenance man (railway maintenance and repair) • Relayer (railways) • Trackman (railways) • Ultrasonic engineer (railway maintenance and repair)
8149 Construction operatives not elsewhere classified	• Asbestos remover • Cable layer • Demolition worker • Dry liner • General handyman • Maintenance man • Thermal insulation engineer
8211 Large goods vehicle drivers	• Haulage contractor • HGV driver • Lorry driver • Owner (heavy goods vehicle) • Tanker driver
8212 Van drivers	• Courier driver • Delivery driver • Driver • Parcel delivery driver • Van driver
8213 Bus and coach drivers	• Bus driver • Coach driver • Coach operator • Minibus driver • PSV driver
8214 Taxi and cab drivers and chauffeurs	• Chauffeur • Mini cab driver • Taxi driver • Taxi owner
8221 Crane drivers	• Crane driver • Crane operator • Haulage engine driver • Winchman

Occupation code	Related job titles
8222 Fork-lift truck drivers	• Fork lift driver • Fork lift truck driver • Fork truck operator • Stacker-driver
8223 Agricultural machinery drivers	• Agricultural machinist • Attendant (agricultural machinery) • Operator (agricultural machinery) • Tractor driver (agriculture)
8229 Mobile machine drivers and operatives not elsewhere classified	• Digger driver • Dredger • Excavator driver • JCB driver • Plant operator • Rig operator
8231 Train and tram drivers	• Train driver • Train operator • Tram driver
8233 Air transport operatives	• Aircraft dispatcher • Baggage handler • Cargo handler (airport) • Ramp agent • Refueller (airport)
8234 Rail transport operatives	• Railway worker • Shunter • Signalman (railways) • Transport supervisor (railways)
8239 Other drivers and transport operatives not elsewhere classified	• Bus inspector • Operations assistant (freight handling) • Test driver (motor vehicle mfr) • Transport supervisor • Yard foreman (road transport)
9111 Farm workers	• Agricultural worker • Farm labourer • Farm worker • Herdsman • Shepherd
9112 Forestry workers	• Forestry contractor • Forestry worker • Lumberjack
9119 Fishing and other elementary agriculture occupations not elsewhere classified – all jobs not listed in Table 1	• Horticultural worker • Labourer (landscape gardening) • Mushroom picker • Nursery worker
9120 Elementary construction occupations	• Electrician's mate (building construction) • Ground worker (building construction) • Hod carrier • Labourer (building construction)
9132 Industrial cleaning process occupations	• Cleaner and greaser • Factory cleaner • Hygiene operator • Industrial cleaner
9134 Packers, bottlers, canners and fillers	• Factory worker (packing) • Packaging operator • Packer • Paint filler
9139 Elementary process plant occupations not elsewhere classified	• Factory worker • Fitter's mate • Labourer (engineering) • Material handler

Occupation code	Related job titles
9211 Postal workers, mail sorters, messengers and couriers	• Courier • Leaflet distributor • Mail sorter • Messenger • Postman
9219 Elementary administration occupations not elsewhere classified	• General assistant • Office junior • Office worker • Reprographic technician
9231 Window cleaners	• Window cleaner • Window cleaning contractor
9232 Street cleaners	• Cleansing operative (street cleaning) • Road sweeper • Street cleaner
9233 Cleaners and domestics	• Chambermaid • Cleaner • Domestic • Home help • School cleaner
9234 Launderers, dry cleaners and pressers	• Carpet cleaner • Dry cleaner • Garment presser • Laundry assistant • Laundry worker
9235 Refuse and salvage occupations	• Binman (local government: cleansing department) • Hopper attendant (refuse destruction) • Refuse disposal operative • Salvage worker
9236 Vehicle valeters and cleaners	• Car wash assistant • Carriage service man (railways) • Motor car polisher (garage) • Vehicle valeter
9239 Elementary cleaning occupations not elsewhere classified	• Amenity block attendant • Chimney cleaner • Sweep (chimney) • Toilet attendant
9241 Security guards and related occupations	• CCTV operator • Park keeper • Private investigator • Security guard • Security officer
9242 Parking and civil enforcement occupations	• Car park attendant • Community warden • Parking attendant • Traffic warden
9244 School midday and crossing patrol occupations	• Dinner lady (schools) • Lollipop man • Lunchtime supervisor • Midday supervisor • School crossing patrol
9249 Elementary security occupations not elsewhere classified	• Bailiff • Commissionaire • Court usher • Door supervisor • Doorman
9251 Shelf fillers	• General assistant (retail trade) • Grocery assistant • Shelf filler • Shelf stacker

Occupation code	Related job titles
9259 Elementary sales occupations not elsewhere classified	• Code controller (wholesale, retail trade) • Home shopper • Order picker (retail trade) • Trolley assistant (wholesale, retail trade)
9260 Elementary storage occupations	• Labourer (haulage contractor) • Order picker • Warehouse assistant • Warehouse operator • Warehouse supervisor • Warehouseman
9271 Hospital porters	• Hospital porter • Porter (hospital service) • Portering supervisor (hospital services)
9272 Kitchen and catering assistants	• Catering assistant • Crew member (fast food outlet) • Kitchen assistant • Kitchen porter
9273 Waiters and waitresses	• Head waiter • Silver service waiter • Steward (catering) • Waiter • Waitress
9274 Bar staff	• Bar supervisor • Barmaid • Barperson • Bartender • Glass collector (public house)
9275 Leisure and theme park attendants	• Arcade assistant • Cinema attendant • Ride operator • Steward (sports ground) • Usher • Usherette
9279 Other elementary services occupations not elsewhere classified	• Bingo caller • Hotel assistant • Night porter • Porter (residential buildings) • Stage hand (entertainment)

Appendix Skilled Worker

The Skilled Worker route is for employers to recruit people to work in the UK in a specific job. A Skilled Worker must have a job offer in an eligible skilled occupation from a Home Office-approved sponsor.

A dependent partner and dependent children can apply on this route. Skilled Worker is a route to settlement.

Validity requirements for a Skilled Worker

SW 1.1.   A person applying for entry clearance or permission to stay as a Skilled Worker must apply online on the gov.uk website on the specified form as follows:

    (a)   for applicants outside the UK, form "Skilled Worker visa"; or

    (b)   for applicants inside the UK, form "Skilled Worker".

SW 1.2.   An application for entry clearance or permission to stay as a Skilled Worker must meet all the following requirements:

    (a)   any fee and Immigration Health Charge must have been paid; and

    (b)   the applicant must have provided any required biometrics; and

    (c)   the applicant must have provided a passport or other travel document which satisfactorily establishes their identity and nationality; and

    (d)   the applicant must have a certificate of sponsorship that was issued to them by their sponsor no more than 3 months before the date of application.

SW 1.3.   The applicant must be aged 18 or over on the date of application.

SW 1.4.   An applicant applying for entry clearance or permission to stay, who has received an award from a Government or international scholarship agency in the 12 months before the date of application which covers both fees and living costs for study in the UK, must have provided written consent to the application from that Government or agency.

SW 1.5.   An applicant who is applying for permission to stay must be in the UK on the date of application and must not have, or have last been granted, permission:

    (a)   as a Visitor; or

    (b)   as a Short-term student; or

    (c)   as a Parent of a Child Student; or

    (d)   as a Seasonal Worker; or

    (e)   as a Domestic Worker in a Private Household; or

    (f)   outside the Immigration Rules.

SW 1.6.   An application which does not meet the validity requirements for a Skilled Worker is invalid and may be rejected and not considered.

Suitability requirements for a Skilled Worker

SW2.1.   The applicant must not fall for refusal under Part 9: grounds for refusal.

SW2.2.   If applying for permission to stay the applicant must not be:

    (a)   in breach of immigration laws, except that where paragraph 39E applies, that period of overstaying will be disregarded; or

    (b)   on immigration bail.

Eligibility requirements for a Skilled Worker

Entry requirements for a Skilled Worker

SW 3.1.   A person seeking to come to the UK as a Skilled Worker must apply for and obtain entry clearance as a Skilled Worker before they arrive in the UK.

SW 3.2.   A person applying for entry clearance as a Skilled Worker must, if paragraph A39 and Appendix T of these rules apply, provide a valid medical certificate confirming that they have undergone screening for active pulmonary tuberculosis and that this tuberculosis is not present in them.

Points requirement for a Skilled Worker

SW 4.1. The applicant must be awarded 50 mandatory points from the table below. Details of how these points are awarded are set out in SW 5.1. to SW 7.4.

Mandatory points requirements	Relevant rules	Points
Sponsorship	SW 5.1. to SW 5.7.	20
Job at an appropriate skill level	SW 6.1. to SW 6.5.	20
English language skills at level B1 (intermediate)	SW 7.1. to SW 7.3.	10

SW 4.2. An applicant must be awarded 20 tradeable points from the table below. An applicant may only be awarded points from one entry in the table. Details of how these points are awarded are set out in SW 8.1. to SW 14.6.

Option	Tradeable points requirements for each option	Relevant rules	Points
A	The applicant's salary equals or exceeds all of the following: • £25,600 per year; • £10.10 per hour; and • the going rate for the occupation code.	SW 8.1. to SW 8.5. and SW 14.1. to SW 14.6.	20
B	Educational qualification: PhD in a subject relevant to the job and the applicant's salary equals or exceeds all of the following: • £23,040 per year; • £10.10 per hour; and • 90% of the going rate for the occupation code. In this entry, 10 points will be awarded for the educational qualification and 10 points will be awarded for the applicant's salary.	SW 9.1. to SW 9.10. and SW 14.1. to SW 14.6.	20
C	Educational qualification: PhD in a STEM subject relevant to the job and the applicant's salary equals or exceeds all of the following: • £20,480 per year; • £10.10 per hour; and • 80% of the going rate for the occupation code.	SW 10.1. to SW 10.6. and SW 14.1. to SW 14.6.	20
D	Job in a shortage occupation and the applicant's salary equals or exceeds all of the following: • £20,480 per year; • £10.10 per hour; and • 80% of the going rate for the occupation code.	SW 11.1. to SW 11.6. and SW 14.1. to SW 14.6.	20
E	Applicant is a new entrant to the labour market and their salary equals or exceeds all of the following: • £20,480 per year; • £10.10 per hour; and • 70% of the going rate for the occupation code.	SW 12.1. to SW 12.7. and SW 14.1. to SW 14.6.	20
F	Job in a listed health or education occupation and the applicant's salary equals or exceeds both: • £20,480 per year; and • the going rate for the occupation code. An applicant with a job in a listed health or education occupation can only be awarded tradeable points from option F.	SW 13.1. to SW 13.7. and SW14.1 to SW 14.6.	20

Points for sponsorship (mandatory)

SW 5.1. The applicant must have a valid Certificate of Sponsorship for the job they are planning to do; which to be valid must:

> (a) confirm the applicant's name, that they are being sponsored as a Skilled Worker, details of the job and salary the sponsor is offering them and PAYE details if HM Revenue and Customs (HMRC) requires income tax and National Insurance for the sponsored job to be paid via PAYE; and
>
> (b) if the application is for entry clearance, have been allocated by the Home Office to that sponsor for the specific job and salary details shown; and
>
> (c) include a start date, stated by the sponsor, which is no more than 3 months after the date of application; and
>
> (d) not have been used in a previous application which was either granted or refused (but can have been used in a previous application which was rejected as invalid, made void or withdrawn); and
>
> (e) not have been withdrawn by the sponsor or cancelled by the Home Office; and
>
> (f) confirm whether or not the Academic Technology Approval Scheme (ATAS) requirement in Appendix ATAS applies.

SW 5.2. The sponsor must be authorised by the Home Office to sponsor the job in question under the Skilled Worker route.

SW 5.3. The sponsor must be listed as A-rated on the Home Office's register of licensed sponsors, unless the applicant was last granted permission as a Skilled Worker and is applying to continue working for the same sponsor as in their last permission.

SW 5.4. The sponsor must have paid in full any required Immigration Skills Charge.

SW 5.5. The decision maker must not have reasonable grounds to believe the job the applicant is being sponsored to do:

> (a) does not exist; or
>
> (b) is a sham; or
>
> (c) has been created mainly so the applicant can apply for entry clearance or permission to stay.

SW 5.6. The decision maker must not have reasonable grounds to believe the job the applicant is being sponsored to do amounts to:

> (a) the hire of the applicant to a third party who is not the sponsor to fill a position with that party, whether temporary or permanent; or
>
> (b) contract work to undertake an ongoing routine role or to provide an ongoing routine service for a third party who is not the sponsor, regardless of the nature or length of any arrangement between the sponsor and the third party.

SW 5.7. If the requirements in SW 5.1. to SW 5.6. are met, the applicant will be awarded 20 mandatory points for sponsorship.

Points for a job at the appropriate skill level (mandatory)

SW 6.1. The applicant must be sponsored for a job in an eligible occupation code listed in Appendix Skilled Occupations, subject to SW 6.2.

SW 6.2. The sponsor must choose an appropriate occupation code, and the decision maker must not have reasonable grounds to believe the sponsor has chosen a less appropriate occupation code for any of the following reasons:

> (a) the most appropriate occupation code is not eligible under the Skilled Worker route; or
>
> (b) the most appropriate occupation code has a higher going rate than the proposed salary; or
>
> (c) the most appropriate occupation code is not a shortage occupation and the applicant is claiming points for a job in a shortage occupation; or
>
> (d) the most appropriate occupation code is not listed as "eligible for PhD points" in Table 1 of Appendix Skilled Occupations and the applicant is claiming points for an educational qualification.

SW 6.3. To support the assessment in SW 6.2., the decision maker may, in particular, consider:

> (a) whether the sponsor has shown a genuine need for the job as described; and
>
> (b) whether the applicant has the appropriate skills, qualifications and experience needed to do the job as described; and
>
> (c) the sponsor's history of compliance with the immigration system including, but not limited to, paying its sponsored workers appropriately; and
>
> (d) any additional information from the sponsor.

SW 6.3A. If the ATAS requirement in Appendix ATAS applies, the applicant must provide a valid ATAS certificate.

SW 6.4.   If the requirements in SW 6.1. to SW 6.3A. are met, an applicant will be awarded 20 mandatory points for a job at the appropriate skill level, subject to SW 6.5.

SW 6.5.   No points will be awarded for a job at the appropriate skill level if the applicant is not also being awarded the 20 mandatory points for sponsorship under SW 5.7.

Points for the English language requirement (mandatory)

SW 7.1.   An applicant must show English language ability on the Common European Framework of Reference for Languages in all 4 components (reading, writing, speaking and listening) of at least level B1 (intermediate).

SW 7.2.   The applicant must show they meet the English language requirement as specified in Appendix English Language.

SW 7.3.   If the requirements in SW 7.1. to SW 7.2. are met, the applicant will be awarded 10 mandatory points for meeting the English language requirement.

Tradeable points option A

SW 8.1.   The applicant must be sponsored for a job in an appropriate eligible occupation code listed in Table 1 of Appendix Skilled Occupations.

SW 8.2.   The salary for the job for which the applicant is being sponsored must equal or exceed all of the following:

(a)   £25,600 per year; and

(b)   £10.10 per hour; and

(c)   the going rate for the occupation code.

SW 8.3.   The salary will be considered as set out in SW 14.1. to SW 14.6.

SW 8.4.   If the requirements in SW 8.1. to SW 8.3. are met, the applicant will be awarded 20 tradeable points for their salary, subject to SW 8.5.

SW 8.5.   No points will be awarded for salary if the applicant is not also being awarded the 20 mandatory points for sponsorship under SW 5.7. and the 20 mandatory points for a job at the appropriate skill level under SW 6.4.

Tradeable points option B

SW 9.1.   The applicant must be sponsored for a job in an appropriate occupation code listed as being "eligible for PhD points" in Table 1 of Appendix Skilled Occupations.

SW 9.2.   The applicant must have a UK PhD or other academic doctoral qualification, or an overseas academic qualification which Ecctis confirms meets the recognised standard of a UK PhD.

SW 9.3.   The applicant's sponsor must provide a credible explanation of how the qualification is relevant to the job for which the applicant is being sponsored.

SW 9.4.   If the applicant has been correctly awarded points for an educational qualification in a previous grant of permission as a Skilled Worker, the applicant does not need to provide evidence of the qualification again, but the sponsor must still provide the explanation in SW 9.3.

SW 9.5.   The applicant may only be awarded points for one qualification.

SW 9.6.   The salary for the job the applicant is being sponsored for must equal or exceed all of the following:

(a)   £23,040 per year; and

(b)   £10.10 per hour; and

(c)   90% of the going rate for the occupation code.

SW 9.7.   The salary will be considered as set out in SW 14.1. to SW 14.6.

SW 9.8.   If the requirements in SW 9.1. to SW 9.5. are met, the applicant will be awarded 10 tradeable points for a relevant educational qualification, subject to SW 9.10.

SW 9.9.   If the requirements SW 9.6. to SW 9.7. are met and the occupation code is listed in Table 1 of Appendix Skilled Occupations, the applicant will be awarded 10 tradeable points for their salary, subject to SW 9.10.

SW 9.10.   No points will be awarded for a relevant educational qualification or salary if the applicant is not also being awarded the 20 mandatory points for sponsorship under SW 5.7. and the 20 mandatory points for a job at the appropriate skill level under SW 6.4.

Tradeable points option C

SW 10.1.   The applicant must meet the requirements in SW 9.1. to SW 9.5.

SW 10.2.   The applicant's sponsor must provide a credible explanation that the qualification in question is in a Science, Technology, Engineering or Mathematics (STEM) subject.

SW 10.3.   The salary for the job the applicant is being sponsored for must equal or exceed all of the following:

    (a)   £20,480 per year; and

    (b)   £10.10 per hour; and

    (c)   80% of the going rate for the occupation code.

SW 10.4.   The salary will be considered as set out in SW 14.1. to SW 14.6.

SW 10.5.   If the requirements in SW 10.1. to SW 10.4. are met, the applicant will be awarded 20 tradeable points for a relevant educational qualification in a STEM subject and their salary, subject to SW 10.6.

SW 10.6.   No points will be awarded for a relevant educational qualification and salary if the applicant is not also being awarded the 20 mandatory points for sponsorship under SW 5.7. and the 20 mandatory points for a job at the appropriate skill level under SW 6.4.

Tradeable points option D

SW 11.1.   The applicant must be sponsored for a job in an appropriate eligible occupation code listed in Appendix Shortage Occupation List as being a shortage occupation in the nation of the UK where that job is based, unless SW 11.2. applies.

SW 11.2.   If, on or before the date the sponsor assigned the Certificate of Sponsorship to the applicant, the applicant's job was removed from Appendix Shortage Occupation List, both of the following conditions must be met:

    (a)   the applicant's most recent permission was as a Skilled Worker in which they were sponsored to work in a shortage occupation under the applicable rules at that time; and

    (b)   the applicant is being sponsored to continue working in the same job for the same sponsor as in their previous permission.

SW 11.3.   The salary for the job the applicant is being sponsored for must equal or exceed all of the following:

    (a)   £20,480 per year; and

    (b)   £10.10 per hour; and

    (c)   80% of the going rate for the occupation code.

SW 11.4.   The salary will be considered as set out in SW 14.1. to SW 14.6.

SW 11.5.   If the requirements in SW 11.1. to SW 11.4. are met, the applicant will be awarded 20 tradeable points for a job in a shortage occupation and their salary, subject to SW 11.6.

SW 11.6.   No points will be awarded for a job in a shortage occupation and salary if the applicant is not also being awarded the 20 mandatory points for sponsorship under SW 5.7. and the 20 mandatory points for a job at the appropriate skill level under SW 6.4.

Tradeable points option E

SW 12.1.   The applicant must be sponsored for a job in an appropriate eligible occupation code listed in Table 1 of Appendix Skilled Occupations.

SW 12.2.   The applicant must meet one or more of the following requirements:

    (a)   the applicant must be under the age of 26 on the date of application; or

    (b)   the job offer must be for a postdoctoral position in any of the following occupation codes:

        • 2111 Chemical scientists

        • 2112 Biological scientists and biochemists

        • 2113 Physical scientists

        • 2114 Social and humanities scientists

        • 2119 Natural and social science professionals not elsewhere classified

        • 2311 Higher education teaching professionals; or

    (c)   the job offer must be in a UK Regulated Profession and the applicant must be working towards a recognised professional qualification for that profession; or

    (d)   the applicant must be working towards full registration or chartered status with the relevant professional body for the job they are being sponsored for; or

    (e)   the application must be for permission to stay and the applicant's most recent permission must have been as a Tier 1 (Graduate Entrepreneur) Migrant; or

    (f)   all of the following conditions apply:

        (i)   the applicant's most recent permission, other than as a visitor, was as a Student: and

        (ii)   that permission is either current or expired less than 2 years before the date of application; and

(iii)   in that permission or any previous permission as a Student, the applicant was sponsored to study one of the following courses (not any other qualifications of an equivalent level):

- a UK bachelor's degree; or

- a UK master's degree; or

- a UK PhD or other doctoral qualification; or

- a Postgraduate Certificate in Education; or

- a Professional Graduate Diploma of Education; and

(iv)   the applicant has completed (or is applying no more than 3 months before they are expected to complete) the course in (iii) above, or the applicant is studying a PhD and has completed at least 12 months study in the UK towards the PhD; or

(g)   the applicant's most recent permission, other than as a visitor, was as a Graduate, and that permission is either current or expired less than 2 years before the date of application.

SW 12.3.   Granting the application must not mean the applicant's combined permission as a Skilled Worker, Graduate and/or Tier 2 Migrant would be more than 4 years in total, whether or not the permission is for a continuous period.

SW 12.4.   The salary for the job the applicant is being sponsored for must equal or exceed all of the following:

(a)   £20,480 per year; and

(b)   £10.10 per hour; and

(c)   70% of the going rate for the occupation code.

SW 12.5.   The salary will be considered as set out in SW 14.1. to SW 14.6.

SW 12.6.   If the requirements in SW 12.1. to SW 12.5. are met, the applicant will be awarded 20 tradeable points for being a new entrant to the labour market and their salary, subject to SW 12.7.

SW 12.7.   No points will be awarded for being a new entrant to the labour market and salary if the applicant is not also being awarded the 20 mandatory points for sponsorship under SW 5.7. and the 20 mandatory points for a job at the appropriate skill level under SW 6.4.

Tradeable points option F

SW 13.1.   The applicant must be sponsored for a job in an appropriate eligible occupation code listed in Table 2 of Appendix Skilled Occupations.

SW 13.2.   The salary for the job for which the applicant is being sponsored must equal or exceed both:

(a)   £20,480 per year; and

(b)   the going rate for the occupation code.

SW 13.3.   The salary will be considered as set out in SW 14.1. to SW 14.5.

SW 13.4.   If the applicant is being sponsored for a job in the occupation code "2231 Nurses" or "2232 Midwives", their salary may be temporarily (for up to 8 months) less than the £20,480 per year required under SW 13.2(a) in either of the following circumstances:

(a)   the applicant has previously held Nursing and Midwifery Council (NMC) registration and is undertaking an NMC-approved programme with a view to returning to practice; or

(b)   the applicant is working towards NMC registration and all of the following conditions apply:

(i)   the applicant has passed the NMC's English language requirements and Computer Based Test of competence, before the date of application; and

(ii)   the applicant will sit an Objective Structured Clinical Examination (OSCE) to obtain NMC registration no later than 3 months after the stated job start date.

SW 13.5.   Where SW 13.4. applies:

(a)   the sponsor must confirm that the applicant will stop being sponsored if they do not achieve full NMC registration within 8 months of the job start date (if the applicant was last granted permission as a as a nurse or midwife on the Skilled Worker route, the 8 months is counted from the start date of the job they were sponsored to do in their most recent permission); and

(b)   during the 8 months in (a), or until the applicant achieves NMC registration (if sooner), the applicant's salary must be at least equal to the appropriate Agenda for Change Band 3 rate, as stated in Table 3 of Appendix Skilled Occupations.

SW 13.6.   If the requirements in SW 13.1. to SW 13.5. are met, the applicant will be awarded 20 tradeable points for a job in a listed health or education occupation and their salary, subject to SW 13.7.

SW 13.7.   No points will be awarded for a job in a listed health or education occupation and salary if the applicant is not also being awarded the 20 mandatory points for sponsorship under SW 5.7. and the 20 mandatory points for a job at the appropriate skill level under SW 6.4.

Consideration of salary (all tradeable points options)

SW 14.1.   Salary only includes guaranteed basic gross pay (before income tax and including employee pension and national insurance contributions).

SW 14.2.   Salary does not include other pay and benefits, such as any of the following:

(a)   pay which cannot be guaranteed because the nature of the job means that hours fluctuate; or

(b)   additional pay such as shift, overtime or bonus pay, (whether or not it is guaranteed); or

(c)   employer pension and employer national insurance contributions; or

(d)   any allowances, such as accommodation or cost of living allowances; or

(e)   in-kind benefits, such as equity shares, health insurance, school or university fees, company cars or food; or

(f)   one-off payments, such as 'golden hellos'; or

(g)   any payments relating to immigration costs, such as the fee or Immigration Health Charge; or

(h)   payments to cover business expenses, including (but not limited to) travel to and from the applicant's country of residence, equipment, clothing, travel or subsistence.

SW 14.3.   If the applicant is being sponsored to work more than 48 hours a week, only the salary for the first 48 hours a week will be considered towards the salary thresholds of £25,600, £23,040 or £20,480 per year referred to in SW 8.1. to SW 13.7.

For example, an applicant who works 60 hours a week for £10 per hour will be considered to have a salary of £24,960 (£10 x 48 x 52) per year and not £31,200 (£10 x 60 x 52).

SW 14.4.   Going rates will be pro-rated, and the £10.10 per hour salary requirement will be calculated, to the applicant's working pattern, as follows:

(a)   going rates for occupation codes listed in Table 1 of Appendix Skilled Occupations are based on a 39-hour week and will be pro-rated as follows:

(the going rate for the occupation code stated in Table 1 of Appendix Skilled Occupations) x (the number of weekly working hours stated by the sponsor ÷ 39)

(b)   where an applicant's salary is required to be 70%, 80% or 90% of the going rate, the resulting figure from the calculation in (a) will be multiplied by 0.7, 0.8 or 0.9 as appropriate, to calculate the required salary; and.

(c)   going rates for the health and education occupation codes listed in Table 2 of Appendix Skilled Occupations will be pro-rated as stated in Appendix Skilled Occupations; and

(d)   the applicant's full weekly hours will be included when checking their salary against the going rate and the £10.10 per hour salary requirement, even if they work more than 48 hours a week.

Transitional arrangements for salary on the Skilled Worker route

SW 14.5.   If the applicant is applying for permission to stay or settlement, the applicant was granted permission as a Tier 2 (General) Migrant and has had continuous permission as a Skilled Worker ever since, the following transitional arrangements apply:

(a)   if the date of application is before 1 December 2026 salary may also include allowances (the other restrictions in SW 14.20 also apply), providing the following conditions are met:

(i)   the applicant is applying to work for the same sponsor as in their previous permission; and

(ii)   the allowances are guaranteed, will be paid for the duration of the applicant's permission, and would be paid to a local settled worker in similar circumstances, such as London weighting; and

(b)   if the date of application is before 24 May 2023 and the applicant had permission as a Tier 2 (General) Migrant based on a certificate of sponsorship given to them by their sponsor before 24 November 2016, the applicant does not need to score 20 tradeable points from options A to F, as set out in SW 8.1. to SW 13.6, instead, 20 tradeable points will be awarded for a salary of £20,800 or above, or at least the going rate for the occupation code, if higher (the other requirements in SW 12.1. to SW 12.4 also apply), but these points will not be awarded if the applicant is not also being awarded the 20 mandatory points for sponsorship under SW 5.7. and the 20 mandatory points for a job at the appropriate skill level under SW 6.4; and

(c)   if the applicant was sponsored to work in one of the occupation codes in the table below at the time they applied for their last permission as a Tier 2 (General) Migrant and has continued to be sponsored in that occupation code ever since (whether as a Tier 2 (General) Migrant and/or as a Skilled Worker), and the date of application is before 1 December 2026, the going rates in the table below apply, instead of the going rates listed in Table 1 of Appendix Skilled Occupations. These going rates are based on a 40-hour working week and must be pro-rated for other working patterns, based on the weekly working hours stated by the applicant's sponsor:

Occupation code	Going rate – option A	90% of going rate – option B	80% of going rate – options C and D	70% of going rate – option E
2113 Physical scientists	£29,000 (£13.94 per hour)	£26,100 (£12.55 per hour)	£23,200 (£11.15 per hour)	£20,300 (£9.76 per hour)
2119 Natural and social science professionals not elsewhere classified	£29,000 (£13.94 per hour)	£26,100 (£12.55 per hour)	£23,200 (£11.15 per hour)	£20,300 (£9.76 per hour)
2311 Higher education teaching professionals	£33,000 (£15.87 per hour)	£29,700 (£14.28 per hour)	£26,400 (£12.69 per hour)	£23,100 (£11.11 per hour)

SW 14.6.   If the applicant was granted permission as a Skilled Worker under the Rules in place before 6 April 2021, and has had continuous permission as a Skilled Worker since then, the £10.10 per hour salary requirement does not apply, but all other salary requirements continue to apply.

Financial requirement (mandatory) for a Skilled Worker

SW 15.1.   If the applicant is applying for permission to stay and has been in the UK with permission for 12 months or longer on the date of application, they will meet the financial requirement and do not need to show funds.

SW 15.2.   If the applicant is applying for entry clearance, or has been in the UK for less than 12 months on the date of application, either:

(a)   the applicant must have funds of at least £1,270; or

(b)   the applicant's A-rated sponsor must certify that they will, if necessary, maintain and accommodate the applicant up to the end of the first month of their employment, to an amount of at least £1,270.

SW 15.3.   If SW 15.2.(a) applies, the applicant must show that they have held the required funds for a 28-day period and as specified in Appendix Finance.

Criminal record certificate requirement (mandatory) for a Skilled Worker

SW 16.1.   If the applicant is applying for entry clearance and is being sponsored for a job in any of the occupation codes listed below, they must provide a criminal record certificate from the relevant authority in any country in which they have been present for 12 months or more (whether continuously or in total) in the 10 years before the date of application, and while aged 18 or over:

- 1181 Health services and public health managers and directors
- 1184 Social services managers and directors
- 1241 Health care practice managers
- 1242 Residential, day and domiciliary care managers and proprietors
- 2211 Medical practitioners
- 2212 Psychologists
- 2213 Pharmacists
- 2214 Ophthalmic opticians
- 2215 Dental practitioners
- 2217 Medical radiographers
- 2218 Podiatrists
- 2219 Health professionals not elsewhere classified
- 2221 Physiotherapists
- 2222 Occupational therapists

- 2223 Speech and language therapists
- 2229 Therapy professionals not elsewhere classified
- 2231 Nurses
- 2232 Midwives
- 2312 Further education teaching professionals
- 2314 Secondary education teaching professionals
- 2315 Primary and nursery education teaching professionals
- 2316 Special needs education teaching professionals
- 2317 Senior professionals of educational establishments
- 2318 Education advisers and school inspectors
- 2319 Teaching and other educational professionals not elsewhere classified
- 2442 Social workers
- 2443 Probation officers
- 2449 Welfare professionals not elsewhere classified
- 3213 Paramedics
- 3216 Dispensing opticians
- 3217 Pharmaceutical technicians
- 3218 Medical and dental technicians
- 3219 Health associate professionals not elsewhere classified
- 3231 Youth and community workers
- 3234 Housing officers
- 3235 Counsellors
- 3239 Welfare and housing associate professionals not elsewhere classified
- 3443 Fitness instructors
- 3562 Human resources and industrial relations officers
- 6121 Nursery nurses and assistants
- 6122 Childminders and related occupations
- 6123 Playworkers
- 6125 Teaching assistants
- 6126 Educational support assistants 6141 Nursing auxiliaries and assistants
- 6143 Dental nurses
- 6144 Houseparents and residential wardens
- 6146 Senior care workers

SW 16.2.   The requirement in SW 16.1. does not apply if the applicant provides a satisfactory explanation why it is not reasonably practicable for them to obtain a criminal record certificate from any or all of the relevant authorities.

Decision on an application as a Skilled Worker

SW 17.1.   If the decision maker is satisfied all the suitability and relevant eligibility requirements for a Skilled Worker are met, the application will be granted, otherwise the application will be refused.

SW 17.2.   If the application is refused, the person can apply for an Administrative Review under Appendix AR: Administrative Review.

Period and conditions of grant for a Skilled Worker

SW 18.1.   The applicant will be granted entry clearance or permission to stay until 14 days after the end date of their certificate of sponsorship (which may be up to a maximum of 5 years after the start date of their certificate of sponsorship).

SW 18.2.   The grant will be subject to all the following conditions:

(a)   no access to public funds; and

(b)   work is permitted only in the job the applicant is being sponsored for, subject to (c) to (e); and

(c)   supplementary employment is permitted, providing the person continues to work in the job for which they are being sponsored; and

(d)   voluntary work is permitted; and

(e)   working out a contractual notice period is permitted, for a job the applicant was lawfully working in on the date of application; and

(f)   study is permitted, subject to the ATAS condition in Appendix ATAS; and

(g)   if Part 10 applies, the applicant will be required to register with the police.

Settlement as a Skilled Worker

Validity requirements for settlement as a Skilled Worker

SW 19.1.   A person applying for settlement as a Skilled Worker must apply online on the gov.uk website on the specified form, "Settle in the UK in various immigration categories: form SET(O)".

SW 19.2.   An application for settlement as a Skilled Worker must meet all the following requirements:

(a)   any fee must have been paid; and

(b)   the applicant must have provided any required biometrics; and

(c)   the applicant must have provided a passport or other travel document which satisfactorily establishes their identity and nationality; and

(d)   the applicant must be in the UK on the date of application.

SW 19.3.   The applicant must have, or have last been granted, permission as a Skilled Worker.

SW 19.4.   An application which does not meet the validity requirements for settlement as a Skilled Worker is invalid and may be rejected and not considered.

Suitability requirements for settlement as a Skilled Worker

SW20.1.   The applicant must not fall for refusal under Part 9: grounds for refusal

SW20.2.   The applicant must not be:

(a)   in breach of immigration laws, except that where paragraph 39E applies, that period of overstaying will be disregarded; or

(b)   on immigration bail.

Eligibility requirements for settlement as a Skilled Worker

Qualifying period requirement for settlement as a Skilled Worker

SW 21.1.   The applicant must have spent a continuous period of 5 years in the UK.

SW 21.2.   The 5-year continuous period must consist of time with permission on any of, or any combination of, the following routes:

(a)   Skilled Worker; or

(b)   Global talent; or

(c)   Innovator; or

(d)   T2 Minister of Religion; or

(e)   International Sportsperson; or

(f)   Representative of an Overseas Business; or

(g)   as a Tier 1 Migrant, other than as a Tier 1 (Graduate Entrepreneur) Migrant; or

(h)   permission on any other route, during the time the applicant was waiting for a decision on their application as a Skilled Worker, providing that application:

(i)   was for permission to stay; and

(ii)   was made between 24 January 2020 and 30 June 2021 (inclusive); and

(iii)   was supported on the date of application by a certificate of sponsorship assigned by a licensed sponsor; and

(iv)   was granted.

Continuous residence requirement for settlement as a Skilled Worker

SW 22.1.   The applicant must meet the continuous residence requirement as set out in Appendix Continuous Residence during the period in SW 21.1.

Knowledge of life in the UK requirement for settlement as a Skilled Worker

SW 23.1   The applicant must meet the knowledge of Life in the UK requirement as set out in Appendix KOL UK.

Sponsorship and salary requirement for settlement as a Skilled Worker

SW 24.1.   The sponsor in the applicant's most recent permission must still be approved by the Home Office to sponsor Skilled Workers on the date of decision.

SW 24.2.   The sponsor must confirm that they still require the applicant to work for them for the foreseeable future, and that the applicant is paid, and will be paid for the foreseeable future, at least the salary in SW 24.3.

SW 24.3.   Subject to SW 24.4, the applicant's salary must equal or exceed all three salary requirements shown in the relevant row of the table below.

•	Applicant's circumstances	General salary	Minimum hourly rate	Going rate
A	All cases where rows B and C do not apply	Salary of at least £25,600 per year	At least £10.10 per hour	At least the going rate
B	The applicant was sponsored in their most recent permission for a job in a shortage occupation or a health or education occupation code listed in Table 2 of Appendix Skilled Occupations	Salary of at least £20,480 per year	At least £10.10 per hour	At least the going rate
C	The 5-year qualifying period for settlement includes time as a Tier 2 (General) Migrant in which the applicant was sponsored for a job in one of the following occupation codes: • 2111 Chemical scientists • 2112 Biological scientists and biochemists • 2113 Physical scientists • 2114 Social and humanities scientists • 2119 Natural and social science professionals not elsewhere classified • 2150 Research and development managers • 2311 Higher education teaching professionals	Salary of at least £20,480 per year	At least £10.10 per hour	At least the going rate in the table at paragraph SW 14.5(c), if the applicant has continued to be sponsored in that occupation code ever since. At least the going rate in Appendix Skilled Occupations, in other cases.

SW 24.4.   Salary under the table in SW 24.3 is subject to the following:

(a)   salary will be considered as set out in SW 14.1. to SW 14.6. (and in SW 14.3., references to the salary thresholds of £25,600 or £20,480 per year should be read as including references in the table in SW 24.3 above); and

(b)   if the applicant is currently absent from work for one of the reasons set out in Part 9 paragraph 9.30.1, or has returned from such an absence within the month before the date of application, consideration will be based on their salary on their return to work, as stated by their sponsor.

Decision on an application for settlement as a Skilled Worker

SW 25.1.   If the decision maker is satisfied all the suitability and eligibility requirements for settlement as a Skilled Worker are met, the applicant will be granted settlement, otherwise the application will be refused.

SW 25.2.   If the application is refused, the person can apply for an Administrative Review under Appendix AR: Administrative Review.

Dependants of a Skilled Worker

Validity requirements for a dependent partner or dependent child of a Skilled Worker

SW 26.1.   A person applying for entry clearance or permission to stay as a dependent partner or dependent child of a Skilled Worker must apply online on the gov.uk website on the specified form as follows:

Location of Partner or Child	Specified form
Applicant outside the UK	Dependant partner visa
	Dependant child visa
Applicant inside the UK	Dependant partner
	Dependant child

SW 26.2.   An application for entry clearance or permission to stay as a dependent partner or dependent child of a Skilled Worker must meet all the following requirements:

(a)   any fee and Immigration Health Charge must have been paid; and

(b)   the applicant must have provided any required biometrics; and

(c)   the applicant must have provided a passport or other travel document which satisfactorily establishes their identity and nationality.

SW 26.3.   If the applicant is applying as a dependent partner they must be aged 18 or over on the date of application.

SW 26.4.   An applicant who is applying for permission to stay as a dependent partner or dependent child of a Skilled Worker must be in the UK on the date of application and must not have, or have last been granted, permission:

(a)   as a Visitor; or

(b)   as a Short-term student; or

(c)   as a Parent of a Child Student; or

(d)   as a Seasonal Worker; or

(e)   as a Domestic Worker in a Private Household; or

(f)   outside the Immigration Rules.

SW 26.5.   An application which does not meet the validity requirements for a dependent partner or dependent child of a Skilled Worker is invalid and may be rejected and not considered.

Suitability requirements for a dependent partner or dependent child of a Skilled Worker

SW 27.1.   The applicant must not fall for refusal under Part 9: grounds for refusal.

SW 27.2.   If applying for permission to stay the applicant must not be:

(a)   in breach of immigration laws, except that where paragraph 39E applies, that period of overstaying will be disregarded; or

(b)   on immigration bail.

Eligibility requirements for a dependent partner or dependent child of a Skilled Worker

Entry requirement for a dependent partner or dependent child of a Skilled Worker

SW 28.1.   A person seeking to come to the UK as a dependent partner or dependent child of a Skilled Worker must apply for and obtain entry clearance as a dependent partner or dependent child of a Skilled Worker before they arrive in the UK.

SW 28.2.   A person applying for entry clearance as the dependent partner or dependent child of a Skilled Worker must, if paragraph A39 and Appendix T of these rules apply, provide a valid medical certificate confirming that they have undergone screening for active pulmonary tuberculosis and that this tuberculosis is not present in them.

Relationship requirement for a dependent partner of a Skilled Worker

SW 29.1.   The applicant must be the partner of a person (P) where one of the following applies:

(a)   P has permission on the Skilled Worker route; or

(b)   P is, at the same time, applying for (and is granted) entry clearance or permission on the Skilled Worker route; or

(c) P is settled or has become a British citizen, providing P had permission on the Skilled Worker route when they settled and the applicant had permission as P's partner at that time.

SW 29.2. If the applicant and their Skilled Worker partner are not married or in a civil partnership, all of the following requirements must be met:

(a) they must have been living together in a relationship similar to marriage or civil partnership for at least the two years before the date of application; and

(b) any previous relationship of the applicant or their Skilled Worker partner with another person must have permanently broken down; and

(c) the applicant and their Skilled Worker partner must not be so closely related that they would not be allowed to marry or form a civil partnership in the UK.

SW 29.3. The relationship between the applicant and their Skilled Worker partner must be genuine and subsisting.

SW 29.4. The applicant and their Skilled Worker partner must intend to live together throughout the applicant's stay in the UK.

Relationship requirement for a dependent child of a Skilled Worker

SW 30.1. The applicant must be the child of a parent (P) where one of the following applies:

(a) P has permission on the Skilled Worker route; or

(b) P is, at the same time, applying for (and is granted) entry clearance or permission on the Skilled Worker route; or

(c) P is settled or has become a British citizen, providing P had permission on the Skilled Worker route when they settled and the applicant had permission as P's child at that time.

SW 30.2. The applicant's parents must each be either applying at the same time as the applicant or have permission to be in the UK (other than as a Visitor) unless:

(a) the parent applying for or with entry clearance or permission to stay as a Skilled Worker is the sole surviving parent; or

(b) the parent applying for or with entry clearance or permission to stay as a Skilled Worker has sole responsibility for the child's upbringing; or

(c) the parent who does not have permission as a Skilled Worker –

(i) is a British citizen or a person who has a right to enter or stay in the UK without restriction; and

(ii) is or will be ordinarily resident in the UK; or

(d) the decision maker is satisfied that there are serious and compelling reasons to grant the child entry clearance or permission to stay with the parent who is applying for or has entry clearance or permission as a Skilled Worker.

SW 30.3. If the applicant is a child born in the UK to a Skilled Worker or their partner, the applicant must provide a full UK birth certificate showing the names of both parents.

Care requirement for a dependent child of a Skilled Worker

SW 31.1. If the applicant is aged under 18 on the date of application, there must be suitable arrangements for the child's care and accommodation in the UK, which must comply with relevant UK legislation and regulations.

Age requirement for a dependent child of a Skilled Worker

SW 32.1. The child must be under the age of 18 on the date of application, unless they were last granted permission as the dependent child of their parent or parents.

SW 32.2. If the child is aged 16 or over at the date of application, they must not be leading an independent life.

Financial requirement for a dependent partner or dependent child of a Skilled Worker

SW 33.1. If the applicant is applying for permission to stay and has been living in the UK with permission for 12 months or longer on the date of application, they will meet the financial requirement and do not need to show funds.

SW 33.2. If the applicant is applying for entry clearance, or has been in the UK for less than 12 months on the date of application, either:

(a) funds of at least the amount required in SW 33.3 must be held collectively by one or more of the following:

i) the applicant; and

ii) the Skilled Worker (P); and

iii)   if the applicant is applying as a dependent child, their parent who is lawfully present in the UK or being granted entry clearance, or permission to stay, at the same time;

or

(b)   the Skilled Worker's A-rated sponsor must certify that they will, if necessary, maintain and accommodate the dependent partner and/or any dependent child as well as the Skilled Worker, up to the end of the first month of each of their grants of permission, to at least the amounts required in SW 33.3.

SW 33.3.   The funds required are:

(a)   £285 for a dependent partner in the UK, or applying for entry clearance; and

(b)   £315 for the first dependent child in the UK, or applying for entry clearance; and

(c)   £200 for any other dependent child in the UK, or applying for entry clearance.

SW 33.4.   If SW 33.2.(a) applies, the funds held for the applicant must be held in addition to any funds required for the Skilled Worker to meet the financial requirement and any other dependants in the UK or applying at the same time.

SW 33.5.   If SW 33.2.(a) applies, the funds must have been held for a 28-day period and as specified in Appendix Finance.

Criminal record certificate requirement for a dependent partner of a Skilled Worker

SW 34.1.   Where a Skilled Worker is being sponsored for a job in an occupation code listed in SW 16.1, an applicant applying for entry clearance as the partner of the Skilled Worker must provide a criminal record certificate from the relevant authority in any country in which they have been present for 12 months or more (whether continuously or in total) in the 10 years before the date of application, and while aged 18 or over.

SW 34.2.   The requirement in SW 34.1. does not apply if the applicant provides a satisfactory explanation why it is not reasonably practicable for them to obtain a criminal record certificate from any or all of the relevant authorities.

Decision on an application as a dependent partner or dependent child of a Skilled Worker

SW 35.1.   If the decision maker is satisfied that all the suitability and eligibility requirements for a dependent partner or dependent child of a Skilled Worker are met, the application will be granted, otherwise the application will be refused.

SW 35.2.   If the application is refused, the person can apply for an Administrative Review under Appendix AR: Administrative Review.

Period and conditions of grant for a dependent partner or dependent child of a Skilled Worker

SW 36.1.   A partner will be granted:

(a)   permission which ends on the same date as their partner's permission as a Skilled Worker; or

(b)   3 years' permission if the Skilled Worker was (or is being) granted settlement as a Skilled Worker.

SW 36.2.   A child will be granted permission which ends on the same date as whichever of their parents' permission ends first, unless both parents have (or are being granted) settlement or British Citizenship, in which case the child will be granted permission for 3 years.

SW 36.3.   The grant will be subject to all the following conditions:

(a)   no access to public funds; and

(b)   work (including self-employment and voluntary work) is permitted, except as a professional sportsperson (including as a sports coach); and

(c)   study is permitted, subject to the ATAS condition in Appendix ATAS, if the applicant is over the age of 18; and

(d)   if Part 10 applies, the applicant will be required to register with the police.

Settlement as a dependent partner or dependent child of a Skilled Worker

Validity requirements for settlement as a dependent partner or dependent child of a Skilled Worker

SW 37.1.   A person applying for settlement as a dependent partner or dependent child of a Skilled Worker must apply online on the gov.uk website on the specified form, "Settle in the UK in various immigration categories: form SET(O)".

SW 37.2.   An application for settlement as a dependent partner or dependent child of a Skilled Worker must meet all the following requirements:

    (a)   any fee must have been paid; and

    (b)   the applicant must have provided any required biometrics; and

    (c)   the applicant must have provided a passport or other travel document which satisfactorily establishes their identity and nationality; and

    (d)   the applicant must be in the UK on the date of application.

SW 37.3.   An application which does not meet the validity requirements for a dependent partner or dependent child of a Skilled Worker is invalid and may be rejected and not considered.

Suitability requirements for settlement as a dependent partner or dependent child of a Skilled Worker

SW38.1.   The applicant must not fall for refusal under Part 9: grounds for refusal.

SW38.2.   The applicant must not be:

    (a)   in breach of immigration laws, except that where paragraph 39E applies, that period of overstaying will be disregarded; or

    (b)   on immigration bail.

Eligibility requirements for settlement as a dependent partner or dependent child of a Skilled Worker

Relationship requirement for settlement for a dependent partner or dependent child of a Skilled Worker

SW 39.1.   The applicant must be the partner or child of a person (P) where one of the following applies:

    (a)   P is, at the same time, being granted settlement as a Skilled Worker; or

    (b)   P is settled in the UK or has become a British citizen, providing P had permission as a Skilled Worker when they settled and the applicant either:

        i)   had permission as P's partner or child at that time; or

        ii)   is applying as a child of P, and was born in the UK before P settled.

SW 39.2.   The applicant must either:

    (a)   have last been granted permission as a dependent partner or dependent child of the person (P) in SW 39.1; or

    (b)   have been born in the UK and be applying as a child of the person (P) in SW 39.1.

SW 39.3.   If applying as a partner, the applicant and the person (P) in SW 39.1. must meet the relationship requirement in SW 29.2. to SW 29.4. and must have met them throughout the 5 years ending on the date of application.

SW 39.4.   If applying as a child, the applicant's other parent (who is not the person (P) in SW 39.1.) must be being granted settlement at the same time, or be settled or a British citizen, unless:

    (a)   the person (P) in SW 39.1. is the applicant's sole surviving parent; or

    (b)   the person (P) in SW 39.1. has sole responsibility for the applicant's upbringing; or

    (c)   the decision maker is satisfied that there are serious and compelling reasons to grant the applicant settlement.

Care requirement for settlement as a dependent child of a Skilled Worker

SW 40.1.   If the applicant is under the age of 18 on the date of application there must be suitable arrangements for the child's care and accommodation in the UK, which must comply with relevant UK legislation and regulations.

Age requirement for settlement as a dependent child of a Skilled Worker

SW 41.1.   The applicant must be under the age of 18 on the date of application, unless they were last granted permission as the dependent child of their parent or parents.

SW 41.2.   If the applicant is aged 16 or over on the date of application, they must not be leading an independent life.

Qualifying period requirement for settlement as a dependent partner of a Skilled Worker

SW 42.1.   The applicant must have spent a continuous period of 5 years in the UK with permission as a dependent partner of the person (P) in SW 39.1.

Continuous residence requirement for settlement as a dependent partner of a Skilled Worker

SW 43.1.   The applicant must meet the continuous residence requirement as set out in Appendix Continuous Residence during the period in SW 42.1.

English language requirement for settlement as a dependent partner or dependent child of a Skilled Worker

SW 44.1.   Unless an exemption applies, the applicant must show English language ability on the Common European Framework of Reference for Languages in speaking and listening to at least level B1.

SW 44.2.   The applicant must show they meet the English language requirement as specified in Appendix English Language.

Knowledge of life in the UK requirement for settlement as a dependent partner or dependent child of a Skilled Worker

SW 45.1.   If the applicant is aged 18 or over on the date of application, they must meet the knowledge of Life in the UK requirement as set out in Appendix KOL UK.

Decision on an application for settlement as a dependent partner or dependent child of a Skilled Worker

SW 46.1.   If the decision maker is satisfied all the suitability and eligibility requirements are met for settlement as a dependent partner or dependent child of a Skilled Worker, the application will be granted, otherwise the application will be refused.

SW 46.2.   If the application is refused the person can apply for an Administrative Review under Appendix AR: Administrative Review.

Appendix Start-up

The Start-up route is for a person seeking to establish a business in the UK for the first time.

The person must have an innovative, viable and scalable business idea which is supported by an endorsing body approved by the Home Office.

A person on the Start-up route can bring a dependent partner and dependent children to the UK.

Start-up is not a route to settlement. A person may be eligible to progress from Start-up to the Innovator route, which is a route to settlement.

Validity requirements for Start-up route

SU 1.1.   A person applying for entry clearance or permission to stay on the Start-up route must apply online on the gov.uk website on the specified form as follows:

Applicant	Specified form
EEA national with a chipped passport	Either:
	• Start-up or Innovator using the UK Immigration: ID Check app (when available); or
	• the forms listed below for applicants outside or inside the UK (as relevant)
Applicants outside the UK	Start-up or Innovator visa
Applicants inside the UK	Start-up or Innovator permission to stay

SU 1.2.   An application for entry clearance or permission to stay on the Start-up route must meet all the following requirements:

(a)   any fee and Immigration Health Charge must have been paid; and

(b)   the applicant must have provided any required biometrics; and

(c)   the applicant must have provided a passport or other travel document which satisfactorily establishes their identity and nationality; and

(d)   the applicant must have been issued with an endorsement letter by an endorsing body dated no more than 3 months before the date of application and that endorsement must not have been withdrawn.

SU 1.3.   The applicant must be aged 18 or over on the date of application.

SU 1.4.   If the applicant has in the last 12 months before the date of application received an award from a Government or international scholarship agency covering both fees and living costs for study in the UK, they must provide written consent to the application from that Government or agency.

SU 1.5.   A person applying for permission to stay must be in the UK and must not have, or have last been granted, permission:

(a)   as a Visitor; or

(b)   as a Short-term Student; or

(c)   as a Parent of a Child Student; or

(d)   as a Seasonal Worker; or

(e)   as a domestic worker in a private household; or

(f)   outside the Immigration Rules.

SU 1.6.   An application which does not meet all the validity requirements for the Start-up route is invalid and may be rejected and not considered.

Suitability requirements for the Start-up route

SU 2.1.   The applicant must not fall for refusal under Part 9: grounds for refusal.

SU 2.2.   If applying for permission to stay the applicant must not be:

(a)   in breach of immigration laws, except that where paragraph 39E applies, that period of overstaying will be disregarded; or

(b)   on immigration bail.

Eligibility requirements for the Start-up route

Entry requirements for the Start-up route

SU 3.1.   A person seeking to come to the UK on the Start-up route must apply for and obtain entry clearance on the Start-up route before they arrive in the UK.

SU 3.2.   A person applying for entry clearance on the Start-up route must, if paragraph A39 and Appendix T of these rules apply, provide a valid medical certificate confirming that they have undergone screening for active pulmonary tuberculosis and that this tuberculosis is not present in them.

Points requirement for Start-up

SU 4.1.   The applicant must be awarded a total of 70 points from the table below.

Requirement (mandatory)	Points available
Business is innovative, viable and scalable.	25
The applicant has not previously established a business in the UK	25
English Language at level B2	10
Financial requirement	10
Total number of points required	**70**

Innovative, viable and scalable business requirement for Start-up route

SU 5.1.   An applicant will meet the innovative, viable and scalable business venture requirement if all the following requirements are met:

(a)   the applicant has a genuine, original business plan that meets new or existing market needs and/or creates a competitive advantage; and

(b)   the applicant's business plan is realistic and achievable based on the applicant's available resources; and

(c)   the applicant has, or is actively developing, the necessary skills, knowledge, experience and market awareness to successfully run the business; and

(d)   there is evidence of structured planning and of potential for job creation and growth into national markets.

No other established business in the UK requirement for Start-up route

SU 6.1.   The applicant must not have previously established any business in the UK which commenced trading, unless this business commenced trading during the applicant's last period of permission and that permission was for any of the following routes:

(a)   Start-up; or

(b)   Tier 1 (Graduate Entrepreneur); or

(c)   Student on the doctorate extension scheme.

Genuine Start-up requirement

SU 7.1.   The applicant must be a genuine Start-up applicant.

Financial requirement for the Start-up route

SU 8.1.   If the applicant is applying for permission to stay and has been living in the UK with permission for 12 months or more on the date of application, they will meet the financial requirement and do not need to show funds.

SU 8.2.   If an applicant is applying for entry clearance or has been in the UK for less than 12 months at the date of application, they must have funds of at least £1,270.

SU 8.3.   The applicant must show that they have held the required level of funds for a 28 day period and as set out in Appendix Finance unless their endorsing body confirms they have been awarded funding of at least the amount in SU 8.2.

English language requirement for the Start-up route

SU 9.1.   The applicant must show English language ability on the Common European Framework of Reference for Languages in all 4 components (reading, writing, speaking and listening) of at least level B2.

SU 9.2.   The applicant must show they meet the English language requirement as specified in Appendix English Language.

Endorsement requirement for the Start-up route

SU 10.1. The applicant must provide a letter from their endorsing body which includes all the following information:

(a) the name of the endorsing body; and

(b) the endorsement reference number; and

(c) the name, telephone number, email and workplace address of a person at the endorsing body who will verify the contents of the letter to the Home Office if requested; and

(d) the date of endorsement; and

(e) the applicant's name, date of birth, nationality and passport or other travel document number; and

(f) a short description of the applicant's business venture and the main products or services it will provide to its customers; and

(g) confirmation that in the view of the endorsing body the applicant's business is innovative, viable and scalable as set out at SU 5.1.; and

(h) confirmation that the endorsing body is satisfied that the applicant will spend the majority of their working time in the UK on developing their business venture; and

(i) confirmation that the endorsing body is satisfied the applicant is either the sole founder of the business or an instrumental member of the founding team; and

(j) confirmation the endorsing body is satisfied that the applicant has created and is relying on their own business plan.

Decision on the Start-up route

SU 11.1. If the decision- maker is satisfied that all the suitability and eligibility requirements are met for the Start-up route, the application will be granted, otherwise the application will be refused.

SU 11.2. If the application is refused the person can apply for Administrative Review under Appendix AR: Administrative Review.

Conditions and period of grant on the Start-up route

SU 12.1. The grant will be subject to all the following conditions:

(a) no access to public funds; and

(b) work (including self-employment and voluntary work) permitted except for employment as a professional sportsperson, including as a sports coach; and

(c) study is permitted, subject to the ATAS condition in Appendix ATAS; and

(d) if Part 10 applies the applicant will be required to register with the police.

SU 12.2. The applicant will be granted permission for a maximum period of 2 years, and a person must not be granted further permission which would result in them spending more than 2 years with permission on the Start-up route, or a combination of the Start-up route and the Tier 1 (Graduate Entrepreneur) route.

Dependants on the Start-up route

Validity requirements for a dependent partner or dependent child on the Start-up route

SU 13.1. An application as a partner or child on the Start-up route must be made online on the gov.uk website on the specified form as follows:

Applicant	Specified form
EEA national with a chipped passport	Either (as applicable): • Dependant partner or dependant child using the UK Immigration: ID Check app; or • the forms listed below for dependant applicants outside or inside the UK as relevant.
Applicants outside the UK	Dependant partner visa Dependant child visa
Applicants inside the UK	If the dependant is applying at the same time as the Start-Up route applicant, they can be included in the form "Start-Up or Innovator permission to stay" where the form allows dependants to be added.
Otherwise:	- Dependant partner - Dependant child

SU 13.2.   An application for entry clearance or permission to stay as a dependent partner or dependent child on the Start-up route must meet all the following requirements:

(a)   any fee and Immigration Health Charge must have been paid; and

(b)   the applicant must have provided any required biometrics; and

(c)   the applicant must have provided a passport or other travel document which satisfactorily establishes their identity and nationality.

SU 13.3.   A person applying as a dependent partner must be aged 18 or over on the date of application.

SU 13.4.   DELETED

SU 13.5.   A person applying for permission to stay must be in the UK and must not have, or have last been granted, permission:

(a)   as a Visitor; or

(b)   as a Short-term Student; or

(c)   as a Parent of a Child Student; or

(d)   as a Seasonal Worker; or

(e)   as a domestic worker in a private household; or

(f)   outside the Immigration Rules.

SU 13.6.   An application which does not meet all the validity requirements is invalid and may be rejected and not considered.

Suitability requirements for a dependent partner or dependent child on the Start-up route

SU 14.1.   The suitability requirements for a partner or child on the Start-up route are that they must not fall for refusal under Part 9: grounds for refusal.

SU 14.2.   If applying for permission to stay the applicant must not be:

(a)   in breach of immigration laws, except that where paragraph 39E applies, that period of overstaying will be disregarded; or

(b)   on immigration bail.

Eligibility requirements for a dependent partner and dependent child on the Start-up route

Entry requirement for a dependent partner and dependent child on the Start-up route

SU 15.1.   A person seeking to come to the UK as a partner or child must apply for and obtain entry clearance as a partner or child before they arrive in the UK.

SU 15.2.   A person applying for entry clearance as a partner or child on the Start-up route must, if paragraph A39 and Appendix T of these rules apply, provide a valid medical certificate confirming that they have undergone screening for active pulmonary tuberculosis and that this tuberculosis is not present in them.

Relationship requirements for a dependent partner on the Start-up route

SU 16.1.   The applicant must be the partner of a person (P) and one of the following must apply:

(a)   P has permission on the Start-up route; or

(b)   P is, at the same time, applying for (and is granted) permission on the Start-up route.

SU 16.2.   If the applicant and their Start-up partner are not married or in a civil partnership, all of the following requirements must be met:

(a)   they must have been living together in a relationship similar to marriage or civil partnership for at least the 2 years before the date of application; and

(b)   any previous relationship of the applicant or their Start-up partner with another person must have permanently broken down; and

(c)   the applicant and their Start-up partner must not be so closely related that they would not be allowed to marry or form a civil partnership in the UK.

SU 16.3.   The relationship between the applicant and their Start-up partner must be genuine and subsisting.

SU 16.4.   The applicant and their Start-up partner must intend to live together throughout the applicant's stay in the UK.

Relationship requirement for a dependent child on the Start-up route

SU 17.1.   The applicant must be the child of a person (P) and one of the following must apply:

(a)   P has permission on the Start-up route; or

(b)   P is, at the same time, applying for (and is granted) entry clearance or permission on the Start-up route.

SU 17.2.   The applicant's parents must each be either applying at the same time as the applicant, or have permission to be in the UK (other than as a Visitor) unless:

(a)   the parent applying for or with entry clearance or permission to stay on the Start-up route is the sole surviving parent; or

(b)   the parent applying for or with entry clearance or permission to stay on the Start-up route has sole responsibility for the child's upbringing; or

(c)   the parent who does not have permission on the Start-up route –

(i)   is a British citizen or a person who has a right to enter or stay in the UK without restriction; and

(ii)   is or will be ordinarily resident in the UK.

(d)   the decision maker is satisfied that there are serious and compelling reasons to grant the child entry clearance or permission to stay with the parent who is applying for or has entry clearance or permission on the Start-up route.

Care requirement for a dependent child on the Start-up route

SU 18.1.   If the applicant is under the age of 18 on the date of application, there must be suitable arrangements for the child's care and accommodation in the UK, which must comply with relevant UK legislation and regulations.

Age requirement for a dependent child on the Start-up route

SU 19.1.   The child must be under the age of 18 at the date of application, unless they were last granted permission as the dependent child of their parent or parents.

SU 19.2.   If the applicant is aged 16 or over at the date of application, they must not be leading an independent life.

Financial requirement for a dependent partner or dependent child on the Start-up route

SU 20.1.   If the applicant is applying for permission to stay and has been living in the UK with permission for 12 months or longer on the date of application, they will meet the financial requirement and do not need to show funds.

SU 20.2A.   The funds required are:

(a)   £285 for a dependent partner in the UK, or applying for entry clearance; and

(b)   £315 for the first dependent child in the UK, or applying for entry clearance; and

(c)   £200 for any other dependent child in the UK, or applying for entry clearance.

SU 20.3.   The funds must be in addition to any funds required by the Start-up applicant to meet the financial requirement and for any dependants in the UK or applying at the same time.

SU 20.4.   The required level of funds must have been held for a 28-day period and as set out in Appendix Finance.

Decision on application for a dependent partner and dependent child on the Start-up route

SU 21.1.   If the decision maker is satisfied that all the suitability and eligibility requirements are met for a dependent partner or dependent child on the Start-up route the application will be granted, otherwise the application will be refused.

SU 21.2.   If the application is refused the person can apply for an Administrative Review under Appendix AR: Administrative Review.

Period and conditions of grant for a dependent partner and dependent child on the Start-up route

SU 22.1.   A partner will be granted permission which ends on the same date as their partner's permission on the Start-up route

SU 22.2.   A child will be granted permission which ends on the same date as whichever of their parents' permission ends first.

SU 22.3.   The grant will be subject to all the following conditions: *(a) no access to public funds; and

(b)   work (including self-employment and voluntary work) permitted; except for employment as a professional sportsperson, including as a sports coach; and

(c)   study is permitted, subject to the ATAs condition in Appendix ATAS; and

(d)   if Part 10 applies the applicant will be required to register with the police.

Appendix Student

Student route

This route is for a person aged 16 or over who wants to study with a sponsor on a course of further or higher education, a pre-sessional English course, a recognised foundation programme, or to take an elected post as a Student Union Sabbatical Officer.

The register of licensed student sponsors can be found at: www.gov.uk/government/publications/register-of-licensed-sponsors-students

A person who is aged 16 or 17 and wants to study with a sponsor that is an Independent School on a course at Regulated Qualifications Framework 3 or Scottish Credit and Qualifications Framework 6 and above can apply as either a Student or as a Child Student (see Appendix Child Student).

A person who wants to study a course for 6 months or less without a student sponsor but with an accredited provider should apply under Appendix V: Visitor. A person aged 16 or over who wants to study an English Language course of 11 months or less without a student sponsor but with an accredited provider, should apply under Appendix Short-term Student.

Some Students can bring a dependent partner and dependent children to the UK, for example if they are studying at postgraduate level or on a government sponsored scheme.

The Student route is not a route to settlement.

Validity requirements for a Student

A person applying for entry clearance or permission to stay as a Student must apply on the specified form on the gov.uk website as follows:

(a)   for out of country, form "Student visa"; or

(b)   for in country, form "Student".

ST 1.2.   An application for entry clearance or permission to stay as a Student must meet all the following requirements:

(a)   any fee and Immigration Health Charge must have been paid; and

(b)   the applicant must have provided any required biometrics; and

(c)   the applicant must have provided a passport or other travel document which satisfactorily establishes their identity and nationality; and

(d)   the applicant must provide a Confirmation of Acceptance for Studies reference number that was issued to them no more than 6 months before the date of application.

ST 1.3.   If the applicant has, in the last 12 months before the date of application, completed a course of studies in the UK for which they have been awarded a scholarship or sponsorship by a Government or international scholarship agency covering both fees and living costs for study in the UK, they must provide written consent in relation to the application from that Government or agency.

ST 1.4.   An applicant who is in the UK on the date of application must not have, or have last been granted, permission:

(a)   as a Visitor; or

(b)   as a Short-term Student; or

(c)   as a Parent of a Child Student; or

(d)   as a Seasonal Worker; or

(e)   as a Domestic Worker in a Private Household; or

(f)   outside the Immigration Rules.

ST 1.5.   The applicant must be at least 16 years old on the date of application.

ST 1.6.   An application which does not meet all the validity requirements for a Student is invalid and may be rejected and not considered.

Suitability requirements for a Student

ST2.1.   The applicant must not fall for refusal under Part 9: grounds for refusal.

ST2.2.   If the applicant is applying for permission to stay, they must not be:

(a)   in the UK in breach of immigration laws, except that where paragraph 39E applies, that period of overstaying will be disregarded; or

(b)   on immigration bail.

Eligibility requirements for a Student

Entry requirements for a Student

ST 3.1.   A person seeking to come to the UK as a Student must apply for and obtain entry clearance as a Student before they arrive in the UK.

ST 3.2.   A person applying for entry clearance as a Student must, if paragraph A39 and Appendix T of these rules apply, provide a valid medical certificate confirming that they have undergone screening for active pulmonary tuberculosis and that this tuberculosis is not present in them.

Date of application requirement for a Student

ST 4.1.   An application for entry clearance must be made no more than 6 months before the start date of the course stated on the Confirmation of Acceptance for Studies.

ST 4.2.   An application for permission to stay must be made no more than 3 months before the start date of the course on the Confirmation of Acceptance for Studies.

ST 4.3.   An application for permission to stay must be for study on a course with a start date no more than 28 days after the expiry date of the applicant's previous permission.

Genuine Student requirement

ST 5.1.   The applicant must be a genuine student.

Points requirement for a Student

ST 6.1.   The applicant must be awarded a total of 70 points based on the table below.

Points type	Relevant requirements to be met	Number of points
Study (must meet all)	• Confirmation of Acceptance for Studies requirement	50
	• Course requirement	
	• Approved qualification requirement	
	• Level of study requirement	
	• Place of study requirement	
Financial	• Financial requirement	10
English language	• English language requirement	10

Confirmation of Acceptance for Studies requirement

ST 7.1.   The Confirmation of Acceptance for Studies must have been issued by a student sponsor whose licence is still valid on the date on which the application is decided.

ST 7.2.   The Confirmation of Acceptance for Studies must not have been used in a previous application which was either granted or refused (but could have been relied on in a previous application which was rejected as invalid, made void or withdrawn).

ST 7.3.   The student sponsor must not have withdrawn the offer to the applicant after the date that the Confirmation of Acceptance for Studies was issued.

ST 7.4.   The Confirmation of Acceptance for Studies must contain the necessary information to confirm all the following requirements are met:

(a)   the course requirement; and

(b)   the approved qualification requirement; and

(c)   the level of study requirement; and

(d)   the place of study requirement.

ST 7.5.   The Confirmation of Acceptance for Studies must state the cost of any accommodation provided by the sponsors and fees (and any payment already made) so that the financial requirement can be assessed.

ST 7.6.   The Confirmation of Acceptance for Studies must show how the English language requirement has been met, and where the sponsor has assessed the applicant's English language ability, must include the information in ST 13.3. and ST 13.4.

Course requirement for a Student

ST 8.1.   The application must be for a single course of study that meets the requirements in ST 8.2. unless it is one of the following:

(a)   a combined pre-sessional course which meets the requirements in ST 15.1. to 15.3.; or

(b)   a full-time, salaried, elected executive position as a Student Union Sabbatical Officer, where the applicant is either part-way through their studies or will fill the position in the academic year immediately after their graduation

ST 8.2.   The application must be for a course which is one of the following:

(a)   a full-time course at degree level or above that leads to an approved qualification; or

(b)   a full-time course below degree level involving a minimum of 15 hours per week of classroom-based daytime study (08:00 to 18:00, Monday to Friday) that leads to an approved qualification; or

(c)   a full-time course involving a minimum of 15 hours per week of classroom-based daytime study that is a pre-sessional course; or

(d)   a part-time course above degree level that leads to an approved qualification where the Confirmation of Acceptance for Studies has been issued by a higher education provider with a track record of compliance; or

(e)   a full-time course at degree level or above that is recognised by UK NARIC as being equivalent to a UK higher education course where the Confirmation of Acceptance for Studies has been assigned by an overseas higher education institution or a higher education provider with a track record of compliance.

ST 8.3.   If the course is an Association of Certified Chartered Accountants (ACCA) qualification or an ACCA Foundations in Accountancy qualification, the student sponsor must be an ACCA approved learning partner – student tuition at either Gold or Platinum level.

ST 8.4.   If the Academic Technology Approval Scheme (ATAS) requirement in Appendix ATAS applies, the applicant must have a valid ATAS certificate and provide it with the application.

Approved qualification requirement for a Student

ST 9.1.   The course of study, unless it is a pre-sessional course, must lead to an approved qualification which is one of the following:

(a)   validated by Royal Charter; or

(b)   awarded by a UK recognised body; or

(c)   covered by a legal agreement between a UK recognised body and another education provider or awarding body, which confirms both:

    (i)   the UK recognised body's independent assessment of the level of the student sponsor's or awarding body's programme compared to the Regulated Qualifications Framework or its equivalents; and

    (ii)   that the UK recognised body would admit any student who successfully completes the education provider's or the awarding body's named course onto a specific or a range of degree-level courses it provides; or

(d)   recognised by one or more recognised bodies through a formal articulation agreement with the awarding body; or

(e)   in England, Wales and Northern Ireland, is at Regulated Qualifications Framework level 3 or above; or in Scotland is accredited at Scottish Credit and Qualifications Framework level 6 or above; or

(f)   an overseas qualification that Ecctis assesses as valid and equivalent to Regulated Qualifications Framework level 3 or above; or

(g)   an aviation licence, rating or certificate issued by the UK's Civil Aviation Authority.

Level of study requirement for a Student

ST 10.1.   If the Confirmation of Acceptance for Studies has been assigned by a probationary sponsor, the course must meet one of the following requirements unless it is a pre-sessional course:

(a)   the course will be studied in England, Wales or Northern Ireland, and the applicant is aged under 18, and the course is at Regulated Qualifications Framework level 3 or above; or

(b)   the course will be studied in England, Wales or Northern Ireland, and the applicant is aged 18 or over, and the course is at Regulated Qualifications Framework level 4 or above; or

(c)   the course will be studied in Scotland, and the applicant is aged under 18, and the course is at Scottish Credit and Qualifications Framework level 6 or above; or

(d)   the course will be studied in Scotland, and the applicant is aged 18 or over and the course is at Scottish Credit and Qualifications Framework level 7 or above.

ST 10.2.   If the Confirmation of Acceptance for Studies has been assigned by a student sponsor, the course must meet one of the following requirements:

    (a)   the course will be studied in England, Wales or Northern Ireland and it is at Regulated Qualifications Framework level 3 or above; or

    (b)   the course will be studied in Scotland and it is at Scottish Credit and Qualifications Framework level 6 or above; or

    (c)   the course is a short-term study abroad programme in the UK as part of the applicant's qualification at an overseas higher education institution outside of the UK, and that qualification is recognised as being at UK bachelor's degree level or above by Ecctis; or

    (d)   the course is a pre-sessional course in English language at level B2 or above of the Common European Framework of Reference for Languages; or

    (e)   the course is a recognised Foundation Programme for postgraduate doctors or dentists; or

    (f)   the course is being delivered under a partnership between a higher education institution and a research institute and is accredited at Regulated Qualifications Framework level 7 or above, or at Scottish Credit and Qualifications Framework Level 11 or above.

Place of study requirement for a Student

ST 11.1.   All study that forms part of the course of study must take place on the premises of the student sponsor or a partner institution unless the applicant is on a course-related work placement, a study abroad programme overseas, or a pre-sessional course.

Financial requirement for a Student

ST 12.1.   If the applicant is applying for permission to stay and has been living in the UK with permission for 12 months or more on the date of application, they will meet the financial requirement and do not need to show funds.

ST 12.2.   If the applicant is applying for entry clearance or permission to stay and is applying as a Student Union Sabbatical Officer or to study on a recognised foundation programme as a doctor or dentist in training, they will meet the financial requirement and do not need to show funds.

ST 12.3.   If ST 12.2. does not apply, and the applicant is applying for entry clearance, or is applying for permission to stay and has been in the UK with permission for less than 12 months, the applicant must have the following funds:

    (a)   Studying in London

Type of Study	Funds required
Residential Independent School	Sufficient funds to pay outstanding fees (course fees and boarding fees) for one academic year
All other cases	Sufficient funds to pay any outstanding course fees as stated on the Confirmation of Acceptance for Studies, and £1334 for each month of the course (up to a maximum of 9 months)

    (b)   Studying outside London

Type of Study	Funds required
Residential Independent School	Sufficient funds to pay outstanding fees (course fees and boarding fees) for one academic year
All other cases	Sufficient funds to pay any outstanding course fees as stated on the Confirmation of Acceptance for Studies, and £1023 for each month of the course (up to a maximum of 9 months)

If the length of the applicant's course includes a part of a month, the time period will be rounded up to the next full month.

ST 12.4.   If the applicant has paid a deposit to the student sponsor for accommodation arranged by the sponsor, this deposit (up to a maximum of £1334) can be offset against the funds required in ST 12.3.

ST 12.5.   If the applicant has paid all or part of their course fees to their student sponsor this must be confirmed on the Confirmation of Acceptance for Studies, or the applicant must provide a receipt issued by the student sponsor confirming the amount of fees paid.

ST 12.6.   Unless the applicant is relying on a student loan or on official financial sponsorship such as an award from a Government or international scholarship agency, they must show that they have held the required level of funds for a 28-day period and as specified in Appendix Finance.

ST.12.7. If the funds held in the applicant's account on the date of decision fall substantially below the level of funds required at ST.12.3, the decision maker must be satisfied that the spent funds have been in part used to pay outstanding course fees or a deposit for accommodation.

English language requirement for a Student

ST 13.1. The applicant must show English language ability on the Common European Framework of Reference for Languages in all 4 components (reading, writing, speaking and listening) of at least:

(a) level B2, where the applicant is studying a course at UK bachelor's degree level or above; or

(b) level B1, where the applicant is studying a pre-sessional course or a course below UK bachelor's degree level.

ST 13.2. The applicant must show they meet the English language requirement as specified in Appendix English Language.

ST 13.3. Where the student sponsor has assessed that the applicant meets the English language requirement, they must state this and the method of assessment on the Confirmation of Acceptance for Studies.

ST 13.4. Where a Secure English Language Test is required, the name of the test provider, the unique reference number for the test and the score for each component tested (reading, writing, listening, speaking) must be included on the Confirmation of Acceptance for Studies.

Academic Progress requirement for a Student

ST 14.1. An applicant who has, or previously had, permission as a Student and is applying for permission to stay as a Student must have successfully completed the course of study for which they were last granted permission as a Student, or one of the following applies:

(a) one of the exceptions in ST 14.4.; or

(b) they are applying to progress to a higher level course as specified in ST 14.3.(a) or (b).; or

(c) they have successfully completed the course of study with their sponsor where the change of course was allowed without applying for further permission on the Student route.

ST 14.2. An applicant who has, or previously had, permission on the Student route and is applying for permission to stay as a Student must show academic progress from the previous courses of study unless one of the exceptions in ST 14.4. applies.

ST 14.3. An applicant will show academic progress if they are applying for any of the following:

(a) to progress from a bachelor's to master's level course which is part of an integrated master's course, where the applicant has been offered a place on a higher-level course by the student sponsor after an assessment of their academic ability; or

(b) to progress from a master's degree to a PhD which is part of an integrated master's and PhD programme, where the applicant has been offered a place on a higher-level course by the student sponsor after an assessment of their academic ability; or

(c) a course which is above the level of the previous course of study for which they were last granted permission unless:

(i) the student sponsor is a higher education provider with a track record of compliance; and

(ii) the course is at degree level or above; and

(iii) the new course is at the same level as the previous course of study; and

(iv) the student sponsor confirms that either:

(a) the new course of study is related to the applicant's previous course of study (meaning that it is either connected to the previous course, part of the same subject group, or involves deeper specialisation); or

(b) the combination of the previous course of study and the new course of study support the applicant's genuine career aspirations.

(c) the applicant has left an integrated master's or PhD programme having successfully completed the course leading to the award of the lower level qualification which formed a part of that programme.

ST 14.4. An applicant does not need to show academic progress where they:

(a) are applying to re-sit examinations or repeat modules under ST 14.5.; or

(b) have previously re-sat examinations or repeated modules under ST 14.5. and are applying to complete the course for which those examinations were re-sat or modules repeated; or

(c)   are applying to continue studying with their current student sponsor for the purpose of completing the PhD or other doctoral qualification for which study was undertaken during their last period of permission as a Student; or

(d)   are making an application to move to a new student sponsor to complete a course of study begun at a student sponsor that has subsequently had its licence revoked; or

(e)   are applying to undertake a role as a Student Union Sabbatical Officer; or

(f)   after undertaking a period as a Student Union Sabbatical Officer are applying to complete the qualification for which the Confirmation of Acceptance for Studies was assigned before that period; or

(g)   are applying for permission to stay or as a postgraduate doctor or dentist on a recognised Foundation Programme; or

(h)   are applying to undertake an intercalated bachelor's or master's degree course or PhD where they are studying medicine, veterinary medicine and science, or dentistry as their principal course of study, or to complete their principal course, having completed a period of intercalation; or

(i)   are applying to undertake a study abroad programme or work placement which is both integral to and assessed as part of the course, or to complete their course, having completed a study abroad programme or work placement.

ST 14.5.   If the applicant is re-sitting examinations or repeating a module of a course, the applicant must not previously have re-sat the same examination or repeated the same module, more than once (they can only do so twice), unless the sponsor is a student sponsor (and is not a probationary sponsor).

Combined Pre-sessional Course requirement for a Student

ST 15.1.   A single Confirmation of Acceptance for Studies can be assigned for a combined pre-sessional course and a main course at degree level or above by a higher education provider with a track record of compliance if:

(a)   the pre-sessional course lasts no longer than 3 months; and

(b)   the main course will begin no more than 1 month after the pre-sessional course ends.

ST 15.2.   If the applicant has been assessed as having language ability of at least level B2 in order to meet the English language requirement at ST 13.1., the Confirmation of Acceptance for Studies must confirm that the applicant has an unconditional offer of a place on the main course.

ST 15.3.   If the applicant has been assessed (which must be by a method other than assessment by the student sponsor) as having language ability of at least level B1 in order to meet the English language requirement at ST 13.1., the Confirmation of Acceptance for Studies must confirm that the student sponsor is satisfied that the applicant will have at least level B2 at the end of the pre-sessional course.

Postgraduate Doctor or Dentist requirement

ST 16.1.   If the applicant is applying to be a postgraduate doctor or dentist on a recognised Foundation Programme, they must have both:

(a)   successfully completed a recognised UK bachelor's degree or above in medicine or dentistry; and

(b)   previously been granted permission as a Student, for at least two academic years, which must include the final year, of their UK bachelor's degree or above in medicine or dentistry.

Work Placement requirement

ST 17.1.   A course that includes a work placement must lead to an approved qualification and the Confirmation of Acceptance for Studies must be assigned by a student sponsor (who is not a probationary sponsor) if the course of study is below degree level.

ST 17.2.   A work placement must be assessed as an integral part of the course and must not be longer than one third of the total length of the course, except when there is a statutory requirement that it must be so, or where ST 17.3. applies.

ST 17.3.   A work placement on a course that is at degree level or above at a higher education provider with a track record of compliance or at an overseas higher education institution must not be longer than half of the total length of the course.

ST 18.1.   DELETED

ST 18.2.   DELETED

Maximum period of study requirement for a Student

ST 19.1.   If the course is below degree level, the grant of permission must not lead to the applicant being granted more than two years' permission as a Student to study courses below degree level from the age of 18 unless ST 19.2. applies.

ST 19.2.   If the course is below degree level but is subject to a regulatory requirement by the Maritime and Coastguard Agency that the applicant must spend at least 12 months at sea as a part of that course, the grant of permission must not lead to the applicant being granted more than 3 years' permission as a Student from the age of 18 to study courses below degree level.

ST 19.3.   If the course is at degree level, the grant of permission must not lead to the applicant being granted more than five years' permission as a Student from the age of 18 to study courses at degree level unless the course of study is one of those listed at ST 19.4.

ST 19.4.   The five-year maximum period of study at degree level in ST 19.3. will not apply if the applicant has a Confirmation of Acceptance for Studies that has been assigned for a course of study in one of the following subjects:

(a)   architecture; or

(b)   medicine; or

(c)   dentistry; or

(d)   veterinary medicine and science; or

(e)   music at a music college that is a member of Conservatoires UK; or

(f)   law, where the applicant has completed a course at degree level or above and is applying for a course of study which is:

(i)   a law conversion course validated by the Solicitors Regulation Authority and the Bar Standards Board in England and Wales; or

(ii)   a Masters in Law (MLaw) in Northern Ireland; or

(iii)   an accelerated graduate LLB in Scotland.

ST 19.5.   If the applicant has previously been granted permission as a postgraduate doctor or dentist, the grant of permission to the applicant must not lead to the applicant having been granted more than 3 years' permission as a postgraduate doctor or dentist.

ST 19.6.   When calculating the period of permission granted under ST 19.1. to ST 19.5., any period of permission as a Student extended under section 3C of the Immigration Act 1971 will count towards the period of permission granted.

Documents used to obtain an offer requirement for a Student

ST 20.1.   The applicant must provide evidence of the qualifications or references they used to obtain the offer of a place on the course of study from the student sponsor, unless either:

(a)   the applicant is applying for a course of study at degree level or above and is sponsored by a higher education provider with a track record of compliance; or

(b)   ST 22.1. applies.

ST 20.2.   The evidence of each qualification must be one of the following:

(a)   the certificate(s) of qualification; or

(b)   the transcript of results; or

(c)   a print out of the qualification or transcript results from the awarding body's online checking service.

ST 20.3.   Where the applicant has provided a print out of qualifications or transcript results from the awarding body's online checking service, the decision maker may require the applicant to provide the certificate of qualification or transcript of results.

Parental consent requirement for a Student

ST 21.1.   If the applicant is aged 16 or 17, they must have written consent from:

(a)   both parents; or

(b)   one parent, if that parent has sole legal responsibility for the applicant; or

(c)   the applicant's legal guardian.

ST 21.2.   The written consent must confirm support for all of the following:

(a)   the application; and

(b)   the applicant's living and care arrangements in the UK; and

(c)   if the application is for entry clearance, the applicant's travel to, and reception arrangements in, the UK.

Differential evidence requirement for a Student

ST 22.1.   Evidence to show that the applicant meets the financial requirement and the requirement to provide documents used to obtain an offer does not need to be provided with the application (but may be required by the decision maker) if the applicant is applying from the country or territory where they are living, or from in the UK, and the applicant either:

(a)   holds a passport which shows they are registered as a British National (Overseas), or which was issued by the competent authorities of Hong Kong SAR, Macau SAR or Taiwan (which includes the number of the identification card issued by the competent authority in Taiwan); or

(b)   is a national of any of the following:

Australia

Austria

Bahrain

Barbados

Belgium

Botswana

Brazil

Brunei

Bulgaria

Cambodia

Canada

Chile

China

Croatia

Republic of Cyprus

Czech Republic

Denmark

The Dominican Republic

Estonia

Finland

France

Germany

Greece

Hungary

Iceland

Indonesia

Ireland

Italy

Japan

Kazakhstan

Kuwait

Latvia

Liechtenstein

Lithuania

Luxembourg

Malaysia

Malta

Mauritius

Mexico

Netherlands

New Zealand

Norway

Oman

Peru

Poland

Portugal

Qatar

Romania

Serbia

Singapore

Slovakia

Slovenia

South Korea

Spain

Sweden

Switzerland

Thailand

Tunisia

United Arab Emirates

United States of America

Information on the Confirmation of Acceptance for Studies requirement

ST 23.1.   The student sponsor must provide all the following information about the course of study on the Confirmation of Acceptance for Studies:

(a)   title of course; and

(b)   academic level of course; and

(c)   course start and end dates; and

(d)   hours of study per week, including confirmation on whether the course is part-time or full-time; and

(e)   the address of the main place of study; and

(f)   the cost of accommodation and fees; and

(g)   if the student sponsor has assessed the applicant by use of one or more references, details of the references assessed; and

(h)   if the course involves a work placement, details of any work placement relating to the course; and

(i)   if the course will be provided by an education provider which is not the student sponsor, details of the partner institution; and

(j)   whether the ATAS requirement in Annex ATAS applies; and

(k)   confirmation if the course is a recognised Foundation Programme for postgraduate doctors or dentists, and requires a certificate from the Postgraduate Dean; and

(l)   a statement of how the student sponsor has assessed the applicant's English language ability including, where relevant, the applicant's English language test scores in all 4 components (reading, writing, speaking and listening); and

(m)   if the course is part of a study abroad programme, the name and address of the partner institution; and

(n)   if the applicant is applying for a full-time, salaried, elected executive position as a Student Union Sabbatical Officer and is part-way through their studies or being sponsored to fill the position in the academic year immediately after their graduation; and

(o)   DELETED

(p)   if the applicant has previously been granted permission as a Student, confirmation that the new course meets the academic progress requirement from the previous course as required by ST 14.1. to ST 14.5.

Decision on application for a Student

ST 24.1.   If the decision maker is satisfied that all the suitability and eligibility requirements for a Student are met, the application will be granted; otherwise, the application will be refused.

ST 24.2.   If the application is refused, the person can apply for an Administrative Review under Appendix AR.

Period and conditions of grant for a Student

ST 25.1.   The grant of permission will be subject to the following conditions:

(a)   no access to public funds; and

(b)   no work, except as specified in ST 26; and

(c)   no study, except as specified in ST 27; and

(d)   if Part 10 applies, the person will be required to register with the police.

ST 25.2.   The applicant will be granted permission for the duration of the course as specified on the Confirmation of Acceptance for Studies plus the relevant periods specified in ST 25.3.

ST 25.3.   The period of permission granted to an applicant before the start of the course who is applying for entry clearance will be either:

(a)   the relevant period before the course date which is set out in the table below, if entry clearance is granted 1 month or more before the start date of the course; or

(b)   7 days before the intended date of travel, if entry clearance is granted less than 1 month before the start date of the course; or

(c)   with immediate effect, if entry clearance is granted less than 7 days before the intended date of travel and less than 1 month before the start date of the course.

The applicant will be granted a period of permission dependent on the type and length of course as in the table below:

Type of Course	Period granted before course start date	Period granted after course end date
A course of 12 months or longer	1 Month	4 Months
A course of 6 months or longer but shorter than 12 months	1 Month	2 Months
A pre-sessional course of less than 6 months	1 Month	1 Month
A course as a Postgraduate doctor or dentist	1 Month	1 Month
A course of less than 6 months in length which is not a pre- sessional course	7 Days	7 Days

Work Conditions for a Student

ST26.1.   The applicant will be granted permission with the following employment conditions:

Type of study	Employment conditions
Student following a full-time course of degree level or above study: • sponsored by a higher education provider with a track record of compliance; or • sponsored by an overseas higher education institution to undertake a short-term study abroad programme in the UK	20 hours per week during term-time (full- time employment permitted outside of term-time)
Student undertaking a full-time course below degree level study sponsored by a higher education provider with a track record of compliance	10 hours per week during term-time (full- time employment permitted outside of term-time)
All other study, including all part-time study	No employment permitted

ST 26.2.   Students are permitted to undertake work related to a work placement, assessed as an integral part of the course, that meets the requirements at ST 17.1. to ST 17.3.

ST 26.3.   Employment as an elected Student Union Sabbatical Officer or elected National Union of Students (NUS) position is permitted for up to 2 years if the Confirmation of Acceptance for Studies was assigned for this purpose.

ST 26.4.   DELETED

ST 26.5.   A Student is not allowed to do any of the following:

      (a)   be self-employed or engage in business activity unless ST 26.8 applies; or

      (b)   work as a professional sportsperson (including as a sports coach); or

      (c)   work as an entertainer; or

      (d)   work in a position which would fill a permanent full-time vacancy unless ST 26.6. applies.

ST 26.6.   If a Student has permission and makes an application for permission to stay under the Skilled Worker route, supported by a Certificate of Sponsorship assigned by a licensed sponsor, the Student can start the employment for which the Certificate of Sponsorship was assigned, for up to 3 months prior to the course completion date, provided:

      (a)   the Student is studying a full-time course of study at degree level or above with a higher education provider with a track record of compliance; and

      (b)   the application as a Skilled Worker was made when the applicant had permission as a Student; and

      (c)   a decision has not been made on the Skilled Worker application, or where a decision has been made, any Administrative Review against a refusal has not been finally determined.

ST 26.7.   A Student may be employed as a postgraduate doctor or dentist if they are on a recognised Foundation Programme.

ST 26.8.   A Student may be self-employed, if:

      (a)   they have applied for permission on the Start-up route; and

      (b)   that application is supported by an endorsement from a Start-up route endorsing body which is a higher education provider with a track record of compliance; and

      (c)   the application was made when the applicant had permission as a Student; and

      (d)   a decision has not been made on the application, or where the application has been refused, any Administrative Review against a refusal has not been finally determined.

Study Conditions

ST 27.1.   A Student must only study with the student sponsor which assigned the Confirmation of Acceptance for Studies unless either:

      (a)   the Student is studying at a partner institution of their student sponsor; or

      (b)   the Student has made an application for permission to stay while they have permission as a Student:

          (i)   which is supported by a valid Confirmation of Acceptance for Studies assigned by a student sponsor; and

          (ii)   the application has not yet been decided, or any Administrative Review against that decision has not been determined; and

          (iii)   the Student will be studying at the student sponsor that assigned the Confirmation of Acceptance for Studies.

ST 27.2.   A Student must only study on the course of study, or courses where a combined pre- sessional course is being taken, for which the Confirmation of Acceptance for Studies was assigned unless ST 27.3. applies.

ST 27.3.   A Student may begin studying on a new course with their current student sponsor if:

      (a)   the student sponsor is a higher education provider with a track record of compliance; and

      (b)   the Student has not completed the course that the Confirmation of Acceptance for Studies was assigned for; and

      (c)   the new course is not at a lower qualification level than the course the Confirmation of Acceptance for Studies was assigned for; and

      (d)   the course is at degree level or above; and

      (e)   any new course at degree level can be completed within the current period of permission; and

      (f)   the student sponsor confirms that new course is related to the course for which the Confirmation of Acceptance for Studies was assigned or supports the Student's genuine career aspirations.

ST 27.4.   The Student may study on a study abroad programme overseas that is an integral and assessed part of the course of study named on the Confirmation of Acceptance for Studies.

ST 27.5.   Supplementary study is permitted.

ST 27.6.   Study is subject to the ATAS condition in Appendix ATAS.

ST 27.7.   The Student must not study at a State School or Academy (except for a voluntary grammar school with boarding in Northern Ireland) but if the Student has been granted permission to study at a student sponsor which becomes a State School or Academy during that period of permission the Student may complete the course for which the Confirmation of Acceptance for Studies was assigned.

Dependants of a Student

Validity requirements for a dependent partner or dependent child of a Student

ST 28.1. A person applying for entry clearance or permission to stay as a partner or child of a Student must apply on the specified form on the gov.uk website as follows:

Location of Partner or Child	Specified form
Applicant outside the UK	Dependant partner visa
	Dependant child visa
Applicant inside the UK	Dependant partner
	Dependant child

ST 28.2. An application for entry clearance or permission to stay as a partner or child of a Student must meet all the following requirements:

(a)   any fee and Immigration Health Charge must have been paid; and

(b)   the applicant must have provided any required biometrics; and

(c)   the applicant must have provided a passport or other travel document which satisfactorily establishes their identity and nationality.

ST 28.3. If the applicant has in the 12 months before the date of application been awarded a scholarship or sponsorship by a Government or international scholarship agency covering both fees and living costs for study in the UK, they must provide written consent to the application from that Government or agency.

ST 28.4. An applicant who is in the UK on the date of application must not have, or have last been granted, permission:

(a)   as a Visitor; or

(b)   as a Short-term Student; or

(c)   as a Parent of a Child Student; or

(d)   as a Seasonal Worker; or

(e)   as a Domestic Worker in a Private Household; or

(f)   outside the Immigration Rules.

ST 28.5. An application which does not meet the validity requirements for a partner or child on the Student route is invalid and may be rejected and not considered.

Suitability requirements for a dependent partner or dependent child of a Student

ST 29.1. The suitability requirements for a partner or child on the Student route are that they must not fall for refusal under Part 9: grounds for refusal.

ST 29.2. A person applying for permission to stay must not be:

(a)   in the UK in breach of immigration laws, except that where paragraph 39E applies, that period of overstaying will be disregarded; or

(b)   on immigration bail.

Eligibility requirements for a dependent partner or dependent child of a Student

Entry requirement for a dependent partner or dependent child of a Student

ST 30.1. A person seeking to come to the UK as a partner or child of a Student must apply for and obtain entry clearance as a partner or child before they arrive in the UK.

ST 30.2. A person applying for entry clearance as a partner or child of a Student must, if paragraph A39 and Appendix T of these rules apply, provide a valid medical certificate confirming that they have undergone screening for active pulmonary tuberculosis and that this tuberculosis is not present in them.

Student course requirement for a dependent partner or dependent child of a Student

ST 31.1. Unless they are a child who meets the requirements in ST 31.2., the applicant must be the partner or child of a person who is:

(a)   a Student who has received an award from a Government and has, or is applying for, permission to study on a full-time course of 6 months or longer; or

(b)   a full-time Student who has, or is applying for, permission to study a postgraduate level course of 9 months or longer at a higher education provider with a track record of compliance; or

(c)   a Student who has permission on the Doctorate Extension Scheme; or

(d)   a Student who has, or had within the last 3 months before the date of application, permission to study on a full-time course of 6 months or longer, and is now applying for permission to study a full-time course of 6 months or longer where either:

    (i)   the partner or child already has, or had within the last 3 months before the date of application, permission as a dependent partner or dependent child of the Student; or

    (ii)   the child was born since the last grant of permission to the Student, where the Student and partner or child are applying at the same time.

ST 31.2.   If the applicant is a child who does not meet the requirement at ST.31.1., they must instead meet one of the following requirements:

(a)   the applicant must have been born during the Student's current period of permission to study a full-time course of 6 months or longer and they are applying for permission during that period; or

(b)   where the Student has permission to re-sit examinations or repeat a module of a full- time course of 6 months or longer, the applicant must have been born either:

    (i)   during the Student's original period of permission; or

    (ii)   during the period of permission granted for re-sitting examinations or to repeat a module; or

(c)   the applicant must have been born no more than 3 months after the expiry of the Student's most recent permission and must be making an application for entry clearance within 6 months of the expiry of their parent's most recent permission.

Relationship requirement for dependent partner of a Student

ST 32.1.   The applicant must be the partner of a Student, or the partner of a person applying at the same time as a Student.

ST 32.2.   Both the applicant and their partner must be aged 18 or over at the date of application.

ST 32.3.   If the applicant and their partner (who must be a Student, or applying at the same time as a Student) are not married or in a civil partnership, all the following requirements must be met:

(a)   they must have been living together in a relationship similar to marriage or civil partnership for at least the 2 years before the date of application; and

(b)   any previous relationship of the applicant and their partner with another person must have permanently broken down; and

(c)   the applicant and their partner must not be so closely related that they would not have been allowed to marry in the UK.

ST 32.4.   The relationship between the applicant and their partner must be genuine and subsisting.

ST 32.5.   The applicant and their partner (who must be a Student, or applying at the same time as a Student) must intend to live together throughout the applicant's stay in the UK.

ST 32.6.   The applicant must not intend to stay in the UK beyond any permission granted to their partner (who must be a Student or applying at the same time as a Student).

Financial requirement for dependent partner of a Student

ST 33.1.   If the applicant is applying for permission to stay and has been living in the UK with permission for 12 months or longer on the date of application, they will meet the financial requirement and do not need to show funds.

ST 33.2.   If the applicant is applying for entry clearance or permission to stay, where they have been in the UK less than 12 months, the applicant or their partner (who must be a Student or applying at the same time as a Student) must have the funds specified in the table below, for a total of 9 months, or for the period of permission applied for by the applicant, whichever is the shorter.

Place of Student's study	Funds required by a dependent partner
Studying in London	£845 per month
Studying outside London	£680 per month

ST 33.3.   The funds must be in addition to the funds required for the Student to meet the financial requirement, and the funds required to meet the financial requirement for any dependent child who is applying at the same time, or is already in the UK as a dependent child of the Student.

ST 33.4.   Unless the applicant is relying on financial sponsorship from a Government or international scholarship agency that covers the living costs of the applicant and the Student, they must show that they have held the required level of funds for a 28-day period and as specified in Appendix Finance.

ST 33.5.   Unless the applicant is applying at the same time as the Student and ST 22.1. applies, the applicant must show that they have the required funds as specified in Appendix Finance.

ST.33.6.   If the funds held in the applicant's account on the date of decision fall substantially below the level of funds required at ST.33.2, the decision maker must be satisfied that the spent funds have been in part used to pay a deposit for accommodation.

Relationship requirement for dependent child of a Student

ST 34.1.   The applicant must be the child of a parent who has, or is at the same time being granted permission as:

(a)   a Student; or

(b)   the partner of a Student.

ST 34.2.   The applicant's parents must each be either applying at the same time as the applicant or have permission to be in the UK (other than as a visitor) unless:

(a)   the parent with permission as a Student or as the partner of a Student is the sole surviving parent; or

(b)   the parent with permission as a Student or as the partner of a Student has sole responsibility for the child's upbringing; or

(c)   the decision maker is satisfied that there are serious and compelling reasons to grant the child entry clearance or permission to stay with the parent who has permission as a Student or as the partner of a Student.

ST 34.3.   If the applicant is a child born in the UK to a Student or their partner, the applicant must provide a full UK birth certificate showing the names of both parents.

Care requirement for dependent child of a Student

ST 35.1.   If the applicant is aged under 18 on the date of application there must be suitable arrangements for the child's care and accommodation in the UK which must comply with relevant UK legislation and regulations.

Age requirement for a dependent child of a Student

ST 36.1.   The child must be under the age of 18 at the date of application, unless they were last granted permission as a dependent child of the parent (P) who has or is applying for entry clearance or permission to stay as a Student or as a partner of a Student (regardless of the route under which the parent (P) had permission at the time the child's last permission was granted).

ST 36.2.   If the child is aged 16 or over on the date of application, they must not be leading an independent life.

Financial requirement for dependent child of a Student

ST 37.1.   If the applicant is applying for permission to stay and has been in the UK with permission for 12 months or longer on the date of application, they will meet the financial requirement and do not need to show funds.

ST 37.2.   Where the applicant is applying for entry clearance, or permission to stay and they have been in the UK less than 12 months on the date of application, the applicant or their parent must have the funds specified in the table below, for a total of 9 months, or for the period of permission applied for by the applicant, whichever is the shorter.

Place of Student's study	Funds required for a dependent child
Studying in London	£845 per month
Studying outside London	£680 per month

ST 37.3.   The funds must be in addition to the funds required for the Student to meet the financial requirement, and the funds required for any dependant of the Student, who is applying at the same time as the applicant or is already in the UK as a dependant of the Student.

ST 37.4.   Where ST 37.2. applies, unless the applicant is relying on financial sponsorship from a Government or international scholarship agency that covers the living costs of the Student and the applicant, the required level of funds must have been held for a 28-day period and as specified in Appendix Finance.

ST.37.5.   If the funds held in the applicant's account on the date of decision fall substantially below the level of funds required at ST.37.2, the decision maker must be satisfied that the spent funds have been in part used to pay a deposit for accommodation.

Decision on application for a dependent partner or dependent child of a Student

ST 38.1.   If the decision maker is satisfied that all the suitability and eligibility requirements for the dependent partner or dependent child of a Student are met, the application will be granted, otherwise the application will be refused.

ST 38.2.   If the application is refused, the person can apply for an Administrative Review under Appendix AR.

Period and conditions of grant for a dependent partner or dependent child of a Student

ST 39.1.   A dependent partner will be granted permission which ends on the same date as the Student's permission.

ST 39.2.   A dependent child will be granted permission which ends on the same date as whichever of their parents' permission ends first.

ST 39.3.   The grant will be subject to all the following conditions:

(a)   no access to public funds; and

(b)   work (including self-employment and voluntary work) is permitted except:

(i)   where the dependant meets the requirement at ST 31.1.(d) and the Student has been granted less than 9 months' permission, unless that is to continue a course of study where they had previously been granted at least 9 months' permission; or

(ii)   where the dependant meets the requirement at ST 31.1.(d) and the Student is studying a course below degree level; or

(iii)   no employment as a professional sportsperson (including as a sports coach); and

(c)   study is permitted, subject to the ATAS condition in Appendix ATAS (if the study will commence when the partner or child is aged over 18); and

(d)   if Part 10 applies the person will be required to register with the police.

Appendix Graduate

This route is for a Student in the UK who wants to work, or look for work, following the successful completion of an eligible course of study at UK bachelor's degree-level or above. The study must have been with a higher education provider with a track record of compliance.

The Graduate route is an unsponsored route.

Individuals who already have permission as a dependant of a Student who is applying on this route can also apply to extend their permission as a dependant on this route; other types of dependants are not permitted on this route.

The Graduate route is not a route to settlement.

Validation requirements for a Graduate

GR 1.1.   A person applying for permission to stay as a Graduate must apply online on the gov.uk website on the specified form "Graduate".

GR 1.2.   An application for permission as a Graduate must meet all the following requirements:

(a)   any fee and Immigration Health Charge must have been paid; and

(b)   the applicant must have provided any required biometrics; and

(c)   the applicant must have provided a passport or other travel document which satisfactorily establishes their identity and nationality; and

(d)   the applicant must be in the UK.

GR 1.3.   The applicant must have, or have last had, permission as a Student.

GR 1.4.   The applicant must not have been previously granted permission under the Doctorate Extension Scheme or as a Graduate.

GR 1.5.   If the applicant has in the 12 months before the date of application been awarded a scholarship or sponsorship by a Government or international scholarship agency covering both fees and living costs for study in the UK, they must provide written consent to the application from that Government or agency.

GR 1.6.   An application which does not meet all the validity requirements for a Graduate is invalid and may be rejected and not considered.

Suitability requirements for a Graduate

GR 2.1.   The applicant must not fall for refusal under Part 9: grounds for refusal.

GR 2.2.   The applicant must not be:

(a)   in the UK in breach of immigration laws, except that where paragraph 39E applies, that period of overstaying will be disregarded; or

(b)   on immigration bail.

Eligibility requirements for a Graduate

Points requirement

GR 3.1.   The applicant must be awarded a total of 70 points based on the table below.

Points type	Relevant requirements to be met	Number of points
Successful course completion	• Successful completion requirement • Qualification requirement • Study in the UK requirement	70

Successful completion requirement

GR 4.1.   The applicant must have last been sponsored by a Student sponsor which is a higher education provider with a track record of compliance on the date of application.

GR 4.2.   The applicant must have successfully completed the course of study which was undertaken during their last grant of permission to study on the Student route (where the applicant was allowed to change their course of study without applying for further permission as a Student, this requirement only applies to the course to which they changed).

GR 4.3.   The student sponsor must have notified the Home Office, by the date of application, that the applicant has successfully completed the course of study in GR 4.2.

Qualification requirement

GR 5.1. The applicant will meet the qualification requirement if they have successfully completed a course of study for which they have been or will be awarded a UK bachelor's degree, a UK postgraduate degree, or successfully completed a relevant qualification listed in GR 5.2.

GR 5.2. A relevant qualification is one of the following:

(a)   a law conversion course validated by the Solicitors Regulation Authority in England and Wales; or

(b)   the Legal Practice Course in England and Wales, the Solicitors Course in Northern Ireland, or a Diploma in Professional Legal Practice in Scotland; or

(c)   the Bar Practice Course in England and Wales, or the Bar Course in Northern Ireland; or

(d)   a foundation programme in Medicine or Dentistry; or

(e)   a Postgraduate Certificate in Education (PGCE) or Postgraduate Diploma in Education (PGDE); or

(f)   a professional course requiring study at UK bachelor's degree level or above in a profession with reserved activities that is regulated by UK law or UK public authority.

GR 5.3. If the name of the applicant's course of study was changed by the Student sponsor, but the course content remained the same, or if an integral and assessed work placement or permitted study abroad programme was added, this will not prevent the applicant being able to meet the qualification requirement.

GR 5.4. The qualification must have been gained during the last grant of permission to study as a Student, or in the period of permission immediately before the applicant's last grant of permission, if the last grant of permission was to undertake a role as a Student Union Sabbatical Officer.

Study in the UK requirement

GR 6.1. The applicant must have studied in the UK for a minimum period of the course for which they were last granted permission to study on the Student route (the relevant period), as in the table below.

Total length of course	Relevant period of Student permission granted during which all study took place in the UK (apart from permitted study abroad programmes)
12 months or less	Full duration of course
Longer than 12 months	At least 12 months

GR 6.2. Where distance learning took place overseas between 24 January 2020 and 27 September 2021, this will not prevent the applicant meeting the requirement to spend the relevant period at GR 6.1. studying in the UK if:

(a)   they began their course in 2020 and entered the UK on or before 21 June 2021 and complete that course of study in the UK with permission as a Student; or

(b)   they began their course in 2021 and entered the UK before 27 September 2021 and complete that course of study in the UK with permission as a Student.

GR 6.3. Any period of distance learning between 24 January 2020 and 27 September 2021 as part of a course of study lasting longer than 12 months whilst the applicant held permission as a Student, will not prevent the applicant from meeting the requirement to spend the relevant period at GR 6.1. studying in the UK.

Decision on application as a Graduate

GR 7.1. If the decision maker is satisfied that all the suitability and eligibility requirements for a Graduate are met the application will be granted, otherwise the application will be refused.

GR 7.2. If the application is refused, the person can apply for an Administrative Review under Appendix AR: Administrative Review.

Period and conditions of grant for a Graduate

GR 8.1. The applicant will be granted the period of permission as set out in the table below dependent on how they met the qualification requirement.

Type of Qualification	Period granted from date of decision
PhD or other doctoral qualification	3 years
All other qualifications	2 years

GR 8.2. The grant will be subject to all the following conditions:

(a)   no access to public funds; and

(b)   work (including self-employment and voluntary work) is permitted, apart from work as a professional sportsperson; and

(c)   study is permitted, except study with an education provider which is a Student sponsor, and which would meet the approved qualification and level of study requirements of the Student route which are set out in Appendix Student; and

(d)   study is subject to the ATAS condition in Appendix ATAS; and

(e)   if Part 10 applies the person will be required to register with the police.

Dependants of a Graduate

Validity requirements for a dependent partner or dependent child of a Graduate

GR 9.1.   A person applying for permission to stay as a partner or child of a Graduate must apply on the specified form on the gov.uk website as follows:

Either (as applicable):

Dependant partner

Dependant child

GR 9.2.   An application for permission to stay as a partner or child of a Graduate must meet all the following requirements:

(a)   any fee and Immigration Health Charge must have been paid; and

(b)   the applicant must have provided any required biometrics; and

(c)   the applicant must have provided a passport or other travel document which satisfactorily establishes their identity and nationality.

GR 9.3.   If the applicant has in the 12 months before the date of application been awarded a scholarship or sponsorship by a Government or international scholarship agency covering both fees and living costs for study in the UK, they must provide written consent to the application from that Government or agency.

GR 9.4.   The applicant must be in the UK on the date of application and must:

(a)   have, or have last been granted, permission as a dependant partner of a Student and that Student is applying for, or has now been granted, permission to stay in the Graduate route; or

(b)   have, or have last been granted, permission as a dependant child of either a Student or dependant partner of the Student and that Student is applying for, or has now been granted, permission to stay in the Graduate route; or

(c)   be a child born in the UK during the last grant of Student permission of a Student and that Student is applying for, or has now been granted, permission to stay in the Graduate route.

GR 9.5.   An application which does not meet the validity requirements for a partner or child on the Graduate route is invalid and may be rejected and not considered.

Suitability requirements for a dependent partner or dependent child of a Graduate

GR 10.1.   The applicant must not fall for refusal under Part 9: grounds for refusal.

GR 10.2.   The applicant must not be:

(a)   in the UK in breach of immigration laws, except that where paragraph 39E applies, that period of overstaying will be disregarded; or

(b)   on immigration bail.

Eligibility requirements for a dependent partner or dependent child of a Graduate

Relationship requirement for dependent partner of a Graduate

GR 11.1.   The relationship between the applicant and their partner must be genuine and subsisting.

GR 11.2.   The applicant and their partner must intend to live together throughout the applicant's stay in the UK.

GR 11.3.   The applicant must not intend to stay in the UK beyond any permission granted to their partner.

Relationship requirement for dependent child of a Graduate

GR 12.1.   The applicant must be a child of a parent who has, or is at the same time being granted permission as:

(a)   a Graduate; or

(b)   the partner of a Graduate.

GR 12.2.   Each of the applicant's parents must either be applying at the same time as the applicant, or have permission to be in the UK (other than as a visitor) unless:

(a)   the parent with permission as a Student or Graduate or as the partner of a Student or Graduate is the sole surviving parent; or

(b)   the parent with permission as a Student or Graduate or as the partner of a Student or Graduate has sole responsibility for the child's upbringing; or

(c)   the decision maker is satisfied that there are serious and compelling reasons to grant the child permission to stay with the parent who is applying for permission as a Graduate or as partner of a Graduate.

GR 12.3.   If the applicant is a child who is born in the UK to a Student or Graduate, or their partner the applicant must provide a full UK birth certificate showing the names of both parents.

Care requirement for dependent child of a Graduate

GR 13.1.   If the applicant is aged under 18 on the date of application there must be suitable arrangements for the child's care and accommodation in the UK which must comply with relevant UK legislation and regulations.

Age requirement for a dependent child of a Graduate

GR 14.1.   The child must be under the age of 18 at the date of application, unless they were last granted permission as a dependent child of a parent (P) who has or is applying for permission to stay as a Graduate or a dependent partner of a Graduate (regardless of the route under which the parent (P) had permission at the time the child's last permission was granted).

GR 14.2.   If the child is aged 16 or over on the date of application, they must not be leading an independent life.

Decision on application for a dependent partner or dependent child of a Graduate

GR 15.1.   If the decision maker is satisfied that all the suitability and eligibility requirements for a dependent partner or dependent child of a Graduate are met, the application will be granted, otherwise the application will be refused.

GR 15.2.   If the application is refused, the person can apply for an Administrative Review under Appendix AR.

Period and conditions of grant for a dependent partner or dependent child of a Graduate

GR 16.1.   A dependent partner will be granted permission which ends on the same date as the Graduate partner's permission.

GR 16.2.   A dependent child will be granted permission which ends on the same date as whichever of their parents' permission ends first.

GR 16.3.   The grant will be subject to all the following conditions:

(a)   no access to public funds; and

(b)   work (including self-employment and voluntary work) is permitted except as a professional sportsperson (including as a sports coach); and

(c)   study is permitted, subject to the ATAS condition in Appendix ATAS (if the study will commence when the person is aged over 18); and (d) if Part 10 applies the person will be required to register with the police.

Appendix UK Ancestry

Immigration Rules for UK Ancestry

The UK Ancestry route is for a Commonwealth citizen aged 17 or over who wants to live and work in the UK and who has a grandparent who was born in the UK or Islands.

A dependent partner and dependent children can apply under this route.

UK Ancestry is a route to settlement.

Validity requirements for UK Ancestry

UKA 1.1.　A person applying for entry clearance or permission to stay on the UK Ancestry route must apply online on the gov.uk website on the specified form as follows:

(a)　for entry clearance, form "UK Ancestry, Right of Abode or Returning Residents visa"; or

(b)　for permission to stay, form "Application to extend stay in the UK: FLR(IR)".

UKA 1.2.　An application for entry clearance or permission to stay on the UK Ancestry route must meet all the following requirements:

(a)　any fee and Immigration Health Charge must have been paid; and

(b)　the applicant must have provided any required biometrics; and

(c)　the applicant must have provided a passport or other travel document which satisfactorily establishes their identity and nationality.

UKA 1.3.　The applicant must be a Commonwealth citizen.

UKA 1.4.　If applying for entry clearance, the applicant must be aged 17 or over on the date of their intended arrival in the UK.

UKA 1.5.　An applicant who is in the UK on the date of application must have previously been granted permission on the UK Ancestry route as a person with UK Ancestry.

UKA 1.6.　An application which does not meet all the validity requirements for the UK Ancestry route is invalid and may be rejected and not considered.

Suitability requirements for UK Ancestry

UKA 2.1.　The applicant must not fall for refusal under Part 9: grounds for refusal.

UKA 2.2.　If applying for permission to stay, the applicant must not be:

(a)　in breach of immigration laws, except that where paragraph 39E applies, that period of overstaying will be disregarded; or

(b)　on immigration bail.

Eligibility requirements for UK Ancestry

Entry requirements for UK Ancestry

UKA 3.1.　A person seeking to come to the UK on the UK Ancestry route must apply for and obtain entry clearance on the UK Ancestry route before they arrive in the UK.

UKA 3.2.　A person applying for entry clearance on the UK Ancestry route must, if paragraph A39 and Appendix T of these rules apply, provide a valid medical certificate confirming that they have undergone screening for active pulmonary tuberculosis and that this tuberculosis is not present in them.

Grandparent born in the UK and Islands requirement

UKA 4.1.　The applicant must have a grandparent born in the UK or Islands.

Financial requirement for UK Ancestry

UKA 5.1.　The decision maker must be satisfied that the applicant can and will adequately maintain and accommodate themselves, and any dependants in the UK, or applying for entry clearance, without recourse to public funds.

UKA 5.2.　Funds must be shown as specified in Appendix Finance.

UKA 5.3.　In assessing whether the applicant meets the financial requirement in UKA 5.1, the decision maker may take into account credible promises of financial support from a third party, such as a relative or friend of the applicant.

Work requirement for UK Ancestry

UKA 6.1.   The applicant must be able to work and intend to seek and take employment in the UK.

Parental consent requirement for UK Ancestry applicant aged under 18

UKA 7.1.   If the applicant is aged under 18 on the date of application, they must have written consent from:

(a)   both parents; or

(b)   one parent, if that parent has sole legal responsibility for the applicant; or

(c)   the applicant's legal guardian.

UKA 7.2.   The written consent must confirm support for all of the following:

(a)   the application; and

(b)   the applicant's living and care arrangements in the UK; and

(c)   if the application is for entry clearance, the applicant's travel to, and reception arrangements in, the UK.

Decision on an application for UK Ancestry

UKA 8.1.   If the decision maker is satisfied that all the suitability and eligibility requirements are met for UK Ancestry, the application will be granted, otherwise the application will be refused.

UKA 8.2.   If the application is refused the person can apply for an Administrative Review under Appendix AR: Administrative Review.

Period and conditions of grant on the UK Ancestry route

UKA 9.1.   The applicant will be granted permission for 5 years.

UKA 9.2.   The grant will be subject to all the following conditions:

(a)   no access to public funds; and

(b)   work is permitted (including self-employment); and

(c)   voluntary work is permitted; and

(d)   study is permitted, subject to the ATAS condition in Appendix ATAS; and

(e)   if Part 10 applies the applicant will be required to register with the police.

Settlement on the UK Ancestry route

Validity requirements for settlement on the UK Ancestry route

UKA 10.1.   A person on the UK Ancestry route who is applying for settlement must apply online on the gov.uk website on the specified form "Settle in the UK in various immigration categories: form SET(O)".

UKA 10.2.   An application for settlement must meet all the following requirements:

(a)   any fee must have been paid; and

(b)   the applicant must have provided any required biometrics; and

(c)   the applicant must have provided a passport or other travel document which satisfactorily establishes their identity and nationality; and

(d)   the applicant must be in the UK.

UKA 10.3.   The applicant must be a Commonwealth citizen on the date of application.

UKA 10.4.   An application which does not meet all the validity requirements for settlement on the UK Ancestry route is invalid and may be rejected and not considered.

Suitability Requirements for settlement on the UK Ancestry route

UKA 11.1.   The applicant must not fall for refusal under Part 9: grounds for refusal.

UKA 11.2.   The applicant must not be:

(a)   in breach of immigration laws, except that where paragraph 39E applies, that period of overstaying will be disregarded; or

(b)   on immigration bail.

Eligibility requirements for settlement on the UK Ancestry route

UKA 12.1.   The applicant must continue to meet the eligibility requirements of UKA 4.1 to UKA 6.1.

Qualifying period requirement for settlement on the UK Ancestry route

UKA 13.1.   The applicant must have spent 5 years in the UK with permission on the UK Ancestry route as a person with UK Ancestry.

Continuous residence requirement for settlement on the UK Ancestry route

UKA 14.1.   The applicant must meet the continuous residence requirement in Appendix Continuous Residence during the period in UKA 13.1.

English language requirement for settlement on the UK Ancestry route

UKA 15.1.   Unless an exemption applies, the applicant must show English language ability on the Common European Framework of Reference for Languages in speaking and listening to at least level B1.

UKA 15.2.   The applicant must show they meet the English language requirement as specified in Appendix English Language.

Knowledge of life in the UK requirement for settlement on the UK Ancestry route

UKA 16.1.   The applicant must meet the knowledge of Life in the UK requirement as specified in Appendix KOL UK.

Decision on an application for settlement on the UK Ancestry route

UKA 17.1.   If the decision maker is satisfied all the suitability and eligibility requirements are met for settlement on the UK Ancestry route, the applicant will be granted settlement, otherwise the application will be refused.

UKA 17.2.   If the application is refused the person can apply for an Administrative Review under Appendix AR: Administrative Review.

Dependants of a person with UK Ancestry

Validity requirements for a dependent partner or dependent child on the UK Ancestry route

UKA 18.1.   A person applying for entry clearance or permission to stay as a dependent partner or dependent child on the UK Ancestry route must apply online on the gov.uk website on the specified form as follows:

    (a)   for entry clearance, "Join or accompany a family member" on the "Find and apply for other visas from outside the UK" form; or

    (b)   for permission to stay, form "Application to extend stay in the UK: FLR(IR)".

UKA 18.2.   An application for entry clearance or permission to stay as a dependent partner or dependent child on the UK Ancestry route must meet all the following requirements:

    (a)   any fee and Immigration Health Charge must have been paid; and

    (b)   the applicant must have provided any required biometrics; and

    (c)   the applicant must have provided a passport or other travel document which satisfactorily establishes their identity and nationality.

UKA 18.3.   An applicant who is applying for permission to stay must be in the UK on the date of application must not have, or have last been granted, permission:

    (a)   as a Visitor; or

    (b)   as a Short-term Student; or

    (c)   as a Parent of a Child Student; or

    (d)   as a Seasonal Worker; or

    (e)   as a Domestic Worker in a Private Household; or

    (f)   outside the Immigration Rules.

UKA 18.4.   An application which does not meet the validity requirements for a partner or child on the UK Ancestry route is invalid and may be rejected and not considered.

Suitability requirements for a dependent partner or dependent child on the UK Ancestry route

UKA 19.1.   The suitability requirements for a dependent partner or dependent child on the UK Ancestry route are that they must not fall for refusal under Part 9: grounds for refusal.

UKA 19.2.   The applicant must not be:

(a) in breach of immigration laws, except that where paragraph 39E applies, that period of overstaying will be disregarded; or

(b) on immigration bail.

Eligibility requirements for a dependent partner or dependent child on the UK Ancestry route

Entry requirement for a dependent partner or dependent child on the UK Ancestry route

UKA 20.1. A person seeking to come to the UK as a partner or child must apply for and obtain an entry clearance as a partner or child before they arrive in the UK.

UKA 20.2. A person applying for entry clearance as a partner or child on the UK Ancestry route must, if paragraph A39 and Appendix T of these rules apply, provide a valid medical certificate confirming that they have undergone screening for active pulmonary tuberculosis and that this tuberculosis is not present in them.

Relationship requirements for a partner on the UK Ancestry route

UKA 21.1. The applicant must be the partner of a person (P) and one of the following must apply:

(a) P has permission on the UK Ancestry route; or

(b) P is, at the same time, applying for (and is granted) permission on the UK Ancestry route; or

(c) if the applicant is applying for permission to stay, P is settled or has become a British citizen, providing P had permission on the UK Ancestry route when they settled.

UKA 21.2. If the applicant and the person with UK Ancestry are not married or in a civil partnership, all of the following requirements must be met:

(a) they must have been living together in a relationship similar to marriage or civil partnership for at least the two years before the date of application; and

(b) any previous relationship of the applicant or of the person with UK Ancestry with another person must have permanently broken down; and

(c) the applicant and the person with UK Ancestry must not be so closely related that they would not be allowed to marry or form a civil partnership in the UK.

UKA 21.3. The relationship between the applicant and the person with UK Ancestry must be genuine and subsisting.

UKA 21.4. The applicant and the person with UK Ancestry must intend to live together throughout the applicant's stay in the UK.

Relationship requirement for a dependent child on the UK Ancestry route

UKA 22.1. The applicant must be the child of a person (P) and one of the following must apply:

(a) P has permission on the UK Ancestry route; or

(b) P is, at the same time, applying for (and is granted) permission on the UK Ancestry route; or

(c) if the applicant is applying for permission to stay, P is settled or has become a British citizen, providing P had permission on the UK Ancestry route when they settled.

UKA 22.2. The applicant's parents must both be either applying at the same time as the applicant, or have permission to be in the UK (other than as a Visitor) unless:

(a) the parent applying for or with entry clearance or permission on the UK Ancestry route is the sole surviving parent; or

(b) the parent applying for or with entry clearance or permission on the UK Ancestry route has sole responsibility for the child's upbringing; or

(c) the parent who does not have permission on the UK Ancestry route –

(i) is a British citizen or a person who has a right to enter or stay in the UK without restriction; and

(ii) is or will be ordinarily resident in the UK; or

(d) the decision maker is satisfied that there are serious and compelling reasons to grant the child entry clearance or permission to stay with the parent who is applying for or has entry clearance or permission on the UK Ancestry route.

Care requirement for a dependent child on the UK Ancestry route

UKA 23.1. If the child is under the age of 18 on the date of application, there must be suitable arrangements for the child's care and accommodation in the UK, which must comply with relevant UK legislation and regulations.

Age requirement for a dependent child on the UK Ancestry route

UKA 24.1.   The child must be under the age of 18 on the date of application, unless they were last granted permission as the dependent child of their parent or parents.

UKA 24.2.   If the child is aged 16 or over on the date of application, they must not be leading an independent life.

Financial requirement for a partner or child on the UK Ancestry route

UKA 25.1.   The decision maker must be satisfied that there will be adequate maintenance and accommodation for the applicant, the person with UK Ancestry, and any other dependants in the UK, without recourse to public funds.

UKA 25.2.   Funds must be shown as specified in Appendix Finance.

UKA 25.3.   In assessing whether the applicant meets the financial requirement in UKA 25.1, the decision maker may take into account credible promises of financial support from a third party, such as a relative or friend of the applicant.

Decision on an application for a dependent partner and dependent child on the UK Ancestry route

UKA 26.1.   If the decision maker is satisfied that all the suitability and eligibility requirements are met for a dependent partner or dependent child on the UK Ancestry route, the application will be granted, otherwise the application will be refused.

UKA 26.2.   If the application is refused the person can apply for an Administrative Review under Appendix AR: Administrative Review.

Period and conditions of grant for a dependent partner and dependent child on the UK Ancestry route

UKA 27.1.   Unless UKA 27.2 applies, the applicant will be granted permission which ends on the same date as the person with UK Ancestry.

UKA 27.2.   If the application is for permission to stay, and the person with UK Ancestry is being, or has been, granted settlement on the UK Ancestry route, or has become a British Citizen having previously had permission on the UK Ancestry route, the applicant will be granted permission to stay for 30 months.

UKA 27.3.   The grant will be subject to all the following conditions:

(a)   no access to public funds; and

(b)   work (including self-employment and voluntary work) permitted; and

(c)   study is permitted, subject to the ATAS condition in Appendix ATAS; and

(d)   if Part 10 applies the applicant will be required to register with the police.

Settlement by a dependent partner and dependent child on the UK Ancestry route

Validity requirements for settlement by a dependent partner or dependent child on the UK Ancestry route

UKA 28.1.   A partner or child on the UK Ancestry route who is applying for settlement must apply online on the gov.uk website on the specified form "Settle in the UK in various immigration categories: form SET(O)".

UKA 28.2.   An application for settlement must meet all the following requirements:

(a)   any fee must have been paid; and

(b)   the applicant must have provided any required biometrics; and

(c)   the applicant must have provided a passport or other travel document which satisfactorily establishes their identity and nationality; and

(d)   the applicant must be in the UK.

UKA 28.3.   The applicant must not have, or have last been granted, permission:

(a)   as a Visitor; or

(b)   as a Short-term Student; or

(c)   as a Parent of a Child Student; or

(d)   as a Seasonal Worker; or

(e)   as a Domestic Worker in a Private Household; or

(f)   outside the Immigration Rules.

UKA 28.4.   An application which does not meet all the validity requirements for settlement as a partner or child on the UK Ancestry route is invalid and may be rejected and not considered.

Suitability requirements for settlement by a dependent partner and dependent child on the UK Ancestry route

UKA 29.1.   The applicant must not fall for refusal under Part 9: grounds for refusal.

UKA 29.2.   The applicant must not be:

(a)   in breach of immigration laws, except that where paragraph 39E applies, that period of overstaying will be disregarded; or

(b)   on immigration bail.

Eligibility requirements for settlement by a dependent partner or dependent child on the UK Ancestry route

Relationship requirement for settlement by a partner or child on the UK Ancestry route

UKA 30.1.   The applicant must be the partner or child of a person (P) where one of the following applies:

(a)   P is, at the same time, being granted settlement on the UK Ancestry route; or

(b)   P is settled or has become a British citizen, providing P had permission on the UK Ancestry route when they settled.

UKA 30.2.   If applying as a partner, and the applicant and the person with UK Ancestry are not married or in a civil partnership, all of the following requirements must be met:

(a)   they must have been living together in a relationship similar to marriage or civil partnership for at least the two years before the date of application; and

(b)   any previous relationship of the applicant or of the person with UK Ancestry with another person must have permanently broken down; and

(c)   the applicant and the person with UK Ancestry must not be so closely related that they would not be allowed to marry or form a civil partnership in the UK.

UKA 30.3.   The relationship between the applicant and the person with UK Ancestry must be genuine and subsisting.

UKA 30.4.   The applicant and the person with UK Ancestry must intend to live together throughout the applicant's stay in the UK.

UKA 30.5.   If applying as a child, the applicant's other parent must be being granted settlement at the same time, or be settled or a British citizen, unless:

(a)   the person (P) in UKA 30.1. is the applicant's sole surviving parent; or

(b)   the person (P) in UKA 30.1. has sole responsibility for the applicant's upbringing; or

(c)   the decision maker is satisfied that there are serious and compelling reasons to grant the applicant settlement.

Care requirement for settlement by a child on the UK Ancestry route

UKA 31.1.   If the applicant is under the age of 18 on the date of application, there must be suitable arrangements for the child's care and accommodation in the UK, which must comply with relevant UK legislation and regulations.

Age requirement for settlement by a child on the UK Ancestry route

UKA 32.1.   The child must be under the age of 18 on the date of application, unless they were last granted permission as the dependent child of their parent or parents.

UKA 32.2.   If the child is aged 16 or over on the date of application, they must not be leading an independent life.

Financial requirement for settlement for a partner or child on the UK Ancestry route

UKA 33.1.   The decision maker must be satisfied that there will be adequate maintenance and accommodation for the applicant, the person with UK Ancestry, and any other dependants in the UK, without recourse to public funds.

UKA 33.2.   Funds must be shown as specified in Appendix Finance.

UKA 33.3.   In assessing whether the applicant meets the financial requirement in UKA 33.1, the decision maker may take into account credible promises of financial support from a third party, such as a relative or friend of the applicant.

English language requirement for settlement by a partner or child on the UK Ancestry route

UKA 34.1.   Unless an exemption applies, the applicant must show English language ability on the Common European Framework of Reference for Languages in speaking and listening of at least level B1.

UKA 34.2.   The applicant must show they meet the English language requirement as specified in Appendix English Language.

Knowledge of life in the UK requirement for settlement by a partner or child on the UK Ancestry route

UKA 35.1   If the applicant is aged 18 or over at the date of application, they must meet the Knowledge of Life in the UK requirement as set out in Appendix KOL UK.

Decision on an application for settlement by a partner or child on the UK Ancestry route

UKA 36.1.   If the decision maker is satisfied all the suitability and eligibility requirements are met for settlement as a dependent partner or dependent child on the UK Ancestry route the applicant will be granted settlement, otherwise the application will be refused.

UKA 36.2.   If the application is refused the person can apply for an Administrative Review under Appendix AR: Administrative Review.

Appendix V: Visitor

Immigration Rules for Visitors

This route is for a person who wants to visit the UK for a temporary period, (usually for up to 6 months), for purposes such as tourism, visiting friends or family, carrying out a business activity, or undertaking a short course of study.

Each Visitor must meet the requirements of the Visitor route, even if they are travelling as, for example, a family group, a tour group or a school party.

A visa national as set out in Appendix Visitor: Visa National list must obtain entry clearance as a Visitor (a visit visa) before arrival in the UK.

A non-visa national can normally seek entry on arrival in the UK.

There are 4 types of Visitor:

- Standard Visitor: for those seeking to undertake the activities set out in Appendix Visitor: Permitted Activities, for example tourism and visiting family, usually for up to 6 months. A Standard Visitor may apply for a visit visa of six months, two, five or 10 years validity, however each stay in the UK must not exceed the permitted length of stay endorsed on the visit visa (usually six months).
- Marriage/Civil Partnership Visitor: for those seeking to come to the UK to marry or form a civil partnership, or give notice of marriage or civil partnership.
- Permitted Paid Engagement Visitor: for experts in their field coming to the UK to undertake specific paid engagements for up to one month.
- Transit Visitor: for those who want to transit the UK on route to another country outside the Common Travel Area and who will enter the UK for up to 48 hours by crossing the UK border unless Appendix Visitor: Transit Without Visa Scheme applies.

Visitors cannot work in the UK unless this is expressly allowed under the permitted activities set out in Appendix Visitor: Permitted Activities.

Further information of how long each Visitor can stay and what they can and cannot do in the UK is set out at V 17.2 and Appendix Visitor: Permitted Activities.

Entry requirements for Visitors

V 1.1.   A person seeking to come to the UK as a Visitor must apply for and obtain entry clearance before they arrive in the UK if they are:

(a)   a visa national, unless V 1.3. (b) applies; or

(b)   seeking to marry or form a civil partnership, or give notice of marriage or civil partnership, in the UK unless they are a "relevant national" as defined in section 62 of the Immigration Act 2014; or

(c)   seeking to come to the UK as a Visitor for more than 6 months.

V 1.2.   Within the period for which the entry clearance is valid, a Visitor may enter and leave the UK multiple times, unless the entry clearance is endorsed as single or dual entry.

V 1.3.   A person seeking to come to the UK as a Visitor may apply for permission to enter on arrival in the UK where they are:

(a)   a non-visa national, unless V 1.1. (b) or (c) apply; or

(b)   a visa national and an exception applies as set out in Appendix Visitor: Visa National list or Appendix Visitor: Transit Without Visa Scheme.

V 1.4.   A child who holds entry clearance as a Visitor on arrival in the UK must either:

(a)   hold a valid entry clearance that states they are accompanied and will be travelling with an adult identified on that entry clearance; or

(b)   hold an entry clearance which states they are unaccompanied; otherwise the child may be refused entry to the UK, unless they meet the requirements of V 5.1. and V 5.2.

Validity requirements for entry clearance or permission to stay as a Visitor

V 2.1.   A person applying for entry clearance as a Visitor must apply online on the gov.uk website on the specified form "Apply for a UK visit visa".

V 2.2.   A person applying for permission to stay as a Visitor must apply online on the gov.uk website on the specified form "Application to extend stay in the UK: FLR(IR)".

V 2.3.   An application for entry clearance or permission to stay as a Visitor must meet all the following requirements:

(a)   any fee must have been paid; and

(b)   the applicant must have provided any required biometrics; and

(c)   the applicant must have provided a passport or other document which satisfactorily establishes their identity and nationality.

V 2.4.   An application for entry clearance as a Visitor must be made while the applicant is outside the UK and to a post designated to accept such applications.

V 2.5.   An application for permission to stay as a Visitor must be made by a person:

(a)   in the UK; and

(b)   with permission as a Standard Visitor or Marriage/Civil Partnership Visitor.

V 2.6.   An application which does not meet all the validity requirements for a Visitor is invalid and may be rejected and not considered.

Suitability requirements for all Visitors

V3.1.   The applicant must not fall for refusal under Part 9: grounds for refusal.

V3.2.   If applying for permission to stay the applicant must not be: (a) in breach of immigration laws, except that where paragraph 39E applies, that period of overstaying will be disregarded; or (b) on immigration bail.

Eligibility requirements for Visitors

V 4.1.   The decision maker must be satisfied that the applicant (unless they are applying for entry clearance or permission to enter as a Transit Visitor) meets all of the eligibility requirements in V 4.2. to V 4.6. and that they meet the specified additional eligibility requirements where the applicant:

(a)   is a child at the date of application, they must also meet the additional requirements at V 5.1. and V 5.2; or

(b)   is coming to the UK under the Approved Destination Status Agreement, they must also meet the requirements at V 6.1; or

(c)   is coming to the UK to receive private medical treatment, they must also meet the additional requirements at V 7.1. to V 7.3; or

(d)   is coming to the UK as an organ donor, they must also meet the additional requirements at V 8.1. to V 8.4; or

(e)   is coming to the UK to study as a Visitor, they must also meet the additional requirements at V 9.1. to V 9.5; or

(f)   is an academic seeking a 12-month entry clearance, they must also meet the additional requirements at V 10.1; or

(g)   is coming to the UK to undertake work related training, they must also meet the additional requirements at V 11.1. to V 11.3; or

(h)   is coming to the UK to marry or form a civil partnership, or give notice of intention to marry or form a civil partnership, they must also meet the additional requirements at V 12.1. and V 12.2; or

(i)   is coming to the UK to undertake permitted paid engagements, they must also meet the additional requirements in V 13.1. to V 13.3; or

(j)   is applying for permission to stay as a Visitor, they must also meet the additional requirements at V 15.1. to V 15.4.

Genuine Visitor requirement

V 4.2.   The applicant must satisfy the decision maker that they are a genuine Visitor, which means the applicant:

(a)   will leave the UK at the end of their visit; and

(b)   will not live in the UK for extended periods through frequent or successive visits, or make the UK their main home; and

(c)   is genuinely seeking entry or stay for a purpose that is permitted under the Visitor route as set out in Appendix Visitor: Permitted Activities and at V 13.3; and

(d)   will not undertake any of the prohibited activities set out in V 4.4. to V 4.6; and

(e)   must have sufficient funds to cover all reasonable costs in relation to their visit without working or accessing public funds, including the cost of the return or onward journey, any costs relating to their dependants, and the cost of planned activities such as private medical treatment. The applicant must show that any funds they rely upon are held in a financial institution permitted under FIN 2.1 in Appendix Finance.

V 4.3.   In assessing whether an applicant has sufficient funds under V 4.2.(e), the applicant's travel, maintenance and accommodation may be provided by a third party only if that third party:

(a)   has a genuine professional or personal relationship with the applicant; and

(b)   is not, or will not be, in breach of immigration laws at the time of the decision or the applicant's entry to the UK as a Visitor; and

(c)   can and will provide support to the applicant for the intended duration of the applicant's stay as a Visitor.

Prohibited activities and payment requirements for Visitors

V 4.4.   The applicant must not intend to:

(a)   work in the UK, which includes:

(i)   taking employment in the UK; and

(ii)   doing work for an organisation or business in the UK; and

(iii)   establishing or running a business as a self-employed person; and

(iv)   doing a work placement or internship; and

(v)   direct selling to the public; and

(vi)   providing goods and services,

unless expressly allowed by the permitted activities in Appendix Visitor: Permitted Activities, Appendix Visitor: Permit Free Festival List or the Permitted Paid Engagements in V 13.3; or

(b)   study in the UK, except as permitted by Appendix Visitor: Permitted Activities (and provided they meet the relevant additional requirements for study); or

(c)   access medical treatment, other than private medical treatment or to donate an organ (for either of these activities they must meet the relevant additional eligibility requirements); or

(d)   get married or form a civil partnership, or give notice of intention to marry or form a civil partnership, unless they are applying for entry clearance as a Marriage/Civil Partnership Visitor or are a relevant national as defined in section 62 of the Immigration Act 2014.

V 4.5.   Permitted activities must not amount to the Visitor undertaking employment, or doing work which amounts to them filling a role or providing short-term cover for a role within a UK based organisation and where the Visitor is already paid and employed outside of the UK they must remain so.

V 4.6.   The Visitor must not receive payment from a UK source for any activities undertaken in the UK, except for the following:

(a)   reasonable expenses to cover the cost of their travel and subsistence, including fees for directors attending board-level meetings; or

(b)   international drivers undertaking activities permitted under PA 9.2.; or

(c)   prize money; or

(d)   billing a UK client for their time in the UK, where the Visitor's overseas employer is contracted to provide services to a UK company, and the majority of the contract work is carried out overseas (payment must be lower than the amount of the applicant's salary); or

(e)   multi-national companies who, for administrative reasons, handle payment of their employees' salaries from the UK; or

(f)   paid performances at a permit free festival as listed in Appendix Visitor: Permit Free Festivals, where the Visitor is an artist, entertainer or musician; or

(g)   Permitted Paid Engagements, where they have permission as a Permitted Paid Engagement Visitor.

Additional eligibility requirements for children

V 5.1.   Adequate arrangements must have been made for a child's travel to, reception and care in the UK.

V 5.2.   If the child is not travelling with a parent or legal guardian, based in their home country or country of ordinary residence, who is responsible for their care, that parent or legal guardian must consent to the child's travel to, reception and care in the UK and, where requested, this consent must be given in writing.

Additional eligibility requirement for Visitors under the Approved Destination Status Agreement

V 6.1.   A person applying for entry clearance as a Visitor under the Approved Destination Status Agreement must:

(a)   be a national of the People's Republic of China; and

(b)   intend to enter, leave and travel within the UK as a member of a tourist group under the Approved Destination Status Agreement.

Additional eligibility requirements for Visitors coming to the UK to receive private medical treatment

V 7.1.   If the applicant is suffering from a communicable disease they must have satisfied the medical inspector that they are not a danger to public health.

V 7.2.   The applicant must have arranged their private medical treatment before they travel to the UK, and must provide either:

(a)   a letter from their doctor or consultant in the UK detailing:

(i)   the medical condition requiring consultation or treatment; and

(ii)   the estimated costs and likely duration of any treatment, which must be of a finite duration; and

(iii)   where the consultation or treatment will take place; or

(b)   if the applicant intends to receive NHS treatment under a reciprocal healthcare arrangement between the UK and another country, an authorisation form issued by the government of that country.

V 7.3.   If the applicant is applying for an 11-month entry clearance for the purposes of private medical treatment they must also:

(a)   provide either:

(i)   evidence from their doctor or consultant in the UK that the proposed treatment is likely to exceed 6 months, but not more than 11 months; or

(ii)   if the applicant intends to receive NHS treatment under a reciprocal healthcare arrangement between the UK and another country, an authorisation form issued by the government of that country which clearly states that the proposed treatment is likely to exceed 6 months, but not more than 11 months; and

(b)   provide a valid medical certificate, if paragraph A39 and Appendix T of these rules apply, confirming that they have undergone screening for active pulmonary tuberculosis and that this tuberculosis is not present in them.

Additional eligibility requirements for Visitors coming to the UK to donate an organ

V 8.1.   The applicant must satisfy the decision maker that they genuinely intend to donate an organ to, or be assessed as a potential organ donor for, an identified recipient in the UK with whom they have a genetic or close personal relationship.

V 8.2.   The applicant must provide written confirmation of medical tests to show that they are a donor match to the identified recipient, or that they are undergoing further tests to be assessed as a potential donor to the identified recipient.

V 8.3.   The applicant must provide a letter, dated no more than 3 months before the applicant's intended date of arrival in the UK from either:

(a)   the lead nurse or coordinator of the UK NHS Trust's Living Donor Kidney Transplant team; or

(b)   a UK registered medical practitioner who holds an NHS consultant post or who appears in the Specialist Register of the General Medical Council;

which confirms that the applicant meets the requirements in V 8.1. and V 8.2. and confirms when and where the planned organ transplant or medical tests will take place.

V 8.4.   The applicant must be able to show, if required to do so, that the identified recipient is lawfully present in the UK, or will be at the time of the planned organ transplant.

Additional eligibility requirements for Visitors coming to the UK to study for up to six months

V 9.1.   Where the applicant is seeking to come to the UK to study, they must have been accepted onto a course of study that is to be provided by an Accredited Institution that is not a State Funded School or Academy.

V 9.2. The course of study referred to in V 9.1. must last no longer than six months unless the course is being undertaken from outside the UK as a Distance Learning Course.

V 9.3. Where the applicant is seeking to come to the UK for up to six months to undertake electives relevant to a course of study abroad, they must:

(a) be aged 16 or over; and

(b) be enrolled on a course of study abroad equivalent to at least degree level study in the UK; and

(c) be studying medicine, veterinary medicine and science, nursing, or dentistry as their principal course of study; and

(d) have been accepted by a UK Higher Education Provider to undertake electives relevant to their course of study provided these are unpaid and involve no treatment of patients; and

(e) provide written confirmation from the UK Higher Education Provider.

V 9.4. Where the applicant is seeking to come to the UK to undertake research or be taught about research (research tuition) for up to six months:

(a) they must be aged 16 or over; and

(b) they must be enrolled on a course of study abroad equivalent to at least degree level study in the UK; and

(c) they must have been accepted by a UK Higher Education Provider to undertake research or be taught about research (research tuition); and

(d) the overseas course provider must confirm that the research or research tuition is part of or relevant to the course of study that they are enrolled on overseas; and

(e) this must not amount to the Visitor being employed at the UK institution.

V 9.5. The research or research tuition referred to in V 9.4. may be undertaken at a UK research institute, providing a formal partnership exists between the research institute and the UK Higher Education Provider for this purpose.

Additional eligibility requirements for academics seeking to come to the UK for more than 6 months

V 10.1. An academic applying for a 12-month entry clearance must:

(a) intend to undertake one (or more) of the permitted activities in Appendix Visitor: Permitted Activities at PA 11.2. for up to 12 months; and

(b) be highly qualified within their own field of expertise; and

(c) currently be working in that field at an academic institution or institution of higher education overseas; and

(d) provide a valid medical certificate, if paragraph A39 and Appendix T of these rules apply, confirming that they have undergone screening for active pulmonary tuberculosis and that this tuberculosis is not present in them.

Additional eligibility requirements for Visitors coming to the UK for work related training

V 11.1. Where the applicant is seeking to come to the UK to undertake a clinical attachment or dental observer post as an overseas graduate from a medical, dental or nursing school, they must provide written confirmation of their offer to take up this post and confirm they have not previously undertaken this activity in the UK.

V 11.2. Where the applicant is seeking to come to the UK to take the Professional and Linguistic Assessment Board test, they must provide written confirmation of this from the General Medical Council.

V 11.3. Where the applicant is seeking to come to the UK to take the Objective Structured Clinical Examinations for overseas, they must provide written confirmation of this from the Nursing and Midwifery Council.

Additional eligibility requirement for Visitors coming to the UK for purpose of marriage or civil partnership

V 12.1. The applicant must be aged 18 or over on the date of application.

V 12.2. The applicant must, within the period for which they are seeking permission as a Visitor:

(a) intend to give notice of marriage or civil partnership in the UK; or

(b) intend to marry or form a civil partnership in the UK;

which is not a sham marriage or civil partnership.

Additional eligibility requirement for Visitors coming to the UK for Permitted Paid Engagements

V 13.1.   An applicant as a Permitted Paid Engagement Visitor must be aged 18 or over on the date of application.

V 13.2.   The applicant must intend to do one (or more) of the permitted paid engagements set out in V 13.3. which must be:

(a)   arranged before the applicant travels to the UK; and

(b)   declared as part of the application for entry clearance or permission to enter the UK; and

(c)   evidenced by a formal invitation, as required by V13.3; and

(d)   relate to the applicant's area of expertise and occupation overseas.

V 13.3.   The following are permitted paid engagements:

(a)   an academic who is highly qualified within their field of expertise, coming to examine students and/or participate in or chair selection panels, and have been invited by a UK higher education institution, or a UK-based research or arts organisation as part of that institution or organisation's quality assurance processes; and

(b)   an expert coming to give lectures in their subject area, where they have been invited by a higher education institution, or a UK-based research or arts organisation, and this does not amount to filling a teaching position for the host organisation; and

(c)   an overseas designated pilot examiner coming to assess UK-based pilots to ensure they meet the national aviation regulatory requirements of other countries, where they have been invited by an approved training organisation based in the UK that is regulated by the UK Civil Aviation Authority for that purpose; and

(d)   a qualified lawyer coming to provide advocacy for a court or tribunal hearing, arbitration or other form of dispute resolution for legal proceedings within the UK, where they have been invited by a client; and

(e)   a professional artist, entertainer, or musician coming to carry out an activity directly relating to their profession, where they have been invited by a creative (arts or entertainment) organisation, agent or broadcaster based in the UK; and

(f)   a Professional Sportsperson coming to carry out an activity directly relating to their profession, where they have been invited by a sports organisation, agent, or broadcaster based in the UK.

Eligibility requirement for Visitors coming to the UK to transit

V 14.1.   A visa national must hold entry clearance as a Standard Visitor, Marriage/Civil Partnership Visitor or Transit Visitor, unless they meet the requirements for admission under Appendix Visitor: Transit Without Visa Scheme, in which case they may apply for permission to enter on arrival in the UK.

V 14.2.   An applicant applying for entry clearance or permission to enter as a Transit Visitor must satisfy the decision maker that they:

(a)   are genuinely in transit to another country outside the Common Travel Area, meaning the main purpose of their visit is to transit the UK (passing through immigration control) and that the applicant is taking a reasonable transit route; and

(b)   will not access public funds or medical treatment, work or study in the UK; and

(c)   genuinely intend and are able to leave the UK within 48 hours after their arrival; and

(d)   are assured entry to their country of destination and any other countries they are transiting on their way there.

Additional eligibility requirements for permission to stay as a Visitor

V 15.1.   Where the applicant is applying for permission to stay as a Visitor for the purpose of receiving private medical treatment they must also:

(a)   satisfy the decision maker that the costs of any medical treatment already received have been met; and

(b)   provide either:

(i)   a letter from a registered medical practitioner, at a private practice or NHS hospital, who holds an NHS consultant post or who appears in the Specialist Register of the General Medical Council, detailing the medical condition requiring further treatment; or

(ii)   if the applicant intends to continue to receive NHS treatment under a reciprocal healthcare arrangement between the UK and another country, an authorisation form issued by the government of that country which authorises further treatment.

V 15.2. Where the applicant applying for permission to stay is an academic (or the accompanying partner or child of such an academic) they must:

(a) continue to intend to do one (or more) of the activities at Appendix Visitor: Permitted Activities at PA 11.2; and

(b) be highly qualified within their own field of expertise; and

(c) have been working in that field at an academic institution or institution of higher education overseas prior to their arrival in the UK.

V 15.3. Where the applicant is applying for permission to stay as a Visitor to resit the Professional and Linguistic Assessment Board Test, they must provide written confirmation of this from the General Medical Council.

V 15.4. Where the applicant is applying for permission to stay as a Visitor and they are an overseas graduate of a medical, dental or nursing school intending to undertake an unpaid clinical attachment or dental observer post, they must have been successful in the Professional and Linguistic Assessment Board test.

Decision

V 16.1. If the decision maker is satisfied that all the suitability requirements are met, and that the relevant eligibility requirements for a Visitor are met, the application will be granted, otherwise the application will be refused.

Period and conditions of grant for Visitors

V 17.1. The grant will be subject to all the following conditions:

(a) no access to public funds; and

(b) no work (which does not prohibit the permitted activities in Appendix Visitor: Permitted Activities, Appendix Visitor: Permit Free Festival List or the Permitted Paid Engagements in V 13.3.); and

(c) no study except where permitted by Appendix Visitor: Permitted Activities at PA 2. and PA 17.

(d) study or research as part of a permitted activity is subject to the ATAS condition in Appendix ATAS.

V 17.2. Entry clearance and permission to enter as a Visitor will be granted for the periods set out in the following table:

	Visitor type	Maximum initial length of stay in the UK
(a)	Standard visitor	up to 6 months except:
		(i) Visitor who is coming to the UK for private medical treatment may be granted entry clearance for up to 11 months;
		(ii) an academic (or the accompanying partner or child of such an academic), who is employed by an overseas institution and is carrying out the specific permitted activities at paragraph PA.11.2., may be granted entry clearance for up to 12 months;
		(iii) a Visitor under the Approved Destination Status Agreement may be granted entry clearance for up to 30 days.
(b)	Marriage / civil partnership Visitor	up to 6 months
(c)	Permitted Paid Engagement (PPE) Visitor	up to 1 month
(d)	Transit Visitor	up to 48 hours, except for permission to enter as a Transit Visitor under the Transit Without Visa Scheme which may be granted until 23:59 hours on the next day after the day the applicant arrived in the UK.

V 17.3. Permission to stay will be granted for the following periods:

(a) a Standard Visitor or a Marriage/Civil Partnership Visitor, who was granted permission for less than 6 months may be granted permission to stay for a period which results in the total period they can remain in the UK (including both the original grant and the extension) not exceeding 6 months; and

(b) a Standard Visitor who is in the UK for private medical treatment may be granted permission to stay as a Visitor for a further 6 months, provided the purpose is for private medical treatment; and

(c) a Standard Visitor who is in the UK to undertake the activities in Appendix Visitor: Permitted Activities at PA 11.2. or the accompanying partner or child of such a Standard Visitor, may be granted permission to stay for a period which results in the total period they can remain in the UK (including both the original grant and the extension) not exceeding 12 months; and

(d)   a Standard Visitor may be granted permission to stay as a Visitor for up to 6 months in order to resit the Professional and Linguistic Assessment Board Test; and

(e)   a Standard Visitor who is successful in the Professional and Linguistic Assessment Board Test may be granted permission to stay as a Visitor to undertake the activities in PA 10.1. (a) for a period which results in the total period they can remain in the UK (including both the original grant and the extension) not exceeding 18 months.

Appendix Visitor: Permit Free Festival List

List of Permit Free Festivals

PFF 1.   An artist, entertainer or musician visiting the UK to perform at one or more of the following permit free festivals may receive payment to do so:

(a)   Aldeburgh Festival

(b)   Barbican Festivals – Live from the Barbican

(c)   Belfast International Arts Festival

(d)   Billingham International Folklore Festival of World Dance

(e)   Boomtown Festival

(f)   Brass

(g)   Breakin' Convention

(h)   Brighton Festival

(i)   Brighton Fringe

(j)   Brouhaha international

(k)   BST Hyde Park

(l)   Cambridge Folk Festival

(m)   Camp Bestival

(n)   Celtic Connections

(o)   Cheltenham Festivals (Jazz, Science, Music & Literature Festivals)

(p)   Cornwall International Male Choral Festival

(q)   Dance Umbrella

(r)   Download

(s)   Edinburgh Festival Fringe

(t)   Edinburgh International Book Festival

(u)   Edinburgh International Festival

(v)   Edinburgh International Jazz and Blues Festival

(w)   Freedom Festival

(x)   Garsington Opera

(y)   Glasgow International Jazz Festival

(z)   Glastonbury

(aa)   Glyndebourne

(bb)   Greenbelt

(cc)   Green Man

(dd)   Greenwich and Docklands International Festival

(ee)   Harrogate International Festivals

(ff)   Hay Festival

(gg)   Huddersfield Contemporary Music Festival

(hh)   Isle of Wight Festival

(ii)   Latitude

(jj)   Leeds Festival

(kk)   Llangollen International Musical Eisteddfod

(ll)   London International Festival of Theatre (LIFT)

(mm)   London Jazz Festival (EFG)

(nn)   Love Supreme

(oo)   Manchester International Festival

(pp)   Meltdown (Southbank Centre)

(qq)   Norfolk & Norwich Festival

(rr)   Out There Festival

(ss)   Parklife

(tt)   Reading Festival

(uu)   Shubbak

(vv)   Snape Proms

(ww)   Southbank Centre Festivals

(xx)   The Royal Edinburgh Military Tattoo

(yy)   The Warehouse Project

(zz)   Wireless Festival

(aaa)   WOMAD

(bbb)   WWE Live

Appendix Visitor: Permitted Activities

Permitted Activities for visitors

PA 1.   Visitors are permitted to undertake the following activities:

	Visitor type	Visitors of this type can
(a)	Standard Visitor	do all permitted activities in Appendix Visitor: Permitted Activities, except Visitors under the Approved Destination Status Agreement may only do the activities in PA 2(a).
(b)	Marriage / Civil Partnership Visitor	marry or form a civil partnership, or give notice of marriage or civil partnership and do all permitted activities in Appendix Visitor: Permitted Activities, other than study as described in PA17.
(c)	Permitted Paid Engagement Visitor	do the permitted paid engagements in Appendix V: Visitor at V13.3. and all permitted activities in Appendix Visitor: Permitted Activities other than study as described in PA 17 and transit as described in PA 18.
(d)	Transit Visitor	transit the UK as described in PA 18.

Tourism and Leisure

PA 2.   A Visitor may:

(a)   visit friends and family and / or come to the UK for a holiday; and

(b)   take part in educational exchanges or visits with a state funded school or academy or independent school; and

(c)   attend recreational courses (not English Language training) for a maximum of 30 days.

Volunteering

PA 3.   A Visitor may undertake volunteering provided it lasts no more than 30 days in total and is for a charity that is registered with either the Charity Commission for England and Wales; the Charity Commission for Northern Ireland; or the Office of the Scottish Charity Regulator.

General Business Activities

PA 4.   A Visitor may:

(a)   attend meetings, conferences, seminars, interviews; and

(b)   give a one-off or short series of talks and speeches provided these are not organised as commercial events and will not make a profit for the organiser; and

(c)   negotiate and sign deals and contracts; and

(d)   attend trade fairs, for promotional work only, provided the Visitor is not directly selling; and

(e)   carry out site visits and inspections; and

(f)   gather information for their employment overseas; and

(g)   be briefed on the requirements of a UK based customer, provided any work for the customer is done outside of the UK.

Intra-corporate Activities

PA 5.   An employee of an overseas based company may:

(a)   advise and consult; and

(b)   trouble-shoot; and

(c)   provide training; and

(d)   share skills and knowledge;

on a specific internal project with UK employees of the same corporate group, provided no work is carried out directly with clients.

PA 6.   An internal auditor may carry out regulatory or financial audits at a UK branch of the same group of companies as the Visitor's employer overseas.

Manufacture and supply of goods to the UK

PA 7.   An employee of an overseas company may install, dismantle, repair, service or advise on machinery, equipment, computer software or hardware (or train UK based workers to provide these services) where there is a contract of purchase, supply or lease with a UK company or organisation and either:

(a)   the overseas company is the manufacturer or supplier; or

(b)   the overseas company is part of a contractual arrangement for after sales services agreed at the time of the sale or lease, including in a warranty or other service contract incidental to the sale or lease.

Clients of UK export companies

PA 8.   A client of a UK export company may be seconded to the UK company in order to oversee the requirements for goods and services that are being provided under contract by the UK company or its subsidiary company, provided the two companies are not part of the same group.

Overseas roles requiring specific activities in the UK

PA 9.1.   Individuals employed outside the UK may visit the UK to take part in the following activities in relation to their employment overseas:

(a)   a translator and/or interpreter may translate and/or interpret in the UK as an employee of an enterprise located overseas; or

(b)   personal assistants and bodyguards may support an overseas business person in carrying out permitted activities, provided they will attend the same event(s) as the business person and are employed by them outside the UK. They must not be providing personal care or domestic work for the business person; or

(c)   a tour group courier, contracted to a company with its headquarters outside the UK, who is entering and departing the UK with a tour group organised by their company; or

(d)   a journalist, correspondent, producer or cameraman gathering information for an overseas publication, programme or film; or

(e)   archaeologists taking part in a one-off archaeological excavation; or

(f)   a professor from an overseas academic institution accompanying students to the UK as part of a study abroad programme, may provide a small amount of teaching to the students at the host organisation providing this does not amount to filling a permanent teaching role for that institution; or

(g)   market researchers and analysts may conduct market research or analysis for an enterprise located outside the UK.

PA 9.2.   Drivers on a genuine international route between the UK and a country outside the UK may:

(a)   deliver or collect goods or passengers from a country outside the UK to the UK; and

(b)   undertake cabotage operations.

PA 9.3.   Drivers under PA 9.2 must be employed or contracted to an operator registered in a country outside the UK or be a self-employed operator and driver based outside the UK and the operator must hold an International Operators Licence or be operating on an own account basis.

Work-related training

PA 10.1.   Overseas graduates from medical, dental or nursing schools may:

(a)   undertake clinical attachments or dental observer posts provided these are unpaid and involve no treatment of patients, where the additional requirements of Appendix V: Visitor at V 11.1. are also met; and

(b)   take the following test/examination in the UK:

(i)   the Professional and Linguistic Assessment Board test, where the additional requirements of Appendix V: Visitor at V 11.2. are also met; or

(ii)   the Objective Structured Clinical Examinations for overseas, where the additional requirements of Appendix V: Visitor at V 11.3. are also met.

PA 10.2.   Employees of an overseas company or organisation may receive training from a UK based company or organisation in work practices and techniques which are required for the Visitor's employment overseas and not available in their home country.

PA 10.3.   An employee of an overseas based training company may deliver a short series of training to employees of a UK based company, where the trainer is employed by an overseas business contracted to deliver global training to the international corporate group to which the UK based company belongs.

Science and academia

PA 11.1.   Scientists and researchers may:

(a)   gather information and facts for a specific project which directly relates to their employment overseas, or conduct independent research; and

(b)   share knowledge or advise on an international project that is being led from the UK, provided the Visitor is not carrying out research in the UK.

PA 11.2.   Academics may:

(a)   take part in formal exchange arrangements with UK counterparts (including doctors); and

(b)   carry out research for their own purposes if they are on sabbatical leave from their home institution; and

(c)   if they are an eminent senior doctor or dentist, take part in research, teaching or clinical practice provided this does not amount to filling a permanent teaching post.

Legal

PA 12.1.   An expert witness may visit the UK to give evidence in a UK court; other witnesses may attend a court hearing in the UK if summoned in person by a UK court.

PA 12.2.   An overseas lawyer may advise a UK based client on specific international litigation and/or an international transaction.

Religion

PA 13.   Religious workers overseas may visit the UK to preach or do pastoral work.

Creative

PA 14.1.   An artist, entertainer, or musician may:

(a)   give performances as an individual or as part of a group; and

(b)   take part in competitions or auditions; and

(c)   make personal appearances and take part in promotional activities; and

(d)   take part in one or more cultural events or festivals on the list of permit free festivals in Appendix Visitor: Permit Free Festival List.

PA 14.2.   Personal or technical staff or members of the production team of an artist, entertainer or musician may support the activities in PA 14.1. or Appendix V: Visitor at V13.3 (e) provided they are attending the same event as the artist, entertainer or musician, and are employed to work for them outside of the UK.

PA.14.3.   Film crew (actor, producer, director or technician) employed by an overseas company may visit the UK to take part in a location shoot for a film or programme or other media content that is produced and financed overseas.

Sports

PA 15.1.   A sports person may:

(a)   take part in a sports tournament or sports event as an individual or part of a team; and

(b)   make personal appearances and take part in promotional activities; and

(c)   take part in trials provided they are not in front of a paying audience; and

(d)   take part in short periods of training provided they are not being paid by a UK sporting body; and

(e)   join an amateur team or club to gain experience in a particular sport if they are an amateur in that sport.

PA 15.2.   Personal or technical staff of the sports person, or sports officials, may support the activities in PA 15.1. or in Appendix V: Visitor at V 13.3.(f), if they are attending the same event as the sports person. Personal or technical staff of the sports person must be employed to work for the sports person outside the UK.

Medical treatment and organ donation

PA 16.1.   A Visitor may receive private medical treatment provided the additional requirements at Appendix V: Visitor at V 7.1. to V 7.3. are also met.

PA.16.2.   A Visitor may act as an organ donor or be assessed as a potential organ donor to an identified recipient in the UK, provided the additional requirements at Appendix V: Visitor at V 8.1. to V 8.4. are also met.

Study as a Visitor

PA 17.   A Visitor may study for up to six months providing the requirements of V 9.1. to V 9.5. are met.

Transit

PA 18.   A Visitor may transit the UK, provided they meet the requirements of Appendix V: Visitor at V 14.1. and V 14.2.

Appendix Visitor: Visa national list

List of nationalities requiring entry clearance prior to travel to the UK as a Visitor, or for any other purpose for less than six months

VN 1.1.   A person who meets one or more of the criteria below needs entry clearance (also referred to as visa) in advance of travel to the UK as a visitor, or for any other purpose for less than six months where there is no mandatory entry clearance requirement, unless they meet one of the exceptions set out in VN 2.1., VN 2.2. (subject to VN 2.3.) or VN 3.1.

(a)   Nationals or citizens of the following countries or territorial entities (a "*" indicates there are exceptions in VN 2.2 to VN 6.5):

Afghanistan

Albania

Algeria

Angola

Armenia

Azerbaijan

Bahrain*

Bangladesh

Belarus

Benin

Bhutan

Bolivia

Bosnia Herzegovina

Burkina Faso

Burundi

Cambodia

Cameroon

Cape Vere

Central African Republic

Chad

People's Republic of China*

Colombia

Comoros

Congo

Côte d'Ivoire (formerly Ivory Coast)

Cuba

Democratic Republic of the Congo

Djibouti

Dominican Republic

Ecuador

Egypt

Equatorial Guinea

Eritrea

Eswatini (formerly Swaziland)

Ethiopia

Fiji

Gabon

Gambia

Georgia

Ghana

Guinea

Guinea Bissau

Guyana

Haiti

India

Indonesia*

Iran

Iraq

Jamaica

Jordan

Kazakhstan

Kenya

Korea (North)

Kosovo

Kuwait*

Kyrgyzstan

Laos

Lebanon

Lesotho

Liberia

Libya

Madagascar

Malawi

Mali

Mauritania

Moldova

Mongolia

Montenegro

Morocco

Mozambique

Myanmar (formerly Burma)

Nepal

Niger

Nigeria

North Macedonia (formerly Macedonia)

Oman*

Pakistan

Peru

Philippines

Qatar*

Russia

Rwanda

São Tomé and Principe

Saudi Arabia

Senegal

Serbia

Sierra Leone

Somalia

South Africa*

South Sudan

Sri Lanka

Sudan

Suriname

Syria

Taiwan*

Tajikistan

Tanzania

Thailand

Togo

Tunisia

Turkey*

Turkmenistan

Uganda

Ukraine

United Arab Emirates*

Uzbekistan

Venezuela

Vietnam*

Yemen

Zambia

Zimbabwe

(b)   stateless people; and

(c)   people travelling on any document other than a national passport, or, in the case of a person to whom paragraphs 11A and 11B of these rules apply, a national identity card, regardless of whether the document is issued by or evidences nationality of a state not listed in VN 1.1. (a), except where that document has been issued by the UK.

Exceptions to the list of visa nationals

Holders of specified travel documents

VN 2.1.   It is not necessary for a Transit Visitor to hold an entry clearance before they travel to the UK if they are travelling on an emergency travel document issued by, and evidencing the nationality of, a country not listed in VN 1.1.(a) and the purpose of their transit is to travel to the country in which they are ordinarily resident.

VN 2.2.   The following people do not need a visit visa before they travel to the UK as a Visitor, other than where VN 2.3. applies:

(a)   nationals or citizens of the People's Republic of China who hold a passport issued by the Hong Kong Special Administrative Region; or

(b)   nationals or citizens of the People's Republic of China who hold a passport issued by the Macao Special Administrative Region; or

(c)   nationals or citizens of Taiwan who hold a passport issued by Taiwan that includes in it the number of the identification card issued by the competent authority in Taiwan; or

(d)   people who hold a Service, Temporary Service or Diplomatic passport issued by the Holy See; or

(e)   nationals or citizens of Oman who hold a diplomatic or special passport issued by Oman; or

(f)   nationals or citizens of Qatar who hold a diplomatic or special passport issued by Qatar; or

(g)   nationals or citizens of the United Arab Emirates who hold a diplomatic or special passport issued by the United Arab Emirates; or

(h)   nationals or citizens of Turkey who hold a diplomatic passport issued by Turkey; or

(i)   nationals or citizens of Kuwait who hold a diplomatic or special passport issued by Kuwait; or

(j)   nationals or citizens of Bahrain who hold a diplomatic or special passport issued by Bahrain; or

(k)   nationals or citizens of South Africa who hold a diplomatic passport issued by South Africa; or

(l)   nationals or citizens of Vietnam who hold a diplomatic passport issued by Vietnam; or

(m)   nationals or citizens of Indonesia who hold a diplomatic passport issued by Indonesia.

VN 2.3.   VN 2.2. does not apply where the person is:

(a)   visiting the UK to marry or to form a civil partnership, or to give notice of marriage or civil partnership, unless they are a "relevant national" as defined in section 62 of the Immigration Act 2014; or

(b)   seeking to visit the UK for more than 6 months.

Exception where the applicant holds an Electronic Visa Waiver (EVW) Document (Kuwait, Oman, Qatar and United Arab Emirates nationals or citizens only)

VN 3.1.   The holder of a valid Electronic Visa Waiver (EVW) Document does not need to obtain a visit visa, or a visa for entry for six months or less where there is no mandatory entry clearance requirement, in advance of arrival in the UK, but can instead apply for permission to enter at the UK border.

VN 3.2.   VN 3.1. will not apply (meaning that the person will normally be refused permission to enter the UK) unless the EVW Document is used in the manner specified in VN 6.1. to VN 6.5.

VN 3.3.   An EVW Document relates to one person and may only be used for one application for permission to enter the UK or, where applicable, one crossing of the land border from the Republic of Ireland to the UK.

Obtaining an Electronic Visa Waiver Document

VN 4.1.   Only passport holders who are nationals or citizens of Kuwait, Oman, Qatar or the United Arab Emirates can obtain and use an EVW document.

VN 4.2.   To obtain an EVW Document, a person must provide the required biographic and travel information at the website established by the UK Government at https://www.electronic-visa-waiver.service.gov.uk/.

VN 4.3.   EVW Documents are issued to the applicant in electronic form.

Validity Requirements for an Electronic Visa Waiver Document

VN 5.1.   To be valid the biographic details on the EVW Document must match those of the holder's passport, except where:

(a)   an apostrophe, space or hyphen is present in the holder's name on their EVW Document but is not present in the holder's name on their passport; or

(b)   an apostrophe, space or hyphen is present in the holder's name on their passport but is not present in the holder's name on their EVW Document.

VN 5.2.   To be valid an EVW Document must be able to be presented by the holder:

(a)   in clear, legible format; and

(b)   in English; and

(c)   electronically or in printed form.

VN 5.3.   To be valid the EVW Document must specify the flight, train or ship on which the holder intends to arrive in the UK, including the port of departure and arrival, and the scheduled date and time of departure and arrival, unless VN 5.4. or VN 5.5. applies.

VN 5.4.   Where the holder of an EVW Document is seeking to arrive in the UK by entering a control zone in France or Belgium or supplementary control zone in France, the EVW must specify the train or ship on which the holder intends to arrive in the UK, including:

(a)   the railway station or port where the holder intends to enter the control zone or supplementary control zone and from which the holder intends to depart for the UK; and

(b)   the railway station or port at which the holder intends to leave the train or ship after arrival in the UK; and

(c)   the scheduled date and time of departure from, and arrival at, the specified railway stations or ports.

VN 5.5.   Where the holder of an EVW Document intends to cross the land border from the Republic of Ireland to the UK by train, car or any other means, the EVW must specify the place at which it is intended to cross the border and the intended date and time of arrival in the UK.

VN 5.6.   For the EVW to be valid the required information must be submitted at least 48 hours before the holder departs on a flight, train or ship to the UK or crosses the UK land border from the Republic of Ireland by train, car or any other means.

VN 5.7.   To be valid the EVW Document must not have been issued more than 3 months before the date of the holder's scheduled departure to the UK as specified on the EVW Document or, where the holder intends to cross the land border with the Republic of Ireland, before the intended date of the holder's arrival in the UK as specified on the EVW Document.

Use of the Electronic Visa Waiver Document

VN 6.1.   The holder must present the EVW Document to an Immigration Officer on request upon the holder's arrival at the UK Border or, where the holder is seeking to arrive in the UK by entering a control zone in France or Belgium or a supplementary control zone in France, upon arrival in that zone.

VN 6.2.   Where the holder has presented a printed copy of the EVW Document, it must be surrendered to an Immigration Officer upon request.

VN 6.3.   The holder must travel on the flight, train or ship specified on the EVW Document unless VN 6.4. or VN 6.5. applies.

VN 6.4.   If the holder travels on a different flight, train or ship from that specified in the EVW Document it must depart from the same port or railway station and arrive at the same UK port or railway station as specified on the EVW Document and either:

(a)   depart after the departure time specified on the EVW Document and arrive in the UK no more than 8 hours after the arrival time specified on the EVW Document; or

(b)   if the holder is seeking to arrive in the UK by entering a control zone in France or Belgium or a supplementary control zone in France, arrive no more than 8 hours after the departure time specified on the EVW Document.

VN 6.5.   If the holder is seeking to arrive in the UK by crossing the land border from the Republic of Ireland, the holder must cross at the time specified on the EVW Document, or no more than 8 hours after the time specified on the EVW Document.

The European Union and Associated States

Member States of the European Union (see Chapter 4)

Austria
Belgium
Bulgaria
Croatia
Cyprus
Czech Republic
Denmark
Estonia
Finland
France
Germany
Greece
Hungary
Republic of Ireland
Italy
Latvia
Lithuania
Luxembourg
Malta
The Netherlands
Poland
Portugal
Romania
Slovakia
Slovenia
Spain
Sweden

Other Members of the European Economic Area (see Chapter 4)

Iceland
Norway
Liechtenstein
(As to Switzerland, see **4.1**)

Directive 2004/38/EC

CHAPTER I – GENERAL PROVISIONS

Article 1 – Subject

This Directive lays down:

(a)   the conditions governing the exercise of the right of free movement and residence within the territory of the Member States by Union citizens and their family members;

(b)   the right of permanent residence in the territory of the Member States for Union citizens and their family members;

(c)   the limits placed on the rights set out in (a) and (b) on grounds of public policy, public security or public health.

Article 2 – Definitions

For the purposes of this Directive:

1.   'Union citizen' means any person having the nationality of a Member State;

2.   'family member' means:

    (a)   the spouse;

    (b)   the partner with whom the Union citizen has contracted a registered partnership, on the basis of the legislation of a Member State, if the legislation of the host Member State treats registered partnerships as equivalent to marriage and in accordance with the conditions laid down in the relevant legislation of the host Member State;

    (c)   the direct descendants who are under the age of 21 or are dependants and those of the spouse or partner as defined in point (b);

    (d)   the dependent direct relatives in the ascending line and those of the spouse or partner as defined in point (b);

3.   'host Member State' means the Member State to which a Union citizen moves in order to exercise his/her right of free movement and residence.

Article 3 – Beneficiaries

1.   This Directive shall apply to all Union citizens who move to or reside in a Member State other than that of which they are a national, and to their family members as defined in point 2 of Article 2 who accompany or join them.

2.   Without prejudice to any right to free movement and residence the persons concerned may have in their own right, the host Member State shall, in accordance with its national legislation, facilitate entry and residence for the following persons:

    (a)   any other family members, irrespective of their nationality, not falling under the definition in point 2 of Article 2 who, in the country from which they have come, are dependants or members of the household of the Union citizen having the primary right of residence, or where serious health grounds strictly require the personal care of the family member by the Union citizen;

    (b)   the partner with whom the Union citizen has a durable relationship, duly attested.

The host Member State shall undertake an extensive examination of the personal circumstances and shall justify any denial of entry or residence to these people.

CHAPTER II – RIGHT OF EXIT AND ENTRY

Article 4 – Right of exit

1.   Without prejudice to the provisions on travel documents applicable to national border controls, all Union citizens with a valid identity card or passport and their family members who are not nationals of a Member State and who hold a valid passport shall have the right to leave the territory of a Member State to travel to another Member State.

2.   No exit visa or equivalent formality may be imposed on the persons to whom paragraph 1 applies.

3.   Member States shall, acting in accordance with their laws, issue to their own nationals, and renew, an identity card or passport stating their nationality.

4.   The passport shall be valid at least for all Member States and for countries through which the holder must pass when travelling between Member States. Where the law of a Member State does not provide for identity cards to be issued, the period of validity of any passport on being issued or renewed shall be not less than five years.

Article 5 – Right of entry

1.   Without prejudice to the provisions on travel documents applicable to national border controls, Member States shall grant Union citizens leave to enter their territory with a valid identity card or passport and shall grant family members who are not nationals of a Member State leave to enter their territory with a valid passport.

    No entry visa or equivalent formality may be imposed on Union citizens.

2.   Family members who are not nationals of a Member State shall only be required to have an entry visa in accordance with Regulation (EC) No 539/2001 or, where appropriate, with national law. For the purposes of this Directive, possession of the valid residence card referred to in Article 10 shall exempt such family members from the visa requirement.

    Member States shall grant such persons every facility to obtain the necessary visas. Such visas shall be issued free of charge as soon as possible and on the basis of an accelerated procedure.

3.   The host Member State shall not place an entry or exit stamp in the passport of family members who are not nationals of a Member State provided that they present the residence card provided for in Article 10.

4.   Where a Union citizen, or a family member who is not a national of a Member State, does not have the necessary travel documents or, if required, the necessary visas, the Member State concerned shall, before turning them back, give such persons every reasonable opportunity to obtain the necessary documents or have them brought to them within a reasonable period of time or to corroborate or prove by other means that they are covered by the right of free movement and residence.

5.   The Member State may require the person concerned to report his/her presence within its territory within a reasonable and non-discriminatory period of time. Failure to comply with this requirement may make the person concerned liable to proportionate and non-discriminatory sanctions.

CHAPTER III – RIGHT OF RESIDENCE

Article 6 – Right of residence for up to three months

1.   Union citizens shall have the right of residence on the territory of another Member State for a period of up to three months without any conditions or any formalities other than the requirement to hold a valid identity card or passport.

2.   The provisions of paragraph 1 shall also apply to family members in possession of a valid passport who are not nationals of a Member State, accompanying or joining the Union citizen.

Article 7 – Right of residence for more than three months

1.   All Union citizens shall have the right of residence on the territory of another Member State for a period of longer than three months if they:

(a)   are workers or self-employed persons in the host Member State; or

(b)   have sufficient resources for themselves and their family members not to become a burden on the social assistance system of the host Member State during their period of residence and have comprehensive sickness insurance cover in the host Member State; or

(c)   —   are enrolled at a private or public establishment, accredited or financed by the host Member State on the basis of its legislation or administrative practice, for the principal purpose of following a course of study, including vocational training; and

—   have comprehensive sickness insurance cover in the host Member State and assure the relevant national authority, by means of a declaration or by such equivalent means as they may choose, that they have sufficient resources for themselves and their family members not to become a burden on the social assistance system of the host Member State during their period of residence; or

(d)   are family members accompanying or joining a Union citizen who satisfies the conditions referred to in points (a), (b) or (c).

2.   The right of residence provided for in paragraph 1 shall extend to family members who are not nationals of a Member State, accompanying or joining the Union citizen in the host Member State, provided that such Union citizen satisfies the conditions referred to in paragraph 1(a), (b) or (c).

3.   For the purposes of paragraph 1(a), a Union citizen who is no longer a worker or self-employed person shall retain the status of worker or self-employed person in the following circumstances:

(a)   he/she is temporarily unable to work as the result of an illness or accident;

(b)   he/she is in duly recorded involuntary unemployment after having been employed for more than one year and has registered as a job-seeker with the relevant employment office;

(c)   he/she is in duly recorded involuntary unemployment after completing a fixed-term employment contract of less than a year or after having become involuntarily unemployed during the first twelve months and has registered as a job-seeker with the relevant employment office. In this case, the status of worker shall be retained for no less than six months;

(d)   he/she embarks on vocational training. Unless he/she is involuntarily unemployed, the retention of the status of worker shall require the training to be related to the previous employment.

4.   By way of derogation from paragraphs 1(d) and 2 above, only the spouse, the registered partner provided for in Article 2(2)(b) and dependent children shall have the right of residence as family members of a Union citizen meeting the conditions under 1(c) above. Article 3(2) shall apply to his/her dependent direct relatives in the ascending lines and those of his/her spouse or registered partner.

Article 8 – Administrative formalities for Union citizens

1.   Without prejudice to Article 5(5), for periods of residence longer than three months, the host Member State may require Union citizens to register with the relevant authorities.

2.   The deadline for registration may not be less than three months from the date of arrival. A registration certificate shall be issued immediately, stating the name and address of the person registering and the date of the registration. Failure to comply with the registration requirement may render the person concerned liable to proportionate and non-discriminatory sanctions.

3.   For the registration certificate to be issued, Member States may only require that

—   Union citizens to whom point (a) of Article 7(1) applies present a valid identity card or passport, a confirmation of engagement from the employer or a certificate of employment, or proof that they are self-employed persons,

—   Union citizens to whom point (b) of Article 7(1) applies present a valid identity card or passport and provide proof that they satisfy the conditions laid down therein,

—   Union citizens to whom point (c) of Article 7(1) applies present a valid identity card or passport, provide proof of enrolment at an accredited establishment and of comprehensive sickness insurance cover and the declaration or equivalent means referred to in point (c) of Article 7(1). Member States may not require this declaration to refer to any specific amount of resources.

4.   Member States may not lay down a fixed amount which they regard as 'sufficient resources', but they must take into account the personal situation of the person concerned. In all cases this amount shall not be higher than the threshold below which nationals of the host Member State become eligible for

social assistance, or, where this criterion is not applicable, higher than the minimum social security pension paid by the host Member State.

5. For the registration certificate to be issued to family members of Union citizens, who are themselves Union citizens, Member States may require the following documents to be presented:

    (a) a valid identity card or passport;

    (b) a document attesting to the existence of a family relationship or of a registered partnership;

    (c) where appropriate, the registration certificate of the Union citizen whom they are accompanying or joining;

    (d) in cases falling under points (c) and (d) of Article 2(2), documentary evidence that the conditions laid down therein are met;

    (e) in cases falling under Article 3(2)(a), a document issued by the relevant authority in the country of origin or country from which they are arriving certifying that they are dependants or members of the household of the Union citizen, or proof of the existence of serious health grounds which strictly require the personal care of the family member by the Union citizen;

    (f) in cases falling under Article 3(2)(b), proof of the existence of a durable relationship with the Union citizen.

Article 9 – Administrative formalities for family members who are not nationals of a Member State

1. Member States shall issue a residence card to family members of a Union citizen who are not nationals of a Member State, where the planned period of residence is for more than three months.

2. The deadline for submitting the residence card application may not be less than three months from the date of arrival.

3. Failure to comply with the requirement to apply for a residence card may make the person concerned liable to proportionate and non-discriminatory sanctions.

Article 10 – Issue of residence cards

1. The right of residence of family members of a Union citizen who are not nationals of a Member State shall be evidenced by the issuing of a document called 'Residence card of a family member of a Union citizen' no later than six months from the date on which they submit the application. A certificate of application for the residence card shall be issued immediately.

2. For the residence card to be issued, Member States shall require presentation of the following documents:

    (a) a valid passport;

    (b) a document attesting to the existence of a family relationship or of a registered partnership;

    (c) the registration certificate or, in the absence of a registration system, any other proof of residence in the host MemberState of the Union citizen whom they are accompanying or joining;

    (d) in cases falling under points (c) and (d) of Article 2(2), documentary evidence that the conditions laid down therein are met;

    (e) in cases falling under Article 3(2)(a), a document issued by the relevant authority in the country of origin or country from which they are arriving certifying that they are dependants or members of the household of the Union citizen, or proof of the existence of serious health grounds which strictly require the personal care of the family member by the Union citizen;

    (f) in cases falling under Article 3(2)(b), proof of the existence of a durable relationship with the Union citizen.

Article 11 – Validity of the residence card

1. The residence card provided for by Article 10(1) shall be valid for five years from the date of issue or for the envisaged period of residence of the Union citizen, if this period is less than five years.

2. The validity of the residence card shall not be affected by temporary absences not exceeding six months a year, or by absences of a longer duration for compulsory military service or by one absence of

a maximum of 12 consecutive months for important reasons such as pregnancy and childbirth, serious illness, study or vocational training, or a posting in another Member State or a third country.

Article 12 – Retention of the right of residence by family members in the event of death or departure of the Union citizen

1. Without prejudice to the second subparagraph, the Union citizen's death or departure from the host Member State shall not affect the right of residence of his/her family members who are nationals of a Member State.

   Before acquiring the right of permanent residence, the persons concerned must meet the conditions laid down in points (a), (b), (c) or (d) of Article 7(1).

2. Without prejudice to the second subparagraph, the Union citizen's death shall not entail loss of the right of residence of his/her family members who are not nationals of a Member State and who have been residing in the host Member State as family members for at least one year before the Union citizen's death.

   Before acquiring the right of permanent residence, the right of residence of the persons concerned shall remain subject to the requirement that they are able to show that they are workers or self-employed persons or that they have sufficient resources for themselves and their family members not to become a burden on the social assistance system of the host Member State during their period of residence and have comprehensive sickness insurance cover in the host Member State, or that they are members of the family, already constituted in the host Member State, of a person satisfying these requirements. 'Sufficient resources' shall be as defined in Article 8(4).

   Such family members shall retain their right of residence exclusively on a personal basis.

3. The Union citizen's departure from the host Member State or his/her death shall not entail loss of the right of residence of his/her children or of the parent who has actual custody of the children, irrespective of nationality, if the children reside in the host Member State and are enrolled at an educational establishment, for the purpose of studying there, until the completion of their studies.

Article 13 – Retention of the right of residence by family members in the event of divorce, annulment of marriage or termination of registered partnership

1. Without prejudice to the second subparagraph, divorce, annulment of the Union citizen's marriage or termination of his/her registered partnership, as referred to in point 2(b) of Article 2 shall not affect the right of residence of his/her family members who are nationals of a Member State.

   Before acquiring the right of permanent residence, the persons concerned must meet the conditions laid down in points (a), (b), (c) or (d) of Article 7(1).

2. Without prejudice to the second subparagraph, divorce, annulment of marriage or termination of the registered partnership referred to in point 2(b) of Article 2 shall not entail loss of the right of residence of a Union citizen's family members who are not nationals of a Member State where:

   (a) prior to initiation of the divorce or annulment proceedings or termination of the registered partnership referred to in point 2(b) of Article 2, the marriage or registered partnership has lasted at least three years, including one year in the host Member State; or

   (b) by agreement between the spouses or the partners referred to in point 2(b) of Article 2 or by court order, the spouse or partner who is not a national of a Member State has custody of the Union citizen's children; or

   (c) this is warranted by particularly difficult circumstances, such as having been a victim of domestic violence while the marriage or registered partnership was subsisting; or

   (d) by agreement between the spouses or partners referred to in point 2(b) of Article 2 or by court order, the spouse or partner who is not a national of a Member State has the right of access to a minor child, provided that the court has ruled that such access must be in the host Member State, and for as long as is required.

   Before acquiring the right of permanent residence, the right of residence of the persons concerned shall remain subject to the requirement that they are able to show that they are workers or self-employed persons or that they have sufficient resources for themselves and their family members not to become a burden on the social assistance system of the host Member State during their period of residence and have comprehensive sickness insurance cover in the host Member State, or that they are members of the family, already constituted in the host Member State, of a person satisfying these requirements. 'Sufficient resources' shall be as defined in Article 8(4).

Such family members shall retain their right of residence exclusively on personal basis.

Article 14 – Retention of the right of residence

1. Union citizens and their family members shall have the right of residence provided for in Article 6, as long as they do not become an unreasonable burden on the social assistance system of the host Member State.

2. Union citizens and their family members shall have the right of residence provided for in Articles 7, 12 and 13 as long as they meet the conditions set out therein.

   In specific cases where there is a reasonable doubt as to whether a Union citizen or his/her family members satisfies the conditions set out in Articles 7, 12 and 13, Member States may verify if these conditions are fulfilled. This verification shall not be carried out systematically.

3. An expulsion measure shall not be the automatic consequence of a Union citizen's or his or her family member's recourse to the social assistance system of the host Member State.

4. By way of derogation from paragraphs 1 and 2 and without prejudice to the provisions of Chapter VI, an expulsion measure may in no case be adopted against Union citizens or their family members if:

   (a) the Union citizens are workers or self-employed persons, or

   (b) the Union citizens entered the territory of the host Member State in order to seek employment. In this case, the Union citizens and their family members may not be expelled for as long as the Union citizens can provide evidence that they are continuing to seek employment and that they have a genuine chance of being engaged.

Article 15 – Procedural safeguards

1. The procedures provided for by Articles 30 and 31 shall apply by analogy to all decisions restricting free movement of Union citizens and their family members on grounds other than public policy, public security or public health.

2. Expiry of the identity card or passport on the basis of which the person concerned entered the host Member State and was issued with a registration certificate or residence card shall not constitute a ground for expulsion from the host Member State.

3. The host Member State may not impose a ban on entry in the context of an expulsion decision to which paragraph 1 applies.

CHAPTER IV – RIGHT OF PERMANENT RESIDENCE

Section I – Eligibility

Article 16 – General rule for Union citizens and their family members

1. Union citizens who have resided legally for a continuous period of five years in the host Member State shall have the right of permanent residence there. This right shall not be subject to the conditions provided for in Chapter III.

2. Paragraph 1 shall apply also to family members who are not nationals of a Member State and have legally resided with the Union citizen in the host Member State for a continuous period of five years.

3. Continuity of residence shall not be affected by temporary absences not exceeding a total of six months a year, or by absences of a longer duration for compulsory military service, or by one absence of a maximum of 12 consecutive months for important reasons such as pregnancy and childbirth, serious illness, study or vocational training, or a posting in another Member State or a third country.

4. Once acquired, the right of permanent residence shall be lost only through absence from the host Member State for a period exceeding two consecutive years.

Article 17 – Exemptions for persons no longer working in the host Member State and their family members

1. By way of derogation from Article 16, the right of permanent residence in the host Member State shall be enjoyed before completion of a continuous period of five years of residence by:

    (a) workers or self-employed persons who, at the time they stop working, have reached the age laid down by the law of that Member State for entitlement to an old age pension or workers who cease paid employment to take early retirement, provided that they have been working in that Member State for at least the preceding twelve months and have resided there continuously for more than three years.

    If the law of the host Member State does not grant the right to an old age pension to certain categories of self-employed persons, the age condition shall be deemed to have been met once the person concerned has reached the age of 60;

    (b) workers or self-employed persons who have resided continuously in the host Member State for more than two years and stop working there as a result of permanent incapacity to work.

    If such incapacity is the result of an accident at work or an occupational disease entitling the person concerned to a benefit payable in full or in part by an institution in the host Member State, no condition shall be imposed as to length of residence;

    (c) workers or self-employed persons who, after three years of continuous employment and residence in the host Member State, work in an employed or self-employed capacity in another Member State, while retaining their place of residence in the host Member State, to which they return, as a rule, each day or at least once a week.

    For the purposes of entitlement to the rights referred to in points (a) and (b), periods of employment spent in the Member State in which the person concerned is working shall be regarded as having been spent in the host Member State.

    Periods of involuntary unemployment duly recorded by the relevant employment office, periods not worked for reasons not of the person's own making and absences from work or cessation of work due to illness or accident shall be regarded as periods of employment.

2. The conditions as to length of residence and employment laid down in point (a) of paragraph 1 and the condition as to length of residence laid down in point (b) of paragraph 1 shall not apply if the worker's or the self-employed person's spouse or partner as referred to in point 2(b) of Article 2 is a national of the host Member State or has lost the nationality of that Member State by marriage to that worker or self-employed person.

3. Irrespective of nationality, the family members of a worker or a self-employed person who are residing with him in the territory of the host Member State shall have the right of permanent residence in that Member State, if the worker or self-employed person has acquired himself the right of permanent residence in that Member State on the basis of paragraph 1.

4. If, however, the worker or self-employed person dies while still working but before acquiring permanent residence status in the host Member State on the basis of paragraph 1, his family members who are residing with him in the host Member State shall acquire the right of permanent residence there, on condition that:

    (a) the worker or self-employed person had, at the time of death, resided continuously on the territory of that Member State for two years; or

    (b) the death resulted from an accident at work or an occupational disease; or

    (c) the surviving spouse lost the nationality of that Member State following marriage to the worker or self-employed person.

Article 18 – Acquisition of the right of permanent residence by certain family members who are not nationals of a Member State

Without prejudice to Article 17, the family members of a Union citizen to whom Articles 12(2) and 13(2) apply, who satisfy the conditions laid down therein, shall acquire the right of permanent residence after residing legally for a period of five consecutive years in the host Member State.

Section II – Administrative formalities

Article 19 – Document certifying permanent residence for Union citizens

1. Upon application Member States shall issue Union citizens entitled to permanent residence, after having verified duration of residence, with a document certifying permanent residence.
2. The document certifying permanent residence shall be issued as soon as possible.

Article 20 – Permanent residence card for family members who are not nationals of a Member State

1. Member States shall issue family members who are not nationals of a Member State entitled to permanent residence with a permanent residence card within six months of the submission of the application. The permanent residence card shall be renewable automatically every 10 years.
2. The application for a permanent residence card shall be submitted before the residence card expires. Failure to comply with the requirement to apply for a permanent residence card may render the person concerned liable to proportionate and non-discriminatory sanctions.
3. Interruption in residence not exceeding two consecutive years shall not affect the validity of the permanent residence card.

Article 21 – Continuity of residence

For the purposes of this Directive, continuity of residence may be attested by any means of proof in use in the host Member State. Continuity of residence is broken by any expulsion decision duly enforced against the person concerned.

CHAPTER V – PROVISIONS COMMON TO THE RIGHT OF RESIDENCE AND THE RIGHT OF PERMANENT RESIDENCE

Article 22 – Territorial scope

The right of residence and the right of permanent residence shall cover the whole territory of the host Member State. Member States may impose territorial restrictions on the right of residence and the right of permanent residence only where the same restrictions apply to their own nationals.

Article 23 – Related rights

Irrespective of nationality, the family members of a Union citizen who have the right of residence or the right of permanent residence in a Member State shall be entitled to take up employment or self-employment there.

Article 24 – Equal treatment

1. Subject to such specific provisions as are expressly provided for in the Treaty and secondary law, all Union citizens residing on the basis of this Directive in the territory of the host Member State shall enjoy equal treatment with the nationals of that Member State within the scope of the Treaty. The benefit of this right shall be extended to family members who are not nationals of a Member State and who have the right of residence or permanent residence.
2. By way of derogation from paragraph 1, the host Member State shall not be obliged to confer entitlement to social assistance during the first three months of residence or, where appropriate, the longer period provided for in Article 14(4)(b), nor shall it be obliged, prior to acquisition of the right of permanent residence, to grant maintenance aid for studies, including vocational training, consisting in student grants or student loans to persons other than workers, self-employed persons, persons who retain such status and members of their families.

Article 25 – General provisions concerning residence documents

1. Possession of a registration certificate as referred to in Article 8, of a document certifying permanent residence, of a certificate attesting submission of an application for a family member residence card, of a residence card or of a permanent residence card, may under no circumstances be made a precondition for the exercise of a right or the completion of an administrative formality, as entitlement to rights may be attested by any other means of proof.

2. All documents mentioned in paragraph 1 shall be issued free of charge or for a charge not exceeding that imposed on nationals for the issuing of similar documents.

Article 26 – Checks

Member States may carry out checks on compliance with any requirement deriving from their national legislation for non-nationals always to carry their registration certificate or residence card, provided that the same requirement applies to their own nationals as regards their identity card. In the event of failure to comply with this requirement, Member States may impose the same sanctions as those imposed on their own nationals for failure to carry their identity card.

CHAPTER VI – RESTRICTIONS ON THE RIGHT OF ENTRY AND THE RIGHT OF RESIDENCE ON GROUNDS OF PUBLIC POLICY, PUBLIC SECURITY OR PUBLIC HEALTH

Article 27 – General principles

1. Subject to the provisions of this Chapter, Member States may restrict the freedom of movement and residence of Union citizens and their family members, irrespective of nationality, on grounds of public policy, public security or public health. These grounds shall not be invoked to serve economic ends.

2. Measures taken on grounds of public policy or public security shall comply with the principle of proportionality and shall be based exclusively on the personal conduct of the individual concerned. Previous criminal convictions shall not in themselves constitute grounds for taking such measures.

   The personal conduct of the individual concerned must represent a genuine, present and sufficiently serious threat affecting one of the fundamental interests of society. Justifications that are isolated from the particulars of the case or that rely on considerations of general prevention shall not be accepted.

3. In order to ascertain whether the person concerned represents a danger for public policy or public security, when issuing the registration certificate or, in the absence of a registration system, not later than three months from the date of arrival of the person concerned on its territory or from the date of reporting his/her presence within the territory, as provided for in Article 5(5), or when issuing the residence card, the host Member State may, should it consider this essential, request the Member State of origin and, if need be, other Member States to provide information concerning any previous police record the person concerned may have. Such enquiries shall not be made as a matter of routine. The Member State consulted shall give its reply within two months.

4. The Member State which issued the passport or identity card shall allow the holder of the document who has been expelled on grounds of public policy, public security, or public health from another Member State to re-enter its territory without any formality even if the document is no longer valid or the nationality of the holder is in dispute.

Article 28 – Protection against expulsion

1. Before taking an expulsion decision on grounds of public policy or public security, the host Member State shall take account of considerations such as how long the individual concerned has resided on its territory, his/her age, state of health, family and economic situation, social and cultural integration into the host Member State and the extent of his/her links with the country of origin.

2. The host Member State may not take an expulsion decision against Union citizens or their family members, irrespective of nationality, who have the right of permanent residence on its territory, except on serious grounds of public policy or public security.

3.   An expulsion decision may not be taken against Union citizens, except if the decision is based on imperative grounds of public security, as defined by Member States, if they:

     (a)   have resided in the host Member State for the previous 10 years; or

     (b)   are a minor, except if the expulsion is necessary for the best interests of the child, as provided for in the United Nations Convention on the Rights of the Child of 20 November 1989.

Article 29 – Public health

1.   The only diseases justifying measures restricting freedom of movement shall be the diseases with epidemic potential as defined by the relevant instruments of the World Health Organisation and other infectious diseases or contagious parasitic diseases if they are the subject of protection provisions applying to nationals of the host Member State.

2.   Diseases occurring after a three-month period from the date of arrival shall not constitute grounds for expulsion from the territory.

3.   Where there are serious indications that it is necessary, Member States may, within three months of the date of arrival, require persons entitled to the right of residence to undergo, free of charge, a medical examination to certify that they are not suffering from any of the conditions referred to in paragraph 1. Such medical examinations may not be required as a matter of routine.

Article 30 – Notification of decisions

1.   The persons concerned shall be notified in writing of any decision taken under Article 27(1), in such a way that they are able to comprehend its content and the implications for them.

2.   The persons concerned shall be informed, precisely and in full, of the public policy, public security or public health grounds on which the decision taken in their case is based, unless this is contrary to the interests of State security.

3.   The notification shall specify the court or administrative authority with which the person concerned may lodge an appeal, the time limit for the appeal and, where applicable, the time allowed for the person to leave the territory of the Member State. Save in duly substantiated cases of urgency, the time allowed to leave the territory shall be not less than one month from the date of notification.

Article 31 – Procedural safeguards

1.   The persons concerned shall have access to judicial and, where appropriate, administrative redress procedures in the host Member State to appeal against or seek review of any decision taken against them on the grounds of public policy, public security or public health.

2.   Where the application for appeal against or judicial review of the expulsion decision is accompanied by an application for an interim order to suspend enforcement of that decision, actual removal from the territory may not take place until such time as the decision on the interim order has been taken, except:

     —   where the expulsion decision is based on a previous judicial decision; or

     —   where the persons concerned have had previous access to judicial review; or

     —   where the expulsion decision is based on imperative grounds of public security under Article 28(3).

3.   The redress procedures shall allow for an examination of the legality of the decision, as well as of the facts and circumstances on which the proposed measure is based. They shall ensure that the decision is not disproportionate, particularly in view of the requirements laid down in Article 28.

4.   Member States may exclude the individual concerned from their territory pending the redress procedure, but they may not prevent the individual from submitting his/her defence in person, except when his/her appearance may cause serious troubles to public policy or public security or when the appeal or judicial review concerns a denial of entry to the territory.

Article 32 – Duration of exclusion orders

1.   Persons excluded on grounds of public policy or public security may submit an application for lifting of the exclusion order after a reasonable period, depending on the circumstances, and in any event after

three years from enforcement of the final exclusion order which has been validly adopted in accordance with Community law, by putting forward arguments to establish that there has been a material change in the circumstances which justified the decision ordering their exclusion.

The Member State concerned shall reach a decision on this application within six months of its submission.

2. The persons referred to in paragraph 1 shall have no right of entry to the territory of the Member State concerned while their application is being considered.

Article 33 – Expulsion as a penalty or legal consequence

1. Expulsion orders may not be issued by the host Member State as a penalty or legal consequence of a custodial penalty, unless they conform to the requirements of Articles 27, 28 and 29.

2. If an expulsion order, as provided for in paragraph 1, is enforced more than two years after it was issued, the Member State shall check that the individual concerned is currently and genuinely a threat to public policy or public security and shall assess whether there has been any material change in the circumstances since the expulsion order was issued.

CHAPTER VII – FINAL PROVISIONS

Article 34 – Publicity

Member States shall disseminate information concerning the rights and obligations of Union citizens and their family members on the subjects covered by this Directive, particularly by means of awareness-raising campaigns conducted through national and local media and other means of communication.

Article 35 – Abuse of rights

Member States may adopt the necessary measures to refuse, terminate or withdraw any right conferred by this Directive in the case of abuse of rights or fraud, such as marriages of convenience. Any such measure shall be proportionate and subject to the procedural safeguards provided for in Articles 30 and 31.

Article 36 – Sanctions

Member States shall lay down provisions on the sanctions applicable to breaches of national rules adopted for the implementation of this Directive and shall take the measures required for their application. The sanctions laid down shall be effective and proportionate. Member States shall notify the Commission of these provisions not later than 30 April 2006 and as promptly as possible in the case of any subsequent changes.

Article 37 – More favourable national provisions

The provisions of this Directive shall not affect any laws, regulations or administrative provisions laid down by a Member State which would be more favourable to the persons covered by this Directive.

Article 38 – Repeals

1. Articles 10 and 11 of Regulation (EEC) No 1612/68 shall be repealed with effect from 30 April 2006.

2. Directives 64/221/EEC, 68/360/EEC, 72/194/EEC, 73/148/EEC, 75/34/EEC, 75/35/EEC, 90/364/EEC, 90/365/EEC and 93/96/EEC shall be repealed with effect from 30 April 2006.

3. References made to the repealed provisions and Directives shall be construed as being made to this Directive.

Article 39 – Report

No later than 30 April 2006 the Commission shall submit a report on the application of this Directive to the European Parliament and the Council, together with any necessary proposals, notably on the opportunity to extend the period of time during which Union citizens and their family members may reside in the territory of the host Member State without any conditions. The Member States shall provide the Commission with the information needed to produce the report.

Article 40 – Transposition

1. Member States shall bring into force the laws, regulations and administrative provisions necessary to comply with this Directive by 30 April 2006.

    When Member States adopt those measures, they shall contain a reference to this Directive or shall be accompanied by such a reference on the occasion of their official publication. The methods of making such reference shall be laid down by the Member States.

2. Member States shall communicate to the Commission the text of the provisions of national law which they adopt in the field covered by this Directive together with a table showing how the provisions of this Directive correspond to the national provisions adopted.

Article 41 – Entry into force

This Directive shall enter into force on the day of its publication in the *Official Journal of the European Union*.

Article 42 – Addressees

This Directive is addressed to the Member States.

Done at Strasbourg, 29 April 2004.

Immigration (European Economic Area) Regulations 2016

PART 1

PRELIMINARY

1. Citation and commencement

(1)   These Regulations may be cited as the Immigration (European Economic Area) Regulations 2016.

(2)   These Regulations come into force—

(a)   for the purposes of this regulation, regulation 44 and Schedule 5 (transitory provisions), on 25th November 2016;

(b)   for all other purposes, on 1st February 2017.

2. General interpretation

(1)   In these Regulations—

"the 1971 Act" means the Immigration Act 1971;

"the 1999 Act" means the Immigration and Asylum Act 1999;

"the 2002 Act" means the Nationality, Immigration and Asylum Act 2002;

"the 2006 Regulations" means the Immigration (European Economic Area) Regulations 2006;

"civil partner" does not include—

(a)   a party to a civil partnership of convenience; or

(b)   the civil partner ("C") of a person ("P") where a spouse, civil partner or durable partner of C or P is already present in the United Kingdom;

"civil partnership of convenience" includes a civil partnership entered into for the purpose of using these Regulations, or any other right conferred by the EU Treaties, as a means to circumvent—

(a)   immigration rules applying to non-EEA nationals (such as any applicable requirement under the 1971 Act to have leave to enter or remain in the United Kingdom); or

(b)   any other criteria that the party to the civil partnership of convenience would otherwise have to meet in order to enjoy a right to reside under these Regulations or the EU Treaties;

"Common Travel Area" has the meaning given in section 1(3) of the 1971 Act;

"decision maker" means the Secretary of State, an immigration officer or an entry clearance officer (as the case may be);

"deportation order" means an order made under regulation 32(3);

"derivative residence card" means a card issued to a person under regulation 20;

"derivative right to reside" means a right to reside under regulation 16;

"document certifying permanent residence" means a document issued under regulation 19(1);

"durable partner" does not include—

(a)   a party to a durable partnership of convenience; or

(b)   the durable partner ("D") of a person ("P") where a spouse, civil partner or durable partner of D or P is already present in the United Kingdom and where that marriage, civil partnership or durable partnership is subsisting;

"durable partnership of convenience" includes a durable partnership entered into for the purpose of using these Regulations, or any other right conferred by the EU Treaties, as a means to circumvent—

(a)   immigration rules applying to non-EEA nationals (such as any applicable requirement under the 1971 Act to have leave to enter or remain in the United Kingdom); or

(b)   any other criteria that the party to the durable partnership of convenience would otherwise have to meet in order to enjoy a right to reside under these Regulations or the EU Treaties;

"EEA decision" means a decision under these Regulations that concerns—

(a)   a person's entitlement to be admitted to the United Kingdom;

(b)   a person's entitlement to be issued with or have renewed, or not to have revoked, an EEA family permit, a registration certificate, residence card, derivative residence card, document certifying permanent residence or permanent residence card (but does not include a decision to reject an application for the above documentation as invalid);

(c)   a person's removal from the United Kingdom; or

(d)   the cancellation, under regulation 25, of a person's right to reside in the United Kingdom,

but does not include a decision to refuse to issue a document under regulation 12(4) (issue of an EEA family permit to an extended family member), 17(5) (issue of a registration certificate to an extended family member) or 18(4) (issue of a residence card to an extended family member), a decision to refuse an application under regulation 26(4) (misuse of a right to reside: material change of circumstances), or any decisions under regulation 33 (human rights considerations and interim orders to suspend removal) or 41 (temporary admission to submit case in person);

"EEA family permit" means a document issued under regulation 12;

"EEA national" means—

(a)   a national of an EEA State who is not also a British citizen; or

(b)   a national of an EEA State who is also a British citizen and who prior to acquiring British citizenship exercised a right to reside as such a national, in accordance with regulation 14 or 15,

save that a person does not fall within paragraph (b) if the EEA State of which they are a national became a member State after that person acquired British citizenship.

"EEA State" means—

(a)   a member State, other than the United Kingdom; or

(b)   Liechtenstein, Iceland, Norway or Switzerland;

"entry clearance" has the meaning given in section 33(1) of the 1971 Act;

"entry clearance officer" means a person responsible for the grant or refusal of entry clearance;

"exclusion order" means an order made under regulation 23(5);

"indefinite leave", "immigration laws" and "immigration rules" have the meanings given in section 33(1) of the 1971 Act;

"marriage of convenience" includes a marriage entered into for the purpose of using these Regulations, or any other right conferred by the EU Treaties, as a means to circumvent—

(a)   immigration rules applying to non-EEA nationals (such as any applicable requirement under the 1971 Act to have leave to enter or remain in the United Kingdom); or

(b)   any other criteria that the party to the marriage of convenience would otherwise have to meet in order to enjoy a right to reside under these Regulations or the EU Treaties;

"military service" means service in the armed forces of an EEA State;

"permanent residence card" means a document issued under regulation 19(2);

"qualifying EEA State residence card" means a valid document called a "Residence card of a family member of a Union Citizen" issued under Article 10 of Council Directive 2004/38/EC (as applied, where relevant, by the EEA agreement) by any EEA State (except Switzerland) to a non-EEA family member of an EEA national as proof of the holder's right of residence in that State;

"registration certificate" means a certificate issued under regulation 17;

"relevant EEA national" in relation to an extended family member has the meaning given in regulation 8(6);

"residence card" means a card issued under regulation 18;

"right to reside" means a right to reside in the United Kingdom under these Regulations (or where so specified, a right to reside under a particular regulation);

"spouse" does not include—

(a)   a party to a marriage of convenience; or

(b)   the spouse ("S") of a person ("P") where a spouse, civil partner or durable partner of S or P is already present in the United Kingdom.

(2)   Section 11 of the 1971 Act (construction of references to entry) applies for the purpose of determining whether a person has entered the United Kingdom for the purpose of these Regulations as it applies for the purpose of determining whether a person has entered the United Kingdom for the purpose of that Act.

Immigration (European Economic Area) Regulations 2016   551

3. **Continuity of residence**

(1)   This regulation applies for the purpose of calculating periods of continuous residence in the United Kingdom under these Regulations.

(2)   Continuity of residence is not affected by—

    (a)   periods of absence from the United Kingdom which do not exceed six months in total in any year;

    (b)   periods of absence from the United Kingdom on compulsory military service; or

    (c)   one absence from the United Kingdom not exceeding twelve months for an important reason such as pregnancy and childbirth, serious illness, study or vocational training or an overseas posting.

(3)   Continuity of residence is broken when—

    (a)   a person serves a sentence of imprisonment;

    (b)   a deportation or exclusion order is made in relation to a person; or

    (c)   a person is removed from the United Kingdom under these Regulations.

(4)   Paragraph (3)(a) applies, in principle, to an EEA national who has resided in the United Kingdom for at least ten years, but it does not apply where the Secretary of State considers that—

    (a)   prior to serving a sentence of imprisonment, the EEA national had forged integrating links with the United Kingdom;

    (b)   the effect of the sentence of imprisonment was not such as to break those integrating links; and

    (c)   taking into account an overall assessment of the EEA national's situation, it would not be appropriate to apply paragraph (3)(a) to the assessment of that EEA national's continuity of residence.

4. **"Worker", "self-employed person", "self-sufficient person" and "student"**

(1)   In these Regulations—

    (a)   "worker" means a worker within the meaning of Article 45 of the Treaty on the Functioning of the European Union;

    (b)   "self-employed person" means a person who is established in the United Kingdom in order to pursue activity as a self-employed person in accordance with Article 49 of the Treaty on the Functioning of the European Union;

    (c)   "self-sufficient person" means a person who has—

        (i)   sufficient resources not to become a burden on the social assistance system of the United Kingdom during the person's period of residence; and

        (ii)   comprehensive sickness insurance cover in the United Kingdom;

    (d)   "student" means a person who—

        (i)   is enrolled, for the principal purpose of following a course of study (including vocational training), at a public or private establishment which is—

            (aa)   financed from public funds; or

            (bb)   otherwise recognised by the Secretary of State as an establishment which has been accredited for the purpose of providing such courses or training within the law or administrative practice of the part of the United Kingdom in which the establishment is located;

        (ii)   has comprehensive sickness insurance cover in the United Kingdom; and

        (iii)   has assured the Secretary of State, by means of a declaration, or by such equivalent means as the person may choose, that the person has sufficient resources not to become a burden on the social assistance system of the United Kingdom during the person's intended period of residence.

(2)   For the purposes of paragraphs (3) and (4) below, "relevant family member" means a family member of a self-sufficient person or student who is residing in the United Kingdom and whose right to reside is dependent upon being the family member of that student or self-sufficient person.

(3)   In sub-paragraphs (1)(c) and (d)—

    (a)   the requirement for the self-sufficient person or student to have sufficient resources not to become a burden on the social assistance system of the United Kingdom during the intended period of residence is only satisfied if the resources available to the student or self-sufficient person and any of their relevant family members are sufficient to avoid the self-sufficient person or student and all their relevant family members from becoming such a burden; and

(b) the requirement for the student or self-sufficient person to have comprehensive sickness insurance cover in the United Kingdom is only satisfied if such cover extends to cover both the student or self-sufficient person and all their relevant family members.

(4) In paragraph (1)(c) and (d) and paragraph (3), the resources of the student or self-sufficient person and, where applicable, any of their relevant family members, are to be regarded as sufficient if—

(a) they exceed the maximum level of resources which a British citizen (including the resources of the British citizen's family members) may possess if the British citizen is to become eligible for social assistance under the United Kingdom benefit system; or

(b) paragraph (a) does not apply but, taking into account the personal circumstances of the person concerned and, where applicable, all their relevant family members, it appears to the decision maker that the resources of the person or persons concerned should be regarded as sufficient.

(5) For the purposes of regulation 16(2) (criteria for having a derivative right to reside), references in this regulation to "family members" includes a "primary carer" as defined in regulation 16(8).

5. **"Worker or self-employed person who has ceased activity"**

(1) In these Regulations, "worker or self-employed person who has ceased activity" means an EEA national who satisfies a condition in paragraph (2), (3), (4) or (5).

(2) The condition in this paragraph is that the person—

(a) terminates activity as a worker or self-employed person and—

(i) had reached the age of entitlement to a state pension on terminating that activity; or

(ii) in the case of a worker, ceases working to take early retirement;

(b) pursued activity as a worker or self-employed person in the United Kingdom for at least 12 months prior to the termination; and

(c) resided in the United Kingdom continuously for more than three years prior to the termination.

(3) The condition in this paragraph is that the person terminates activity in the United Kingdom as a worker or self-employed person as a result of permanent incapacity to work; and—

(a) had resided in the United Kingdom continuously for more than two years immediately prior to the termination; or

(b) the incapacity is the result of an accident at work or an occupational disease that entitles the person to a pension payable in full or in part by an institution in the United Kingdom.

(4) The condition in this paragraph is that the person—

(a) is active as a worker or self-employed person in an EEA State but retains a place of residence in the United Kingdom and returns, as a rule, to that place at least once a week; and

(b) immediately prior to becoming so active in the EEA State, had been continuously resident and continuously active as a worker or self-employed person in the United Kingdom for at least three years.

(5) A person who satisfied the condition in paragraph (4)(a) but not the condition in paragraph (4)(b) must, for the purposes of paragraphs (2) and (3), be treated as being active and resident in the United Kingdom during any period during which that person is working or self-employed in the EEA State.

(6) The conditions in paragraphs (2) and (3) as to length of residence and activity as a worker or self-employed person do not apply in relation to a person whose spouse or civil partner is a British citizen.

(7) Subject to regulation 6(2), periods of—

(a) inactivity for reasons not of the person's own making;

(b) inactivity due to illness or accident; and

(c) in the case of a worker, involuntary unemployment duly recorded by the relevant employment office,

must be treated as periods of activity as a worker or self-employed person, as the case may be.

6. **"Qualified person"**

(1) In these Regulations—

"jobseeker" means an EEA national who satisfies conditions A, B and, where relevant, C;

"qualified person" means a person who is an EEA national and in the United Kingdom as—

    (a)   a jobseeker;

    (b)   a worker;

    (c)   a self-employed person;

    (d)   a self-sufficient person; or

    (e)   a student;

"relevant period" means—

    (a)   in the case of a person retaining worker status under paragraph (2)(b) or self-employed person status under paragraph (4)(b), a continuous period of six months;

    (b)   in the case of a jobseeker, 91 days, minus the cumulative total of any days during which the person concerned previously enjoyed a right to reside as a jobseeker, not including any days prior to a continuous absence from the United Kingdom of at least 12 months.

(2)   A person who is no longer working must continue to be treated as a worker provided that the person—

    (a)   is temporarily unable to work as the result of an illness or accident;

    (b)   is in duly recorded involuntary unemployment after having been employed in the United Kingdom for at least one year, provided the person—

        (i)   has registered as a jobseeker with the relevant employment office; and

        (ii)   satisfies conditions A and B;

    (c)   is in duly recorded involuntary unemployment after having been employed in the United Kingdom for less than one year, provided the person—

        (i)   has registered as a jobseeker with the relevant employment office; and

        (ii)   satisfies conditions A and B;

    (d)   is involuntarily unemployed and has embarked on vocational training; or

    (e)   has voluntarily ceased working and has embarked on vocational training that is related to the person's previous employment.

(3)   A person to whom paragraph (2)(c) applies may only retain worker status for a maximum of six months.

(4)   A person who is no longer in self-employment must continue to be treated as a self-employed person provided that the person—

    (a)   is temporarily unable to engage in activities as a self-employed person as the result of an illness or accident;

    (b)   is in duly recorded involuntary unemployment after having worked as a self-employed person in the United Kingdom for at least one year provided the person—

        (i)   has registered as a jobseeker with the relevant employment office; and

        (ii)   satisfies conditions D and E;

    (c)   is in duly recorded involuntary unemployment after having worked as a self-employed person in the United Kingdom for less than one year, provided the person—

        (i)   has registered as a jobseeker with the relevant employment office; and

        (ii)   satisfies conditions D and E;

    (d)   is involuntarily no longer in self-employment and has embarked on vocational training; or

    (e)   has voluntarily ceased self-employment and has embarked on vocational training that is related to the person's previous occupation.

(4A)   A person to whom paragraph (4)(c) applies may only retain self-employed person status for a maximum of six months.

(4B)   Condition D is that the person—

    (a)   entered the United Kingdom as a self-employed person or in order to seek employment as a self-employed person; or

    (b)   is present in the United Kingdom seeking employment or self-employment, immediately after enjoying a right to reside under sub-paragraphs (c) to (e) of the definition of qualified person in paragraph (1) (disregarding any period during which self-employed status was retained pursuant to paragraph (4)(b) or (c)).

(4C)   Condition E is that the person provides evidence of seeking employment or self-employment and having a genuine chance of being engaged.

(5)   Condition A is that the person—

    (a)   entered the United Kingdom in order to seek employment; or

    (b)   is present in the United Kingdom seeking employment, immediately after enjoying a right to reside under sub-paragraphs (b), (d) or (e) of the definition of qualified person in paragraph (1) (disregarding any period during which worker status was retained pursuant to paragraph (2)(b) or (c)).

(6)   Condition B is that the person provides evidence of seeking employment and having a genuine chance of being engaged.

(7)   A person may not retain the status of—

    (a)   a worker under paragraph (2)(b);

    (b)   a jobseeker; or

    (c)   a self-employed person under paragraph (4)(b);

for longer than the relevant period without providing compelling evidence of continuing to seek employment and having a genuine chance of being engaged.

(8)   Condition C applies where the person concerned has, previously, enjoyed a right to reside under this regulation as a result of satisfying conditions A and B or, as the case may be, conditions D and E—

    (a)   in the case of a person to whom paragraph (2)(b) or (c) or (4)(b) or (c) applied, for at least six months; or

    (b)   in the case of a jobseeker, for at least 91 days in total,

unless the person concerned has, since enjoying the above right to reside, been continuously absent from the United Kingdom for at least 12 months.

(9)   Condition C is that the person has had a period of absence from the United Kingdom.

(10)   Where condition C applies—

    (a)   paragraph (7) does not apply; and

    (b)   condition B or, as the case may be, condition E has effect as if "compelling" were inserted before "evidence".

7.   "Family member"

(1)   In these Regulations, "family member" means, in relation to a person ("A")—

    (a)   A's spouse or civil partner;

    (b)   A's direct descendants, or the direct descendants of A's spouse or civil partner who are either—

        (i)   aged under 21; or

        (ii)   dependants of A, or of A's spouse or civil partner;

    (c)   dependent direct relatives in A's ascending line, or in that of A's spouse or civil partner.

(2)   Where A is a student residing in the United Kingdom otherwise than under regulation 13 (initial right of residence), a person is not a family member of A under paragraph (1)(b) or (c) unless—

    (a)   in the case of paragraph (1)(b), the person is the dependent child of A or of A's spouse or civil partner; or

    (b)   A also falls within one of the other categories of qualified person mentioned in regulation 6(1).

(3)   A person ("B") who is an extended family member and has been issued with an EEA family permit, a registration certificate or a residence card must be treated as a family member of A, provided—

    (a)   B continues to satisfy the conditions in regulation 8(1A), 8(2), (3), (4) or (5); and

    (b)   the EEA family permit, registration certificate or residence card remains in force.

(4)   A must be an EEA national unless regulation 9 applies (family members of British citizens).

8.   "Extended family member"

(1)   In these Regulations "extended family member" means a person who is not a family member of an EEA national under regulation 7(1)(a), (b) or (c) and who satisfies a condition in paragraph (1A), (2), (3), (4) or (5).

(1A)   The condition in this paragraph is that the person—

    (a)   is under the age of 18;

    (b)   is subject to a non-adoptive legal guardianship order in favour of an EEA national that is recognised under the national law of the state in which it was contracted;

    (c)   has lived with the EEA national since their placement under the guardianship order;

    (d)   has created family life with the EEA national; and

    (e)   has a personal relationship with the EEA national that involves dependency on the EEA national and the assumption of parental responsibility, including legal and financial responsibilities, for that person by the EEA national.

(2)   The condition in this paragraph is that the person is—

    (a)   a relative of an EEA national; and

    (b)   residing in a country other than the United Kingdom and is dependent upon the EEA national or is a member of the EEA national's household; and either—

        (i)   is accompanying the EEA national to the United Kingdom or wants to join the EEA national in the United Kingdom; or

        (ii)   has joined the EEA national in the United Kingdom and continues to be dependent upon the EEA national, or to be a member of the EEA national's household.

(3)   The condition in this paragraph is that the person is a relative of an EEA national and on serious health grounds, strictly requires the personal care of the EEA national or the spouse or civil partner of the EEA national.

(4)   The condition in this paragraph is that the person is a relative of an EEA national and would meet the requirements in the immigration rules (other than those relating to entry clearance) for indefinite leave to enter or remain in the United Kingdom as a dependent relative of the EEA national.

(5)   The condition in this paragraph is that the person is the partner (other than a civil partner) of, and in a durable relationship with, an EEA national, or the spouse or civil partner of the EEA national and is able to prove this to the decision maker.

(6)   In these Regulations, "relevant EEA national" means, in relation to an extended family member—

    (a)   referred to in paragraph (2), (3) or (4), the EEA national to whom the extended family member is related;

    (b)   referred to in paragraph (5), the EEA national who is the durable partner of the extended family member.

(7)   In paragraphs (2), (3) and (4), "relative of an EEA national" includes a relative of the spouse or civil partner of an EEA national.

(8)   Where an extensive examination of the personal circumstances of the applicant is required under these Regulations, it must include examination of the following—

    (a)   the best interests of the applicant, particularly where the applicant is a child;

    (b)   the character and conduct of the applicant; and

    (c)   whether an EEA national would be deterred from exercising their free movement rights if the application was refused.

9. Family members of British citizens

(1)   If the conditions in paragraph (2) are satisfied, these Regulations apply to a person who is the family member ("F") of a British citizen ("BC") as though the BC were an EEA national.

(2)   The conditions are that—

    (a)   BC—

        (i)   is residing in an EEA State as a worker, self-employed person, self-sufficient person or a student, or so resided immediately before returning to the United Kingdom; or

        (ii)   has acquired the right of permanent residence in an EEA State;

    (b)   F and BC resided together in the EEA State;

    (c)   F and BC's residence in the EEA State was genuine; and

    (d)   either—

        (i)   F was a family member of BC during all or part of their joint residence in the EEA State;

        (ii)   F was an EFM of BC during all or part of their joint residence in the EEA State, during which time F was lawfully resident in the EEA State; or

        (iii)   EFM was an EFM of BC during all or part of their joint residence in the EEA State, during which time EFM was lawfully resident in the EEA State;

    (e)   genuine family life was created or strengthened during their joint residence in the EEA State; and

(f)   the conditions in sub-paragraphs (a), (b) and (c) have been met concurrently.

(3)   Factors relevant to whether residence in the EEA State is or was genuine include—

(a)   whether the centre of BC's life transferred to the EEA State;

(b)   the length of F and BC's joint residence in the EEA State;

(c)   the nature and quality of the F and BC's accommodation in the EEA State, and whether it is or was BC's principal residence;

(d)   the degree of F and BC's integration in the EEA State;

(e)   whether F's first lawful residence in the EU with BC was in the EEA State.

(4)   This regulation does not apply—

(a)   where the purpose of the residence in the EEA State was as a means for circumventing any immigration laws applying to non-EEA nationals to which F would otherwise be subject (such as any applicable requirement under the 1971 Act to have leave to enter or remain in the United Kingdom); or

(b)   to a person who is only eligible to be treated as a family member as a result of regulation 7(3) (extended family members treated as family members).

(5)   Where these Regulations apply to F, BC is to be treated as holding a valid passport issued by an EEA State for the purposes of the application of these Regulations to F.

(6)   In paragraph (2)(a)(ii), BC is only to be treated as having acquired the right of permanent residence in the EEA State if such residence would have led to the acquisition of that right under regulation 15, had it taken place in the United Kingdom.

(7)   For the purposes of determining whether, when treating the BC as an EEA national under these Regulations in accordance with paragraph (1), BC would be a qualified person—

(a)   any requirement to have comprehensive sickness insurance cover in the United Kingdom still applies, save that it does not require the cover to extend to BC;

(b)   in assessing whether BC can continue to be treated as a worker under regulation 6(2)(b) or (c), BC is not required to satisfy condition A;

(c)   in assessing whether BC can be treated as a jobseeker as defined in regulation 6(1), BC is not required to satisfy conditions A and, where it would otherwise be relevant, condition C.

9A.   Dual national: national of an EEA State who acquires British citizenship

(1)   In this regulation "DN" means a person within paragraph (b) of the definition of "EEA national" in regulation 2(1).

(2)   DN who comes within the definition of "qualified person" in regulation 6(1) is only a qualified person for the purpose of these Regulations if DN—

(a)   came within the definition of "qualified person" at the time of acquisition of British citizenship; and

(b)   has not at any time subsequent to the acquisition of British citizenship lost the status of qualified person.

(3)   Regulation 15 only applies to DN, or to the family member of DN who is not an EEA national, if DN satisfies the condition in paragraph (4).

(4)   The condition in this paragraph is that at the time of acquisition of British citizenship DN either—

(a)   was a qualified person; or

(b)   had acquired a right of permanent residence in accordance with these Regulations.

10.   "Family member who has retained the right of residence"

(1)   In these Regulations, "family member who has retained the right of residence" means, subject to paragraphs (8) and (9), a person who satisfies a condition in paragraph (2), (3), (4) or (5).

(2)   The condition in this paragraph is that the person—

(a)   was a family member of a qualified person or of an EEA national with a right of permanent residence when the qualified person or the EEA national with the right of permanent residence died;

(b)   resided in the United Kingdom in accordance with these Regulations for at least the year immediately before the death of the qualified person or the EEA national with a right of permanent residence; and

    (c)   satisfies the condition in paragraph (6).

(3)   The condition in this paragraph is that the person—

    (a)   is the direct descendant of—

        (i)   a qualified person or an EEA national with a right of permanent residence who has died;

        (ii)   a person who ceased to be a qualified person on ceasing to reside in the United Kingdom;

        (iii)   the spouse or civil partner of the qualified person or EEA national described in sub-paragraph (i) immediately preceding that qualified person or EEA national's death; or

        (iv)   the spouse or civil partner of the person described in sub-paragraph (ii); and

    (b)   was attending an educational course in the United Kingdom immediately before the qualified person or the EEA national with a right of permanent residence died, or ceased to be a qualified person, and continues to attend such a course.

(4)   The condition in this paragraph is that the person is the parent with actual custody of a child who satisfies the condition in paragraph (3).

(5)   The condition in this paragraph is that the person ("A")—

    (a)   ceased to be a family member of a qualified person or an EEA national with a right of permanent residence on the initiation of proceedings for the termination of the marriage or civil partnership of A;

    (b)   was residing in the United Kingdom in accordance with these Regulations at the date of the termination;

    (c)   satisfies the condition in paragraph (6); and

    (d)   either—

        (i)   prior to the initiation of the proceedings for the termination of the marriage or the civil partnership, the marriage or civil partnership had lasted for at least three years and the parties to the marriage or civil partnership had resided in the United Kingdom for at least one year during its duration;

        (ii)   the former spouse or civil partner of the qualified person or the EEA national with a right of permanent residence has custody of a child of that qualified person or EEA national;

        (iii)   the former spouse or civil partner of the qualified person or the EEA national with a right of permanent residence has the right of access to a child of that qualified person or EEA national, where the child is under the age of 18 and where a court has ordered that such access must take place in the United Kingdom; or

        (iv)   the continued right of residence in the United Kingdom of A is warranted by particularly difficult circumstances, such as where A or another family member has been a victim of domestic violence whilst the marriage or civil partnership was subsisting.

(6)   The condition in this paragraph is that the person—

    (a)   is not an EEA national but would, if the person were an EEA national, be a worker, a self-employed person or a self-sufficient person under regulation 6; or

    (b)   is the family member of a person who falls within paragraph (a).

(7)   In this regulation, "educational course" means a course within the scope of Article 10 of Council Regulation (EU) No. 492/2011.

(8)   A person ("P") does not satisfy a condition in paragraph (2), (3), (4) or (5) if, at the first time P would otherwise have satisfied the relevant condition, P had a right of permanent residence under regulation 15.

(9)   A family member who has retained the right of residence ceases to enjoy that status on acquiring a right of permanent residence under regulation 15.

PART 2
EEA RIGHTS

11. **Right of admission to the United Kingdom**

(1)   An EEA national must be admitted to the United Kingdom on arrival if the EEA national produces a valid national identity card or passport issued by an EEA State.

(2)   A person who is not an EEA national must be admitted to the United Kingdom if that person is—

(a)   a family member of an EEA national and produces on arrival a valid passport and qualifying EEA State residence card, provided the conditions in regulation 23(4) (family member of EEA national must accompany or join EEA national with right to reside) are met; or

(b)   a family member of an EEA national, a family member who has retained the right of residence, a person who meets the criteria in paragraph (5) or a person with a right of permanent residence under regulation 15 and produces on arrival—

(i)   a valid passport; and

(ii)   a valid EEA family permit, residence card, derivative residence card or permanent residence card.

(3)   An immigration officer must not place a stamp in the passport of a person admitted to the United Kingdom under this regulation who is not an EEA national if the person produces a residence card, a derivative residence card, a permanent residence card or a qualifying EEA State residence card.

(4)   Before an immigration officer refuses admission to the United Kingdom to a person under this regulation because the person does not produce on arrival a document mentioned in paragraph (1) or (2), the immigration officer must provide every reasonable opportunity for the document to be obtained by, or brought to, the person or allow the person to prove by other means that the person is—

(a)   an EEA national;

(b)   a family member of an EEA national with a right to accompany that EEA national or join that EEA national in the United Kingdom;

(c)   a person who meets the criteria in paragraph (5); or

(d)   a family member who has retained the right of residence or a person with a right of permanent residence under regulation 15.

(5)   The criteria in this paragraph are that a person ("P")—

(a)   previously resided in the United Kingdom under regulation 16(3) and would be entitled to reside in the United Kingdom under that regulation were P in the country;

(b)   is accompanying an EEA national to, or joining an EEA national in, the United Kingdom and P would be entitled to reside in the United Kingdom under regulation 16(2) were P and the EEA national both in the United Kingdom;

(c)   is accompanying a person ("the relevant person") to, or joining the relevant person in, the United Kingdom and—

(i)   the relevant person is residing, or has resided, in the United Kingdom under regulation 16(3); and

(ii)   P would be entitled to reside in the United Kingdom under regulation 16(4) were P and the relevant person both in the United Kingdom;

(d)   is accompanying a person who meets the criteria in sub-paragraph (b) or (c) ("the relevant person") to the United Kingdom and—

(i)   P and the relevant person are both—

(aa)   seeking admission to the United Kingdom in reliance on this paragraph for the first time; or

(bb)   returning to the United Kingdom having previously resided there pursuant to the same provisions of regulation 16 in reliance on which they now base their claim to admission; and

(ii)   P would be entitled to reside in the United Kingdom under regulation 16(6) were P and the relevant person there; or

(e)   is accompanying a British citizen to, or joining a British citizen in, the United Kingdom and P would be entitled to reside in the United Kingdom under regulation 16(5) were P and the British citizen both in the United Kingdom.

(6)   Paragraph (7) applies where—

(a)   a person ("P") seeks admission to the United Kingdom in reliance on paragraph (5)(b), (c) or (e); and

(b)   if P were in the United Kingdom, P would have a derived right to reside under regulation 16(8)(b)(ii).

(7)   Where this paragraph applies a person ("P") must only be regarded as meeting the criteria in paragraph (5)(b), (c) or (e) where P—

    (a)   is accompanying the person with whom P would on admission to the United Kingdom jointly share care responsibility for the purpose of regulation 16(8)(b)(ii); or

    (b)   has previously resided in the United Kingdom pursuant to regulation 16(2), (4) or (5) as a joint primary carer and seeks admission to the United Kingdom in order to reside there again on the same basis.

(8)   But this regulation is subject to regulations 23(1), (2), (3) and (4) and 31.

(9)   A person is not entitled to be admitted by virtue of this regulation where that person is subject to a decision under regulation 23(6)(b) (removal decision).

12.   Issue of EEA family permit

(1)   An entry clearance officer must issue an EEA family permit to a person who applies for one if the person is a family member of an EEA national and—

    (a)   the EEA national—

        (i)   is residing in the United Kingdom in accordance with these Regulations; or

        (ii)   will be travelling to the United Kingdom within six months of the date of the application and will be an EEA national residing in the United Kingdom in accordance with these Regulations on arrival in the United Kingdom; and

    (b)   the family member will be accompanying the EEA national to the United Kingdom or joining the EEA national there.

(2)   An entry clearance officer must issue an EEA family permit to a person who applies and provides evidence demonstrating that, at the time at which the person first intends to use the EEA family permit, the person—

    (a)   would be entitled to be admitted to the United Kingdom because that person would meet the criteria in regulation 11(5); and

    (b)   will (save in the case of a person who would be entitled to be admitted to the United Kingdom because that person would meet the criteria for admission in regulation 11(5)(a)) be accompanying to, or joining in, the United Kingdom any person from whom the right to be admitted to the United Kingdom under the criteria in regulation 11(5) is derived.

(3)   An entry clearance officer must issue an EEA family permit to—

    (a)   a family member who has retained the right of residence; or

    (b)   a person who is not an EEA national but who has acquired the right of permanent residence under regulation 15.

(4)   An entry clearance officer may issue an EEA family permit to an extended family member of an EEA national (the relevant EEA national) who applies for one if—

    (a)   the relevant EEA national satisfies the condition in paragraph (1)(a);

    (b)   the extended family member wants to accompany the relevant EEA national to the United Kingdom or to join that EEA national there; and

    (c)   in all the circumstances, it appears to the entry clearance officer appropriate to issue the EEA family permit.

(5)   Where an entry clearance officer receives an application under paragraph (4) an extensive examination of the personal circumstances of the applicant must be undertaken by the Secretary of State and if the application is refused, the entry clearance officer must give reasons justifying the refusal unless this is contrary to the interests of national security.

(5A)   An EEA family permit issued under this regulation may be issued in electronic form.

(6)   An EEA family permit issued under this regulation must be issued free of charge and as soon as possible.

(7)   But an EEA family permit must not be issued under this regulation if the applicant or the EEA national concerned is not entitled to be admitted to the United Kingdom as a result of regulation 23(1), (2) or (3) or falls to be excluded in accordance with regulation 23(5).

(8)   An EEA family permit must not be issued under this regulation to a person ("A") who is the spouse, civil partner or durable partner of a person ("B") where a spouse, civil partner or durable partner of A or B holds a valid EEA family permit.

13. Initial right of residence

(1)   An EEA national is entitled to reside in the United Kingdom for a period not exceeding three months beginning on the date of admission to the United Kingdom provided the EEA national holds a valid national identity card or passport issued by an EEA State.

(2)   A person who is not an EEA national but is a family member who has retained the right of residence or the family member of an EEA national residing in the United Kingdom under paragraph (1) is entitled to reside in the United Kingdom provided that person holds a valid passport.

(3)   An EEA national or the family member of an EEA national who is an unreasonable burden on the social assistance system of the United Kingdom does not have a right to reside under this regulation.

(4)   A person who otherwise satisfies the criteria in this regulation is not entitled to a right to reside under this regulation where the Secretary of State or an immigration officer has made a decision under regulation 23(6)(b) (decision to remove on grounds of public policy, public security or public health), 24(1) (refusal to issue residence documentation etc), 25(1) (cancellation of a right of residence), 26(3) (misuse of right to reside) or 31(1) (revocation of admission), or an order under regulation 23(5) (exclusion order) or 32(3) (deportation order), unless that decision or order, as the case may be, is set aside, revoked or otherwise no longer has effect.

14. Extended right of residence

(1)   A qualified person is entitled to reside in the United Kingdom for as long as that person remains a qualified person.

(2)   A person ("P") who is a family member of a qualified person residing in the United Kingdom under paragraph (1) or of an EEA national with a right of permanent residence under regulation 15 is entitled to remain in the United Kingdom for so long as P remains the family member of that person or EEA national.

(3)   A family member who has retained the right of residence is entitled to reside in the United Kingdom for so long as that person remains a family member who has retained the right of residence.

(4)   A person who otherwise satisfies the criteria in this regulation is not entitled to a right to reside in the United Kingdom under this regulation where the Secretary of State or an immigration officer has made a decision under regulation 23(6)(b), 24(1), 25(1), 26(3) or 31(1), or an order under regulation 23(5) (exclusion order) or 32(3) (deportation order), unless that decision or order, as the case may be, is set aside, revoked or otherwise no longer has effect.

15. Right of permanent residence

(1)   The following persons acquire the right to reside in the United Kingdom permanently—

(a)   an EEA national who has resided in the United Kingdom in accordance with these Regulations for a continuous period of five years;

(b)   a family member of an EEA national who is not an EEA national but who has resided in the United Kingdom with the EEA national in accordance with these Regulations for a continuous period of five years;

(c)   a worker or self-employed person who has ceased activity;

(d)   the family member of a worker or self-employed person who has ceased activity, provided—

(i)   the person was the family member of the worker or self-employed person at the point the worker or self-employed person ceased activity; and

(ii)   at that point, the family member enjoyed a right to reside on the basis of being the family member of that worker or self-employed person;

(e)   a person who was the family member of a worker or self-employed person where—

(i)   the worker or self-employed person has died;

(ii)   the family member resided with the worker or self-employed person immediately before the death; and

(iii)   the worker or self-employed person had resided continuously in the United Kingdom for at least two years immediately before dying or the death was the result of an accident at work or an occupational disease;

(f)   a person who—

(i)   has resided in the United Kingdom in accordance with these Regulations for a continuous period of five years; and

(ii)   was, at the end of the period, a family member who has retained the right of residence.

(2)   Residence in the United Kingdom as a result of a derivative right to reside does not constitute residence for the purpose of this regulation.

(3)   The right of permanent residence under this regulation is lost through absence from the United Kingdom for a period exceeding two years.

(4)   A person who satisfies the criteria in this regulation is not entitled to a right to permanent residence in the United Kingdom where the Secretary of State or an immigration officer has made a decision under regulation 23(6)(b), 24(1), 25(1), 26(3) or 31(1), or an order under regulation 23(5) (exclusion order) or 32(3) (deportation order), unless that decision or order, as the case may be, is set aside, revoked or otherwise no longer has effect.

16.   **Derivative right to reside**

(1)   A person has a derivative right to reside during any period in which the person—

(a)   is not an exempt person; and

(b)   satisfies each of the criteria in one or more of paragraphs (2) to (6).

(2)   The criteria in this paragraph are that—

(a)   the person is the primary carer of an EEA national; and

(b)   the EEA national—

(i)   is under the age of 18;

(ii)   resides in the United Kingdom as a self-sufficient person; and

(iii)   would be unable to remain in the United Kingdom if the person left the United Kingdom for an indefinite period.

(3)   The criteria in this paragraph are that—

(a)   any of the person's parents ("PP") is an EEA national who resides or has resided in the United Kingdom;

(b)   both the person and PP reside or have resided in the United Kingdom at the same time, and during such a period of residence, PP has been a worker in the United Kingdom; and

(c)   the person is in education in the United Kingdom.

(4)   The criteria in this paragraph are that—

(a)   the person is the primary carer of a person satisfying the criteria in paragraph (3) ("PPP"); and

(b)   PPP would be unable to continue to be educated in the United Kingdom if the person left the United Kingdom for an indefinite period.

(5)   The criteria in this paragraph are that—

(a)   the person is the primary carer of a British citizen ("BC");

(b)   BC is residing in the United Kingdom; and

(c)   BC would be unable to reside in the United Kingdom or in another EEA State if the person left the United Kingdom for an indefinite period.

(6)   The criteria in this paragraph are that—

(a)   the person is under the age of 18;

(b)   the person does not have leave to enter, or remain in, the United Kingdom under the 1971 Act;

(c)   the person's primary carer is entitled to a derivative right to reside in the United Kingdom under paragraph (2), (4) or (5); and

(d)   the primary carer would be prevented from residing in the United Kingdom if the person left the United Kingdom for an indefinite period.

(7)   In this regulation—

(a)   "education" excludes nursery education but does not exclude education received before the compulsory school age where that education is equivalent to the education received at or after the compulsory school age;

(b)   "worker" does not include a jobseeker or a person treated as a worker under regulation6(2);

(c)   an "exempt person" is a person—

(i)   who has a right to reside under another provision of these Regulations;

(ii)   who has the right of abode under section 2 of the 1971 Act;

(iii)   to whom section 8 of the 1971 Act, or an order made under subsection (2) of that section, applies; or

(iv)   who has indefinite leave to enter or remain in the United Kingdom.

(8)   A person is the "primary carer" of another person ("AP") if—

(a)   the person is a direct relative or a legal guardian of AP; and

(b)   either—

(i)   the person has primary responsibility for AP's care; or

(ii)   shares equally the responsibility for AP's care with one other person.

(9)   In paragraph (2)(b)(iii), (4)(b) or (5)(c), if the role of primary carer is shared with another person in accordance with paragraph (8)(b)(ii), the words "the person" are to be read as "both primary carers".

(10)   Paragraph (9) does not apply if the person with whom care responsibility is shared acquired a derivative right to reside in the United Kingdom as a result of this regulation prior to the other person's assumption of equal care responsibility.

(11)   A person is not be regarded as having responsibility for another person's care for the purpose of paragraph (8) on the sole basis of a financial contribution towards that person's care.

(12)   A person does not have a derivative right to reside where the Secretary of State or an immigration officer has made a decision under regulation 23(6)(b), 24(1), 25(1), 26(3) or 31(1), unless that decision is set aside or otherwise no longer has effect.

PART 3
RESIDENCE DOCUMENTATION

17.   Issue of registration certificate

(1)   The Secretary of State must issue a registration certificate to a qualified person immediately on application and production of—

(a)   a valid national identity card or passport issued by an EEA State; and

(b)   proof that the applicant is a qualified person.

(2)   In the case of a worker, confirmation of the worker's engagement from the worker's employer or a certificate of employment is sufficient proof for the purposes of paragraph (1)(b).

(3)   The Secretary of State must issue a registration certificate to an EEA national who is the family member of a qualified person or of an EEA national with a right of permanent residence under regulation 15 immediately on application and production of—

(a)   a valid national identity card or passport issued by an EEA State; and

(b)   proof that the applicant is such a family member.

(4)   The Secretary of State must issue a registration certificate to an EEA national who is a family member who has retained the right of residence on application and production of—

(a)   a valid national identity card or passport; and

(b)   proof that the applicant is a family member who has retained the right of residence.

(5)   The Secretary of State may issue a registration certificate to an extended family member not falling within regulation 7(3) who is an EEA national on application if—

(a)   the application is accompanied or joined by a valid national identity card or passport;

(b)   the relevant EEA national is a qualified person or an EEA national with a right of permanent residence under regulation 15; and

(c)   in all the circumstances it appears to the Secretary of State appropriate to issue the registration certificate.

(6)   Where the Secretary of State receives an application under paragraph (5) an extensive examination of the personal circumstances of the applicant must be undertaken by the Secretary of State and if the application is refused, the Secretary of State must give reasons justifying the refusal unless this is contrary to the interests of national security.

(7)   A registration certificate issued under this regulation must state the name and address of the person registering and the date of registration.

(8)   A registration certificate is—

(a)   proof of the holder's right to reside on the date of issue;

(b)   no longer valid if the holder ceases to have a right to reside under these Regulations;

(c)   invalid if the holder never had a right to reside under these Regulations.

(9)   This regulation is subject to regulations 24 (refusal to issue or renew and revocation of residence documentation) and 25 (cancellation of a right of residence).

18. Issue of residence card

(1)   The Secretary of State must issue a residence card to a person who is not an EEA national and is the family member of a qualified person or of an EEA national with a right of permanent residence under regulation 15 on application and production of—

(a)   a valid passport; and

(b)   proof that the applicant is such a family member.

(2)   The Secretary of State must issue a residence card to a person who is not an EEA national but who is a family member who has retained the right of residence on application and production of—

(a)   a valid passport; and

(b)   proof that the applicant is a family member who has retained the right of residence.

(3)   On receipt of an application under paragraph (1) or (2) and the documents that are required to accompany the application the Secretary of State must immediately issue the applicant with a certificate of application for the residence card and the residence card must be issued no later than six months after the date on which the application and documents are received.

(4)   The Secretary of State may issue a residence card to an extended family member not falling within regulation 7(3) who is not an EEA national on application if—

(a)   the application is accompanied or joined by a valid passport;

(b)   the relevant EEA national is a qualified person or an EEA national with a right of permanent residence under regulation 15; and

(c)   in all the circumstances it appears to the Secretary of State appropriate to issue the residence card.

(5)   Where the Secretary of State receives an application under paragraph (4) an extensive examination of the personal circumstances of the applicant must be undertaken by the Secretary of State and if the application is refused, the Secretary of State must give reasons justifying the refusal unless this is contrary to the interests of national security.

(6)   A residence card issued under this regulation is valid for—

(a)   five years from the date of issue; or

(b)   in the case of a residence card issued to the family member or extended family member of a qualified person, the envisaged period of residence in the United Kingdom of the qualified person,

whichever is the shorter.

(7)   A residence card—

(a)   must be called "Residence card of a family member of a Union citizen";

(b)   is proof of the holder's right to reside on the date of issue;

(c)   is no longer valid if the holder ceases to have a right to reside under these Regulations;

(d)   is invalid if the holder never had a right to reside under these Regulations.

(8)   This regulation is subject to regulations 24 and 25.

19. Issue of a document certifying permanent residence and a permanent residence card

(1)   The Secretary of State must, as soon as possible, issue an EEA national with a right of permanent residence under regulation 15 with a document certifying permanent residence on application and the production of—

(a)   a valid national identity card or passport issued by an EEA State; and

(b)   proof that the EEA national has a right of permanent residence.

(2)   The Secretary of State must issue a person who is not an EEA national who has a right of permanent residence under regulation 15 with a permanent residence card no later than six months after an application is received and the production of—

(a)   a valid passport; and

(b)   proof that the person has a right of permanent residence.

(3)   Subject to paragraph (4) a permanent residence card is valid for ten years from the date of issue and must be renewed on application.

(4)   A document certifying permanent residence and a permanent residence card is—

(a)   proof that the holder had a right to reside under regulation 15 on the date of issue;

(b)   no longer valid if the holder ceases to have a right of permanent residence under regulation 15;

(c)   invalid if the holder never had a right of permanent residence under regulation 15.

(5)   This regulation is subject to regulations 24 and 25.

20.   Issue of a derivative residence card

(1)   The Secretary of State must issue a person with a derivative residence card on application and on production of—

(a)   a valid national identity card issued by an EEA State or a valid passport; and

(b)   proof that the applicant has a derivative right to reside under regulation 16.

(2)   On receipt of an application under paragraph (1) the Secretary of State must issue the applicant with a certificate of application as soon as possible.

(3)   A derivative residence card issued under paragraph (1) is valid until—

(a)   the date five years from the date of issue; or

(b)   any earlier date specified by the Secretary of State when issuing the derivative residence card.

(4)   A derivative residence card issued under paragraph (1) must be issued as soon as practicable.

(5)   A derivative residence card is—

(a)   proof of the holder's derivative right to reside on the day of issue;

(b)   no longer valid if the holder ceases to have a derivative right to reside under regulation 16;

(c)   invalid if the holder never had a derivative right to reside under regulation 16.

(6)   This regulation is subject to regulations 24 and 25.

21.   Procedure for applications for documentation under this Part and regulation 12

(1)   An application for documentation under this Part, or for an EEA family permit under regulation 12, must be made—

(a)   online, submitted electronically using the relevant pages of www.gov.uk; or

(b)   by post or in person, using the relevant application form specified by the Secretary of State on www.gov.uk.

(2)   All applications must—

(a)   be accompanied by the evidence or proof required by this Part or regulation 12, as the case may be, as well as that required by paragraph (5), within the time specified by the Secretary of State on www.gov.uk; and

(b)   be complete.

(3)   An application for a residence card or a derivative residence card must be submitted while the applicant is in the United Kingdom.

(4)   When an application is submitted otherwise than in accordance with the requirements in this regulation, it is invalid and must be rejected.

(4A)   An application for documentation under this Part, or for an EEA family permit under regulation 12, is invalid where the person making the application is subject to a removal decision made under regulation 23(6)(b), a deportation order made under regulation 32(3) or an exclusion order made under regulation 23(5).

(5)   Where an application for documentation under this Part is made by a person who is not an EEA national on the basis that the person is or was the family member of an EEA national or an extended family member of an EEA national, the application must be accompanied by a valid national identity card or passport in the name of that EEA national.

(6)   Where—

(a)   there are circumstances beyond the control of an applicant for documentation under this Part; and

(b)   as a result, the applicant is unable to comply with the requirements to submit an application online or using the application form specified by the Secretary of State, the Secretary of State may accept an application submitted by post or in person which does not use the relevant application form specified by the Secretary of State.

22. **Verification of a right of residence**

(1)   This regulation applies where the Secretary of State—

(a)   has reasonable doubt as to whether a person ("A") has a right to reside or a derivative right to reside; or

(b)   wants to verify the eligibility of a person ("A") to apply for an EEA family permit or documentation issued under Part 3.

(2)   Where this regulation applies, the Secretary of State may invite A to—

(a)   provide evidence to support the existence of a right to reside or a derivative right to reside (as the case may be), or to support an application for an EEA family permit or documentation under this Part; or

(b)   attend an interview with the Secretary of State.

(3)   If A purports to have a right to reside on the basis of a relationship with another person ("B"), (including, where B is a British citizen, through having lived with B in another EEA State), the Secretary of State may invite B to—

(a)   provide information about their relationship or residence in another EEA State; or

(b)   attend an interview with the Secretary of State.

(4)   If without good reason A or B (as the case may be)—

(a)   fails to provide the information requested;

(b)   on at least two occasions, fails to attend an interview if so invited;

the Secretary of State may draw any factual inferences about A's entitlement to a right to reside as appear appropriate in the circumstances.

(5)   The Secretary of State may decide following the drawing of an inference under paragraph (4) that A does not have or ceases to have a right to reside.

(6)   But the Secretary of State must not decide that A does not have or ceases to have a right to reside on the sole basis that A failed to comply with this regulation.

(7)   This regulation may not be invoked systematically.

PART 4
REFUSAL OF ADMISSION AND REMOVAL ETC

23. **Exclusion and removal from the United Kingdom**

(1)   A person is not entitled to be admitted to the United Kingdom by virtue of regulation 11 if a refusal to admit that person is justified on grounds of public policy, public security or public health in accordance with regulation 27.

(2)   A person is not entitled to be admitted to the United Kingdom by virtue of regulation 11 if that person is subject to a deportation or exclusion order, except where the person is temporarily admitted pursuant to regulation 41.

(3)   A person is not entitled to be admitted to the United Kingdom by virtue of regulation 11 if the Secretary of State considers there to be reasonable grounds to suspect that the person's admission would lead to the misuse of a right to reside under regulation 26(1).

(4)   A person is not entitled to be admitted to the United Kingdom as the family member of an EEA national under regulation 11(2) unless, at the time of arrival—

(a)   that person is accompanying the EEA national or joining the EEA national in the United Kingdom; and

(b)   the EEA national has a right to reside.

(5)   If the Secretary of State considers that the exclusion of the EEA national or the family member of an EEA national is justified on the grounds of public policy, public security or public health in accordance with regulation 27 the Secretary of State may make an order prohibiting that person from entering the United Kingdom.

(6)   Subject to paragraphs (7) and (8), an EEA national who has entered the United Kingdom or the family member of such a national who has entered the United Kingdom may be removed if—

(a)   that person does not have or ceases to have a right to reside under these Regulations;

(b)   the Secretary of State has decided that the person's removal is justified on grounds of public policy, public security or public health in accordance with regulation 27; or

(c)   the Secretary of State has decided that the person's removal is justified on grounds of misuse of rights under regulation 26(3).

(7)   A person must not be removed under paragraph (6)—

(a)   as the automatic consequence of having recourse to the social assistance system of the United Kingdom; or

(b)   if that person has leave to remain in the United Kingdom under the 1971 Act unless that person's removal is justified on the grounds of public policy, public security or public health in accordance with regulation 27.

(8)   A decision under paragraph (6)(b) must state that upon execution of any deportation order arising from that decision, the person against whom the order was made is prohibited from entering the United Kingdom—

(a)   until the order is revoked; or

(b)   for the period specified in the order.

(9)   A decision taken under paragraph (6)(b) or (c) has the effect of terminating any right to reside otherwise enjoyed by the individual concerned.

24.   Refusal to issue or renew and revocation of residence documentation

(1)   The Secretary of State may refuse to issue, revoke or refuse to renew a registration certificate, a residence card, a document certifying permanent residence or a permanent residence card if the refusal or revocation is justified on grounds of public policy, public security or public health, or on grounds of misuse of rights in accordance with regulation 26(3).

(2)   A decision under regulation 23(6) or 32(4) to remove a person from the United Kingdom, or a decision under regulation 31 to revoke a person's admission to the United Kingdom invalidates a registration certificate, residence card, document certifying permanent residence or permanent residence card held by that person or an application made by that person for such a certificate, card or document.

(3)   The Secretary of State may revoke or refuse to renew a registration certificate or a residence card if the holder of the certificate or card has ceased to have, or never had, a right to reside under these Regulations.

(4)   The Secretary of State may revoke or refuse to renew a document certifying permanent residence or a permanent residence card if the holder of the certificate or card has ceased to have, or never had, a right of permanent residence under regulation 15.

(5)   An immigration officer may, at the time of a person's arrival in the United Kingdom—

(a)   revoke that person's residence card if the person is not at that time the family member of a qualified person or of an EEA national who has a right of permanent residence under regulation 15, a family member who has retained a right of residence or a person with a right of permanent residence under regulation 15;

(b)   revoke that person's permanent residence card if the person is not at that time a person with a right of permanent residence under regulation 15.

(6)   An entry clearance officer or an immigration officer may at any time revoke a person's EEA family permit, including one issued in electronic form, if—

(a)   the revocation is justified on grounds of public policy, public security or public health; or

(b)   the person is not at that time the family member of an EEA national with the right to reside in the United Kingdom under these Regulations or is not accompanying that EEA national or joining that EEA national in the United Kingdom.

(7)   Any action taken under this regulation on grounds of public policy, public security or public health must be in accordance with regulation 27.

25.   Cancellation of a right of residence

(1)   Where the conditions in paragraph (2) are met the Secretary of State may cancel a person's right to reside.

(2)   The conditions in this paragraph are met where—

(a)   a person has a right to reside in the United Kingdom as a result of these Regulations;

(b)   the Secretary of State has decided that the cancellation of that person's right to reside in the United Kingdom is justified on the grounds of public policy, public security or public health in accordance with regulation 27 or on grounds of misuse of rights in accordance with regulation 26(3);

(c)   the circumstances are such that the Secretary of State cannot make a decision under regulation 24(1); and`

(d)   it is not possible for the Secretary of State to remove the person from the United Kingdom under regulation 23(6)(b) or (c).

26.   Misuse of a right to reside

(1)   The misuse of a right to reside occurs where a person—

(a)   observes the requirements of these Regulations in circumstances which do not achieve the purpose of these Regulations (as determined by reference to Council Directive 2004/38/EC and the EU Treaties); and

(b)   intends to obtain an advantage from these Regulations by engaging in conduct which artificially creates the conditions required to satisfy the criteria set out in these Regulations.

(2)   Such misuse includes attempting to enter the United Kingdom within 12 months of being removed under regulation 23(6)(a), where the person attempting to do so is unable to provide evidence that, upon re-entry to the United Kingdom, the conditions for a right to reside, other than the initial right of residence under regulation 13, will be met.

(3)   The Secretary of State may take an EEA decision on the grounds of misuse of rights where there are reasonable grounds to suspect the misuse of a right to reside and it is proportionate to do so.

(4)   Where, as a result of paragraph (2), the removal of a person under regulation 23(6)(a) may prevent that person from returning to the United Kingdom during the 12 month period following removal, during that 12 month period the person who was removed may apply to the Secretary of State to have the effect of paragraph (2) set aside on the grounds that there has been a material change in the circumstances which justified that person's removal under regulation 23(6)(a).

(5)   An application under paragraph (4) may only be made whilst the applicant is outside the United Kingdom.

(6)   This regulation may not be invoked systematically.

27.   Decisions taken on grounds of public policy, public security and public health

(1)   In this regulation, a "relevant decision" means an EEA decision taken on the grounds of public policy, public security or public health.

(2)   A relevant decision may not be taken to serve economic ends.

(3)   A relevant decision may not be taken in respect of a person with a right of permanent residence under regulation 15 except on serious grounds of public policy and public security.

(4)   A relevant decision may not be taken except on imperative grounds of public security in respect of an EEA national who—

(a)   has a right of permanent residence under regulation 15 and who has resided in the United Kingdom for a continuous period of at least ten years prior to the relevant decision; or

(b)   is under the age of 18, unless the relevant decision is in the best interests of the person concerned, as provided for in the Convention on the Rights of the Child adopted by the General Assembly of the United Nations on 20th November 1989.

(5)   The public policy and public security requirements of the United Kingdom include restricting rights otherwise conferred by these Regulations in order to protect the fundamental interests of society, and where a relevant decision is taken on grounds of public policy or public security it must also be taken in accordance with the following principles—

(a)   the decision must comply with the principle of proportionality;

(b)   the decision must be based exclusively on the personal conduct of the person concerned;

(c)   the personal conduct of the person must represent a genuine, present and sufficiently serious threat affecting one of the fundamental interests of society, taking into account past conduct of the person and that the threat does not need to be imminent;

(d)   matters isolated from the particulars of the case or which relate to considerations of general prevention do not justify the decision;

(e)   a person's previous criminal convictions do not in themselves justify the decision;

(f)   the decision may be taken on preventative grounds, even in the absence of a previous criminal conviction, provided the grounds are specific to the person.

(6)   Before taking a relevant decision on the grounds of public policy and public security in relation to a person ("P") who is resident in the United Kingdom, the decision maker must take account of considerations such as the age, state of health, family and economic situation of P, P's length of residence in the United Kingdom, P's social and cultural integration into the United Kingdom and the extent of P's links with P's country of origin.

(7)   In the case of a relevant decision taken on grounds of public health—

(a)   a disease that does not have epidemic potential as defined by the relevant instruments of the World Health Organisation or is not a disease listed in Schedule 1 to the Health Protection (Notification) Regulations 2010; or

(b)   if the person concerned is in the United Kingdom, any disease occurring after the three month period beginning on the date on which the person arrived in the United Kingdom,

does not constitute grounds for the decision.

(8)   A court or tribunal considering whether the requirements of this regulation are met must (in particular) have regard to the considerations contained in Schedule 1 (considerations of public policy, public security and the fundamental interests of society etc.).

28.   Application of Part 4 to a person with a derivative right to reside

(1)   This regulation applies where a person—

(a)   would, but for this Part of these Regulations, be entitled to a derivative right to reside (other than a derivative right to reside conferred by regulation 16(3));

(b)   holds a derivative residence card; or

(c)   has applied for a derivative residence card.

(2)   Where this regulation applies, this Part of these Regulations applies as though—

(a)   references to "the family member of an EEA national" referred instead to "a person with a derivative right to reside";

(b)   references to a registration certificate, a residence card, a document certifying permanent residence or a permanent residence card referred instead to a "derivative residence card";

(c)   regulation 24(5) instead conferred on an immigration officer the power to revoke a derivative residence card where the holder is not at that time a person with a derivative right to reside; and

(d)   regulations 24(4) and 27(3) and (4) were omitted.

PART 5
PROCEDURE IN RELATION TO EEA DECISIONS

29.   Person claiming right of admission

(1)   This regulation applies to a person who claims a right of admission to the United Kingdom under regulation 11 as—

(a)   a person, not being an EEA national, who—

(i)   is a family member of an EEA national;

(ii)   is a family member who has retained the right of residence;

(iii)   has a derivative right to reside;

(iv)   has a right of permanent residence under regulation 15; or

(v)   is in possession of a qualifying EEA State residence card;

(b)   an EEA national, where there is reason to believe that the EEA national may be a person to whom regulation 23(1), (2), (3) or (4) applies; or

(c)   a person to whom regulation 41 applies (temporary admission to submit case in person).

(2)   A person to whom this regulation applies is to be treated as if that person were a person seeking leave to enter the United Kingdom under the 1971 Act for the purposes of paragraphs 2, 3, 4, 7, 16 to 18A and 21 to 24 of Schedule 2 to the 1971 Act (administrative provisions as to control on entry etc), except that—

    (a)   the reference in paragraph 2(1) to the purpose for which the immigration officer may examine any persons who have arrived in the United Kingdom is to be read as a reference to the purpose of determining whether the person is to be granted admission under these Regulations;

    (b)   the references in paragraphs 3, 7 and 16(1) to a person who is, or may be, given leave to enter are to be read as references to a person who is, or may be, granted admission under these Regulations; and

    (c)   a medical examination is not to be carried out under paragraph 2 or paragraph 7 as a matter of routine and may only be carried out within three months of the person's arrival in the United Kingdom.

(3)   For so long as a person to whom this regulation applies is detained, or temporarily admitted or released whilst liable to detention, under the powers conferred by Schedule 2 to the 1971 Act, that person is deemed not to have been admitted to the United Kingdom.

30. Person refused admission

(1)   This regulation applies to a person who is in the United Kingdom and has been refused admission to the United Kingdom—

    (a)   because that person does not meet the requirements of regulation 11 (including where that person does not meet those requirements because that person's EEA family permit, residence card, derivative residence card or permanent residence card has been revoked by an immigration officer in accordance with regulation 24); or

    (b)   in accordance with regulation 23(1), (2), (3) or (4).

(2)   A person to whom this regulation applies, is to be treated as if the person were a person refused leave to enter under the 1971 Act for the purpose of paragraphs 8, 10, 10A, 11, 16 to 19 and 21 to 24 of Schedule 2 to the 1971 Act, except that the reference in paragraph 19 to a certificate of entitlement, entry clearance or work permit is to be read as a reference to an EEA family permit, residence card, derivative residence card, a qualifying EEA State residence card, or a permanent residence card.

31. Revocation of admission

(1)   This regulation applies to a person admitted to the United Kingdom under regulation 11 in circumstances where, under regulation 23(1), (2) or (3) that person was not entitled to be admitted.

(2)   Paragraph 6(2) of Schedule 2 to the 1971 Act (administrative provisions as to control on entry: refusal of leave to enter) applies to a person to whom this regulation applies, as though the references:

    (a)   to that person's examination under paragraph 2 of Schedule 2 to the 1971 Act were to that paragraph as applied by regulation 29(2)(a) and (c);

    (b)   to notices of leave to enter the United Kingdom were to a decision to admit that person to the United Kingdom under these Regulations; and

    (c)   to the cancellation of such a notice and the refusal of leave to enter were to revocation of the decision to admit that person to the United Kingdom under this regulation.

(3)   Where a person's admission to the United Kingdom is revoked, that person is to be treated as a person to whom admission to the United Kingdom has been refused and regulation 30 applies accordingly.

32. Person subject to removal

(1)   If there are reasonable grounds for suspecting that a person is someone who may be removed from the United Kingdom under regulation 23(6)(b), that person may be detained under the authority of the Secretary of State pending a decision whether or not to remove the person under that regulation, and paragraphs 17 to 18A of Schedule 2 to the 1971 Act apply in relation to the detention of such a person as those paragraphs apply in relation to a person who may be detained under paragraph 16 of that Schedule.

(2)   Where a decision is taken to remove a person under regulation 23(6)(a) or (c), the person is to be treated as if the person were a person to whom section 10(1) of the 1999 Act applies, and section 10 of that Act (removal of certain persons unlawfully in the United Kingdom) is to apply accordingly.

(3)   Where a decision is taken to remove a person under regulation 23(6)(b), the person is to be treated as if the person were a person to whom section 3(5)(a) of the 1971 Act (liability to deportation) applies, and section 5 of that Act (procedure for deportation) and Schedule 3 to that Act (supplementary provision as to deportation) are to apply accordingly.

(4)   A person who enters the United Kingdom in breach of a deportation or exclusion order, or in circumstances where that person was not entitled to be admitted under regulation 23(1) or (3), is removable as an illegal entrant under Schedule 2 to the 1971 Act and the provisions of that Schedule apply accordingly.

(5)   Where a deportation order is made against a person but the person is not removed under the order during the two year period beginning on the date on which the order is made, the Secretary of State may only take action to remove the person under the order at the end of that period if, having assessed whether there has been any material change in circumstances since the deportation order was made, the Secretary of State considers that the removal continues to be justified on the grounds of public policy, public security or public health.

(6)   A person to whom this regulation applies must be allowed one month to leave the United Kingdom, beginning on the date on which the decision to remove is communicated before being removed because of that decision except—

   (a)   in duly substantiated cases of urgency;

   (b)   where the person is detained pursuant to the sentence or order of any court;

   (c)   where the person is a person to whom paragraph (4) applies.

(7)   Paragraph (6) does not apply where a decision has been taken under regulation 23(6) on the basis that the relevant person—

   (a)   has ceased to have a derivative right to reside; or

   (b)   is a person who would have had a derivative right to reside but for the effect of a decision to remove under regulation 23(6)(b).

33.   Human rights considerations and interim orders to suspend removal

(1)   This regulation applies where the Secretary of State intends to give directions for the removal of a person ("P") to whom regulation 32(3) applies, in circumstances where—

   (a)   P has not appealed against the EEA decision to which regulation 32(3) applies, but would be entitled, and remains within time, to do so from within the United Kingdom (ignoring any possibility of an appeal out of time with permission); or

   (b)   P has so appealed but the appeal has not been finally determined.

(2)   The Secretary of State may only give directions for P's removal if the Secretary of State certifies that, despite the appeals process not having been begun or not having been finally determined, removal of P to the country or territory to which P is proposed to be removed, pending the outcome of P's appeal, would not be unlawful under section 6 of the Human Rights Act 1998 (public authority not to act contrary to Human Rights Convention).

(3)   The grounds upon which the Secretary of State may certify a removal under paragraph (2) include (in particular) that P would not, before the appeal is finally determined, face a real risk of serious irreversible harm if removed to the country or territory to which P is proposed to be removed.

(4)   If P applies to the appropriate court or tribunal (whether by means of judicial review or otherwise) for an interim order to suspend enforcement of the removal decision, P may not be removed from the United Kingdom until such time as the decision on the interim order has been taken, except—

   (a)   where the removal decision is based on a previous judicial decision;

   (b)   where P has had previous access to judicial review; or

   (c)   where the removal decision is based on imperative grounds of public security.

(5)   In this regulation, "finally determined" has the same meaning as in Part 6.

34.   Revocation of deportation and exclusion orders

(1)   An exclusion order remains in force unless it is revoked by the Secretary of State under this regulation.

(2)   A deportation order remains in force—

   (a)   until the order is revoked under this regulation; or

   (b)   for the period specified in the order.

(3)   A person who is subject to a deportation or exclusion order may only apply to the Secretary of State to have it revoked on the basis that there has been a material change in the circumstances that justified the making of the order.

(4)   An application under paragraph (3) must set out the material change in circumstances relied upon by the applicant and may only be made whilst the applicant is outside the United Kingdom.

(5)   On receipt of an application under paragraph (3), the Secretary of State must revoke the order if the Secretary of State considers that the criteria for making such an order are no longer satisfied.

(6)   The Secretary of State must take a decision on an application under paragraph (2) no later than six months after the date on which the application is received.

PART 6
APPEALS UNDER THESE REGULATIONS

35.   Interpretation of Part 6

(1)   In this Part—

"the 1997 Act" means the Special Immigration Appeals Commission Act 1997;

"Commission" has the same meaning as in the 1997 Act.

(2)   For the purposes of this Part, and subject to paragraphs (3) and (4), an appeal is to be treated as pending during the period when notice of appeal is given and ending when the appeal is finally determined, withdrawn or abandoned.

(3)   An appeal is not to be treated as finally determined while a further appeal may be brought; and, if such a further appeal is brought, the original appeal is not to be treated as finally determined until the further appeal is determined, withdrawn or abandoned.

(4)   A pending appeal is not to be treated as abandoned solely because the appellant leaves the United Kingdom.

36.   Appeal rights

(1)   The subject of an EEA decision may appeal against that decision under these Regulations.

(2)   If a person claims to be an EEA national, that person may not appeal under these Regulations without producing a valid national identity card or passport issued by an EEA State.

(3)   If a person claims to be in a durable relationship with an EEA national, that person may not appeal under these Regulations without producing—

(a)   a valid passport; and

(b)   either—

    (i)   an EEA family permit; or

    (ii)   sufficient evidence to satisfy the Secretary of State that the person is in a relationship with the EEA national.

(4)   If a person to whom paragraph (2) does not apply claims to be the family member of an EEA national under regulation 7, the relative of an EEA national who is an extended family member under regulation 8, or a family member who has retained the right of residence under regulation 10, that person may not appeal under these Regulations without producing—

(a)   a valid passport; and

(b)   either—

    (i)   an EEA family permit

    (ii)   a qualifying EEA State residence card;

    (iii)   in the case of a person claiming to be the family member of an EEA national, proof that the definition of 'family member' in regulation 7(1) is met;

    (iv)   in the case of a person claiming to be a family member who has retained the right of residence, proof that the definition of 'family member who has retained the right of residence' in regulation 10(1) is met; or

    (v)   in the case of a person claiming to be the relative of an EEA national who is an extended family member, proof that the definition of 'extended family member' in regulation 8(1) is met.

(5)   If a person ("P") claims to have a derivative right to reside, P may not appeal under these Regulations unless P produces a valid national identity card issued by an EEA State or a valid passport, and either—

(a)   an EEA family permit; or

(b)   where P claims to have a derivative right to reside as a result of—

    (i)   regulation 16(2), proof that P is a direct relative or legal guardian of an EEA national who is under the age of 18;

(ii) regulation 16(3), proof that P is the child of an EEA national;

(iii) regulation 16(4), proof that P is a direct relative or legal guardian of the child of an EEA national;

(iv) regulation 16(5), proof that P is a direct relative or legal guardian of a British citizen;

(v) regulation 16(6), proof that P is under the age of 18 and is a dependant of a person satisfying the criteria in paragraph (i), (iii) or (iv).

(6) If a person claims to be entitled to a right to reside under regulation 9 (family members of British citizens), that person may not appeal without producing a valid passport and either—

(a) an EEA family permit; or

(b) a qualifying EEA State residence card; and

(i) ...

(ii) proof that the British citizen is residing, or did reside, in another EEA State as a worker, self-employed person, self-sufficient person or student.

(7) The Secretary of State or an immigration officer may certify a ground for the purposes of paragraph (8) if it has been considered in a previous appeal brought under these Regulations or under section 82(1) of the 2002 Act.

(8) A person may not bring an appeal under these Regulations on a ground certified under paragraph (7) or rely on such a ground in an appeal brought under these Regulations.

(9) Except where an appeal lies to the Commission, an appeal under these Regulations lies to the First-tier Tribunal.

(10) The provisions of, or made under, the 2002 Act referred to in Schedule 2 have effect for the purposes of an appeal under these Regulations to the First-tier Tribunal in accordance with that Schedule.

(11) Nothing in this Part prevents a person who has a right of appeal under this regulation from appealing to the First-tier Tribunal under section 82(1) of the 2002 Act (right of appeal to the Tribunal), or, where relevant, to the Commission pursuant to section 2 of the 1997 Act (jurisdiction of the Commission: appeals), provided the criteria for bringing such an appeal under those Acts are met.

(12) Where there is a requirement under this regulation to produce an EEA family permit—

(a) where notice of appeal is given electronically, the permit may be produced either in paper or electronic form;

(b) in all other cases, the permit must be produced in paper form.

37. Out of country appeals

(1) Subject to paragraph (2), a person may not appeal under regulation 36 whilst in the United Kingdom against an EEA decision—

(a) to refuse to admit that person to the United Kingdom;

(b) to revoke that person's admission to the United Kingdom;

(c) to make an exclusion order against that person;

(d) to refuse to revoke a deportation or exclusion order made against the person;

(e) to refuse to issue the person with an EEA family permit;

(f) to revoke, or to refuse to issue or renew any document under these Regulations where that decision is taken at a time when the person is outside the United Kingdom; or

(g) to remove the person from the United Kingdom following entry to the United Kingdom in breach of a deportation or exclusion order, or in circumstances where that person was not entitled to be admitted pursuant to regulation 23(1), (2), (3) or (4).

(2) Sub-paragraphs (a) to (c) of paragraph (1) do not apply where the person is in the United Kingdom and—

(a) the person, not being a person who is deemed not to have been admitted to the United Kingdom under regulation 29(3)—

(i) holds a valid EEA family permit, registration certificate, residence card, derivative residence card, document certifying permanent residence, permanent residence card or qualifying EEA State residence card on arrival in the United Kingdom; or

(ii) can otherwise prove that the person is resident in the United Kingdom; or"

    (b)   the person is deemed not to have been admitted to the United Kingdom under regulation 29(3) but at the date on which notice of the decision to refuse admission is given the person has been in the United Kingdom for at least 3 months.

38. Appeals to the Commission

(1)   An appeal against an EEA decision lies to the Commission where paragraph (2) or (4) applies.

(2)   This paragraph applies if the Secretary of State certifies that the EEA decision was taken—

    (a)   by the Secretary of State wholly or partly on a ground listed in paragraph (3); or

    (b)   in accordance with a direction of the Secretary of State which identifies the person to whom the decision relates and which is given wholly or partly on a ground listed in paragraph (3).

(3)   The ground mentioned in paragraph (2) are that the person's exclusion or removal from the United Kingdom is—

    (a)   in the interests of national security; or

    (b)   in the interests of the relationship between the United Kingdom and another country.

(4)   This paragraph applies if the Secretary of State certifies that the EEA decision was taken wholly or partly in reliance on information which the Secretary of State considers must not be made public—

    (a)   in the interests of national security;

    (b)   in the interests of the relationship between the United Kingdom and another country; or

    (c)   otherwise in the public interest.

(5)   In paragraphs (2) and (4) the reference to the Secretary of State is a reference to the Secretary of State acting in person.

(6)   Where a certificate is issued under paragraph (2) or (4) in respect of a pending appeal to the First-tier Tribunal or Upper Tribunal the appeal must lapse.

(7)   An appeal against an EEA decision lies to the Commission where an appeal lapses by virtue of paragraph (6).

(8)   The 1997 Act applies to an appeal to the Commission under this regulation as it applies to an appeal under section 2 of that Act.

(9)   Where the 1997 Act applies to an appeal to the Commission under this regulation, section 2(2) of that Act is to be treated as though it applies the 2002 Act to that appeal in the form modified by Schedule 2 to these Regulations.

39. National Security: EEA Decisions

(1)   Section 97A of the 2002 Act applies to an appeal against an EEA decision where the Secretary of State has certified under regulation 38(2) or (4) that the EEA decision was taken in the interests of national security.

(2)   Where section 97A so applies, it has effect as if—

    (a)   the references in that section to a deportation order were to an EEA decision;

    (b)   subsections (1), (1A), (2)(b) and (4) were omitted;

    (c)   the reference in subsection (2)(a) to section 79 were a reference to regulations 37(2) and 40 of these Regulations; and

    (d)   in subsection (2A) for sub-paragraphs (a) and (b), "against an EEA decision" were substituted.

40. Effect of appeals to the First-tier Tribunal or Upper Tribunal

(1)   This regulation applies to appeals under these Regulations made to the First-tier Tribunal or Upper Tribunal.

(2)   If a person in the United Kingdom appeals against an EEA decision refusing admission to the United Kingdom (other than a decision under regulation 23(1), (2), or (5)), any directions for that person's removal from the United Kingdom previously given by virtue of the refusal cease to have effect, except in so far as they have already been carried out, while the appeal is pending.

(3)   If a person in the United Kingdom appeals against an EEA decision concerning that person's removal from the United Kingdom (other than a decision under regulation 23(6)(b)), any directions for removal given under section 10 of the 1999 Act or Schedule 3 to the 1971 Act are to have no effect, except in so far as they have already been carried out, while the appeal is pending.

(4)   The provisions of Part 1 of Schedule 2, or as the case may be, Schedule 3 to the 1971 Act concerning detention and persons liable to detention, apply to a person appealing against a refusal of admission, a

decision to revoke admission, or a removal decision as if there were in force directions for that person's removal from the United Kingdom, except that the person may not be detained on board a ship or aircraft so as to compel that person to leave the United Kingdom while the appeal is pending.

(5)   In paragraph (4), the words "except that the person" to the end do not apply to an EEA decision to which regulation 33 applies (human rights considerations and interim orders to suspend removal).

(6)   In calculating the period of two months limited by paragraph 8(2) of Schedule 2 to the 1971 Act for—

(a)   the giving of directions under that paragraph for the removal of a person from the United Kingdom; and

(b)   the giving of a notice of intention to give such directions,

any period during which there is an appeal pending by that person is to be disregarded (except in cases where the EEA decision was taken under regulation 23(1), (2), (5) and (6)(b).

(7)   Paragraph 29 of Schedule 2 to the 1971 Act (grant of bail pending appeal) applies to a person who has an appeal pending under these Regulations as it applies to a person who has an appeal pending under section 82(1) of the 2002 Act.

41.   Temporary admission to submit case in person

(1)   This regulation applies where—

(a)   a person ("P") is subject to a decision to remove made under regulation 23(6)(b);

(b)   P has appealed against the decision referred to in sub-paragraph (a);

(c)   a date for P's appeal has been set by the First-tier Tribunal or Upper Tribunal;

(d)   P wants to make submissions before the First-tier Tribunal or Upper Tribunal in person; and

(e)   P is outside the United Kingdom.

(2)   P may apply to the Secretary of State for permission to be temporarily admitted (within the meaning of paragraphs 21 to 24 of Schedule 2 to the 1971 Act, as applied by this regulation) to the United Kingdom in order to make submissions in person.

(3)   The Secretary of State must grant P permission, except when P's appearance may cause serious troubles to public policy or public security.

(4)   When determining when P is entitled to be given permission, and the duration of P's temporary admission should permission be granted, the Secretary of State must have regard to the dates upon which P will be required to make submissions in person.

(5)   Where—

(a)   P is temporarily admitted to the United Kingdom pursuant to this regulation;

(b)   a hearing of P's appeal has taken place; and

(c)   the appeal is not finally determined,

P may be removed from the United Kingdom pending the remaining stages of the appeal (but P may apply to return to the United Kingdom to make submissions in person during the remaining stages of the appeal in accordance with this regulation).

(6)   Where the Secretary of State grants P permission to be temporarily admitted to the United Kingdom under this regulation, upon such admission P is to be treated as if P were a person refused leave to enter under the 1971 Act for the purposes of paragraphs 8, 10, 10A, 11, 16 to 18A and 21 to 24 of Schedule 2 to the 1971 Act.

(7)   Where Schedule 2 to the 1971 Act so applies, it has effect as if—

(a)   the reference in paragraph 8(1) to leave to enter were a reference to admission to the United Kingdom under these Regulations; and

(b)   the reference in paragraph 16(1) to detention pending a decision regarding leave to enter or remain in the United Kingdom were to detention pending submission of P's case in person in accordance with this regulation.

(8)   P is deemed not to have been admitted to the United Kingdom during any time during which P is temporarily admitted pursuant to this regulation.

42.   Alternative evidence of identity and nationality

(1)   Subject to paragraph (2), where a provision of these Regulations requires a person to hold or produce a valid national identity card issued by an EEA State or a valid passport, the Secretary of State may accept alternative evidence of identity and nationality where the person is unable to obtain or produce the required document due to circumstances beyond the person's control.

(2)   This regulation does not apply to regulation 11.

SCHEDULE 1

CONSIDERATIONS OF PUBLIC POLICY, PUBLIC SECURITY AND THE
FUNDAMENTAL INTERESTS OF SOCIETY ETC.

Regulation 27

Considerations of public policy and public security

1.   The EU Treaties do not impose a uniform scale of public policy or public security values: member States enjoy considerable discretion, acting within the parameters set by the EU Treaties, applied where relevant by the EEA agreement, to define their own standards of public policy and public security, for purposes tailored to their individual contexts, from time to time.

Application of paragraph 1 to the United Kingdom

2.   An EEA national or the family member of an EEA national having extensive familial and societal links with persons of the same nationality or language does not amount to integration in the United Kingdom; a significant degree of wider cultural and societal integration must be present before a person may be regarded as integrated in the United Kingdom.

3.   Where an EEA national or the family member of an EEA national has received a custodial sentence, or is a persistent offender, the longer the sentence, or the more numerous the convictions, the greater the likelihood that the individual's continued presence in the United Kingdom represents a genuine, present and sufficiently serious threat affecting of the fundamental interests of society.

4.   Little weight is to be attached to the integration of an EEA national or the family member of an EEA national within the United Kingdom if the alleged integrating links were formed at or around the same time as—

(a)   the commission of a criminal offence;

(b)   an act otherwise affecting the fundamental interests of society;

(c)   the EEA national or family member of an EEA national was in custody.

5.   The removal from the United Kingdom of an EEA national or the family member of an EEA national who is able to provide substantive evidence of not demonstrating a threat (for example, through demonstrating that the EEA national or the family member of an EEA national has successfully reformed or rehabilitated) is less likely to be proportionate.

6.   It is consistent with public policy and public security requirements in the United Kingdom that EEA decisions may be taken in order to refuse, terminate or withdraw any right otherwise conferred by these Regulations in the case of abuse of rights or fraud, including—

(a)   entering, attempting to enter or assisting another person to enter or to attempt to enter, a marriage, civil partnership or durable partnership of convenience; or

(b)   fraudulently obtaining or attempting to obtain, or assisting another to obtain or to attempt to obtain, a right to reside under these Regulations.

The fundamental interests of society

7.   For the purposes of these Regulations, the fundamental interests of society in the United Kingdom include—

(a)   preventing unlawful immigration and abuse of the immigration laws, and maintaining the integrity and effectiveness of the immigration control system (including under these Regulations) and of the Common Travel Area;

(b)   maintaining public order;

(c)   preventing social harm;

(d)   preventing the evasion of taxes and duties;

(e)   protecting public services;

(f)   excluding or removing an EEA national or family member of an EEA national with a conviction (including where the conduct of that person is likely to cause, or has in fact caused, public offence) and maintaining public confidence in the ability of the relevant authorities to take such action;

(g)   tackling offences likely to cause harm to society where an immediate or direct victim may be difficult to identify but where there is wider societal harm (such as offences related to the misuse of drugs or crime with a cross-border dimension as mentioned in Article 83(1) of the Treaty on the Functioning of the European Union);

(h)   combating the effects of persistent offending (particularly in relation to offences, which if taken in isolation, may otherwise be unlikely to meet the requirements of regulation 27);

(i)   protecting the rights and freedoms of others, particularly from exploitation and trafficking;

(j)   protecting the public;

(k)   acting in the best interests of a child (including where doing so entails refusing a child admission to the United Kingdom, or otherwise taking an EEA decision against a child);

(l)   countering terrorism and extremism and protecting shared values.

SCHEDULE 2   Regulation 36

APPEALS TO THE FIRST-TIER TRIBUNAL

1.   The following provisions of, or made under, the 2002 Act have effect in relation to an appeal under these Regulations to the First-tier Tribunal as if it were an appeal against a decision of the Secretary of State under section 82(1) of the 2002 Act (right of appeal to the Tribunal)—

section 84 (grounds of appeal), as though the sole permitted grounds of appeal were that the decision breaches the appellant's rights under the EU Treaties in respect of entry to or residence in the United Kingdom ("an EU ground of appeal");

section 85 (matters to be considered), as though—

(a)   the references to a statement under section 120 of the 2002 Act include, but are not limited to, a statement under that section as applied by paragraph 2; and

(b)   a "matter" in subsection (2) and a "new matter" in subsection (6) include a ground of appeal of a kind listed in section 84 of the 2002 Act and an EU ground of appeal;

section 86 (determination of appeal);

section 105 and any regulations made under that section; and

section 106 and any rules made pursuant to that section.

2.   (1)   Section 92(3) of the 2002 Act has effect as though an additional basis upon which an appeal under section 82(1)(b) of that Act (human rights claim appeal) must be brought from outside the United Kingdom were that—

(a)   the claim to which that appeal relates arises from an EEA decision or the consequences of an EEA decision; and

(b)   the removal of that person from the United Kingdom has been certified under regulation 33 (human rights considerations and interim orders to suspend removal).

(2)   Section 120 of the 2002 Act applies to a person ("P") if an EEA decision has been taken or may be taken in respect of P and, accordingly, the Secretary of State or an immigration officer may by notice require a statement from P under subsection (2) of that section, and that notice has effect for the purpose of section 96(2) of the 2002 Act.

(3)   Where section 120 of the 2002 Act so applies, it has effect as though—

(a)   subsection (3) also provides that a statement under subsection (2) need not repeat reasons or grounds relating to the EEA decision under challenge previously advanced by P;

(b)   subsection (5) also applies where P does not have a right to reside.

(4)   For the purposes of an appeal brought under section 82(1) of the 2002 Act, subsections (2) and (6)(a) of section 85 (matters to be considered) have effect as though section 84 included a ground of appeal that the decision appealed against breaches the appellant's right under the EU Treaties in respect of entry into or residence in the United Kingdom.

3.   Tribunal Procedure Rules made under section 22 of the Tribunals, Courts and Enforcement Act 2007 have effect in relation to appeals under these Regulations.

SCHEDULE 3   Regulation 43

EFFECT ON OTHER LEGISLATION

1.   **Leave under the 1971 Act**

Where a person has leave to enter or remain under the 1971 Act which is subject to conditions and that person also has a right to reside under these Regulations, those conditions do not have effect for as long as the person has that right to reside.

2. **Person not subject to restriction on the period for which they may remain**

   (1) For the purposes of the 1971 Act and British Nationality Act 1981, a person who has a right of permanent residence under regulation 15 must be regarded as a person who is in the United Kingdom without being subject under the immigration laws to any restriction on the period for which the person may remain.

   (2) But a qualified person, the family member of a qualified person, a person with a derivative right to reside and a family member who has retained the right of residence must not, by virtue of that status, be so regarded for those purposes.

3. **Carriers' liability under the 1999 Act**

   For the purposes of satisfying a requirement to produce a visa under section 40(1)(b) of the 1999 Act (charges in respect of passenger without proper documents), "a visa of the required kind" includes an EEA family permit, a residence card, a derivative residence card, a qualifying EEA State residence card, or a permanent residence card required for admission under regulation 11(2), or permission to be temporarily admitted under regulation 41.

Extracts from the European Convention on Human Rights

Article 2 – right to life

1.   Everyone's right to life shall be protected by law. No one shall be deprived of his life intentionally save in the execution of a sentence of a court following his conviction of a crime for which this penalty is provided by law.

2.   Deprivation of life shall not be regarded as inflicted in contravention of this Article when it results from the use of force which is no more than absolutely necessary:

Article 3 – prohibition of torture

No one shall be subjected to torture or to inhuman or degrading treatment or punishment.

Article 5 – right to liberty and security

1.   Everyone has the right to liberty and security of person. No one shall be deprived of his liberty save in the following cases and in accordance with a procedure prescribed by law:
     (a)   the lawful detention of a person after conviction by a competent court;
     (b)   the lawful arrest or detention of a person for non-compliance with the lawful order of a court or in order to secure the fulfilment of any obligation prescribed by law;
     (c)   the lawful arrest or detention of a person effected for the purpose of bringing him before the competent legal authority on reasonable suspicion of having committed an offence or when it is reasonably considered necessary to prevent his committing an offence or fleeing after having done so;
     (d)   the detention of a minor by lawful order for the purpose of educational supervision or his lawful detention for the purpose of bringing him before the competent legal authority;
     (e)   the lawful detention of persons for the prevention of the spreading of infectious diseases, of persons of unsound mind, alcoholics or drug addicts or vagrants;
     (f)   the lawful arrest or detention of a person to prevent his effecting an unauthorised entry into the country or of a person against whom action is being taken with a view to deportation or extradition.

2.   Everyone who is arrested shall be informed promptly, in a language which he understands, of the reasons for his arrest and of any charge against him.

3.   Everyone arrested or detained in accordance with the provisions of paragraph 1(c) of this Article shall be brought promptly before a judge or other officer authorised by law to exercise judicial power and shall be entitled to trial within a reasonable time or to release pending trial. Release may be conditioned by guarantees to appear for trial.

4.   Everyone who is deprived of his liberty by arrest or detention shall be entitled to take proceedings by which the lawfulness of his detention shall be decided speedily by a court and his release ordered if the detention is not lawful.

5.   Everyone who has been the victim of arrest or detention in contravention of the provisions of this Article shall have an enforceable right to compensation.

Article 6 – right to a fair trial

1.   In the determination of his civil rights and obligations or of any criminal charge against him, everyone is entitled to a fair and public hearing within a reasonable time by an independent and impartial tribunal established by law. Judgment shall be pronounced publicly but the press and public may be excluded from all or part of the trial in the interest of morals, public order or national security in a democratic society, where the interests of juveniles or the protection of the private life of the parties so

require, or to the extent strictly necessary in the opinion of the court in special circumstances where publicity would prejudice the interests of justice.

2. Everyone charged with a criminal offence shall be presumed innocent until proved guilty according to law.

3. Everyone charged with a criminal offence has the following minimum rights:

    (a) to be informed promptly, in a language which he understands and in detail, of the nature and cause of the accusation against him;

    (b) to have adequate time and facilities for the preparation of his defence;

    (c) to defend himself in person or through legal assistance of his own choosing or, if he has not sufficient means to pay for legal assistance, to be given it free when the interests of justice so require;

    (d) to examine or have examined witnesses against him and to obtain the attendance and examination of witnesses on his behalf under the same conditions as witnesses against him;

    (e) to have the free assistance of an interpreter if he cannot understand or speak the language used in court.

Article 8 – right to respect for private and family life

1. Everyone has the right to respect for his private and family life, his home and his correspondence.

2. There shall be no interference by a public authority with the exercise of this right except such as is in accordance with the law and is necessary in a democratic society in the interests of national security, public safety or the economic well-being of the country, for the prevention of disorder or crime, for the protection of health or morals, or for the protection of the rights and freedoms of others.

Article 9 – freedom of thought, conscience and religion

1. Everyone has the right to freedom of thought, conscience and religion; this right includes freedom to change his religion or belief and freedom, either alone or in community with others and in public or private, to manifest his religion or belief, in worship, teaching, practice and observance.

2. Freedom to manifest one's religion or beliefs shall be subject only to such limitations as are prescribed by law and are necessary in a democratic society in the interests of public safety, for the protection of public order, health or morals, or for the protection of the rights and freedoms of others.

Article 10 – freedom of expression

1. Everyone has the right to freedom of expression. This right shall include freedom to hold opinions and to receive and impart information and ideas without interference by public authority and regardless of frontiers. This Article shall not prevent States from requiring the licensing of broadcasting, television or cinema enterprises.

2. The exercise of these freedoms, since it carries with it duties and responsibilities, may be subject to such formalities, conditions, restrictions or penalties as are prescribed by law and are necessary in a democratic society, in the interests of national security, territorial integrity or public safety, for the prevention of disorder or crime, for the protection of health or morals, for the protection of the reputation or rights of others, for preventing the disclosure of information received in confidence, or for maintaining the authority and impartiality of the judiciary.

Article 11 – freedom of assembly and association

1. Everyone has the right to freedom of peaceful assembly and to freedom of association with others, including the right to form and to join trade unions for the protection of his interests.

2. No restrictions shall be placed on the exercise of these rights other than such as are prescribed by law and are necessary in a democratic society in the interests of national security or public safety, for the prevention of disorder or crime, for the protection of health or morals or for the protection of the rights and freedoms of others. This Article shall not prevent the imposition of lawful restrictions on the exercise of these rights by members of the armed forces, of the police or of the administration of the State.

Article 12 – right to marry

Men and women of marriageable age have the right to marry and to found a family, according to the national laws governing the exercise of this right.

Article 14 – prohibition of discrimination

The enjoyment of the rights and freedoms set forth in this Convention shall be secured without discrimination on any ground such as sex, race, colour, language, religion, political or other opinion, national or social origin, association with a national minority, property, birth or other status.

The First Protocol, Article 1 – protection of property

Every natural or legal person is entitled to the peaceful enjoyment of his possessions. No one shall be deprived of his possessions except in the public interest and subject to the conditions provided for by law and by the general principles of international law.

The preceding provisions shall not, however, in any way impair the right of a State to enforce such laws as it deems necessary to control the use of property in accordance with the general interest or to secure the payment of taxes or other contributions or penalties.

British Citizenship: A Summary

The BNA 1981 sets out some basic rules for determining who is a British citizen. The following series of questions can be used to work out if a person may be a British citizen. However, remember that nationality law can be complex, and you will not always be able to work out if a person is a British citizen or not without detailed research of the law and facts.

Q1. When was the person born?

(a) Before [1st January] 1983: go to Q2.

(b) After [31st December] 1982: go to Q9.

Q2. Where was the person born?

(a) In the UK: he is a British citizen otherwise than by descent (see **2.2.1**).

(b) Outside the UK: go to Q3.

Q3. Was the person's father born [or registered/naturalised before he was born] in the UK?

(a) Yes: go to Q4.

(b) No: go to Q5.

Q4. Was the person's father married to their mother? [If after the child's birth, did that marriage legitimise the child?]

(a) Yes: he is a British citizen by descent (see **2.2.2**).

(b) No: go to Q5.

Q5. Was the person's mother born [or registered/naturalised before he was born] in the UK?

(a) Yes: go to Q6.

(b) No: go to Q7.

Q6. Did the person's mother register him as a British citizen?

(a) Yes: he is a British citizen by descent (see **2.2.6.2**).

(b) No: go to Q7.

Q7. Has the person registered as a British citizen?

(a) Yes: he is a British citizen by descent (see **2.2.6.2**).

(b) No: go to Q8.

Q8. Has the person naturalised in the UK as a British citizen?

(a) Yes: he is a British citizen otherwise than by descent (see **2.2.7**).

(b) No: he is not a British citizen under these rules but a detailed analysis of law and facts is required.

Q9. Was the person born in the UK?

(a) Yes: go to Q10.

(b) No: go to Q13.

Q10. Was either of the person's parents a British citizen or settled in the UK when he was born?

(a) Yes: he is a British citizen otherwise than by descent (see **2.2.3**).

(b) No: go to Q11.

Q11. Did either of the person's parents subsequently become a British citizen or settled in the UK?

(a) Yes: he can apply to register as a British citizen otherwise than by descent (see **2.2.6.1**).

(b) No: go to Q12.

Q12. Has the person remained in the UK for the first 10 years of his life and not been absent for more than 90 days?

(a) Yes: he is a British citizen otherwise than by descent (see **2.2.6.1**).

(b) No: he is not a British citizen under these rules but a detailed analysis of law and facts is required.

Q13. Was one of the person's parents a British citizen otherwise than by descent by birth, registration or naturalisation in the UK before he was born?

(a)   Yes: he is a British citizen by descent (see **2.2.4**).

(b)   No: he is not a British citizen under these rules but a detailed analysis of the law and facts is required.

Note 1: a parent in this context may include the father of an illegitimate child but only if certain conditions are met (see **2.2.3** and **2.2.4**).

Note 2: as to second generation children born outside UK, see **2.2.5**.

Naturalisation: A Summary

The following series of questions can be used to work out if a person may be eligible to apply for naturalisation as a British citizen.

Q1. Is the person settled in the UK?

    (a)   Yes: go to Q2.

    (b)   No: ineligible.

Q2. Is the person married to a British citizen or in a civil partnership with a British citizen?

    (a)   Yes: go to Q3.

    (b)   No: go to Q7.

Q3. Has the person been living in the UK legally for three years continuously before making the application?

    (a)   Yes: go to Q4.

    (b)   No: ineligible.

Q4. Has the person been absent for less than 270 days in total and not more than 90 days in the year immediately before the application?

    (a)   Yes: go to Q5.

    (b)   No: ineligible but check Home Office policy.

Q5. Can the person produce written evidence to show sufficient knowledge of English (Welsh or Scottish Gaelic) and Life in the UK?

    (a)   Yes: go to Q6.

    (b)   No: ineligible but check to see if Home Office might waive this requirement.

Q6. Can the person show good character?

    (a)   Yes: may be granted naturalisation as a British citizen at discretion of Home Secretary.

    (b)   No: application will be refused.

Q7. Has the person been settled in the UK for at least one year before making the application?

    (a)   Yes: go to Q8.

    (b)   No: ineligible.

Q8. Has the person been living in the UK legally for five years continuously before making the application?

    (a)   Yes: go to Q9.

    (b)   No: ineligible.

Q9. Has the person been absent for less than 450 days in total and not more than 90 days in the year immediately before the application?

    (a)   Yes: go to Q10.

    (b)   No: ineligible but check Home Office policy.

Q10. Can the person produce written evidence to show sufficient knowledge of English (Welsh or Scottish Gaelic) and Life in the UK?

    (a)   Yes: go to Q11.

    (b)   No: ineligible but check to see if Home Office might waive this requirement.

Q11. Can the person show good character?

    (a)   Yes: go to Q12.

    (b)   No: application will be refused.

Q12. Can the person show an intention to live in the UK?

    (a)   Yes: may be granted naturalisation as a British citizen at discretion of Home Secretary.

    (b)   No: application will be refused.

Criminality grounds

9.4.1 An application for entry clearance, permission to enter or permission to stay must be refused where the applicant:

(a) has been convicted of a criminal offence in the UK or overseas for which they have received a custodial sentence of 12 months or more; or

(b) is a persistent offender who shows a particular disregard for the law; or

(c) has committed a criminal offence, or offences, which caused serious harm.

9.4.2 Entry clearance or permission held by a person must be cancelled where the person:

(a) has been convicted of a criminal offence in the UK or overseas for which they have received a custodial sentence of 12 months or more; or

(b) is a persistent offender who shows a particular disregard for the law; or

(c) has committed a criminal offence, or offences, which caused serious harm.

9.4.3 An application for entry clearance, permission to enter or permission to stay may be refused (where paragraph 9.4.2. and 9.4.4. do not apply) where the applicant:

(a) has been convicted of a criminal offence in the UK or overseas for which they have received a custodial sentence of less than 12 months; or

(b) has been convicted of a criminal offence in the UK or overseas for which they have received a non-custodial sentence, or received an out-of-court disposal that is recorded on their criminal record.

9.4.4 An application for entry clearance or permission to enter under Appendix V: Visitor, or where a person is seeking entry on arrival in the UK for a stay for less than 6 months, must be refused where the applicant:

(a) has been convicted of a criminal offence in the UK or overseas for which they have received a custodial sentence of less than 12 months, unless more than 12 months have passed since the end of the custodial sentence; or

(b) has been convicted of a criminal offence in the UK or overseas for which they have received a non-custodial sentence, or received an out-of-court disposal that is recorded on their criminal record, unless more than 12 months have passed since the date of conviction.

9.4.5 Entry clearance or permission held by a person may be cancelled (where paragraph 9.4.2. does not apply) where the person:

(a) has been convicted of a criminal offence in the UK or overseas for which they have received a custodial sentence of less than 12 months; or

(b) has been convicted of a criminal offence in the UK or overseas for which they have received a non-custodial sentence, or received an out-of-court disposal that is recorded on their criminal record.

Commonwealth Citizens

Citizens of the following countries are currently Commonwealth citizens according to Sch 3 to the British Nationality Act 1981 (as amended).

Antigua and Barbuda	Mozambique
Australia	Namibia
The Bahamas	Nauru
Bangladesh	New Zealand
Barbados	Nigeria
Belize	Pakistan
Botswana	Papua New Guinea
Brunei	Saint Christopher and Nevis
Cameroon	Saint Lucia
Canada	Saint Vincent and the Grenadines
Republic of Cyprus	Seychelles
Dominica	Sierra Leone
Fiji	Singapore
The Gambia	Solomon Islands
Ghana	South Africa
Grenada	Sri Lanka
Guyana	Swaziland
India	Tanzania
Jamaica	Tonga
Kenya	Trinidad and Tobago
Kiribati	Tuvalu
Lesotho	Uganda
Malawi	Vanuatu
Malaysia	Western Samoa
Maldives	Zambia
Malta	Zimbabwe
Mauritius	

Note that British citizens, and some other categories of British Nationals (including British dependent territories citizens and British overseas citizens) are Commonwealth citizens by virtue of s 37 of the 1981 Act.

It is important to note that as Cameroon, Mozambique, Namibia, Pakistan and South Africa were not members of the Commonwealth on 31 December 1982, then nationals of those countries cannot take advantage of the provisions dealt with at **2.3.**

Commonwealth Citizen with Right of Abode: A Summary

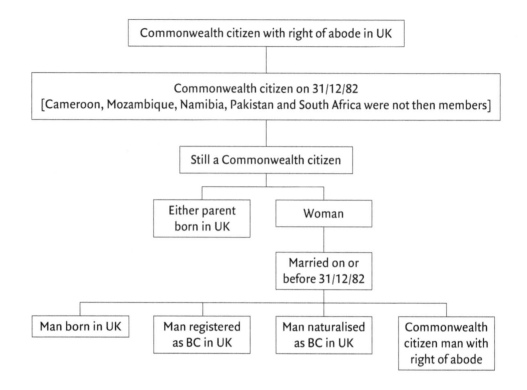

British Overseas Territories

The following are currently British Overseas Territories according to Sch 6 to the British Nationality Act 1981 (as amended).

Anguilla

Bermuda

British Antarctic Territory

British Indian Ocean Territory

Cayman Islands

Gibraltar

Montserrat

Pitcairn, Henderson, Ducie and Oeno Islands

St Helena and Dependencies

South Georgia

South Sandwich Islands

The Sovereign Base Areas of Akrotiri and Dhekelia

Turks and Caicos Islands

Virgin Islands

Note that people from the Falkland Islands were made into full British citizens under the British Nationality (Falkland Islands) Act 1983.

APPENDIX 12

Active and trading UK registered companies

The Home Office definition of 'active and trading UK registered companies' means companies which:

(i)   are registered with Companies House in the UK;

(ii)   are registered with HM Revenue and Customs for corporation tax and PAYE;

(iii)   have accounts and a UK business bank account, both showing regular trading of its own goods or services; and

(iv)   have at least two UK-based employees who are not its directors.

Refugee or Person in Need of International Protection (Qualification) Regulations 2006

SI 2006/2525

1.   Citation and commencement

(1)   These Regulations may be cited as The Refugee or Person in Need of International Protection (Qualification) Regulations 2006 and shall come into force on 9th October 2006.

(2)   These Regulations apply to any application for asylum which has not been decided and any immigration appeal brought under the Immigration Acts (as defined in section 64(2) of the Immigration, Asylum and Nationality Act 2006) which has not been finally determined.

2.   Interpretation

In these Regulations—

'application for asylum' means the request of a person to be recognised as a refugee under the Geneva Convention;

'Geneva Convention' means the Convention Relating to the Status of Refugees done at Geneva on 28 July 1951 and the New York Protocol of 31 January 1967;

'immigration rules' means rules made under section 3(2) of the Immigration Act 1971;

'persecution' means an act of persecution within the meaning of Article 1(A) of the Geneva Convention;

'person eligible for humanitarian protection' means a person who is eligible for a grant of humanitarian protection under the immigration rules;

'refugee' means a person who falls within Article 1(A) of the Geneva Convention and to whom regulation 7 does not apply;

'residence permit' means a document confirming that a person has leave to enter or remain in the United Kingdom whether limited or indefinite;

'serious harm' means serious harm as defined in the immigration rules;

'person' means any person who is not a British citizen.

3.   Actors of persecution or serious harm

In deciding whether a person is a refugee or a person eligible for humanitarian protection, persecution or serious harm can be committed by:

(a)   the State;

(b)   any party or organisation controlling the State or a substantial part of the territory of the State;

(c)   any non-State actor if it can be demonstrated that the actors mentioned in paragraphs (a) and (b), including any international organisation, are unable or unwilling to provide protection against persecution or serious harm.

4.   Actors of protection

(1)   In deciding whether a person is a refugee or a person eligible for humanitarian protection, protection from persecution or serious harm can be provided by:

(a)   the State; or

(b)   any party or organisation, including any international organisation, controlling the State or a substantial part of the territory of the State.

(2)   Protection shall be regarded as generally provided when the actors mentioned in paragraph (1)(a) and (b) take reasonable steps to prevent the persecution or suffering of serious harm by operating an effective legal system for the detection, prosecution and punishment of acts constituting persecution or serious harm, and the person mentioned in paragraph (1) has access to such protection.

(3)   In deciding whether a person is a refugee or a person eligible for humanitarian protection the Secretary of State may assess whether an international organisation controls a State or a substantial part of its territory and provides protection as described in paragraph (2).

5.   Act of persecution

(1)   In deciding whether a person is a refugee an act of persecution must be:

(a)   sufficiently serious by its nature or repetition as to constitute a severe violation of a basic human right, in particular a right from which derogation cannot be made under Article 15 of the Convention for the Protection of Human Rights and Fundamental Freedoms; or

(b)   an accumulation of various measures, including a violation of a human right which is sufficiently severe as to affect an individual in a similar manner as specified in (a).

(2)   An act of persecution may, for example, take the form of:

(a)   an act of physical or mental violence, including an act of sexual violence;

(b)   a legal, administrative, police, or judicial measure which in itself is discriminatory or which is implemented in a discriminatory manner;

(c)   prosecution or punishment, which is disproportionate or discriminatory;

(d)   denial of judicial redress resulting in a disproportionate or discriminatory punishment;

(e)   prosecution or punishment for refusal to perform military service in a conflict, where performing military service would include crimes or acts falling under regulation 7.

(3)   An act of persecution must be committed for at least one of the reasons in Article 1(A) of the Geneva Convention.

6.   Reasons for persecution

(1)   In deciding whether a person is a refugee:

(a)   the concept of race shall include consideration of, for example, colour, descent, or membership of a particular ethnic group;

(b)   the concept of religion shall include, for example, the holding of theistic, non-theistic and atheistic beliefs, the participation in, or abstention from, formal worship in private or in public, either alone or in community with others, other religious acts or expressions of view, or forms of personal or communal conduct based on or mandated by any religious belief;

(c)   the concept of nationality shall not be confined to citizenship or lack thereof but shall include, for example, membership of a group determined by its cultural, ethnic, or linguistic identity, common geographical or political origins or its relationship with the population of another State;

(d)   a group shall be considered to form a particular social group where, for example:

(i)   members of that group share an innate characteristic, or a common background that cannot be changed, or share a characteristic or belief that is so fundamental to identity or conscience that a person should not be forced to renounce it, and

(ii)   that group has a distinct identity in the relevant country, because it is perceived as being different by the surrounding society;

(e)   a particular social group might include a group based on a common characteristic of sexual orientation but sexual orientation cannot be understood to include acts considered to be criminal in accordance with national law of the United Kingdom;

(f)   the concept of political opinion shall include the holding of an opinion, thought or belief on a matter related to the potential actors of persecution mentioned in regulation 3 and to their policies or methods, whether or not that opinion, thought or belief has been acted upon by the person.

(2)   In deciding whether a person has a well-founded fear of being persecuted, it is immaterial whether he actually possesses the racial, religious, national, social or political characteristic which attracts the persecution, provided that such a characteristic is attributed to him by the actor of persecution.

7.   Exclusion

(1)   A person is not a refugee, if he falls within the scope of Article 1D, 1E or 1F of the Geneva Convention.

(2)   In the construction and application of Article 1F(b) of the Geneva Convention:

    (a)   the reference to serious non-political crime includes a particularly cruel action, even if it is committed with an allegedly political objective;

    (b)   the reference to the crime being committed outside the country of refuge prior to his admission as a refugee shall be taken to mean the time up to and including the day on which a residence permit is issued.

(3)   Article 1F(a) and (b) of the Geneva Convention shall apply to a person who instigates or otherwise participates in the commission of the crimes or acts specified in those provisions.

Pre-Action Protocol for Judicial Review

INTRODUCTION

1. This Protocol applies to proceedings within England and Wales only. It does not affect the time limit specified by Rule 54.5(1) of the Civil Procedure Rules (CPR), which requires that any claim form in an application for judicial review must be filed promptly and in any event not later than 3 months after the grounds to make the claim first arose. Nor does it affect the shorter time limits specified by Rules 54.5(5) and (6), which set out that a claim form for certain planning judicial reviews must be filed within 6 weeks and the claim form for certain procurement judicial reviews must be filed within 30 days.[1]

2. This Protocol sets out a code of good practice and contains the steps which parties should generally follow before making a claim for judicial review.

3. The aims of the protocol are to enable parties to prospective claims to—

    (a) understand and properly identify the issues in dispute in the proposed claim and share information and relevant documents;

    (b) make informed decisions as to whether and how to proceed;

    (c) try to settle the dispute without proceedings or reduce the issues in dispute;

    (d) avoid unnecessary expense and keep down the costs of resolving the dispute; and

    (e) support the efficient management of proceedings where litigation cannot be avoided.

4. Judicial review allows people with a sufficient interest in a decision or action by a public body to ask a judge to review the lawfulness of—

    • an enactment; or

    • a decision, action or failure to act in relation to the exercise of a public function.[2]

5. Judicial review should only be used where no adequate alternative remedy, such as a right of appeal, is available. Even then, judicial review may not be appropriate in every instance. Claimants are strongly advised to seek appropriate legal advice as soon as possible when considering proceedings. Although the Legal Aid Agency will not normally grant full representation before a letter before claim has been sent and the proposed defendant given a reasonable time to respond, initial funding may be available, for eligible claimants, to cover the work necessary to write this. (See Annex C for more information.)

6. This protocol will not be appropriate in very urgent cases. In this sort of case, a claim should be made immediately. Examples are where directions have been set for the claimant's removal from the UK or where there is an urgent need for an interim order to compel a public body to act where it has unlawfully refused to do so, such as where a local housing authority fails to secure interim accommodation for a homeless claimant. A letter before claim, and a claim itself, will not stop the implementation of a disputed decision, though a proposed defendant may agree to take no action until its response letter has been provided. In other cases, the claimant may need to apply to the court for an urgent interim order. Even in very urgent cases, it is good practice to alert the defendant by telephone and to send by email (or fax) to the defendant the draft Claim Form which the claimant intends to issue. A claimant is also normally required to notify a defendant when an interim order is being sought.

7. All claimants will need to satisfy themselves whether they should follow the protocol, depending upon the circumstances of the case. Where the use of the protocol is appropriate, the court will normally expect all parties to have complied with it in good time before proceedings are issued and will take into account compliance or non-compliance when giving directions for case management of proceedings or when making orders for costs.[3]

8. The Upper Tribunal Immigration and Asylum Chamber (UTIAC) has jurisdiction in respect of judicial review proceedings in relation to most immigration decisions.[4] The President of UTIAC has issued a Practice Statement to the effect that, in judicial review proceedings in UTIAC, the parties will be expected to follow this protocol, where appropriate, as they would for proceedings in the High Court.

Alternative Dispute Resolution

9. The courts take the view that litigation should be a last resort. The parties should consider whether some form of alternative dispute resolution ('ADR') or complaints procedure would be more suitable than litigation, and if so, endeavour to agree which to adopt. Both the claimant and defendant may be required by the court to provide evidence that alternative means of resolving their dispute were considered. Parties are warned that if the protocol is not followed (including this paragraph) then the court must have regard to such conduct when determining costs. However, parties should also note that a claim for judicial review should comply with the time limits set out in the Introduction above. Exploring ADR may not excuse failure to comply with the time limits. If it is appropriate to issue a claim to ensure compliance with a time limit, but the parties agree there should be a stay of proceedings to explore settlement or narrowing the issues in dispute, a joint application for appropriate directions can be made to the court.

10. It is not practicable in this protocol to address in detail how the parties might decide which method to adopt to resolve their particular dispute. However, summarised below are some of the options for resolving disputes without litigation which may be appropriate, depending on the circumstances—

    • Discussion and negotiation.

    • Using relevant public authority complaints or review procedures.

    • Ombudsmen – the Parliamentary and Health Service and the Local Government Ombudsmen have discretion to deal with complaints relating to maladministration. The British and Irish Ombudsman Association provide information about Ombudsman schemes and other complaint handling bodies and this is available from their website at www.bioa.org.uk. Parties may wish to note that the Ombudsmen are not able to look into a complaint once court action has been commenced.

    • Mediation – a form of facilitated negotiation assisted by an independent neutral party.

11. The Civil Justice Council and Judicial College have endorsed The Jackson ADR Handbook by Susan Blake, Julie Browne and Stuart Sime (2013, Oxford University Press). The Citizens Advice Bureaux website also provides information about ADR: http://www.adviceguide.org.uk/england/law_e/law_legal_system_e/law_taking_legal_action_e/alternatives_to_court.htm.

    Information is also available at: http://www.civilmediation.justice.gov.uk/

12. If proceedings are issued, the parties may be required by the court to provide evidence that ADR has been considered. A party's silence in response to an invitation to participate in ADR or refusal to participate in ADR might be considered unreasonable by the court and could lead to the court ordering that party to pay additional court costs.

Requests for information and documents at the pre-action stage

13. Requests for information and documents made at the pre-action stage should be proportionate and should be limited to what is properly necessary for the claimant to understand why the challenged decision has been taken and/or to present the claim in a manner that will properly identify the issues. The defendant should comply with any request which meets these requirements unless there is good reason for it not to do so. Where the court considers that a public body should have provided relevant documents and/or information, particularly where this failure is a breach of a statutory or common law requirement, it may impose costs sanctions.

The letter before claim

14. In good time before making a claim, the claimant should send a letter to the defendant. The purpose of this letter is to identify the issues in dispute and establish whether they can be narrowed or litigation can be avoided.

15. Claimants should normally use the suggested standard format for the letter outlined at Annex A. For Immigration, Nationality and Asylum cases, the Home Office has a standardised form which can be used. It can be found online at: https://www.gov.uk/government/publications/chapter-27-judicial-review-guidance-part-1

16. The letter should contain the date and details of the decision, act or omission being challenged, a clear summary of the facts and the legal basis for the claim. It should also contain the details of any information that the claimant is seeking and an explanation of why this is considered relevant. If the claim is considered to be an Aarhus Convention claim (see Rules 45.41 to 45.44 and Practice Direction 45), the letter should state this clearly and explain the reasons, since specific rules as to costs apply to such claims. If the claim is

considered appropriate for allocation to the Planning Court and/or for classification as "significant" within that court, the letter should state this clearly and explain the reasons.

17.   The letter should normally contain the details of any person known to the claimant who is an Interested Party. An Interested Party is any person directly affected by the claim.[5] They should be sent a copy of the letter before claim for information. Claimants are strongly advised to seek appropriate legal advice when considering proceedings which involve an Interested Party and, in particular, before sending the letter before claim to an Interested Party or making a claim.

18.   A claim should not normally be made until the proposed reply date given in the letter before the claim has passed, unless the circumstances of the case require more immediate action to be taken. The claimant should send the letter before claim in good time so as to enable a response which can then be taken into account before the time limit for issuing the claim expires, unless there are good reasons why this is not possible.

19.   Any claimant intending to ask for a protective costs order (an order that the claimant will not be liable for the costs of the defendant or any other party or to limit such liability) should explain the reasons for making the request, including an explanation of the limit of the financial resources available to the claimant in making the claim.

The letter of response

20.   Defendants should normally respond within 14 days using the standard format at Annex B. Failure to do so will be taken into account by the court and sanctions may be imposed unless there are good reasons.[6] Where the claimant is a litigant in person, the defendant should enclose a copy of this Protocol with its letter.

21.   Where it is not possible to reply within the proposed time limit, the defendant should send an interim reply and propose a reasonable extension, giving a date by which the defendant expects to respond substantively. Where an extension is sought, reasons should be given and, where required, additional information requested. This will not affect the time limit for making a claim for judicial review[7] nor will it bind the claimant where he or she considers this to be unreasonable. However, where the court considers that a subsequent claim is made prematurely it may impose sanctions.

22.   If the claim is being conceded in full, the reply should say so in clear and unambiguous terms.

23.   If the claim is being conceded in part or not being conceded at all, the reply should say so in clear and unambiguous terms, and—

    (a)   where appropriate, contain a new decision, clearly identifying what aspects of the claim are being conceded and what are not, or, give a clear timescale within which the new decision will be issued;

    (b)   provide a fuller explanation for the decision, if considered appropriate to do so;

    (c)   address any points of dispute, or explain why they cannot be addressed;

    (d)   enclose any relevant documentation requested by the claimant, or explain why the documents are not being enclosed;

    (e)   where documents cannot be provided within the time scales required, then give a clear timescale for provision. The claimant should avoid making any formal application for the provision of documentation/information during this period unless there are good grounds to show that the timescale proposed is unreasonable;

    (f)   where appropriate, confirm whether or not they will oppose any application for an interim remedy; and

    (g)   if the claimant has stated an intention to ask for a protective costs order, the defendant's response to this should be explained.

    If the letter before claim has stated that the claim is an Aarhus Convention claim but the defendant does not accept this, the reply should state this clearly and explain the reasons. If the letter before claim has stated that the claim is suitable for the Planning Court and/or categorisation as "significant" within that court but the defendant does not accept this, the reply should state this clearly and explain the reasons.

24.   The response should be sent to all Interested Parties[8] identified by the claimant and contain details of any other persons who the defendant considers are Interested Parties.

ANNEX A

Letter before claim

Section 1. Information required in a letter before claim

1 Proposed claim for judicial review

To

(Insert the name and address of the proposed defendant – see details in section 2.)

2 The claimant

(Insert the title, first and last name and the address of the claimant.)

3 The defendant's reference details

(When dealing with large organisations it is important to understand that the information relating to any particular individual's previous dealings with it may not be immediately available, therefore it is important to set out the relevant reference numbers for the matter in dispute and/or the identity of those within the public body who have been handling the particular matter in dispute – see details in section 3.)

4 The details of the claimants' legal advisers, if any, dealing with this claim

(Set out the name, address and reference details of any legal advisers dealing with the claim.)

5 The details of the matter being challenged

(Set out clearly the matter being challenged, particularly if there has been more than one decision.)

6 The details of any Interested Parties

(Set out the details of any Interested Parties and confirm that they have been sent a copy of this letter.)

7 The issue

(Set out a brief summary of the facts and relevant legal principles, the date and details of the decision, or act or omission being challenged, and why it is contended to be wrong.)

8 The details of the action that the defendant is expected to take

(Set out the details of the remedy sought, including whether a review or any interim remedy are being requested.)

9 ADR proposals

(Set out any proposals the claimant is making to resolve or narrow the dispute by ADR.)

10 The details of any information sought

(Set out the details of any information that is sought which is related to identifiable issues in dispute so as to enable the parties to resolve or reduce those issues. This may include a request for a fuller explanation of the reasons for the decision that is being challenged.)

11 The details of any documents that are considered relevant and necessary

(Set out the details of any documentation or policy in respect of which the disclosure is sought and explain why these are relevant.)

12 The address for reply and service of court documents

(Insert the address for the reply.)

13 Proposed reply date

(The precise time will depend upon the circumstances of the individual case. However, although a shorter or longer time may be appropriate in a particular case, 14 days is a reasonable time to allow in most circumstances.)

Section 2. Address for sending the letter before claim

Public bodies have requested that, for certain types of cases, in order to ensure a prompt response, letters before claim should be sent to specific addresses.

- Where the claim concerns a decision in an Immigration, Asylum or Nationality case (including in relation to an immigration decision taken abroad by an Entry Clearance Officer)— The claim should be sent electronically to the following Home Office email address: UKVIPAP@homeoffice.gsi.gov.uk

Alternatively the claim may be sent by post to the following Home Office postal address:

Litigation Allocation Unit
6, New Square

Bedfont Lakes
Feltham, Middlesex
TW14 8HA

The Home Office has a standardised form which claimants may find helpful to use for communications with the Home Office in Immigration, Asylum or Nationality cases pursuant to this Protocol, to assist claimants to include all relevant information and to promote speedier review and response by the Home Office. The Home Office form may be filled out in electronic or hard copy format. It can be found online at: https://www.gov.uk/government/publications/chapter-27-judicial-review-guidance-part-1

- Where the claim concerns a decision by the Legal Aid Agency—
  The address on the decision letter/notification;
  Legal Director
  Corporate Legal Team
  Legal Aid Agency
  102 Petty France
  London SW1H 9AJ

- Where the claim concerns a decision by a local authority—
  The address on the decision letter/notification; and
  their legal department[9]

- Where the claim concerns a decision by a department or body for whom Treasury Solicitor acts and Treasury Solicitor has already been involved in the case a copy should also be sent, quoting the Treasury Solicitor's reference, to—
  The Treasury Solicitor,
  102 Petty France,
  Westminster,
  London SW1H 9GL

- Where the claim concerns a decision by Her Majesty's Revenue and Customs—
  the address on the letter notifying the decision; and
  The General Counsel and Solicitor to HM Revenue and Customs,
  HM Revenue and Customs,
  South West Wing,
  Bush House,
  Strand,
  London WC2B 4RD

In all other circumstances, the letter should be sent to the address on the letter notifying the decision.

Section 3. Specific reference details required

Public bodies have requested that the following information should be provided, if at all possible, in order to ensure prompt response. Where the claim concerns an Immigration, Asylum or Nationality case, dependent upon the nature of the case—

- The Home Office reference number;
- The Port reference number;
- The Asylum and Immigration Tribunal reference number;
- The National Asylum Support Service reference number; or, if these are unavailable:
- The full name, nationality and date of birth of the claimant.

Where the claim concerns a decision by the Legal Aid Agency—

- The certificate reference number.

ANNEX B

Response to a letter before claim

Information required in a response to a letter before claim

1 The claimant

(Insert the title, first and last names and the address to which any reply should be sent.)

2 From

(Insert the name and address of the defendant.)

3 Reference details

(Set out the relevant reference numbers for the matter in dispute and the identity of those within the public body who have been handling the issue.)

4 The details of the matter being challenged

(Set out details of the matter being challenged, providing a fuller explanation of the decision, where this is considered appropriate.)

5 Response to the proposed claim

(Set out whether the issue in question is conceded in part, or in full, or will be contested. Where an interim reply is being sent and there is a realistic prospect of settlement, details should be included. If the claimant is a litigant in person, a copy of the Pre-Action Protocol should be enclosed with the letter.)

6 Details of any other Interested Parties

(Identify any other parties who you consider have an interest who have not already been sent a letter by the claimant.)

7 ADR proposals

(Set out the defendant's position on any ADR proposals made in the letter before claim and any ADR proposals by the defendant.)

8 Response to requests for information and documents

(Set out the defendant's answer to the requests made in the letter before claim including reasons why any requested information or documents are not being disclosed.)

9 Address for further correspondence and service of court documents

(Set out the address for any future correspondence on this matter)

ANNEX C

Notes on public funding for legal costs in judicial review

Public funding for legal costs in judicial review is available from legal professionals and advice agencies which have contracts with the Legal Aid Agency. Funding may be provided for—

- Legal Help to provide initial advice and assistance with any legal problem; or
- Legal Representation to allow you to be represented in court if you are taking or defending court proceedings. This is available in two forms—

Investigative Help is limited to funding to investigate the strength of the proposed claim. It includes the issue and conduct of proceedings only so far as is necessary to obtain disclosure of relevant information or to protect the client's position in relation to any urgent hearing or time limit for the issue of proceedings. This includes the work necessary to write a letter before claim to the body potentially under challenge, setting out the grounds of challenge, and giving that body a reasonable opportunity, typically 14 days, in which to respond.

Full Representation is provided to represent you in legal proceedings and includes litigation services, advocacy services, and all such help as is usually given by a person providing representation in proceedings, including steps preliminary or incidental to proceedings, and/or arriving at or giving effect to a compromise to avoid or bring to an end any proceedings. Except in emergency cases, a proper letter before claim must be sent and the other side must be given an opportunity to respond before Full Representation is granted.

Further information on the type(s) of help available and the criteria for receiving that help may be found in the Legal Aid Agency's pages on the Ministry of Justice website at: https://www.justice.gov.uk/legal-aid

A list of contracted firms and Advice Agencies may be found at: http://find-legal-advice.justice.gov.uk"

Footnotes

1. The court has a discretion to extend time. It cannot be taken that compliance with the protocol will of itself be sufficient to excuse delay or justify an extension of time, but it may be a relevant factor. Under rule 54.5(2), judicial review time limits cannot be extended by agreement between the parties. However, a court will take account of a party's agreement 'not to take a time point' so far as concerns delay while they were responding to a letter before claim.

2. Civil Procedure Rules, Rule 54.1(2).

3. Civil Procedure Rules, Practice Directions 44-48.

4. See the Direction made by the Lord Chief Justice dated 21 August 2013 (as amended on 17 October 2014), available in the UTIAC section of the www. justice.gov.uk website. Also, the High Court can order the transfer of judicial review proceedings to the UTIAC.

5. See Civil Procedure Rules, Rule 54.1(2).

6. See Civil Procedure Rules, Practice Direction – Pre-Action Conduct and Protocols, paragraphs 2-3.

7. See Civil Procedure Rules, Rule 54.5(1).

8. See Civil Procedure Rules, Rule 54.1(2)(f).

9. The relevant address should be available from a range of sources such as the Phone Book; Business and Services Directory, Thomson's Local Directory, CAB, etc.

Index